CHERRYPICKERS' GUIDE

to Rare Die Varieties of United States Coins

Sixth Edition • Volume I
Half Cents Through Nickel Five-Cent Pieces

1982 Zinc Small Date
Doubled-Die Reverse Lincoln Cent
Regular 1982 Zinc Small Date value, MS-63: 50¢.
1982 Zinc Small Date Doubled-Die variety value, MS-63: $1,000.

Bill Fivaz • J.T. Stanton

edited by Mike Ellis

forewords by Q. David Bowers and Kenneth Bressett

Atlanta, Georgia

CHERRYPICKERS' GUIDE

to Rare Die Varieties of United States Coins

Sixth Edition • Volume I

Reprinted 2024

3101 Clairmont Road • Suite C • Atlanta, GA 30329

Correspondence concerning this book may be directed to the publisher, Attn: CPG, at the address above.

ISBN: 0794843182
Printed in China

Disclaimer: Expert opinion should be sought in any significant numismatic purchase. This book is presented as a guide only. No warranty or representation of any kind is made concerning the completeness of the information presented. The authors are professional numismatists who regularly buy, trade, and sometimes hold certain of the items discussed in this book.

Caveat: The price estimates given are subject to variation and differences of opinion. Before making decisions to buy or sell, consult the latest information. Past performance of the rare coin market or any coin or series within that market is not necessarily an indication of future performance, as the future is unknown. Such factors as changing demand, popularity, grading interpretations, strength of the overall coin market, and economic conditions will continue to be influences.

Advertisements within this book: Whitman Publishing, LLC, does not endorse, warrant, or guarantee any of the products or services of its advertisers. All warranties and guarantees are the sole responsibility of the advertiser.

About the Cover: The two featured coins are each legendary varieties. The 1873 doubled-die obverse Indian Head cent (FS-01-1873-101) is known for the dramatic doubling on LIBERTY on the headdress (see the top-center inset) and is one of the most popular—not to mention valuable—varieties in the series. The 1939 doubled-die reverse Jefferson nickel (FS-05-1939-801) also shows impressive doubling, most noticeable on MONTICELLO (see the bottom-right inset) and FIVE CENTS. Both of these coins are prominent enough to be listed in *A Guide Book to United States Coins* (the "Red Book"), as well as its new, expanded *Deluxe Edition*. The other coins pictured include (top left) a 1921 "Two Feathers" Buffalo nickel (FS-05-1921-401); (top right) an 1867 doubled-die obverse two-cent piece (FS-02-1867-101); (bottom left) a 2009 doubled-die reverse Lincoln cent (FS-01-2009-803); and (bottom center) an 1873 repunched date Shield nickel (FS-05-1873-1301).

If you enjoy the *Cherrypickers' Guide*, you'll also enjoy these books (in Whitman's Bowers Series of numismatic references): *A Guide Book of Morgan Silver Dollars; A Guide Book of Double Eagle Gold Coins; A Guide Book of United States Type Coins; A Guide Book of Modern United States Proof Coin Sets; A Guide Book of Shield and Liberty Head Nickels; A Guide Book of Buffalo and Jefferson Nickels; A Guide Book of Flying Eagle and Indian Head Cents; A Guide Book of Washington and State Quarters; A Guide Book of United States Commemorative Coins; A Guide Book of Lincoln Cents; A Guide Book of United States Tokens and Medals; A Guide Book of Gold Dollars; A Guide Book of Peace Dollars A Guide Book of Franklin and Kennedy Half Dollars; A Guide Book of the Official Red Book of United States Coins; A Guide Book of Civil War Tokens; A Guide Book of Hard Times Tokens; A Guide Book of Half Cents and Large Cents; A Guide Book of Mercury Dimes, Standing Liberty Quarters, and Liberty Walking Half Dollars; A Guide Book of Barber Silver Coins;* and *A Guide Book of Liberty Seated Silver Coins.*

For a complete catalog of numismatic reference books, supplies, and storage products, visit Whitman Publishing online at www.whitman.com.

WCG™ OCG™

DEDICATION

James Wiles

This volume of the *Cherrypickers' Guide* is dedicated to Dr. James Wiles, who, like many of us, started collecting coins as a boy and made it a life-long passion. Throughout his career in numismatics, James has demonstrated what the *Cherrypickers' Guide* is all about: promoting enthusiasm for collecting. Through his steadfast dedication and service to Combined Organizations of Numismatic Error Collectors of America (CONECA), James has promoted the hobby by writing, speaking, teaching, and leading.

James began by collecting die cracks and die breaks. His interests soon progressed to repunched mintmarks and doubled dies. In the mid-1980s, he began to seriously study these die varieties and to share his knowledge through books and articles that have become key reference sources for hobbyists across the country. He published *The Error Index* in 1990, cataloging a vast quantity of Lincoln cent repunched mintmarks. By 1994, he had created *The Official CONECA Doubled Die Master Listing*. After that, James's numismatic writing credits mounted year after year. In 1997 he was commissioned by the American Numismatic Association to author *The Modern Minting Process; U.S. Minting Errors and Varieties: An ANA Correspondence Course*, now in its second edition, which serves as the curriculum for the annual Modern Minting Process course at the ANA Summer Seminar. James considers his most significant contribution to the hobby to be the CONECA Attribution Series, an entire library of attribution guides covering every denomination of 20th-century U.S. coinage. He continues to expand this series, which includes the following:

The Lincoln Cent RPM Book, Vol. 1 (1909–1958) and *Vol. 2 (1959–1989)*
The Lincoln Cent Doubled Die Book, Vol. 1 (1909–1958)
The Jefferson Nickel RPM Book: An Attribution and Pricing Guide
The Washington Quarter Dollar Book: Volumes 1–3, 1932–1949
The Kennedy Half Dollar Book: An Attribution and Pricing Guide
CONECA Attribution Guide to Eisenhower Dollar Die Varieties
Ultra Modern Doubled Dies: The Single Squeeze Era (1996–2012)
What are Die Varieties?

James served two terms as president of CONECA, in addition to many years filling various supporting roles on the CONECA board of directors. In recognition of his writing and various other contributions to the hobby, he has often been the recipient of notable CONECA awards, including the Alan Herbert Best Column Award, the Lonesome John Photography Award, and the Kenny Knapp Membership Recruiting Award. In 1996 James was honored with CONECA's highest recognition, the Dr. Lyndon King Award. For a lifetime of service to the club, he was inducted into the CONECA Hall of Fame in 2011.

In 1997 the ANA awarded James the M. Vernon Sheldon Memorial Audio/Visual Award. And in 2010 the ANA recognized him with a Presidential award.

James's enthusiasm for the hobby is contagious, and he continues to spread that enthusiasm through his publications, through his teaching at the annual ANA Summer Seminar, and through his Web site, www.varietyvista.com, a treasure trove of knowledge for the die-variety collector.

J.T. Stanton, CONECA past president and *Cherrypickers' Guide* editor Mike Ellis, and Bill Fivaz pose with the *Cherrypickers' Guide* at the American Numismatic Association's summer show, Denver, Colorado, 2006.

CONTENTS

FOREWORD

Q. David Bowers

Time was when relatively few interesting die varieties were known to the coin-collecting fraternity. The *Guide Book of United States Coins* (the hobby's popular "Red Book," first issued in 1946) listed certain of these, after which ensuing editions listed more. Today the Red Book offers a few hundred, mostly devoted to early coinage issues. Examples include the 1794 copper cent with 94 five-pointed stars on the reverse, one of the most curious varieties of all time; and the cent of 1801 with the reverse having three errors—II and ITED instead of UNITED, one stem missing from the wreath, and the fraction expressed as the mathematically meaningless 1/000. A variety of 1800 silver dollar is called the AMERICAI, because of the extraneous I at the end of the word. Then we have various doubled-die coins, led by the famous 1955 doubled-die Lincoln cent, and joined by the 1916 doubled-die Buffalo nickel and others. With relatively few exceptions, these varieties listed in the Red Book are at once scarce and very expensive.

As interesting as these Red Book–listed coins may be, they are only the tip of the iceberg!

A great change came to the hobby in 1963 when Frank G. Spadone published his *Major Variety and Error Guide.* This popular book was, for lack of a better expression, for the "common man"—listing many varieties not found in the Red Book, but interesting to collect, and dating mainly from the modern era. Today, Spadone's pioneering work is little remembered, but it remains important as a foundation.

Enter Bill Fivaz and J.T. Stanton and their *Cherrypickers' Guide to Rare Die Varieties.* Greatly expanding the field of opportunity, the authors studied coins mainly from the 20th century and compiled a veritable encyclopedia of interesting repunchings, misaligned mintmarks, and the like. Armed with a copy of this book a collector, with magnifying glass in hand, could review a dealer's stock of seemingly ordinary Lincoln cents and find curious and interesting varieties—mintmarks misaligned or punched over each other, oddities in the lettering, and more. A very nice collection could be formed at modest cost, all the while offering the thrill of the chase.

Today the latest volume of the *Cherrypickers' Guide,* now with well-known expert Mike Ellis building upon the work of Fivaz and Stanton, is the latest and most extensive passport to finding treasures. Coin conventions, shops, Internet listings, and even pocket change are the hunting field for varieties that in all instances are fascinating to own, and, in some cases, are very valuable. Recently a 1969-S doubled-die cent in MS-64 was sold for $80,500 in an online auction! You might not find a coin that will enable you to tour the world in grand style for a year, but with the *Cherrypickers' Guide* the chances are very good that you will capture many different coin varieties and enjoy them all.

The treasure map is now in your hands. Good luck!

Q. David Bowers
Wolfeboro, New Hampshire

Since 1953, Q. David Bowers—the "Dean of American Numismatics"—has been active in the hobby as an award-winning author, coin dealer, auctioneer, and researcher. He is chairman emeritus of Stack's Bowers Galleries and numismatic director of Whitman Publishing, and serves as research editor of the Guide Book of United States Coins.

FOREWORD

Kenneth Bressett

There are many different ways to enjoy the hobby of numismatics. Nearly every collector has some uniquely personal motivation as to what is important or how to achieve their goals. The number of different coins available to hobbyists seems endless. The reasons for wanting to acquire, preserve, and classify these coins are equally numerous and complex.

For some collectors it is the thrill of the hunt, for others the pride of ownership or the satisfaction of completing a set or series. For most there is an underlying pleasure in knowing that acquiring a special coin was not only prudent but also profitable. Even the most altruistic collector takes pleasure in seeing that an investment of time and money has paid dividends.

When it comes to selecting coins to fit any collecting agenda, *saber es poder*—knowledge is power. Whatever your objectives are it is vitally important to know that each coin is genuine and to correctly interpret what you are seeing when you examine it. With that thought in mind, the *Cherrypickers' Guide* was written. This book is a gateway to understanding, classifying, and appreciating the many unusual—albeit sometimes minuscule—varieties of United States coins that are often misunderstood or ignored by a vast majority of collectors.

What originally began as a basic listing of valuable varieties that might be disregarded by the casual or traditional collector has, in the latest expanded volume of this book, morphed into a new sphere of specialization that is of interest to thousands of collectors. Taking a more careful look at *all* coins is no longer something reserved for specialists, but a necessity for anyone interested in learning about how coins are made, what can go wrong in the minting process, and why some seemingly unimportant variations can make a difference of hundreds of dollars in value.

Selecting which varieties belong in a specialized book like this is no easy task. Some of the pieces listed here are included to illustrate abnormal coins even though they have little or no premium value. Most listings, however, show which varieties have a numismatic premium that might otherwise go unnoticed by the casual observer. Learning to identify the kinds of variations that are included in this catalog will arm even the most novice hobbyist with a knowledge of what to look for in discovering similar valuable varieties and perhaps open a whole new world of collectible coins.

We are fortunate to have this extensive listing by some of the country's leading experts to guide us through this exciting field of collecting. People frequently asked why certain of these coins are not listed in the *Guide Book of United States Coins* (the "Red Book"). Or why some are there while others are not. The reason is there would never be enough room to include them all in the Red Book, and thus this specialized catalog has been produced. I am sure you will find it entertaining, educational, and useful in a thousand ways.

Kenneth Bressett
Colorado Springs, Colorado

Kenneth Bressett, longtime editor of the best-selling Guide Book of United States Coins *(the "Red Book"), has been active in numismatics since the 1940s. His accomplishments—research, writing, and serving in hobby organizations, including as president of the American Numismatic Association—have earned him nearly every important award in the hobby.*

PREFACE

Numismatist Bill Fivaz, by mid-1989, was well known for his curious habit of searching collections and dealers' inventories for neat coin varieties. Around June of that year, J. Woodside of Scotsman Coins in St. Louis, Missouri, suggested to Bill that he should write a book telling other collectors about his interest. Bill called a friend and fellow variety enthusiast, printer J.T. Stanton, to talk about the idea, and they agreed that such a reference was needed by the hobby community.

Bill and J.T. were very experienced in numismatics, but both were novices when it came to publishing—and certainly not prepared for the monumental project they were about to undertake. Their first thought was to include about 100 of the most significant coinage varieties—the ones that any collector would want. Those 100 varieties quickly grew into more than 160. With that, the two collectors worked out a format for the book, and the first *Cherrypickers' Guide* blossomed.

J.T. was well established in the printing business, so he handled the book's production. The U.S. Postal Service was kept busy as copy was shuttled back and forth between Bill, in Dunwoody, Georgia, and J.T., 275 miles away in Savannah. They sent the final laid-out pages to press in November 1989, hoping to have the book printed, bound, and ready for distribution in time for the Florida United Numismatists (FUN) convention the first weekend of January 1990. On his way to that show in Tampa, J.T. stopped by the bindery in Jacksonville, Florida. His plan was to pick up about 500 copies—a sufficient quantity for the show, they felt, not quite sure how well the book would be received and how brisk its sales would be.

When they left Tampa that Sunday, they had sold all 500 copies, and had a backlog of orders for more to be shipped and mailed as soon as possible.

That first edition of the *Cherrypickers' Guide* was a great learning experience for Bill and J.T. both. They didn't expect to sell the entire initial print run of 3,000 copies, and actually felt lucky when they sold out in less than 10 months. Before long they planned a second edition, with more listings and the addition of retail values, along with other improvements. Thanks to coverage in the numismatic press and word-of-mouth publicity among variety enthusiasts, excitement grew for the second edition. Dealers and wholesalers wanted the book to offer to their customers. The new edition's print run of 5,000 copies sold out in about six months.

Bill and J.T. were very pleased with the hobby's acceptance of the *Cherrypickers' Guide*—and the fact that grading services were using the Fivaz-Stanton (FS) attribution numbers on their slabs. (To the best of the authors' knowledge, ANACS was the first to recognize a coin with a Fivaz-Stanton designation.) It seemed that Bill and J.T. had luckily stumbled onto a book with the right topic at the right time.

The second edition was made in both regular and spiral-bound formats. "The *Cherrypickers' Guide* might well have been the first mainstream numismatic book to be offered with the spiral or coil binding," says Stanton. This format is perfect for collectors: they can lay the book open to a particular variety without struggling to keep the book flat, leaving their hands free to hold a coin and magnifying glass.

For the third edition, the entire print run was published in the spiral format.

When it was time for that third edition, the authors had a big hurdle to overcome: J.T. simply didn't have time to handle the production. So they set out to find a willing publisher. Several were contacted, and several were interested, with Bowers and Merena being the authors' ultimate choice. They worked to provide the hobby community what would become their best effort yet. The third edition featured about five times as many varieties as the first; it went to six printings and more than 28,000 copies before the fourth edition finally came out.

Since J.T. was in the business of printing (and by this time some publishing), he and Bill asked famous numismatist Q. David Bowers (a principal of Bowers and Merena) if they could produce the fourth edition themselves. Being the gentleman everyone knows, Bowers immediately agreed—if that's what they wanted, that's what he wanted.

The fourth edition became by far the duo's largest effort to that date, so large in fact that it had to be divided into two volumes to accommodate the spiral binding. Volume I included half cents through nickels. Volume II (later published by Whitman Publishing in 2006) picked up with half dimes and bigger denominations. The division was a natural one. Volume I contained all minor coinage, and there are a lot of people who collect only cents and nickels. Volume II included other popular series comprising silver half dimes through dollars (including Bust and Liberty Seated series), federal gold coinage, and commemoratives. For collectors' convenience, volume II introduced a newly simplified Fivaz-Stanton numbering system.

The fifth edition, volume I, was published in 2009. It carried on the *Cherrypickers'* tradition, with updated market information, new varieties, a new appendix on the minting process, and other improvements. It continued the new Fivaz-Stanton numbering system introduced in the previous volume. An appendix cross-referenced the old numbering system, allowing collectors and dealers to bring their listings up to date.

With the fifth edition, volume II, published in 2012, Bill Fivaz and J.T. Stanton remained involved in the book's production while passing the torch to a new editor, Ken Potter. Well known in the hobby as a coin dealer, a published researcher, and the consummate die-variety specialist, Potter has his finger constantly on the pulse of the variety-collecting segment of numismatics. Thanks to Ken's coordination and management, the fifth edition, volume II, included dozens of upgraded photographs, more than 100 new listings, updated content, and even a whole new section on silver, gold, and platinum bullion-coin varieties. Ken brought together a team of pricing experts and analysts to provide the most accurate market pricing on the coins listed. The book was 32 pages longer than the fourth edition's volume II, and it featured nearly 800 unique varieties—about five times the coverage of the first edition published twenty-some years earlier.

Today, with the sixth edition, volume I, a new cycle starts with the *Cherrypickers' Guide*. Longtime die-variety specialist, hobby educator, writer, and CONECA Hall of Famer Michael Ellis was brought on as the editor for this book. For die-variety collectors, Mike needs no introduction; he edited the fourth edition, volume I, of the *Guide*, which earned him a 2001 "Extraordinary Merit" award from the Numismatic Literary Guild. Mike has grabbed the baton carried by Fivaz, Stanton, and Potter, and run with it, upgrading photos, conferencing with series specialists to bring the old listings up to date and add more than 140 new varieties, and making sure hobbyists get all the information they need to build a great collection. Thanks to his coordination and the work of a team of experts, with Bill Fivaz providing constant support, 48 pages have been added to this new volume.

"The *Cherrypickers' Guide* proves that there are times when someone can get lucky, and tackle the right subject at the right time," Bill and J.T. have said. "We've enjoyed the experience of creating the book, and hope our readers have learned a lot from the contributions of all the people who have made it possible—those who have provided varieties and information, and who have made other contributions, including values, rarity data, and other vital details."

This year, 2015, marks the 25th anniversary of the *Cherrypickers' Guide*. If collector enthusiasm is any gauge, it will continue to serve the hobby for generations to come.

CREDITS AND ACKNOWLEDGMENTS

Bill Fivaz and J.T. Stanton are the authors of the *Cherrypickers' Guide*—and now Mike Ellis has joined the team as the book's editor—but the backbone of the book is the contributions of hundreds of coin collectors, dealers, and specialists over the years. Without those very important people offering new listings, detailed descriptions, rarity information, market values (updated on a constant basis), and detailed knowledge of a variety or series, the *Cherrypickers' Guide* would not have become the popular and indispensable reference that it is today.

Dedicatee **James Wiles** provided extensive information—including corrections, additions, pricing, and images—for the Lincoln cent, Buffalo nickel, and Jefferson nickel sections.

Bob Grellman reviewed the half cent and large cent sections, making changes to prices, rarities, and descriptions as needed.

Rick Snow lent his expertise for the Flying Eagle and Indian Head cent sections, revising the pricing of existing varieties, describing new additions, and submitting coin photos.

Marlon Green and **Alan Meghrig** proved invaluable by supplying revisions and additions, including images, for the two-cent piece section.

Howard Spindel offered much time and effort to revamp the Shield nickel section, including making additions, pricing coins, and providing new images.

Ron Pope helped update prices and provide accurate descriptions and photos for the Buffalo nickel section.

Brian Raines also assisted with the Buffalo nickel section—especially the market values of varieties.

In addition to the above, the following individuals assisted with revisions, additions, and pricing feedback on various sections within the book: **Ken Potter**; **Chris** and **Charity Welch**; **David W. Lange**; **Tom DeLorey**; **Sam Gelberd**; **Larry Briggs**; **Michael Fey**; and **Brian Greer.**

There are numerous other collectors, dealers, and specialists who have contributed since the first edition of the *Cherrypickers' Guide*. We wish to thank all those variety enthusiasts who are willing to share their coins, photographs, knowledge, and experience. Those who have contributed to this and previous volumes are noted here. If we have missed anyone it is with our most sincere apologies.

Bill Affanato
Leonard Albrecht
Roger Alexander
Brian Alford
Brian Allen
Matt Allman
Gary Alt
ANACS
Walter Anderson
Guy Araby
Richard Austin
Chuck Avery
Saverio Barbieri
Richard Bateson
Frank Baumann*
Joe Beaupied
Ed Becker
Roger Beckner
Steve Bernatowicz
Jack Beymer
David Biglow
Dick Bland
Al Blythe*
Cliff Bolling
Don Bonser
John Bordner*
Q. David Bowers
Charlie Boyd*
Mike Bozovich
Dan Brady
Jym Braun
Kenneth Bressett
Larry Briggs
David Brody
Robert Bruce*
Gene Bruder
Mike Bruggeman
Paul Bucerel
Bill Bugert
B. Buholtz
Vincent Burke
Ty Buxton
Cameo Coin Gallery
David J. Camire
Will Camp
Terry Campbell*
Donald Cantrell
Rick Carpenter

* **deceased**

Jennifer Casazza
Charles Cataldo Jr.
Ken Chylinski
Nicholas Ciancio
Ted Clark*
Clem Clement
Mark Clewell
Tim Clough
Blaine Coffey
Coin World
Lou Coles
Frank Colletti
CONECA
Jim Conrad*
Edward Cook
Bert Corkhill
José Cortez
Billy Crawford
David Crawford
Whaden Curtis
Charles Daughtrey
Dave's DCW Collection
Ray Davis
Lee Day
Tom DeLorey
George Derwart
Rick DeSanctis
Daniel Dodge
J.T. Donahue
David Druzisky
Justin Duane
Elliott Durann
Edgewood Coin Co.
Brian Edwards
Harry Ellis*
Mike Ellis
Larry Emard
Bill Erdokos
Richard Evans
Rob Ezerman
Michael "Skip" Fazzari
Joe Feld
Ronn Fern
Michael Fey
Gerald Fishman
Jason Fishman
Ed Fletcher
Gerry Fortin
Geoffrey Fults
Paul Funaiole
Bill Gase
Paul Geiserbach
Sam Gelberd
Ray Gelewski
Jack Gorby*
Don Gordon*
Rudy Gos
Mike Gourley
Peter Goydos
Jane Gray
Marlon Green
David Greenfelder
Brian Greer
Bob Grellman
Robert Griffiths
Linda Hagopian
Richard Hana
Joe Haney
Rob Hanks Jr.
Lloyd Hanson*
B.D. Harding
Tim Hargis
Linda Harp
Ash Harrison
Tom Hart
Donald Hauser
James W. Hay
Dennis Heard
Doug Heisler
Richard Helbig
John Hemphill
Alan Herbert*
Ronald Hickman*
Lee Hiemke
Doug Hill
Ken Hill
Mike Holstein
ICG
The Ike Group
Adrian Jellinek
Jim Jones
Martin Jordan
Matt Juppo
Mike Jurek
Carl Kanoff
Gary Kelly
Jerry Kennison
Jonathan Kern
Jeff Kierstead
Derry King
Joe Kirchgessner
Keith Klopfenstein*
Robert Knauss
Gerald Kochel
Bud Kolanda
Martin Krashoc
James Kropp
Harold Kuykendall
L&C Coins
Jim Lafferty
Rick Lajoie
David W. Lange
Frank Leone
Akio Lis
Fred Lindsey
Don Lommler
Mark Lowers
Carl R. Loyd
Lee Lydston
Lee Maples
Aimee McCabe
Steve McCabe
Mark McWherter
Roy Maines
Ross Manning
Arnold Margolis*
J.P. Martin
Kip Mecum
R.A. Medina
Alan Meghrig
Tom Mendonca
Anthony Mesaros
Michael Mesaros
Michael Michel
Ed Miller
Joe Miller
John Miller
Tom Miller
Ward Miller
Warren Mills
Mike Mizak
MMNS
Michael Morris
David Moss
Wali Motorwalla
Allan C. Murphy
Dan Murray
BJ Neff
NGC
Gene Nichols
Neil Niederman
P. Nilson
John Nogosek
Charlie Nowack
Numismatic News
Numismedia.com
Jim O'Donnell*
Old Pueblo Coin Exchange
Dick Osborne
Lynn Ourso
Jeff Oxman
Dick Painter
Mike Paradis
Brett Parrish
Dennis Paulsen
George Pauwells
Richard Pawley
Daniel Pazsint
PCGS
Ben Peters
Karen Peterson*
Larry Philbrick*
Bob Piazza
Chris Pilliod
Denny Polly
Ron Pope
Ken Potter
Colleen Prebish
Andrew Prechtl*
Al Raddi
Brian Raines

* deceased

Wayne Rattray
RCNH
Roger Reiner
Paul Reitmeir
Doug Riley
Mike Ringo*
Joe Rizdy
John Roberts
Emory Robinson
Rogers' Coins
Del Romines*
Lee Roschen
Gary Rosner
P. Scott Rubin
Tony Russo
Bob Ryan
Rick Rybicki
Jerry Sajbel
Steve Santangelo
Charles Schaefer
George Schaetzle
Steve Schmidt
Terry Searcy*
SEGS
Mark Serafine
Gary Shaffstall
Blaise Sidor
Rich Sisti
Sue Sisti
E.O. Smith
Jim Smith
Les Leroy Smith
Ruben Smith
Richard Snow
Art Snyder
Terry Souder
Max Spiegel
Howard Spindel
Jeff Stahl
John Starr
Larry Steve
Suzanne Stewart
Bob Stimax
Tom Stott
Jim Stoutjesdyk
Eric Striegel
Dave Stutzman
Andrew Suchan
Kevin Swan
Norm Talbert*
Sol Taylor
David Thacker
Dave Thomas
Jeff Thomas
Carson Torpey
Lee Tucker
Andy Turnbull
Leroy Van Allen
Marilyn Van Allen
John L. Veach
Kyle Vick
Michael Volz
Gary Wagnon
Dan Walker
W.O. Walker
Mike Wallace
J.R. Walters
Jonathan Warren
Troy Watkins
Richard Watts
Val Webb
Charity Welch
Chris Welch
David Welch
John Wells
Dave Welsh
Michael Werda
Vic West
John Wexler
Paul Wheeler
Bill White
Bob White
C.C. Whitaker
John Whitworth
James Wiles
Dave Wilson
Steve Wilson
Al Windholtz
Chuck Wishon
Tim Wissert
Andy Wong
Jay Woodside
Hank Woods
C.L. Wyatt
Jerry Wysong
Vicken Yegparian
Dan Zaporra
Frank M. Zapushek
Anthony Zito

* deceased

HOW TO USE THIS BOOK

As do most technical reference books (especially those involving numismatics), the *Cherrypickers' Guide* frequently uses abbreviations, acronyms, and numbering systems to identify and attribute its listings as clearly as possible. Most experienced collectors will recognize and understand the format used herein. However, novices will find this section very helpful.

Symbols Used in This Book

The *Pocket Change* symbol indicates a variety that may reasonably be expected to be found in circulation today. Pocket Change varieties typically are cents dated after 1959, Jefferson nickels (other than silver wartime issues), dimes and quarters minted after 1964, half dollars minted after 1970, and some circulation-strike modern dollars.

The *Red Book* symbol indicates a variety that is listed in the most recent edition of R.S. Yeoman's *Guide Book of United States Coins* (popularly known as the "Red Book"), the best-selling annual price guide of U.S. coins.

The *Red Book: Deluxe Edition* symbol indicates a variety that is listed in the most recent edition of R.S. Yeoman's *Guide Book of United States Coins, Deluxe Edition* (a greatly expanded version of the classic known as the "Red Book").

The *Young Numismatists* symbol indicates a variety that young and/or emerging collectors might want to focus on. Many of these fall into the Pocket Change category as well. In most cases, coins marked with the YN symbol are varieties of coins that are very inexpensive when found in their "normal" format, either in Mint State or high circulated grades. They usually can be sold for significant premiums through private sale or through auctions. Finding these varieties can help finance the collection of a numismatist with modest funds.

The *New Listing* symbol indicates that a variety is newly listed in this edition of the *Cherrypickers' Guide*. It also appears when some, but not all, of the entries in a new Group Variety Listing are new to this edition.

Abbreviations Used in This Book

DDO	doubled-die obverse
DDR	doubled-die reverse
I	Interest Factor
L	Liquidity Factor
LD	Large Date
MPD	misplaced date
n/a	not available
NA	No Arrows
ND	No Drapery
N/L	not listed
OMM	over mintmark
PF	Proof
PUP	Pick-Up Point (see text)
R	rarity
RPD	repunched date
RPM	repunched mintmark
SD	Small Date
SMS	Special Mint Set
TDO	tripled-die obverse
TDR	tripled-die reverse
URS	Universal Rarity Scale
WA	With Arrows
WD	With Drapery
WDC	Wrong Denomination Clash

PICK-UP POINTS (PUPS)

A variety's *Pick-Up Point* is its area most prone to exhibit whatever characteristic(s) makes the variety unique. In most cases, this will be the date, the mintmark, or legends. Other PUPs include denticles, stars, designer's initials, and various design elements.

VARIETY VALUE AND NORMAL VALUE

Throughout the guide we offer values for varieties in several grades of preservation. (For more information on grading, refer to the *Official American Numismatic Association Grading Standards for United States Coins* and *Grading Coins by Photographs: An Action Guide for the Collector and Investor*.)

Sources for the values of varieties include:

- actual sales (retail or auction) reported to us, with the most recent sales bearing the most weight;
- our assessments comparing one variety to another similar in rarity, collectibility, interest, and other factors; and
- recommendation by those who specialize in particular series or denominations.

Note that cells left blank within pricing charts indicate that the variety is not known to exist in that grade; cells containing a dash (—) indicate that the variety is so rare in that grade that sales records are rarely found; and cells with italicized figures indicate that the market for that variety in that grade is unsettled.

Also included in this volume are fair-market values for each variety's *normal*-version coin. These values are derived from the *Guide Book of United States Coins* (the "Red Book") and the *Guide Book of United States Coins, Deluxe Edition*, first edition. They reflect actual retail sales from some of the most respected dealers across the country. These "normal coin" values provide an easy comparison for the amount or percentage of premium each variety can command.

As with any price guide, the values listed should be used strictly as a reference. Although great pains are taken to ensure as much accuracy as possible, values can and do change, especially among varieties that trade frequently.

Factors Affecting Value

Always keep in mind the two major factors affecting the value of any item: supply and demand. That advice has never been proven wrong. If 10 people want a particular variety and only 6 examples are available, the value will be far greater than a similar variety desired by 10 people with 20 examples available.

With numismatic varieties especially, add to those two factors a very important third: *eye appeal!* As a general rule (there may be very few exceptions), the more visually dramatic a variety, the greater its value. For instance, compare two different repunched dates, with similar rarity and in similar grade, on two 1868 Shield nickels—one with a wide degree of separation and one with a very close separation. The variety with the wide separation will always command a greater price.

Values are subject to change whenever a variety becomes more readily available or more desirable. Variety values certainly change with the normal fluctuations of the numismatic market. Remember that, generally speaking, **the higher the numismatic value of a particular coin, the lower the premium associated with its varieties**. For example, a nice doubled die on an Uncirculated Liberty Head $20 gold coin will (generally) command little, if any, premium for the knowledgeable collector.

A variety's die state (or stage) can also play an important part in pricing. Earlier die states that show sharper doubling than later die states (where the doubling may be subdued or nearly gone) typically sell for higher prices. Exceptions exist where a later die state may actually be stronger, or other variations to the die may create greater demand, but as a general rule, the earlier the die state, the more the coin is worth to a specialist.

Values for Actively Traded Varieties

Some of the varieties listed in the *Cherrypickers' Guide* are also noted in other hobby price guides that are updated on a regular basis. The values for these varieties, such as the 1955 doubled-die obverse Lincoln cent, fluctuate quite often as a result of market trends. In these instances, we highly recommend that you refer to other *current* price guides to obtain an up-to-date value for the variety. Values for these varieties are included in the *Cherrypickers' Guide* for reference only. Collectors and dealers can compare the prices noted with current prices and use the difference as a guide for possibly adjusting other similar varieties.

The Fivaz-Stanton (FS) Numbering System

The Fivaz-Stanton (FS) numbering system dramatically changed in the fourth edition, volume II (published in 2006).

In the older system, adding new listings was problematic as additional decimal places were required in many instances. Furthermore, an attribution number such as FS-05-003.752, or even FS-10c-0.008 was very complicated, and not within the normal thought processes of most collectors. The older system simply left no room for additions. The current system allows for additions to the listings on an ongoing basis, and *without any limitation!*

Reading the Fivaz-Stanton Number

With the Fivaz-Stanton numbering system, the complete listing number includes

- the **denomination,** followed by
- the **date** and **mintmark** (if there is a mintmark), and finally
- the sequential **"identifier" number**.

The identifiers essentially denote the type of variety, and/or the location of its point of interest. This number is usually three digits, but can be four digits.

There is one major exception in the identifier number system. The Morgan and Peace dollar series use their Van Allen–Mallis (VAM) numbers (when available) as the identifier. This is more convenient for VAM enthusiasts and for the grading services. For instance, with an 1878 VAM-44, the FS number is FS-S1-1878-044.

Most third-party grading services will gladly change an existing slab with the old FS number for a new slab with the newer FS numbering system. A fee for this service can be expected, but it will usually be lower than a normal submission.

Identifiers for Fivaz-Stanton Numbers

The following are the identifiers for the Fivaz-Stanton numbers and their related meanings. Any coin with an obverse and reverse variety will be identified with two ID numbers separated with a slash.

101–299	obverse doubled die
301–399	obverse date variety
401–499	obverse variety, miscellaneous
501–699	mintmark variety
701–799	miscellaneous variety
801–899	reverse doubled die
901–999	reverse variety, miscellaneous

A four-digit identifier is used for dates that include two or more major types. For instance, a date variety on an 1867 With Rays Shield nickel might be FS-05-1867-301, yet a date variety on an 1867 No Rays Shield nickel might be FS-05-1867-1301. There are a few instances when there are three or more distinctive types, such as the 1864 Indian Head cent (copper-nickel, bronze No L, and bronze With L). In these cases the first type will be three digits, with the second and third types will be four digits, such as 1301 and 2301.

With two major types, such as the 1867 With Rays and 1867 No Rays nickels, the With Rays varieties would have three digits, such as 301. The No Rays varieties would have four digits, such as 1301. The 1 at the beginning of the No Rays varieties differentiates the second type from the first.

Note: As mentioned, Morgan and Peace dollar varieties have Van Allen–Mallis (VAM) numbers as the primary number sequence of their identifiers.

Old Fivaz-Stanton Numbers Included in the Listings

For this volume some old FS numbers are included as a cross-reference. The new FS number is primary, and the old FS number (when available) is secondary, in parentheses.

Abbreviations for Denominations

HC	half cent	S1	silver dollar
LC	large cent	T1	trade dollar
01	small cent	C1	clad dollar / golden dollar
02	two-cent piece	G1	gold dollar
3S	three-cent piece (silver)	G2.5	$2.50 gold piece
3N	three-cent piece (nickel)	G5	$5 gold piece
05	nickel five-cent piece	G10	$10 gold piece
H10	half dime	G20	$20 gold piece
10	dime	C50	commemorative half dollar
20	twenty-cent piece	P25	$25 platinum piece
25	quarter dollar	P100	$100 platinum piece
50	half dollar	SE	$1 Silver Eagle

Rarity Factor

The rarity factors used in the *Cherrypickers' Guide* are based upon the Universal Rarity Scale developed by Q. David Bowers. This is the only rarity scale available that is reasonably accurate for die varieties of the late-19th, 20th, and 21st centuries. Following you will find a background of the older Sheldon rarity scale, and details of Bowers's Universal Rarity Scale.

The Sheldon Scale

For many years, the only method of reasonably identifying rarity was with the use of the Sheldon scale, designed by numismatic author Dr. William H. Sheldon to identify the rarity of large-cent varieties. Put to that use, the Sheldon scale worked very well, as most varieties ranged from scarce to very rare. It was further adapted for use with grading and rarity of many other coin series and denominations, as it was the only common scale in existence. However, it was not quite appropriate for most series, most varieties, or most errors.

The Sheldon scale was simply a progression of eight levels into which the populations of all large-cent varieties were to fall. Each level was prefaced with the letter R, for Rarity:

R-1 common
R-2 not so common
R-3 scarce
R-4 very scarce (est. 76–200 pieces in existence)
R-5 rare (31–75 pieces)
R-6 very rare (13–30 pieces)
R-7 extremely rare (4–12 pieces)
R-8 unique, or nearly so (1–3 pieces)

Numismatic writers adopted this scale to represent coins that were considered scarce or rare. However, as one can imagine, the scale is not appropriate for many coins, especially those of the late-19th, 20th, and 21st centuries, with their high mintages. For instance, using this scale, the 1955 Doubled-Die Lincoln cent would be considered "common" or "not so common." Yet we know it is in fact scarce or rare.

Bowers's Universal Rarity Scale (URS)

Clearly, another scale was needed by the hobby community for indicating rarity of all coins. Leave it to numismatic historian Q. David Bowers to recognize the need and develop a method that could be used for any series, and any rarity. (In fact, it can be used not only for coins, but for virtually anything whose rarity, scarcity, or availability is important.) Bowers developed the Universal Rarity Scale (URS), which, as its name implies, is universal for any coin or item. He outlined this scale in the June 1992 issue of *The Numismatist*. It has been adopted by many writers and catalogers and is used throughout the *Cherrypickers' Guide*.

The URS is simple and reasonable in its mathematical progression:

URS-0	none	URS-12	1,001 to 2,000
URS-1	1; unique	URS-13	2,001–4,000
URS-2	2	URS-14	4,001–8,000
URS-3	3 or 4	URS-15	8,001–16,000
URS-4	5–8	URS-16	16,001–32,000
URS-5	9–16	URS-17	32,001–65,000
URS-6	17–32	URS-18	65,001–125,000
URS-7	33–64	URS-19	125,001–250,000
URS-8	65–125	URS-20	250,001–500,000
URS-9	126–250	URS-21	500,001–1,000,000
URS-10	251–500	URS-22	1,000,001–2,000,000
URS-11	501–1,000	(etc.)	

When using rarity numbers with coins, there are a couple important factors to remember:

1. **Rarity generally differs from one grade to another.** If a coin is listed as URS-13 (2,001 to 4,000 known) it might be relatively common. However, if there are only two pieces known in grades above About Uncirculated, it would be a true rarity (URS-2) in MS-63. Such is the case with the 1888-O Morgan dollar, Hot Lips variety. These are fairly common in Very Good and Fine, but virtually unknown above About Uncirculated. Such a coin is often referred to as a *condition rarity*.
2. **Rarity and value are not always as closely related as one might expect.** If there are 10 known examples of a particular variety, but only seven or eight collectors are interested in it, the coin would certainly be rare, but because of a relatively low Interest Factor (low demand), it would not command much of a premium. Conversely, there could be 10,000 pieces known of a variety, but if 20,000 collectors are interested in obtaining one, the premium over the normal value of the coin would be much greater, due to the high Interest Factor (high demand). This brings us back to the age-old law of supply and demand.

INTEREST FACTOR

Interest Factor is a term we use to indicate just how much demand a particular coin or variety has.

- A variety with a very high Interest Factor is in high demand, with several thousands of collectors desiring it.
- A medium Interest Factor may indicate that the variety is desired by hundreds or a few thousand people.
- A low Interest Factor might indicate that the coin is sought by just a handful of collectors.

In this guide, we rate each variety's Interest Factor as follows:

I-5	very high interest (most general collectors interested)
I-4	high interest (most variety collectors interested)
I-3	moderate interest (most series collectors interested)
I-2	minimal interest (some collectors interested)
I-1	very low interest (only very specialized collectors interested)

The Interest Factor, combined with the rarity, helps to determine the value of a variety or error. However, eye appeal is also a very important factor and must be considered in the final evaluation. A critical part of eye appeal for a variety or error is the relative strength or visibility of its defining characteristic—how easily can it be seen?

As a variety receives more publicity within the numismatic press, its Interest Factor might rise as demand increases. This can cause the price or value to increase without any change in the estimated quantity available.

Liquidity Factor

The Liquidity Factor indicates how quickly or how easily a coin or variety *should* sell, given normal market conditions.

- A coin with a high Liquidity Factor would be expected to sell right away, generally commanding full or inflated values.
- A coin with a low Liquidity Factor would not normally sell very easily or quickly, and then usually at a discount from suggested values.

Hot or highly active market conditions can inflate the Liquidity Factor of any coin, with a cold market having the opposite effect.

Our Liquidity Factor scale is as follows:

L-5 will sell easily, and often above listed value

L-4 will usually sell quickly at listed value (for variety enthusiasts)

L-3 will often sell in a reasonable time period, often to specialists

L-2 might sell in time, maybe at a discounted price

L-1 might sell provided the right buyer is available, but at a discount

Other Numbers and Abbreviations

Identification numbers and abbreviations appear more frequently in the study of mint errors (and especially die varieties) than within the regular segment of the hobby. Some are easy methods of precisely identifying different varieties. Others are used to describe rarity, or even a certain class or type of variety. The important fact is with the use of these numbers, most specialists will know right away exactly which variety is being discussed. At the very least, a dealer or collector can consult a reference and find the corresponding number along with photos or detailed descriptions, which can easily and accurately identify a certain variety.

Most of these identification systems are simply numbers listed after the date, mintmark, and denomination. Some are more complex identification listings and include letters or symbols to further identify the variety or error.

CONECA Abbreviations Used in This Edition

The CONECA die variety files originated in the 1970s under the leadership of Alan Herbert and John Wexler as an independent effort. When Wexler retired from the hobby in the mid-1980s, he sold the doubled-die portion to CONECA. The RPM files went into private hands, where they stayed until 1997, when they too were sold to CONECA.

Since then CONECA has maintained and expanded the files under the leadership of Dr. James Wiles, who has developed them into the most comprehensive set of die variety files available with almost 10,000 listings and more than 60,000 published photos. The club's ownership of the files guarantees their perpetual existence. Therefore, the *Cherrypickers' Guide* has chosen to cross reference to the CONECA files for all 20th- and 21st-century die varieties.

These three letter acronyms have been adopted by CONECA to indicate the various variety types. They are followed by a number to indicate listing sequence (e.g. DDO-001). Additional information about the CONECA numbering system can be found at www.varietyvista.com.

Note that just because a variety is listed as 001 does not suggest that it is the strongest, the most desirable, or the most valuable (although this is often the case). Note also that some previous editions (third edition and volume I of the fourth and fifth editions) of the *Cherrypickers' Guide* incorporated different CONECA numbers for doubled-die varieties which included the class and spread of the doubling; this information can also be found on www.varietyvista.com.

DDO	Doubled-Die Obverse	MPD	Misplaced Date
DDR	Doubled-Die Reverse	ODV	Obverse Design Variety
IMM	Inverted Mintmark	OMM	Over Mintmark
MAD	Misaligned Die Clash	RDV	Reverse Design Variety
MDO	Master Die Doubled Obverse	RED	Re-Engraved Design
MDR	Master Die Doubled Reverse	RPD	Repunched Date
MMO	Mintmark Omission	RPM	Repunched Mintmark
MMS	Mintmark Style	WDC	Wrong Denominational Clash

NUMBERING SYSTEMS FROM OTHER PUBLICATIONS

Other numbers are used from time to time in this book to indicate how a variety is cataloged in another reference book. The list below might not be comprehensive, as new books and reference works are being produced constantly.

Breen	*Walter Breen's Complete Encyclopedia of U.S. and Colonial Coins*
F (Fletcher)	Edward Fletcher, *The Shield Five Cent Series*
Greer	Brian Greer, *Complete Guide to Liberty Seated Dimes*
L	David Lawrence's books on Barber coinage (as mentioned in the text)
Leone	Frank Leone, *Longacre's Two-Cent Piece—An Attribution Guide*
S (Snow)	Rick Snow, *The Flying Eagle & Indian Cent Attribution Guide*
S1, S2, S3, S4, S5	Howard Spindel, *Shield Nickel Viewer*
VAM (Van Allen–Mallis)	*Comprehensive Catalog and Encyclopedia of Morgan and Peace Dollars*
WB (Wiley-Bugert)	*Complete Guide to Liberty Seated Half Dollars*

AVERAGE DIE LIFE

The list below indicates the average number of strikes measured for dies of recent coin designs. These figures, which are for circulation-strike dies, are presented as a range, as there is considerable variance. Dies can and do last longer, and some may be retired earlier due to damage.

Dies can be repaired depending on the severity of the damage, but in the end, most dies are retired for cracks or die chips due to metal fatigue. The number of strikes needed to produce a metal fatigue failure vary widely from 50,000 to more than 2 million strikes. Retirement can also occur if an abnormality—such as doubling or another inaccuracy—is discovered on a die.

Lincoln cent, 1996–2008 (Memorial reverse)	800,000–2,000,000
Lincoln cent, 2009 (four Centennial reverses)	250,000–550,000
Lincoln cent, 2010–2014 (Shield reverse)	400,000–800,000
Jefferson nickel, 2011–2014	400,000–700,000
Roosevelt dime, 2011–2014	400,000–800,000
Washington quarter, 1932–1998 (Eagle reverse)	350,000
Washington quarter, 1999–2009 (56 State and Territory reverses)	150,000–350,000
Washington quarter, 2010–2014 (25 America the Beautiful reverses)	250,000–1,200,000
Kennedy half dollar, 1964–2006*	160,000
Sacagawea and Native American dollars, 2000–2011**	250,000
Presidential dollars, 2007–2011** (20 designs)	250,000–800,000

*The Mint has not produced circulating half dollars since 2006.
** The Mint has not produced circulating dollar coins since 2011.

A coin's redesign will negatively affect the expected life of a die by some 30 to 70 percent. The average will improve slightly over time, as technicians analyze problems from the preceding year and "tweak" dies to address cracking issues. Once a new design is in operation for three to five years, Mint personnel will have improved die life to its maximum.

Also note that from 2010 through 2011, the mint facilities changed how the stamping process was lubricated. Lubrication is now added during the blank-washing process instead of using stamping oil at the press. This caused die life to increase for nickel, dime, and quarter.

Whitman Publishing would like to thank Thomas Jurkowsky, Director of Corporate Communications for the U.S. Mint, and the Mint's manufacturing technicians, for their contributions to this section.

Changes to This Volume of the *Cherrypickers' Guide*

Cataloging changes for the sixth edition, volume I, include:

Treatment of New Variety Listings

In the *Cherrypickers' Guide,* fifth edition, volume II, we chose to not include rarity, interest, liquidity, and pricing information for newly listed varieties, because the very act of listing a new variety can increase collector demand and, therefore, market value. Now, in the sixth edition, volume I, we have changed our policy and are instead providing this information when possible. Readers should note that this information is considered reliable at the time of publication, and it may vary over time—sometimes dramatically, and sometimes very soon after publication.

Also with regards to new varieties: each section now features a chart of all newly listed varieties within that denomination or coin type. This chart can be found directly after the introductory text.

Treatment of Low-Interest and Debunked Varieties

As in the fifth edition, volume II, we have identified certain varieties in the sixth edition, volume I, that have proven over time to be of low collector interest, and we have slated these for future removal from the coin-by-coin listings in order to make room for other, more significant, varieties. They will remain *Cherrypickers' Guide* varieties (as opposed to being "deleted," as such); for example, they will continue to be cross-referenced and summarized in Appendix I. An exception to this policy would be varieties debunked as counterfeit or which later research revealed to be erroneous classifications. These will be removed entirely.

Coins slated to be removed from the coin-by-coin listings and those varieties that have been debunked will be listed in a chart following each section's introduction.

Grouped Variety Listings

Another new feature in this volume: varieties that are very similar and occur either on a single date issue or several dates of a series are compiled in a single entry that covers all the variety as a group. For example, all Two Feathers Buffalo nickels are now gathered for study on pages 307–310.

Half Cents, 1793–1857

The foundation of the half-cent section of this book—its text, rarity ratings, detailed descriptions, and images—is the work of copper specialist J.R. "Bob" Grellman. Other numismatists have added to his research over the years.

Most of the specialists in this area are already very familiar with these varieties. However, we hope by including these listings a spark of interest may develop for newcomers to the field.

There are a couple of books that are well worth adding to your numismatic library for further study of the series:

> *The Half Cent Die State Book, 1793–1857,* by Ronald P. Manley, is one of the best books available today. Edited by Bob Grellman, the book contains hundreds of excellent photographs, very detailed descriptions, die-state census information, and much more. Well worth the retail price for a large, hardbound reference.
>
> *Walter Breen's Encyclopedia of United States Half Cents, 1793–1857,* by Walter Breen, is another excellent reference for the specialists. Like the Manley book, hundreds of photos are included with very detailed information on die marriages, die states, and even some pedigree information for some of the rarer varieties. With more than 500 pages and many color plates, this again is well worth the retail price for a deluxe, hardbound edition.
>
> *A Guide Book of Half Cents and Large Cents,* by Q. David Bowers, is a newer entry to the field (copyright 2015). Bowers has drawn on his own considerable experience as well as the expertise of today's specialists to study and illustrate (in full color) more than 800 half cent and large cent varieties, along with history and market advice presented in the engaging Bowers style.

For specialty clubs there is none better than Early American Coppers (EAC), a non-profit group of the most devoted numismatists studying the early copper coins of the United States. Founded in 1967, EAC is dedicated to the advancement and study of U.S. colonial coins, half cents, large cents, and Hard Times tokens. Its award-winning quarterly magazine is *Penny-Wise*. More information and a membership application can be obtained at www.eacs.org.

1804 — FS-HC-1804-301 (001)

Variety: Date Orientation — Cohen-2

PUP: Date

URS-6 • I-5 • L-5

Description: ***Obverse***—This obverse is the same as FS-HC-1804-302 (002). The 4 of the date is low and tilted slightly to the left. The digits are closely spaced, especially the 0 and 4. ***Reverse***—The zeroes on the denominator are very close. The left side is always weakly struck.

	G-4	VG-8
Variety	$10,000	$20,000
Normal	$70	$90

1804 — FS-HC-1804-302 (002)

Variety: Date Orientation — Cohen-4

PUP: Date

URS-7 • I-4 • L-4

Description: ***Obverse***—This obverse is the same as FS-HC-1804-301 (001). The 4 of the date is low and tilted slightly to the left. The digits are closely spaced, especially the 0 and 4. ***Reverse***—The digits in the denominator are widely spaced.

	G-4	VG-8
Variety	$600	$2,500
Normal	$70	$90

1805 — FS-HC-1805-301 (003)

Variety: Date Orientation — Cohen-2
PUP: Date, T of LIBERTY
URS-6 • I-5 • L-5

Description: *Obverse*—This obverse is the same as Cohen-3. There is a small 5 in the date. The T in LIBERTY has no feet. ***Reverse***—There are stems on the reverse. The leaf tip is under the center of the O in OF. (On the more common Stems reverse, this leaf tip is under the right side of the O in OF.)

	G-4	VG-8
Variety	$3,000	$7,000
Normal	$70	$90

1806 — FS-HC-1806-301 (004)

Variety: Date Orientation — Cohen-3
PUP: Date
URS-6 • I-5 • L-5

Description: *Obverse*—The 6 of the date is small and high. The space between the 0 and 6 is equal to the space between the 8 and 0. (On the more common "Small 6 Without Stems" variety, the 0 and 6 are closely spaced.) ***Reverse***—There are stems on the wreath. A few are known with a cud die break on the rim at ICA in AMERICA.

	G-4	VG-8
Variety	$3,000	$7,000
Normal	$70	$90

1808 — FS-HC-1808-301 (005)

VARIETY: Overdate — COHEN-1

PUP: Date

URS-5 • I-5 • L-5

Description: ***Obverse***— This obverse is the same as Cohen-2. This is the Overdate, 8 Over 7. ***Reverse***—The leaf tip is close under the upright of the D in UNITED. (On the common reverse, this leaf tip is distant and left of the upright.) The die is usually cracked through tops of TED and STATES.

	AG-3	G-4
VARIETY	$9,500	$16,500
NORMAL	$35	$75

1809 — FS-HC-1809-301 (006)

VARIETY: Date Orientation — COHEN-1

PUP: Date, T of LIBERTY

URS-8 • I-5 • L-5

Description: ***Obverse***—This obverse is the same as Cohen-2. It has a close, straight date without any digits recut. ***Reverse***—The berry is centered under the upright of the T in UNITED. The tip of the leaf is under the right edge of the second S in STATES. Two are well known for a cud die break joining MERI to the rim above.

	G-4	VG-8
VARIETY	$1,000	$2,000
NORMAL	$55	$65

Large Cents, 1793–1857

A section on large cents first appeared in the second edition of the *Cherrypickers' Guide.* As with the half cent section, the data and photos were provided by J.R. "Bob" Grellman, and have been reviewed and updated by Grellman and other specialists over the years.

As with U.S. half cents, most large cent specialists are already very familiar with these varieties. However, we hope by including them a spark of interest may develop for new collectors.

Unlike for some of the other coin types listed, die varieties are the primary focus for most serious copper specialists. As a result of this interest and demand, some of the rarest varieties will bring huge premiums, often within an hour of their discovery. During an American Numismatic Association convention in Orlando, a rare large-cent variety was spotted and quietly purchased by a knowledgeable collector. The coin was subsequently sold within just an hour for a tidy $12,000—not bad for a $12 purchase!

Note that many of the diagnostics listed for this series are difficult to see except on very high-grade circulated, and/or Mint State, coins.

There are several excellent books highly recommended for further study of the series. A detailed and easy to use reference is *The Die Varieties of U.S. Large Cents, 1840–1857*, by J.R. "Bob" Grellman. The "must have" and the foundation for variety collecting is *Penny Whimsy*, by William H. Sheldon. Originally published in 1958, updated versions are currently available for $60 or less. Other excellent books for the series are also available. The dates covered and authors are noted as follows: for the years 1793 to 1814, *United States Large Cents 1793–1814* (Bill Noyes), *Walter Breen's Encyclopedia of Early United States Cents 1793–1814* (Breen and Mark Borckardt); for the years 1816 to 1839, *United States Large Cents 1816–1839* (Noyes) and *The Cent Book 1816–1839* (John D. Wright). Q. David Bowers's *Guide Book of Half Cents and Large Cents* covers all years of both early copper denominations.

For specialty clubs there is none better than Early American Coppers (EAC). This non-profit group includes the most dedicated numismatists studying the early copper coins of the United States. Founded in 1967, it promotes the advancement and study of U.S. colonial coins, half cents, large cents, and Hard Time tokens. Its quarterly journal, *Penny-Wise*, is an entertaining and well-researched publication. New members are always welcome. More information and a membership application can be obtained at www.eacs.org.

1843 FS-LC-1843-301 (001)

VARIETY: Date Orientation NEWCOMB-17
PUP: Date
URS-8 • I-4 • L-4

Description: ***Obverse***—This is a Head of 1844 variety. The point of the lowest curl is slightly to the right of the inner right curve of the 8 in the date. The 1 is closer to the denticles than to the bust. At least two apparent digits appear in the denticles below the 8 and 4. ***Reverse***—This is the reverse of 1844. There are two points down to the right from the base of the N in ONE; and another up to the left at the same angle from the left top of that N.

	F-12	VF-20
VARIETY	$200	$350
NORMAL	$30	$45

1846 — FS-LC-1846-301 (002)

VARIETY: Date Orientation — NEWCOMB-23

PUP: Date

URS-7 • I-4 • L-4

Description: ***Obverse***—This is a Tall Date coin. There is a horizontal line through center of the 1, strongest on left side of the upright. There are points down from the inner bun, main curl, neck, throat, and jaw (strongest from the main curl). There is a coarse vertical line moving up from between the denticles to the right of the 6 in the date. ***Note:*** This obverse die comes matched with four different reverse dies, two of which resulted in rare pairings. ***Reverse***—There are points down and slightly to the right from ONE and ENT, with some rough lines on the same angle between the N and E of ONE and the N of CENT. There are heavy, rough lines from the denticles to the T in UNITED, the second T in STATES, and the R in AMERICA.

Comments: Three examples are known with a strong rim break over TES.

	F-12	VF-20
VARIETY	$250	$500
NORMAL	$35	$50

1846 — FS-LC-1846-302 (002.5)

Variety: Date Orientation — **Newcomb-25**
PUP: Date
URS-7 • I-4 • L-4

Description: ***Obverse***—This obverse is the same as FS-LC-1846-301 (002). It is a Tall Date coin. There is a horizontal line through the center of the 1, strongest on the left side. There are points down from the inner bun, main curl, neck, throat, and jaw (strongest from the main curl). There is a coarse vertical line moving up from between the denticles to the right of the 6 in the date.
Reverse—Early examples have fine lapping lines, pointing down and very slightly to the right, over most of the die, strongest on the right side. The tops of CE are connected by shallow crumbling, and minor crumbling is visible on the underside of the crossbar on the N in UNITED. There is a strong line from the denticles to the top left of the N in UNITED and a strong, short, dull line up from the top right of the first T in STATES. Another fine line moves down to the right from the denticles and passes into the E of AMERICA; another, wider line, at a different angle, goes from the denticles down to the top of that letter. The denticles below the point of the stem are crumbling at their bases.

	F-12	VF-20
Variety	$400	$800
Normal	$35	$50

1847 — FS-LC-1847-301 (003)

Variety: Date Orientation — **Newcomb-36**
PUP: Date
URS-7 • I-4 • L-4

Description: *Obverse*—The points of the lowest curl are slightly to the left of the right edge of the 8. The field is rough, especially in the area in front of the face, down to the bottom of the neck. Additional roughness is evident in the field from the 18 to star five (strongest around star four). The date is rather weak, especially at the 8 and 4. The top of the 1 does not touch the base. ***Reverse***—There are many points up slightly to the left around ONE CENT; another up from the berry left of the C in CENT. There are additional points down and slightly to the right from ONE CENT (strongest from the right top of N in CENT). The points up from CENT reach nearly halfway up to the bases of ON in ONE. ***Note:*** This reverse die also comes matched to a common obverse on which the 1 touches the bust.

	F-12	VF-20
Variety	$225	$400
Normal	$30	$40

1847 FS-LC-1847-302 (004)

VARIETY: Date Orientation NEWCOMB-43
PUP: Date, reverse
URS-1 • I-5 • L-5

Description: ***Obverse***—The point of the lowest curl is slightly to the right of the inner right curve of the 8 in the date. The base of the 1 is strongly repunched below. ***Note:*** This obverse die also comes mated with a common reverse without the fine lines at NE in ONE. ***Reverse***—Many nearly horizontal lines and points are behind ONE CENT, strongest at NE, with some lines reaching the leaf and berry to the right of the T. A few lines on the same angle connect the wreath to the N and E of UNITED.

	F-12	VF-20
VARIETY	(unique)	
NORMAL	$30	$40

1849 — FS-LC-1849-301 (005)

Variety: Date Orientation — **Newcomb-25**
PUP: Date
URS-4 • I-5 • L-5

Description: *Obverse*—The point of the lowest curl is slightly to the right side of the 8 in the date. Lines point up to the left from the denticles below star 12 to below the date; others point down slightly to the left from the denticles between stars seven and eight; and some weaker ones point down from the denticles right of star 10. There are short spikes to the right from the denticles at stars three, four, five, and six. Fine lines point up and to the right from the inner curl and main curl just below the inner bun. All stars show crumbling or swelling (strongest on the side closest to Miss Liberty). The edge and entire field are wavy and irregular, as if the die was improperly hardened. The denticles are sharp, indicating this is not a worn die. There is a rust lump on the center of Liberty's cheek. ***Reverse***—A rough line points up and to the right from the top of the N in UNITED to the denticles. There are fine lines over AME (nearly horizontal to the top of the M), and lumps on the edges of ONE CENT (strongest on the tops of C and T, very similar to Newcomb-10). The fields are wavy and irregular, similar to the obverse. The field around ERICA, extending to the stem tip, is extremely rough. The reverse die is not double hubbed (as seen on Newcomb-10 and 27).

Comments: Eight examples are known as of this writing.

	F-12	VF-20
Variety	$2,000	$3,000
Normal	$30	$35

1850 FS-LC-1850-301 (005.5)

Variety: Date Orientation Newcomb-24
PUP: Date, reverse
URS-8 • I-3 • L-3

Description: ***Obverse***—The obverse is the same as Newcomb-23. This is an Open 5 coin. The date is now very weak, especially the top right of the 0. There is a curved line under the top right serif of the T. The top points up to the right from the inner curl, seen on Newcomb-18 and 23, are obscured by roughness around the inner curl. There is a small dot near the hair right of the eyebrow; another weaker one left of the Y, almost touching that letter; and one below the eye, even with the front edge of the eyeball. ***Reverse***—There are points up and slightly to the right from ONE and ENT; a few stronger ones point down to the left from the bases of NE. Lines point down to the left inside NE and EN. There is a long, strong, slightly curved line near the denticles over UNI (strongest over the top left of N). There are also other minor lines and points on the U and around the wreath in early die states.

	F-12	VF-20
Variety	$75	$150
Normal	$30	$35

1851 — FS-LC-1851-301 (006)

VARIETY: Date Orientation — NEWCOMB-42
PUP: Date, reverse
URS-1 • I-5 • L-5

Description: ***Obverse***—The point of the lowest curl sits slightly to the right of the inner right curve of the 8 in the date. Three heavy, nearly vertical lines point down from the denticles left of star four. Many lines point down and to the right at different angles over most of the die, strongest from the lowest curl to star thirteen. ***Note:*** This obverse die also comes mated with a common reverse die without the lines from E in ONE. ***Reverse***—Four lines point up and to the left from the top of the E in ONE. There is a short point up from the top left of the E in CENT, and others up and to the right from the top of the ribbon below the EN in CENT. The reverse die is buckled, with wavy fields from improper die preparation.

Comments: This variety is still unique as of this writing. No sales have been reported.

	F-12	VF-20
VARIETY	(unique)	
NORMAL	$30	$35

1851 FS-LC-1851-302 (006.5)

Variety: Date Orientation Newcomb-44
PUP: Date
URS-4 • I-5 • L-5

Description: ***Obverse***—The date is heavily punched into the die, with both 1's repunched several times. The most prominent evidence of repunching is a horizontal dash below the left half of the base of the first 1; two more dashes to the right from its upright; a dash to the left from the bottom of the base of the second 1; and a dash to the left of its upright. There are short points up to the right from the denticles below the 5 and 1. A long, dull vertical line points down from the curls over the space between the 5 and 1; a similar line points up from the denticles to the right of the date. There is a strong point up from the hair on the forehead; and others up from the hair and coronet, below star six. Minor die scratches point up to the right at different angles from the inner curl. The die is sinking, causing the fields to "puff out" slightly, most likely the result of improper die hardening. ***Reverse***—There are fine lines up and to the left on top of the E in ONE; others exist at the same angle from the left at the right of that E. There are short points up from the left top of the E in CENT; others move up from the top of the T in UNITED. There are two points up to the right from the top of the ribbon below the EN in CENT and another point up to the right from the stem close to the top. The die is sinking, causing the fields to "puff out" slightly, most likely the result of improper die hardening.

Comments: Six examples are known as of this writing.

	F-12	VF-20
Variety	$2,500	$5,000
Normal	$30	$35

1856 — FS-LC-1856-301 (007)

Variety: Date Orientation — **Newcomb-22**

PUP: Date

URS-8 • I-3 • L-3

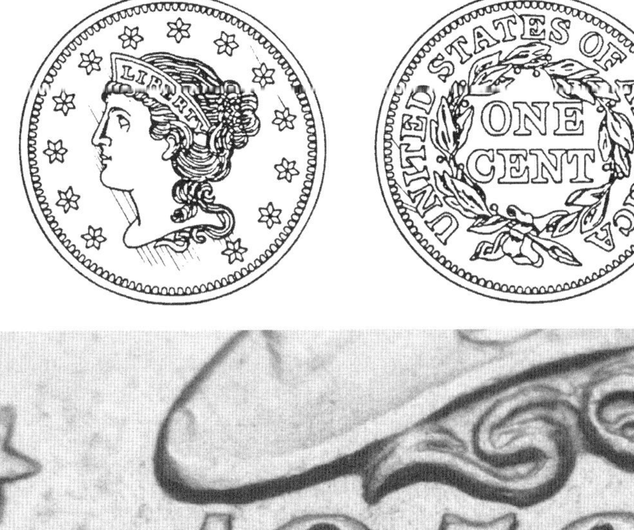

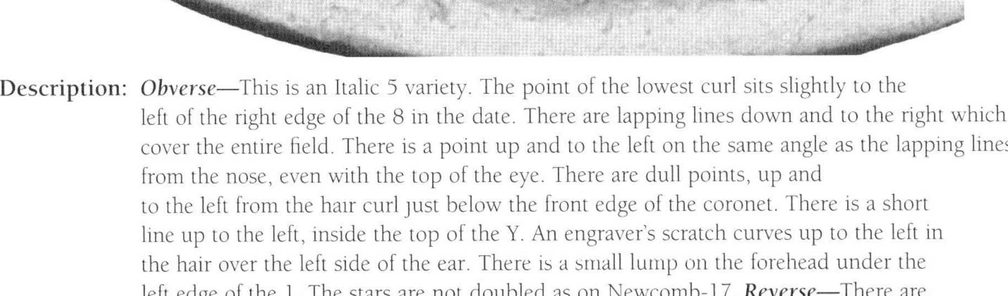

Description: ***Obverse***—This is an Italic 5 variety. The point of the lowest curl sits slightly to the left of the right edge of the 8 in the date. There are lapping lines down and to the right which cover the entire field. There is a point up and to the left on the same angle as the lapping lines from the nose, even with the top of the eye. There are dull points, up and to the left from the hair curl just below the front edge of the coronet. There is a short line up to the left, inside the top of the Y. An engraver's scratch curves up to the left in the hair over the left side of the ear. There is a small lump on the forehead under the left edge of the 1. The stars are not doubled as on Newcomb-17. ***Reverse***—There are lapping lines down and to the right which cover most of the die, strongest at NIT, the E in STATES, and the E in AMERICA.

	F-12	VF-20
Variety	$100	$175
Normal	$30	$35

Flying Eagle Cents, 1856–1858

Although the Flying Eagle series was very short-lived, there are many exciting varieties that can be found within it. Cents of the first year, 1856, were produced in three separate striking periods in both Proof and non-Proof formats. At least five collectible die pairs exist, but these are the realm of specialists and are well detailed in Rick Snow's *Flying Eagle and Indian Cent Attribution Guide,* third edition, 2014.

The varieties of 1857 are varied and numerous. The wrong-denominational die clashes are very popular and are highly sought after. There are numerous doubled dies and repunched dates, as well. The best of these are detailed here in the *Cherrypickers' Guide*; for a complete list of all the varieties known, we again recommend Rick Snow's *Attribution Guide*. Another important collectors' guide is *A Guide Book of Flying Eagle and Indian Head Cents*, also by Snow; this excellent general-purpose reference details the history of the series and features the mainstream varieties. Still other good reference books have been published and are easy to locate through numismatic book and supply dealers.

The 1858 issue is also filled with numerous opportunities for finding exciting varieties. The year is broken down between the Large Letters and Small Letters obverse designs. The Small Letters is a low-relief redesign that was meant to prolong die life. Both the eagle and the letters were changed. The reverse design was also changed, giving collectors the opportunity to cherrypick scarce design combinations. The High Leaves reverse is the design held over from 1857. The Low Leaves reverse is the low-relief redesign. The scarcer design combinations are listed in this edition.

Additional resources are available for series specialists. The Flying Eagle and Indian Cent Collectors Society is a very active club for collectors of these coins. Commonly referred to as the "Fly-In Club," the organization has a Web site at www.fly-inclub.org and publishes an award-winning full-color magazine for collectors, *Longacre's Ledger*.

Also available via the Web is a wiki devoted to these coins, www.indiancent.wikispaces.com. There you will find the latest condition census and sales information for all the varieties listed. Rick Snow maintains the site and all are free to contribute. If you need information that is not presented, you can contact Rick at rick@indiancent.com.

The varieties presented in this edition of *Cherrypickers' Guide* are the best of the best and the list should not be considered complete.

Our thanks go to Rick Snow for his generous and invaluable contributions to this section.

Newly Listed Varieties

Fivaz-Stanton Number	Variety	Page No.
FS-01-1858-901	Low Leaves	25
FS-01-1858-1901	High Leaves	25

1857 — FS-01-1857-101 (002)

VARIETY: Doubled-Die Obverse (DDO-002) — SNOW-4

PUP: Beak, eye, last A of AMERICA, wing tip

URS-9 • I-4 • L-3

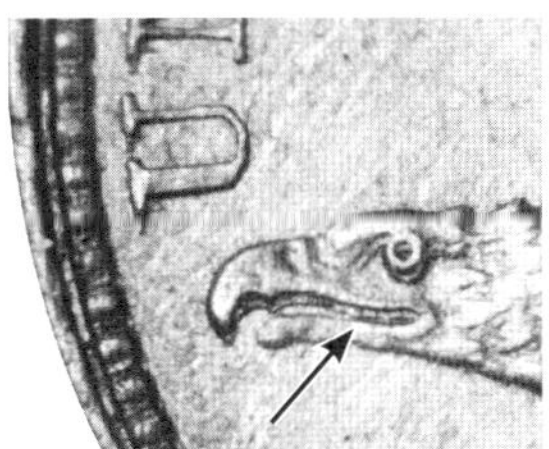

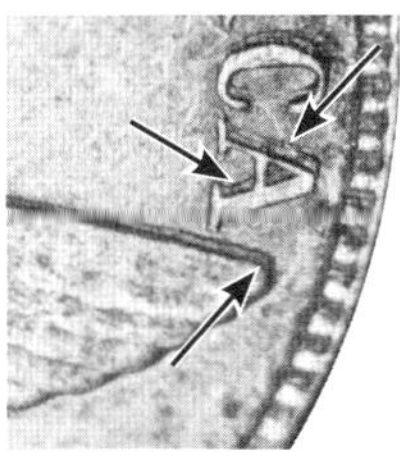

Description: There is doubling on the eagle's beak, eye, and tail feathers, and the letters of UNITED STATES OF AMERICA, with the spread increasing in strength from left to right. The eagle is missing a wing tip. This is a defect on the hub that is found on a few dies.

Comments: FS-105 and 101 are very similar, with 105 having a broken wing tip, while 101 has a missing wing tip.

	EF-40	AU-50	MS-60	MS-63	MS-65
VARIETY	$250	$500	$750	$1,000	$5,000
NORMAL	$150	$225	$380	$900	$4,000

1857 — FS-01-1857-102 (002.3)

VARIETY: Doubled-Die Obverse (DDO-003) — SNOW-15

PUP: Beak, eye, last A of AMERICA, wing tip

URS-8 • I-4 • L-3

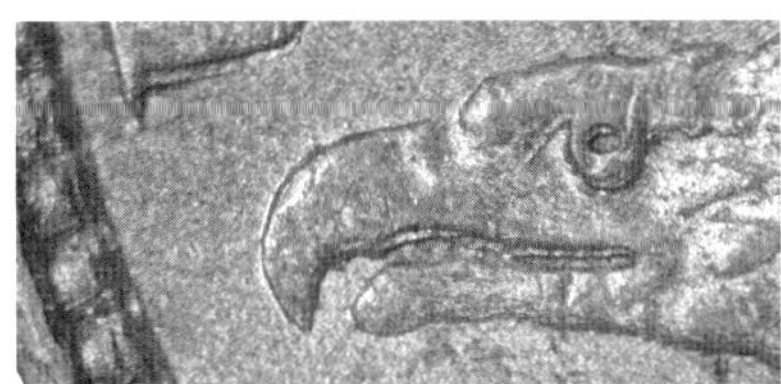

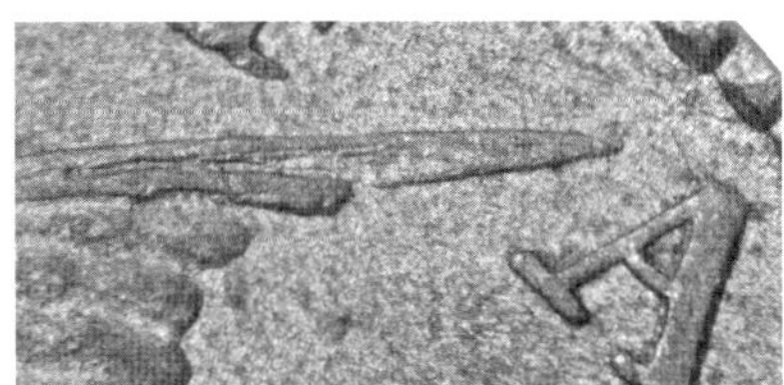

Description: The doubling is evident on the eagle's eye and tail, and UNITED STATES OF AMERICA. Although not as strong as the other two listings, this variety is nonetheless exciting to locate.

Comments: This doubled die is very similar to FS-101 and 105. This one has the missing wing tip corrected by hand engraving of the die.

	EF-40	AU-50	MS-60	MS-63	MS-65
VARIETY	$200	$350	$600	$1,000	$4,300
NORMAL	$150	$225	$380	$900	$4,000

1857 — FS-01-1857-103 (002.7)

Variety: Repunched Date, Doubled-Die Obverse (DDO-006) — Snow-10
PUP: Beak, eye, last A of AMERICA, wing tip
URS-6 • I-4 • L-4

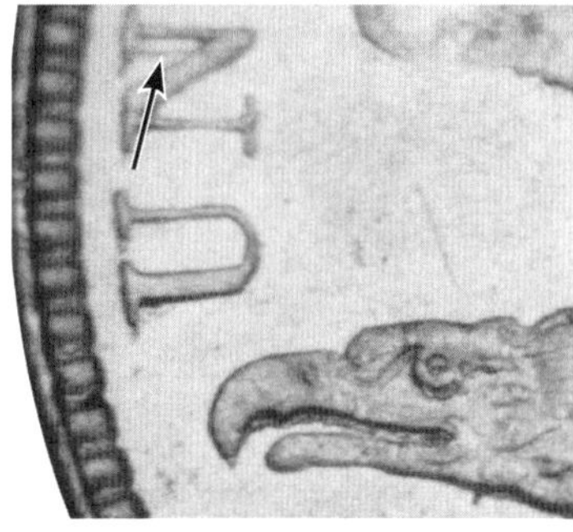

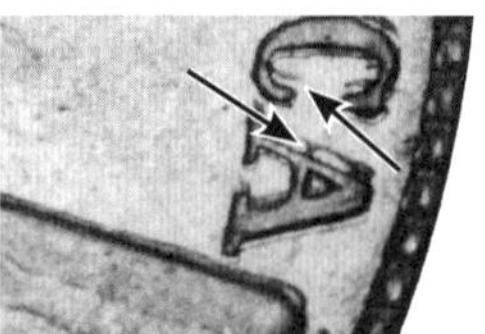

Description: Doubling is evident on UNITED STATES OF AMERICA and the eagle's eye and beak. A bold repunched date is evident as secondary digits below the primary 5 and 7.

Comments: This is similar to many other doubled dies this year, but the repunched date makes it much more desirable! This is unusual, due to the few repunched dates found this year. Late-die-state specimens have a reverse cud from the left leaves to the rim, and are worth an additional premium.

	EF-40	AU-50	MS-60	MS-63	MS-65
Variety	$300	$700	$1,500	$2,500	$6,000
Normal	$150	$225	$380	$900	$4,000

1857 — FS-01-1857-104 (002.8)

Variety: Doubled-Die Obverse (DDO-005) — Snow-5
PUP: Beak, UNITED STATES OF AMERICA
URS-6 • I-4 • L-4

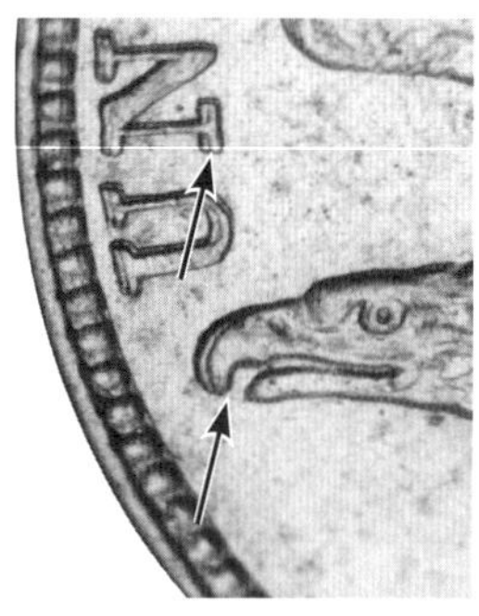

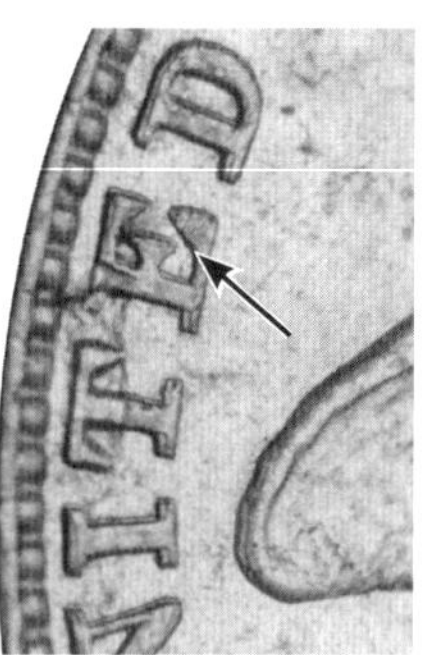

Description: Strong doubling is evident on UNITED STATES OF AMERICA and the eagle's eye, beak, and wing fold. Unlike the previous doubled dies for this date, the doubling on this variety is spread toward the center, away from the rim.

Comments: This doubled die is scarcer than others of the date.

	EF-40	AU-50	MS-60	MS-63	MS-65
Variety	$500	$1,000	$1,250	$2,000	$5,000
Normal	$150	$225	$380	$900	$4,000

1857 FS-01-1857-105 (002)

Variety: Doubled-Die Obverse (DDO-008) Snow-3
PUP: Beak, eye, last A of AMERICA, wing tip
URS-9 • I-4 • L-3

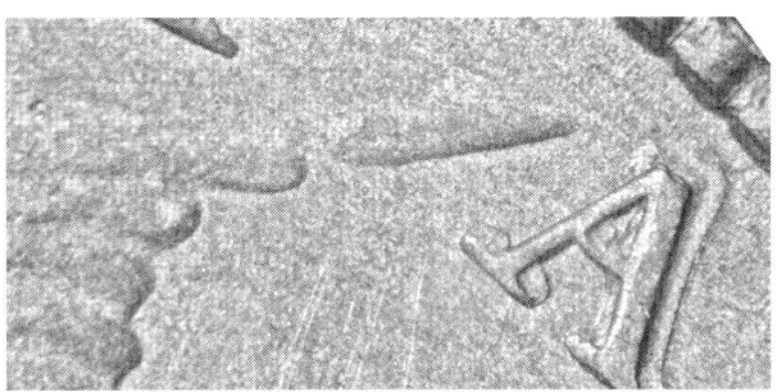

Description: There is doubling on the eagle's beak, eye, and tail feathers, and the letters of UNITED STATES OF AMERICA, with the spread increasing in strength from left to right. The obverse also has a broken wing tip—this is the same hub that produced the 1858, 8 Over 7, FS-301 (Snow-1).

Comments: FS-105 and 101 are very similar, with 105 having a broken wing tip, while 101 has a missing wing tip.

	EF-40	AU-50	MS-60	MS-63	MS-65
Variety	$250	$500	$750	$1,000	$5,000
Normal	$150	$225	$380	$900	$4,000

1857 FS-01-1857-301 (001.5)

Variety: Repunched Date (RPD-003) Snow-11
PUP: Date
URS-6 • I-3 • L-3

Description: The digits from an initial date punch are evident south of the primary digits.

Comments: The weaker or secondary image is usually difficult to observe in specimens below EF-40, primarily due to the weakness of the initial date punch.

	EF-40	AU-50	MS-60	MS-63	MS-65
Variety	$250	$500	$900	$1,800	$5,500
Normal	$150	$225	$380	$900	$4,000

1857 — FS-01-1857-401a (001)

VARIETY: Type of 1856, Repunched Date (RPD-001) — SNOW-1
PUP: Date, letters of UNITED STATES OF AMERICA
URS-10 • I-5 • L-5

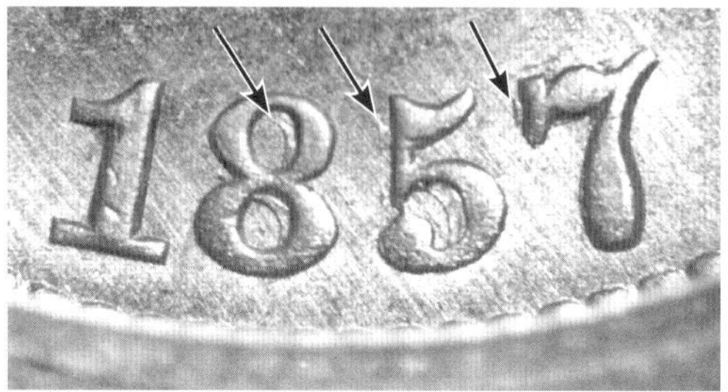

Description: Early die states show repunching on all of the digits in the date. Later die states show repunching only on the 8 and 5. The obverse lettering (UNITED STATES OF AMERICA) of this variety is the same as that on the 1856 pattern cent. The opening of the letter O in OF is rectangular instead of round or oval, the serifs in the letters E and F are longer than on other 1857's, and the lower center point of the M is almost bulbous.

Comments: The early-die-state pieces are prooflike. An MS-66 prooflike example sold for $40,000 in 2007. At least five other obverse dies were made using the hub of 1856 (see next listing).

	EF-40	AU-50	MS-60	MS-63	MS-65
VARIETY	$400	$900	$1,500	$4,000	$15,000
NORMAL	$150	$225	$380	$900	$4,000

1857 — FS-01-1857-401b (001)

VARIETY: Type of 1856 — SNOW-2
PUP: Letters of UNITED STATES OF AMERICA
URS-12 • I-5 • L-5

Description: The obverse lettering (UNITED STATES OF AMERICA) of this variety is the same as that on the 1856 pattern cent. The opening of the letter O in OF is rectangular instead of round or oval, the serifs in the letters E and F are longer than on other 1857's, and the lower center point of the M is almost bulbous.

Comments: At least five obverse dies were made using the hub of 1856. It is believed by Flying Eagle researcher Richard Snow that these dies were made at the same time as the other 1856 obverse dies, but were left undated until 1857.

	EF-40	AU-50	MS-60	MS-63	MS-65
VARIETY	$250	$500	$900	$1,500	$4,500
NORMAL	$150	$225	$380	$900	$4,000

1857 — FS-01-1857-402 (003)

VARIETY: Obverse Clashed Die (with Liberty Seated 50¢) — CONECA: WDC-003, SNOW-9

PUP: Apparent retained cud through AMERICA

URS-12 • I-5 • L-5

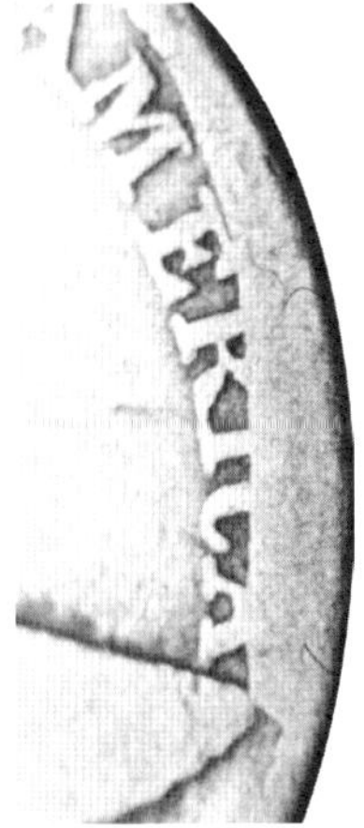

Description: The obverse die of this 1857 Flying Eagle cent was clashed with the obverse die of a Liberty Seated half dollar. The clash is most evident through the word AMERICA.

Comments: Die researcher Chris Pilliod discovered that these clashes were probably caused while the dies in the press were being changed from half dollars to cents. In the process, the press was cycled through once and clashed the half dollar obverse die with the cent obverse die. Why are the dies head-to-head? Chris has shown through die cud research that the Flying Eagle dies were installed in the press with the obverse die in the anvil (lower) position, while Liberty Seated half dollars had their obverse die in the hammer (upper) position.

	EF-40	AU-50	MS-60	MS-63	MS-65
VARIETY	$250	$600	$1,200	$1,750	$6,000
NORMAL	$150	$225	$380	$900	$4,000

1857 — FS-01-1857-403 (004)

Variety: Obverse Clashed Die (with Liberty Head $20) — **CONECA:** WDC-001, Snow-7

PUP: Profile of Liberty of the obverse right side

URS-7 • I-5 • L-5

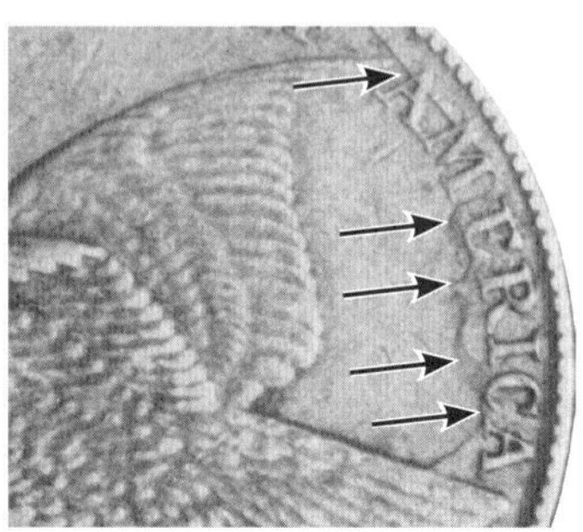

Description: The obverse die of this 1857 Flying Eagle cent was clashed with the obverse die of a Liberty Head double eagle.

Comments: No Mint State specimens of this variety are known as of 2015. These were caused the same way the half dollar clash of 1857 occurred. Many collectors actively search for the three multi-denominational die clashes of the 1857 cents. An AU-58 example sold for $15,000 in 2003. (See also FS-402 and 901.)

	EF-40	AU-50	MS-60	MS-63	MS-65
Variety	$6,000	$8,000			
Normal	$150	$225	$380	$900	$4,000

1857 — FS-01-1857-901 (005)

Variety: Reverse Clashed Die (with Liberty Seated 25¢) — **CONECA:** WDC-002, Snow-8

PUP: Field on reverse above ONE

URS-9 • I-5 • L-5

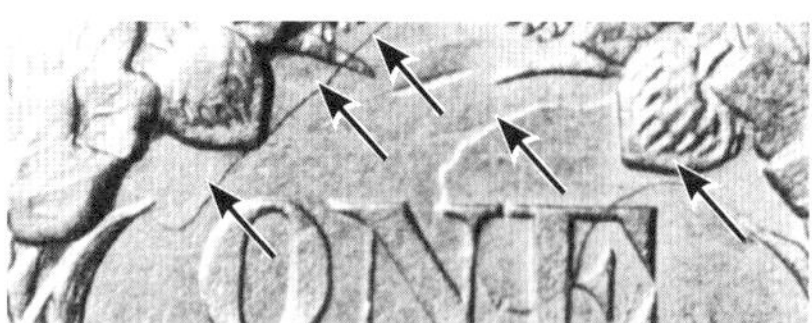

Description: The reverse die of this 1857 Flying Eagle cent was clashed with the reverse die of a Liberty Seated quarter. The outline of the eagle's head is evident above the word ONE on the reverse.

Comments: Like FS-402 and 403, Chris Pilliod theorized that these clashes were probably caused during the die change from cents to quarter dollars. In this case, the Flying Eagle dies were installed in the press with the reverse die in the hammer position, while Liberty Seated quarter dollars had their reverse die in the anvil position in the press. The matching 1857 quarter with the reverse cent clash exists and is a very popular addition to the cent clash set. An MS-64 example of this coin sold for $12,500 in 2007.

	EF-40	AU-50	MS-60	MS-63	MS-65
Variety	$750	$1,000	$2,000	$3,000	$15,000
Normal	$150	$225	$380	$900	$4,000

1858, Large Letters — FS-01-1858-101 (005.5)

VARIETY: Doubled-Die Obverse (DDO-002) SNOW-2
PUP: AMERICA
URS-7 • I-4 • L-3

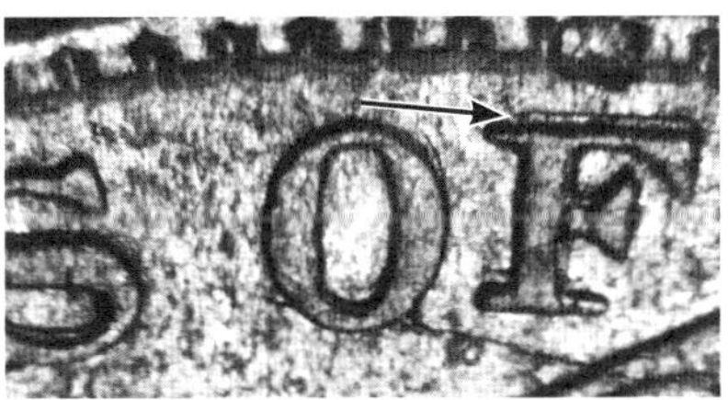

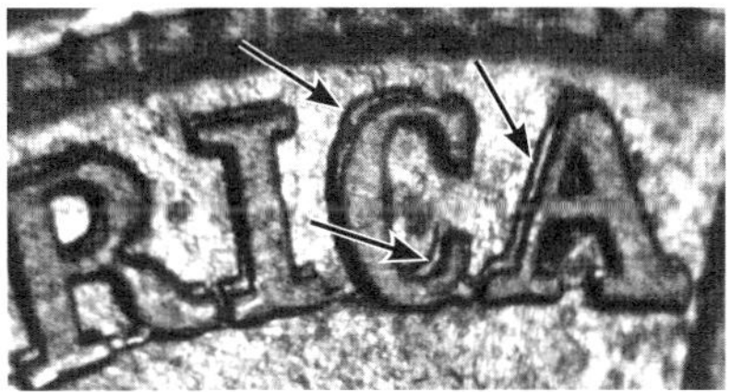

Description: The doubling is evident on UNITED STATES OF AMERICA, with increasing strength of spread from left to right.

Comments: This doubled die is rarely encountered. The interest and liquidity might actually be higher than stated. These have been under-appreciated, as previous sales have not been at large premiums.

	EF-40	AU-50	MS-60	MS-63	MS-65
VARIETY	$400	$550	$750	$1,500	$4,500
NORMAL	$150	$225	$375	$900	$4,000

1858, Large Letters — FS-01-1858-301 (006)

VARIETY: Overdate (RPD-001) SNOW-1
PUP: Date
URS-10 • I-5 • L-5

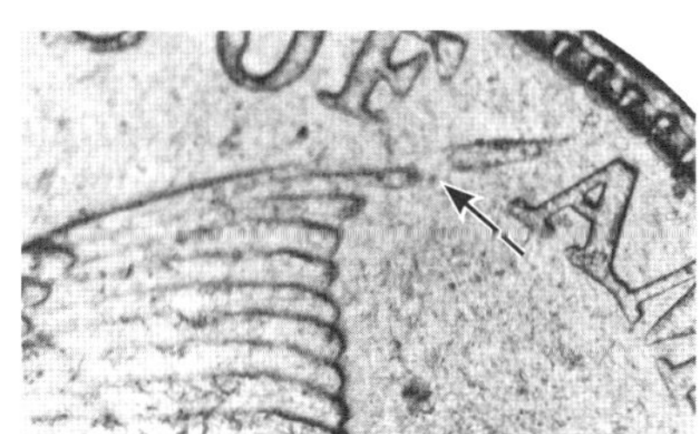

Description: The last 8 was punched over a 7. It is not known at this time whether a four-digit logo punch was used, or a three-digit logo punch in addition to a single-digit punch. The flag of the upper right corner of a 7 can be seen above the second 8. There is a raised triangular-shaped dot in the field above the first 8. This die marker is the only confirming diagnostic. A secondary diagnostic for this variety is the "broken" right wing of the eagle. However, this diagnostic is also known for dies without the overdate, including other 1857's. The flag of the 7 may not be evident on later-die-state specimens, but the raised dot above the first 8 is virtually always visible.

Comments: Some specialists believe the triangular dot in the field is the remaining portion of an errantly punched 1. There is always weakness on the upper right area of the wreath on the reverse. An early-die-state MS-65 specimen sold for $130,000 in 2015. Note that late-die-state specimens are always considered much less valuable than earlier die states. A major third-party grading service is identifying early-die-state coins as "strong" and late-die-state coins as "weak."

	F-12	VF-20	EF-40	AU-50	MS-60	MS-63	MS-65
VARIETY	$500	$900	$1,500	$2,500	$5,000	$12,000	$100,000+
LATE DIE STATE	$100	$150	$250	$400	$700	$1,000	$5,500
NORMAL	$50	$60	$150	$225	$375	$900	$4,000

1858, Large Letters — FS-01-1858-302 (006.1)

Variety: Overdate, Doubled-Die Obverse (DDO-007) — Snow-7
PUP: Date, UNITED
URS-5 • I-5 • L-5

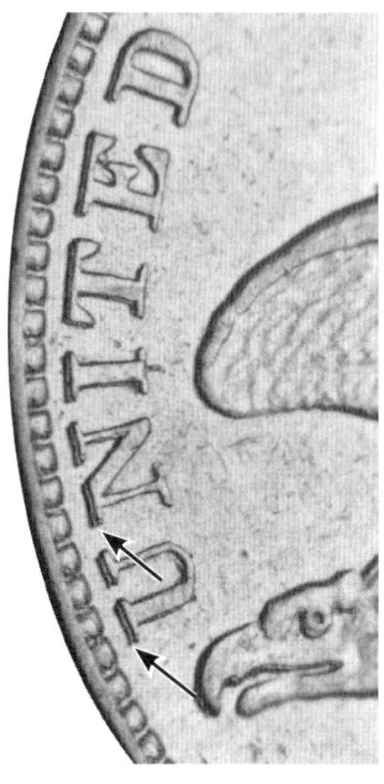

Description: This overdate is likely the result of two differently dated logo punches: the first an 1857-dated punch and the second and primary date 1858. The flag of the upper right of a 7 is evident outside the top right of the second 8, and the flag of a secondary 1 is evident just left of the primary 1. Unlike FS-301, this variety is not found in various die states. However, the overdate is rather light and difficult to spot without knowing what to look for. This overdate also exhibits a strong Class II doubled die, evident on UNITED STATES OF AMERICA.

Comments: This variety is much rarer than FS-301, but much less known. It was discovered by Mark McWherter. The lightness of the overdate and difficulty in detection present a great cherrypicking opportunity.

	F-12	VF-20	EF-40	AU-50	MS-60	MS-63	MS-65
Variety	$300	$500	$1,000	$2,000	$4,500	$7,500	$25,000
Normal	$50	$60	$150	$225	$375	$900	$4,000

1858, Large Letters — FS-01-1858-901

VARIETY: Low Leaves

PUP: Leaves inside wreath on reverse at C and T of CENT

URS-16 • I-4 • L-4

Description: The wreath is a low-relief design with many elements that are slightly different from the design carried over from 1857. The easiest design difference to notice are the short leaves by the C and T of CENT. The tips of these leaves end below the base of the letters.

Comments: The 1858, Large Letters, are typically found paired with the High Leaves reverse. Four design combinations exist for this year—Large Letters with High Leaves and Low Leaves reverses and Small Letters with High Leaves and Low Leaves reverses.

	EF-40	AU-50	MS-60	MS-63	MS-65
VARIETY	$200	$400	$700	$1,000	$4,250
NORMAL	$150	$225	$375	$900	$4,000

1858, Small Letters — FS-01-1858-1901

VARIETY: High Leaves

PUP: Leaves inside wreath on reverse at C and T of CENT

URS-16 • I-4 • L-4

Description: The wreath is a high-relief design carried over from 1857. The easiest design difference to notice are the long leaves by the C and T of CENT. The tips of these leaves end above the base of the letters.

Comments: The 1858, Small Letters, are typically found paired with the Low Leaves reverse. Four design combinations exist for this year—Large Letters with High Leaves and Low Leaves reverses and Small Letters with High Leaves and Low Leaves reverses.

	EF-40	AU-50	MS-60	MS-63	MS-65
VARIETY	$200	$400	$700	$1,000	$4,500
NORMAL	$150	$225	$400	$950	$4,000

Indian Head Cents, 1859–1909

Indian Head cent varieties are one of the most actively collected series in numismatics. Primarily through the efforts of Rick Snow, including his books and the club he co-founded, The Fly-In Club, the series is well researched and has a very strong following. Almost every year of production has interesting repunched dates, doubled dies, misplaced digits, and other types of strange and interesting varieties.

Indian Head cents will always be tied to the Flying Eagle cent series, due in part to the fact that they were the first two small-cent types and were each designed by James B. Longacre. There are several excellent references for these series, most notably by Rick Snow. The first is *The Flying Eagle & Indian Cent Attribution Guide,* third edition, 2014. This 900-page, two-volume opus covers everything about these series that is known. Every premium-value variety is listed with large images and detailed descriptions. Another resource, also by Snow, is *A Guide Book of Flying Eagle and Indian Cents*. This is part of Whitman Publishing's "Bowers Series" and gives readers a detailed history and date-by-date collecting guide to these series. The basic well-known varieties are listed in this book.

Additional resources are available for series specialists. The Flying Eagle and Indian Cent Collectors Society is a very active club for collectors of these coins. Commonly referred to as the "Fly-In Club," the organization has a Web site at www.fly-inclub.org. It publishes an award-winning magazine for collectors, *Longacre's Ledger*.

Also available online is a wiki devoted to these coins, www.indiancent.wikispaces.com. There you will find the latest condition census and sales information for all the varieties listed. Rick Snow maintains the site and all are welcome to participate. If you need information that is not presented, you can contact Rick at rick@indiancent.com.

Our thanks go to Rick Snow for his generous and invaluable contributions to this section.

Newly Listed Varieties

Fivaz-Stanton Number	Variety	Page No.	Fivaz-Stanton Number	Variety	Page No.
FS-01-1862-802	DDR	30	FS-01-1871-301	MPD	54
FS-01-1864-1401	Lathe Lines	34	FS-01-1873-1302	MPD	58
FS-01-1867-303	RPD	45	FS-01-1882-301	Broken 2	63
FS-01-1868-302/901	RPD / Die Gouge	48	FS-01-1883-404	Misaligned Die Clash	65
FS-01-1869-303	RPD	50	FS-01-1889-302	RPD / MPD	70
FS-01-1870-303	Die Gouge ("Pick-Axe")	53	FS-01-1889-901	Misaligned Die Clash	72

Fivaz-Stanton Number	Variety	Page No.
FS-01-1890-901	Misaligned Die Clash	74
FS-01-1895-303	RPD	79
FS-01-1896-302	Date Variety	80
FS-01-1907-304	RPD	92

Varieties to be Delisted

Fivaz-Stanton Number	Variety	Page No.
FS-01-1888-305	MPD	69
FS-01-1890-302	MPD	73

1859 — FS-01-1859-301 (006.3)

Variety: Repunched Date (RPD-001) — Snow-1
PUP: Date
URS-7 • I-5 • L-4

Description: This is a strong repunched date, with all secondary digits evident to the southwest of the primary digits. The flag of a secondary 1 is quite evident below the flag of the primary 1.

Comments: This repunched date is considered to be rarer than the next listing, and due to the spread of the secondary digits should be considered worth a great premium.

	EF-40	AU-50	MS-60	MS-63	MS-65
Variety	$800	$1,250	$2,000	$4,000	$10,000
Normal	$110	$200	$285	$600	$3,500

1859 FS-01-1859-302 (006.2)

Variety: Repunched Date (RPD-002) Snow-2
PUP: Date
URS-8 • I-4 • L-4

Description: This repunched date is evident with a secondary digit to the south on the 1 and 8, and very slightly on the 5.

Comments: Any repunched date on an 1859 cent is generally considered very scarce to rare and is usually in reasonably high demand.

	EF-40	AU-50	MS-60	MS-63	MS-65
Variety	$165	$300	$500	$1,750	$5,000
Normal	$110	$200	$285	$600	$3,500

1859 FS-01-1859-303 (006.35)

Variety: Repunched Date (RPD-003) Snow-3
PUP: Date
URS-7 • I-3 • L-3

Description: This repunched date is evident with secondary digits to the south of the 1 and very slightly on the 8. Minor repunching is also visible north above the 5 and in the upper loop of the 9.

Comments: This particular repunched date is not as valuable, nor in such high demand, as the previous two listings, but it is scarcer.

	EF-40	AU-50	MS-60	MS-63	MS-65
Variety	$250	$350	$750	$1,200	$4,000
Normal	$110	$200	$285	$600	$3,500

1860 FS-01-1860-401 (006.4)

VARIETY: Transitional
PUP: Point of bust
URS-13 • I-4 • L-4

Description: This extremely important transitional obverse is evident from the pointed bust, typical of those dies of 1859. The bust of 1860 has a more rounded point than that of 1859. This is sometimes labeled as Type 1 (T1).

Comments: There are at last count six minutely different dies comprising this variety. It is getting more accepted as a regular member of the basic Indian Head cent collection. Presently it is priced similarly to the 1859, but it is much scarcer. A repunched date variety is known, with minute repunching on the 1 (Snow-T1-1).

	EF-40	AU-50	MS-60	MS-63	MS-65
VARIETY	$100	$200	$300	$750	$5,500
NORMAL	$65	$100	$185	$250	$1,200

1861 FS-01-1861-301 (006.45)

VARIETY: Repunched Date (RPD-001) SNOW-1
PUP: Date
URS-7 • I-3 • L-3

Description: This repunched date is evident with the second 1 having a weaker secondary digit slightly to the south of the primary 1.

Comments: This variety is quite scarce. Very few sales are noted.

	EF-40	AU-50	MS-60	MS-63	MS-65
VARIETY	$200	$300	$400	$900	$3,000
NORMAL	$110	$175	$225	$325	$1,100

1862 — FS-01-1862-301

Variety: Misplaced Date (MPD-002) Snow-2
PUP: Denticles below date
URS-4 • I-3 • L-3

Description: This misplaced date exhibits the remnants of two digits protruding from the denticles below the date.

Comments: This variety is relatively new and very few have been located.

	VF-20	EF-40	AU-50	MS-60	MS-63	MS-65
Variety	$40	$70	$100	$125	$500	$1,200
Normal	$30	$50	$75	$110	$200	$1,000

1862 — FS-01-1862-801, 802

Variety: Doubled-Die Reverse (DDR-001) Snow-5, Snow-6
PUP: Arrow shafts, ribbon knot
URS-3 • I-3 • L-3

Description: FS-801 is a very bold doubled die, with doubling on the arrow shafts. FS-802 can be identified by bold doubling primarily on the wreath knot.

Comments: Both of these varieties are presently very rare. An example of FS-802 was cherrypicked from the famed Eric Newman collection. As more collectors turn over their coins, perhaps more will show up.

	VF-20	EF-40	AU-50	MS-60	MS-63	MS-65
Variety, FS-801	$300	$500	$800	$1,250	$3,000	
Variety, FS-802	$750	$1,250	$2,000			
Normal	$30	$50	$75	$110	$200	$1,000

1863 — FS-01-1863-301

Variety: Repunched Date (RPD-002) — Snow-2
PUP: Date
URS-6 • I-3 • L-3

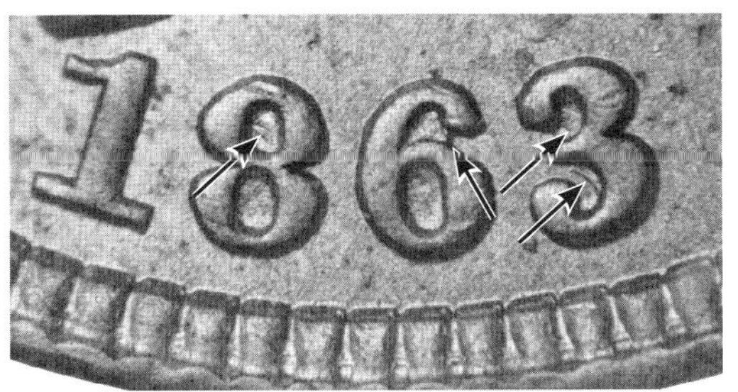

Description: Secondary digits are evident to the south on the last three digits. The secondary 8 is apparent within the upper loop of the primary 8, a secondary 6 within the upper loop of the 6, and the secondary 3 within both loops of the 3. Some collectors may feel this is an overdate (3 Over 2), but the curve within the primary 3 too closely matches that of a 3.

Comments: This variety is very scarce.

	VF-20	EF-40	AU-50	MS-60	MS-63	MS-65
Variety	$50	$75	$150	$200	$500	$2,000
Normal	$30	$50	$75	$110	$200	$1,000

1863 — FS-01-1863-302

Variety: Misplaced Date — Snow-20
PUP: Neck at necklace
URS-4 • I-3 • L-3

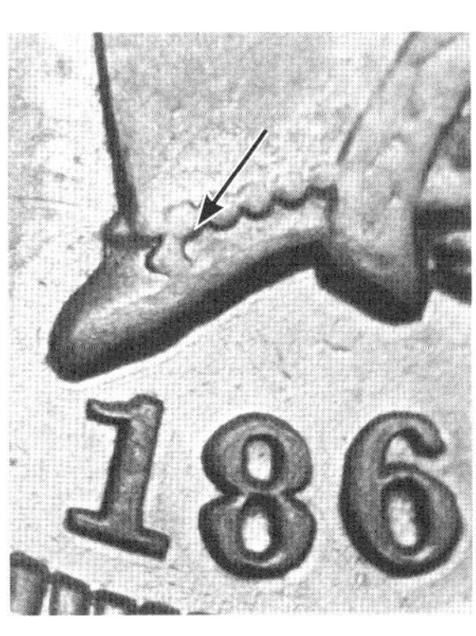

Description: A portion of a digit (likely a 1) is evident by the front of the neck at the necklace.

	VF-20	EF-40	AU-50	MS-60	MS-63	MS-65
Variety	$75	$150	$175	$250	$500	$1,250
Normal	$30	$50	$75	$110	$200	$1,000

1863 FS-01-1863-801 (006.46)

Variety: Doubled-Die Reverse (DDR-001) Snow-10
PUP: Right leaves
URS-3 • I-3 • L-4

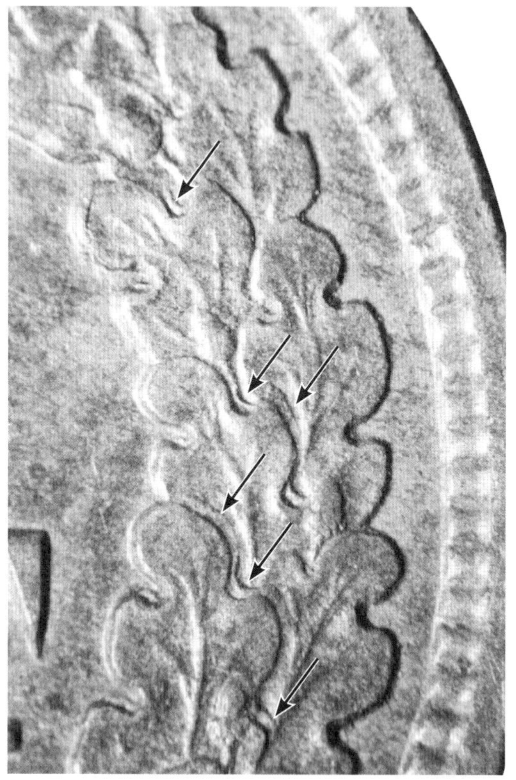

Description: Strong doubling is evident on the right leaves of the wreath and to a lesser degree on the upper left leaves.

Comments: Discovered in 1999 (by Mike Ellis), this variety remains very scarce.

	EF-40	AU-50	MS-60	MS-63	MS-65
Variety	$250	$500	$750	$1,000	$3,000
Normal	$50	$75	$110	$200	$1,000

1864, Copper-Nickel — FS-01-1864-401

VARIETY: Die File Marks — SNOW-5

PUP: Ear

URS-8 • I-2 • L-2

Description: Strong die file marks are evident above and through the ear.

Comments: This variety's true rarity is unknown, and its value remains very subjective. Eventually its popularity may wane.

	VF-20	EF-40	AU-50	MS-60	MS-63	MS-65
VARIETY	*$65*	*$125*	*$175*	*$250*	*$400*	*$1,800*
NORMAL	$55	$100	$150	$200	$325	$1,600

1864, Bronze — FS-01-1864-1101 (006.47)

VARIETY: Doubled-Die Obverse, Repunched Date (DDO-001, RPD-004) — SNOW-4

PUP: LIBERTY

URS-6 • I-4 • L-4

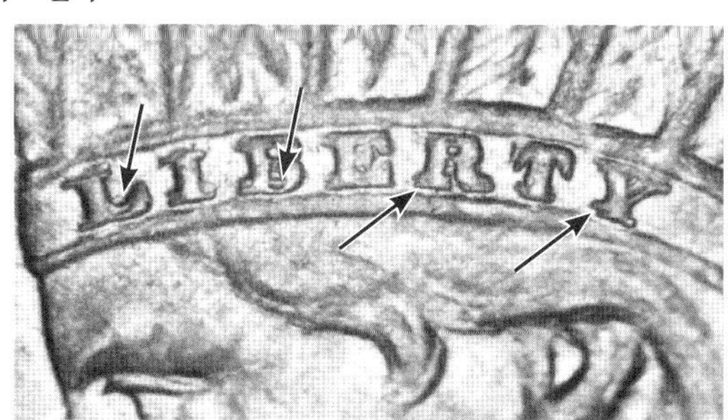

Description: Strong doubling is evident on LIBERTY and portions of the hair and headdress. There is repunching on the 4.

Comments: This is an 1864 Bronze, No L, cent. The variety was first reported by Bob Stimax in 1993. It is very scarce and desirable. Most examples are rather mushy, possibly due to improper hardening of the dies. Early die states are rare.

	VF-20	EF-40	AU-50	MS-60	MS-63	MS-65
VARIETY	$250	$400	$500	$1,250	$2,500	$6,000
NORMAL	$45	$70	$90	$115	$150	$400

Note: Values listed for MS-60 and higher are for RB (red and brown) specimens. Full red Uncirculated specimens command higher prices.

1864, Bronze — FS-01-1864-1301 (006.48)

Variety: Repunched Date (RPD-002) — Snow-2
PUP: Date
URS-10 • I-3 • L-3

Description: Secondary digits of the 8, 6, and 4 are evident to the south of the primary digits.

Comments: This is not as strong as some other repunched dates for this date. Many 1864, No L dies, (both copper-nickel and bronze) show apparent repunching on the 4. This is due to a defect on the digit punch.

	VF-20	EF-40	AU-50	MS-60	MS-63	MS-65
Variety	$50	$75	$100	$150	$250	$450
Normal	$45	$70	$90	$115	$150	$400

Note: Values listed for MS-60 and higher are for RB (red and brown) specimens. Full red Uncirculated specimens command higher prices.

1864 Bronze — FS-01-1864-1401

Variety: Lathe Lines — Snow-11
PUP: Portrait
URS-8 • I-3 • L-3

Description: Concentric circular raised lines are seen on the portrait of Miss Liberty. These are believed by Rick Snow to have been lathe lines on the blank die that were pushed farther into the die when the design was hubbed (sunk into) the die.

Comments: This is an interesting and unusual class of die variety. Later die states show the lines weaker.

	VF-20	EF-40	AU-50	MS-60	MS-63	MS-65
Variety	$50	$100	$175	$250	$300	$500
Normal	$45	$70	$90	$115	$150	$400

Note: Values listed for MS-60 and higher are for RB (red and brown) specimens. Full red Uncirculated specimens command higher prices.

1864, With L — FS-01-1864-2301 (006.7)

VARIETY: Repunched Date (RPD-003) SNOW-1
PUP: Date
URS-6 • I-4 • L-4

Description: The strongly repunched date, evident to the southeast, is possibly a tripled date. Secondary digits are most evident below the primary 1 and 8.

Comments: The savvy collector will look at all 1864-dated cents; there are numerous repunched dates.

	VF-20	EF-40	AU-50	MS-60	MS-63	MS-65
VARIETY	$250	$400	$500	$750	$1,250	$2,000
NORMAL	$200	$275	$350	$450	$600	$1,800

Note: Values listed for MS-60 and higher are for RB (red and brown) specimens. Full red Uncirculated specimens command higher prices.

1864, With L — FS-01-1864-2302 (006.71)

VARIETY: Repunched Date (RPD-003) SNOW-3
PUP: Date
URS-6 • I-4 • L-4

Description: Secondary images of the 1, 8, and 6 are evident to the northwest of the primary digits.

Comments: There is likely a digit in the denticles immediately below the 8, too.

	VF-20	EF-40	AU-50	MS-60	MS-63	MS-65
VARIETY	$250	$300	$400	$500	$750	$1,950
NORMAL	$200	$275	$350	$450	$600	$1,800

Note: Values listed for MS-60 and higher are for RB (red and brown) specimens. Full red Uncirculated specimens command higher prices.

1864, With L — FS-01-1864-2303 (006.72)

Variety: Repunched Date (RPD-004) — Snow-4
PUP: Date
URS-6 • I-4 • L-4

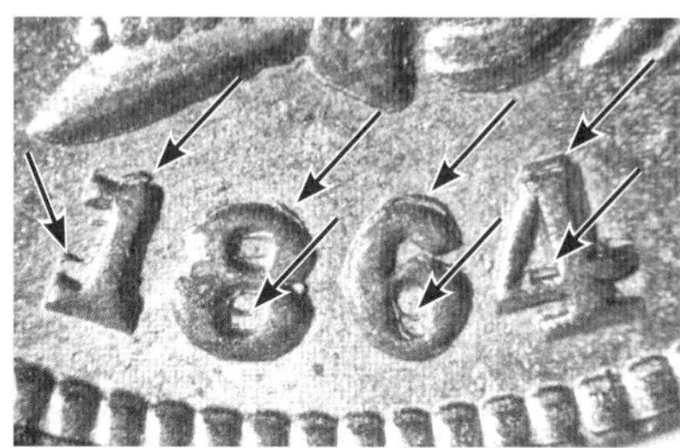

Description: Secondary digits are evident to the north on all four digits.

Comments: This is one of the more popular repunched dates for this date.

	VF-20	EF-40	AU-50	MS-60	MS-63	MS-65
Variety	$300	$300	$400	$500	$750	$2,200
Normal	$200	$275	$350	$450	$600	$1,800

Note: Values listed for MS-60 and higher are for RB (red and brown) specimens. Full red Uncirculated specimens command higher prices.

1864, With L — FS-01-1864-2304 (006.5, 006.55)

Variety: Repunched Date — Snow-5
PUP: Date
URS-10 • I-3 • L-3

Description: Secondary digits on the 1 and 8 are evident slightly to the north of the primary digits. The 1 is actually tripled, with yet another secondary digit evident slightly to the south of the primary.

Comments: This variety was at one time considered to be a "With L" type over a "Without L" type, but that is no longer considered plausible.

	VF-20	EF-40	AU-50	MS-60	MS-63	MS-65
Variety	$300	$400	$500	$600	$750	$2,200
Normal	$200	$275	$350	$450	$600	$1,800

Note: Values listed for MS-60 and higher are for RB (red and brown) specimens. Full red Uncirculated specimens command higher prices.

1864, With L — FS-01-1864-2305

VARIETY: Repunched Date (RPD-002) — SNOW-2
PUP: Date
URS-6 • I-4 • L-4

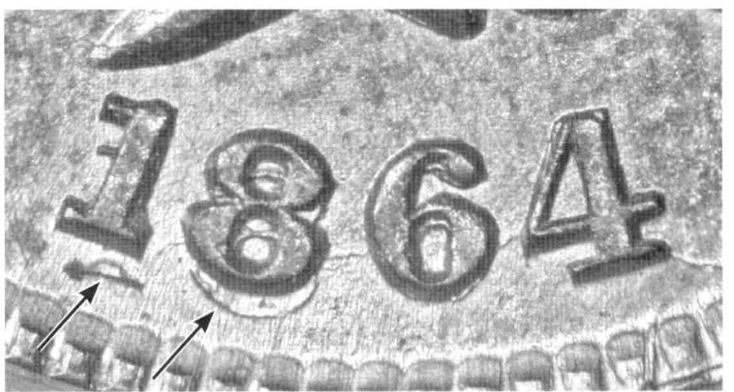

Description: The strongly repunched date, evident to the southwest, is possibly a tripled date. Secondary digits are most evident below the primary 1 and 8.

Comments: This variety is very similar to FS-2301.

	VF-20	EF-40	AU-50	MS-60	MS-63	MS-65
VARIETY	$250	$350	$450	$600	$1,000	
NORMAL	$200	$275	$350	$450	$600	$1,800

Note: Values listed for MS-60 and higher are for RB (red and brown) specimens. Full red Uncirculated specimens command higher prices.

1864, With L — FS-01-1864-2306 (006.73)

VARIETY: Repunched Date (RPD-009) — SNOW-10
PUP: Date
URS-10 • I-3 • L-3

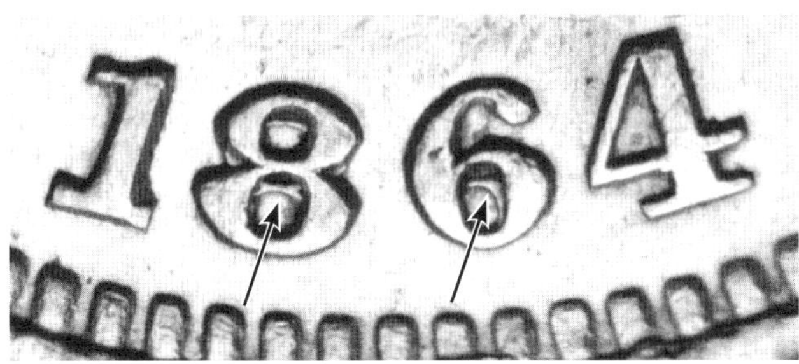

Description: Secondary digits are evident to the south of the primary date, but primarily within the lower loops of the 8 and the 6.

Comments: There are several other repunched dates for this date, known on copper-nickel, bronze, and "With L" types.

	VF-20	EF-40	AU-50	MS-60	MS-63	MS-65
VARIETY	$250	$350	$500	$600	$750	$2,000
NORMAL	$200	$275	$350	$450	$600	$1,800

Note: Values listed for MS-60 and higher are for RB (red and brown) specimens. Full red Uncirculated specimens command higher prices.

1865, Plain 5 FS-01-1865-301 (007.4)

VARIETY: Repunched Date (RPD-001) SNOW-1
PUP: Date
URS-7 • I-3 • L-3

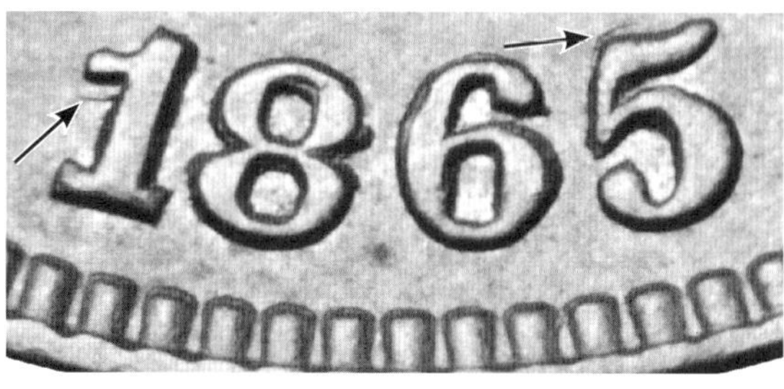

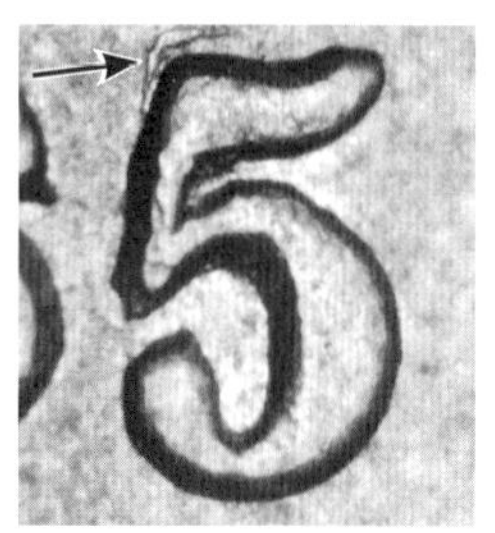

Description: Remnants of secondary digits are evident to the south on the 1 and 8, and to the north on the 5.

Comments: This variety was once considered to be a 5 Over 4 overdate. However, during an Atlanta coin show in the mid-1990s, J.T. Stanton realized this is possibly a Plain 5 Over Fancy 5 variety. This die is found on some copper-nickel pattern strikes (see J-406 in ***United States Pattern Coins***).

	VF-20	EF-40	AU-50	MS-60	MS-63	MS-65
VARIETY	$75	$100	$200	$500	$750	$1,700
NORMAL	$30	$45	$65	$90	$150	$600

Note: Values listed for MS-60 and higher are for RB (red and brown) specimens. Full red Uncirculated specimens command higher prices.

1865, Plain 5 FS-01-1865-302 (007.45)

VARIETY: Repunched Date SNOW-4
PUP: Date
URS-9 • I-3 • L-3

Description: Secondary digits are evident to the north of the 1 and 8, and very slightly within the upper loop of the 6.

Comments: This variety is primarily of interest to variety specialists and Indian Head cent collectors. On late-die-state pieces, a large cud forms above the shield. These are worth a significant premium.

	VF-20	EF-40	AU-50	MS-60	MS-63	MS-65
VARIETY	$40	$75	$100	$200	$250	$750
NORMAL	$30	$45	$65	$90	$150	$600

Note: Values listed for MS-60 and higher are for RB (red and brown) specimens. Full red Uncirculated specimens command higher prices.

1865, Plain 5 — FS-01-1865-303 (007.5)

VARIETY: Repunched Date (RPD-003) — SNOW-3

PUP: Date

URS-7 • I-4 • L-3

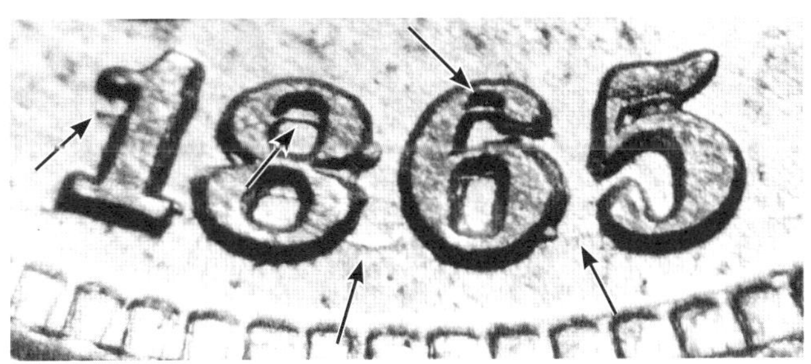

Description: Secondary digits are evident to the south of the 1, 8, and 6, with evidence of a secondary digit on the 5.

Comments: There are some slightly curved lines between the 8 and 6. These are widely repunched digits with the base of either the 8 or 6 showing.

	VF-20	EF-40	AU-50	MS-60	MS-63	MS-65
VARIETY	$100	$150	$200	$400	$650	$1,500
NORMAL	$30	$45	$65	$90	$150	$600

Note: Values listed for MS-60 and higher are for RB (red and brown) specimens. Full red Uncirculated specimens command higher prices.

1865, Plain 5 — FS-01-1865-304 (007.56)

VARIETY: Repunched Date, Misplaced Date (RPD-002, MPD-001) — SNOW-2

PUP: Date

URS-9 • I-4 • L-3

Description: A secondary 1 is evident under the right side of the 8, and a secondary 5 to the south of the primary 5. The tops of four digits are evident protruding from the denticles below the date. Some specialists believe there are two sets of digits in the denticles.

	VF-20	EF-40	AU-50	MS-60	MS-63	MS-65
VARIETY	$100	$200	$300	$500	$1,000	$1,700
NORMAL	$30	$45	$65	$90	$150	$600

Note: Values listed for MS-60 and higher are for RB (red and brown) specimens. Full red Uncirculated specimens command higher prices.

1865, Fancy 5 — FS-01-1865-1301 (007.3)

VARIETY: Digit Punch — SNOW-1
PUP: Date
URS-7 • I-3 • L-3

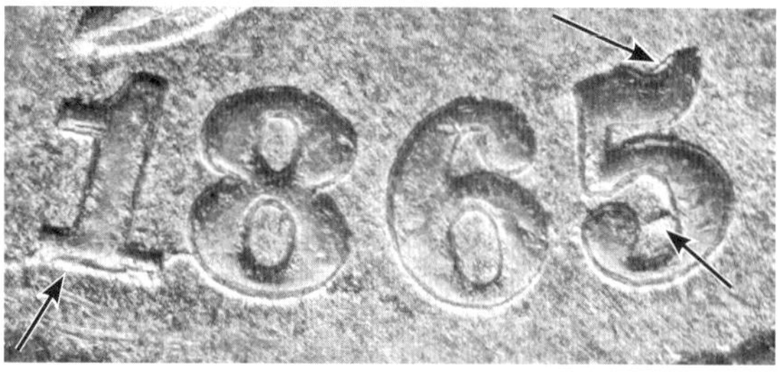
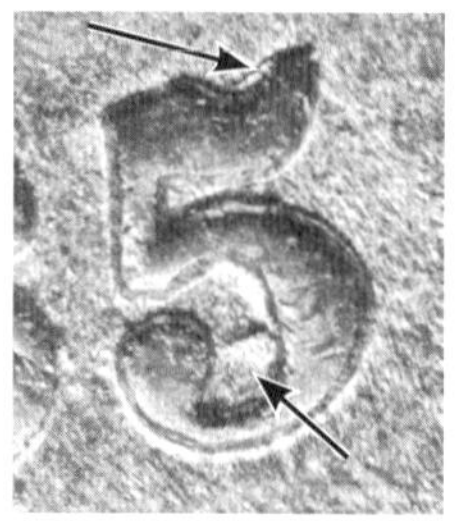

Description: A secondary 1 and 5 are visible, the 1 to the south of the primary 1 and the 5 very slightly to the north of the primary 5.

Comments: This variety was once considered to be a 5 Over 4 overdate. However, photographic overlays disprove the theory, and show this to be a defective logo punch, similar to another known on an 1865 two-cent piece. Two different dies are known, with one of them having additional repunching on the 1.

	VF-20	EF-40	AU-50	MS-60	MS-63	MS-65
VARIETY	$75	$100	$125	$300	$500	$800
NORMAL	$30	$45	$65	$90	$150	$600

Note: Values listed for MS-60 and higher are for RB (red and brown) specimens. Full red Uncirculated specimens command higher prices.

1865, Fancy 5 — FS-01-1865-1302 (007.55)

VARIETY: Repunched Date (RPD-011) — SNOW-4
PUP: Date
URS-5 • I-3 • L-3

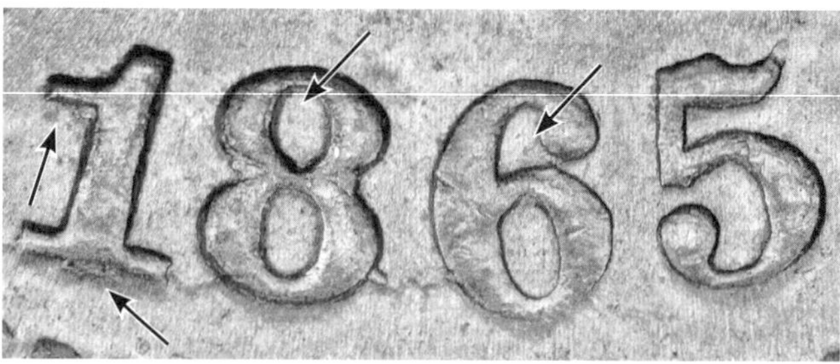

Description: Secondary digits are evident to the south of the 1, and slightly to the southwest of the 8 and 6.

Comments: This variety is very rare, although more may surface as collectors look more closely.

	VF-20	EF-40	AU-50	MS-60	MS-63	MS-65
VARIETY	$100	$200	$300	$500	$750	
NORMAL	$30	$45	$65	$90	$150	$600

Note: Values listed for MS-60 and higher are for RB (red and brown) specimens. Full red Uncirculated specimens command higher prices.

1865, Fancy 5 — FS-01-1865-1401 (007.2)

VARIETY: Die Gouge — SNOW-14
PUP: Headdress
URS-5 • I-5 • L-4

Description: There is a very strong die gouge through Miss Liberty's headdress. The perfect arc of the die gouge makes this very interesting, although there is no known definitive cause for the aberration.

Comments: This variety is believed to have been created by a heavy lathe line which was on the blank die and then "pushed into" the die.

	VF-20	EF-40	AU-50	MS-60	MS-63	MS-65
Variety	$300	$450	$800	$1,500	$2,750	
Normal	$30	$45	$65	$90	$150	$600

Note: Values listed for MS-60 and higher are for RB (red and brown) specimens. Full red Uncirculated specimens command higher prices.

1865, Fancy 5 — FS-01-1865-1801 (007)

VARIETY: Doubled-Die Reverse (DDR-001) — SNOW-2
PUP: ONE CENT, left side of shield
URS-7 • I-5 • L-5

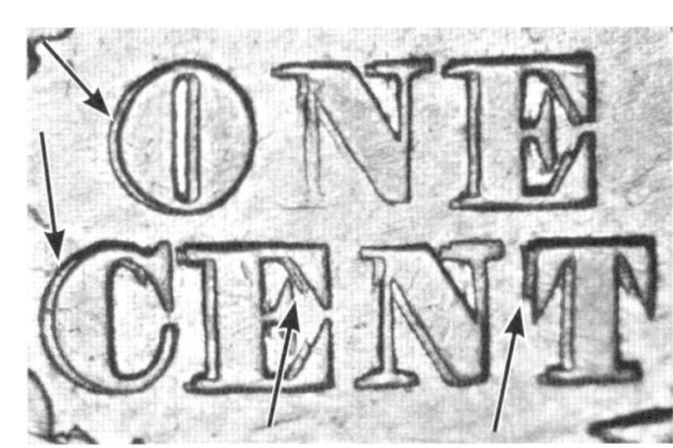

Description: This doubled-die reverse is strongly doubled, primarily on the left side. The doubling is most evident on the letters of ONE CENT.

Comments: With relatively few known specimens, this is one of the more popular varieties of the entire series. An MS-64RB specimen sold for $18,500 in 2012.

	VF-20	EF-40	AU-50	MS-60	MS-63	MS-65
Variety	$750	$1,500	$2,000	$5,000	$7,500	
Normal	$30	$45	$65	$90	$150	$600

Note: Values listed for MS-60 and higher are for RB (red and brown) specimens. Full red Uncirculated specimens command higher prices.

1866 FS-01-1866-101 (007.6)

Variety: Doubled Die, Misplaced Digit (DDO-001, MPD-001) Snow-1

PUP: Date, pearls, LIBERTY

URS-10 • I-4 • L-4

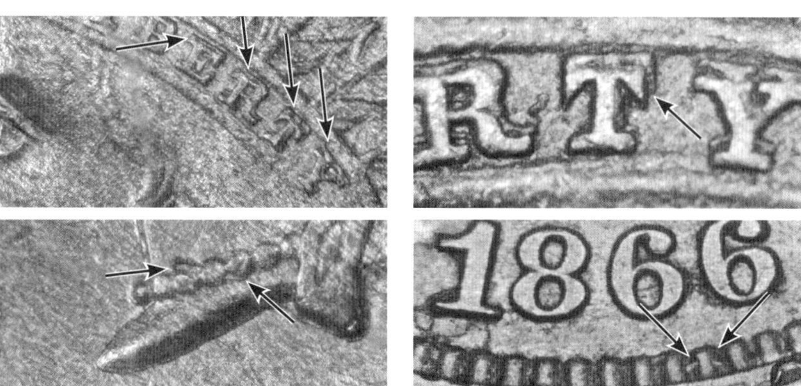

Description: There is wide doubling on LIBERTY and elsewhere. The base of a 1 is visible in the necklace and there are digits in the denticles.

Comments: This is one of the top varieties in the Indian Head cent series. The multiple varieties are very interesting to collectors.

	VF-20	EF-40	AU-50	MS-60	MS-63	MS-65
Variety	$200	$350	$600	$750	$1,200	$3,500
Normal	$100	$190	$250	$290	$380	$1,500

Note: Values listed for MS-60 and higher are for RB (red and brown) specimens. Full red Uncirculated specimens command higher prices.

1866 FS-01-1866-301 (007.7)

Variety: Repunched Date (RPD-001) Snow-2

PUP: Date

URS-8 • I-2 • L-2

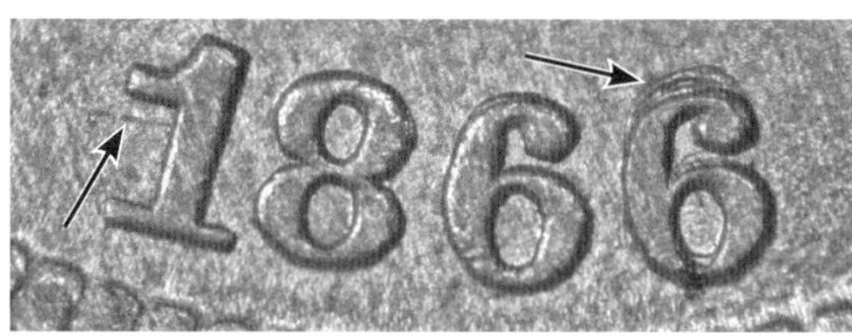

Description: A secondary 1 is visible to the south of the primary 1, with the flag evident below the primary flag. This is usually visible on higher-grade specimens. The top of a secondary 6 is evident to the north of the primary 6 and can be detected on lower grades.

Comments: This variety is in demand mostly from those trying to complete a variety set of the series. It can be easily confused with Snow-4, 5, and 7 of this date.

	VF-20	EF-40	AU-50	MS-60	MS-63	MS-65
Variety	$150	$250	$300	$400	$550	$2,000
Normal	$100	$190	$250	$290	$380	$1,500

Note: Values listed for MS-60 and higher are for RB (red and brown) specimens. Full red Uncirculated specimens command higher prices.

1866 — FS-01-1866-302 (007.9)

Variety: Repunched Date (RPD-002) — Snow-3
PUP: Date
URS-5 • I-2 • L-2

Description: A secondary 1 is evident to the left of the primary 1.

Comments: Early-die-state specimens may also show other digits repunched. On some examples, a reverse die cud shows between eight o'clock and nine o'clock, from the wreath to the rim.

	VF-20	EF-40	AU-50	MS-60	MS-63	MS-65
Variety	$200	$300	$400	$600	$800	
Normal	$100	$190	$250	$290	$380	$1,500

Note: Values listed for MS-60 and higher are for RB (red and brown) specimens. Full red Uncirculated specimens command higher prices.

1866 — FS-01-1866-303 (007.8)

Variety: Repunched Date (RPD-008) — Snow-9
PUP: Date
URS-8 • I-2 • L-2

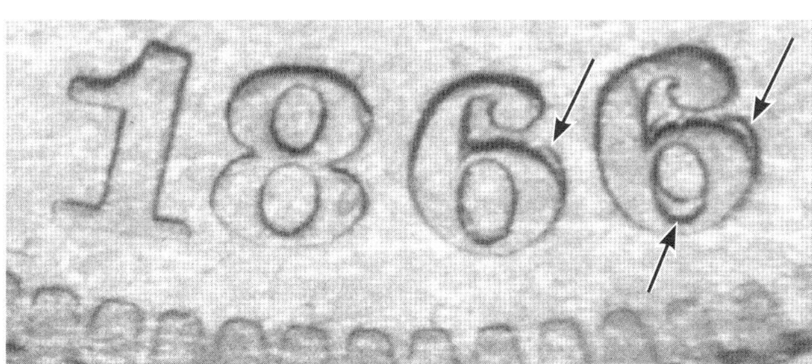

Description: Secondary 6's are evident to the east of the primary digits.

Comments: Although scarcer than FS-301, this variety is in demand mostly from those trying to complete a variety set of the series. Some coins seen have a bright, brassy look, probably due to a different alloy content.

	VF-20	EF-40	AU-50	MS-60	MS-63	MS-65
Variety	$200	$275	$350	$500	$700	$1,600
Normal	$100	$190	$250	$290	$380	$1,500

Note: Values listed for MS-60 and higher are for RB (red and brown) specimens. Full red Uncirculated specimens command higher prices.

1867 — FS-01-1867-301 (008)

VARIETY: Repunched Date (RPD-001) — SNOW-1

PUP: Date

URS-10 • I-5 • L-5

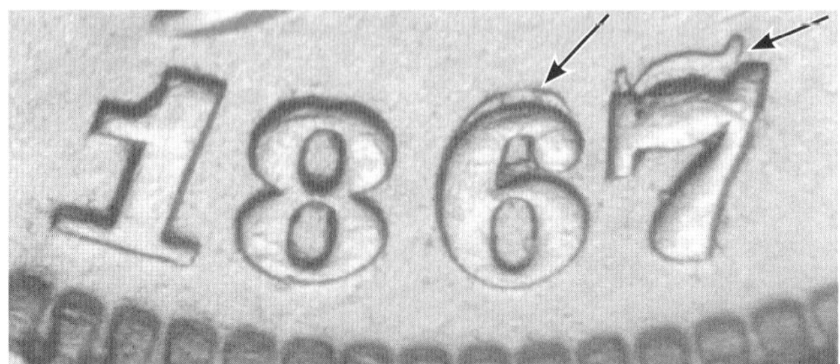

Description: Secondary digits are strongly evident to the north of the primary 6 and 7.

Comments: This is a very popular variety, but still can be cherrypicked. It is much easier to find in lower grades, which are less in demand.

	VF-20	EF-40	AU-50	MS-60	MS-63	MS-65
VARIETY	$500	$600	$800	$1,000	$1,500	$5,000
NORMAL	$135	$230	$275	$300	$400	$1,600

Note: Values listed for MS-60 and higher are for RB (red and brown) specimens. Full red Uncirculated specimens command higher prices.

1867 — FS-01-1867-302 (008.1)

VARIETY: Repunched Date (RPD-004) — SNOW-4

PUP: Date

URS-6 • I-3 • L-3

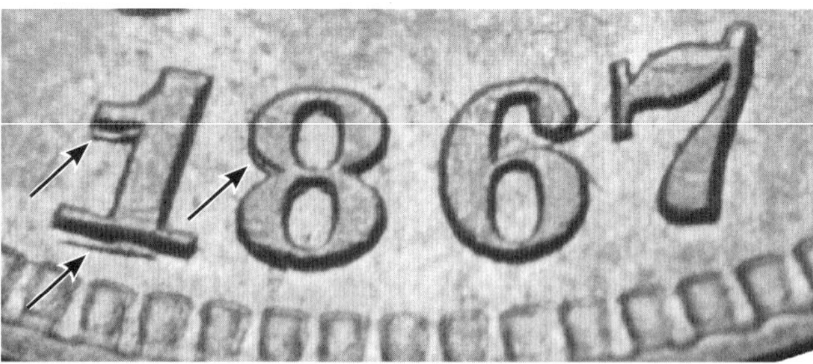

Description: The 1 exhibits a secondary digit to the south of the primary digit, and the 8 exhibits a secondary digit slightly to the west of the primary.

Comments: This variety is primarily of interest to specialists and Indian Head cent collectors. It seems to be quite scarce.

	VF-20	EF-40	AU-50	MS-60	MS-63	MS-65
VARIETY	$200	$250	$300	$450	$675	$2,000
NORMAL	$135	$230	$275	$300	$400	$1,600

Note: Values listed for MS-60 and higher are for RB (red and brown) specimens. Full red Uncirculated specimens command higher prices.

1867 FS-01-1867-303

VARIETY: Repunched Date (RPD-002) SNOW-2
PUP: Date
URS-10 • I-3 • L-3

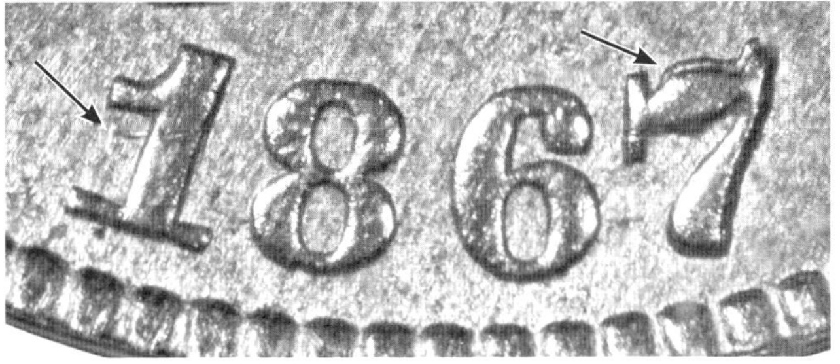

Description: Secondary digits are evident above the 7. Repunching is also visible under the flag of the 1.

Comments: While not as strong as FS-301, this repunched date is quite dramatic.

	VF-20	EF-40	AU-50	MS-60	MS-63	MS-65
VARIETY	$150	$300	$375	$450	$600	$1,800
NORMAL	$135	$230	$275	$300	$400	$1,600

Note: Values listed for MS-60 and higher are for RB (red and brown) specimens. Full red Uncirculated specimens command higher prices.

1868 FS-01-1868-101 (008.2)

VARIETY: Doubled-Die Obverse (DDO-001) SNOW-1
PUP: LIBERTY
URS-10 • I-4 • L-4

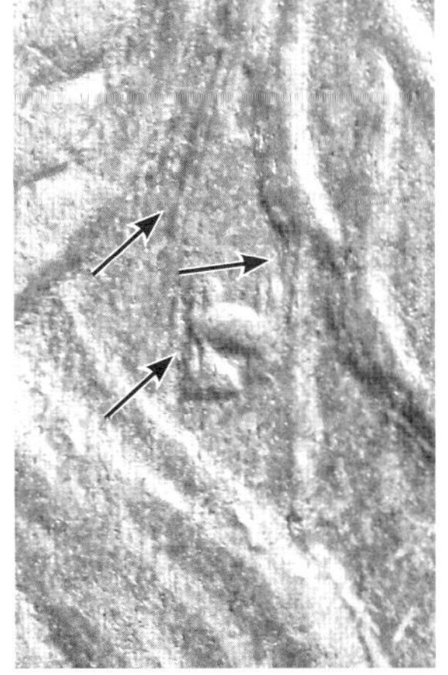

Description: Doubling is evident on the RTY of LIBERTY and on the ribbon, especially at the L.

Comments: This variety is very popular among specialists. It was discovered by Larry Steve.

	VF-20	EF-40	AU-50	MS-60	MS-63	MS-65
VARIETY	$200	$300	$350	$450	$600	$1,750
NORMAL	$125	$170	$220	$250	$360	$925

Note: Values listed for MS-60 and higher are for RB (red and brown) specimens. Full red Uncirculated specimens command higher prices.

1868 — FS-01-1868-102 (008.26)

VARIETY: Doubled-Die Obverse, Repunched Date (DDO-002, RPD-004) — SNOW-4

PUP: LIBERTY, date

URS-4 • I-3 • L-3

Description: Doubling is evident on LIBERTY and other portions of the headdress. The repunched date exhibits secondary digits within the upper loops of both 8's, and just above the lower loop of the 6.

Comments: This variety is different from FS-103. It is one of those "it's got it all" varieties, and is very popular among collectors. It is also scarce.

	VF-20	EF-40	AU-50	MS-60	MS-63	MS-65
VARIETY	$190	$250	$300	$450	$650	$1,250
NORMAL	$125	$170	$220	$250	$360	$925

Note: Values listed for MS-60 and higher are for RB (red and brown) specimens. Full red Uncirculated specimens command higher prices.

1868 — FS-01-1868-103 (008.25)

Variety: Doubled-Die Obverse, Repunched Date, Misplaced Date (DDO-003, RPD-005, MPD-001) — Snow-5

PUP: LIBERTY, date

URS-5 • I-4 • L-4

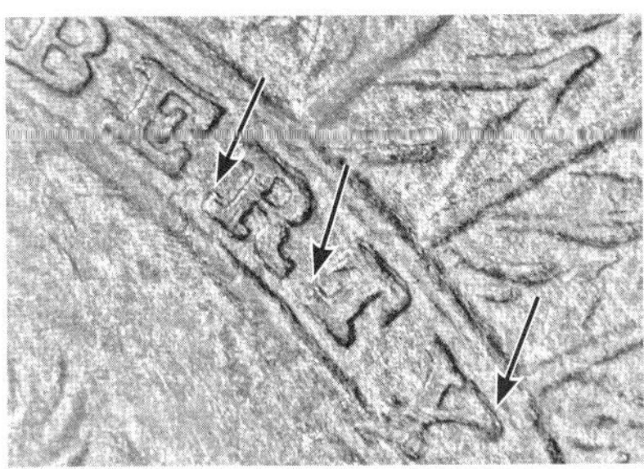

Description: The doubled die is evident on LIBERTY and is especially strong on the RTY. The repunched date is apparent with a secondary 8 slightly to the north of the primary 8. The misplaced date exhibits digits in the denticles below the 6—very likely a misplaced 6.

Comments: This variety is different from FS-102. It's another one of those "it's got it all" varieties. It is both very scarce and very popular among collectors.

	VF-20	EF-40	AU-50	MS-60	MS-63	MS-65
Variety	$200	$300	$400	$500	$800	$1,750
Normal	$125	$170	$220	$250	$360	$925

Note: Values listed for MS-60 and higher are for RB (red and brown) specimens. Full red Uncirculated specimens command higher prices.

1868 — FS-01-1868-301 (008.23)

VARIETY: Misplaced Date (MPD-002) — SNOW-8
PUP: Date
URS-4 • I-3 • L-3

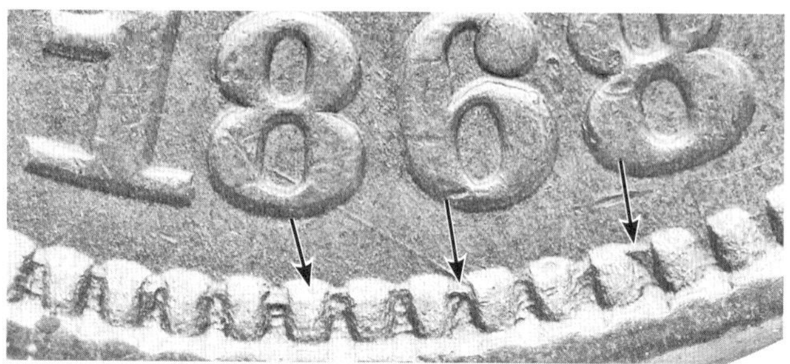

Description: There are three digits in the denticles below the date, very likely the 8, 6, and 8 of the primary date punch.

Comments: This variety is primarily of interest to specialists and Indian Head cent collectors. It is scarce.

	VF-20	EF-40	AU-50	MS-60	MS-63	MS-65
VARIETY	$200	$300	$350	$500	$600	$1,500
NORMAL	$125	$170	$220	$250	$360	$925

Note: Values listed for MS-60 and higher are for RB (red and brown) specimens. Full red Uncirculated specimens command higher prices.

1868 — FS-01-1868-302/901

VARIETY: Repunched Date, Die Gouge — SNOW-13
PUP: Shield
URS-3 • I-4 • L-3

Description: A heavy die gouge is seen in certain areas: through the shield, the O of ONE, the E of CENT, and parts of the wreath. Light repunching of the date can be seen to the south on the 1 and to the north inside the lower loops of the 6 and the second 8.

Comments: This variety is very rare and dramatic. It is believed by Rick Snow that this was damage to the blank die that was effaced in some areas but not in others.

	VF-20	EF-40	AU-50	MS-60	MS-63	MS-65
VARIETY	$400	$500	$750	$1,000		
NORMAL	$125	$170	$220	$250	$360	$925

1869 FS-01-1869-301 (008.3)

Variety: Repunched Date (RPD-003) **Snow-3**
PUP: Date
URS-12 • I-5 • L-5

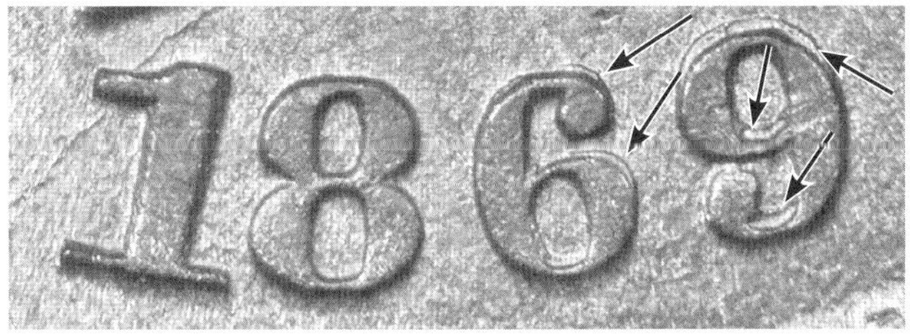

Description: Secondary digits are evident to the north of the 6 and 9, with a spread stronger on the 9 than the 6.

Comments: This variety was once considered an 1869, 9 Over 8 overdate, but the truth prevailed that it is simply a repunched date. Still, it is often listed in regular coin price guides, and is frequently considered a mainstay of the series. There is tremendous demand for circulated examples, especially because of the inclusion of this variety in popular coin albums. It is relatively common and found paired with eight different reverse dies! Several die states exist. This variety is very similar to FS-303; coins should be examined carefully for correct attribution.

	VF-20	EF-40	AU-50	MS-60	MS-63	MS-65
Variety	$500	$700	$800	$1,000	$1,200	$2,250
Normal	$335	$445	$550	$600	$700	$1,800

Note: Values listed for MS-60 and higher are for RB (red and brown) specimens. Full red Uncirculated specimens command higher prices.

1869 FS-01-1868-302 (008.5)

Variety: Repunched Date (RPD-001) **Snow-1**
PUP: Date
URS-6 • I-3 • L-3

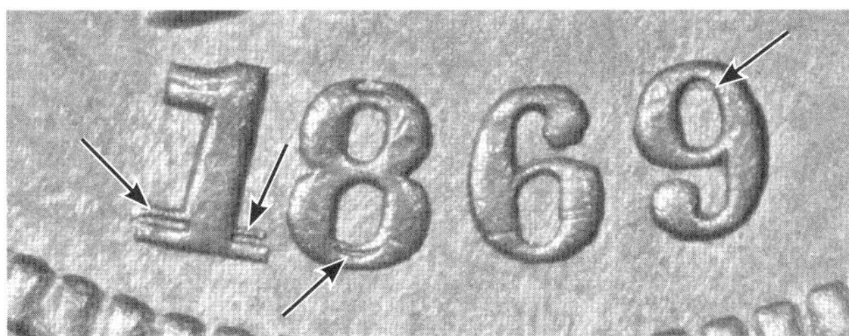

Description: Secondary digits are evident to the north of the 1 and 8, with a spread stronger on the 1 than the 8. Light repunching can also be seen at the top of the upper loop of the 9.

Comments: Generally speaking, die varieties of coins with a relatively high numismatic value rarely command much premium over the normal coin's value. This variety offers an exception. Only a single Mint State example is known. In circulated grades, too, it is very scarce.

	VF-20	EF-40	AU-50	MS-60	MS-63	MS-65
Variety	$500	$750	$800	*$1,200*	*$2,000*	*$5,000*
Normal	$335	$445	$550	$600	$700	$1,800

Note: Values listed for MS-60 and higher are for RB (red and brown) specimens. Full red Uncirculated specimens command higher prices.

1869 FS-01-1869-303

VARIETY: Repunched Date (RPD-004) SNOW-4
PUP: Date
URS-12 • I-3 • L-4

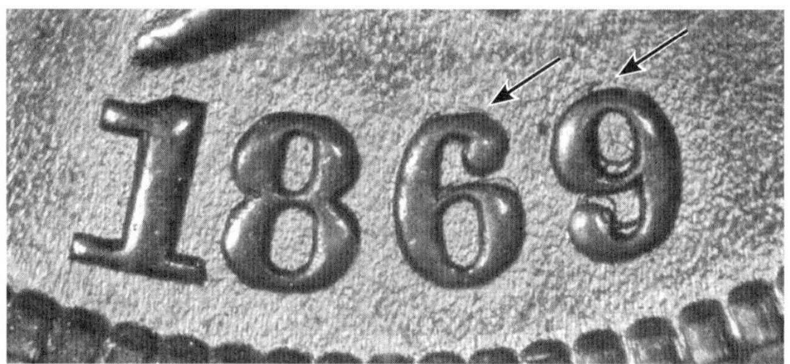

Description: This variety exhibits repunching above the 6 and the 9.

Comments: The repunching is less dramatic than on FS-301, but it looks more like the 1869, 9 Over 8 overdate that was once thought to exist.

	VF-20	EF-40	AU-50	MS-60	MS-63	MS-65
VARIETY	$400	$600	$750	$900	$1,100	$2,200
NORMAL	$335	$445	$550	$600	$700	$1,800

Note: Values listed for MS-60 and higher are for RB (red and brown) specimens. Full red Uncirculated specimens command higher prices.

1870 FS-01-1870-101 (008.6)

VARIETY: Doubled-Die Obverse, Repunched Date (DDO-001, RPD-001) SNOW-1, S-2, S-13, S-22, S-28, S-33 (COMMON OBVERSE, DIFFERENT REVERSES)
PUP: TY of LIBERTY
URS-8 • I-3 • L-3

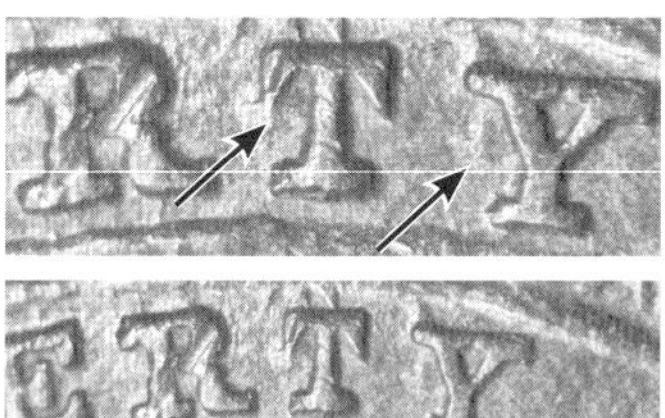

Description: Doubling is evident on the TY of LIBERTY, with a huge spread. The TY has a spread of half a letter's height. The top of the secondary T and Y are well into the ribbon. The coin also exhibits a minor repunched date, with a secondary 0 to the north, evidenced at the lower portion of the inside loop.

Comments: This obverse doubled die is paired with several different reverse dies, some of which are themselves major doubled dies.

	VF-20	EF-40	AU-50	MS-60	MS-63	MS-65
VARIETY	$400	$500	$600	$750	$1,000	$2,000
NORMAL	$280	$375	$450	$500	$850	$1,300

Note: Values listed for MS-60 and higher are for RB (red and brown) specimens. Full red Uncirculated specimens command higher prices.

1870 FS-01-1870-102 (008.82)

Variety: Doubled-Die Obverse, Repunched Date, Misplaced Date (DDO-003, RPD-003, MPD-001) Snow-5

PUP: LIBERTY, date

URS-5 • I-3 • L-3

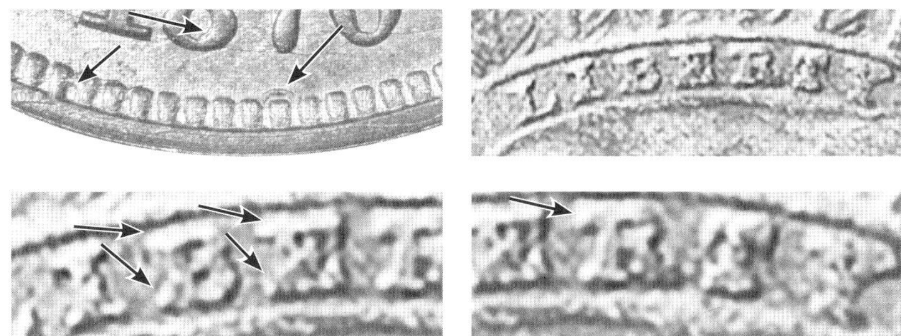

Description: Doubling is evident on LIBERTY, with the secondary letters to the north of the primary letters. A portion of a 0 is evident protruding from the denticles below the 7. A secondary 8 is visible within the loops of the primary 8.

Comments: This variety is highly sought after by collectors of the series.

	VF-20	EF-40	AU-50	MS-60	MS-63	MS-65
Variety	$1,500	$2,000	$2,500	$4,000	$7,500	
Normal	$280	$375	$450	$500	$850	$1,300

Note: Values listed for MS-60 and higher are for RB (red and brown) specimens. Full red Uncirculated specimens command higher prices.

1870 FS-01-1870-301 (008.81)

Variety: Repunched Date (RPD-002) Snow-4

PUP: Date

URS-5 • I-2 • L-2

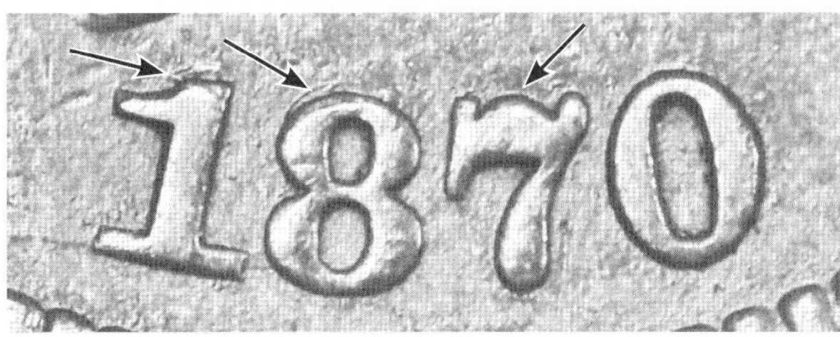

Description: Secondary digits are evident to the north of the primary 1 and 8.

Comments: This coin is primarily of interest to variety specialists and Indian Head cent collectors. It is very scarce.

	VF-20	EF-40	AU-50	MS-60	MS-63	MS-65
Variety	$500	$600	$800	$1,100	$1,500	$2,500
Normal	$280	$375	$450	$500	$850	$1,300

Note: Values listed for MS-60 and higher are for RB (red and brown) specimens. Full red Uncirculated specimens command higher prices.

1870 — FS-01-1870-302 (008.8)

VARIETY: Misplaced Date, Doubled-Die Reverse (MPD-002, DDR-011) — SNOW-8, SNOW-44

PUP: Denticles below date

URS-6 • I-4 • L-5

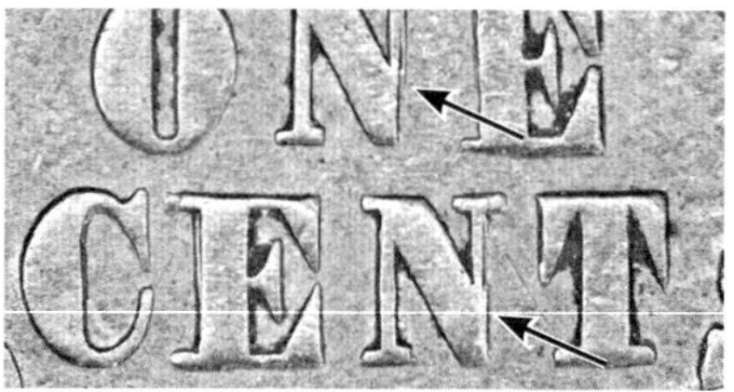

Description: Portions of several numbers are evident within the denticles below the date. Some specialists believe there are as many as 12 numbers present. The doubled-die reverse is evident to the right of the letters NE of ONE and EN of CENT.

Comments: This is one of the wildest misplaced dates known in the Indian Head cent series and likely one of the wildest of any series. This variety is fairly easily detected in lower grades.

	VF-20	EF-40	AU-50	MS-60	MS-63	MS-65
VARIETY	$500	$700	$1,000	$1,250	$2,000	
NORMAL	$280	$375	$450	$500	$850	$1,300

Note: Values listed for MS-60 and higher are for RB (red and brown) specimens. Full red Uncirculated specimens command higher prices.

1870 — FS-01-1870-303

VARIETY: Die Gouge ("Pick-Axe") — SNOW-7a, S-7b, S-17, S-18, S-27, S-41

PUP: Ribbon by lower hair curl

URS-10 • I-4 • L-4

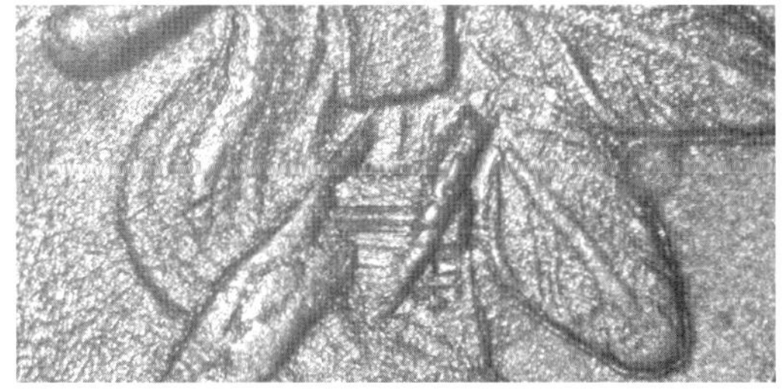

Description: Some kind of die damage left a mark that looks like a small pick-axe.

Comments: This is very popular with collectors. Rick Snow identified six different reverse dies: two with Shallow N (Snow-7a and 7b), three with a minor doubled die (Snow-17, 18, and 27), and one with a Bold N reverse (Snow-41).

	VF-20	EF-40	AU-50	MS-60	MS-63	MS-65
VARIETY	$300	$400	$550	$650	$1,000	$2,000
NORMAL	$280	$375	$450	$500	$850	$1,300

Note: Values listed for MS-60 and higher are for RB (red and brown) specimens. Full red Uncirculated specimens command higher prices.

1870 — FS-01-1870-801 (008.7)

VARIETY: Doubled-Die Reverse — SNOW-2, S-3, S-14

PUP: ONE CENT

URS-9 • I-4 • L-5

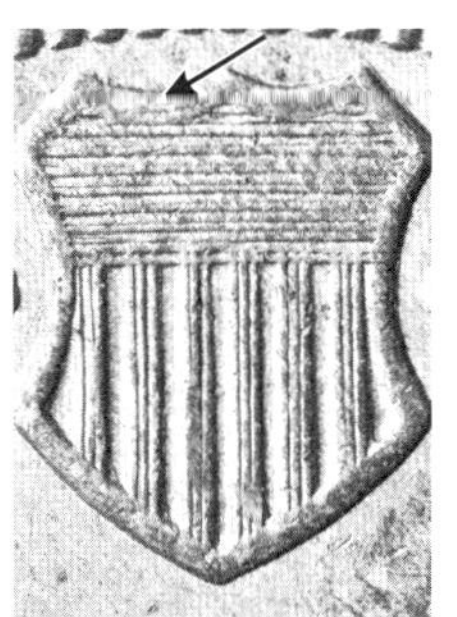

Description: This is a very popular doubled die, with the doubling evident on ONE CENT, both sides of the wreath, and the top of the shield.

Comments: Some specimens exhibit a small die crack from 11:30 to the wreath at two o'clock. One of the obverse dies paired with this reverse is also listed as FS-101 (Snow-2), making that variety a double find! This is the strongest doubled-die reverse of several of this date.

	VF-20	EF-40	AU-50	MS-60	MS-63	MS-65
VARIETY	$500	$700	$1,000	$1,200	$1,500	$2,500
NORMAL	$280	$375	$450	$500	$850	$1,300

Note: Values listed for MS-60 and higher are for RB (red and brown) specimens. Full red Uncirculated specimens command higher prices.

1870 FS-01-1870-901

VARIETY: Reverse of 1869 (Shallow N)
PUP: ONE CENT
URS-14 • I-5 • L-5

Description: This variety has the reverse design from 1869 with a shallow N in ONE. The E's in ONE CENT have T-shaped centers.

Comments: William Barber redesigned the reverse die in 1870. The new version has a bold N in ONE and trumpet-shaped centers of the E's in ONE CENT. These are slightly scarce, but little premium is presently due them. This may change as demand increases.

	VF-20	EF-40	AU-50	MS-60	MS-63	MS-65
VARIETY	$310	$415	$495	$550	$935	$1,430
NORMAL	$280	$375	$450	$500	$850	$1,300

Note: Values listed for MS-60 and higher are for RB (red and brown) specimens. Full red Uncirculated specimens command higher prices.

1871 FS-01-1871-301

VARIETY: Date Variety
PUP: Date
URS-3 • I-4 • L-4

Description: The 7 and 1 of the date touch. This is a Bold N reverse coin.

Comments: This variety has been known for a long time, as it was listed by Breen in 1977. Very few have come to light since then. Proof examples with a Shallow N reverse are not worth the premium stated here. An MS-63RB example sold for $10,000 in 2014.

	VF-20	EF-40	AU-50	MS-60	MS-63	MS-65
VARIETY	$1,000	$2,000	$3,000	$5,000	$10,000	
NORMAL	$350	$475	$525	$550	$800	$2,350

Note: Values listed for MS-60 and higher are for RB (red and brown) specimens. Full red Uncirculated specimens command higher prices.

1871 FS-01-1871-901

Variety: Reverse of 1869 (Shallow N) Snow-4, S-5
PUP: ONE CENT
URS-7 • I-4 • L-5

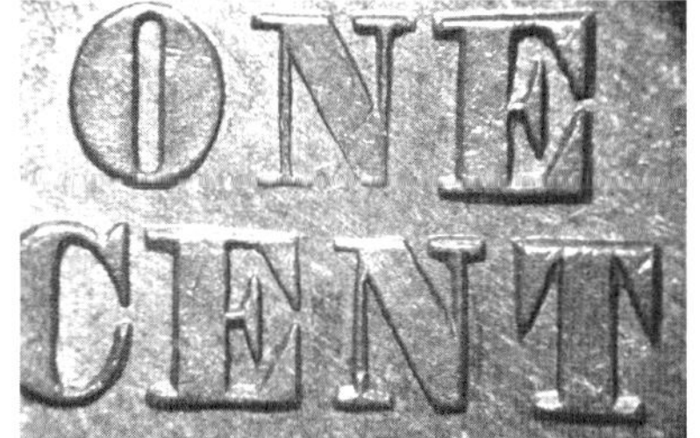

Description: This variety has the reverse design from 1869 with a shallow N in ONE. The E's in ONE CENT have T-shaped centers.

Comments: William Barber redesigned the reverse die in 1870. The new version has a bold N in ONE and trumpet-shaped centers of the E's in ONE CENT. The shallow N's are quite rare for this date, and as more collectors desire to add them to their sets they will become even rarer. An MS-65RB sold for $13,000 in 2005. Proofs do not command these premiums.

	VF-20	EF-40	AU-50	MS-60	MS-63	MS-65
Variety	$650	$850	$1,300	$2,000	$3,000	$6,500
Normal	$350	$475	$525	$550	$800	$2,350

Note: Values listed for MS-60 and higher are for RB (red and brown) specimens. Full red Uncirculated specimens command higher prices.

1872 FS-01-1872-301 (008.9)

Variety: Repunched Date (RPD-001) Snow-1
PUP: Date
URS-7 • I-3 • L-3

Description: A secondary image is evident to the north of the primary 1 and 2. There is no visible doubling evident on the 8 or 7.

Comments: This variety is highly sought by collectors of the series. Premiums are small, due to the high value of the date.

	VF-20	EF-40	AU-50	MS-60	MS-63	MS-65
Variety	$500	$600	$750	$850	$1,300	$4,400
Normal	$375	$500	$650	$785	$1,150	$4,000

Note: Values listed for MS-60 and higher are for RB (red and brown) specimens. Full red Uncirculated specimens command higher prices.

1872 FS-01-1872-901

VARIETY: Reverse of 1869 (Shallow N) SNOW-10, S-13, S-14

PUP: ONE CENT

URS-9 • I-5 • L-5

RB DE

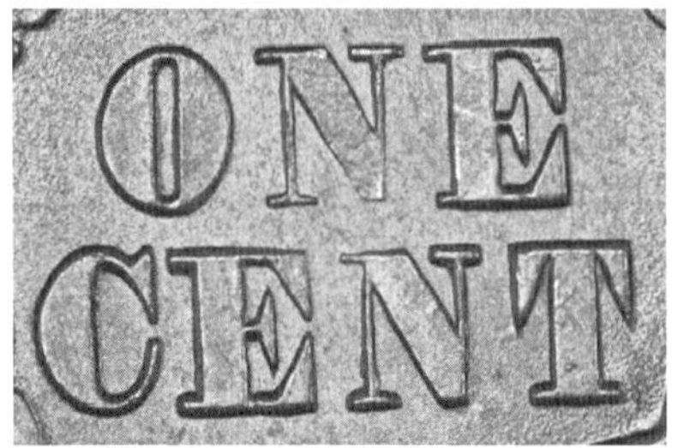

Description: This variety has the reverse design from 1869 with a shallow N in ONE. The E's in ONE CENT have T-shaped centers.

Comments: William Barber redesigned the reverse die in 1870. The new version has a bold N in ONE and trumpet-shaped centers of the E's in ONE CENT. These are quite scarce, and as more collectors desire to add them to their sets they will become even rarer. No Proofs were struck with the Shallow N reverse. An MS-65RB sold for $6,500 in 2005.

	VF-20	EF-40	AU-50	MS-60	MS-63	MS-65
VARIETY	$550	$750	$1,000	$1,500	$2,200	$5,000
NORMAL	$375	$500	$650	$785	$1,150	$4,000

Note: Values listed for MS-60 and higher are for RB (red and brown) specimens. Full red Uncirculated specimens command higher prices.

1873, Close (or Closed) 3 FS-01-1873-101 (009)

VARIETY: Doubled-Die Obverse (DDO-001) SNOW-1

PUP: LIBERTY

URS-9 • I-5 • L-5

RB RB DE

Description: This strong doubled die is evident by the doubling on LIBERTY, the entire headdress, the feather spines, and even the eye. This is a Close 3 (often referred to as a "Closed 3") variety.

Comments: This variety, considered the "chief" of all Indian Head cent varieties, is in very high demand. It is always sought by collectors, in all grades. An MS-65RB sold in 2005 for $69,000. An MS-64RD sold for more than $100,000 in 1998. In lower grades, this coin can more easily be identified by the doubling on the eye and lips.

	VF-20	EF-40	AU-50	MS-60	MS-63	MS-65
VARIETY	$2,000	$3,000	$4,000	$7,500	$14,000	$70,000
NORMAL	$125	$185	$235	$410	$550	$2,500

Note: Values listed for MS-60 and higher are for RB (red and brown) specimens. Full red Uncirculated specimens command higher prices.

1873, Close (or Closed) 3 — FS-01-1873-102 (009.1)

VARIETY: Doubled-Die Obverse (DDO-002) — SNOW-2

PUP: LIBERTY

URS-8 • I-4 • L-4

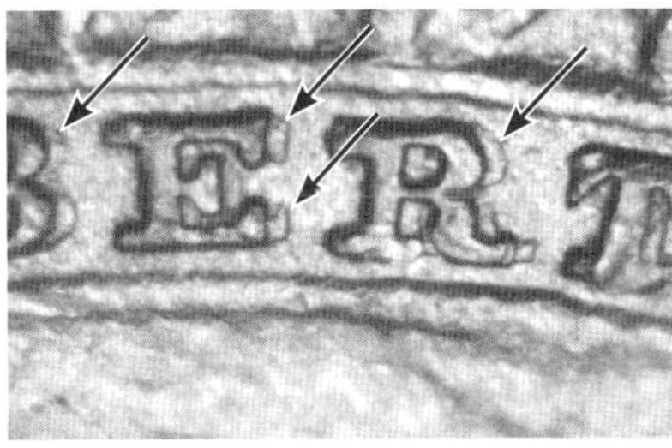

Description: This is another strong doubled die; the letters of LIBERTY show a secondary image slightly to the right of the primary image.

Comments: This variety is well known among Indian Head cent specialists and die-variety enthusiasts, but is often confused with the "biggie" (FS-101) by novice variety collectors. Prices have declined since publication of the fourth edition of the ***Cherrypickers' Guide*** due to more examples surfacing.

	VF-20	EF-40	AU-50	MS-60	MS-63	MS-65
VARIETY	$250	$350	$500	$750	$2,000	$5,000
NORMAL	$125	$185	$235	$410	$550	$2,500

Note: Values listed for MS-60 and higher are for RB (red and brown) specimens. Full red Uncirculated specimens command higher prices.

1873, Open 3 — FS-01-1873-1301 (009.3)

VARIETY: Repunched Date (RPD-001) — SNOW-1

PUP: Date

URS-5 • I-5 • L-4

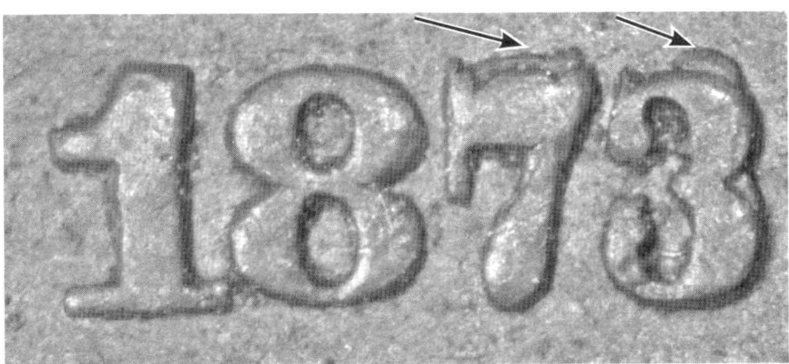

Description: This is a strong repunched date to the north of the 7 and 3.

Comments: Due to the repunching on the 3, it appears to be a Close 3 (or Closed 3) rather than an Open 3. This variety is very scarce.

	VF-20	EF-40	AU-50	MS-60	MS-63	MS-65
VARIETY	$200	$300	$600	$800	$1,200	
NORMAL	$85	$160	$190	$250	$325	$1,250

Note: Values listed for MS-60 and higher are for RB (red and brown) specimens. Full red Uncirculated specimens command higher prices.

1873, Open 3 — FS-01-1873-1302

VARIETY: Misplaced Date (MPD-001) — SNOW-6
PUP: First pearl in the necklace
URS-8 • I-3 • L-3

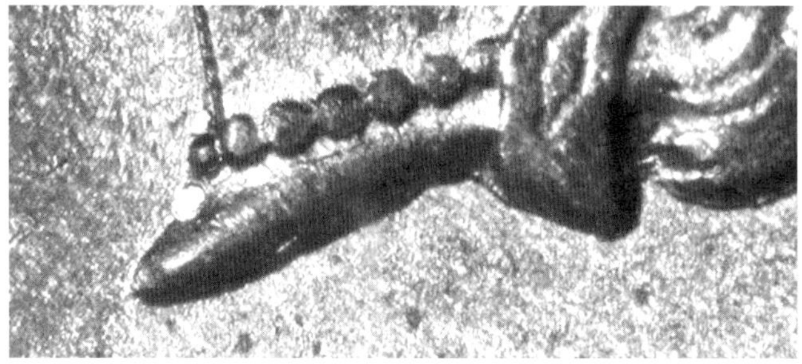

Description: A 3 is punched into the first pearl.

Comments: This is a very dramatic misplaced digit. A coin of this variety was used to make a counterfeit die. These counterfeits were made in the 1960s and will likely have very sharp edges.

	VF-20	EF-40	AU-50	MS-60	MS-63	MS-65
VARIETY	$150	$300	$375	$450	$750	$2,000
NORMAL	$85	$160	$190	$250	$325	$1,250

Note: Values listed for MS-60 and higher are for RB (red and brown) specimens. Full red Uncirculated specimens command higher prices.

1874 — FS-01-1874-101 (009.33)

VARIETY: Doubled-Die Obverse (DDO-001) — SNOW-1
PUP: LIBERTY
URS-7 • I-4 • L-3

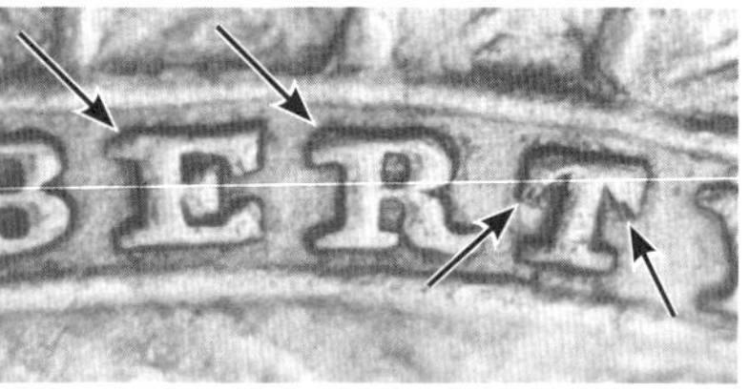

Description: Doubling is evident on LIBERTY, the designer's initials, the feathers, and the eye. The secondary image of LIBERTY is spread to the left of the primary image.

Comments: This variety is well known among Indian Head cent specialists and die-variety enthusiasts. It is considered by most to be highly collectible.

	VF-20	EF-40	AU-50	MS-60	MS-63	MS-65
VARIETY	$150	$400	$600	$800	$1,000	$3,500
NORMAL	$65	$100	$150	$225	$250	$725

Note: Values listed for MS-60 and higher are for RB (red and brown) specimens. Full red Uncirculated specimens command higher prices.

1875 — FS-01-1875-301

Variety: Repunched Date (RPD-001) — Snow-1
PUP: Date
URS-7 • I-4 • L-3

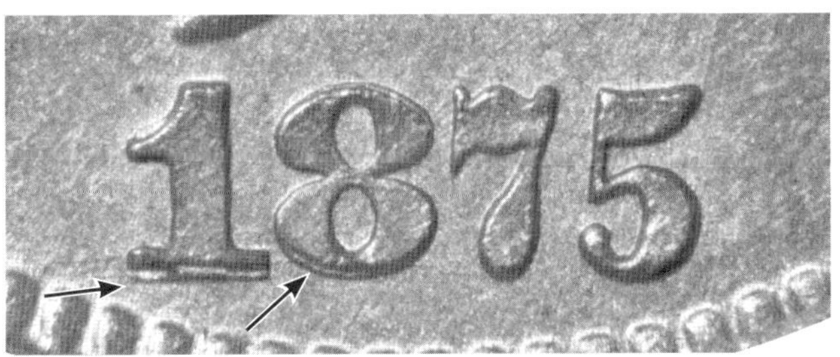

Description: Repunching is evident on the bases of the 1 and the 8.

Comments: This is a fairly bold repunched date. The variety is very similar to FS-303.

	VF-20	EF-40	AU-50	MS-60	MS-63	MS-65
Variety	$100	$150	$200	$300	$450	$1,000
Normal	$75	$120	$160	$235	$265	$900

Note: Values listed for MS-60 and higher are for RB (red and brown) specimens. Full red Uncirculated specimens command higher prices.

1875 — FS-01-1875-302

Variety: Repunched Date (RPD-002) — Snow-2
PUP: Date
URS-9 • I-4 • L-3

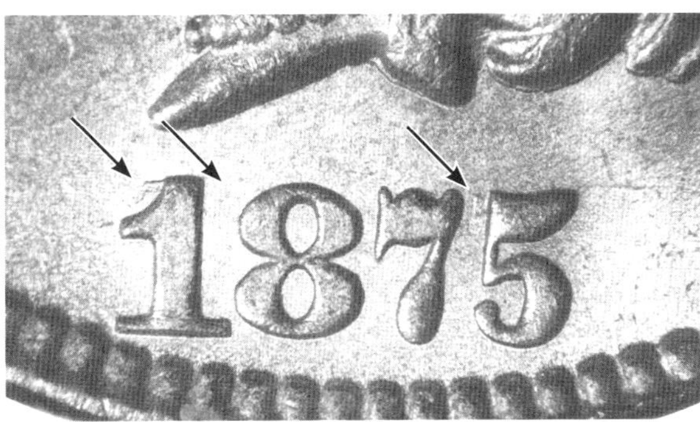

Description: The date is repunched far to the left of the primary 1. The initial date was started with the base of the 1 into the denticles. It was then corrected.

Comments: This is a dramatic repunched date.

	VF-20	EF-40	AU-50	MS-60	MS-63	MS-65
Variety	$100	$150	$200	$300	$450	$1,000
Normal	$75	$120	$160	$235	$265	$900

Note: Values listed for MS-60 and higher are for RB (red and brown) specimens. Full red Uncirculated specimens command higher prices.

1875 — FS-01-1875-303

VARIETY: Repunched Date (RPD-003) — SNOW-3

PUP: Date

URS-8 • I-4 • L-3

Description: Repunching is evident on the base of the 1.

Comments: This is a fairly bold repunched date, very similar to FS-301.

	VF-20	EF-40	AU-50	MS-60	MS-63	MS-65
VARIETY	$100	$150	$200	$300	$450	$1,000
NORMAL	$75	$120	$160	$235	$265	$900

Note: Values listed for MS-60 and higher are for RB (red and brown) specimens. Full red Uncirculated specimens command higher prices.

1875 — FS-01-1875-801

VARIETY: Possible Die Alteration — SNOW-16

PUP: N in ONE

URS-5 • I-5 • L-5

RB DE

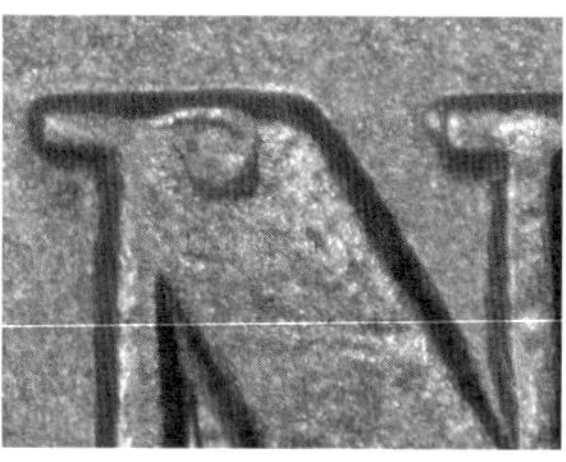

Description: A crude dot is raised at the top of the diagonal of the N in ONE.

Comments: This is a great "story coin" within the Indian Head cent series. In 1875, Mint officials may have secretly modified a reverse die by gouging a small dot into the N in ONE. Allegedly, the die was put into production one morning in order to catch an employee of 50-plus years' standing who was suspected of stealing coins. Late that morning the employee was called aside and asked to empty his pockets, which contained 33 of the marked cents. At first he insisted his pocket change was from his son, but when confronted with the secretly marked die, he admitted his guilt, and tendered his resignation in disgrace. An MS-65RD example sold for $15,000 in recent years.

	VF-20	EF-40	AU-50	MS-60	MS-63	MS-65
VARIETY	$150	$200	$300	$500	$1,000	
NORMAL	$75	$120	$160	$235	$265	$900

Note: Values listed for MS-60 and higher are for RB (red and brown) specimens. Full red Uncirculated specimens command higher prices.

1878 — FS-01-1878-301 (009.4)

VARIETY: Misplaced Date (MPD-001) — SNOW-2
PUP: Denticles below date
URS-5 • I-3 • L-2

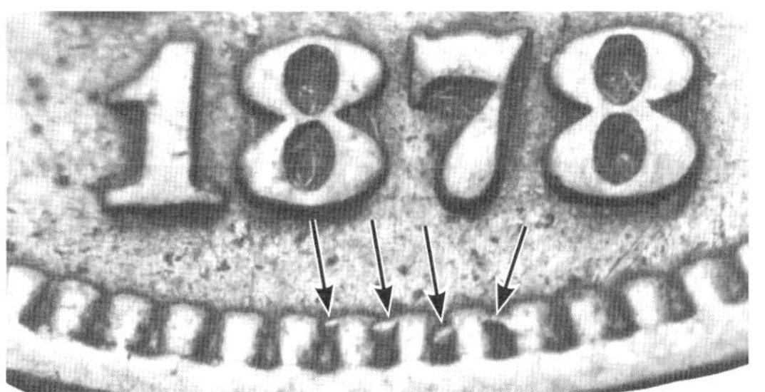

Description: The tops of three numbers (likely all 8's) are evident protruding from the denticles below the 8 and 7 of the date.

Comments: This misplaced date is fairly bold. Very few specimens have been found.

	VF-20	EF-40	AU-50	MS-60	MS-63	MS-65
VARIETY	$300	$400	$550	$750	$850	$1,140
NORMAL	$110	$200	$275	$325	$380	$950

Note: Values listed for MS-60 and higher are for RB (red and brown) specimens. Full red Uncirculated specimens command higher prices.

THE CHERRYPICKERS' GUIDE HELPFUL HINTS

Over time, certain Cherrypickers' Guide *varieties have proven to be of low collector interest, and we have slated these for removal from the listings. However, these varieties will retain their Fivaz-Stanton number and continue to be listed in future editions' cross-reference appendix. Other varieties have been "debunked"—that is, they have been proven by experts to either not be true varieties, not be legitimate Mint issues, or not exist at all. These have been removed from the listings in this edition and will not retain their Fivaz-Stanton number. A full list of varieties either slated to be removed or debunked appears after the introductory text of each section.*

1880 — FS-01-1880-101 (009.41)

VARIETY: Doubled-Die Obverse (DDO-001), Misaligned Die Clash (MAD-001) — SNOW-1

PUP: Shield, upper-right segment of wreath

URS-8 • I-5 • L-5

Description: The clashed impression of the denticles and OF from the obverse die is evident through the wreath to the center of the die. A minor doubled die is visible on the obverse by LIBERTY.

Comments: This is one of the most dramatic misaligned clashed dies that is known. Rick Snow believes that the die clash was made by hand on a softened blank die as a quick hardness test. The die maker might have struck the blank die with a hardened die by hand to see if it was softened enough, which it apparently was. The hubbing process pushed the marks deeper into the die. They appear between the wreath and the E in ONE, and more marks are visible inside the E in ONE, which is well below the field on the die.

	VF-20	EF-40	AU-50	MS-60	MS-63	MS-65
VARIETY	$150	$250	$400	$750	$1,500	$3,500
NORMAL	$12	$30	$60	$80	$130	$400

Note: Values listed for MS-60 and higher are for RB (red and brown) specimens. Full red Uncirculated specimens command higher prices.

1882 — FS-01-1882-301

VARIETY: Broken 2 — SNOW-2

PUP: Date

URS-10 • I-4 • L-4

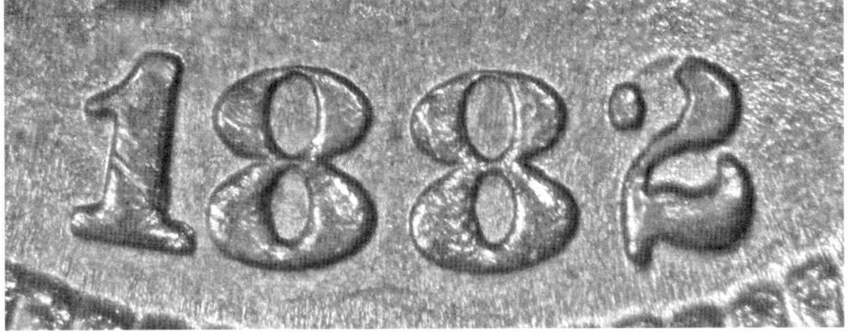

Description: The top of the 2 is broken, leaving a gap between the base and the ball at the top.

Comments: This is a very dramatic digit punch variety. While it is possible that many dies could have this anomaly, only one die is identified.

	VF-20	EF-40	AU-50	MS-60	MS-63	MS-65
VARIETY	$50	$75	$100	$180	$300	$600
NORMAL	$10	$25	$35	$60	$90	$315

Note: Values listed for MS-60 and higher are for RB (red and brown) specimens. Full red Uncirculated specimens command higher prices.

1882 — FS-01-1882-302 (009.43)

VARIETY: Misplaced Date (MPD-001) — SNOW-6

PUP: Necklace

URS-6 • I-5 • L-4

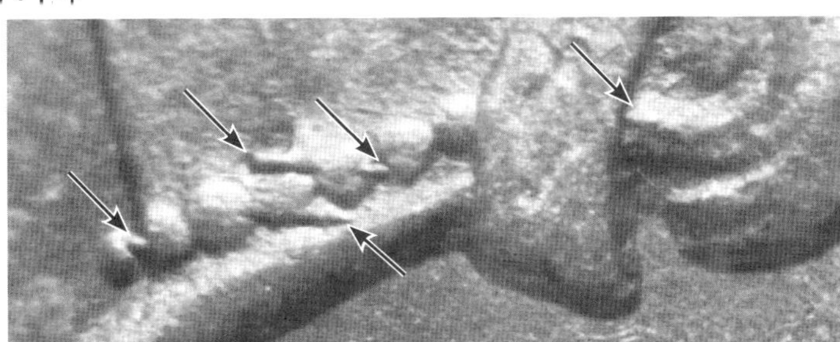

Description: The bases of at least four 1's are evident within the pearls of the necklace.

Comments: This is one of the most popular misplaced dates of the series. It was first reported by W.O. Walker and has since proven to be very rare, with very few examples coming to light.

	VF-20	EF-40	AU-50	MS-60	MS-63	MS-65
VARIETY	$200	$300	$500	$1,000	$2,500	$6,000
NORMAL	$10	$25	$35	$60	$90	$315

Note: Values listed for MS-60 and higher are for RB (red and brown) specimens. Full red Uncirculated specimens command higher prices.

1883 FS-01-1883-301 (009.45)

Variety: Misplaced Date (MPD-002) Snow-8
PUP: Denticles below date
URS-7 • I-3 • L-3

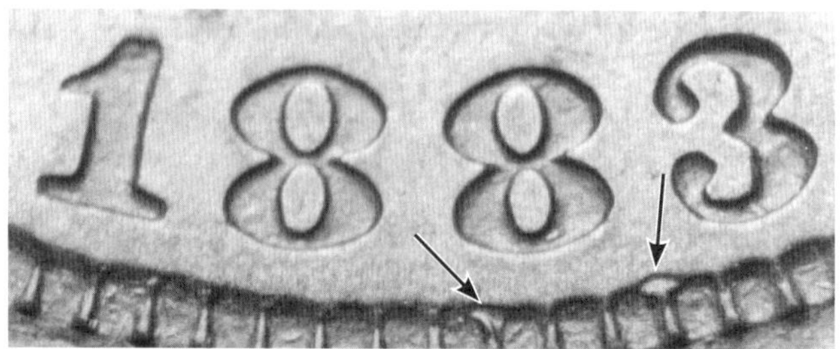

Description: The tops of two digits (likely an 8 and a 3) are evident protruding from the denticles below the date.

Comments: The misplaced digit in this variety is very obvious and therefore quite popular.

	VF-20	EF-40	AU-50	MS-60	MS-63	MS-65
Variety	$75	$100	$200	$350	$500	$1,250
Normal	$10	$25	$35	$60	$90	$315

Note: Values listed for MS-60 and higher are for RB (red and brown) specimens. Full red Uncirculated specimens command higher prices.

1883 FS-01-1883-302

Variety: Misplaced Date (MPD-003) Snow-7
PUP: Pearls
URS-5 • I-4 • L-4

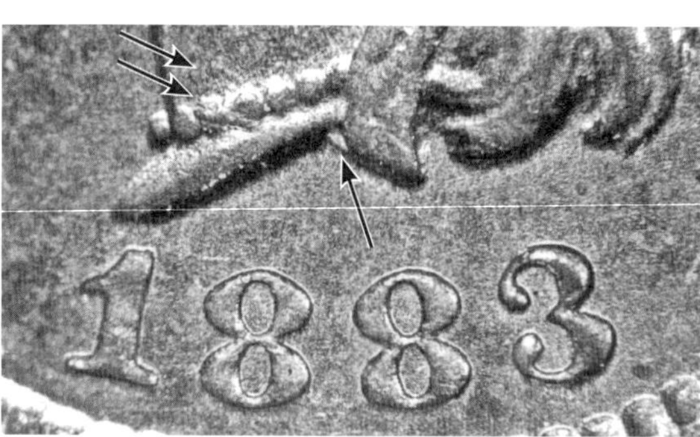

Description: The base of a 1 is visible at the third and fourth pearls, and the possible base of an 8 is visible between the edge of the ribbon and the bottom of the neck.

Comments: Collector interest in misplaced digits increases when they are very visible, such as this one.

	VF-20	EF-40	AU-50	MS-60	MS-63	MS-65
Variety	$100	$150	$250	$400	$750	$1,500
Normal	$10	$25	$35	$60	$90	$315

Note: Values listed for MS-60 and higher are for RB (red and brown) specimens. Full red Uncirculated specimens command higher prices.

1883 — FS-01-1883-303

VARIETY: Misplaced Date (MPD-001) — SNOW-1
PUP: Neck
URS-8 • I-4 • L-4

Description: The base of a 1 digit is sticking out of the neck, below the pearls.

Comments: Collector interest in misplaced digits increases when they are easily visible, such as this one.

	VF-20	EF-40	AU-50	MS-60	MS-63	MS-65
VARIETY	$100	$200	$300	$500	$750	$1,500
NORMAL	$10	$25	$35	$60	$90	$315

Note: Values listed for MS-60 and higher are for RB (red and brown) specimens. Full red Uncirculated specimens command higher prices.

1883 — FS-01-1883-401

VARIETY: Misaligned Die Clash — SNOW-11
PUP: Field below the A in STATES
URS-7 • I-5 • L-4

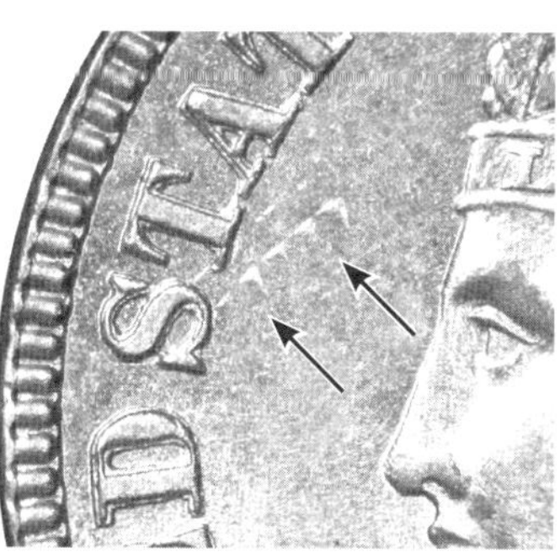

Description: A series of triangle-shaped marks are in the field area between the portrait and STATES. These are clash marks from the denticles of another die.

Comments: Off-center clash marks are widely collected as their own type of die variety. Rick Snow proposes these types of clashed dies are caused by an impromptu hardness test. If you strike a soft die with a hardened die, you will make a mark on the soft die and discover that it is too soft to strike coins.

	VF-20	EF-40	AU-50	MS-60	MS-63	MS-65
VARIETY	$100	$200	$350	$700	$1,200	$2,000
NORMAL	$10	$25	$35	$60	$90	$315

Note: Values listed for MS-60 and higher are for RB (red and brown) specimens. Full red Uncirculated specimens command higher prices.

1883 FS-01-1883-801 (009.46)

VARIETY: Doubled-Die Reverse (DDR-002) SNOW-6

PUP: Ribbon ends, arrowheads

URS-5 • I-4 • L-4

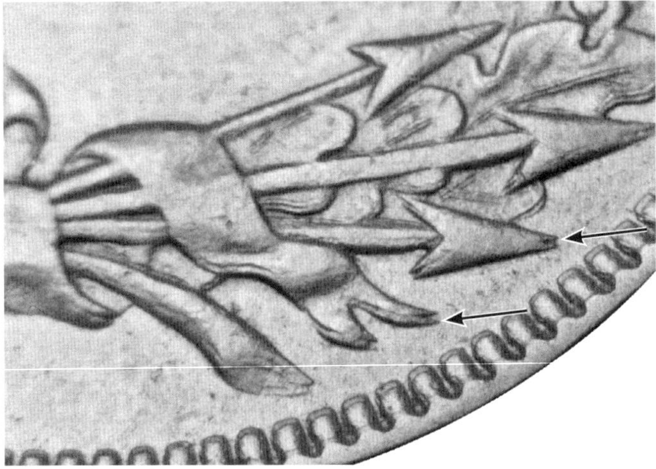

Description: The doubling is evident on the wreath veins, leaves, arrowheads, and ribbon ends.

Comments: Very few examples of this variety have been reported. As more collectors look at the reverse dies, perhaps more will show up.

	VF-20	EF-40	AU-50	MS-60	MS-63	MS-65
VARIETY	$100	$150	$250	$300	$500	$1,000
NORMAL	$10	$25	$35	$60	$90	$315

Note: Values listed for MS-60 and higher are for RB (red and brown) specimens. Full red Uncirculated specimens command higher prices.

1884 — FS-01-1884-301/901 (009.48)

VARIETY: Misplaced Date (MPD-001), Reverse Die Damage — SNOW-1

PUP: Denticles below date

URS-6 • I-2 • L-2

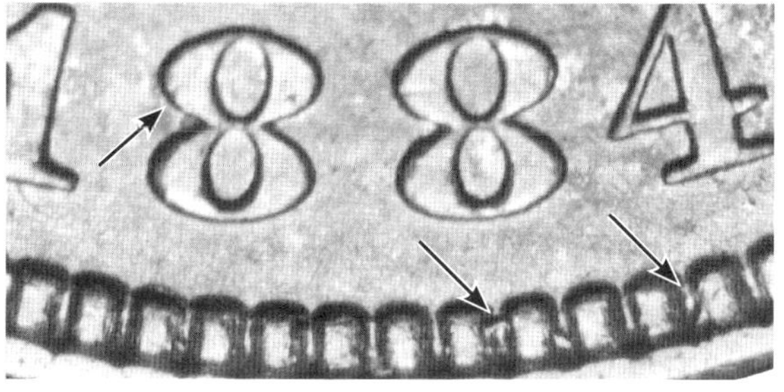

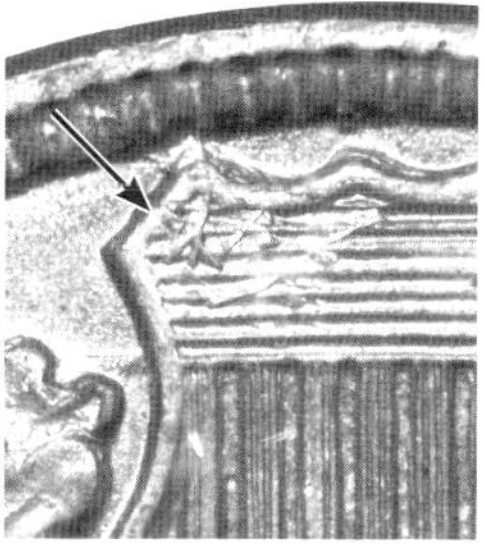

Description: The tops of an 8 and 4 are evident protruding from the denticles below the date. On the reverse, there is damage in the upper left of the shield resembling stars.

Comments: This coin is primarily of interest to variety specialists and Indian Head cent collectors.

	VF-20	EF-40	AU-50	MS-60	MS-63	MS-65
VARIETY	$25	$50	$75	$100	$150	$500
NORMAL	$14	$27	$40	$75	$120	$450

Note: Values listed for MS-60 and higher are for RB (red and brown) specimens. Full red Uncirculated specimens command higher prices.

1887 — FS-01-1887-101 (009.5)

VARIETY: Doubled-Die Obverse (DDO-001) — SNOW-1

PUP: AMERICA

URS-9 • I-5 • L-5

Description: Very strong doubling is evident on UNITED STATES OF AMERICA, with the doubling increasing from left to right.

Comments: This is easily one of the strongest doubled dies in the Indian Head cent series. It's a very impressive variety, especially in high grade.

	VF-20	EF-40	AU-50	MS-60	MS-63	MS-65
VARIETY	$100	$250	$400	$800	$1,800	$8,000
NORMAL	$8	$18	$28	$55	$80	$575

Note: Values listed for MS-60 and higher are for RB (red and brown) specimens. Full red Uncirculated specimens command higher prices.

1888 FS-01-1888-301 (010)

Variety: Overdate (RPD-001) Snow-1
PUP: Date
URS-7 • I-5 • L-5

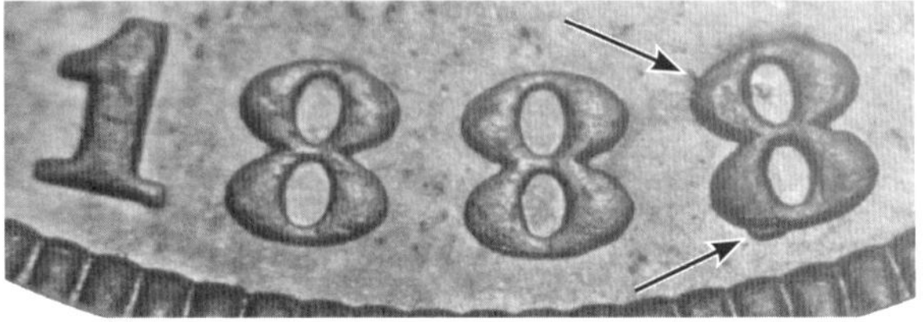

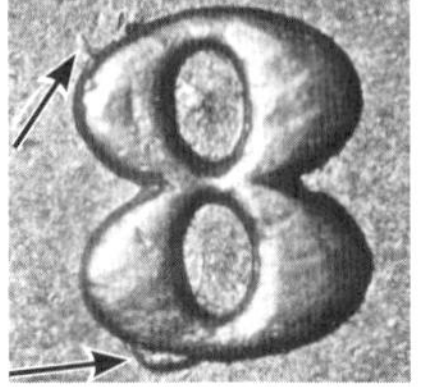

Description: The upper left portion of a 7 is evident protruding from the upper left of the last 8, and the base of that 7 protrudes from the lower left. A portion of the upper-left crossbar may be seen inside the upper loop of the 8 on high-grade specimens.

Comments: Most, if not all, specimens have a small cud (die break) over UNITED, which is usually not visible in grades lower than Extremely Fine. No coins above Very Good have been seen without this cud. This variety is the No. 1 cherrypick among Indian Head cents. About 30 examples are known and demand is very high. An MS-63BN example sold for $74,750 in 2007.

	G-4	VG-8	F-12	VF-20	EF-40	AU-50
Variety	$2,000	$3,000	$5,000	$7,500	$14,000	$20,000
Normal	$3	$4	$5	$8	$22	$27

Note: Values listed for MS-60 and higher are for RB (red and brown) specimens. Full red Uncirculated specimens command higher prices.

1888 FS-01-1888-302 (010.7)

Variety: Repunched Date (PRD-002) Snow-2
PUP: Date
URS-9 • I-5 • L-4

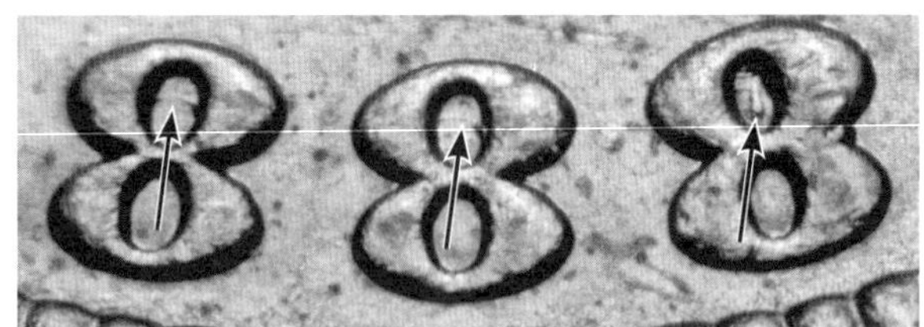

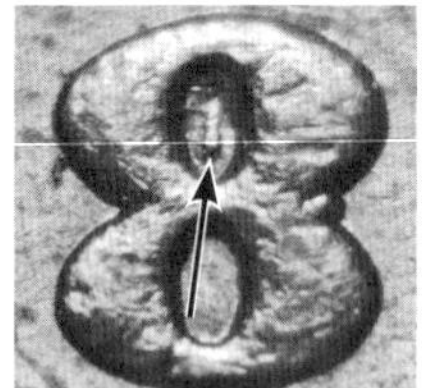

Description: There is repunching on all digits to the north. A die line appears inside the upper loop of the last 8.

Comments: This was originally listed as a second overdate for 1888. Overlays have disproven this attribution, but it is still a very popular and actively sought-after variety.

	VF-20	EF-40	AU-50	MS-60	MS-63	MS-65
Variety	*$300*	*$500*	*$800*	*$1,750*	*$2,500*	
Normal	$8	$22	$27	$65	$130	$725

Note: Values listed for MS-60 and higher are for RB (red and brown) specimens. Full red Uncirculated specimens command higher prices.

1888 FS-01-1888-303 (010.73)

VARIETY: Misplaced Date SNOW-27
PUP: Bottom of ribbon
URS-4 • I-2 • L-2

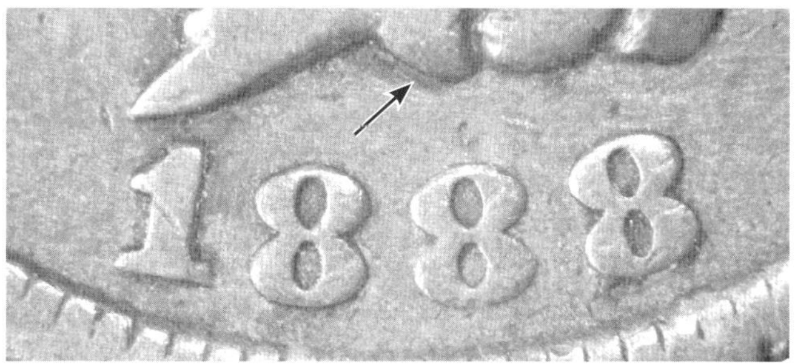

Description: What is believed to be the base of a 1 is evident protruding from the base of the ribbon.

Comments: It is now commonly believed that the misplaced digits are remnants of a quick hardness test employed by Mint die makers. This variety seems to be quite rare, although it is not well known.

	VF-20	EF-40	AU-50	MS-60	MS-63	MS-65
VARIETY	$40	$75	$100	$200		
NORMAL	$8	$22	$27	$65	$130	$725

Note: Values listed for MS-60 and higher are for RB (red and brown) specimens. Full red Uncirculated specimens command higher prices.

1888 FS-01-1888-305 (010.75)

VARIETY: Misplaced Date SNOW-32
PUP: Lower hair curls
URS-4 • I-2 • L-2

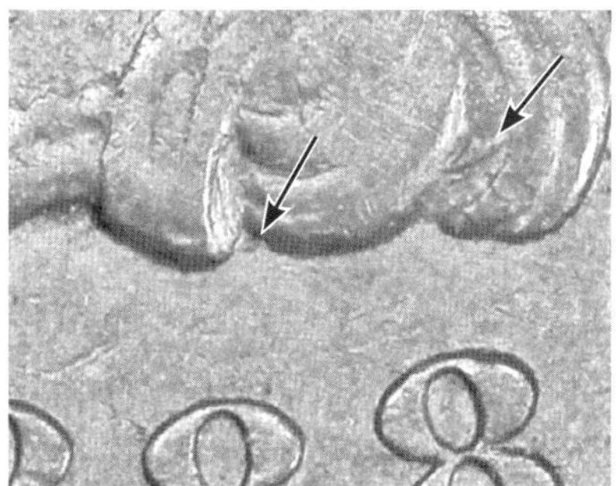

Description: What is believed to be the bases of two 8's are evident within the lower hair curls.

Comments: Many minor misplaced digits are known for this year.

Note: This variety is slated to be removed from the coin-by-coin listings of future editions of the ***Cherrypickers' Guide*** due to lack of interest and/or unavailability. It will retain its Fivaz-Stanton number and continue to be listed in future editions' cross-reference appendix. **A full list of varieties slated to be removed from each section appears after the introductory text of that section.**

1889 FS-01-1889-301 (010.8)

Variety: Repunched Date (RPD-011) Snow-12
PUP: Date
URS-9 • I-2 • L-1

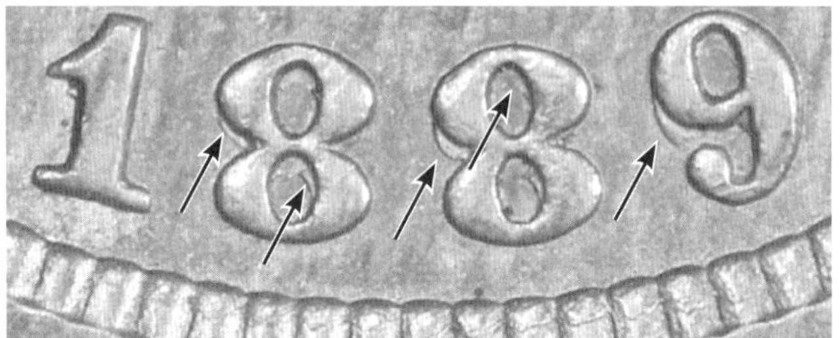

Description: Secondary digits are evident to the southwest of the primary digits on both of the 8's and the 9.

Comments: This has proven to be a relatively easy variety to locate.

	VF-20	EF-40	AU-50	MS-60	MS-63	MS-65
Variety	$10	$25	$50	$75	$150	$650
Normal	$7	$18	$30	$60	$80	$400

Note: Values listed for MS-60 and higher are for RB (red and brown) specimens. Full red Uncirculated specimens command higher prices.

1889 FS-01-1889-302

Variety: Repunched Date Snow-4
PUP: Date, denticles below date
URS-7 • I-3 • L-3

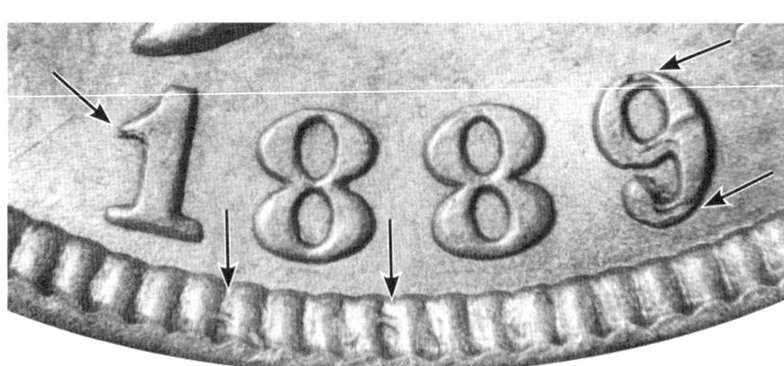

Description: There is repunching on the 9. Digits appear in the denticles.

Comments: This is a very scarce and dramatic repunched date.

	VF-20	EF-40	AU-50	MS-60	MS-63	MS-65
Variety	$25	$40	$50	$120	$250	$600
Normal	$7	$18	$30	$60	$80	$400

Note: Values listed for MS-60 and higher are for RB (red and brown) specimens. Full red Uncirculated specimens command higher prices.

1889 — FS-01-1889-801 (010.81)

VARIETY: Doubled-Die Reverse (DDR-001) SNOW-1
PUP: Date
URS-6 • I-4 • L-3

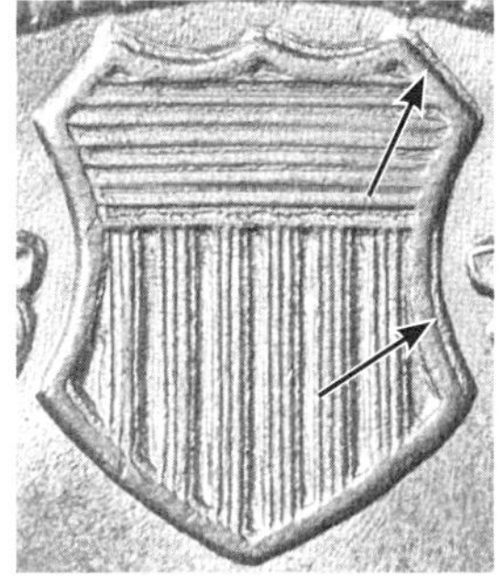
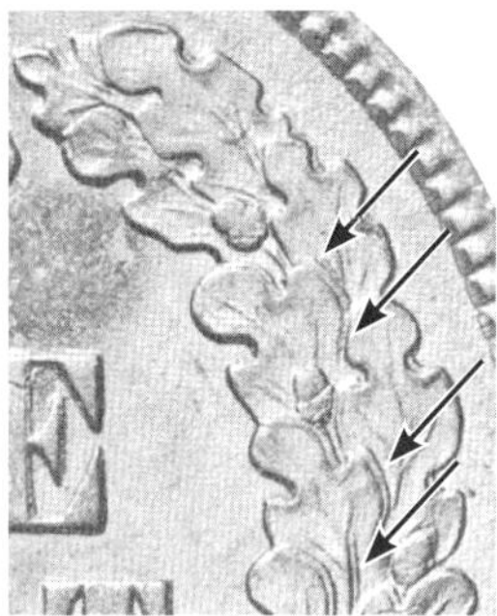

Description: There is strong doubling to the northwest on the shield, the right side of the wreath, and the upper-left segment of the wreath. The doubling is strongest in the upper-right segment of the wreath.

Comments: This is a very bold doubled die.

	VF-20	EF-40	AU-50	MS-60	MS-63	MS-65
VARIETY	$30	$50	$125	$250	$400	$1,000
NORMAL	$7	$18	$30	$60	$80	$400

Note: Values listed for MS-60 and higher are for RB (red and brown) specimens. Full red Uncirculated specimens command higher prices.

1889 — FS-01-1889-802

VARIETY: Doubled-Die Reverse (DDR-002) SNOW-11
PUP: Date
URS-6 • I-4 • L-3

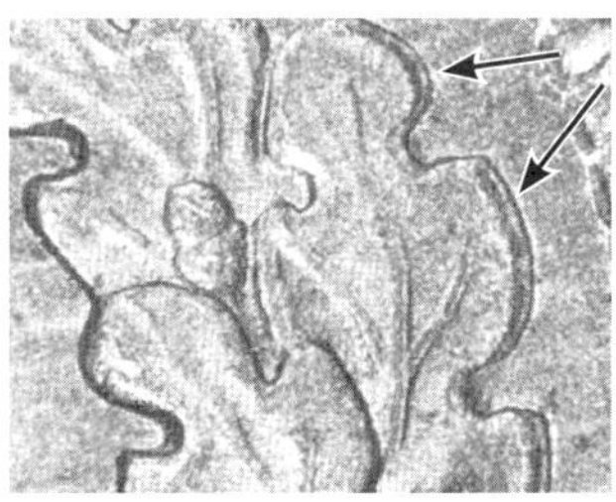
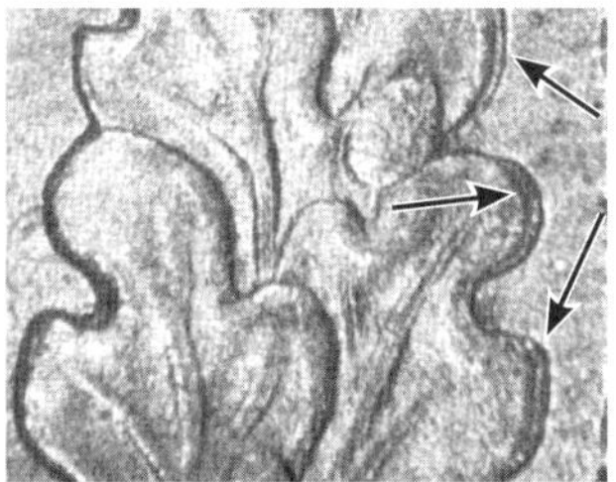

Description: There is strong doubling on the right side of the wreath.

Comments: This is another doubled-die reverse for this year—not as dramatic as FS-801, but scarcer.

	VF-20	EF-40	AU-50	MS-60	MS-63	MS-65
VARIETY	$30	$50	$150	$300	$400	$1,000
NORMAL	$7	$18	$30	$60	$80	$400

Note: Values listed for MS-60 and higher are for RB (red and brown) specimens. Full red Uncirculated specimens command higher prices.

1889 FS-01-1889-901

VARIETY: Misaligned Die Clash SNOW-31
PUP: Field around the letters of ONE
URS-7 • I-4 • L-4

Description: Two sets of clash marks from the denticles of another die appear on the reverse. One clash is inside the O in ONE, and the second clash is to the left of the E in ONE.

Comments: Off-center clash marks are widely collected as their own type of die variety. Rick Snow proposes that these types of clashed dies are caused by an impromptu hardness test.

	VF-20	EF-40	AU-50	MS-60	MS-63	MS-65
VARIETY	$250	$400	$600	$800	$1,250	$2,000
NORMAL	$7	$18	$30	$60	$80	$400

Note: Values listed for MS-60 and higher are for RB (red and brown) specimens. Full red Uncirculated specimens command higher prices.

1890 FS-01-1890-101 (010.85)

VARIETY: Tripled-Die Obverse (TDO-001) SNOW-1
PUP: UNITED STATES OF AMERICA
URS-7 • I-5 • L-5

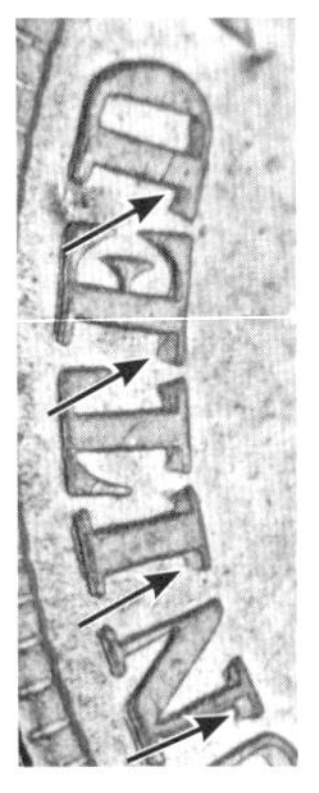

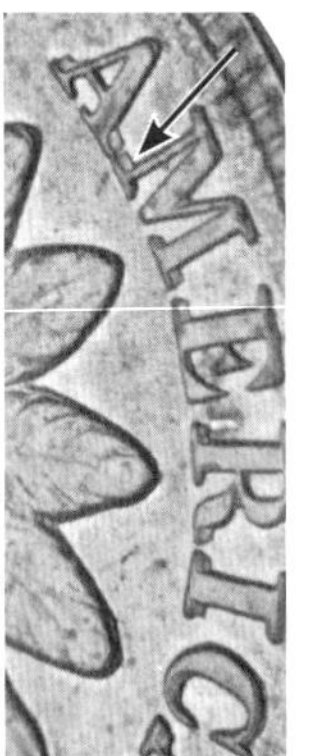

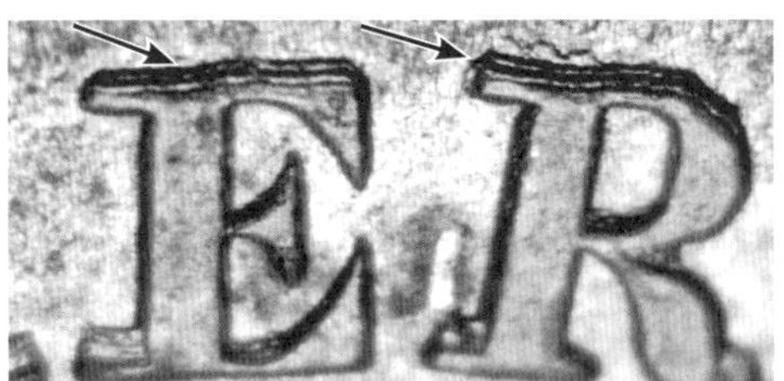

Description: This is one of the more popular Indian Head cent varieties. A tripled image is evident, spread toward the center on all letters of UNITED STATES OF AMERICA.

Comments: This variety was caused by the design spreading with each successive impression of the hub.

	VF-20	EF-40	AU-50	MS-60	MS-63	MS-65
VARIETY	$50	$100	$200	$300	$500	
NORMAL	$7	$16	$30	$60	$80	$450

Note: Values listed for MS-60 and higher are for RB (red and brown) specimens. Full red Uncirculated specimens command higher prices.

1890 — FS-01-1890-301 (010.82)

VARIETY: Misplaced Date (MPD-004) — SNOW-3
PUP: Neck
URS-7 • I-3 • L-3

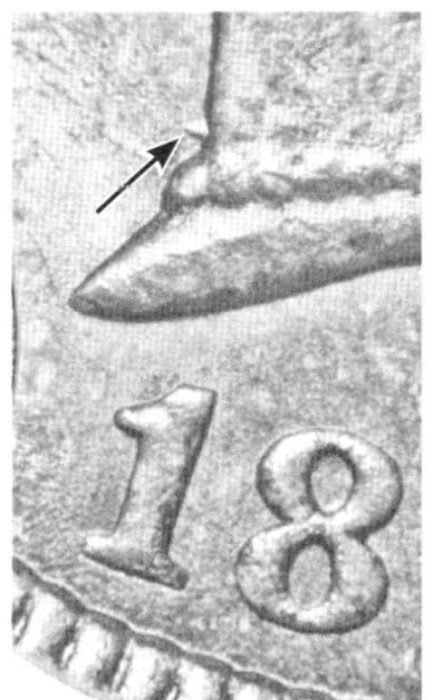

Description: The flag of a 1 is evident protruding from the neck, just above the necklace.

Comments: The digit in the neck is quite prominent.

	VF-20	EF-40	AU-50	MS-60	MS-63	MS-65
VARIETY	$15	$30	$75	$100	$200	$750
NORMAL	$7	$16	$30	$60	$80	$450

Note: Values listed for MS-60 and higher are for RB (red and brown) specimens. Full red Uncirculated specimens command higher prices.

1890 — FS-01-1890-302 (010.84)

VARIETY: Misplaced Date (MPD-001) — SNOW-6
PUP: Denticles below date
URS-7 • I-2 • L-2

Description: A portion of a digit (likely a 0) can be seen within the denticles below the 9 of the date.

Comments: Misplaced digits get more interest the more prominent they are.

Note: This variety is slated to be removed from the coin-by-coin listings of future editions of the ***Cherrypickers' Guide*** due to lack of interest and/or unavailability. It will retain its Fivaz-Stanton number and continue to be listed in future editions' cross-reference appendix. **A full list of varieties slated to be removed from each section appears after the introductory text of that section.**

1890 FS-01-1890-901

VARIETY: Misaligned Die Clash SNOW-16
PUP: Below the N in ONE
URS-6 • I-4 • L-3

Description: A clash mark from the denticles of another die are in the field area below the N in ONE.

Comments: Off-center clash marks are widely collected as their own type of die variety. Rick Snow proposes that these types of clashed dies are caused by an impromptu hardness test.

	VF-20	EF-40	AU-50	MS-60	MS-63	MS-65
VARIETY	$120	$180	$275	$450	$850	$1,200
NORMAL	$7	$16	$30	$60	$80	$450

Note: Values listed for MS-60 and higher are for RB (red and brown) specimens. Full red Uncirculated specimens command higher prices.

1891 FS-01-1891-101 (010.88)

VARIETY: Doubled-Die Obverse (DDO-001) SNOW-1
PUP: Date
URS-7 • I-5 • L-5

Description: The doubling on this variety is evident on LIBERTY and the words STATES OF AMERICA, where the spread decreases from left to right.

Comments: This variety also exhibits a minor repunched date on some higher-grade specimens. It is one of the top Indian Head cent varieties.

	VF-20	EF-40	AU-50	MS-60	MS-63	MS-65
VARIETY	$150	$250	$400	$1,000	$1,750	$3,500
NORMAL	$7	$15	$30	$60	$80	$400

Note: Values listed for MS-60 and higher are for RB (red and brown) specimens. Full red Uncirculated specimens command higher prices.

1891 — FS-01-1891-301 (010.87)

Variety: Repunched Date (RPD-001) — Snow-3
PUP: Date
URS-9 • I-3 • L-3

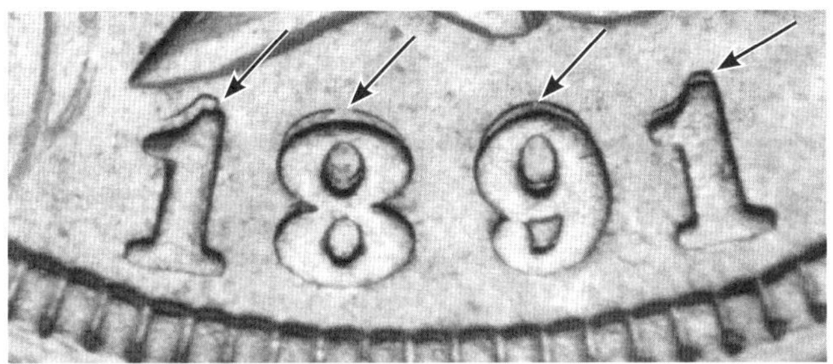

Description: Secondary digits are evident to the north of all four primary digits.

Comments: This variety exhibits wide repunching.

	VF-20	EF-40	AU-50	MS-60	MS-63	MS-65
Variety	$20	$50	$100	$150	$250	$750
Normal	$7	$15	$30	$60	$80	$400

Note: Values listed for MS-60 and higher are for RB (red and brown) specimens. Full red Uncirculated specimens command higher prices.

1892 — FS-01-1892-301 (010.89)

Variety: Repunched Date (RPD-008) — Snow-8
PUP: Date
URS-7 • I-4 • L-4

Description: Secondary digits are evident to the east of the 8 and 2 in the date. Earlier die states may exhibit secondary digits on the 1 and/or 9 as well.

Comments: This variety is quite popular, primarily due to the width of the spread of the secondary digits.

	VF-20	EF-40	AU-50	MS-60	MS-63	MS-65
Variety	$25	$50	$150	$200	$300	$800
Normal	$8	$20	$30	$60	$80	$375

Note: Values listed for MS-60 and higher are for RB (red and brown) specimens. Full red Uncirculated specimens command higher prices.

1892 — FS-01-1892-302 (010.9)

VARIETY: Repunched Date, Doubled-Die Reverse (RPD-002, DDR-001) — SNOW-1

PUP: Date

URS-5 • I-4 • L-4

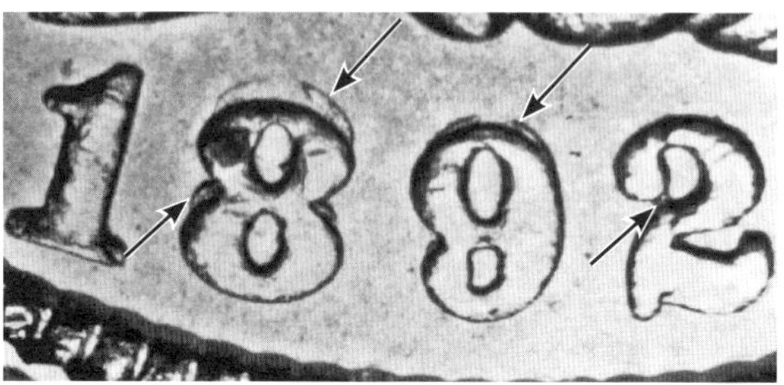

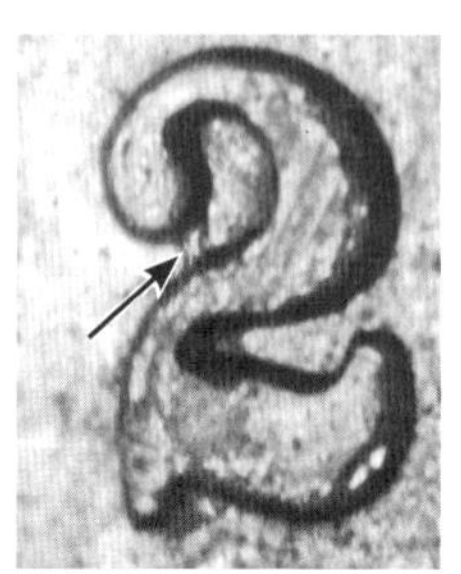

Description: Secondary digits are evident to the north of the 8 and 9. There is a vertical bar, within the opening of the 2, which some believe is a 1. However, most specialists believe this is nothing more than a damaged date punch. A very minor doubled-die reverse is paired with this obverse die.

Comments: This is a very dramatic repunched date and is very scarce.

	VF-20	EF-40	AU-50	MS-60	MS-63	MS-65
VARIETY	$30	$50	$100	$175	$250	$750
NORMAL	$8	$20	$30	$60	$80	$375

Note: Values listed for MS-60 and higher are for RB (red and brown) specimens. Full red Uncirculated specimens command higher prices.

1892 — FS-01-1892-401 (010.91)

VARIETY: Heavy Die Scratches ("Scarface") — SNOW-14

PUP: Cheek

URS-4 • I-4 • L-4

Description: Heavy scratches and/or gouges are evident on the face, neck, and headdress, and slightly into the left field. The origin of these deep scratches is unknown.

Comments: This is affectionately referred to as the "Scarface" variety.

	VF-20	EF-40	AU-50	MS-60	MS-63	MS-65
VARIETY	$75	$150	$300	$750	$1,000	
NORMAL	$8	$20	$30	$60	$80	$375

Note: Values listed for MS-60 and higher are for RB (red and brown) specimens. Full red Uncirculated specimens command higher prices.

1893 FS-01-1893-301 (010.95)

Variety: Repunched Date (RPD-002) Snow-2
PUP: Date
URS-7 • I-3 • L-3

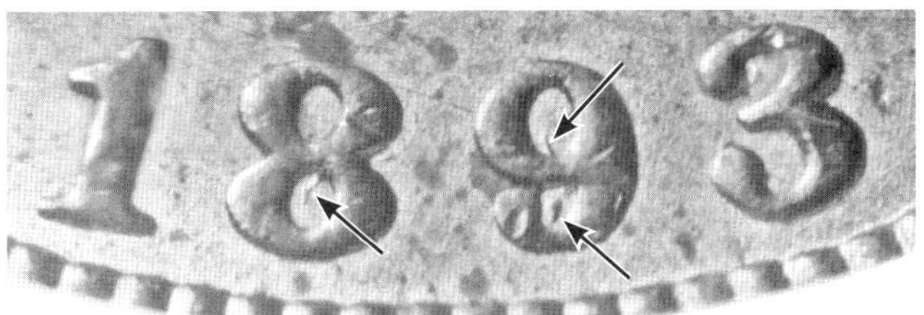

Description: Secondary digits are evident in the lower loop of the 8, in both loops of the 9, and within the upper loop of the 3.

Comments: Lower grades or late die states don't exhibit the secondary image of the 3. A partial roll of these coins was located in the late 1990s.

	VF-20	EF-40	AU-50	MS-60	MS-63	MS-65
Variety	$11	$26	$39	$78	$105	$455
Normal	$8	$20	$30	$60	$80	$350

Note: Values listed for MS-60 and higher are for RB (red and brown) specimens. Full red Uncirculated specimens command higher prices.

1894 FS-01-1894-301 (011)

Variety: Repunched Date (RPD-001) Snow-1
PUP: Date
URS-9 • I-5 • L-5

Description: This massive repunched date is one of the top five varieties in the Indian Head cent series. Secondary digits are vividly evident to the east of the primary digits, with the secondary 4 to the north and east of the primary 4. The repunching can be detected in low grades, and is still saleable down to G-4.

Comments: Don't pass on this variety in any grade. Values have continued to rise over the years as popularity and demand have increased.

	VF-20	EF-40	AU-50	MS-60	MS-63	MS-65
Variety	$250	$400	$600	$1,000	$1,500	$5,000
Normal	$20	$50	$70	$85	$115	$385

Note: Values listed for MS-60 and higher are for RB (red and brown) specimens. Full red Uncirculated specimens command higher prices.

1894 — FS-01-1894-402 (011.2)

VARIETY: Misplaced Digits (MPD-001) — SNOW-2

PUP: Date

URS-6 • I-3 • L-3

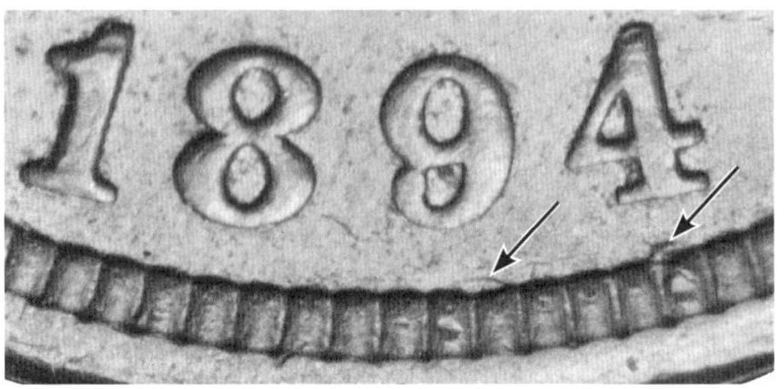

Description: The very top portions of a 9 and a 4 are evident protruding from the denticles below the primary numbers.

Comments: This variety has proven elusive for many years.

	VF-20	EF-40	AU-50	MS-60	MS-63	MS-65
VARIETY	$35	$75	$100	$200	$400	$1,250
NORMAL	$20	$50	$70	$85	$115	$385

Note: Values listed for MS-60 and higher are for RB (red and brown) specimens. Full red Uncirculated specimens command higher prices.

1895 — FS-01-1895-301 (011.3)

VARIETY: Repunched Date (RPD-003) — SNOW-1

PUP: Date

URS-8 • I-3 • L-3

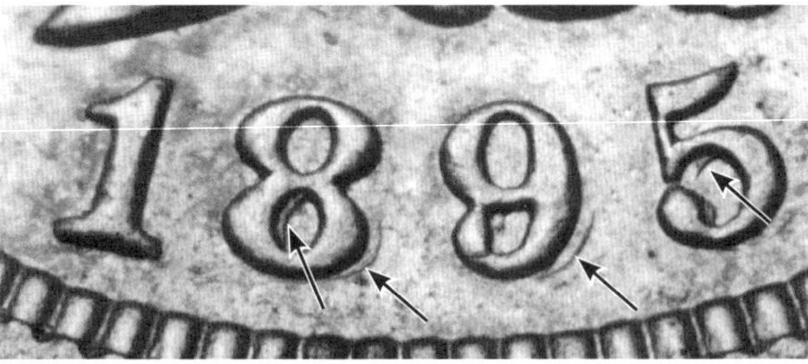

Description: Secondary digits are evident to the right of the primary digits on the 8, 9, and 5.

Comments: There are other, less obvious repunched dates for this date.

	VF-20	EF-40	AU-50	MS-60	MS-63	MS-65
VARIETY	$15	$25	$50	$90	$150	$375
NORMAL	$8	$15	$25	$40	$65	$200

Note: Values listed for MS-60 and higher are for RB (red and brown) specimens. Full red Uncirculated specimens command higher prices.

1895 — FS-01-1895-302 (011.31)

Variety: Repunched Date (RPD-009) — Snow-9
PUP: Date
URS-5 • I-3 • L-3

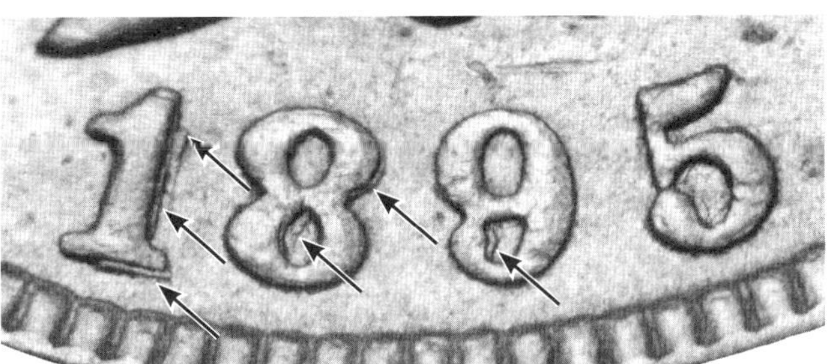

Description: The 1 of the date is tripled, with the two secondary images evident to the right of the primary 1. A secondary 8, 9, and 5 are also evident to the right of the primary.

Comments: This variety is interesting with the tripled 1. It is very rarely seen.

	VF-20	EF-40	AU-50	MS-60	MS-63	MS-65
Variety	$15	$25	$75	$150	$300	$500
Normal	$8	$15	$25	$40	$65	$200

Note: Values listed for MS-60 and higher are for RB (red and brown) specimens. Full red Uncirculated specimens command higher prices.

1895 — FS-01-1895-303

Variety: Repunched Date — Snow-20
PUP: Date
URS-9 • I-4 • L-4

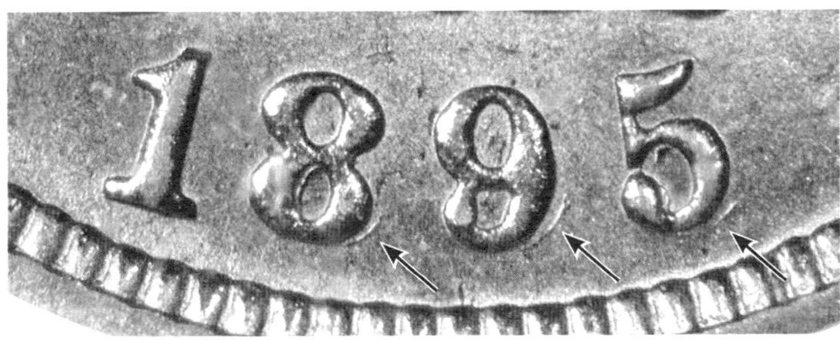

Description: This variety exhibits bold repunching on the 8, 9, and 5.

Comments: This is a very dramatic repunched date. The same die struck Proofs.

	VF-20	EF-40	AU-50	MS-60	MS-63	MS-65
Variety	$75	$100	$150	$200	$400	$500
Normal	$8	$15	$25	$40	$65	$200

Note: Values listed for MS-60 and higher are for RB (red and brown) specimens. Full red Uncirculated specimens command higher prices.

1896 — FS-01-1896-301 (011.4)

Variety: Repunched Date (RPD-001) — Snow-1
PUP: Date
URS-8 • I-3 • L-3

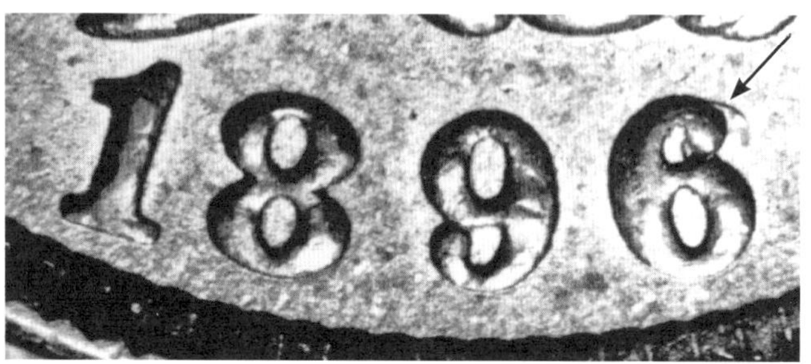

Description: The top of a secondary 6 is evident fairly wide to the right.

Comments: Varieties such as this, wherein only a single digit shows evidence of repunching, are not that uncommon, especially from the 19th century. A similar die (Snow-13) has additional repunching on the 1.

	VF-20	EF-40	AU-50	MS-60	MS-63	MS-65
Variety	$30	$50	$100	$175	$250	$500
Normal	$8	$15	$25	$40	$65	$220

Note: Values listed for MS-60 and higher are for RB (red and brown) specimens. Full red Uncirculated specimens command higher prices.

1896 — FS-01-1896-302

Variety: Date Variety — Snow-21
PUP: Date
URS-1 • I-4 • L-4

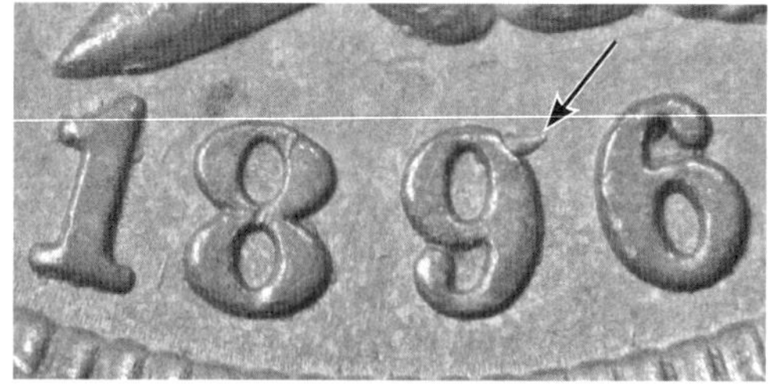

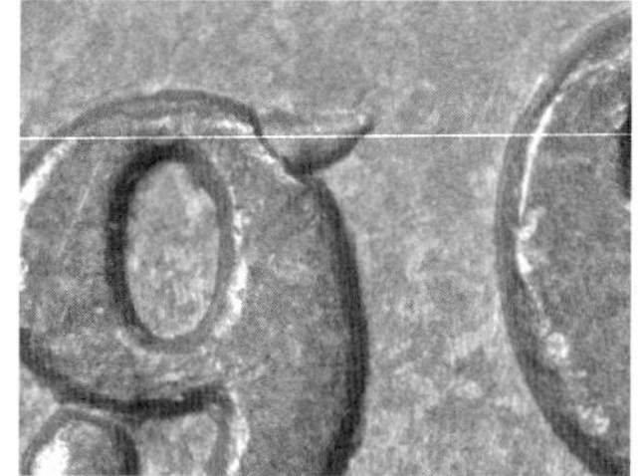

Description: Although this aberration appears to be the flag of a 5, the cause is still undetermined. More research is necessary on this very interesting variety.

Comments: This was discovered by Doug Hill and to date is unique. The boldness of the "horn" would make it visible even in lower grades, and it is surprising it has not been reported until now.

	VF-20	EF-40	AU-50	MS-60	MS-63	MS-65
Variety	(unique)					
Normal	$8	$15	$25	$40	$65	$220

Note: Values listed for MS-60 and higher are for RB (red and brown) specimens. Full red Uncirculated specimens command higher prices.

1897 — FS-01-1897-401 (011.5)

VARIETY: Misplaced Date (MPD-001) — SNOW-1

PUP: Front of neck

URS-9 • I-5 • L-5

Description: The numeral 1 is evident protruding from the front of the neck.

Comments: This variety, although popular, is fairly easy to locate in lower grades. Mint State pieces, though, are very hard to locate. An MS-65RB example sold for $7,500 in 2007.

	VF-20	EF-40	AU-50	MS-60	MS-63	MS-65
VARIETY	$200	$350	$750	$1,000	$2,500	
NORMAL	$8	$15	$25	$40	$65	$200

Note: Values listed for MS-60 and higher are for RB (red and brown) specimens. Full red Uncirculated specimens command higher prices.

1897 — FS-01-1897-402 (011.6)

VARIETY: Repunched Date (RPD-008) — SNOW-8

PUP: Date

URS-6 • I-4 • L-3

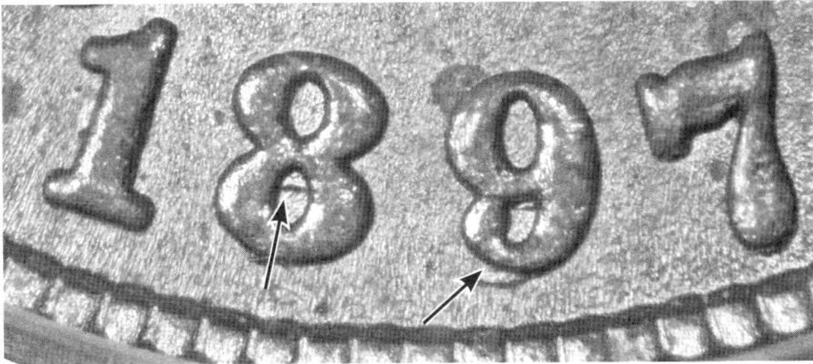

Description: A portion of a loop of the secondary 8 is evident just below the primary center bar, and the lower loop of a secondary 9 is evident just to the south of the primary 9.

Comments: This variety is scarce and dramatic but not as popular as many other repunched dates of the Indian Head cent series.

	VF-20	EF-40	AU-50	MS-60	MS-63	MS-65
VARIETY	$15	$25	$40	$60	$90	$300
NORMAL	$8	$15	$25	$40	$65	$200

Note: Values listed for MS-60 and higher are for RB (red and brown) specimens. Full red Uncirculated specimens command higher prices.

1898 FS-01-1898-401 (011.65)

Variety: Misplaced Date (MPD-012) Snow-12
PUP: Denticles below date
URS-6 • I-2 • L-2

Description: The top of a digit, likely an 8, is evident protruding from the denticles below the second 8.

Comments: This is just one of the many misplaced dates within the series. This one has turned out to be rather scarce in high grades.

	VF-20	EF-40	AU-50	MS-60	MS-63	MS-65
Variety	$10	$20	$40	$60	$150	$400
Normal	$8	$15	$25	$40	$65	$195

Note: Values listed for MS-60 and higher are for RB (red and brown) specimens. Full red Uncirculated specimens command higher prices.

1898 FS-01-1898-402 (011.66)

Variety: Misplaced Date (MPD-003) Snow-5
PUP: Denticles below date
URS-7 • I-3 • L-2

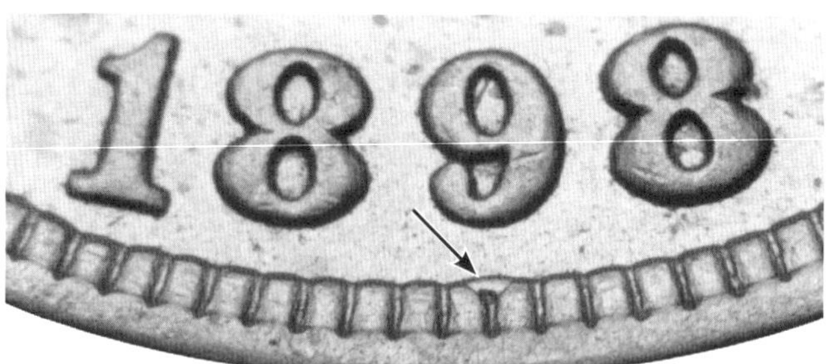

Description: The top of a digit, likely a 9, is evident protruding from the denticles below the primary 9.

Comments: This variety has slightly better eye appeal than the previous. When misplaced dates are visible without magnification, such as this one, they get more interest from collectors.

	VF-20	EF-40	AU-50	MS-60	MS-63	MS-65
Variety	$40	$75	$125	$200	$300	$750
Normal	$8	$15	$25	$40	$65	$195

Note: Values listed for MS-60 and higher are for RB (red and brown) specimens. Full red Uncirculated specimens command higher prices.

1899 — FS-01-1899-301 (011.7)

Variety: Repunched Date (RPD-001) — Snow-1
PUP: Date
URS-7 • I-3 • L-3

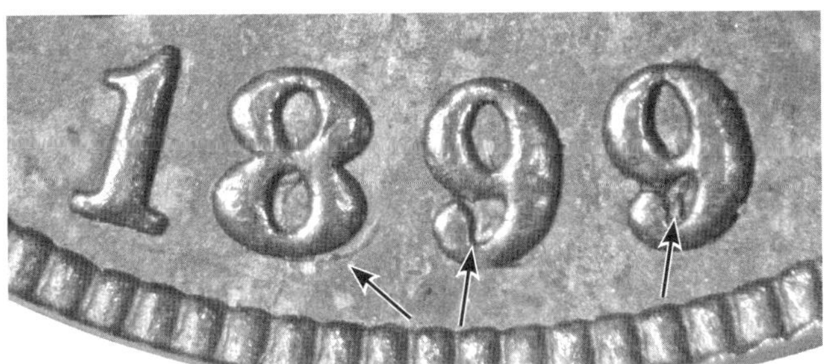

Description: A secondary 8 is evident to the east of the primary 8, and secondary 9's can be detected within the lower loops of both of the primary digits.

Comments: This repunched date is primarily of interest to variety specialists and Indian Head cent collectors.

	VF-20	EF-40	AU-50	MS-60	MS-63	MS-65
Variety	$15	$25	$50	$75	$100	$250
Normal	$8	$15	$25	$40	$65	$195

Note: Values listed for MS-60 and higher are for RB (red and brown) specimens. Full red Uncirculated specimens command higher prices.

1899 — FS-01-1899-302 (011.75)

Variety: Repunched Date (RPD-013) — Snow-13
PUP: Date
URS-8 • I-3 • L-3

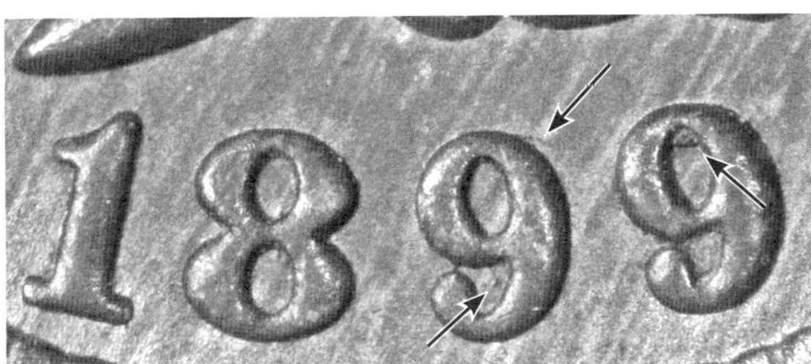

Description: The first 9 is lightly repunched, with the secondary digit visible to the right of the upper portion. There is also a metal fill in the top of the second 9.

Comments: This repunched date is listed by Breen as an overdate, but there is not enough evidence to support that listing in the opinion of most specialists. The variety is primarily of interest to specialists and Indian Head cent collectors.

	VF-20	EF-40	AU-50	MS-60	MS-63	MS-65
Variety	$20	$30	$50	$100	$200	$500
Normal	$8	$15	$25	$40	$65	$195

Note: Values listed for MS-60 and higher are for RB (red and brown) specimens. Full red Uncirculated specimens command higher prices.

1899 FS-01-1899-303

VARIETY: Repunched Date (RPD-009) SNOW-9
PUP: Date
URS-8 • I-3 • L-3

Description: The 1 is repunched, with the secondary digit to the south. The final 9 is also repunched, with the secondary digit to the north.

Comments: This repunched date is primarily of interest to variety specialists and Indian Head cent collectors.

	VF-20	EF-40	AU-50	MS-60	MS-63	MS-65
VARIETY	$15	$20	$35	$60	$100	$300
NORMAL	$8	$15	$25	$40	$65	$195

Note: Values listed for MS-60 and higher are for RB (red and brown) specimens. Full red Uncirculated specimens command higher prices.

1900 FS-01-1900-301 (011.751)

VARIETY: Repunched Date (RPD-001) SNOW-1
PUP: Date
URS-6 • I-4 • L-4

Description: The primary second 0 exhibits a secondary 0 to the northeast.

Comments: This is a dramatic repunched date.

	VF-20	EF-40	AU-50	MS-60	MS-63	MS-65
VARIETY	$20	$30	$50	$100	$225	$500
NORMAL	$6	$10	$20	$35	$60	$170

Note: Values listed for MS-60 and higher are for RB (red and brown) specimens. Full red Uncirculated specimens command higher prices.

1900 FS-01-1900-302

VARIETY: Repunched Date (RPD-003) SNOW-3
PUP: Date
URS-8 • I-4 • L-2

Description: Repunching is visible inside the 9 and to the south. There is also repunching on the 0, to the north.

Comments: This is an easy-to-spot variety—fairly scarce, though.

	VF-20	EF-40	AU-50	MS-60	MS-63	MS-65
VARIETY	$20	$30	$35	$80	$150	$300
NORMAL	$6	$10	$20	$35	$60	$170

Note: Values listed for MS-60 and higher are for RB (red and brown) specimens. Full red Uncirculated specimens command higher prices.

1901 FS-01-1901-301

VARIETY: Repunched Date (RPD-019) SNOW-19
PUP: Date
URS-2 • I-4 • L-2

Description: The first 1 is repunched to the south. The second 1 is repunched to the north.

Comments: This is a fairly bold repunched date. It's easy to spot, but tough to find.

	VF-20	EF-40	AU-50	MS-60	MS-63	MS-65
VARIETY	$25	$50	$75	$150		
NORMAL	$6	$10	$20	$35	$60	$170

Note: Values listed for MS-60 and higher are for RB (red and brown) specimens. Full red Uncirculated specimens command higher prices.

1902 — FS-01-1902-401

VARIETY: Die Gouge — SNOW-4
PUP: Eye
URS-8 • I-5 • L-4

Description: A bold die gouge is under the eye.

Comments: This is a very interesting die gouge. Like the 1870 "Pick-Axe" die gouge, collectors really like it.

	VF-20	EF-40	AU-50	MS-60	MS-63	MS-65
VARIETY	$30	$50	$75	$125	$250	$500
NORMAL	$6	$10	$20	$35	$55	$170

Note: Values listed for MS-60 and higher are for RB (red and brown) specimens. Full red Uncirculated specimens command higher prices.

1903 — FS-01-1903-301 (011.76)

VARIETY: Misplaced Date (MPD-002) — SNOW-10
PUP: Denticles below date
URS-4 • I-3 • L-3

Description: The tops of three digits are evident within the denticles below the date.

Comments: This misplaced date is primarily of interest to variety specialists and Indian Head cent collectors.

	VF-20	EF-40	AU-50	MS-60	MS-63	MS-65
VARIETY	$10	$15	$35	$50	$80	$250
NORMAL	$6	$10	$20	$35	$60	$170

Note: Values listed for MS-60 and higher are for RB (red and brown) specimens. Full red Uncirculated specimens command higher prices.

1903 — FS-01-1903-302 (011.765)

Variety: Misplaced Date (MPD-007) — Snow-6
PUP: Denticles below date
URS-5 • I-3 • L-3

Description: The top of a digit (likely a 0) is evident within the denticles below and right of the primary 0.

Comments: This misplaced date is primarily of interest to variety specialists and Indian Head cent collectors.

	VF-20	EF-40	AU-50	MS-60	MS-63	MS-65
Variety	$10	$15	$35	$50	$80	$250
Normal	$6	$10	$20	$35	$60	$170

Note: Values listed for MS-60 and higher are for RB (red and brown) specimens. Full red Uncirculated specimens command higher prices.

1903 — FS-01-1903-303

Variety: Repunched Date (RPD-006) — Snow-7
PUP: Date
URS-4 • I-4 • L-2

Description: Repunching is evident to the right of the base of the 1, as well as above and to the left of the top of the 1.

Comments: This is a scarce repunched date, but easy to spot.

	VF-20	EF-40	AU-50	MS-60	MS-63	MS-65
Variety	$20	$30	$35	$80	$150	$300
Normal	$6	$10	$20	$35	$60	$170

Note: Values listed for MS-60 and higher are for RB (red and brown) specimens. Full red Uncirculated specimens command higher prices.

1903 — FS-01-1903-304

Variety: Repunched Date (RPD-003) — Snow-3
PUP: Date
URS-6 • I-4 • L-2

Description: Repunching is apparent on the base of all the digits, to the southeast.

Comments: This is a dramatic repunched date.

	VF-20	EF-40	AU-50	MS-60	MS-63	MS-65
Variety	$20	$30	$35	$80	$150	$300
Normal	$6	$10	$20	$35	$60	$170

Note: Values listed for MS-60 and higher are for RB (red and brown) specimens. Full red Uncirculated specimens command higher prices.

1904 — FS-01-1904-301

Variety: Repunched Date (RPD-010) — Snow-10
PUP: Date
URS-6 • I-4 • L-3

Description: Repunching is apparent on the tops of the 0 and 4.

Comments: This is a very noticeable variety.

	VF-20	EF-40	AU-50	MS-60	MS-63	MS-65
Variety	$20	$30	$50	$100	$175	$350
Normal	$6	$10	$20	$40	$60	$170

Note: Values listed for MS-60 and higher are for RB (red and brown) specimens. Full red Uncirculated specimens command higher prices.

1905 — FS-01-1905-301

Variety: Repunched Date (RPD-301) — Snow-1
PUP: Date
URS-8 • I-4 • L-2

Description: Repunching is evident below the 5.

Comments: This is an obvious variety—and very scarce.

	VF-20	EF-40	AU-50	MS-60	MS-63	MS-65
Variety	$20	$30	$35	$80	$150	$300
Normal	$6	$10	$20	$35	$60	$170

Note: Values listed for MS-60 and higher are for RB (red and brown) specimens. Full red Uncirculated specimens command higher prices.

1906 — FS-01-1906-301

Variety: Repunched Date (RPD-001) — Snow-7
PUP: Date
URS-7 • I-4 • L-2

Description: Repunching is apparent below the 1 and 9 and inside the top of the 0.

Comments: There are many minor repunched dates among Indian Head cents of this year. This is one of the more pronounced varieties.

	VF-20	EF-40	AU-50	MS-60	MS-63	MS-65
Variety	$20	$30	$35	$80	$150	$300
Normal	$6	$10	$20	$35	$55	$170

Note: Values listed for MS-60 and higher are for RB (red and brown) specimens. Full red Uncirculated specimens command higher prices.

1906 — FS-01-1906-302

VARIETY: Misplaced Date, Repunched Date (MPD-002, RPD-014) — SNOW-14
PUP: Date, denticles
URS-5 • I-4 • L-2

Description: Repunching is evident inside the top of the 0. The tops of two digits in the denticles are also visible below and slightly left of the 0 and 6.

Comments: Multiple types add desirability to this variety.

	VF-20	EF-40	AU-50	MS-60	MS-63	MS-65
VARIETY	$20	$30	$35	$80	$150	$300
NORMAL	$6	$10	$20	$35	$55	$170

Note: Values listed for MS-60 and higher are for RB (red and brown) specimens. Full red Uncirculated specimens command higher prices.

1906 — FS-01-1906-303

VARIETY: Repunched Date (RPD-017) — SNOW-20
PUP: Date
URS-6 • I-4 • L-2

Description: Bold repunching is evident in the lower loop of the 6, with minor repunching on the 1 and 9 to the south.

Comments: This variety is easy to spot.

	VF-20	EF-40	AU-50	MS-60	MS-63	MS-65
VARIETY	$20	$30	$35	$80	$150	$300
NORMAL	$6	$10	$20	$35	$55	$170

Note: Values listed for MS-60 and higher are for RB (red and brown) specimens. Full red Uncirculated specimens command higher prices.

1907 FS-01-1907-301

VARIETY: Repunched Date (RPD-001) SNOW-1
PUP: Date
URS-8 • I-4 • L-3

Description: Repunching is evident on the base of the 0 and 7 and inside the 9. A minor misplaced digit is visible in the denticles under the 0.

Comments: This is a bold and interesting repunched date.

	VF-20	EF-40	AU-50	MS-60	MS-63	MS-65
VARIETY	$20	$30	$50	$100	$175	$350
NORMAL	$6	$10	$20	$40	$60	$170

Note: Values listed for MS-60 and higher are for RB (red and brown) specimens. Full red Uncirculated specimens command higher prices.

1907 FS-01-1907-302

VARIETY: Repunched Date (RPD-002) SNOW-2
PUP: Date
URS-6 • I-4 • L-3

Description: Very bold repunching is visible inside the 9 and 0.

Comments: This is a very interesting repunched date, although rarely seen.

	VF-20	EF-40	AU-50	MS-60	MS-63	MS-65
VARIETY	$40	$65	$100	$150	$250	$400
NORMAL	$6	$10	$20	$40	$60	$170

Note: Values listed for MS-60 and higher are for RB (red and brown) specimens. Full red Uncirculated specimens command higher prices.

1907 FS-01-1907-303

Variety: Repunched Date (RPD-018) Snow-20
PUP: Date
URS-6 • I-4 • L-2

Description: Wide repunching is apparent inside the bottom of the 9 and 0, to the east.

Comments: This is an obvious repunched date. The variety is tough to locate.

	VF-20	EF-40	AU-50	MS-60	MS-63	MS-65
Variety	$20	$30	$35	$80	$150	$300
Normal	$6	$10	$20	$40	$60	$170

Note: Values listed for MS-60 and higher are for RB (red and brown) specimens. Full red Uncirculated specimens command higher prices.

1907 FS-01-1907-304

Variety: Repunched Date Snow-27
PUP: Date
URS-9 • I-4 • L-4

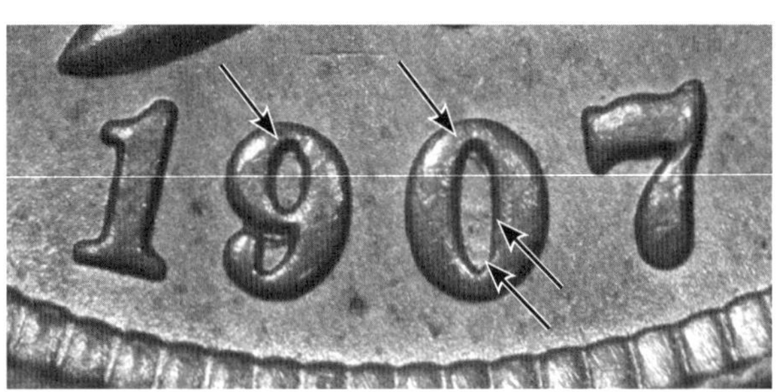

Description: Bold repunching is evident inside the 9 and 0.

Comments: There are multiple digits visible inside the 9 and 0. This is the top variety of the year.

	VF-20	EF-40	AU-50	MS-60	MS-63	MS-65
Variety	$20	$35	$50	$80	$120	$250
Normal	$6	$10	$20	$40	$60	$170

Note: Values listed for MS-60 and higher are for RB (red and brown) specimens. Full red Uncirculated specimens command higher prices.

1908 — FS-01-1908-301 (011.77)

VARIETY: Misplaced Date (MPD-002) — SNOW-4
PUP: Denticles below date
URS-7 • I-3 • L-3

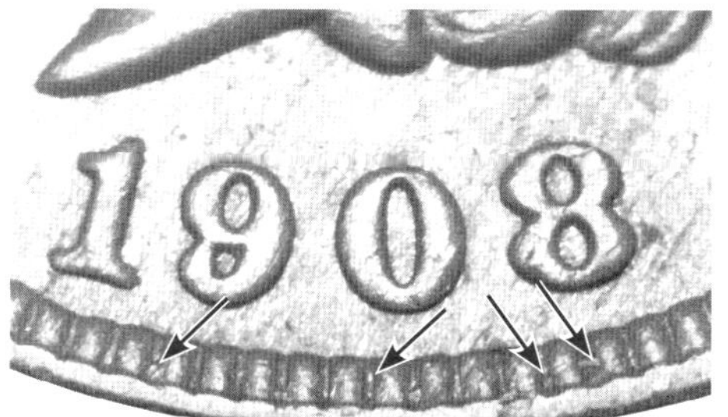
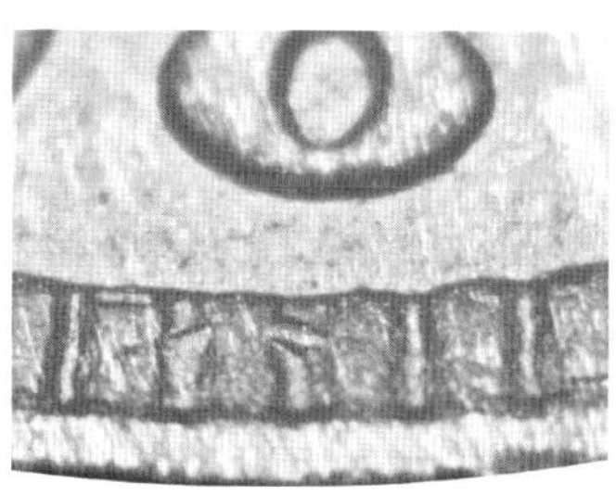

Description: The upper portion of a complete date is evident within the denticles below and slightly left of the primary date. The misplaced date is most prominent under the 8.

Comments: This misplaced date is primarily of interest to variety specialists and Indian Head cent collectors.

	VF-20	EF-40	AU-50	MS-60	MS-63	MS-65
VARIETY	$10	$20	$35	$50	$75	$225
NORMAL	$6	$10	$20	$40	$60	$170

Note: Values listed for MS-60 and higher are for RB (red and brown) specimens. Full red Uncirculated specimens command higher prices.

1908 — FS-01-1908-302 (011.79)

VARIETY: Misplaced Date (MPD-003) — SNOW-9
PUP: Denticles below date
URS-7 • I-3 • L-3

Description: The upper portions of two digits (likely a 9 and 0) are evident within the denticles below the primary 0 and 8.

Comments: This misplaced date is primarily of interest to variety specialists and Indian Head cent collectors.

	VF-20	EF-40	AU-50	MS-60	MS-63	MS-65
VARIETY	$20	$30	$50	$75	$125	$275
NORMAL	$6	$10	$20	$40	$60	$170

Note: Values listed for MS-60 and higher are for RB (red and brown) specimens. Full red Uncirculated specimens command higher prices.

1908-S — FS-01-1908S-501

VARIETY: Repunched Mintmark (RPM-001) — SNOW-1
PUP: Denticles below date
URS-10 • I-5 • L-4

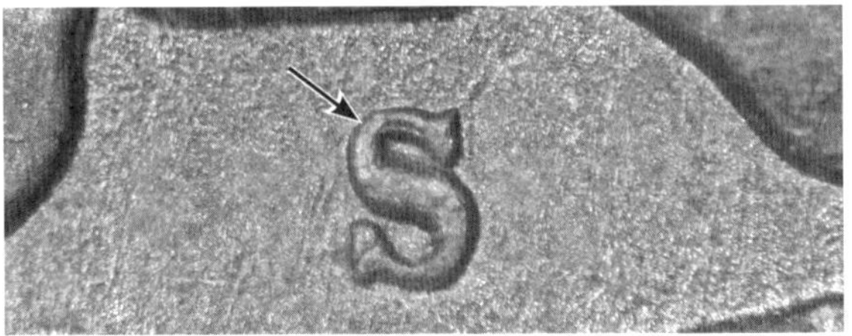

Description: Repunching is visible on the top portion of the mintmark.

Comments: As the only repunched mintmark of the Indian Head cent series, this is quite popular. One variety of 1908-S Indian Head cent shows a straight die line in the upper loop of the S. This is not a repunched date. Regular 1908-S cents with strike doubling may show outlines on the mintmark as well as the base of the wreath.

	VF-20	EF-40	AU-50	MS-60	MS-63	MS-65
VARIETY	$150	$250	$375	$650	$800	$2,500
NORMAL	$145	$175	$250	$290	$400	$850

Note: Values listed for MS-60 and higher are for RB (red and brown) specimens. Full red Uncirculated specimens command higher prices.

1909 — FS-01-1909-101 (011.9)

VARIETY: Doubled-Die Obverse — SNOW-1
PUP: Designer's initial
URS-12 • I-2 • L-2

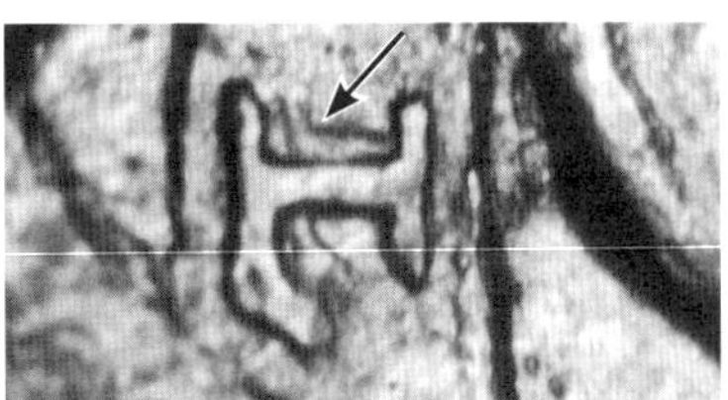

Description: The designer's initial, L, is doubled, giving the illusion of a large L over a small L, though this is not the case. The doubling was apparently on a master die, as many of the working dies have been identified as having this abnormality.

Comments: This variety was once considered more collectible than it is now, due to the false belief that the doubling was, in fact, a "large L over small L." About a quarter of the existing 1909 Indian Head cents show this effect.

	VF-20	EF-40	AU-50	MS-60	MS-63	MS-65
VARIETY	$26	$33	$39	$59	$85	$230
NORMAL	$20	$25	$30	$45	$65	$175

Note: Values listed for MS-60 and higher are for RB (red and brown) specimens. Full red Uncirculated specimens command higher prices.

Lincoln Cents, 1909 to Date

Lincoln cent die varieties are, without a doubt, the most widely collected in today's numismatics. While some varieties in other series might be somewhat difficult to sell, that is not necessarily the case with Lincoln cents. They are always popular, and always in demand. The series is alive and kickin', with new die varieties being brought to the hobby's attention every year. We encourage collectors to dig into this rich field.

A list of the books that we highly recommend for further study of varieties would have to begin with *The Authoritative Reference on Lincoln Cents*, by John A. Wexler et al. Loaded with photos of varieties, this is a treasure trove for the enthusiast. Others include *The RPM Book, Second Edition: Lincoln Cents*, by James Wiles; *The Complete Price Guide and Cross Reference to Lincoln Cent Mint Mark Varieties*, by John A. Wexler and Brian Allen; *A Quick Reference to the Top Lincoln Cent Die Varieties*, by Gary Wagnon et al.; *The Lincoln Cent Doubled Die Book, Vol. 1: 1908–1958*, by James Wiles; *The Lincoln Cent RPM Book, Vol. 1, 1908–1958*, third ed., by James Wiles; *The Lincoln Cent RPM Book, Vol. 2, 1959–1989*, third ed., by James Wiles; and *Ultra Modern Doubled Dies 1996–2012*, by James Wiles.

If you're interested in more general books on the Lincoln cent, an excellent one is *The Complete Guide to Lincoln Cents*, by David W. Lange. Sol Taylor's *Standard Guide to the Lincoln Cent*, fourth edition, and Q. David Bowers's *Guide Book of Lincoln Cents* are also both wonderful choices.

As of press time there is no national club or organization dedicated to the Lincoln cent—an opportunity for enthusiastic cherrypickers to start one up and make their mark on the hobby! However, there has been some discussion of the Society of Lincoln Cent Collectors starting up again.

Longtime specialist Chuck Daughtrey maintains www.coppercoins.com, billed as the largest and most comprehensive catalog of Lincoln cent die varieties ever published.

Lincoln cents and their die varieties are often discussed in online forums like the Collectors Universe Message Boards (forums.collectors.com) and the Collectors Society Message Boards (boards.collectors-society.com). The Lincoln Cent Forum (www.lincolncentforum.com) is an active online community for all kinds of related discussion. James Wiles's "Variety Vista" Web site (www.varietyvista.com) is a resource for ongoing research on many kinds of die varieties, and the Lincoln Cent Resource (www.lincolncentresource.com) is devoted specifically to Lincoln cent doubled dies, repunched mintmarks, over mintmarks, large and small dates, wide AM's, and other varieties in the series.

NEWLY LISTED VARIETIES

FIVAZ-STANTON NUMBER	VARIETY	PAGE NO.
FS-01-1934D-101	DDO	109
FS-01-1942-101	DDO	116
FS-01-1942-104	DDO	117
FS-01-1943-801	DDR	120
FS-01-1944D-101	DDO	122
FS-01-1945-101	DDO	125
FS-01-1946S-501	IMM	125
FS-01-1949S-101	DDO	128
FS-01-1953-401	Re-Engraved Die	132
FS-01-1953-402	Re-Engraved Die	132
FS-01-1953D-502	RPM	133
FS-01-1955-103/801	DDO / DDR	136
FS-01-1956-101	DDO	138
FS-01-1956-801	DDR	139
FS-01-1956D-502	RPM	140
FS-01-1960-801	DDR	145
FS-01-1960D-502	RPM	146
FS-01-1962-801	DDR	147
FS-01-1963-801	DDR	147
FS-01-1966-801	DDR	150
FS-01-1979S-501	Type 2 MM	166
FS-01-1981S-501	Type 2 MM	166
FS-01-1983-802	DDR	170
FS-01-1983D-101	DDO	171
FS-01-1987D-501	DDO	173
FS-01-1988-101	DDO	173
FS-01-1988-901	PF Rev	174
FS-01-1988D-901	PF Rev	174
FS-01-1992-901	Circ Rev	175
FS-01-1998S-901	Circ Rev	175
FS-01-1996-101	DDO	178
FS-01-2004-801	DDR	179
FS-01-2006-101	DDO	179
FS-01-2009-801	DDR	180–181
FS-01-2009-802	DDR	180–181
FS-01-2009-803	DDR	180–181
FS-01-2009-804	DDR	180–181
FS-01-2009-805	DDR	180–181
FS-01-2009-806	DDR	180–181
FS-01-2009-807	DDR	180–181
FS-01-2009-808	DDR	180–181
FS-01-2009S-801	DDR	180–181
FS-01-2014-101	DDO	182

DEBUNKED VARIETIES

FIVAZ-STANTON NUMBER	VARIETY
FS-01-1951D-521	Misplaced MM
FS-01-1955D-511	RPM
FS-01-1964-803	DDR
FS-01-1969D-901	Missing Designer's Initial
FS-01-1971-102	DDO
FS-01-1980D-000	OMM
FS-01-2000S-901	Circulation Rev

1909, V.D.B. — FS-01-1909-1101 (012)

VARIETY: Doubled-Die Obverse — CONECA: DDO-001
PUP: Date, RTY of LIBERTY
URS-13 • I-3 • L-3

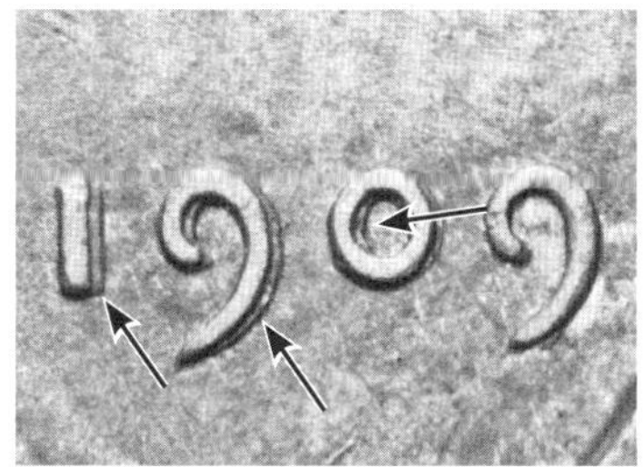

Description: Doubling is evident on the RTY of LIBERTY and on all four digits of the date, with the secondary image east of the primary image.

Comments: This variety can be located in Uncirculated grades with some looking. Values have more than doubled in recent years.

	VF-20	EF-40	AU-50	MS-60	MS-63	MS-65
VARIETY	$25	$40	$60	$90	$150	$225
NORMAL	$18	$19	$20	$25	$30	$100

Note: Values listed for MS-60 and higher are for RB (red and brown) specimens. Full red Uncirculated specimens command higher prices.

1909, V.D.B. — FS-01-1909-1102 (012.1)

VARIETY: Doubled-Die Obverse — CONECA: DDO-002
PUP: Date, R of LIBERTY
URS-12 • I-2 • L-3

Description: The doubling on this variety is evident as extra thickness on all obverse letters and numbers, but it is most noticeable on the date. The upright strokes of the letters of LIBERTY are also thicker than normal, and there is a die chip within the upper loop of the R. The die chip also occurs on coins without the doubled-die obverse.

Comments: This variety is scarcer than FS-01-1909-1101, but less evident and usually more difficult to sell.

	VF-20	EF-40	AU-50	MS-60	MS-63	MS-65
VARIETY	$20	$25	$40	$75	$100	$150
NORMAL	$18	$19	$20	$25	$30	$100

Note: Values listed for MS-60 and higher are for RB (red and brown) specimens. Full red Uncirculated specimens command higher prices.

1909-S FS-01-1909S-1501 (012.2)

Variety: Repunched Mintmark CONECA: RPM-001
PUP: Mintmark
URS-10 • I-3 • L-4

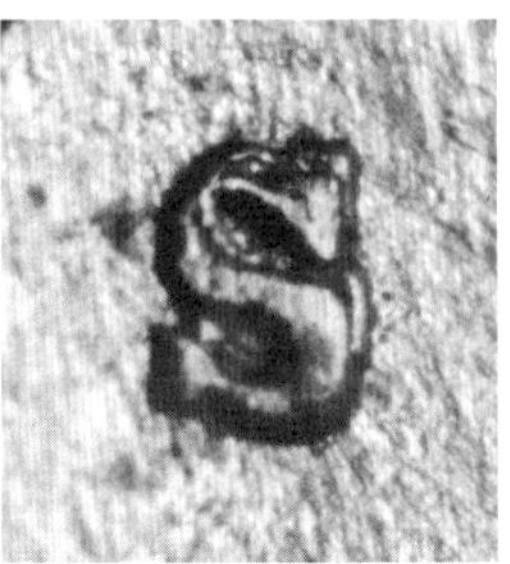

Description: A secondary S is evident slightly north of the primary S.

Comments: Though not as well known as the S Over Horizontal S variety (next listing), this repunched mintmark is scarcer and in much more demand by specialists than the well-known variety.

	VF-20	EF-40	AU-50	MS-60	MS-63	MS-65
Variety	$200	$300	$350	$400	$600	$850
Normal	$150	$225	$275	$325	$365	$650

Note: Values listed for MS-60 and higher are for RB (red and brown) specimens. Full red Uncirculated specimens command higher prices.

1909-S FS-01-1909S-1502 (012.3)

Variety: Repunched Mintmark CONECA: RPM-002
PUP: Mintmark
URS-12 • I-4 • L-5

Description: A secondary S is evident north of the primary S, but orientated horizontally.

Comments: This is a relatively easy variety to purchase, as many examples have already been located and authenticated. Late die states make the horizontal orientation of the secondary S difficult to view, yet the fact that there is a repunched mintmark is still evident.

	VF-20	EF-40	AU-50	MS-60	MS-63	MS-65
Variety	$175	$250	$300	$350	$400	$750
Normal	$150	$225	$275	$325	$365	$650

Note: Values listed for MS-60 and higher are for RB (red and brown) specimens. Full red Uncirculated specimens command higher prices.

1910-S — FS-01-1910S-501

VARIETY: Repunched Mintmark — CONECA: RPM-001
PUP: Mintmark
URS-7 • I-2 • L-2

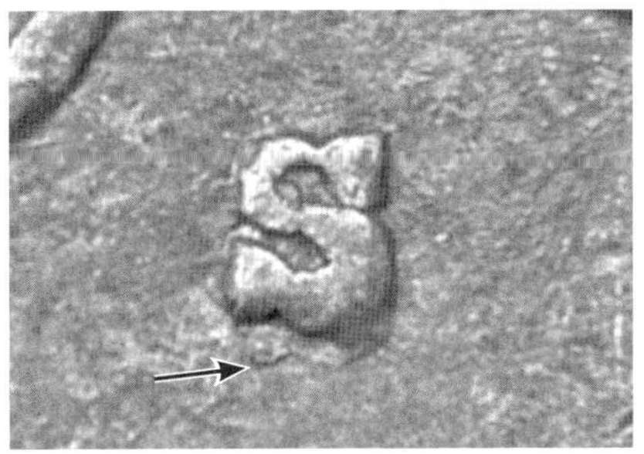

Description: A secondary S is evident south of the primary S.

Comments: Primarily due to the relatively high value of the normal coins, any premium associated with this variety in higher grades will generally be minimal.

	VF-20	EF-40	AU-50	MS-60	MS-63	MS-65
VARIETY	$50	$75	$125	$150	$200	$500
NORMAL	$25	$45	$80	$100	$120	$400

Note: Values listed for MS-60 and higher are for RB (red and brown) specimens. Full red Uncirculated specimens command higher prices.

1910-S — FS-01-1910S-502 (012.7)

VARIETY: Repunched Mintmark — CONECA: RPM-002
PUP: Mintmark
URS-8 • I-4 • L-4

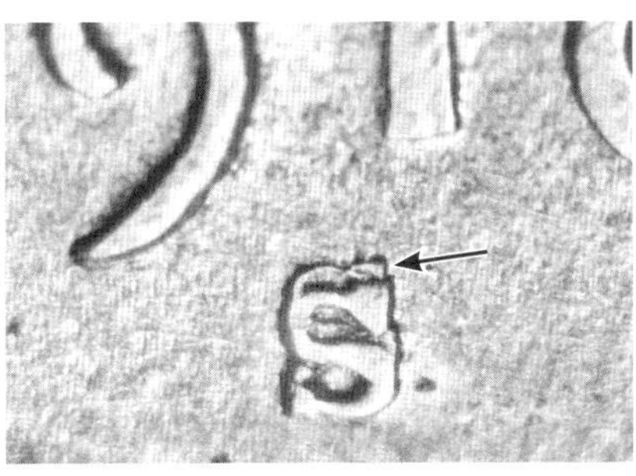

Description: A secondary S is evident north of the primary S.

Comments: This variety may be slightly easier to sell than the previous repunched mintmark, primarily due to its popularity. Interest in this particular variety has been rising.

	VF-20	EF-40	AU-50	MS-60	MS-63	MS-65
VARIETY	$40	$50	$95	$125	$175	$450
NORMAL	$25	$45	$80	$100	$120	$400

Note: Values listed for MS-60 and higher are for RB (red and brown) specimens. Full red Uncirculated specimens command higher prices.

1911-D — FS-01-1911D-501 (012.8)

Variety: Repunched Mintmark — CONECA: RPM-001
PUP: Mintmark
URS-4 • I-3 • L-3

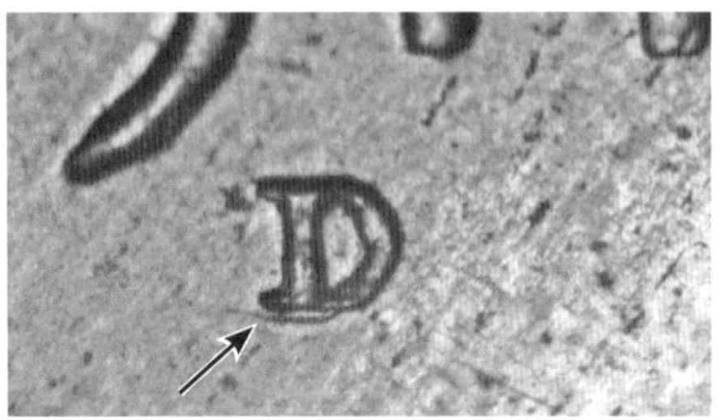

Description: A secondary D is evident southwest of the primary D.

Comments: Primarily due to the relatively high value of the regular coins, Extremely Fine and About Uncirculated specimens may be easier to sell than higher grades.

	VF-20	EF-40	AU-50	MS-60	MS-63	MS-65
Variety	$35	$75	$100	$150	$200	$850
Normal	$20	$50	$75	$95	$125	$650

Note: Values listed for MS-60 and higher are for RB (red and brown) specimens. Full red Uncirculated specimens command higher prices.

1911-D — FS-01-1911D-502 (012.81)

Variety: Repunched Mintmark — CONECA: RPM-002
PUP: Mintmark
URS-3 • I-3 • L-4

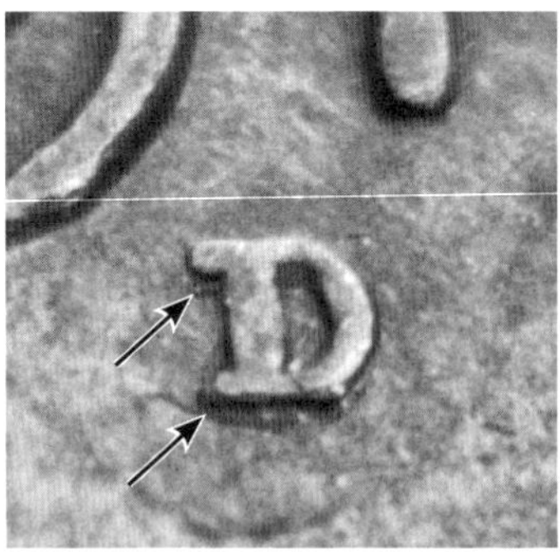

Description: A secondary D is evident to the southwest of the primary D. The vertical bar of the secondary D is evident slightly west of the primary D.

Comments: As of this writing, there are no known Mint State specimens. Primarily due to the relatively high value of the regular coins, Extremely Fine and About Uncirculated specimens may be easier to sell than higher grades.

	VF-20	EF-40	AU-50	MS-60	MS-63	MS-65
Variety	$35	$75	$100			
Normal	$20	$50	$75	$95	$125	$650

1911-D — FS-01-1911D-503 (012.82)

VARIETY: Repunched Mintmark — CONECA: RPM-003
PUP: Mintmark
URS-2 • I-3 • L-4

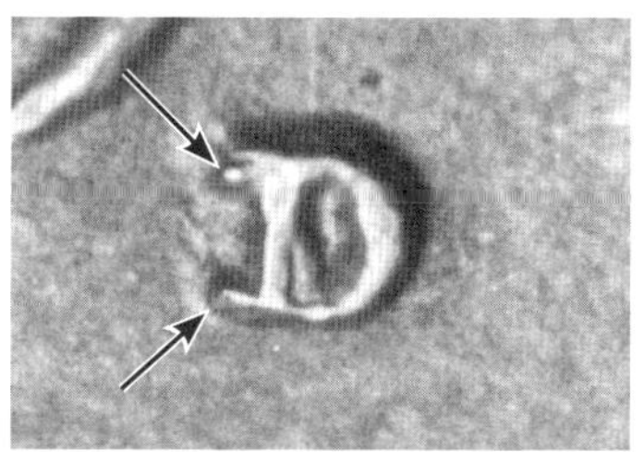

Description: The secondary D mintmark is rotated slightly counterclockwise in relation to the primary D. The top serif of the weaker D is evident just south of the primary upper serif, and a portion of the secondary D's vertical bar is evident within the loop of the primary D.

	VF-20	EF-40	AU-50	MS-60	MS-63	MS-65
VARIETY	$42	$90	$120	$180	$240	$950
NORMAL	$20	$50	$75	$95	$125	$650

Note: Values listed for MS-60 and higher are for RB (red and brown) specimens. Full red Uncirculated specimens command higher prices.

1911-D — FS-01-1911D-504 (012.83)

VARIETY: Repunched Mintmark — CONECA: RPM-004
PUP: Mintmark
URS-3 • I-3 • L-4

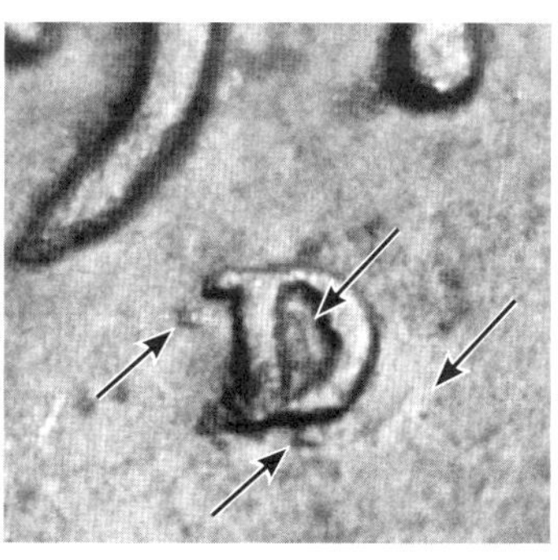

Description: This variety is actually a triple-punched mintmark, with portions of the secondary mintmarks evident south and southeast of the primary D.

Comments: Very few examples of this variety are known, with no Mint State examples reported.

	VF-20	EF-40	AU-50	MS-60	MS-63	MS-65
VARIETY	$35	$75	$100			
NORMAL	$20	$50	$75	$95	$125	$650

1911-S FS-01-1911S-501 (012.85)

VARIETY: Repunched Mintmark CONECA: RPM-001
PUP: Mintmark
URS-4 • I-3 • L-3

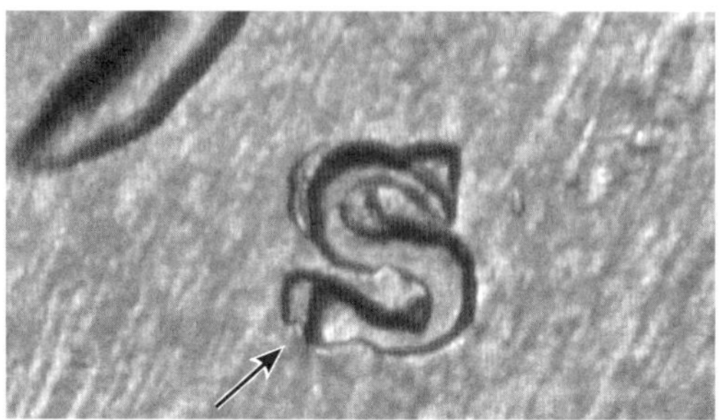

Description: A secondary S mintmark is evident to the west of the primary mintmark.

Comments: This variety is highly sought after by serious Lincoln cent collectors. RPM-002 is very similar, though positioned higher.

	VF-20	EF-40	AU-50	MS-60	MS-63	MS-65
VARIETY	$75	$100	$125	$200	$325	$1,000
NORMAL	$65	$85	$110	$185	$235	$900

Note: Values listed for MS-60 and higher are for RB (red and brown) specimens. Full red Uncirculated specimens command higher prices.

1917 FS-01-1917-101 (013)

VARIETY: Doubled-Die Obverse CONECA: DDO-001
PUP: Date, TRUST
URS-8 • I-5 • L-5

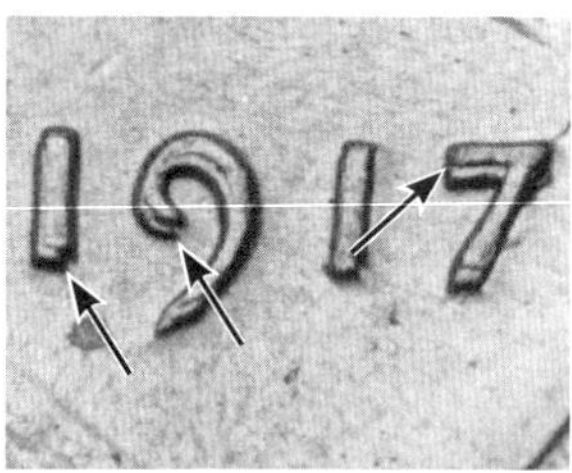

Description: The doubling on this very popular variety is evident on the date and GOD WE TRUST. The earliest-die-state specimens will exhibit slight doubling on the RTY of LIBERTY.

Comments: This variety has finally become arguably the most sought-after of the early Lincoln cent varieties. Grades as low as G-4 are easily sold, and higher-grade examples may command prices higher than those listed here.

	VF-20	EF-40	AU-50	MS-60	MS-63	MS-65
VARIETY	$600	$1,000	$2,000	$3,500	$7,000	$15,000
NORMAL	$2	$4	$10	$16	$32	$140

Note: Values listed for MS-60 and higher are for RB (red and brown) specimens. Full red Uncirculated specimens command higher prices.

1922-(D) FS-01-1922-401, 402 (013.2)

VARIETY: "No D" Mintmark, "Weak D" Mintmark CONECA: N/L
PUP: Mintmark area
URS-11 • I-5 • L-5

Die pair #1

Die pair #2

Die pair #3

Description: The mintmark from this working die was omitted.

Comments: There is only one die pair for the "No D" variety universally recognized, commonly referred to as die pair #2. While all three die pairings have been referred to in the past as a "No D," only die pair #2 had the D mintmark completely obliterated. The other two die pairs (#1 and #3) had a D mintmark at varying times, with the D being either partially or completely obliterated either during heavy die polishing, or resulting from a filled die. Die pair #2 is identified by several markers: (1) the second 2 in the date is sharper than the first, (2) all letters of TRUST are very sharp, (3) WE is only slightly mushy, and (4) the reverse is very sharp. Die pairs #1 and #3 are known for their weak reverses, dates, and mottoes and resulted in coins of the "Weak D" variety. Any specimen should be authenticated by a reputable third-party service.

	VF-20	EF-40	AU-50	MS-60	MS-63	MS-65
Variety, "No D"	$1,300	$2,650	$4,925	$10,500	$26,500	$72,500
Variety, "Weak D"	$70	$160	$200	$350	$1,000	$7,500
Normal	$27	$40	$75	$110	$165	$465

Note: Values listed for MS-60 and higher are for RB (red and brown) specimens. Full red Uncirculated specimens command higher prices.

1925-S — FS-01-1925S-101 (013.3)

VARIETY: Doubled-Die Obverse — CONECA: DDO-001
PUP: Date, LIBERTY, motto
URS-5 • I-3 • L-3

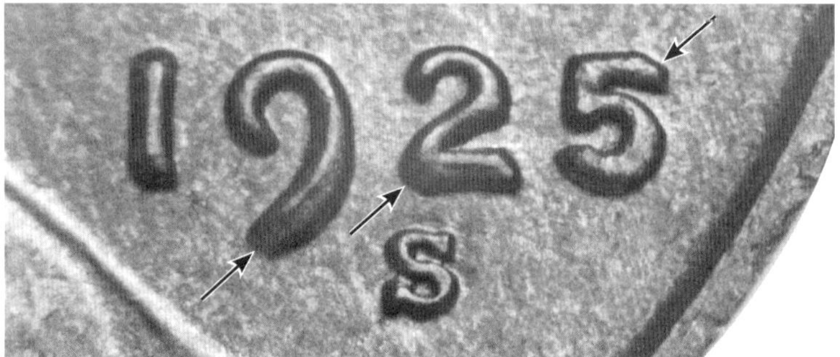

Description: Strong doubling is evident on all obverse letters and numbers. Most of the doubling is evident as extra thickness, though some separation can be detected on the digits of the date.

Comments: This variety was first published in the April 1988 issue of ***ErrorScope***.

	VF-20	EF-40	AU-50	MS-60	MS-63	MS-65
VARIETY	$25	$50	$90	$250	$500	$3,750
NORMAL	$2.75	$12	$30	$90	$200	$3,400

Note: Values listed for MS-60 and higher are for RB (red and brown) specimens. Full red Uncirculated specimens command higher prices.

1925-S — FS-01-1925S-501 (013.31)

VARIETY: Repunched Mintmark — CONECA: RPM-001
PUP: Mintmark
URS-8 • I-3 • L-3

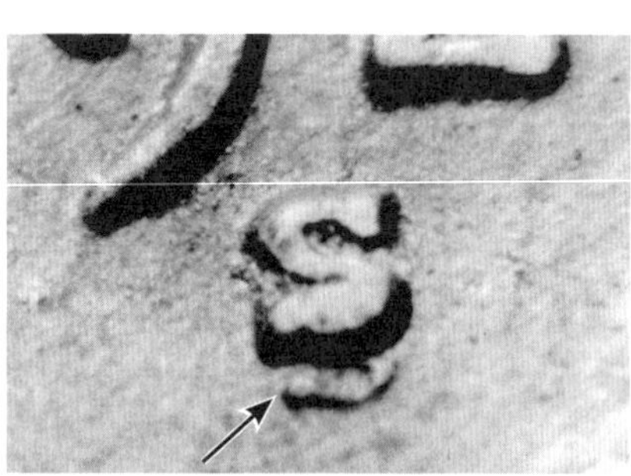

Description: The remains of a secondary S are evident to the south of the primary mintmark.

Comments: This is a fairly popular repunched mintmark, highly sought after by variety specialists and Lincoln cent collectors.

	VF-20	EF-40	AU-50	MS-60	MS-63	MS-65
VARIETY	$20	$35	$90	$250	$500	$3,750
NORMAL	$2.75	$12	$30	$90	$200	$3,400

Note: Values listed for MS-60 and higher are for RB (red and brown) specimens. Full red Uncirculated specimens command higher prices.

1927 — FS-01-1927-101 (013.5)

VARIETY: Doubled-Die Obverse — CONECA: DDO-001
PUP: Motto, date, LIBERTY
URS-8 • I-3 • L-3

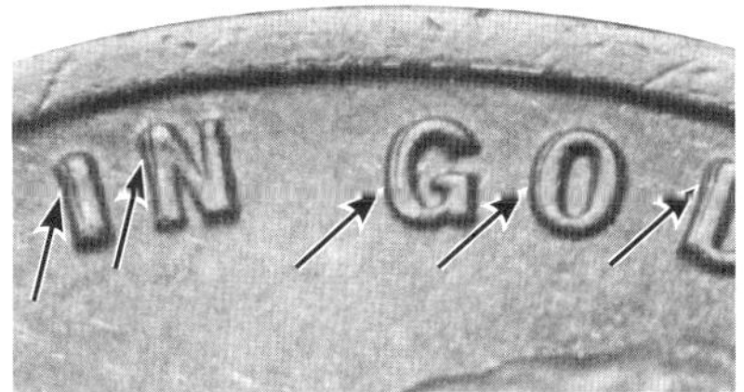

Description: Moderate doubling is evident on the LIBE of LIBERTY, IN GOD WE TRUST, and slightly on the date.

Comments: Although the doubling is not very evident on later die states, this variety is very collectible among Lincoln cent specialists.

	VF-20	EF-40	AU-50	MS-60	MS-63	MS-65
VARIETY	$10	$25	$50	$75	$150	$300
NORMAL	$0.60	$2	$4	$10	$20	$40

Note: Values listed for MS-60 and higher are for RB (red and brown) specimens. Full red Uncirculated specimens command higher prices.

1927-D — FS-01-1927D-501 (013.51)

VARIETY: Repunched Mintmark — CONECA: RPM-001
PUP: Mintmark
URS-8 • I-4 • L-3

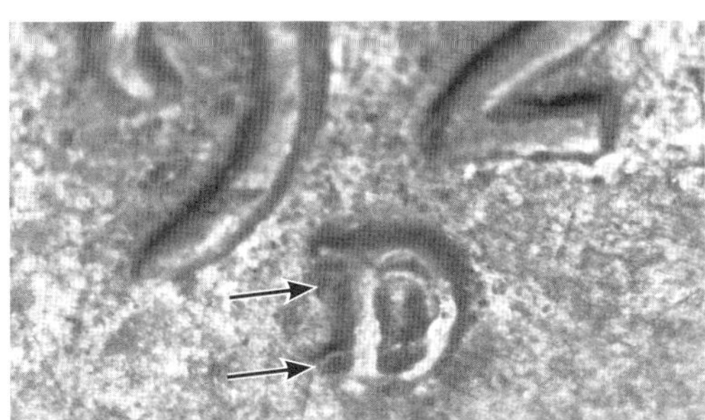

Description: This strong repunched mintmark is evident with the secondary D visible to the north of the primary D.

Comments: This die also exhibits a very minor doubled-die obverse with a doubled eyelid, listed as CONECA DDO-001. This may appear to be a Large D Over Small D (or vice versa) to many, but it is simply a nice repunched mintmark.

	VF-20	EF-40	AU-50	MS-60	MS-63	MS-65
VARIETY	$10	$25	$50	$75	$250	$650
NORMAL	$3.75	$7.50	$25	$62	$85	$575

Note: Values listed for MS-60 and higher are for RB (red and brown) specimens. Full red Uncirculated specimens command higher prices.

1928-S — FS-01-1928S-501 (013.6)

Variety: Large S Mintmark — CONECA: MMS-003
PUP: Mintmark
URS-14 • I-3 • L-3

Small mintmark

Large mintmark

Description: The common mintmark for this date is relatively small. This large S mintmark is very scarce and highly collectible.

Comments: All Lincoln cent mintmark varieties are growing rapidly in popularity.

	VF-20	EF-40	AU-50	MS-60	MS-63	MS-65
Variety	$15	$25	$50	$95	$150	$950
Normal	$3.75	$9.50	$30	$75	$100	$875

Note: Values listed for MS-60 and higher are for RB (red and brown) specimens. Full red Uncirculated specimens command higher prices.

1929-S — FS-01-1929S-501 (013.65)

Variety: Repunched Mintmark — CONECA: RPM-001
PUP: Mintmark
URS-6 • I-3 • L-3

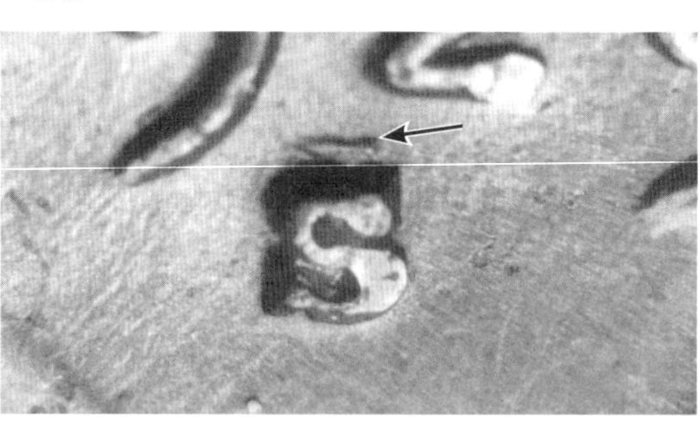

Description: The secondary S mintmark is evident north of the primary mintmark.

Comments: This repunched mintmark is considered rare, and is tough to locate in any grade.

	VF-20	EF-40	AU-50	MS-60	MS-63	MS-65
Variety	$10	$25	$40	$60	$100	$250
Normal	$2.35	$5.80	$14	$21	$29	$185

Note: Values listed for MS-60 and higher are for RB (red and brown) specimens. Full red Uncirculated specimens command higher prices.

1930-D — FS-01-1930D-501

VARIETY: Repunched Mintmark — CONECA: RPM-001
PUP: Mintmark
URS-8 • I-3 • L-3

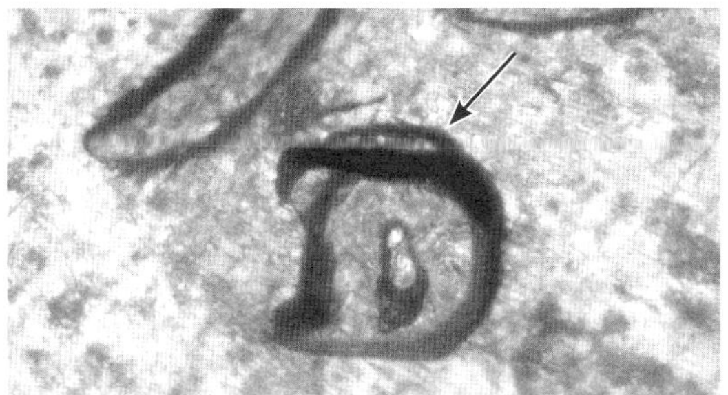

Description: The secondary mintmark is evident north of the primary D.

Comments: This is another very popular repunched mintmark.

	VF-20	EF-40	AU-50	MS-60	MS-63	MS-65
VARIETY	$10	$25	$40	$60	$100	$175
NORMAL	$0.55	$2.50	$4	$12	$28	$45

Note: Values listed for MS-60 and higher are for RB (red and brown) specimens. Full red Uncirculated specimens command higher prices.

1930-D — FS-01-1930D-502 (013.7)

VARIETY: Repunched Mintmark — CONECA: RPM-002
PUP: Mintmark
URS-8 • I-3 • L-3

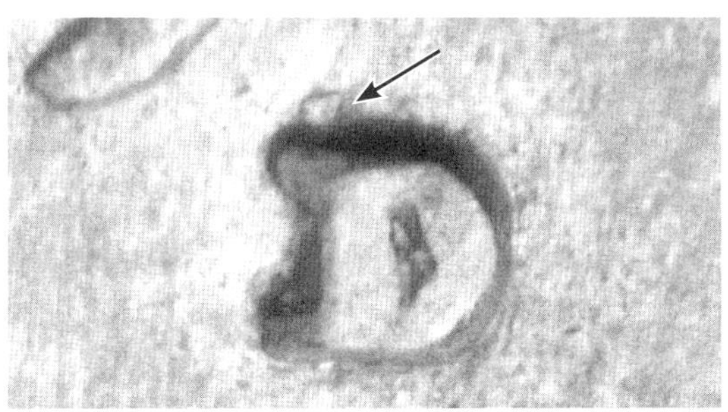

Description: The secondary mintmark is evident north of the primary D.

Comments: This is yet another very popular repunched mintmark.

	VF-20	EF-40	AU-50	MS-60	MS-63	MS-65
VARIETY	$10	$25	$40	$60	$100	$175
NORMAL	$0.55	$2.50	$4	$12	$28	$45

Note: Values listed for MS-60 and higher are for RB (red and brown) specimens. Full red Uncirculated specimens command higher prices.

1930-S — FS-01-1930S-501 (013.73)

Variety: Repunched Mintmark — CONECA: RPM-001
PUP: Mintmark
URS-8 • I-3 • L-3

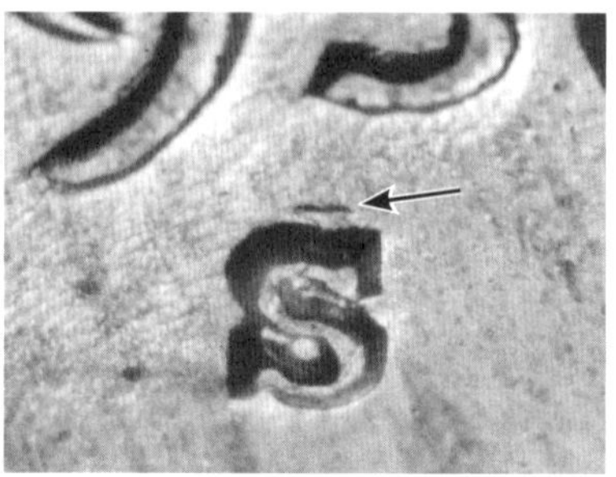

Description: The secondary S is evident north of the primary S.

Comments: This is a well-known and highly collected repunched mintmark.

	VF-20	EF-40	AU-50	MS-60	MS-63	MS-65
Variety	$5	$10	$15	$25	$45	$75
Normal	$0.60	$1.75	$6	$10	$12	$29

Note: Values listed for MS-60 and higher are for RB (red and brown) specimens. Full red Uncirculated specimens command higher prices.

1934 — FS-01-1934-101 (013.79)

Variety: Doubled-Die Obverse — CONECA: DDO-004
PUP: Field below date
URS-4 • I-4 • L-4

Description: The remains of a secondary 9 and 3 are evident below the primary digits.

Comments: Since this was first reported by Lee Day, very few additional specimens have been found.

	VF-20	EF-40	AU-50	MS-60	MS-63	MS-65
Variety	$150	$225	$300	$450	$750	$1,500
Normal	$0.30	$1	$4	$6	$7	$16

Note: Values listed for MS-60 and higher are for RB (red and brown) specimens. Full red Uncirculated specimens command higher prices.

1934-D — FS-01-1934D-101

VARIETY: Doubled-Die Obverse — CONECA: DDO-001
PUP: Date, all lettering
URS-6 • I-3 • L-3

Description: This variety exhibits extreme extra thickness on all lettering and date.

Comments: The extra thickness is caused by the flattening of the hub, either through wear or improper annealing.

	VF-20	EF-40	AU-50	MS-60	MS-63	MS-65
VARIETY	$10	$20	$35	$50	$75	$125
NORMAL	$0.75	$2.25	$7.50	$13.75	$20	$48

Note: Values listed for MS-60 and higher are for RB (red and brown) specimens. Full red Uncirculated specimens command higher prices.

1934-D — FS-01-1934D-503 (013.81)

VARIETY: Repunched Mintmark (D/D/D/D) — CONECA: RPM-003
PUP: Mintmark
URS-8 • I-3 • L-3

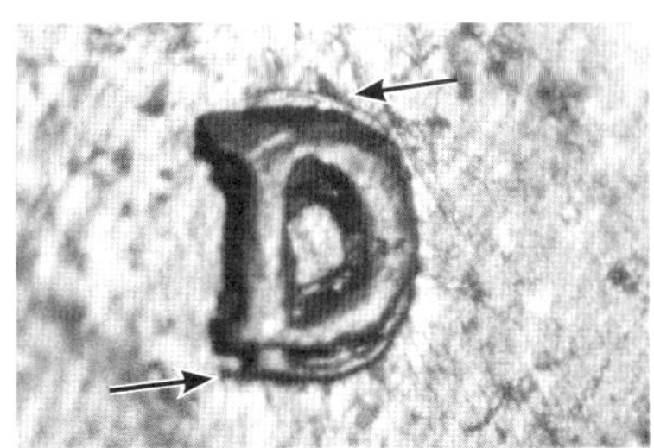

Description: This is a quadruple-punched mintmark, with one secondary D evident to the northwest of the primary D, and two other secondary D's evident to the south of the primary D.

Comments: This repunched mintmark was long thought to be a triple-punched repunched mintmark, but a recent discovery of an early-die-state specimen expanded the known attributes.

	VF-20	EF-40	AU-50	MS-60	MS-63	MS-65
VARIETY	$5	$8	$15	$20	$25	$75
NORMAL	$0.75	$2.25	$7.50	$13.75	$20	$48

Note: Values listed for MS-60 and higher are for RB (red and brown) specimens. Full red Uncirculated specimens command higher prices.

1934-D — FS-01-1934D-504 (013.8)

Variety: Repunched Mintmark — CONECA: RPM-004
PUP: Mintmark
URS-8 • I-3 • L-3

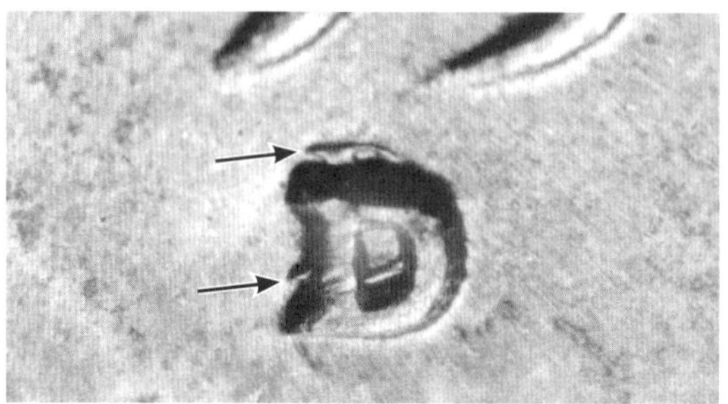

Description: The secondary mintmark is evident to the north of the primary D.

Comments: This variety may appear to be a large over small mintmark, but it is believed to be a normal repunched mintmark with the same-sized letter punches.

	VF-20	EF-40	AU-50	MS-60	MS-63	MS-65
Variety	$5	$8	$15	$20	$25	$75
Normal	$0.75	$2.25	$7.50	$13.75	$20	$48

Note: Values listed for MS-60 and higher are for RB (red and brown) specimens. Full red Uncirculated specimens command higher prices.

1935 — FS-01-1935-101 (013.9)

Variety: Doubled-Die Obverse — CONECA: DDO-001
PUP: Date
URS-6 • I-4 • L-3

Description: Moderate doubling is evident on the date and IN GOD WE TRUST.

Comments: This variety is extremely scarce overall, and exceptionally rare in Mint State. It is well known to Lincoln cent and variety specialists, yet very few specimens have been located.

	VF-20	EF-40	AU-50	MS-60	MS-63	MS-65
Variety	$10	$20	$50	$150	$250	$500
Normal	$0.25	$0.50	$1	$3	$5	$28

Note: Values listed for MS-60 and higher are for RB (red and brown) specimens. Full red Uncirculated specimens command higher prices.

1936 — FS-01-1936-101 (014)

VARIETY: Doubled-Die Obverse — CONECA: DDO-001
PUP: Date, LIBERTY
URS-10 • I-4 • L-5

Description: Very strong doubling is evident on the date, LIBERTY, and IN GOD WE TRUST.

Comments: This is the first of three significant doubled dies for this date. This listing and the following (FS-102) are the strongest and most desirable. However, the third is no slouch, and is in very high demand. Collectors like to assemble all three of the 1936-dated varieties. This variety is extremely rare in Mint State.

	VF-20	EF-40	AU-50	MS-60	MS-63	MS-65
Variety	$75	$100	$250	$500	$2,000	$9,000
Normal	$0.50	$1.50	$2.60	$5	$10	$14

Note: Values listed for MS-60 and higher are for RB (red and brown) specimens. Full red Uncirculated specimens command higher prices.

1936 — FS-01-1936-102 (015)

VARIETY: Doubled-Die Obverse — CONECA: DDO-002
PUP: IN GOD WE TRUST
URS-10 • I-4 • L-4

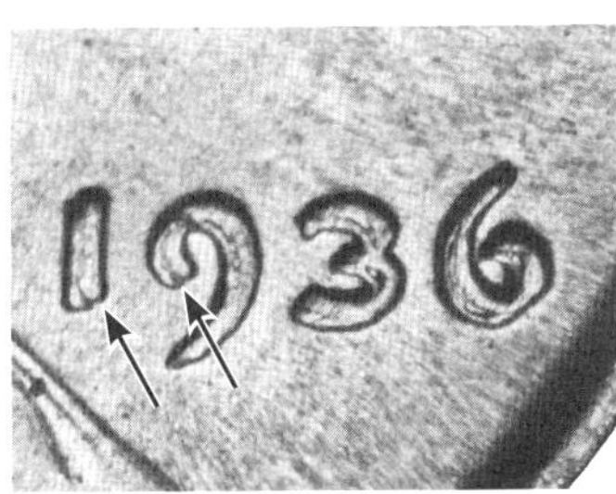

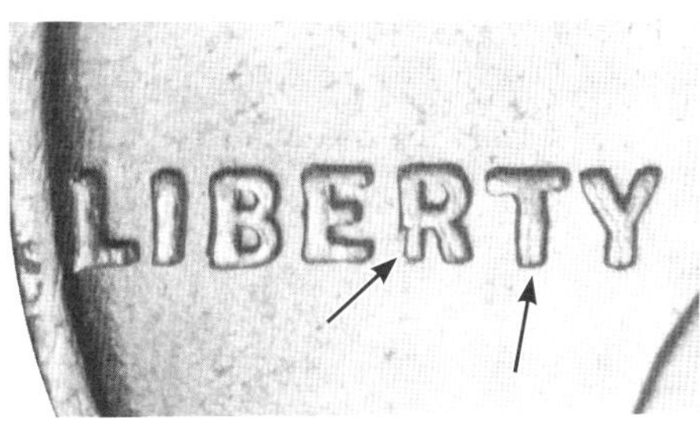

Description: Strong doubling is evident on the date, IN GOD WE TRUST, and LIBERTY.

Comments: One of the working hubs for the 1936 cents had a broken left leg of the R in LIBERTY. This listing was first hubbed by that broken-leg-R hub, then had a second hubbing with a normal-R hub.

	VF-20	EF-40	AU-50	MS-60	MS-63	MS-65
Variety	$75	$100	$200	$300	$1,000	$2,000
Normal	$0.50	$1.50	$2.60	$5	$10	$14

Note: Values listed for MS-60 and higher are for RB (red and brown) specimens. Full red Uncirculated specimens command higher prices.

1936 — FS-01-1936-103 (016)

Variety: Doubled-Die Obverse — CONECA: DDO-003
PUP: IN GOD WE TRUST
URS-7 • I-4 • L-4

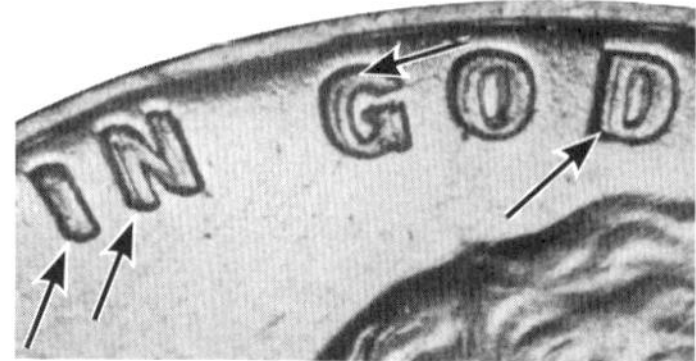

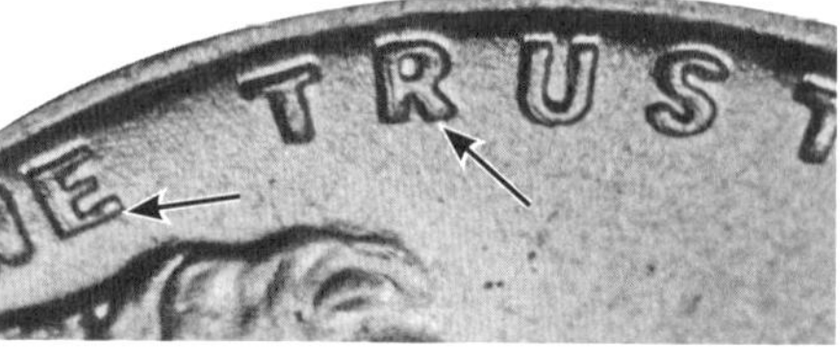

Description: Strong doubling is evident on IN GOD WE TRUST and LIBERTY, with a slight rotation of the secondary image counterclockwise to the primary image.

Comments: This is the third of the major 1936 doubled dies.

	VF-20	EF-40	AU-50	MS-60	MS-63	MS-65
Variety	$25	$50	$75	$100	$250	$500
Normal	$0.50	$1.50	$2.60	$5	$10	$14

Note: Values listed for MS-60 and higher are for RB (red and brown) specimens. Full red Uncirculated specimens command higher prices.

1938-D — FS-01-1938D-501 (016.4)

Variety: Repunched Mintmark — CONECA: RPM-001
PUP: Mintmark
URS-10 • I-2 • L-2

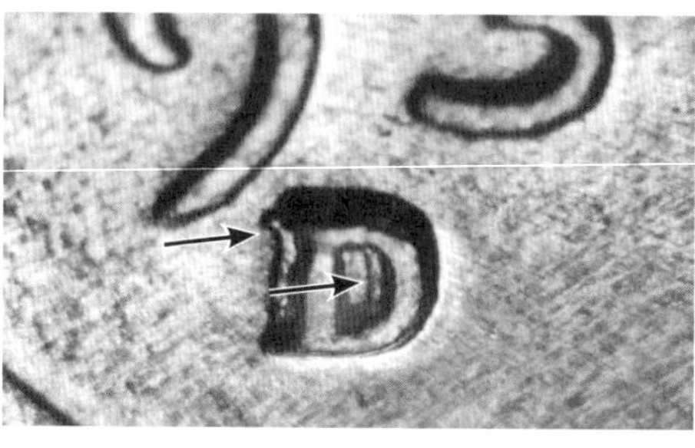

Description: The secondary mintmark is evident west of the primary D.

Comments: Although this repunched mintmark is obtainable and only scarce, demand remains fairly high.

	VF-20	EF-40	AU-50	MS-60	MS-63	MS-65
Variety	$5	$7.50	$10	$15	$25	$35
Normal	$0.80	$1.25	$3	$4	$7	$13

Note: Values listed for MS-60 and higher are for RB (red and brown) specimens. Full red Uncirculated specimens command higher prices.

1938-S FS-01-1938S-501 (016.51)

VARIETY: Repunched Mintmark CONECA: RPM-001
PUP: Mintmark
URS-10 • I-3 • L-3

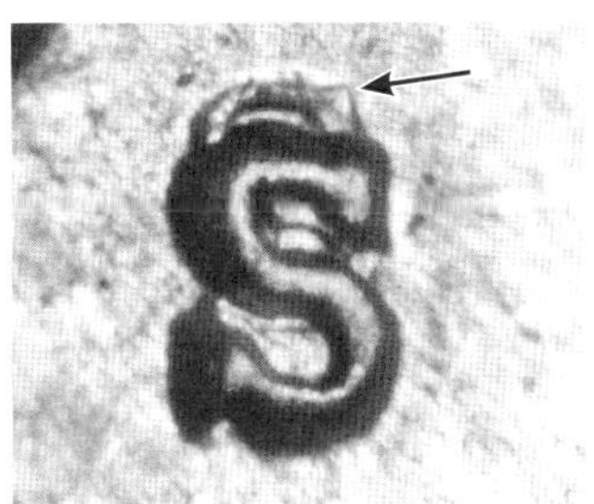

Description: The secondary S mintmark is evident north of the primary S.

Comments: This is one of the more popular repunched mintmarks in the Lincoln series—much scarcer than the next listing, which is better known. The early-die-state specimens (shown here) are very easy to sell.

	VF-20	EF-40	AU-50	MS-60	MS-63	MS-65
VARIETY	$5	$7.50	$10	$15	$25	$35
NORMAL	$0.75	$1.10	$3	$4	$6	$14

Note: Values listed for MS-60 and higher are for RB (red and brown) specimens. Full red Uncirculated specimens command higher prices.

1938-S FS-01-1938S-502 (016.5)

VARIETY: Repunched Mintmark (S/S/S) CONECA: RPM-002
PUP: Mintmark
URS-11 • I-3 • L-3

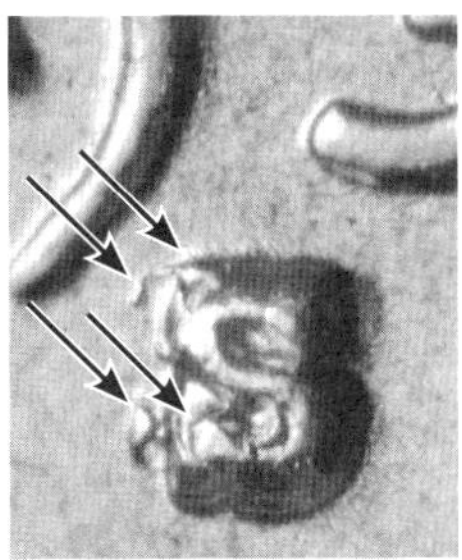

Description: This is a popular triple-punched mintmark, with both secondary images northwest of the primary S. All three S mintmarks are clearly visible, especially on Mint State examples.

Comments: Though this is a very popular repunched mintmark, supply seems to at least equal demand.

	VF-20	EF-40	AU-50	MS-60	MS-63	MS-65
VARIETY	$5	$7.50	$10	$15	$25	$35
NORMAL	$0.75	$1.10	$3	$4	$6	$14

Note: Values listed for MS-60 and higher are for RB (red and brown) specimens. Full red Uncirculated specimens command higher prices.

1939 — FS-01-1939-101 (017)

VARIETY: Doubled-Die Obverse — CONECA: DDO-001

PUP: Date, LIBERTY

URS-8 • I-3 • L-2

Description: Although the first hubbing was weak, the spread of the doubling is strong on the 1 and 9 of the date, BERTY of LIBERTY, the eyelid, and the ear.

Comments: This variety proves to be fairly scarce and difficult to find. The popularity of the coin has grown in recent years.

	VF-20	EF-40	AU-50	MS-60	MS-63	MS-65
VARIETY	$24	$30	$36	$45	$75	$150
NORMAL	$0.25	$0.50	$1	$2	$3	$8

Note: Values listed for MS-60 and higher are for RB (red and brown) specimens. Full red Uncirculated specimens command higher prices.

1941 — FS-01-1941-101 (018)

VARIETY: Doubled-Die Obverse — CONECA: DDO-001

PUP: LIBERTY, TRUST

URS-11 • I-4 • L-4

Description: The doubling is strongest on LIBERTY and IN GOD WE TRUST. The spread of the doubling is strong; however, the first hubbing was very weak in that the hub was set shallow in the die.

Comments: This is one of the "old school" doubled dies and has been known by specialists for decades. It can still be cherrypicked from time to time.

	VF-20	EF-40	AU-50	MS-60	MS-63	MS-65
VARIETY	$25	$50	$75	$100	$200	$300
NORMAL	$0.30	$0.60	$1.50	$2	$3	$14

Note: Values listed for MS-60 and MS-63 are for RB (red and brown) specimens; values listed for MS-65 specimens are for full red specimens.

1941 — FS-01-1941-102 (018.1)

VARIETY: Doubled-Die Obverse — CONECA: DDO-002
PUP: IN GOD WE TRUST
URS-10 • I-4 • L-4

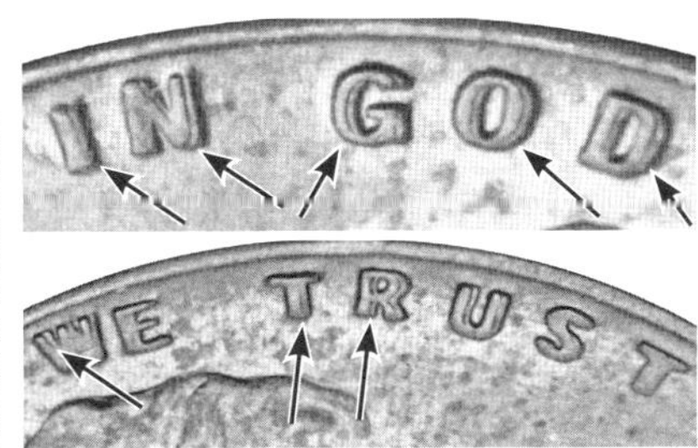

Description: This is similar to FS-01-1941-101; the doubling is evident on LIBERTY and IN GOD WE TRUST, and slightly on the date. The first hubbing was almost as strong as the second, which creates the primary difference between this listing and the previous.

Comments: This variety is in slightly greater demand than the previous listing.

	VF-20	EF-40	AU-50	MS-60	MS-63	MS-65
VARIETY	$25	$50	$75	$100	$200	$300
NORMAL	$0.30	$0.60	$1.50	$2	$3	$14

Note: Values listed for MS-60 and MS-63 are for RB (red and brown) specimens; values listed for MS-65 specimens are for full red specimens.

1941 — FS-01-1941-103 (018.3)

VARIETY: Doubled-Die Obverse — CONECA: DDO-005
PUP: Ear, LIBERTY, 1 and 9 of the date
URS-9 • I-4 • L-3

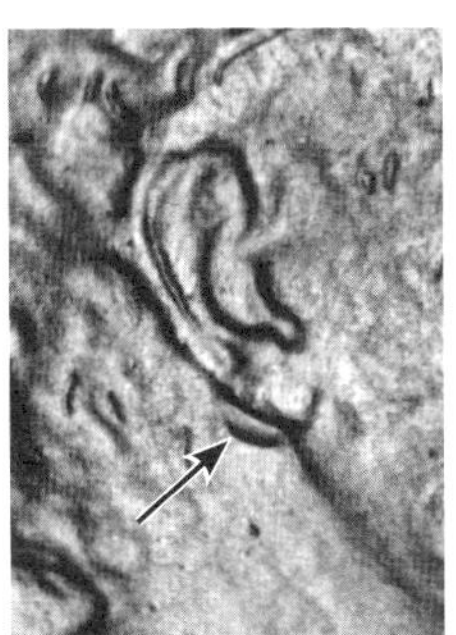

Description: The doubling is particularly evident as a second earlobe to the south, and also in the 1 and 9 of the date and the TY of LIBERTY.

Comments: The first hubbing was very weak and may be visible only on higher-grade specimens.

	VF-20	EF-40	AU-50	MS-60	MS-63	MS-65
VARIETY	$25	$50	$75	$100	$200	$300
NORMAL	$0.30	$0.60	$1.50	$2	$3	$14

Note: Values listed for MS-60 and MS-63 are for RB (red and brown) specimens; values listed for MS-65 specimens are for full red specimens.

1942 FS-01-1942-101

Variety: Doubled-Die Obverse CONECA: DDO-002
PUP: Eye, date
URS-6 • I-3 • L-3

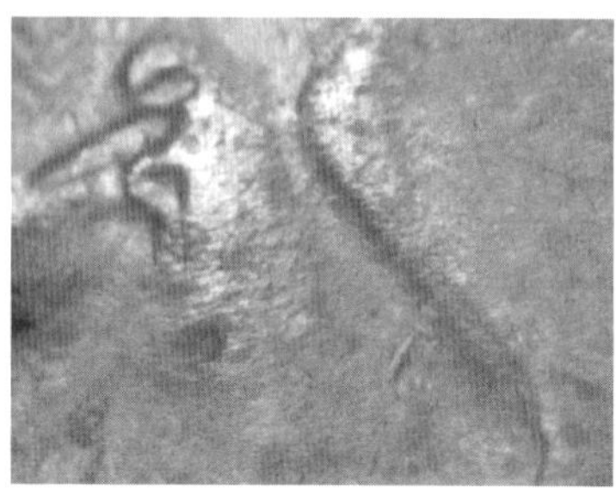

Description: There is a strong spread southwest on the 1 and 9 of the date, as well as at Lincoln's tie, eyelid, upper hair, and profile.

Comments: This is one of four strong doubled-eye varieties for this date. Can you collect them all?

	VF-20	EF-40	AU-50	MS-60	MS-63	MS-65
Variety	$10	$15	$25	$70	$100	$150
Normal	$0.25	$0.50	$0.75	$1	$2	$14

Note: Values listed for MS-60 and MS-63 are for RB (red and brown) specimens; values listed for MS-65 are for full red specimens.

1942 FS-01-1942-102 (018.7)

Variety: Doubled-Die Obverse CONECA: DDO-004
PUP: LIBERTY, 1 of the date
URS-4 • I-2 • L-3

Description: The first hubbing, although somewhat weak, is visible to the north on LIBERTY and the 1 of the date.

Comments: This variety was discovered years ago by Del Romines.

	VF-20	EF-40	AU-50	MS-60	MS-63	MS-65
Variety	$10	$15	$25	$70	$100	$150
Normal	$0.25	$0.50	$0.75	$1	$2	$14

Note: Values listed for MS-60 and MS-63 are for RB (red and brown) specimens; values listed for MS-65 specimens are for full red specimens.

1942 FS-01-1942-103 (018.9)

Variety: Doubled-Die Obverse CONECA: DDO-006
PUP: Eyelid, TRUST
URS-4 • I-3 • L-2

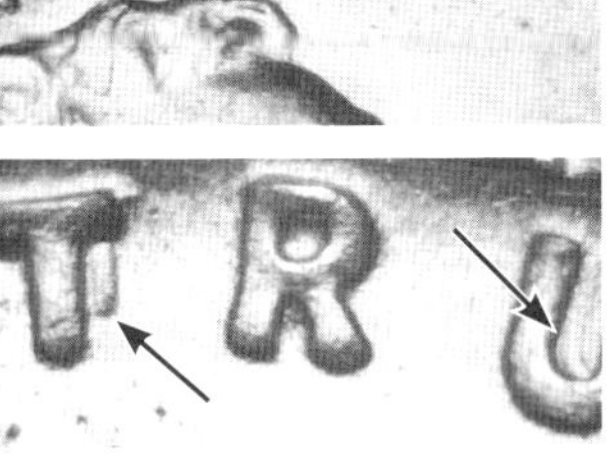
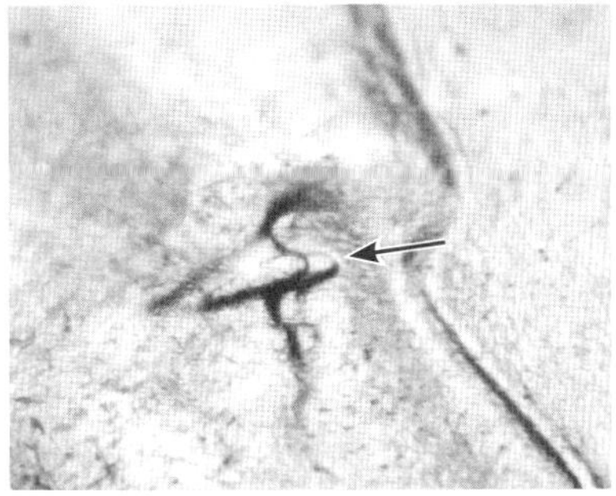

Description: Faint doubling is evident on IN GOD WE TRUST, LIBERTY, and the date, though a strong spread can be detected on high-grade specimens. Very strong doubling is evident on the eyelid.

Comments: Due to the weakness of the secondary image, look for the doubled eyelid. There are several known doubled dies for this date with a doubled eyelid, but only this variety also has strong doubling on TRUST.

	VF-20	EF-40	AU-50	MS-60	MS-63	MS-65
Variety	$10	$15	$25	$70	$100	$150
Normal	$0.25	$0.50	$0.75	$1	$2	$14

Note: Values listed for MS-60 and MS-63 are for RB (red and brown) specimens; values listed for MS-65 specimens are for full red specimens.

1942 FS-01-1942-104

Variety: Doubled-Die Obverse CONECA: DDO-008
PUP: Eye, nose
URS-4 • I-4 • L-3

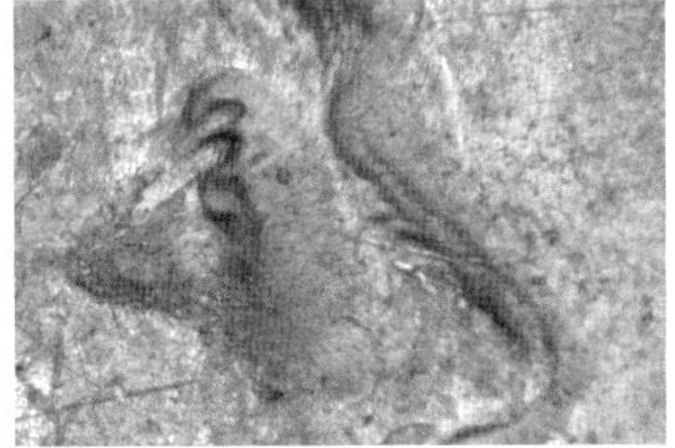

Description: This variety exhibits astrong spread south on the 1 and 9 of the date, as well as at Lincoln's tie, eye, nose, and top of head.

Comments: This variety has been known for some time, but is exceptionally difficult to obtain and is eagerly sought after.

	VF-20	EF-40	AU-50	MS-60	MS-63	MS-65
Variety	$10	$15	$25	$70	$100	$150
Normal	$0.25	$0.50	$0.75	$1	$2	$14

Note: Values listed for MS-60 and MS-63 are for RB (red and brown) specimens; values listed for MS-65 are for full red specimens.

1942-D FS-01-1942D-502 (018.91)

Variety: Repunched Mintmark CONECA: RPM-002
PUP: Mintmark
URS-8 • I-3 • L-3

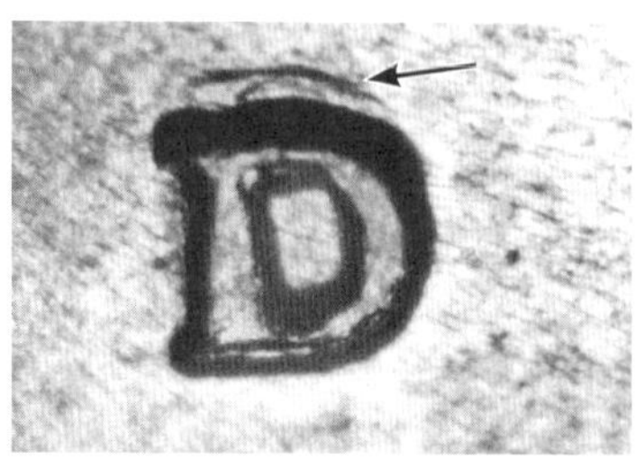

Description: The secondary D is evident to the north of the primary D.

Comments: There are several nice, collectible repunched mintmarks for this series in the 1940s.

	VF-20	EF-40	AU-50	MS-60	MS-63	MS-65
Variety	$5	$8	$10	$15	$20	$35
Normal	$0.25	$0.50	$0.85	$1	$2	$14

Note: Values listed for MS-60 and MS-63 are for RB (red and brown) specimens; values listed for MS-65 specimens are for full red specimens.

1942-D FS-01-1942D-504 (018.92)

Variety: Repunched Mintmark CONECA: RPM-004
PUP: Mintmark
URS-6 • I-3 • L-3

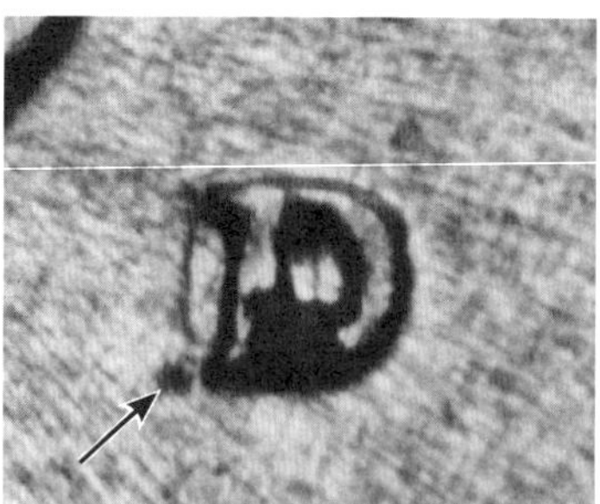

Description: The secondary D is evident to the west of the primary D.

Comments: This is another of several nice, collectible repunched mintmarks for this series in the 1940s.

	VF-20	EF-40	AU-50	MS-60	MS-63	MS-65
Variety	$5	$8	$10	$15	$20	$35
Normal	$0.25	$0.50	$0.85	$1	$2	$14

Note: Values listed for MS-60 and MS-63 are for RB (red and brown) specimens; values listed for MS-65 specimens are for full red specimens.

1942-S FS-01-1942S-101/301 (018.94)

VARIETY: Doubled-Die Obverse, Repunched Mintmark CONECA: DDO-001/RPM-001
PUP: LIBERTY, date, mintmark
URS-9 • I-3 • L-3

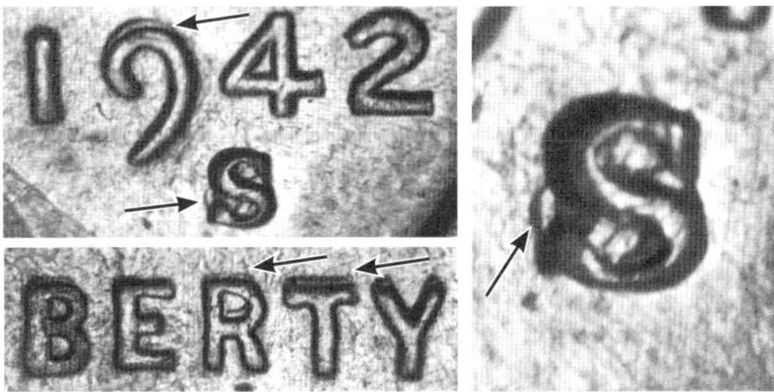

Description: The doubling on this variety is evident to the north on LIBERTY, IN GOD, the eyelid, and the 1 and 9 of the date. The mintmark is also repunched, with the secondary S evident to the west of the primary S.

Comments: This variety is difficult to locate.

	VF-20	EF-40	AU-50	MS-60	MS-63	MS-65
VARIETY	$15	$35	$50	$120	$150	$300
NORMAL	$0.85	$1.25	$5.50	$7	$11	$17

Note: Values listed for MS-60 and MS-63 are for RB (red and brown) specimens; values listed for MS-65 specimens are for full red specimens.

1942-S FS-01-1942S-512 (018.93)

VARIETY: Repunched Mintmark (S/S/S) CONECA: RPM-012
PUP: Mintmark
URS-4 • I-4 • L-3

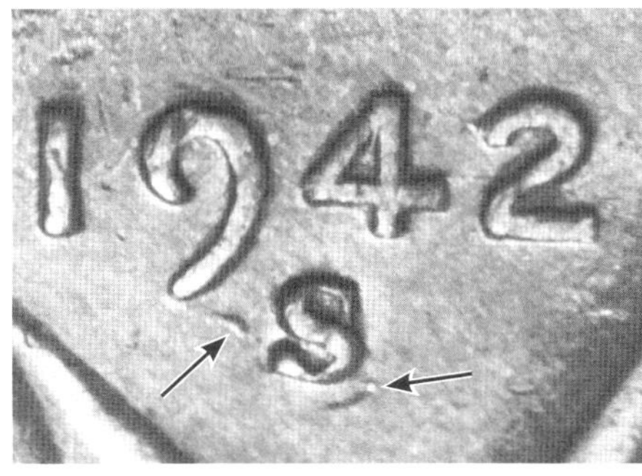

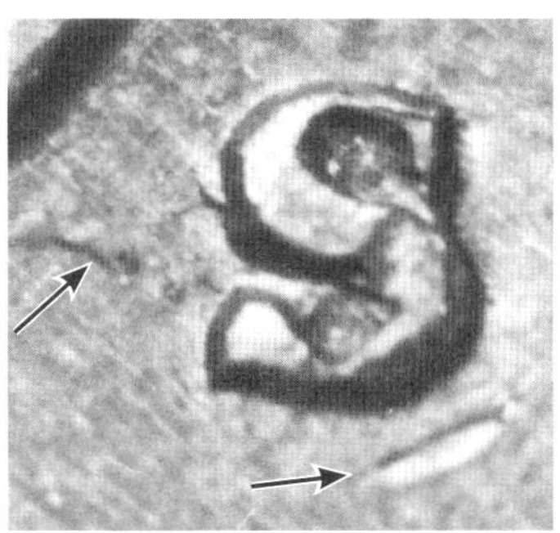

Description: This is a popular triple-punched mintmark, with secondary letters to the west and northwest of the primary S. The image to the west is totally separated from the primary S.

Comments: This is one of the very few repunched mintmarks with a totally separated mintmark.

	VF-20	EF-40	AU-50	MS-60	MS-63	MS-65
VARIETY	$15	$30	$60	$75	$100	$150
NORMAL	$0.85	$1.25	$5.50	$7	$11	$17

Note: Values listed for MS-60 and MS-63 are for RB (red and brown) specimens; values listed for MS-65 specimens are for full red specimens.

1943 — FS-01-1943-101 (018.97)

Variety: Doubled-Die Obverse — CONECA: DDO-001

PUP: Date, LIBERTY

URS-7 • I-4 • L-3

Description: The doubling is evident as extremely thick letters on LIBERTY and IN GOD WE TRUST, and very thick digits on the date.

Comments: This is one of the strongest Class VI doubled dies in the series, and it has always been very popular among Lincoln cent specialists.

	VF-20	EF-40	AU-50	MS-60	MS-63	MS-65
Variety	$100	$200	$350	$500	$900	$1,500
Normal	$0.35	$0.40	$0.50	$1.50	$2.50	$8

1943 — FS-01-1943-801

Variety: Doubled-Die Reverse — CONECA: DDR-001

PUP: E PLURIBUS UNUM

URS-6 • I-4 • L-3

Description: There is extreme extra thickness on E PLURIBUS UNUM, both wheat ears and stems, ONE CENT, and UNITED STATES OF AMERICA.

Comments: This one makes a nice match to the doubled-die obverse listed above.

	VF-20	EF-40	AU-50	MS-60	MS-63	MS-65
Variety	$20	$40	$60	$100	$200	$300
Normal	$0.35	$0.40	$0.50	$1.50	$2.50	$8

1943-D — FS-01-1943D-501 (019)

VARIETY: Repunched Mintmark — CONECA: RPM-001
PUP: Mintmark
URS-9 • I-5 • L-5

Description: The secondary D is evident to the southwest of the primary D.

Comments: This repunched mintmark is extremely tough to locate. This variety will be very easy to sell at a significant premium.

	VF-20	EF-40	AU-50	MS-60	MS-63	MS-65
VARIETY	$100	$200	$350	$500	$750	$2,000
NORMAL	$0.40	$0.45	$0.75	$1.75	$3	$10

1943-D — FS-01-1943D-513 (019.1)

VARIETY: Repunched Mintmark — CONECA: RPM-013
PUP: Mintmark
URS-1 • I-4 • L-4

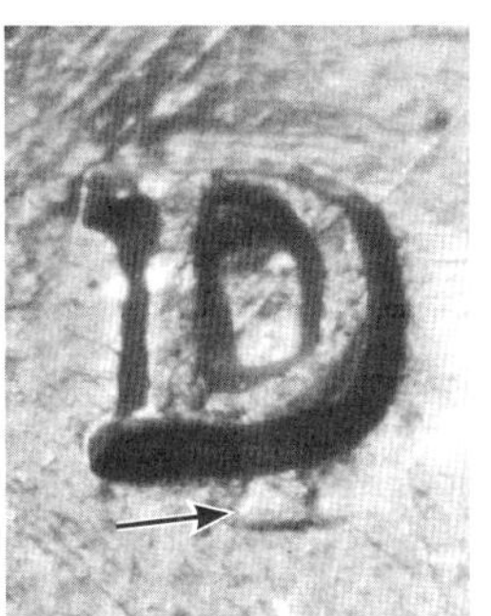

Description: The secondary D is evident to the southeast of the primary D.

Comments: This is a relatively new repunched mintmark. Only one example has been reported. A high-grade example will sell easily, especially to Lincoln cent variety enthusiasts.

	VF-20	EF-40	AU-50	MS-60	MS-63	MS-65
VARIETY	(unique)					
NORMAL	$0.40	$0.45	$0.75	$1.75	$3	$10

1943-S — FS-01-1943S-101 (019.5)

Variety: Doubled-Die Obverse — CONECA: DDO-001
PUP: Date, eyelid
URS-9 • I-3 • L-3

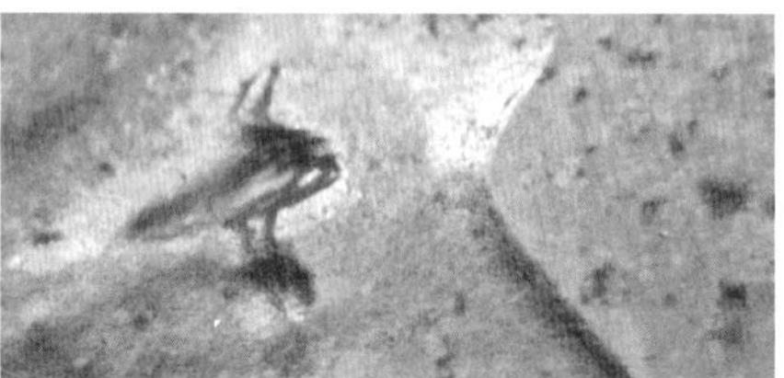

Description: Doubling is evident on the date, Lincoln's bowtie and eye, IN GOD WE TRUST, and LIBERTY.

Comments: Steel cent varieties are fast becoming very popular in their own right.

	VF-20	EF-40	AU-50	MS-60	MS-63	MS-65
Variety	$15	$45	$75	$105	$150	$285
Normal	$0.65	$0.75	$1	$3	$6	$20

1944-D — FS-01-1944D-101

Variety: Doubled-Die Obverse — CONECA: DDO-001
PUP: Date, LIBERTY
URS-7 • I-3 • L-3

Description: This variety shows extreme extra thickness on the date, LIBERTY, and IN GOD WE TRUST.

Comments: Several dies are known with extra thickness in the date. Check with the attribution guides for distinguishing markers.

	EF-40	AU-50	MS-60	MS-63	MS-65
Variety	$10	$20	$30	$50	$75
Normal	$0.20	$0.35	$0.50	$0.85	$14

Note: Values listed for MS-60 and MS-63 are for RB (red and brown) specimens; values listed for MS-65 are for full red specimens.

1944-D — FS-01-1944D-502 (021.1)

VARIETY: Repunched Mintmark — CONECA: RPM-002
PUP: Mintmark
URS-9 • I-2 • L-2

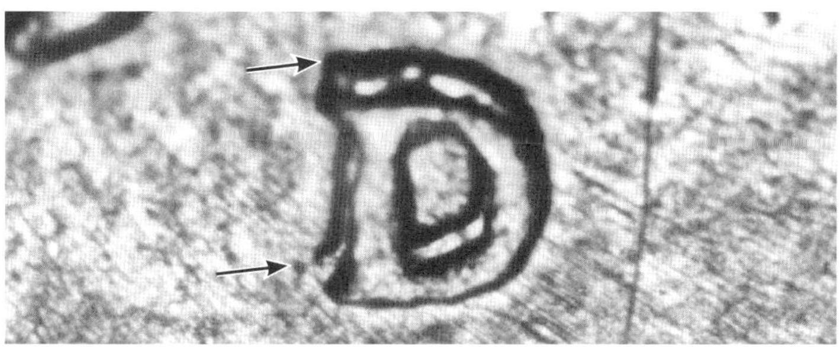

Description: The secondary D is evident to the north of the primary D.

Comments: There are several nice, collectible repunched mintmarks for this series in the 1940s. Note that several varieties of D Over D repunched mintmarks are mistaken for D Over S over mintmarks.

	EF-40	AU-50	MS-60	MS-63	MS-65
VARIETY	$3	$5	$8	$15	$35
NORMAL	$0.20	$0.35	$0.50	$0.85	$14

Note: Values listed for MS-60 and MS-63 are for RB (red and brown) specimens; values listed for MS-65 specimens are for full red specimens.

1944-D — FS-01-1944D-507 (021.11)

VARIETY: Repunched Mintmark — CONECA: RPM-007
PUP: Mintmark
URS-8 • I-3 • L-3

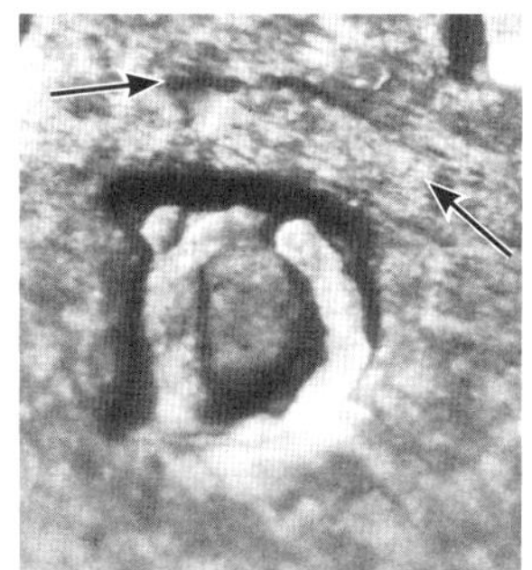

Description: The secondary D is evident to the northeast of the primary D.

Comments: This is the most popular repunched mintmark for the date. Note that several varieties of D Over D repunched mintmarks are mistaken for D Over S over mintmarks.

	EF-40	AU-50	MS-60	MS-63	MS-65
VARIETY	$8	$10	$15	$25	$50
NORMAL	$0.20	$0.35	$0.50	$0.85	$14

Note: Values listed for MS-60 and MS-63 are for RB (red and brown) specimens; values listed for MS-65 specimens are for full red specimens.

1944-D FS-01-1944D-511 (020)

VARIETY: Over Mintmark (D Over S) CONECA: OMM-001
PUP: Mintmark
URS-12 • I-5 • L-5

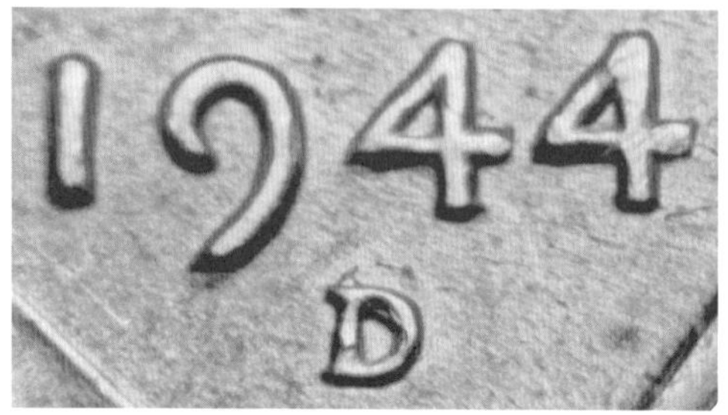

Description: This is a strong variety, listed by CONECA as OMM-001. The secondary S is evident clearly protruding from the top of the D.

Comments: This variety is the 1944-D, D Over S, that is generally quoted in various price guides. This variety is much rarer than the next listing.

	EF-40	AU-50	MS-60	MS-63	MS-65
VARIETY	$150	$165	$275	$375	$900
NORMAL	$0.20	$0.35	$0.50	$0.85	$14

Note: Values listed for MS-60 and MS-63 are for RB (red and brown) specimens; values listed for MS-65 specimens are for full red specimens.

1944-D FS-01-1944D-512 (021)

VARIETY: Over Mintmark (D Over S) CONECA: OMM-002
PUP: Mintmark
URS-12 • I-4 • L-4

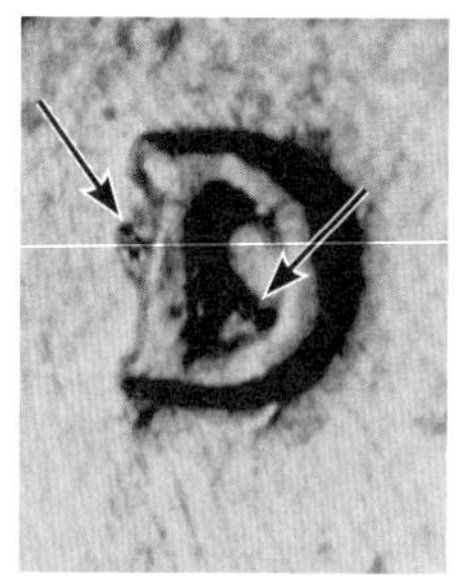

Description: The S is evident centered behind the primary D. On high-grade specimens, the diagonal of the center S crossbar can be seen within the opening of the primary D. On lower-grade specimens, the left curve of the upper loop of the S can be detected to the left of the upright of the D.

Comments: This variety is much more available than the previous listing and does not command the high premiums as the former.

	EF-40	AU-50	MS-60	MS-63	MS-65
VARIETY	$75	$95	$150	$300	$600
NORMAL	$0.20	$0.35	$0.50	$0.85	$14

Note: Values listed for MS-60 and MS-63 are for RB (red and brown) specimens; values listed for MS-65 specimens are for full red specimens.

1945 — FS-01-1945-101

Variety: Doubled-Die Obverse — **CONECA: DDO-013**
PUP: LIBERTY
URS-4 • I-4 • L-3

Description: This variety has a strong spread on LIBERTY and the date, with extra thickness on Lincoln's eye, ear, beard, and tie.

Comments: This variety was recently reported and is now eagerly sought after.

	EF-40	AU-50	MS-60	MS-63	MS-65
Variety	$10	$20	$30	$50	$75
Normal	$0.20	$0.35	$0.50	$0.85	$10

Note: Values listed for MS-60 and MS-63 are for RB (red and brown) specimens; values listed for MS-65 are for full red specimens.

1946-S — FS-01-1946S-501

Variety: Inverted Mintmark — **CONECA: IMM-001**
PUP: Mintmark
URS-6 • I-3 • L-3

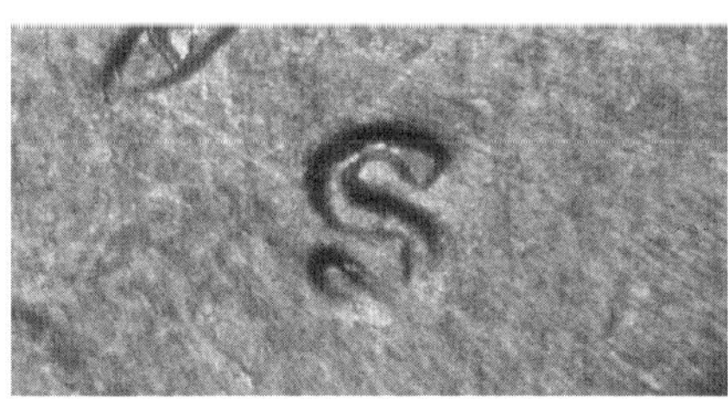

Description: This variety is identified by its inverted ball serif style mintmark.

Comments: The normal position has the flattened ball on the bottom. This is the rarest of the three mintmark styles found on the 1946-S cents.

	EF-40	AU-50	MS-60	MS-63	MS-65
Variety	$10	$20	$30	$50	$75
Normal	$0.20	$0.35	$0.45	$0.60	$10

Note: Values listed for MS-60 and MS-63 are for RB (red and brown) specimens; values listed for MS-65 are for full red specimens.

1946-S FS-01-1946S-511 (021.2)

VARIETY: Over Mintmark (S Over D) CONECA: OMM-001
PUP: Mintmark
URS-9 • I-4 • L-5

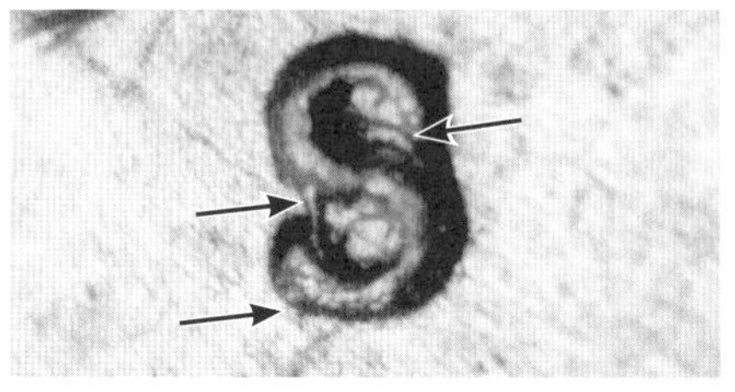

Description: The underlying D mintmark is evident centered below the primary S. The vertical bar of the D is visible in the lower opening of the S. The top curved bar of the D is visible within the upper opening of the S.

Comments: This excellent variety was discovered in the mid-1990s, which is evidence neat varieties are still out there yet to be discovered!

	EF-40	AU-50	MS-60	MS-63	MS-65
VARIETY	$75	$95	$225	$450	$750
NORMAL	$0.20	$0.35	$0.45	$0.60	$10

Note: Values listed for MS-60 and MS-63 are for RB (red and brown) specimens; values listed for MS-65 specimens are for full red specimens.

1947 FS-01-1947-101 (021.3)

VARIETY: Doubled-Die Obverse CONECA: DDO-001
PUP: Date, TRUST
URS-6 • I-4 • L-3

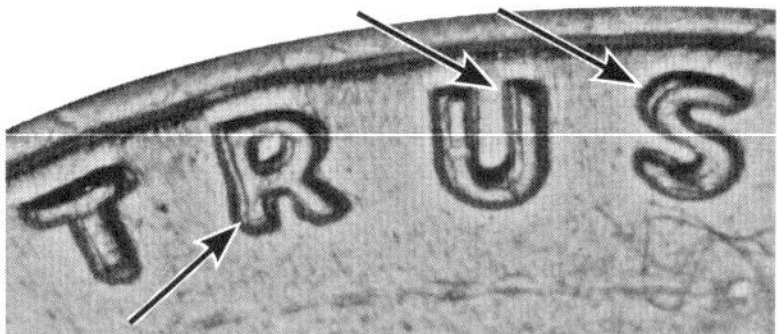

Description: Doubling is visible on LIBERTY, IN GOD WE TRUST, the date, the eye, and the vest.

Comments: This excellent variety was discovered in the mid-1990s, which is evidence neat varieties are still out there yet to be discovered!

	EF-40	AU-50	MS-60	MS-63	MS-65
VARIETY	$60	$75	$135	$225	$285
NORMAL	$0.20	$0.40	$0.70	$1	$15

Note: Values listed for MS-60 and MS-63 are for RB (red and brown) specimens; values listed for MS-65 specimens are for full red specimens.

1947-S — FS-01-1947S-504 (021.31)

Variety: Repunched Mintmark (Sans Over Serif) — **CONECA:** RPM-004
PUP: Mintmark
URS-7 • I-4 • L-4

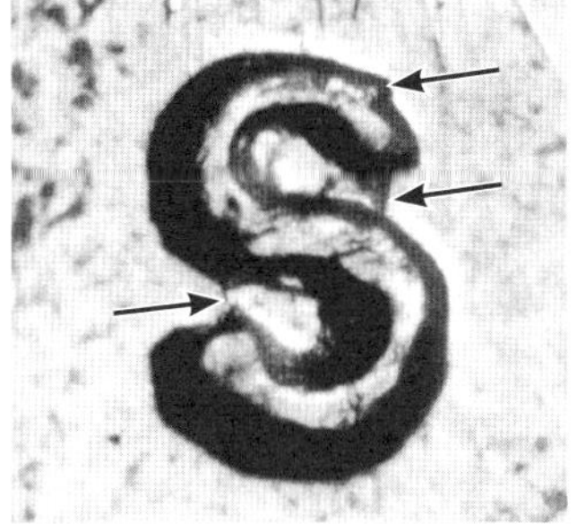

Description: The secondary S is evident squarely underneath the primary S mintmark. The significance of this repunched mintmark is that the first punch was with a trumpet-tail S, and the primary S is the sans serif type.

Comments: This is a very popular repunched mintmark among specialists, primarily for the two different mintmark types.

	EF-40	AU-50	MS-60	MS-63	MS-65
Variety	$25	$75	$125	$250	$500
Normal	$0.25	$0.50	$0.65	$0.85	$10

Note: Values listed for MS-60 are for RB (red and brown) specimens; values listed for MS-63 and MS-65 specimens are for full red specimens.

1949-D — FS-01-1949D-501 (021.33)

Variety: Repunched Mintmark — **CONECA:** RPM-001
PUP: Mintmark
URS-7 • I-3 • L-3

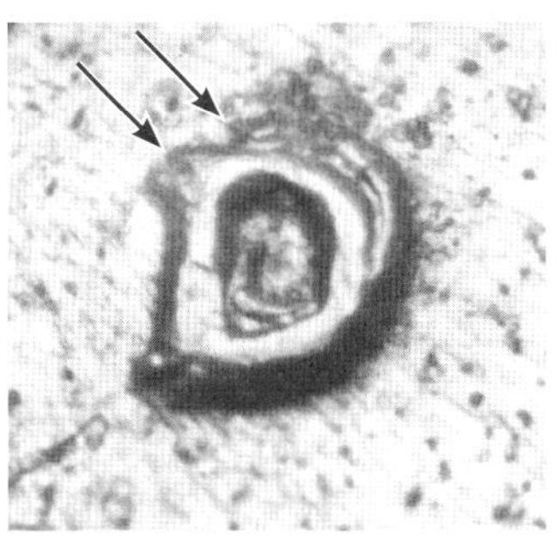

Description: The mintmark is triple-punched, with one of the weaker images to the northeast and one to the south of the primary mintmark.

Comments: This coin is difficult to find in Mint State and early die states.

	EF-40	AU-50	MS-60	MS-63	MS-65
Variety	$4	$7	$10	$15	$35
Normal	$0.20	$0.35	$0.65	$1	$10

Note: Values listed for MS-60 are for RB (red and brown) specimens; values listed for MS-63 and MS-65 specimens are for full red specimens.

1949-S FS-01-1949S-101

VARIETY: Doubled-Die Obverse CONECA: DDO-001
PUP: Date
URS-6 • I-3 • L-3

Description: The doubling shows as a blunt 4 over a pointed 4 in the date.

Comments: Three dies are known with this type of doubling. Check the attribution guides for distinguishing features.

	EF-40	AU-50	MS-60	MS-63	MS-65
VARIETY	$10	$20	$30	$50	$75
NORMAL	$0.30	$0.35	$1.15	$2	$15

Note: Values listed for MS-60 and MS-63 are for RB (red and brown) specimens; values listed for MS-65 are for full red specimens.

1950-S FS-01-1950S-504 (021.34)

VARIETY: Repunched Mintmark CONECA: RPM-004
PUP: Mintmark
URS-7 • I-3 • L-3

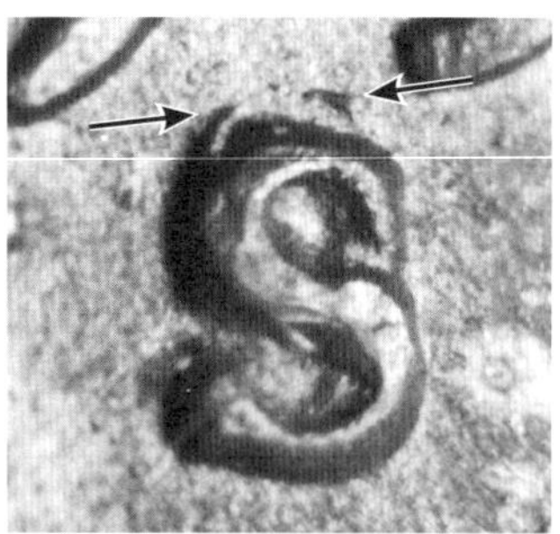

Description: The secondary S is clearly evident north of the primary S. This is actually a triple-punched S mintmark. Another S is visible to the north of, but very close to, the primary S.

	EF-40	AU-50	MS-60	MS-63	MS-65
VARIETY	$4	$7	$10	$15	$35
NORMAL	$0.25	$0.35	$0.50	$0.85	$15

Note: Values listed for MS-60 are for RB (red and brown) specimens; values listed for MS-63 and MS-65 specimens are for full red specimens.

1951 Proof — FS-01-1951-101 (021.35)

VARIETY: Doubled-Die Obverse — CONECA: DDO-001

PUP: IN GOD WE TRUST

URS-6 • I-3 • L-2

Description: There is a strong spread evident on IN GOD WE TRUST.

Comments: This variety can be located with some looking. Examples are known with and without doubled-die reverses.

	PF-63	PF-65	PF-66
VARIETY	$50	$95	$150
NORMAL	$35	$65	$85

Note: Values listed for Proof Lincoln cents are for full red specimens. Red-and-brown and all-brown specimens command less. Cameo and deep cameo specimens should command much greater prices.

1951-D — FS-01-1951D-101 (021.4)

VARIETY: Doubled-Die Obverse — CONECA: DDO-001

PUP: LIBERTY, IN GOD WE TRUST

URS-11 • I-3 • L-3

Description: Moderate doubling is evident on the motto and LIBERTY.

Comments: This is one of those varieties that is highly visible.

	EF-40	AU-50	MS-60	MS-63	MS-65
VARIETY	$8	$10	$30	$50	$100
NORMAL	$0.12	$0.35	$0.45	$0.60	$9

Note: Values listed for MS-60 and MS-63 are for RB (red and brown) specimens; values listed for MS-65 specimens are for full red specimens.

1951-D FS-01-1951D-511 (021.5)

VARIETY: Over Mintmark (D Over S) CONECA: OMM-001

PUP: Mintmark

URS-9 • I-4 • L-4

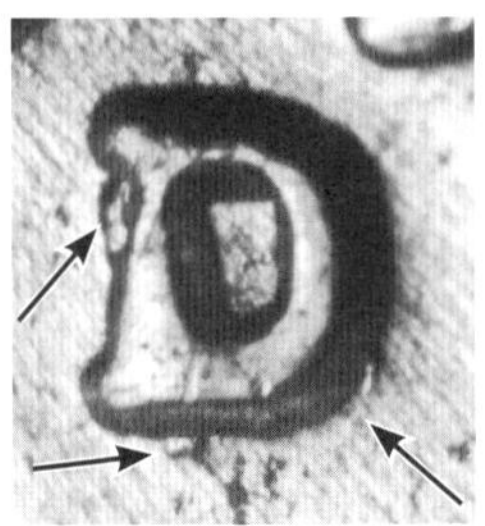

Description: The primary D mintmark was punched squarely over the secondary S. The upper left curve of the S is evident protruding from the upper left of the D's upright, and the lower loop of the S is evident slightly south of the primary D. A portion of the lower serif of the S is evident protruding from the D on earlier-die-state specimens.

Comments: This is a well-known and very popular variety and will usually sell easily at fair prices.

	EF-40	AU-50	MS-60	MS-63	MS-65
VARIETY	$25	$40	$60	$100	$150
NORMAL	$0.12	$0.35	$0.45	$0.60	$9

Note: Values listed for MS-60 and MS-63 are for RB (red and brown) specimens; values listed for MS-65 specimens are for full red specimens.

1951-D FS-01-1951D-512 (021.52)

VARIETY: Over Mintmark (D Over S) CONECA: OMM-002

PUP: Mintmark

URS-9 • I-4 • L-4

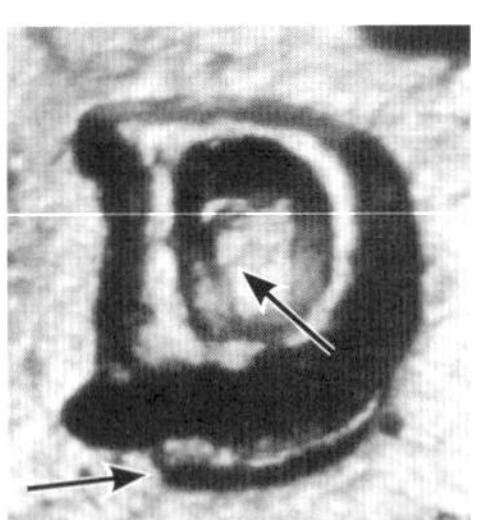

Description: The secondary, underlying S mintmark is evident protruding from the lower portion of the primary D. The lower serif of the underlying S is visible protruding from the lower portion of the primary D.

Comments: This is another well-known and very popular variety that will usually sell easily at fair prices. Values will usually be close to the previous listing.

	EF-40	AU-50	MS-60	MS-63	MS-65
VARIETY	$25	$40	$60	$100	$150
NORMAL	$0.12	$0.35	$0.45	$0.60	$9

Note: Values listed for MS-60 and MS-63 are for RB (red and brown) specimens; values listed for MS-65 specimens are for full red specimens.

1952-D — FS-01-1952D-511 (021.6)

VARIETY: Over Mintmark (D Over S) — CONECA: OMM-001
PUP: Mintmark
URS-9 • I-4 • L-4

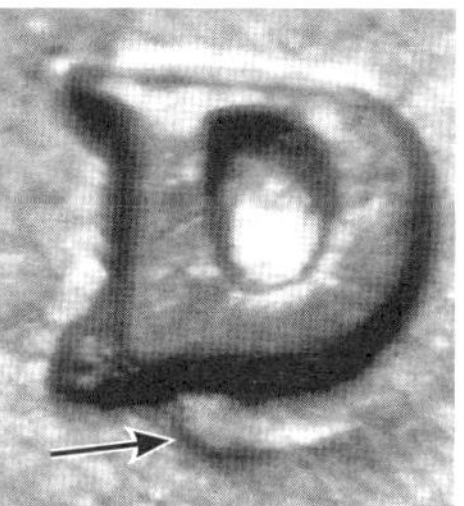

Description: The primary D mintmark was punched into the die over a previously punched S. The lower curve of the S is evident south of the D.

Comments: This over mintmark has received confirmation from all major variety specialists.

	EF-40	AU-50	MS-60	MS-63	MS-65
VARIETY	$25	$40	$60	$100	$150
NORMAL	$0.15	$0.25	$0.50	$0.75	$9

Note: Values listed for MS-60 and MS-63 are for RB (red and brown) specimens; values listed for MS-65 specimens re for full red specimens.

1953 Proof — FS-01-1953-101 (021.7)

VARIETY: Doubled-Die Obverse — CONECA: DDO-001
PUP: Date
URS 6 • I 3 • L 3

Description: There is a strong spread west on the date, and doubling is also evident on the RTY of LIBERTY. Extra thickness from the doubled die is evident on the remainder of the lettering.

Comments: This is another nice doubled die on a Lincoln Proof.

	PF-63	PF-65	PF-66
VARIETY	$30	$65	$100
NORMAL	$15	$30	$40

Note: Values listed for Proof Lincoln cents are for full red specimens. Red-and-brown and full brown specimens command less. Cameo and deep cameo specimens should command much greater prices.

1953 Proof — FS-01-1953-401

Variety: Re-Engraved Design — CONECA: RED-001
PUP: Upper vest line
URS-3 • I-3 • L-3

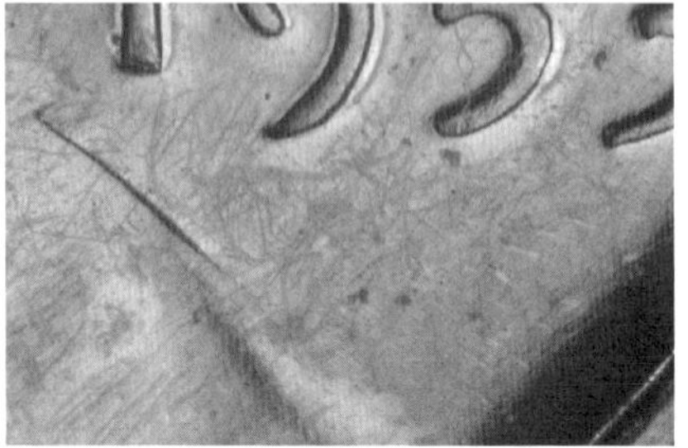

Description: There is a short, raised straight line on the upper vest edge.

Comments: This is one of two dies known with re-engraved vest lines.

	PF-63	PF-65	PF-66
Variety	$150	$250	$300
Normal	$15	$30	$40

Note: Values listed for Proof Lincoln cents are for full red specimens. Red-and-brown and all-brown specimens command less. Cameo and deep cameo specimens should command much greater prices.

1953 Proof — FS-01-1953-402

Variety: Re-Engraved Design — CONECA: RED-002
PUP: Lower vest line
URS-3 • I-3 • L-3

Description: There is a long, raised line down the lower vest edge.

Comments: This is the stronger of the two known re-engraved dies for the 1953 Lincoln cent. Apparently a few more Proof cents were needed and a couple of worn-out dies were touched up to finish the job.

	PF-63	PF-65	PF-66
Variety	$175	$300	$400
Normal	$15	$30	$40

Note: Values listed for Proof Lincoln cents are for full red specimens. Red-and-brown and all-brown specimens command less. Cameo and deep cameo specimens should command much greater prices.

1953-D FS-01-1953D-501 (021.73)

VARIETY: Repunched Mintmark CONECA: RPM-001

PUP: Mintmark

URS-10 • I-3 • L-3

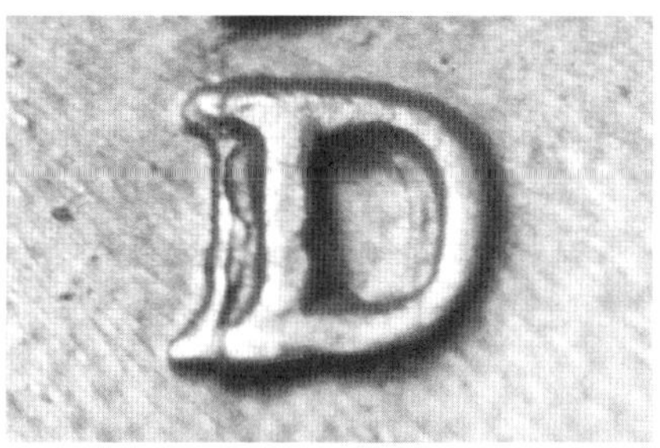

Description: The secondary D is evident west of the primary D. Portions of the underlying D are also evident inside the opening of the primary D.

	EF-40	AU-50	MS-60	MS-63	MS-65
VARIETY	$5	$10	$15	$20	$35
NORMAL	$0.15	$0.20	$0.35	$0.50	$11

Note: Values listed for MS-60 and MS-63 are for RB (red and brown) specimens; values listed for MS-65 specimens are for full red specimens.

1953-D FS-01-1953D-502

VARIETY: Repunched Mintmark CONECA: RPM-028

PUP: Mintmark in vest

URS-5 • I-4 • L-3

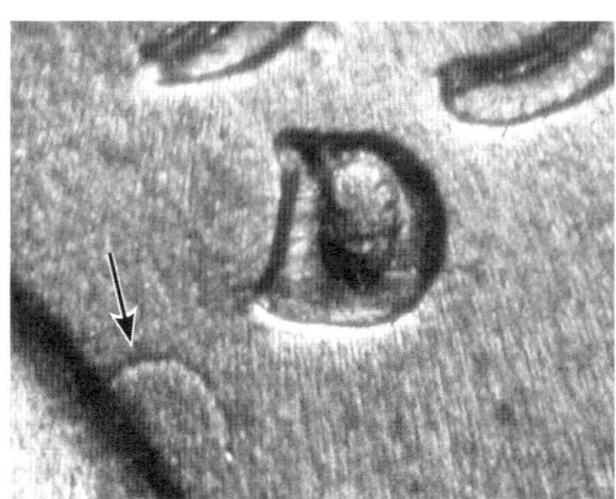

Description: The secondary D mintmark is on the edge of the vest.

Comments: There are five separated repunched mintmarks listed in the CONECA files. Can you collect all five?

	EF-40	AU-50	MS-60	MS-63	MS-65
VARIETY	$30	$50	$75	$100	$125
NORMAL	$0.15	$0.20	$0.35	$0.50	$11

Note: Values listed for MS-60 and MS-63 are for RB (red and brown) specimens; values listed for MS-65 are for full red specimens.

1954-D — FS-01-1954D-501 (021.76)

VARIETY: Repunched Mintmark (D/D/D) — CONECA: RPM-001

PUP: Mintmark

URS-10 • I-3 • L-3

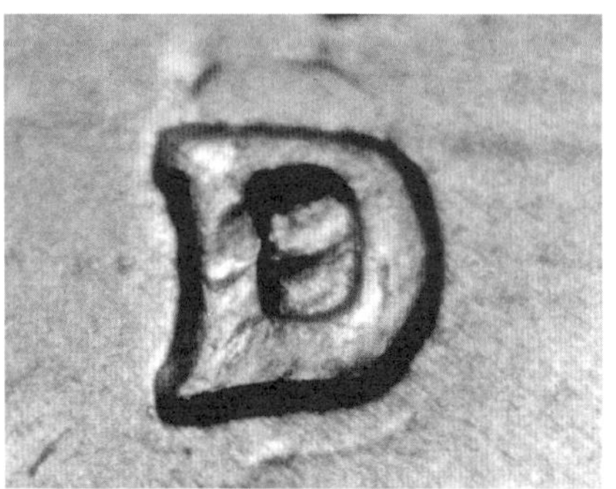

Description: This is a tripled mintmark, with secondary D's evident to the north and south of the primary D.

Comments: This is a very popular repunched mintmark.

	EF-40	AU-50	MS-60	MS-63	MS-65
VARIETY	$5	$10	$20	$30	$50
NORMAL	$0.12	$0.20	$0.35	$0.50	$10

Note: Values listed for MS-60 and MS-63 are for RB (red and brown) specimens; values listed for MS-65 specimens are for full red specimens.

THE CHERRYPICKERS' GUIDE HELPFUL HINTS

The sixth edition, volume I of the Cherrypickers' Guide *introduces a new symbol for use in the coin-by-coin listings. Coins marked with the symbol to the right are listed in the most recent edition of R.S. Yeoman's* Guide Book of United States Coins, Deluxe Edition *(a greatly expanded version of the classic known as the "Red Book").*

RB DE

1955 FS-01-1955-101 (021.8)

VARIETY: Doubled-Die Obverse CONECA: DDO-001
PUP: LIBERTY, date, motto
URS-15 • I-5 • L-5

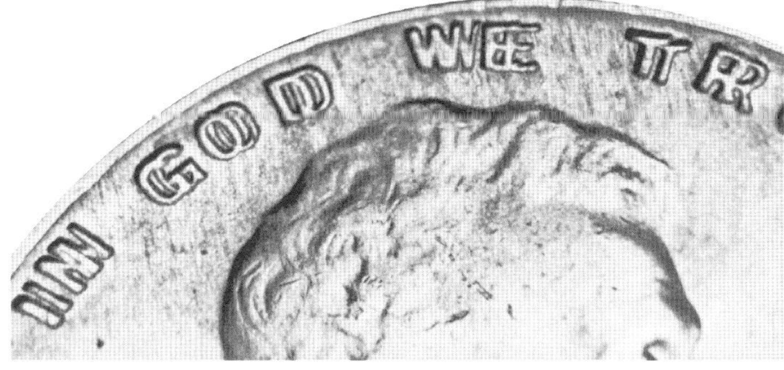

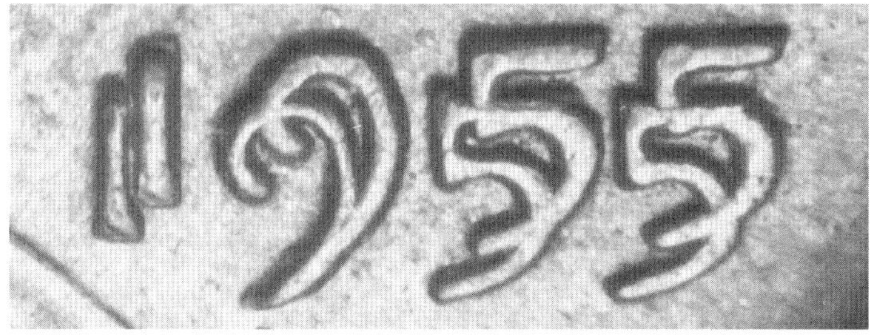

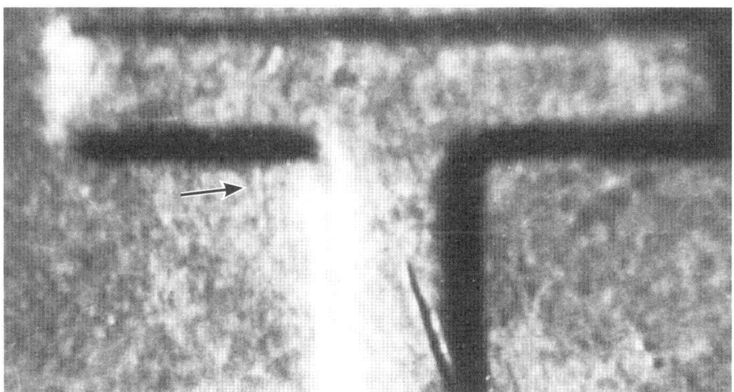

Description: There is very strong doubling on all lettering and the date.

Comments: Although very well known and not considered cherrypickable, this book would not be complete without this listing. Plus, it is helpful for all collectors to be very familiar with the die markers for the genuine coin, as there are many counterfeits available. Check for a faint die scratch under the left horizontal bar of the T of CENT to establish authenticity.

	EF-40	AU-50	MS-60	MS-63	MS-65RB	MS-65RD
VARIETY	$1,700	$2,000	$2,200	$2,300	$30,000	$40,000
NORMAL	$0.12	$0.15	$0.25	$0.35	$1	$19

Note: Values listed for MS-60 and MS-63 are for RB (red and brown) specimens; values listed for MS-65 are shown for red-and-brown and full red specimens.

1955 — FS-01-1955-102 (021.9)

VARIETY: Doubled-Die Obverse — CONECA: DDO-002
PUP: Motto, date, LIBERTY
URS-6 • I-4 • L-4

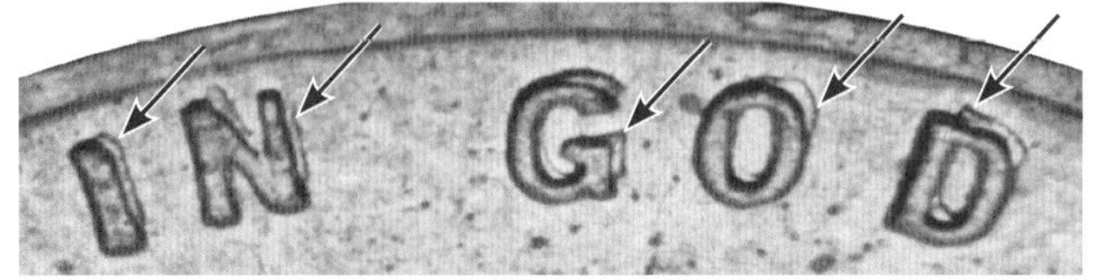

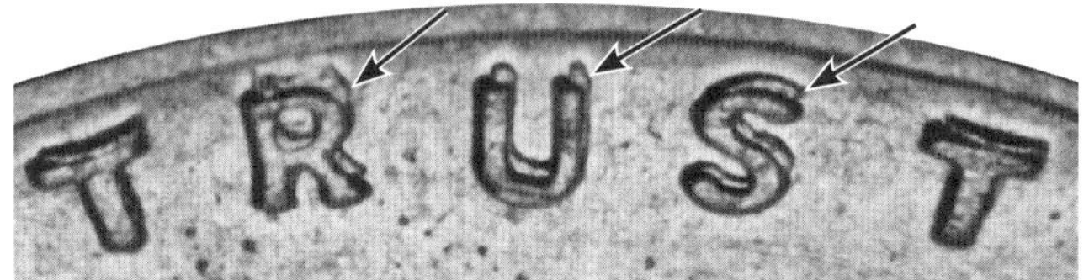

Description: Very strong doubling is evident on the motto, with some slight doubling visible on LIBERTY. The spread is strong, though the secondary hubbing was somewhat weak.

Comments: This is an extremely popular variety among Lincoln cent and variety specialists. Were it not for the previous listing, this would be considered a fantastic doubled die. The photos above show an early-die-state example. Later die states are less distinct.

	EF-40	AU-50	MS-60	MS-63	MS-65
VARIETY	$75	$95	$175	$250	$500
NORMAL	$0.12	$0.15	$0.25	$0.35	$19

Note: Values listed for MS-60 and MS-63 are for RB (red and brown) specimens; values listed for MS-65 are for full red specimens.

1955 Proof — FS-01-1955-103/801

VARIETY: Doubled-Die Obverse and Reverse — CONECA: DDO-004/DDR-004
PUP: Date, E PLURIBUS UNUM
URS-6 • I-4 • L-4

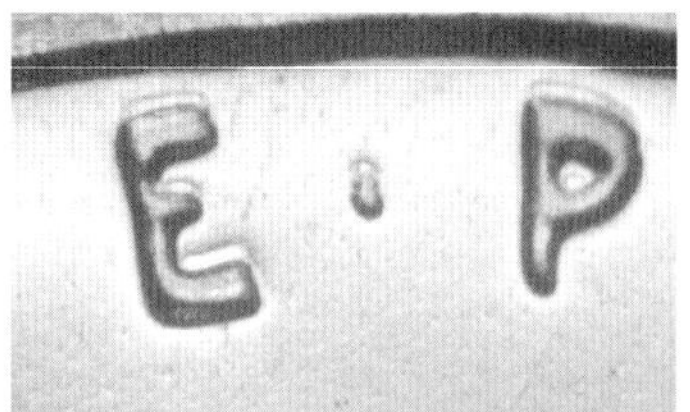

Description: The obverse shows a medium spread on the date, IN GOD WE TRUST, and LIBERTY. The reverse shows a strong spread on E PLURIBUS UNUM and the wheat ears.

Comments: This is a very nice combination doubled-die obverse and doubled-die reverse, often used as a substitute for the big doubled-die obverse.

	PF-63	PF-65	PF-66
VARIETY	$100	$300	$400
NORMAL	$8	$18	$30

Note: Values listed for Proof Lincoln cents are for full red specimens. Red-and-brown and all-brown specimens command less. Cameo and deep cameo specimens should command much greater prices.

1955-D — FS-01-1955D-101 (021.93)

VARIETY: Doubled-Die Obverse — CONECA: DDO-001
PUP: Date, eye
URS-9 • I-3 • L-3

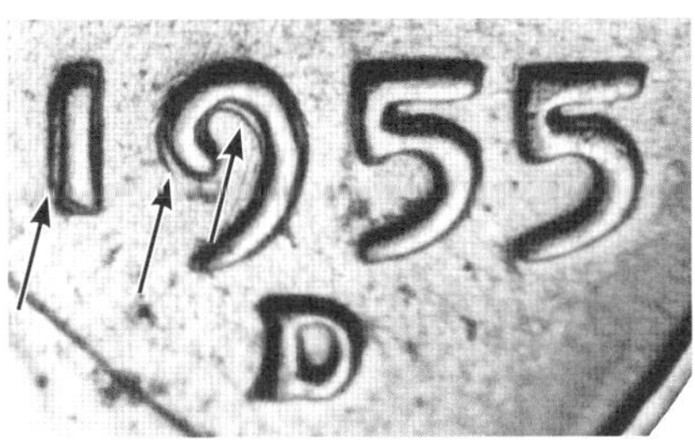

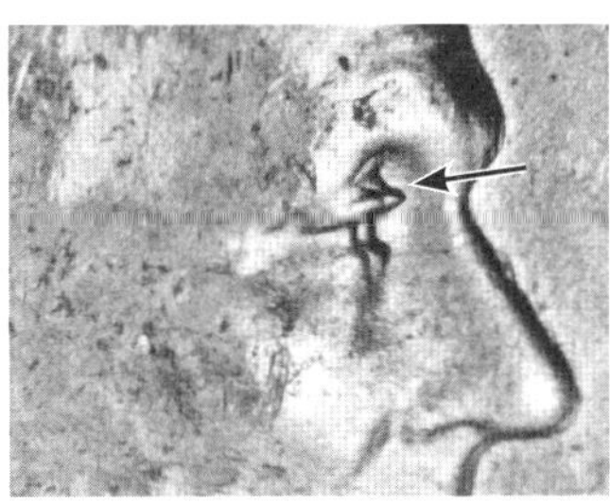

Description: Strong doubling is evident on the 1 and 9 of the date and at Lincoln's eye.

Comments: Another well-known variety among specialists, this variety would be fairly easy to sell when located.

	EF-40	AU-50	MS-60	MS-63	MS-65
VARIETY	$8	$10	$15	$35	$50
NORMAL	$0.12	$0.15	$0.25	$0.35	$10

Note: Values listed for MS-60 and MS-63 are for RB (red and brown) specimens; values listed for MS-65 are for full red specimens.

1955-D — FS-01-1955D-503 (021.94)

VARIETY: Repunched Mintmark — CONECA: RPM-003
PUP: Mintmark
URS-9 • I-3 • L-3

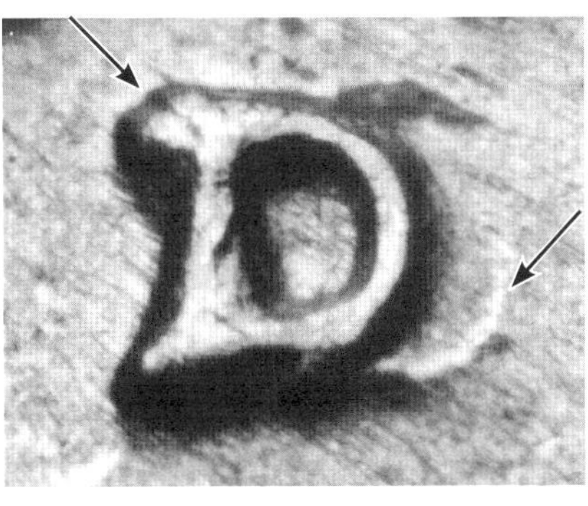

Description: The secondary D is evident widely to the east of the primary D.

Comments: This is a widely spaced repunched mintmark.

	EF-40	AU-50	MS-60	MS-63	MS-65
VARIETY	$8	$10	$15	$35	$50
NORMAL	$0.12	$0.15	$0.25	$0.35	$10

Note: Values listed for MS-60 and MS-63 are for RB (red and brown) specimens; values listed for MS-65 are for full red specimens.

1955-S — FS-01-1955S-501 (021.97)

Variety: Repunched Mintmark (S/S/S) — **CONECA:** RPM-001
PUP: Mintmark
URS-8 • I-3 • L-3

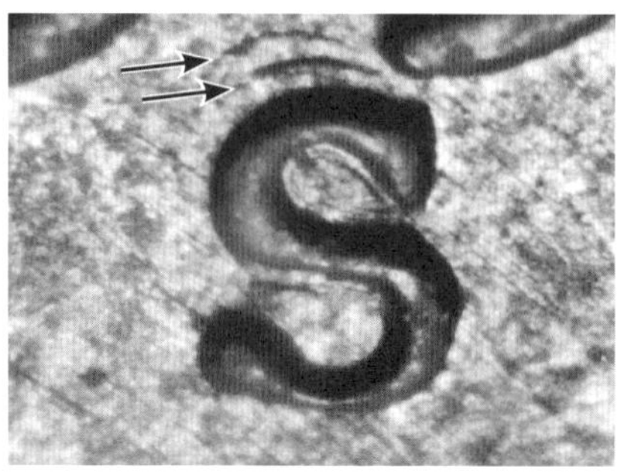

Description: This is a triple-punched mintmark—both secondary S's are evident to the north of the primary S.

Comments: This is a very popular repunched mintmark among specialists.

	EF-40	AU-50	MS-60	MS-63	MS-65
Variety	$8	$10	$15	$25	$50
Normal	$0.30	$0.40	$0.60	$0.85	$8

Note: Values listed for MS-60 and MS-63 are for RB (red and brown) specimens; values listed for MS-65 are for full red specimens.

1956 Proof — FS-01-1956-101

Variety: Doubled-Die Obverse — **CONECA:** DDO-002
PUP: Date, LIBERTY
URS-6 • I-3 • L-3

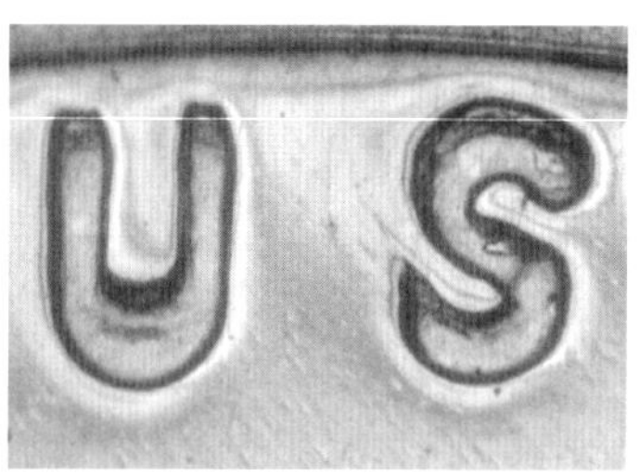

Description: This variety exhibits a strong spread on the date, LIBERTY, and IN GOD WE TRUST.

Comments: Note the semicircle die gouge on the rim at seven o'clock.

	PF-63	PF-65	PF-66
Variety	$50	$100	$125
Normal	$5	$10	$25

Note: Values listed for Proof Lincoln cents are for full red specimens. Red-and-brown and all-brown specimens command less. Cameo and deep cameo specimens should command much greater prices.

1956 Proof — FS-01-1956-801

VARIETY: Doubled-Die Reverse — CONECA: DDR-004
PUP: Lower wheat stems, UNITED STATES OF AMERICA
URS-6 • I-3 • L-3

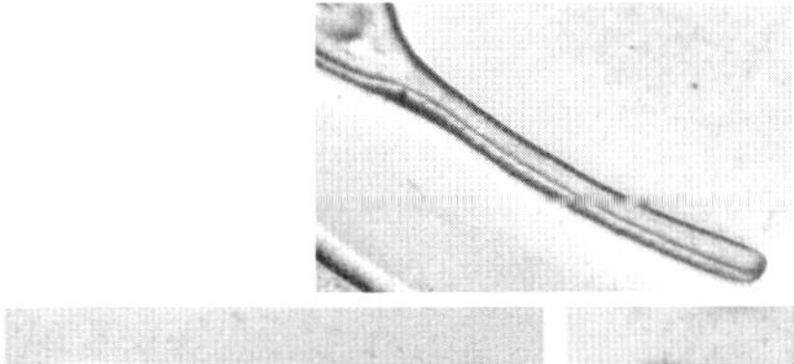

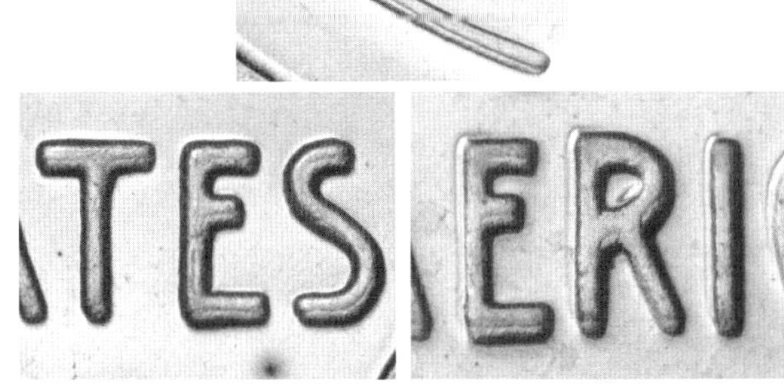

YN

Description: There is a strong spread on UNITED STATES OF AMERICA and the lower wheat stems, with a light spread on E PLURIBUS UNUM.

Comments: This variety is super nice, especially in early die state.

	PF-63	PF-65	PF-66
VARIETY	$50	$100	$125
NORMAL	$5	$10	$25

Note: Values listed for Proof Lincoln cents are for full red specimens. Red-and-brown and all-brown specimens command less. Cameo and deep cameo specimens should command much greater prices.

1956-D — FS-01-1956D-501 (022.1)

VARIETY: Repunched Mintmark — CONECA: RPM 001
PUP: Mintmark
URS-10 • I-3 • L-3

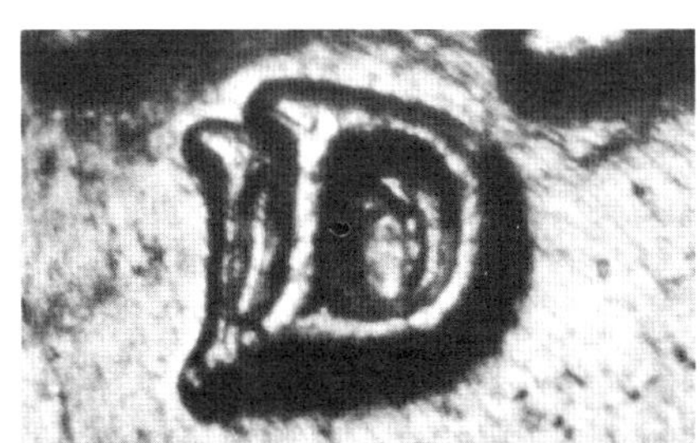

Description: This is a very strong repunched mintmark, with the secondary D evident to the west of the primary D.

	EF-40	AU-50	MS-60	MS-63	MS-65
VARIETY	$8	$10	$15	$20	$50
NORMAL	$0.12	$0.15	$0.20	$0.30	$9

Note: Values listed for MS-60 and MS-63 are for RB (red and brown) specimens; values listed for MS-65 are for full red specimens.

1956-D FS-01-1956D-502

Variety: Repunched Mintmark CONECA: RPM-016
PUP: Mintmark in tail of 9
URS-6 • I-4 • L-3

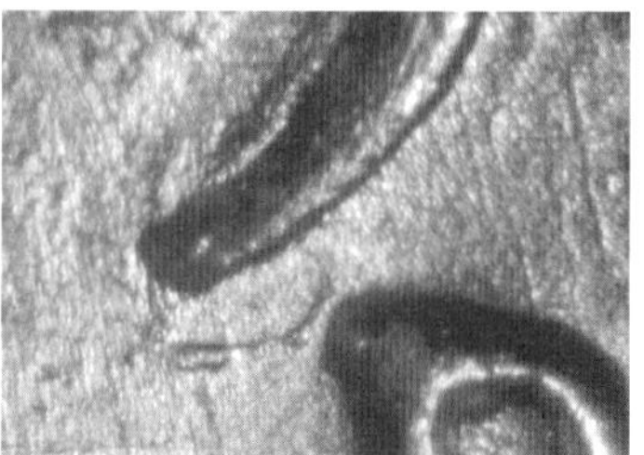

Description: The secondary D mintmark is in the tail of the 9.

Comments: There are three separated repunched mintmarks for the 1956-D Lincoln cent listed in the CONECA files. Can you collect all three?

	EF-40	AU-50	MS-60	MS-63	MS-65
Variety	$50	$75	$100	$125	$200
Normal	$0.12	$0.15	$0.20	$0.30	$9

Note: Values listed for MS-60 and MS-63 are for RB (red and brown) specimens; values listed for MS-65 are for full red specimens.

1956-D FS-01-1956D-508 (022)

Variety: Repunched Mintmark CONECA: RPM-008
PUP: Mintmark
URS-11 • I-4 • L-4

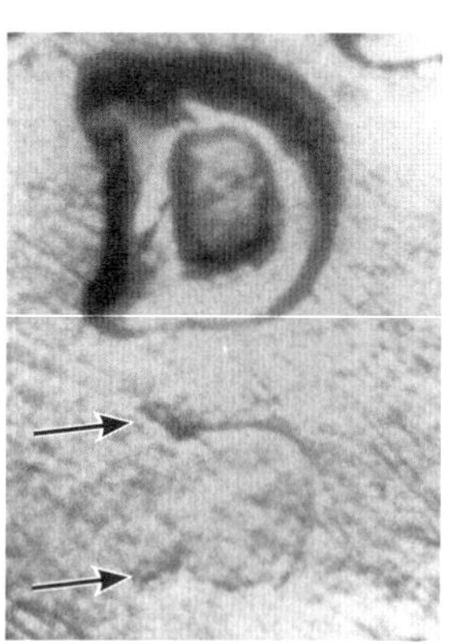

Description: This is a very well-known and popular variety, with a totally separated mintmark; the remains of a secondary D are evident in the field below the primary D.

Comments: Early-die-state specimens, which show a complete D, are very rare and will command a premium. The photo above is of an early-die-state example.

	EF-40	AU-50	MS-60	MS-63	MS-65
Variety	$20	$25	$50	$90	$150
Normal	$0.12	$0.15	$0.20	$0.30	$9

Note: Values listed for MS-60 and MS-63 are for RB (red and brown) specimens; values listed for MS-65 are for full red specimens.

1958 — FS-01-1958-101 (022.15)

Variety: Doubled-Die Obverse — **CONECA:** DDO-001
PUP: All obverse lettering
URS-2 • I-5 • L-5

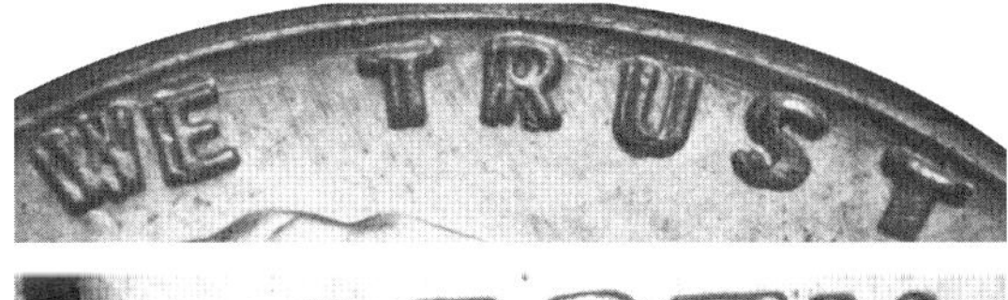

Description: This is a very strong doubled-die obverse, with obvious separation on all letters and numbers. The weakest doubling is on the date.

Comments: The authors feel this variety has never reached the general population. To the best of our knowledge, the only known specimens came either directly or indirectly from an employee of the U.S. Mint in Philadelphia. The variety was first reported during ERRORAMA in Cherry Hill, New Jersey (suburban Philadelphia), in 1983 or 1984. No specimens have been reported being found in circulation, Wheat cent bags, Brilliant Uncirculated rolls, or other means that would lead to credibility of a true accidental release from the Mint. We would caution the purchase of any specimen.

	EF-40	AU-50	MS-60	MS-63	MS-65
Variety					*$40,000*
Normal	$0.12	$0.15	$0.20	$0.30	$9

Note: Value listed for MS-65 is for full red specimens.

1959 FS-01-1959-101 (022.2)

VARIETY: Doubled-Die Obverse CONECA: DDO-001
PUP: Date
URS-9 • I-3 • L-3

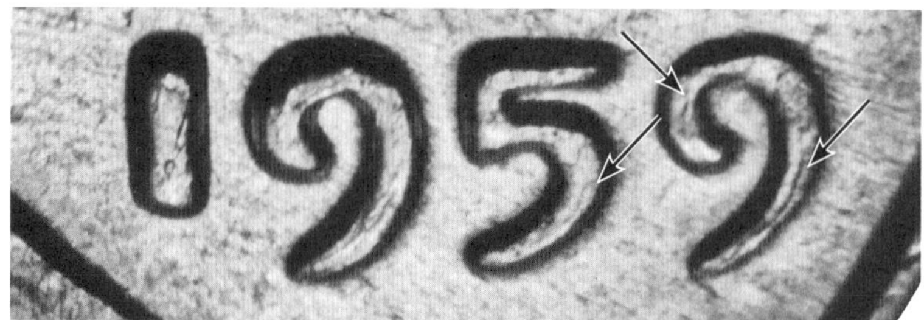

Description: The doubling is evident on the date as notable extra thickness. There are separation lines evident on the 5 and 9 of the date.

Comments: Early-die-state specimens show separation lines on the 9, 5, and 9 of the date and should command a slight premium.

	EF-40	AU-50	MS-60	MS-63	MS-65
VARIETY	$3	$5	$10	$15	$35
NORMAL	$0.01	$0.02	$0.05	$0.20	$0.30

Note: Values for MS-60 and MS-63 coins are for RB (red and brown) specimens; values for MS-65 are for full red specimens.

1959 FS-01-1959-104 (022.3)

VARIETY: Doubled-Die Obverse CONECA: DDO-004
PUP: LIBERTY
URS-9 • I-2 • L-2

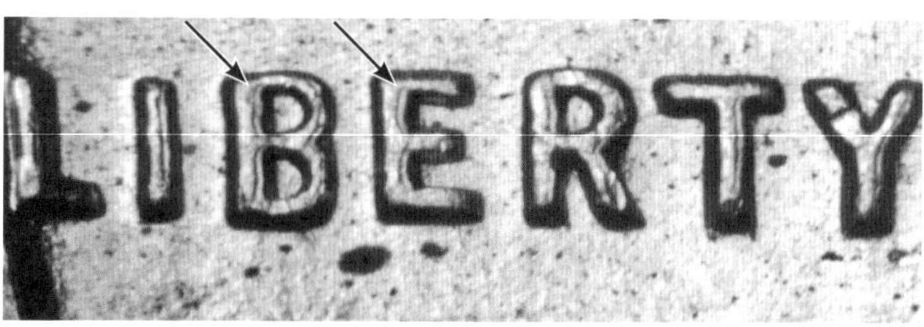

Description: Doubling is evident on LIBERTY, with slight notching evident on IN GOD WE TRUST.

Comments: Although not a big doubled die, variety specialists do have interest in this coin.

	EF-40	AU-50	MS-60	MS-63	MS-65
VARIETY	$3	$5	$8	$10	$25
NORMAL	$0.01	$0.02	$0.05	$0.20	$0.30

Note: Values for MS-60 and MS-63 coins are for RB (red and brown) specimens; values for MS-65 are for full red specimens.

1959-D — FS-01-1959D-501 (022.5)

VARIETY: Repunched Mintmark — CONECA: RPM-001
PUP: Mintmark
URS-12 • I-4 • L-4

Description: This is a very nice triple-punched mintmark, with secondary D's evident to the west and east of the primary D.

Comments: This variety is fairly easy to locate. Look for original rolls to search.

	EF-40	AU-50	MS-60	MS-63	MS-65
VARIETY	$3	$5	$8	$10	$20
NORMAL	$0.02	$0.03	$0.10	$0.50	$0.55

Note: Values for MS-60 and MS-63 coins are for RB (red and brown) specimens; values for MS-65 are for full red specimens.

1960 Proof — FS-01-1960-101 (025)

VARIETY: Doubled-Die Obverse — CONECA: DDO-001
PUP: Date
URS-9 • I-5 • L-5

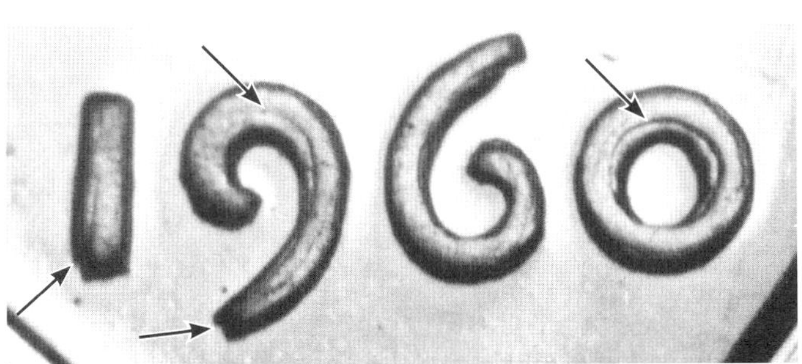

Description: This is best known for being a Large Date Over Small Date Proof. There is also doubling evident to the southwest on BERTY of LIBERTY.

Comments: This is the first of three known doubled dies for the Proof versions involving both sizes of the date.

	PF-63	PF-65	PF-66	PF-67
VARIETY	$250	$450	$600	$750
NORMAL	$1	$2	$12	$25

Note: Values listed for Proof Lincoln cents are for full red specimens. Red-and-brown and full brown specimens command less. Cameo and deep cameo specimens should command much greater prices.

1960 Proof — FS-01-1960-102 (024)

Variety: Doubled-Die Obverse — CONECA: DDO-002
PUP: Date
URS-9 • I-5 • L-5

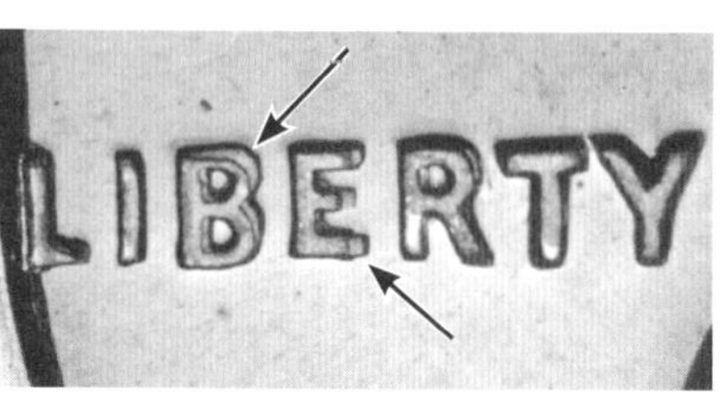

Description: This is best known for being a Small Date Over Large Date Proof. There is also doubling evident to the west on BER of LIBERTY and minor doubling evident on the tops of some letters of IN GOD WE TRUST.

Comments: This is the second of three known doubled dies for the Proof versions involving both sizes of the date.

	PF-63	PF-65	PF-66	PF-67
Variety	$250	$450	$600	$750
Normal	$1	$2	$12	$25

Note: Values listed for Proof Lincoln cents are for full red specimens. Red-and-brown and full brown specimens command less. Cameo and deep cameo specimens should command much greater prices.

1960 Proof — FS-01-1960-103 (023)

Variety: Tripled-Die Obverse — CONECA: DDO-003
PUP: Date
URS-9 • I-5 • L-5

YN

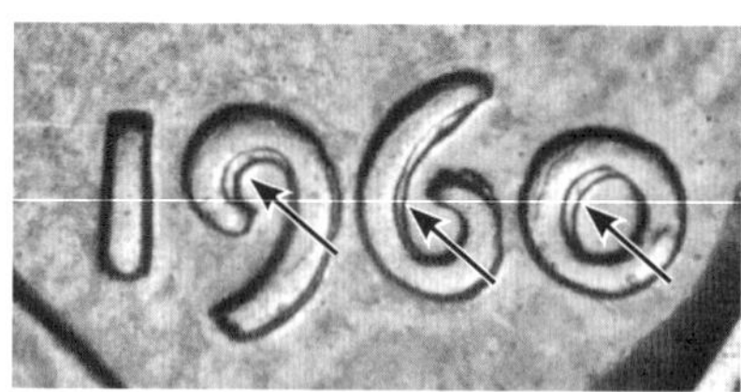

Description: This is best known for being a Large Date Over Large Date Over Small Date Proof. There is also doubling evident on LIBERTY and IN GOD WE TRUST.

Comments: This is the third of three known doubled dies for the Proof versions involving both sizes of the date. However, this one is distinguished by being a tripled date.

	PF-63	PF-65	PF-66	PF-67
Variety	$250	$450	$600	$750
Normal	$1	$2	$12	$25

Note: Values listed for Proof Lincoln cents are for full red specimens. Red-and-brown and full brown specimens command less. Cameo and deep cameo specimens should command much greater prices.

1960 Proof — FS-01-1960-801

VARIETY: Doubled-Die Reverse — CONECA: DDR-009
PUP: Right upper building
URS-6 • I-3 • L-3

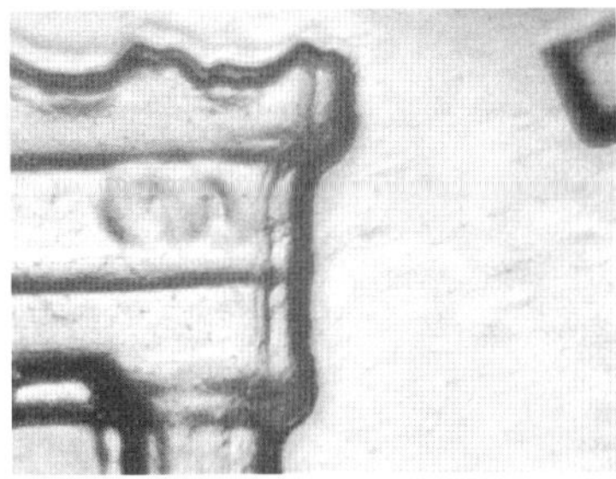

Description: This variety has a medium spread on ONE CENT and at both building edges.

Comments: This is the strongest of the 1960 doubled-die reverses.

	PF-63	PF-65	PF-66	PF-67
VARIETY	$40	$60	$80	$100
NORMAL	$1	$2	$12	$25

Note: Values listed for Proof Lincoln cents are for full red specimens. Red-and-brown and all-brown specimens command less. Cameo and deep cameo specimens should command much greater prices.

1960-D — FS-01-1960D-101/501 (025.5)

VARIETY: Doubled-Die Obverse — CONECA: DDO-001/RPM-100
PUP: Date, mintmark
URS-9 • I-5 • L-5

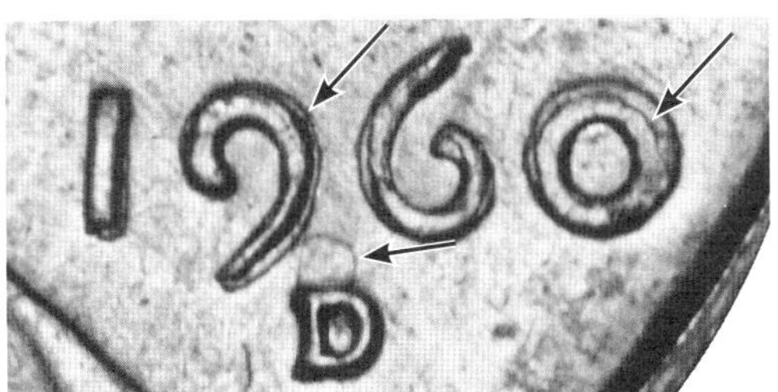

Description: The doubling is evident as a Small Date Over Large Date. There is also a very wide repunched mintmark, with the secondary D far north of the primary D, actually touching the 9 of the date.

Comments: In the not-so-distant past, this coin would sell for $25 in MS-63. Due to increased exposure and popularity, with fewer examples being found, prices have increased tenfold.

	AU-50	MS-60	MS-63	MS-65
VARIETY	$100	$150	$250	$500
NORMAL	$0.01	$0.05	$0.20	$0.30

Note: Values for MS-60 and MS-63 coins are for RB (red and brown) specimens; values for MS-65 are for full red specimens.

1960-D FS-01-1960D-502

Variety: Repunched Mintmark CONECA: RPM-001
PUP: Mintmark
URS-11 • I-3 • L-3

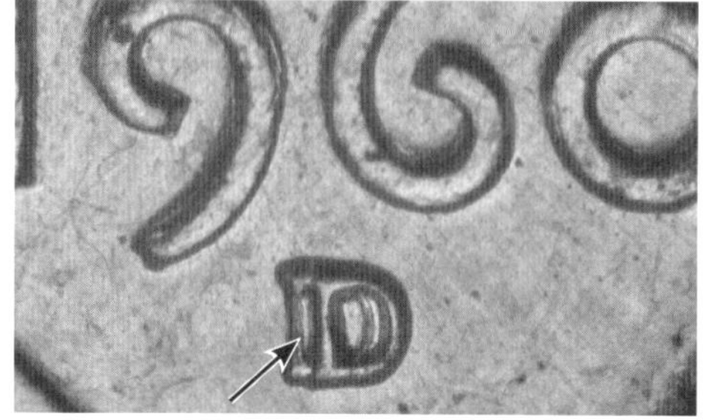

Description: This is a Large Date variety. The secondary D mintmark is west of the primary D.

Comments: These coins can be found in Mint sets. There are many other repunched mintmark varieties of this issue as well.

	AU-50	MS-60	MS-63	MS-65
Variety	$5	$10	$20	$35
Normal	$0.01	$0.05	$0.20	$0.30

Note: Values listed for MS-60 and MS-63 are for RB (red and brown) specimens; values listed for MS-65 are for full red specimens.

1961-D FS-01-1961D-501

Variety: Repunched Mintmark CONECA: RPM-001
PUP: Mintmark
URS-14 • I-4 • L-4

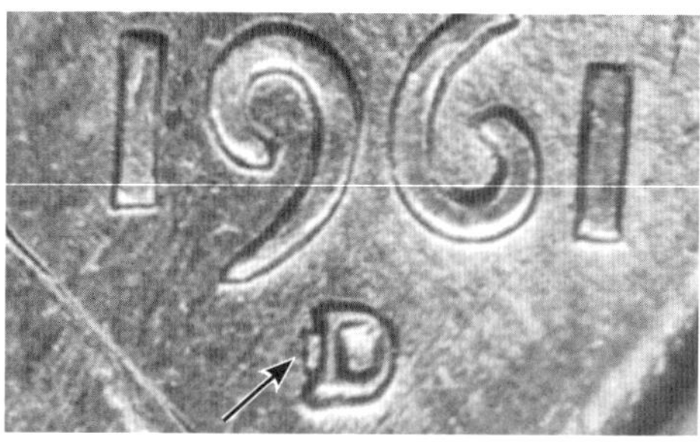

Description: The secondary D is evident in a horizontal orientation protruding left of the primary D.

Comments: This has long been a very popular variety and is well known. There are also enough specimens available to meet current demand, which is keeping the values down for a relatively neat variety.

	AU-50	MS-60	MS-63	MS-65
Variety	$2	$5	$10	$35
Normal	$0.01	$0.05	$0.15	$0.30

Note: Values for MS-60 and MS-63 coins are for RB (red and brown) specimens; values for MS-65 are for full red specimens.

1962 Proof — FS-01-1962-801

VARIETY: Doubled-Die Reverse — CONECA: DDR-020
PUP: AMERICA
URS-5 • I-3 • L-3

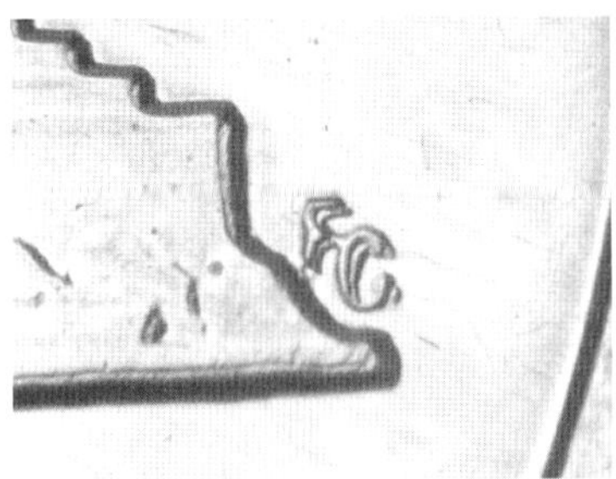

Description: A strong spread is seen on STATES OF AMERICA, the designer's initials, and ONE CENT.

Comments: There are many Proof doubled-die reverses, so check the attribution guides for diagnostic details.

	PF-63	PF-65	PF-66	PF-67
VARIETY	$40	$60	$80	$100
NORMAL	$1	$2	$5	$10

Note: Values listed for Proof Lincoln cents are for full red specimens. Red-and-brown and all-brown specimens command less. Cameo and deep cameo specimens should command much greater prices.

1963 Proof — FS-01-1963-801

VARIETY: Doubled-Die Reverse — CONECA: DDR-006
PUP: AMERICA
URS-6 • I-3 • L-3

Description: This variety shows a very strong spread on all lettering, both sides of the building, and the designer's initials.

Comments: This is probably the strongest of all the Proof Memorial doubled-die reverses.

	PF-63	PF-65	PF-66	PF-67
VARIETY	$50	$100	$150	$250
NORMAL	$1	$2	$5	$10

Note: Values listed for Proof Lincoln cents are for full red specimens. Red-and-brown and all-brown specimens command less. Cameo and deep cameo specimens should command much greater prices.

1963-D FS-01-1963D-101 (025.8)

VARIETY: Doubled-Die Obverse CONECA: DDO-001
PUP: Date
URS-13 • I-3 • L-2

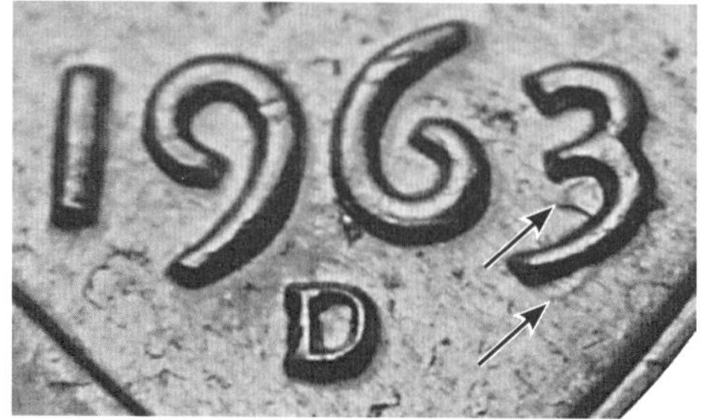

Description: The only significant marker for this doubled die is a secondary 3 evident inside the lower opening of the primary 3, and trailing slightly below the primary 3.

Comments: This doubled die is relatively common, in that it is readily available. Due to large numbers available, sales of any finds may be slow.

	AU-50	MS-60	MS-63	MS-65
VARIETY	$2	$5	$8	$45
NORMAL	$0.01	$0.05	$0.15	$0.30

Note: Values for MS-60 and MS-63 coins are for RB (red and brown) specimens; values for MS-65 are for full red specimens.

1964 FS-01-1964-801 (026)

VARIETY: Doubled-Die Reverse CONECA: DDR-001
PUP: UNITED STATES OF AMERICA
URS-12 • I-3 • L-3

Description: A very strong spread is evident on the letters of UNITED STATES OF AMERICA and E PLURIBUS UNUM, and to a lesser degree on ONE CENT and the designer's initials.

Comments: This doubled die has been known for many years, yet can still be cherrypicked.

	AU-50	MS-60	MS-63	MS-65
VARIETY	$20	$25	$35	$95
NORMAL	$0.01	$0.05	$0.15	$0.30

Note: Values for MS-60 and MS-63 coins are for RB (red and brown) specimens; values for MS-65 are for full red specimens.

1964 — FS-01-1964-802 (027)

VARIETY: Doubled-Die Reverse — CONECA: DDR-020

PUP: AMERICA

URS-7 • I-2 • L-2

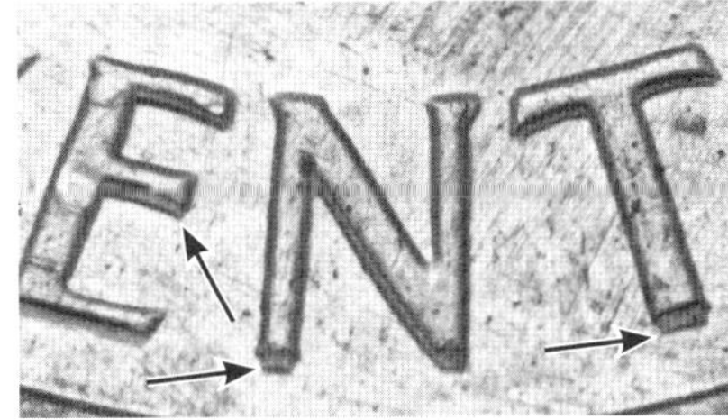

Description: A very strong spread is evident on UNITED STATES OF AMERICA and on ONE CENT, with slight doubling evident on the lower edges of the building.

Comments: This variety is known in two distinct die states, the earlier being more desirable and rare. This is a fairly strong doubled die.

	AU-50	MS-60	MS-63	MS-65
VARIETY	$25	$35	$50	$125
NORMAL	$0.01	$0.05	$0.15	$0.30

Note: Values for MS-60 and MS-63 coins are for RB (red and brown) specimens; values for MS-65 are for full red specimens.

1966 — FS-01-1966-101

VARIETY: Doubled-Die Obverse — CONECA: DDO-001

PUP: Date, IN GOD WE TRUST

URS-4 • I-3 • L-3

Description: Moderate doubling is evident on IN GOD WE TRUST and the date.

Comments: This is another popular variety that has proven difficult to find.

	AU-50	MS-60	MS-63	MS-65
VARIETY	$25	$50	$75	$100
NORMAL	$0.01	$0.05	$0.20	$0.50

Note: Values for MS-60 and MS-63 coins are for RB (red and brown) specimens; values for MS-65 are for full red specimens.

1966 — FS-01-1966-801

Variety: Doubled-Die Reverse — CONECA: DDR-001
PUP: ONE CENT
URS-3 • I-4 • L-4

Description: This variety exhibits a medium spread on ONE CENT, the designer's initials, and UNITED STATES OF AMERICA.

Comments: This is not a Special Mint Set issue. It is very hard to obtain, with many specialists eager to add one to their collections.

	AU-50	MS-60	MS-63	MS-65
Variety	$125	$250	$500	$750
Normal	$0.01	$0.05	$0.20	$0.50

Note: Values listed for MS-60 and MS-63 are for RB (red and brown) specimens; values listed for MS-65 are for full red specimens.

1968-D — FS-01-1968D-501 (027.3)

Variety: Repunched Mintmark — CONECA: RPM-001
PUP: Mintmark
URS-7 • I-3 • L-3

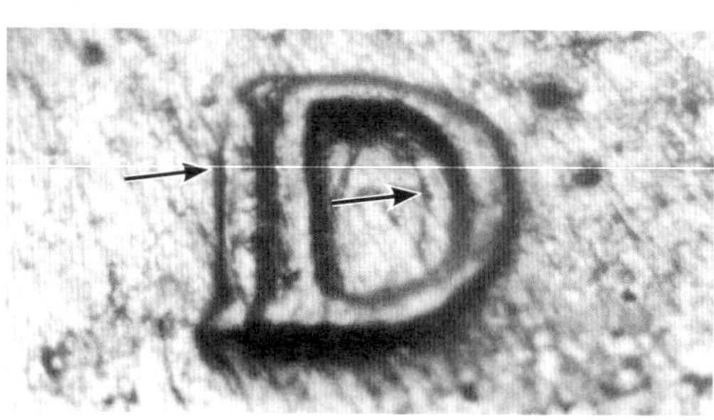

Description: The secondary D is evident to the west of the primary D.

Comments: This has long been a very popular variety and is well known. There are also enough specimens available to meet current demand, which is keeping the values down for a relatively neat variety.

	AU-50	MS-60	MS-63	MS-65
Variety	$2	$5	$10	$25
Normal	$0.01	$0.05	$0.15	$0.40

Note: Values for MS-60 and MS-63 coins are for RB (red and brown) specimens; values for MS-65 are for full red specimens.

1968-D — FS-01-1968D-801 (027.4)

VARIETY: Doubled-Die Reverse — CONECA: DDR-001

PUP: AMERICA

URS-4 • I-3 • L-3

Description: Moderate doubling is evident on STATES OF AMERICA, E PLURIBUS UNUM, and the designer's initials.

Comments: Increased publicity has popularized this variety, but few have been found.

	AU-50	MS-60	MS-63	MS-65
VARIETY	$25	$50	$100	$250
NORMAL	$0.01	$0.05	$0.15	$0.40

Note: Values for MS-60 and MS-63 coins are for RB (red and brown) specimens; values for MS-65 are for full red specimens.

1968-S Proof — FS-01-1968S-101 (027.5)

VARIETY: Doubled-Die Obverse — CONECA: DDO-005

PUP: Date, LIBERTY

URS-9 • I-3 • L-3

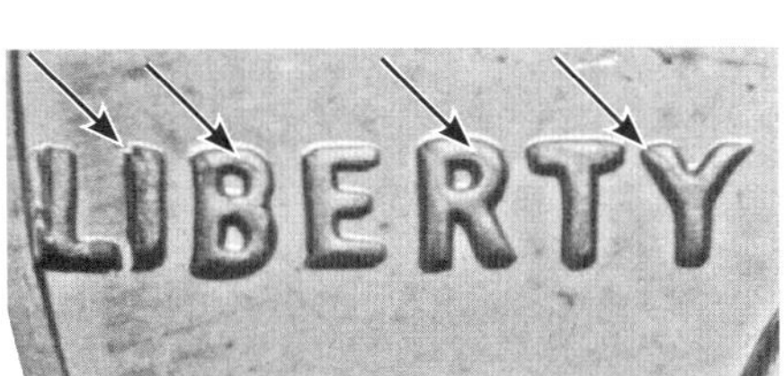

Description: Strong doubling is evident on the date, LIBERTY, and IN GOD WE TRUST.

Comments: This is another underrated variety.

	PF-63	PF-65	PF-66	PF-67
VARIETY	$10	$25	$35	$75
NORMAL	$0.50	$1	$5	$15

Note: Values listed for Proof Lincoln cents are for full red specimens. Red-and-brown and full brown specimens command less. Cameo and deep cameo specimens should command much greater prices.

1969-S FS-01-1969S-101 (028)

Variety: Doubled-Die Obverse CONECA: DDO-001
PUP: Date
URS-6 • I-5 • L-5

Description: Extremely strong doubling is evident on all obverse lettering and numbers.

Comments: The publicity this coin has received over its lifetime has been enormous, hence the very high values, which are well deserved. This is a very rare, strong doubled die. Beware of examples that are strike doubling, which are essentially worth face value. Compare the photos below with those of the true doubled die. A PCGS MS-64RB example sold for $130,000 in 2008.

	EF-40	AU-50	MS-60	MS-63	MS-65
Variety	$15,000	$25,000	$50,000	$75,000	
Normal	$0.01	$0.01	$0.05	$0.15	$0.50

Note: Values for Mint State coins are for RB (red and brown) specimens.

The photos below are NOT a 1969-S doubled die. Read below.

The photo on the left shows the date area of a 1969-S cent with strike doubling. On the right is a photo of LIBERTY on the same coin. Compare these photos with the photos above. This coin with strike doubling has no value above that of a normal coin. Do not be fooled into thinking this is the doubled die. Please read the section on page 371 comparing true die doubling with strike doubling.

1970-S, Large Date — FS-01-1970S-101 (029)

VARIETY: Doubled-Die Obverse — CONECA: DDO-001

PUP: TRUST

URS-5 • I-5 • L-5

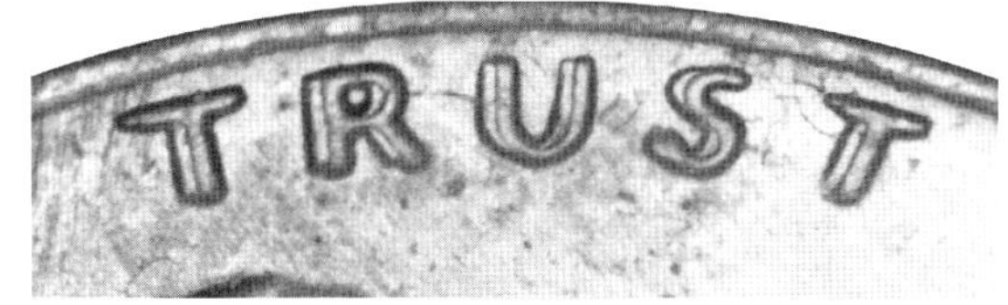

Description: Extremely strong doubling is evident on the date, LIBERTY, and IN GOD WE TRUST.

Comments: This very strong doubled die is extremely rare. To this point, fewer examples are known than the previous listing, the 1969-S. However, this variety has not received the same publicity as the previous, thus the lower values.

	EF-40	AU-50	MS-60	MS-63	MS-65
VARIETY	$750	$1,250	$6,500	$10,000	$18,000
NORMAL	$0.01	$0.01	$0.05	$0.20	$0.50

Note: Values for Mint State coins are for RB (red and brown) specimens.

1970-S Proof, Large Date — FS-01-1970S-102 (030)

VARIETY: Doubled-Die Obverse — CONECA: DDO-003

PUP: Date

URS-9 • I-4 • L-4

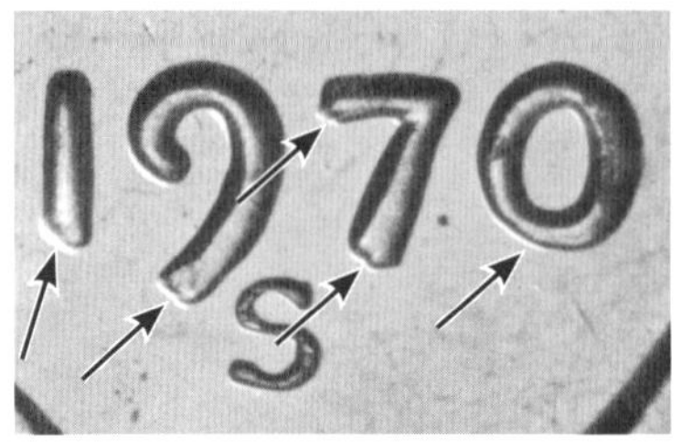

Description: Strong doubling is evident on the date, LIBERTY, and IN GOD WE TRUST. This is actually a Large Date Over Small Date.

Comments: This was long considered a typical Class VI doubled die. In the late 1990s, eagle-eyed Mike Ellis realized (correctly) this was a doubled die created by the use of a small-dated hub and then a large-dated hub.

	PF-63	PF-65	PF-66	PF-67
VARIETY	$125	$300	$500	$650
NORMAL	$0.50	$1	$5	$15

Note: Values listed for Proof Lincoln cents are for full red specimens. Red-and-brown and full brown specimens command less. Cameo and deep cameo specimens should command much greater prices.

1970-S, Large Date — FS-01-1970S-103 (030.1)

VARIETY: Doubled-Die Obverse — CONECA: DDO-005

PUP: Date

URS-13 • I-2 • L-2

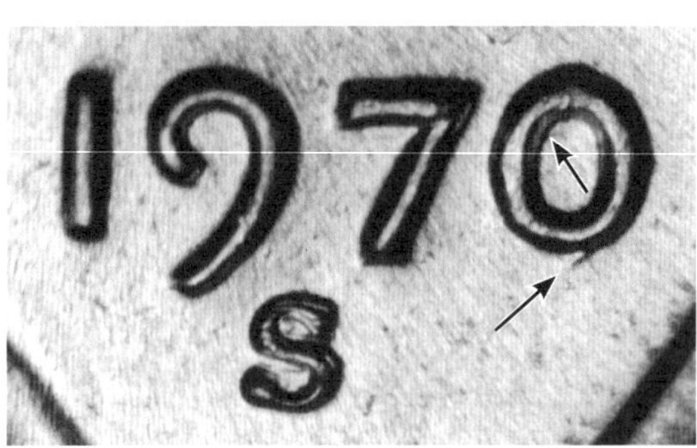

Description: This doubled die is evident only by the secondary bar visible below the primary 0. Similar doubling is also known on Philadelphia and Denver mint coins.

Comments: A relatively minor doubled die, but this is interesting to many collectors.

	AU-50	MS-60	MS-63	MS-65RB
VARIETY	$3	$5	$10	$20
NORMAL	$0.01	$0.05	$0.20	$0.50

Note: Values for MS-60 and MS-63 coins are for RB (red and brown) specimens; values for MS-65 are for full red specimens.

1970-S Proof, Large Date — FS-01-1970S-107 (030.4)

VARIETY: Tripled-Die Obverse — CONECA: DDO-007
PUP: Date, LIBERTY
URS-8 • I-3 • L-3

Description: The tripling is evident on all obverse lettering and numbers. It is stronger toward the rim on the date and LIBERTY.

Comments: This was first discovered by J.T. Stanton during the Blue Ridge convention in 1985.

	PF-63	PF-65	PF-66	PF-67
VARIETY	$35	$75	$125	$150
NORMAL	$0.50	$1	$5	$15

Note: Values listed for Proof Lincoln cents are for full red specimens. Red-and-brown and full brown specimens command less. Cameo and deep cameo specimens should command much greater prices.

1970-S Proof, Large Date — FS-01-1970S-113 (030.6)

VARIETY: Doubled-Die Obverse — CONECA: DDO-013
PUP: Date, TRUST
URS-6 • I-3 • L-3

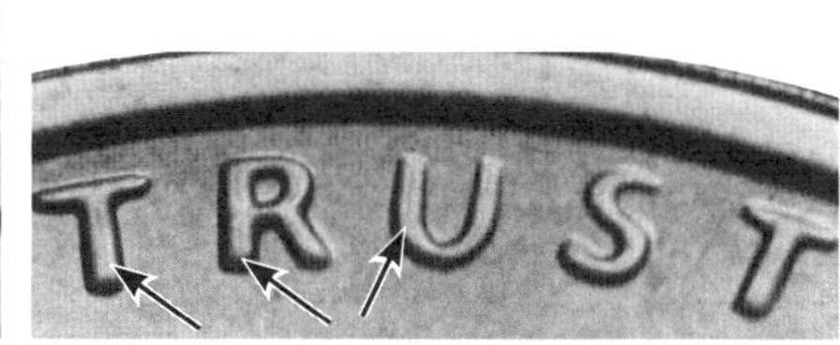

Description: Strong doubling is evident on the date, LIBERTY, and IN GOD WE TRUST.

Comments: This variety is at least as rare as previously thought, and is very difficult to locate.

	PF-63	PF-65	PF-66	PF-67
VARIETY	$75	$125	$175	$225
NORMAL	$0.50	$1	$5	$15

Note: Values listed for Proof Lincoln cents are for full red specimens. Red-and-brown and full brown specimens command less. Cameo and deep cameo specimens should command much greater prices.

1970-S, Small Date — FS-01-1970S-1401 (030.2)

VARIETY: Small Date — CONECA: N/L

PUP: Date

URS-18 • I-5 • L-5

Small Date

Large Date

Description: The date on some 1970-S–dated cents is smaller than the "normal" or Large Date coin. Compare the photos.

Comments: Many collectors miss this variety when looking only at the date. The easiest way to distinguish the Small Date cents of 1970 is actually the word LIBERTY, which weakens dramatically from left to right. Compare the photos above.

	AU-50	MS-60	MS-63	MS-65RB
VARIETY	$13	$17	$20	$28
NORMAL	$0.01	$0.05	$0.20	$0.50

Note: Values for MS-60 and MS-63 coins are for RB (red and brown) specimens; values for MS-65 are for full red specimens.

1970-S Proof, Small Date FS-01-1970S-1402 (030.2)

VARIETY: Small Date CONECA: N/L

PUP: Date

URS-18 • I-5 • L-5

Small Date

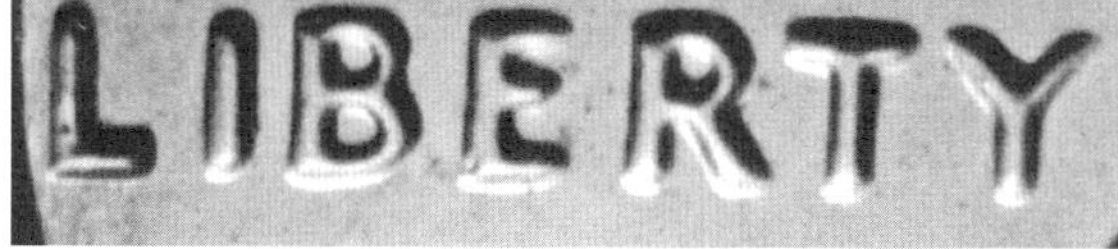

Large Date

Description: The date on some 1970-S–dated cents is smaller than the "normal" or Large Date coin. Compare the photos.

Comments: Many collectors miss this variety when looking only at the date. The easiest way to distinguish the Small Date cents of 1970 is actually the word LIBERTY, which weakens dramatically from left to right. Compare the photos above.

	PF-65	PF-66	PF-67
VARIETY	$75	$100	$125
NORMAL	$1	$5	$15

Note: Values listed for Proof Lincoln cents are for full red specimens. Red-and-brown and full brown specimens command less. Cameo and deep cameo specimens should command much greater prices.

1971 — FS-01-1971-101 (031)

Variety: Doubled-Die Obverse — CONECA: DDO-001
PUP: LIBERTY
URS-9 • I-4 • L-4

Description: Strong doubling is evident on LIBERTY and IN GOD WE TRUST, with slight doubling on the date.

Comments: This variety can be spotted in a dealer's case from 3 feet away! The obverse die was also slightly misaligned, which makes it appear slightly off center.

	AU-50	MS-60	MS-63	MS-65
Variety	$50	$75	$150	$300
Normal	$0.01	$0.05	$0.25	$0.60

Note: Values for MS-60 and MS-63 coins are for RB (red and brown) specimens; values for MS-65 are for full red specimens.

1971-S Proof — FS-01-1971S-101 (032)

Variety: Doubled-Die Obverse — CONECA: DDO-001
PUP: LIBERTY
URS-8 • I-5 • L-5

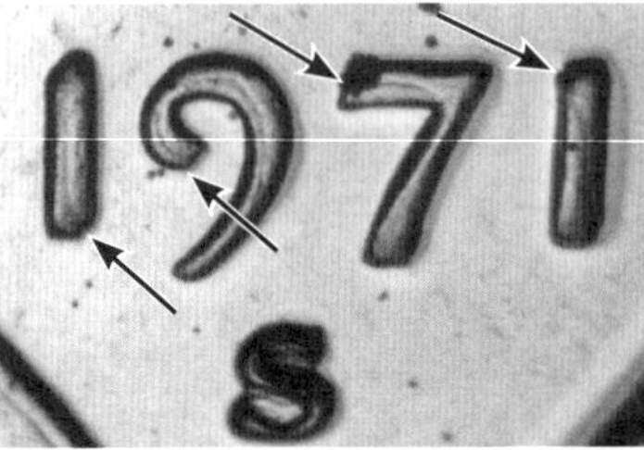

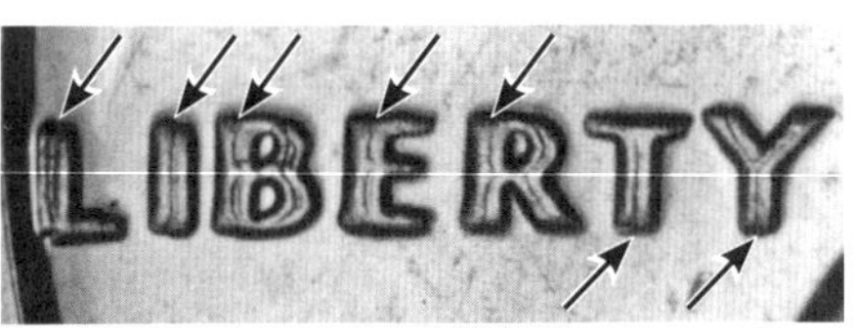

Description: Strong doubling is evident on IN GOD, TRUST, and LIBERTY; there is slight doubling on the date.

Comments: There is little, if any, doubling on WE. This is a popular doubled die, but not as rare as the next listing.

	PF-63	PF-65	PF-66	PF-67
Variety	$250	$450	$600	$750
Normal	$0.50	$1	$6	$18

Note: Values listed for Proof Lincoln cents are for full red specimens. Red-and-brown and full brown specimens command less. Cameo and deep cameo specimens should command much greater prices.

1971-S Proof — FS-01-1971S-102 (033)

VARIETY: Doubled-Die Obverse — CONECA: DDO-002

PUP: LIBERTY

URS-6 • I-5 • L-5

Description: Strong doubling is evident on IN GOD WE TRUST and LIBERTY. There is no doubling on the date.

Comments: This is by far one of the rarest Proof doubled dies in the Lincoln cent series. While this and the previous listing are both strong in terms of the doubling, this variety commands far greater premiums.

	PF-63	PF-65	PF-66	PF-67
VARIETY	$500	$750	$1,100	$1,500
NORMAL	$0.50	$1	$6	$18

Note: Values listed for Proof Lincoln cents are for full red specimens. Red-and-brown and full brown specimens command less. Cameo and deep cameo specimens should command much greater prices.

1971-S Proof — FS-01-1971S-103 (033.1)

VARIETY: Doubled-Die Obverse — CONECA: DDO-004

PUP: LIBERTY, GOD

URS-6 • I-3 • L-3

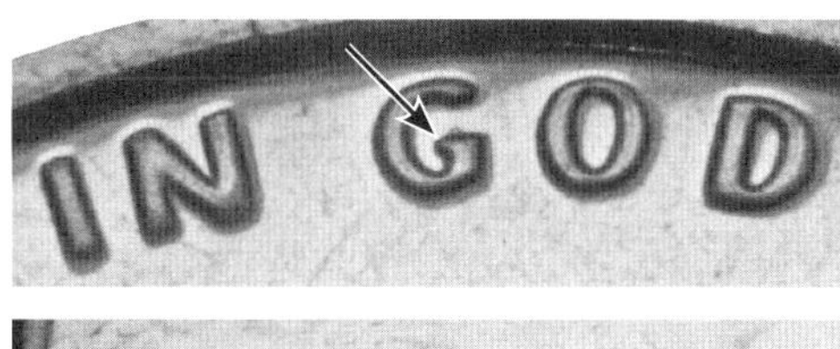

Description: Moderate doubling is evident on LIBERTY and IN GOD WE TRUST, but only very slightly on the date.

Comments: This variety is just another reason to check the 1971 Proof sets.

	PF-63	PF-65	PF-66	PF-67
VARIETY	$35	$75	$125	$150
NORMAL	$0.50	$1	$6	$18

Note: Values listed for Proof Lincoln cents are for full red specimens. Red-and-brown and full brown specimens command less. Cameo and deep cameo specimens should command much greater prices.

1972 FS-01-1972-101 (033.3)

VARIETY: Doubled-Die Obverse CONECA: DDO-001
PUP: Date, lettering
URS-16 • I-5 • L-5

Description: Very strong doubling is evident on the date, LIBERTY, and IN GOD WE TRUST. The secondary image is spread clockwise to the primary image.

Comments: This is the most popular doubled die for the year. Genuine examples exhibit a small die gouge on the reverse near the rim above the D of UNITED. This is the first of many different obverse doubled dies for this date, none of which are this strong.

	AU-50	MS-60	MS-63	MS-65
VARIETY	$240	$300	$400	$600
NORMAL	$0.01	$0.05	$0.15	$0.30

Note: Values for MS-60 and MS-63 coins are for RB (red and brown) specimens; values for MS-65 are for full red specimens.

THE CHERRYPICKERS' GUIDE HELPFUL HINTS

The state of the die at the time the coin was struck can be important. Almost across the board, early-die-state (EDS) coins are much more desirable and will sell for higher prices.

1972 — FS-01-1972-102 (033.52)

VARIETY: Doubled-Die Obverse — CONECA: DDO-002

PUP: LIBERTY

URS-14 • I-3 • L-3

YN

PC

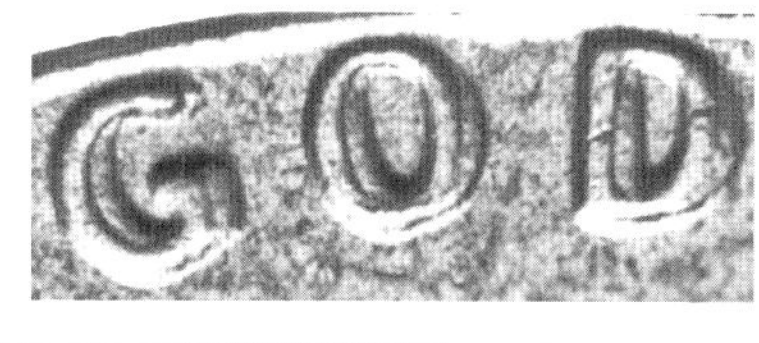

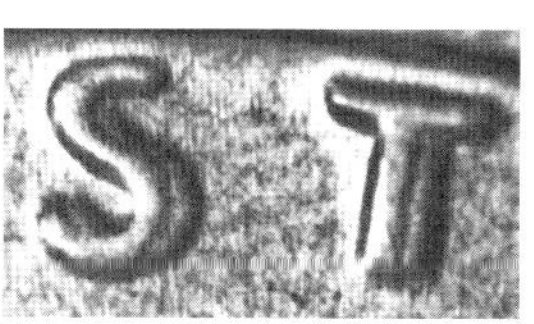

Description: Very strong doubling is evident on the date, LIBERTY, and IN GOD WE TRUST. The secondary image is spread clockwise to the primary image.

Comments: This is the second of the many obverse doubled dies for this year. Many people want to assemble a set of the many examples.

	AU-50	MS-60	MS-63	MS-65
VARIETY	$20	$50	$70	$100
NORMAL	$0.01	$0.05	$0.15	$0.30

Note: Values for MS-60 and MS-63 coins are for RB (red and brown) specimens; values for MS-65 are for full red specimens.

1972 — FS-01-1972-103 (033.53)

VARIETY: Doubled-Die Obverse — CONECA: DDO-003
PUP: LIBERTY
URS-15 • I-3 • L-3

Description: Very strong doubling is evident on the date, LIBERTY, and IN GOD WE TRUST. The secondary image is spread counterclockwise to the primary image.

Comments: This is the third of the many obverse doubled dies for this year. Many people want to assemble a set of the many examples.

	AU-50	MS-60	MS-63	MS-65
VARIETY	$9	$18	$30	$50
NORMAL	$0.01	$0.05	$0.15	$0.30

Note: Values for MS-60 and MS-63 coins are for RB (red and brown) specimens; values for MS-65 are for full red specimens.

1972 — FS-01-1972-104 (033.54)

VARIETY: Doubled-Die Obverse — CONECA: DDO-004
PUP: LIBERTY
URS-4 • I-5 • L-5

Description: Very strong doubling is evident on the date, LIBERTY, and IN GOD WE TRUST. The secondary image is spread clockwise to the primary image. Very early die states may not have die chips near LIBERTY.

Comments: This is the fourth of the many obverse doubled dies for this year. Many people want to assemble a set of the many examples. This is by far the rarest of the 1972 doubled dies.

	AU-50	MS-60	MS-63	MS-65
VARIETY	$150	$400	$900	$1,500
NORMAL	$0.01	$0.05	$0.15	$0.30

Note: Values for MS-60 and MS-63 coins are for RB (red and brown) specimens; values for MS-65 are for full red specimens.

1972 — FS-01-1972-105 (033.55)

VARIETY: Doubled-Die Obverse — CONECA: DDO-005
PUP: LIBERTY
URS-6 • I-3 • L-3

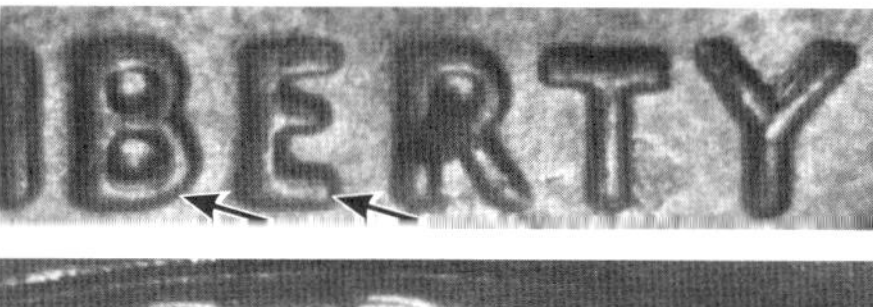

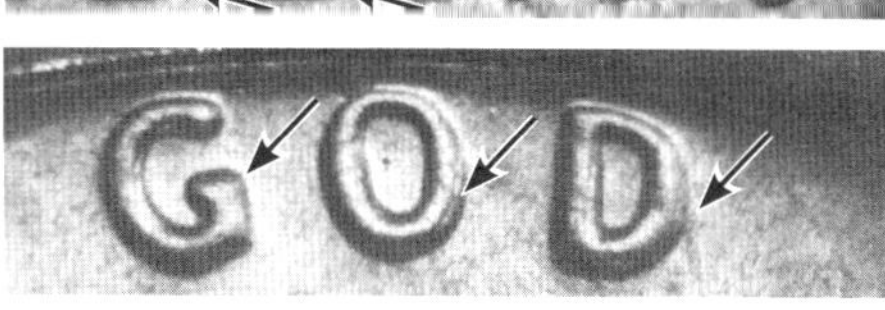

Description: Noticeable doubling is evident on the date, LIBERTY, and IN GOD WE TRUST. The secondary image is spread counterclockwise to the primary image.

Comments: This is the fifth of the many obverse doubled dies for this year. Many people want to assemble a set of the many examples. This is the weakest and least obvious of the many examples.

	AU-50	MS-60	MS-63	MS-65
VARIETY	$9	$18	$30	$50
NORMAL	$0.01	$0.05	$0.15	$0.30

Note: Values for MS-60 and MS-63 coins are for RB (red and brown) specimens; values for MS-65 are for full red specimens.

1972 — FS-01-1972-106 (033.56)

VARIETY: Doubled-Die Obverse — CONECA: DDO-006
PUP: LIBERTY
URS-13 • I-3 • L-3

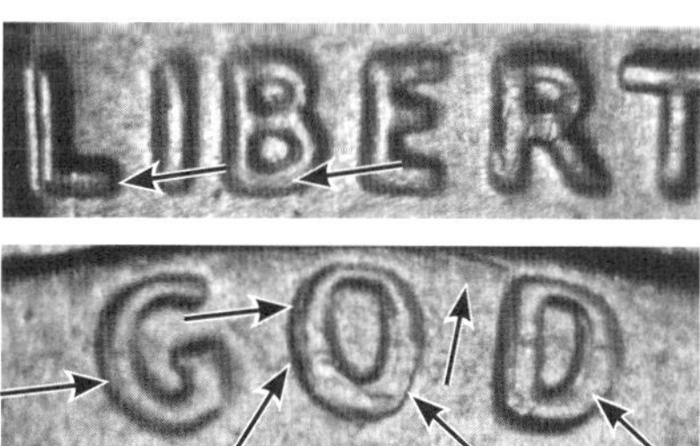

Description: Noticeable doubling is evident on the date, LIBERTY, and IN GOD WE TRUST. The secondary image is spread counterclockwise to the primary image.

Comments: This is the sixth of the many obverse doubled dies for this year. Many people want to assemble a set of the many examples.

	AU-50	MS-60	MS-63	MS-65
VARIETY	$9	$18	$30	$50
NORMAL	$0.01	$0.05	$0.15	$0.30

Note: Values for MS-60 and MS-63 coins are for RB (red and brown) specimens; values for MS-65 are for full red specimens.

1972 — FS-01-1972-107 (033.57)

VARIETY: Doubled-Die Obverse — CONECA: DDO-007
PUP: LIBERTY
URS-13 • I-3 • L-3

Description: Moderate doubling is evident on the date, LIBERTY, and IN GOD WE TRUST. The secondary image is spread clockwise to the primary image.

Comments: This is the seventh of the many obverse doubled dies for this year. Many people want to assemble a set of the many examples.

	AU-50	MS-60	MS-63	MS-65
VARIETY	$9	$18	$30	$50
NORMAL	$0.01	$0.05	$0.15	$0.30

Note: Values for MS-60 and MS-63 coins are for RB (red and brown) specimens; values for MS-65 are for full red specimens.

1972 — FS-01-1972-108 (033.58)

VARIETY: Doubled-Die Obverse — CONECA: DDO-008
PUP: LIBERTY
URS-14 • I-3 • L-3

Description: Strong doubling is evident on the date, LIBERTY, and IN GOD WE TRUST. The secondary image is spread counterclockwise to the primary image.

Comments: This is the eighth of the many obverse doubled dies for this year. Many people want to assemble a set of the many examples.

	AU-50	MS-60	MS-63	MS-65
VARIETY	$9	$15	$24	$75
NORMAL	$0.01	$0.05	$0.15	$0.30

Note: Values for MS-60 and MS-63 coins are for RB (red and brown) specimens; values for MS-65 are for full red specimens.

1972 — FS-01-1972-109 (033.59)

VARIETY: Doubled-Die Obverse — **CONECA:** DDO-009
PUP: Date
URS-11 • I-3 • L-3

Description: This variety is totally different from the others. The only doubling visible is on the tail of the 2, where a secondary tail is evident protruding. This is the strongest of several varieties with a double-tailed 2.

Comments: This is the ninth of the many obverse doubled dies for this year. Many people want to assemble a set of the many examples.

	AU-50	MS-60	MS-63	MS-65
VARIETY	$9	$15	$24	$75
NORMAL	$0.01	$0.05	$0.15	$0.30

Note: Values for MS-60 and MS-63 coins are for RB (red and brown) specimens; values for MS-65 are for full red specimens.

1972-S Proof — FS-01-1972S-101 (033.7)

VARIETY: Doubled-Die Obverse — **CONECA:** DDO-001
PUP: LIBERTY
URS-7 • I-3 • L-3

Description: Moderate doubling is evident on IN GOD WE TRUST and LIBERTY. Slight doubling is visible on the date.

Comments: This variety takes a back seat to the two major 1971-S doubled dies, but is a very collectible variety nonetheless.

	PF-63	PF-65	PF-66	PF-67
VARIETY	$100	$195	$275	$350
NORMAL	$0.50	$1	$5	$15

Note: Values listed for Proof Lincoln cents are for full red specimens. Red-and-brown and full brown specimens command less. Cameo and deep cameo specimens should command much greater prices.

1979-S, 1981-S Proof — FS-01-[Year]S-501

VARIETY: Type 2 Mintmark — CONECA: MMS-009, MMS-010
PUP: Mintmark
URS-14 • I-3 • L-3

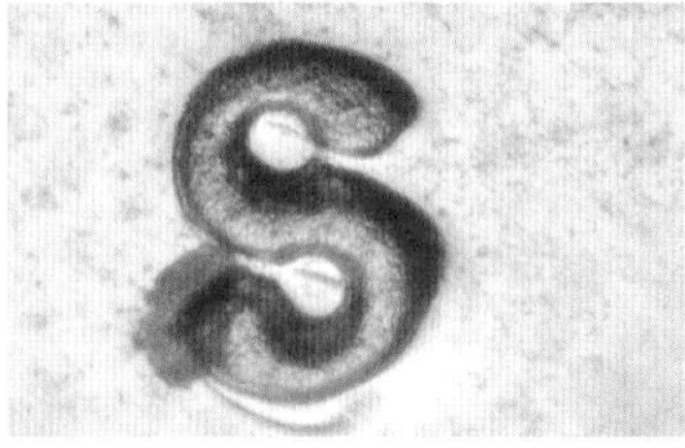

1979-S Type 2 Mintmark

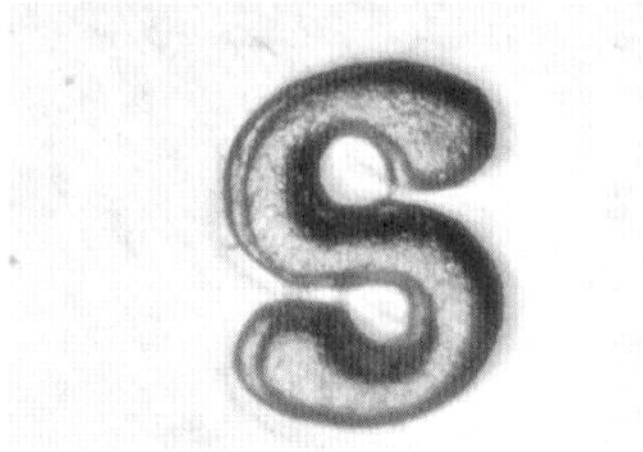

1981-S Type 2 Mintmark

Description: Two S mintmark styles were used on both 1979 and 1981 Proof Lincoln cents. For both years, the second mintmark style used (referred to as "Type 2") is rarer and more valuable than the first.

Comments: Interestingly, the Type 2 mintmark of 1979 is the same style as the Type 1 on 1981.

1979-S, FS-01-1979S-501

	PF-63	PF-65	PF-66	PF-67
Variety, Type 2 MM	$4	$6	$10	$17
Normal, Type 1 MM	$3	$5	$7	$11

1981-S, FS-01-1981S-501

	PF-63	PF-65	PF-66	PF-67
Variety, Type 2 MM	$10	$20	$24	$30
Normal, Type 1 MM	$1.50	$3	$5	$10

1980 — FS-01-1980-101 (034)

VARIETY: Doubled-Die Obverse — CONECA: DDO-001
PUP: Date
URS-11 • I-3 • L-3

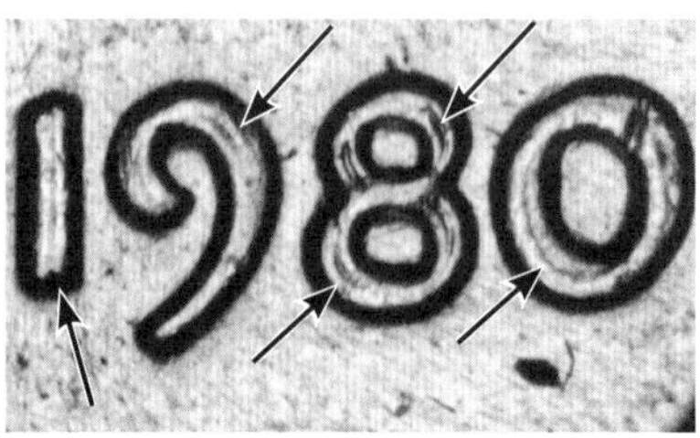

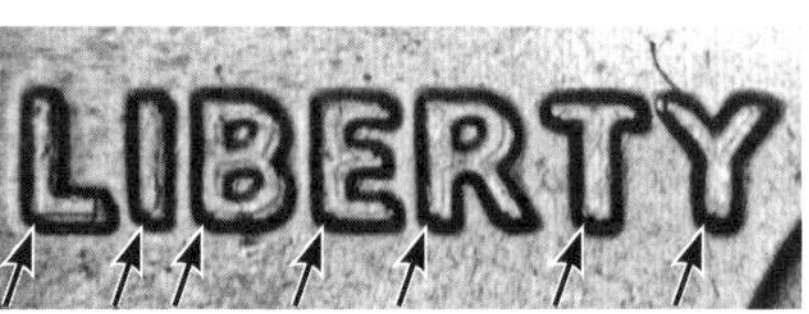

Description: Another very popular variety in the series, strong doubling is evident on the date and LIBERTY. Virtually no doubling is visible on IN GOD WE TRUST.

Comments: Early-die-state specimens exhibit heavy die polish on the reverse just below the memorial.

	AU-50	MS-60	MS-63	MS-65
Variety	$100	$150	$225	$350
Normal	$0.01	$0.03	$0.15	$0.30

Note: Values for MS-60 and MS-63 coins are for RB (red and brown) specimens; values for MS-65 are for full red specimens.

1982, Copper Large Date — FS-01-1982-101 (034.5)

VARIETY: Doubled-Die Obverse — CONECA: DDO-002
PUP: IN GOD WE TRUST
URS-10 • I-3 • L-3

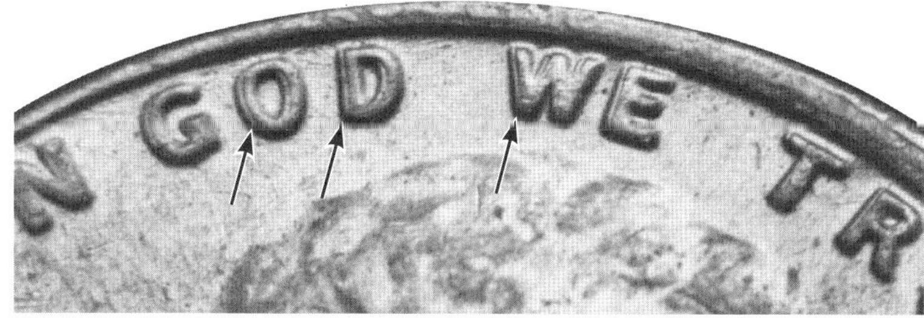

Description: Strong doubling is evident on IN GOD WE TRUST.

Comments: This is the only obverse doubled die for this date that is worth a significant premium. Later die states tend to be less distinct.

	AU-50	MS-60	MS-63	MS-65
VARIETY	$15	$25	$50	$95
NORMAL	$0.01	$0.03	$0.20	$0.35

Note: Values for MS-60 and MS-63 coins are for RB (red and brown) specimens; values for MS-65 are for full red specimens.

1982, Zinc Small Date — FS-01-1982-1801

VARIETY: Doubled-Die Reverse — CONECA: DDR-001
PUP: E PLURIBUS UNUM
URS-3 • I-4 • L-4

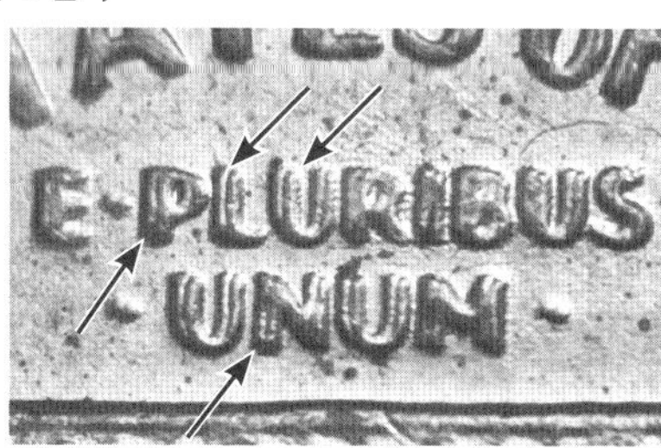

Description: Strong doubling is evident on UNITED STATES OF AMERICA, E PLURIBUS UNUM, and ONE CENT.

Comments: If ever there was a prime example that a significant new variety can still be discovered, check this out. This variety was discovered in the summer of 2007, 25 years after production!

	AU-50	MS-60	MS-63	MS-65
VARIETY	$400	$750	$1,000	$1,500
NORMAL	$0.01	$0.03	$0.50	$0.85

Note: Values for MS-60 and MS-63 coins are for RB (red and brown) specimens; values for MS-65 are for full red specimens.

1983 — FS-01-1983-101 (035)

VARIETY: Doubled-Die Obverse — CONECA: DDO-001
PUP: LIBERTY
URS-9 • I-3 • L-3

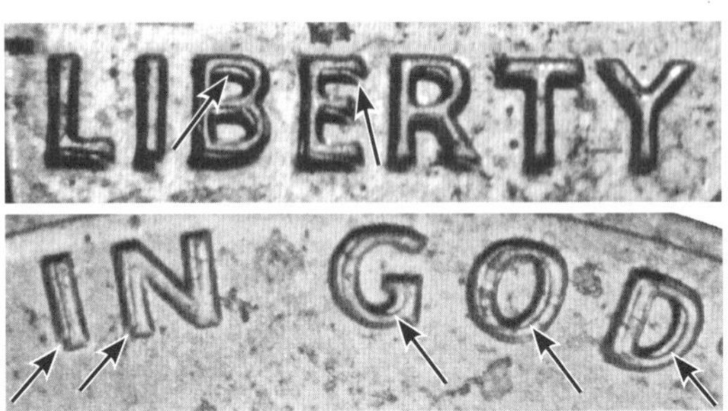

Description: Moderate doubling is evident on LIBERTY and IN GOD WE TRUST, and there is slight doubling on the date.

Comments: Relatively few collectors are aware of the obverse doubled dies for this date. Compare this listing with the next three.

	AU-50	MS-60	MS-63	MS-65
VARIETY	$10	$15	$25	$75
NORMAL	$0.01	$0.03	$0.15	$0.30

Note: Values for MS-60 and MS-63 coins are for RB (red and brown) specimens; values for MS-65 are for full red specimens.

1983 — FS-01-1983-102 (035.1)

VARIETY: Doubled-Die Obverse — CONECA: DDO-002
PUP: LIBERTY
URS-9 • I-3 • L-3

Description: Moderate doubling is evident on the date, with slightly lesser doubling on IN GOD WE TRUST and LIBERTY.

Comments: Relatively few collectors are aware of the obverse doubled dies for this date.

	AU-50	MS-60	MS-63	MS-65
VARIETY	$10	$15	$25	$45
NORMAL	$0.01	$0.03	$0.15	$0.30

Note: Values for MS-60 and MS-63 coins are for RB (red and brown) specimens; values for MS-65 are for full red specimens.

1983 — FS-01-1983-103 (035.2)

VARIETY: Doubled-Die Obverse — CONECA: DDO-003
PUP: IN GOD WE TRUST
URS-9 • I-3 • L-3

Description: Light doubling is evident on IN GOD WE TRUST and LIBERTY.

Comments: Relatively few collectors are aware of the obverse doubled dies for this date.

	AU-50	MS-60	MS-63	MS-65
VARIETY	$10	$15	$25	$45
NORMAL	$0.01	$0.03	$0.15	$0.30

Note: Values for MS-60 and MS-63 coins are for RB (red and brown) specimens; values for MS-65 are for full red specimens.

1983 — FS-01-1983-401 (035.3)

VARIETY: Obverse Die Counterclash — CONECA: N/L
PUP: Field above date
URS-6 • I-3 • L-3

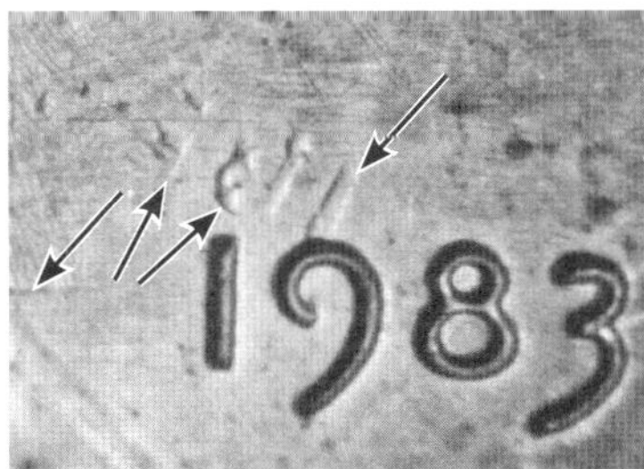

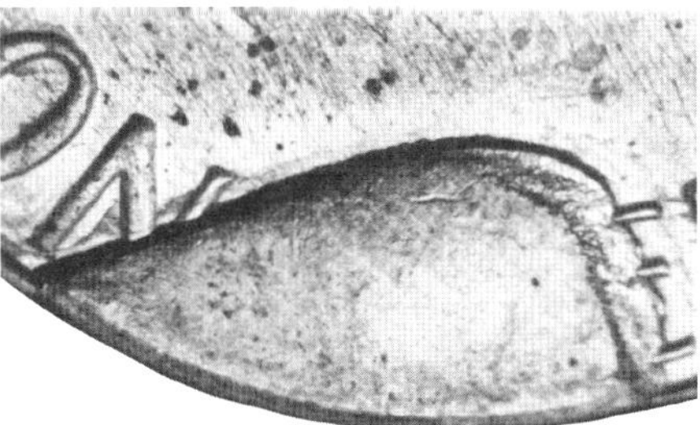

Description: Some weak impressions of the letters from the word LIBERTY appear above the date.

Comments: The letters of LIBERTY above the date are not the result of a doubled die, but a counterclash. The variety is also paired with a major reverse die break (cud) which may hold some key to the images on the obverse.

	AU-50	MS-60	MS-63	MS-65
VARIETY	$100	$150	$350	$500
NORMAL	$0.01	$0.03	$0.15	$0.30

Note: Values for MS-60 and MS-63 coins are for RB (red and brown) specimens; values for MS-65 are for full red specimens.

1983 — FS-01-1983-801 (036)

Variety: Doubled-Die Reverse — CONECA: DDR-001
PUP: ONE CENT
URS-14 • I-5 • L-5

Description: All reverse lettering is strongly doubled, including UNITED STATES OF AMERICA, E PLURIBUS UNUM, and ONE CENT. Also doubled are the designer's initials and portions of the memorial.

Comments: This is a well-known doubled-die reverse for the date. We suggest checking current price guides for constantly changing prices.

	AU-50	MS-60	MS-63	MS-65
Variety	*$75*	*$100*	*$250*	*$400*
Normal	$0.01	$0.03	$0.15	$0.30

Note: Values for MS-60 and MS-63 coins are for RB (red and brown) specimens; values for MS-65 are for full red specimens.

1983 — FS-01-1983-802

Variety: Doubled-Die Reverse — CONECA: DDR-002
PUP: UNITED
URS-6 • I-3 • L-3

Description: This variety shows a medium spread on UNITED, with a light spread on STATES and ONE.

Comments: This coin is nowhere near the strength of the big one, but has a nice localized spread nonetheless.

	AU-50	MS-60	MS-63	MS-65
Variety	$20	$30	$50	$75
Normal	$0.01	$0.03	$0.15	$0.30

Note: Values listed for MS-60 and MS-63 are for RB (red and brown) specimens; values listed for MS-65 are for full red specimens.

1983-D — FS-01-1983D-101

VARIETY: Doubled-Die Obverse — CONECA: DDO-001

PUP: Ear

URS-4 • I-4 • L-3

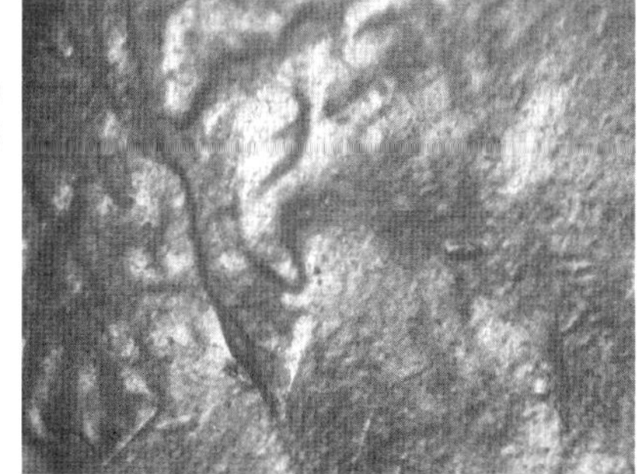

Description: There is a strong spread south appearing as an extra lower earlobe.

Comments: This is another doubled ear, highly sought after by specialists.

	AU-50	MS-60	MS-63	MS-65
VARIETY	$30	$50	$100	$125
NORMAL	$0.01	$0.03	$0.15	$0.30

Note: Values listed for MS-60 and MS-63 are for RB (red and brown) specimens; values listed for MS-65 are for full red specimens.

1984 — FS-01-1984-101 (037)

VARIETY: Doubled-Die Obverse — CONECA: DDO-001

PUP: Ear

URS-15 • I-5 • L-5

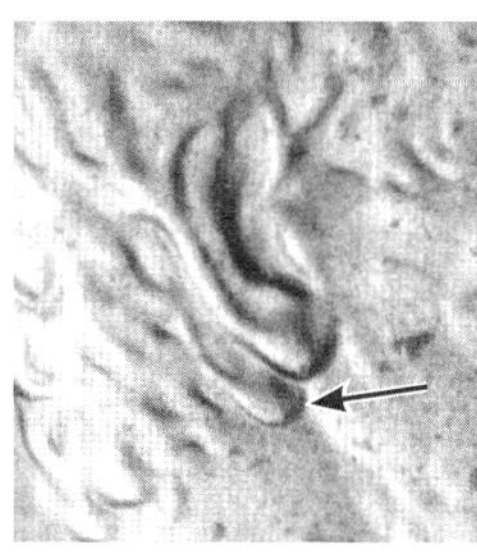

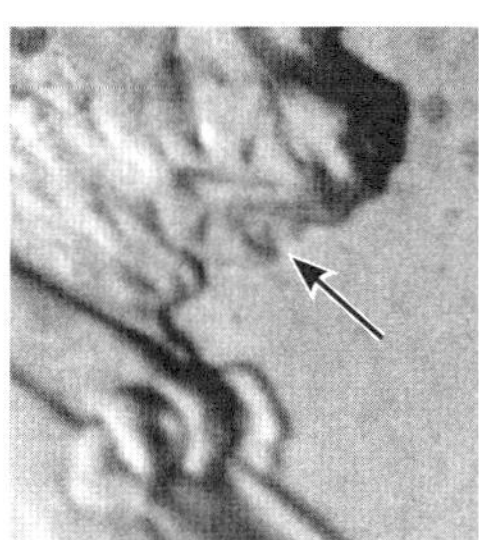

Description: Strong doubling is evident on the ear of Lincoln, with additional doubling on the beard and bowtie.

Comments: This variety is extremely popular among even regular collectors. It was discovered by Richard Austin in 1984.

	AU-50	MS-60	MS-63	MS-65
VARIETY	$85	$105	$135	$200
NORMAL	$0.01	$0.03	$0.15	$0.30

Note: Values for MS-60 and MS-63 coins are for RB (red and brown) specimens; values for MS-65 are for full red specimens.

1984 — FS-01-1984-102 (038)

VARIETY: Doubled-Die Obverse — CONECA: DDO-002

PUP: Date

URS-8 • I-3 • L-3

Description: Moderate doubling is evident on the date and LIBERTY.

Comments: Most of the reported examples of this coin are spotted. A true MS-65 specimen will be a quick sell.

	AU-50	MS-60	MS-63	MS-65
VARIETY	$35	$50	$75	$95
NORMAL	$0.01	$0.03	$0.15	$0.30

Note: Values for MS-60 and MS-63 coins are for RB (red and brown) specimens; values for MS-65 are for full red specimens.

1984-D — FS-01-1984D-101 (039)

VARIETY: Doubled-Die Obverse — CONECA: DDO-001

PUP: Date

URS-8 • I-3 • L-3

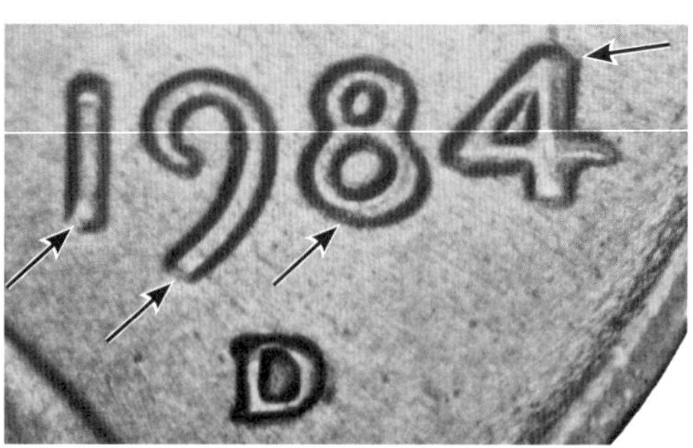

Description: Doubling is evident on the date, with slight doubling on LIBERTY.

Comments: This variety is popular with Lincoln cent specialists and could be a neat find for you Westerners.

	AU-50	MS-60	MS-63	MS-65
VARIETY	$15	$25	$35	$45
NORMAL	$0.01	$0.03	$0.15	$0.30

Note: Values for MS-60 and MS-63 coins are for RB (red and brown) specimens; values for MS-65 are for full red specimens.

1987-D — FS-01-1987D-501

Variety: Repunched Mintmark — **CONECA:** RPM-003
PUP: Mintmark
URS-4 • I-3 • L-3

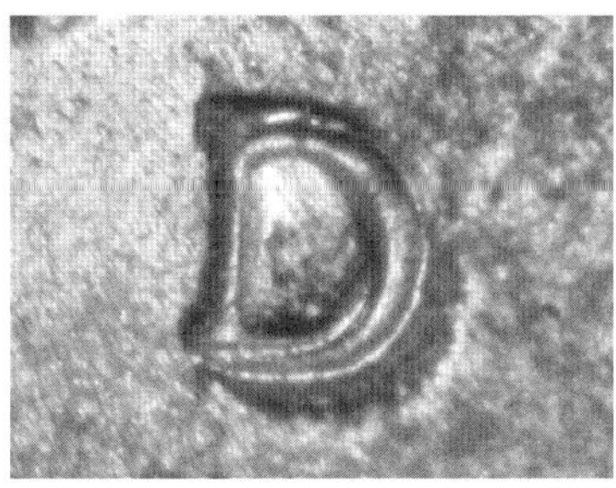

Description: The secondary D mintmark is north of the primary D.

Comments: All repunched mintmarks from the 1980s are difficult to obtain. This is one of the nicest.

	AU-50	MS-60	MS-63	MS-65
Variety	$25	$40	$60	$75
Normal	$0.01	$0.02	$0.15	$0.30

Note: Values listed for vMS-60 and MS-63 are for RB (red and brown) specimens; values listed for MS-65 are for full red specimens.

1988 — FS-01-1988-101

Variety: Doubled-Die Obverse — **CONECA:** DDO-003
PUP: Ear
URS-2 • I-4 • L-4

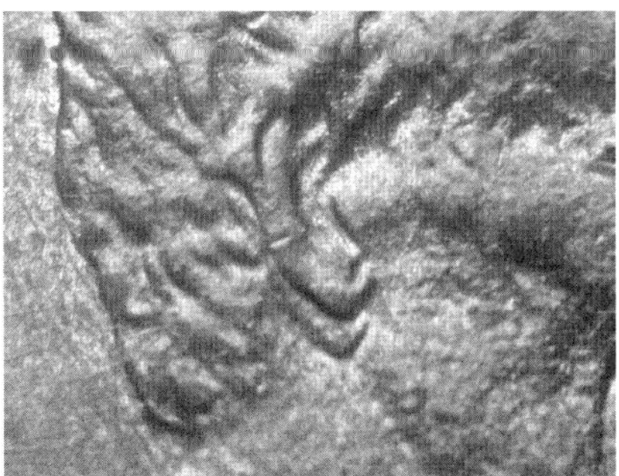

Description: This variety is identified by a strong spread south appearing as an extra lower earlobe.

Comments: This coin is difficult to find, and is highly sought after by specialists.

	AU-50	MS-60	MS-63	MS-65
Variety	$75	$100	$200	$300
Normal	$0.01	$0.02	$0.15	$0.30

Note: Values listed for MS-60 and MS-63 are for RB (red and brown) specimens; values listed for MS-65 are for full red specimens.

1988–2000 FS-01-[Year]-901

VARIETY: Reverse Design Change CONECA: RDV-006
PUP: Wide AM of AMERICA, designer's initials
URS-11 • I-3 • L-3

Description: The reverse Proof design was inadvertently used on some circulation-strike coins. The AM of AMERICA is spaced apart and the G of FG (the designer's initials) has a flared vertical bar.

Comments: Several dies are known for each date/mint and are individually listed by other attributers. Currently, the rarest of the group is the 1999, followed by the 1988-D.

1988, FS-01-1988-901 (CONECA: RDV-006)

	AU-50	MS-60	MS-63	MS-65
VARIETY	$10	$20	$30	$50
NORMAL	$0.01	$0.02	$0.15	$0.30

1988-D, FS-01-1988D-901 (CONECA: RDV-006)

	AU-50	MS-60	MS-63	MS-65
VARIETY	$20	$40	$60	$90
NORMAL	$0.01	$0.02	$0.15	$0.30

1998, FS-01-1998-901 (CONECA: RDV-006)

	AU-50	MS-60	MS-63	MS-65
VARIETY	$20	$25	$35	$50
NORMAL	$0.01	$0.02	$0.15	$0.30

1999, FS-01-1999-901 (CONECA: RDV-006)

	AU-50	MS-60	MS-63	MS-65
VARIETY	$150	$200	$300	$400
NORMAL	$0.01	$0.02	$0.15	$0.30

2000, FS-01-2000-901 (CONECA: RDV-006)

	AU-50	MS-60	MS-63	MS-65
VARIETY	$20	$25	$35	$50
NORMAL	$0.01	$0.02	$0.15	$0.30

Note: Values listed for MS-60 and MS-63 are for RB (red and brown) specimens; values listed for MS-65 are for full red specimens.

1992–1999-S — FS-01-[Year]-901

VARIETY: Reverse Design Change — CONECA: RDV-007
PUP: Close AM of AMERICA, designer's initials
URS-9 • I-3 • L-3

Circulation-strike varieties

Proof varieties

Description: The reverse design of 1993 was inadvertently used on some circulation-strike coins of 1992 (both Philadelphia issues and Denver issues). The AM of AMERICA is closely spaced, and the G of FG (the designer's initials) has a straight vertical bar. This same design was accidently used on some Proof coins from 1998 and 1999.

Comments: Only one die is known for each of the 1992 mints, but multiple dies are associated with the two Proof dates. Currently the most common is the 1999-S, followed by the 1998-S.

1992, FS-01-1992-901 (CONECA: RDV-007)

	AU-50	MS-60	MS-63	MS-65
VARIETY	$250	$500	$750	$1,000
NORMAL	$0.01	$0.02	$0.15	$0.30

1992-D, FS-01-1992D-901 (CONECA: RDV-007)

	AU-50	MS-60	MS-63	MS-65
VARIETY	$250	$500	$750	$1,000
NORMAL	$0.01	$0.02	$0.15	$0.30

1998-S PROOF, FS-01-1998S-901 (CONECA: RDV-007)

	PF-64	PF-65	PF-66	PF-67
VARIETY	$100	$200	$250	$300
NORMAL	$7	$9	$9.50	$10

1999-S PROOF, FS-01-1999S-901 (CONECA: RDV-007)

	PF-64	PF-65	PF-66	PF-67
VARIETY	$75	$100	$125	$150
NORMAL	$5	$6	$7.50	$9

Note: Values listed for MS-60 and MS-63 are for RB (red and brown) specimens; values listed for MS-65 are for full red specimens.

1990-(S) Proof — FS-01-1990-101

VARIETY: No S Mintmark — CONECA: MMO-001
PUP: Mintmark area
URS-6 • I-5 • L-5

Description: The S mintmark is missing.

Comments: These can still be picked, as evidenced by an eagle-eyed cherrypicker who found two sets at the 2008 FUN Convention and sold them shortly afterward for an $11,000 profit.

	PF-65	PF-66	PF-67
VARIETY	$4,500	$5,500	$6,250
NORMAL	$5	$7	$10

Note: Values listed for Proof Lincoln cents are for full red specimens. Red-and-brown and full brown specimens command less. Cameo and deep cameo specimens should command much greater prices.

1994 — FS-01-1994-801 (039.9)

VARIETY: Doubled-Die Reverse — CONECA: DDR-001
PUP: Last three columns of memorial
URS-5 • I-3 • L-3

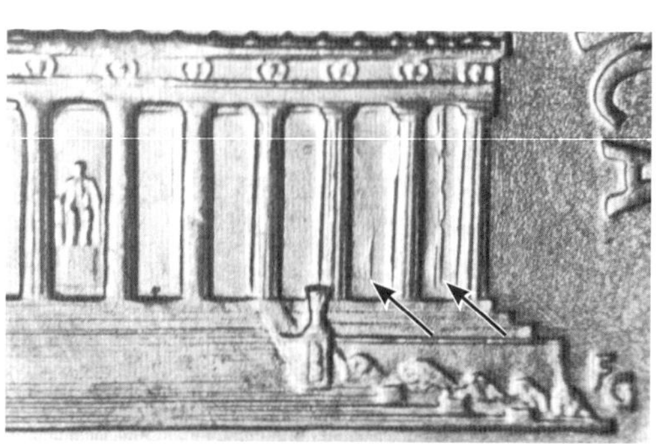

Description: Doubling is evident as two extra columns within the three final columns.

Comments: This variety was first reported by James Mattaliano.

	AU-50	MS-60	MS-63	MS-65
VARIETY	$50	$70	$100	$150
NORMAL	$0.01	$0.02	$0.15	$0.30

Note: Values for MS-60 and MS-63 coins are for RB (red and brown) specimens; values for MS-65 are for full red specimens.

1995 — FS-01-1995-101 (040)

VARIETY: Doubled-Die Obverse — CONECA: DDO-001

PUP: LIBERTY

URS-21 • I-4 • L-3

Description: Very strong doubling is evident on LIBERTY and IN GOD WE TRUST, with minor doubling on the date.

Comments: First reported by Felix Dausilio, this variety received rapid recognition when it appeared on the front page of ***USA Today***, sending all of us on a nationwide treasure hunt.

	AU-50	MS-60	MS-63	MS-65
VARIETY	$25	$30	$35	$45
NORMAL	$0.01	$0.02	$0.15	$0.30

Note: Values for MS-60 and MS-63 coins are for RB (red and brown) specimens; values for MS-65 are for full red specimens.

1995-D — FS-01-1995D-103 (041)

VARIETY: Doubled-Die Obverse — CONECA: DDO-003

PUP: LIBERTY

URS-5 • I-4 • L-4

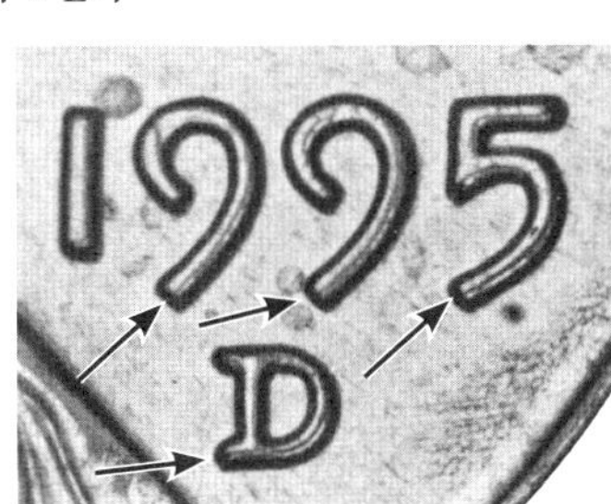

Description: Strong doubling is evident on IN GOD WE TRUST and to a lesser degree on the date, the mintmark, and LIBERTY.

Comments: This variety is the direct result of the Philadelphia Mint specimen being reported. This is also interesting, as the Mint started to include the mintmarks on the master hubs during this time, hence the like doubling on the mintmark.

	AU-50	MS-60	MS-63	MS-65
VARIETY	$175	$250	$350	$500
NORMAL	$0.01	$0.02	$0.15	$0.30

Note: Values for MS-60 and MS-63 coins are for RB (red and brown) specimens; values for MS-65 are for full red specimens.

1996 — FS-01-1996-101

VARIETY: Doubled-Die Obverse — CONECA: DDO-001
PUP: Date
URS-5 • I-3 • L-3

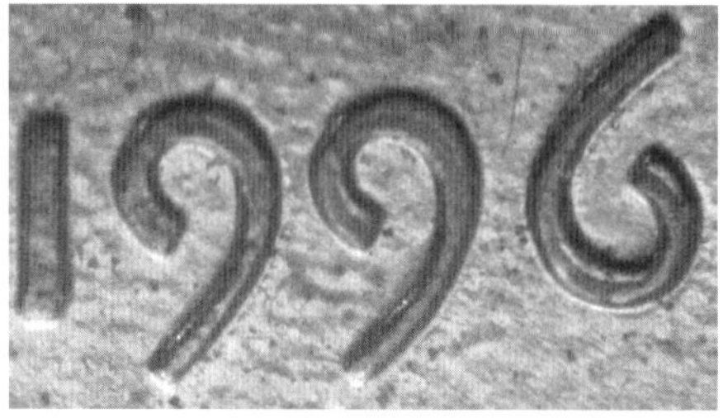

Description: This coin shows a medium spread on the date, the vest, and WE TRUST.

Comments: This is the last date possible for doubled dies produced by the multiple hubbing process, with the exception of the 1999 Susan B. Anthony dollar.

	AU-50	MS-60	MS-63	MS-65
VARIETY	$50	$100	$200	$300
NORMAL	$0.01	$0.02	$0.15	$0.30

Note: Values listed for MS-60 and MS-63 are for RB (red and brown) specimens; values listed for MS-65 are for full red specimens.

1997 — FS-01-1997-101 (043)

VARIETY: Doubled Ear — CONECA: DDO-001
PUP: Ear
URS-9 • I-3 • L-3

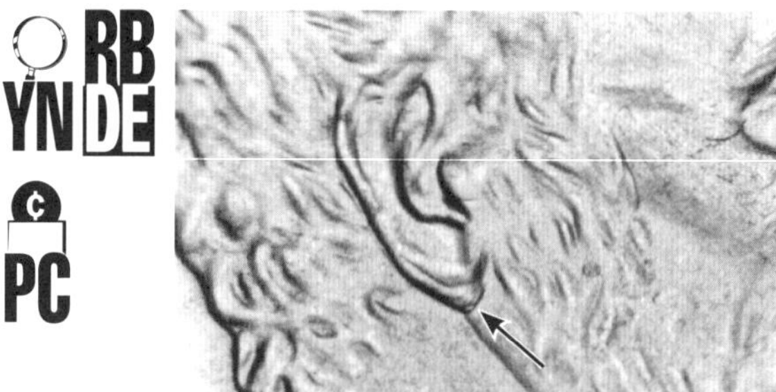

Description: Doubling on the ear gives the appearance of a second earlobe.

Comments: This coin was first reported by Larry Philbrick. It is a neat variety.

	AU-50	MS-60	MS-63	MS-65
VARIETY	$75	$100	$200	$300
NORMAL	$0.01	$0.02	$0.15	$0.30

Note: Values for MS-60 and MS-63 coins are for RB (red and brown) specimens; values for MS-65 are for full red specimens.

2004 FS-01-2004-801

VARIETY: Doubled-Die Reverse CONECA: DDR-001
PUP: E PLURIBUS UNUM
URS-7 • I-3 • L-3

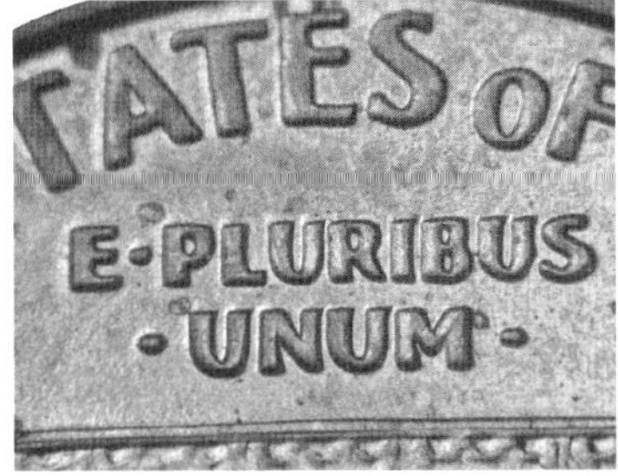

Description: This variety shows a medium spread and extra thickness on E PLURIBUS UNUM and UNITED STATES OF AMERICA.

Comments: Known for a few years now, this coin is often found by roll searchers. 2004-D Lincoln cents can also be found with doubled-die reverses.

	AU-50	MS-60	MS-63	MS-65
VARIETY	$25	$40	$60	$100
NORMAL	$0.01	$0.02	$0.15	$0.30

Note: Values listed for MS-60 and MS-63 are for RB (red and brown) specimens; values listed for MS-65 are for full red specimens.

2006 FS-01-2006-101

VARIETY: Doubled-Die Obverse CONECA: DDO-004
PUP: Ear
URS-7 • I-3 • L-3

Description: The extra-strong spread is seen as a separated earlobe and lower beard.

Comments: This one can be confused with a plating bubble, so check for the additional doubling in the beard. There are many other double-die reverse varieties of this issue as well.

	AU-50	MS-60	MS-63	MS-65
VARIETY	$20	$30	$50	$75
NORMAL	$0.01	$0.02	$0.15	$0.30

Note: Values listed for MS-60 and MS-63 are for RB (red and brown) specimens; values listed for MS-65 are for full red specimens.

2009, 2009-S Proof — FS-01-2009(S)-80X

Variety: Doubled-Die Reverse
PUP: Fingers
URS-3 • I-3 • L-3

Description: Numerous doubled-die reverses appear on Lincoln cents of the Formative Years design. These are localized on the left hand, most often resulting in what appears to be an extra index finger or thumb.

Comments: Those circulation-strike doubled-die reverses listed here all exhibit either a strong or very strong spread. The Proof doubled-die reverse listed here is the strongest of the four listed Proof doubled-die reverses in the CONECA files.

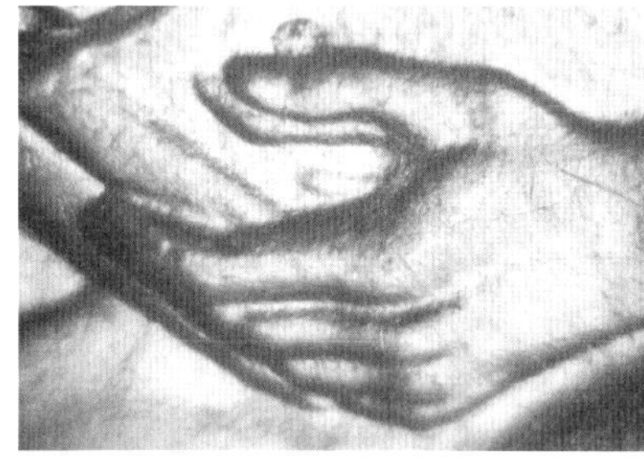

FS-01-2009-801 (DDR-043)

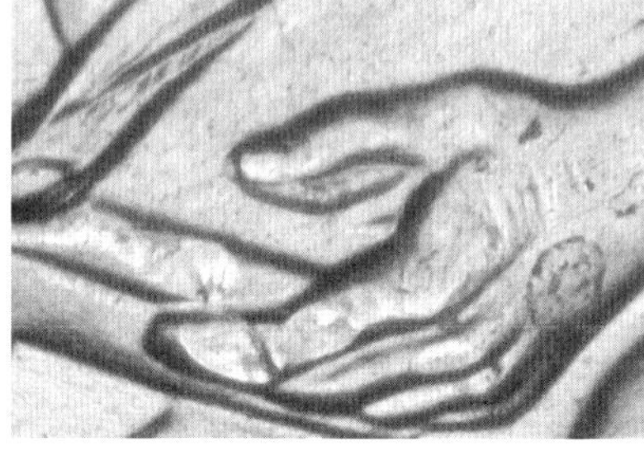

FS-01-2009-802 (DDR-001)

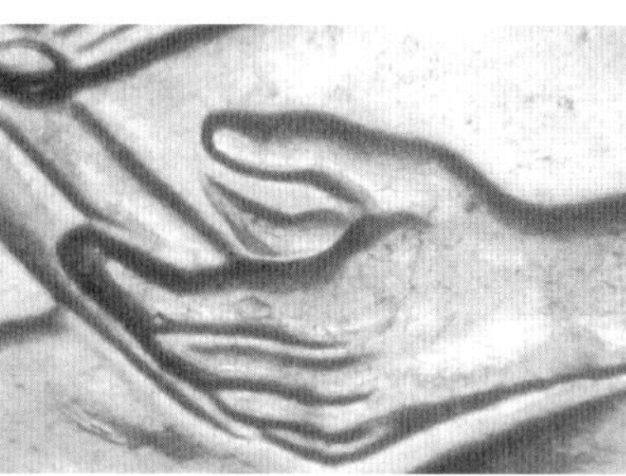

FS-01-2009-803 (DDR-002)

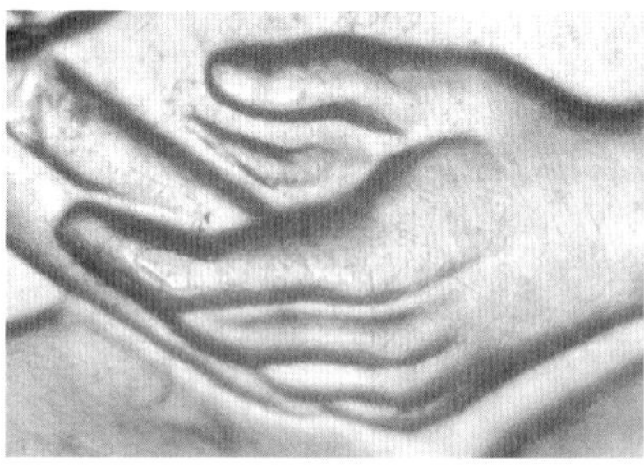

FS-01-2009-804 (DDR-050)

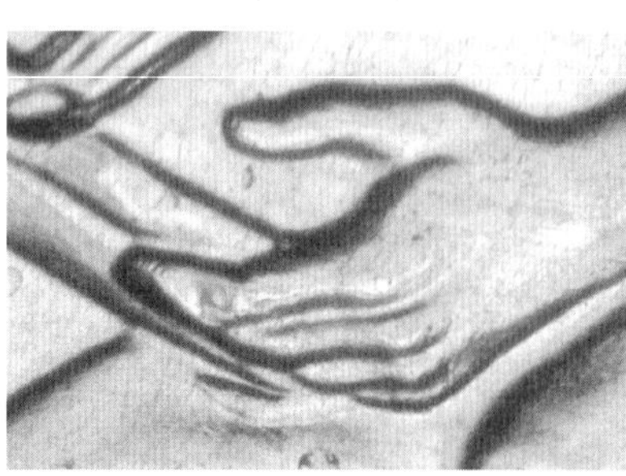

FS-01-2009-805 (DDR-026)

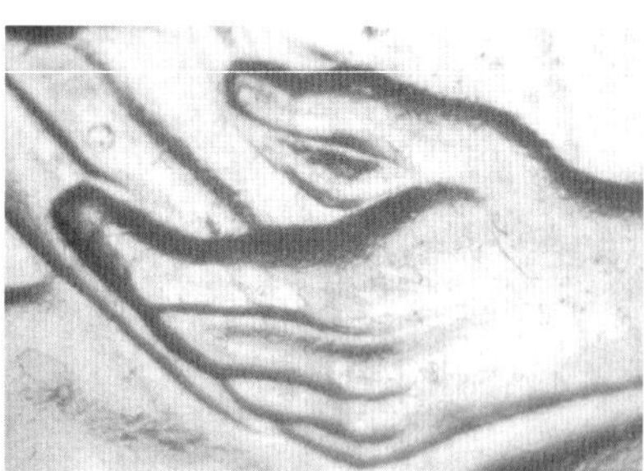

FS-01-2009-806 (DDR-021)

2009, 2009-S Proof (continued) FS-01-2009(S)-80X

VARIETY: Doubled-Die Reverse
PUP: Fingers
URS-3 • I-3 • L-3

FS-01-2009-807 (DDR-012)

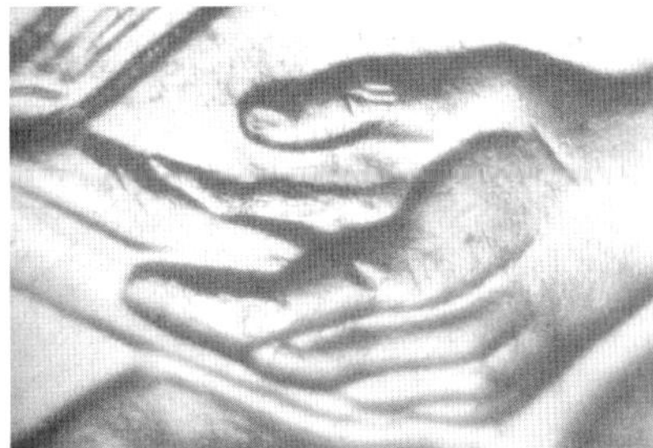

FS-01-2009-808 (DDR-009)

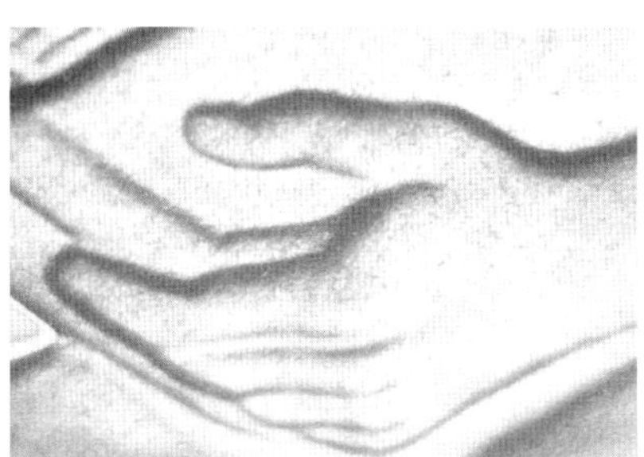

FS-01-2009S-801 (DDR-003)

	AU-50	MS-60	MS-63	MS-65
VARIETY, FS-801	*$5*	*$10*	*$20*	*$40*
VARIETY, FS-802	*$5*	*$10*	*$20*	*$40*
VARIETY, FS-803	*$5*	*$10*	*$20*	*$40*
VARIETY, FS-804	*$5*	*$10*	*$20*	*$40*
VARIETY, FS-805	*$5*	*$10*	*$20*	*$40*
VARIETY, FS-806	*$5*	*$10*	*$20*	*$40*
VARIETY, FS-807	*$5*	*$10*	*$20*	*$40*
VARIETY, FS-808	*$5*	*$10*	*$20*	*$40*
NORMAL	$0.01	$0.02	$0.15	$0.30

Note: Values listed for MS-60 and MS-63 are for RB (red and brown) specimens; values listed for MS-65 are for full red specimens.

	PF-63	PF-65	PF-66	PF-67
VARIETY, PROOF, FS-801	*$75*	*$150*	*$250*	*$350*
NORMAL	$3	$4	$6	$7

Note: Values listed for Proof Lincoln cents are for full red specimens. Red-and-brown and all-brown specimens command less. Cameo and deep cameo specimens should command much greater prices.

2014 FS-01-2014-101

Variety: Doubled-Die Obverse CONECA: DDO-001
PUP: Date
URS-4 • I-4 • L-3

Description: This variety exhibits strong extra thickness on LIBERTY and the date, with light extra thickness on WE TRUST.

Comments: This doubled-die obverse was recently reported and is eagerly sought after by specialists.

	AU-50	MS-60	MS-63	MS-65
Variety	$15	$30	$50	$75
Normal	$0.01	$0.02	$0.05	$0.15

Note: Values listed for MS-60 and MS-63 are for RB (red and brown) specimens; values listed for MS-65 are for full red specimens.

The Cherrypickers' Guide HELPFUL HINTS

Prices provided for varieties are for raw (unslabbed) coins. Varieties correctly attributed, certified, and graded by a third-party grading service may command higher premiums—but not necessarily. Ultimately, the marketplace of variety collectors determines a coin's value.

Two-Cent Pieces, 1864–1873

The two-cent piece has increased in popularity among variety collectors since the first edition of the *Cherrypickers' Guide* was published. This section of the book has grown slowly but steadily as interest has increased within the hobby community. Collectors will find new varieties have been added in this most recent volume.

Several *Cherrypickers' Guide* varieties are listed in the *Guide Book of United States Coins* (the hobby's best-selling annual price guide, known as the "Red Book") and in the *Deluxe Edition* of the Red Book. This kind of publicity in mass-market books helps get the word out about die varieties.

A recommended book for specialists and serious collectors is Frank Leone's *Longacre's Two-Cent Piece—An 1864 Attribution Guide*.

As of press date, there is no collector's club devoted specifically to the two-cent piece. If you're a fan of these neat little bronze coins, and have a mind for organization, this might be a golden opportunity to start a new numismatic society.

Related articles occasionally appear in the larger hobby publications, such as *The Numismatist* (www.money.org/the-numismatist), *Coin World* (www.coinworld.com), *Numismatic News* (www.numismaticnews.net), *COINage Magazine* (www.coinagemag.com), and *Coins Magazine*, and the denomination and its die varieties are sometimes discussed in online forums like the Collectors Universe Message Boards (forums.collectors.com) and the Collectors Society Message Boards (boards.collectors-society.com).

Newly Listed Varieties

Fivaz-Stanton Number	Variety	Page No.
FS-02-1864-1303	RPD	186
FS-02-1864-1304	RPD	186
FS-02-1864-1401/1902	Obv / Rev Die Clash	187
FS-02-1865-102	DDO	188
FS-02-1865-401/901	Obv / Rev Die Clash	189

Fivaz-Stanton Number	Variety	Page No.
FS-02-1865-1305	MPD	192
FS-02-1866-801	DDR	192
FS-02-1868-303	RPD	194
FS-02-1871-103	DDO	197
FS-02-1871-301	RPD	198

Varieties to be Delisted

Fivaz-Stanton Number	Variety	Page No.
FS-02-1869-101	DDR	195
FS-02-1871-102	DDO	197

Debunked Varieties

Fivaz-Stanton Number	Variety
FS-02-1871-101	DDO

1864, Small Motto FS-02-1864-401 (000.5)

VARIETY: Small Motto
PUP: Motto
URS-11 • I-5 • L-5

Description: The motto for the earlier 1864 two-cent pieces was small compared to later issues.

Comments: One of the authors has fairly recently cherrypicked this variety. It can still be done!

	VF-20	EF-40	AU-50	MS-60	MS-63	MS-65
VARIETY	$500	$800	$1,000	$1,750	$2,000	$4,000
NORMAL	$30	$50	$80	$110	$175	$650

Note: Values for MS-60 and MS-63 coins are for brown specimens; values for MS-65 coins are for red and brown specimens. Full red specimens command far greater premiums.

1864, Large Motto FS-02-1864-1101 (001)

VARIETY: Doubled-Die Obverse LEONE: 64LG-06G
PUP: Motto
URS-7 • I-3 • L-3

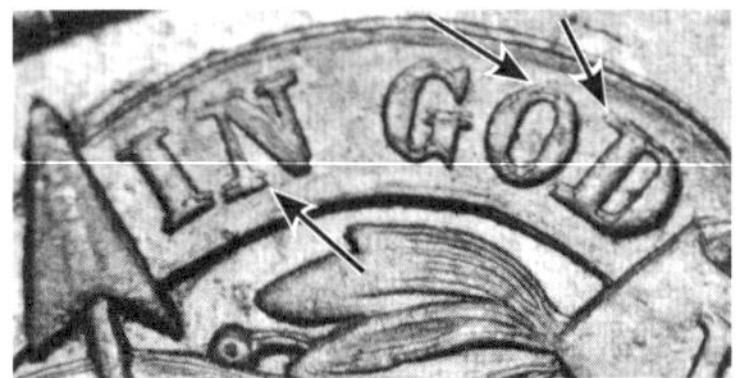

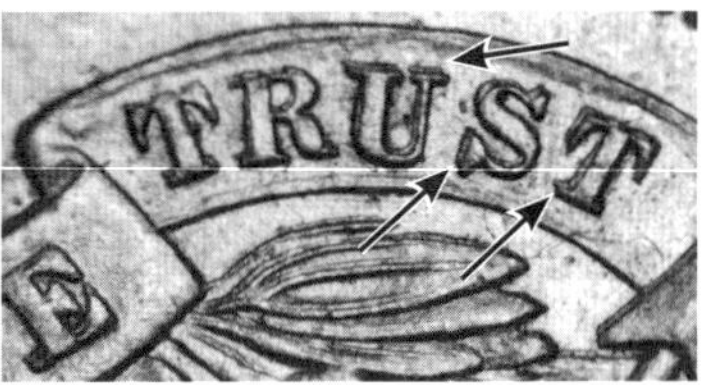

Description: The doubling is most evident on the upper half of the coin, including IN GOD WE TRUST, the upper leaves, and the banner itself.

Comments: A small horizontal die gouge appears over the left side of the banner above IN. Later die states exhibit a cud (die break) at eight o'clock on the obverse.

	VF-20	EF-40	AU-50	MS-60	MS-63	MS-65
VARIETY	$75	$100	$150	$200	$500	$1,000
NORMAL	$30	$50	$80	$110	$175	$650

Note: Values for MS-60 and MS-63 coins are for brown specimens; values for MS-65 coins are for red and brown specimens. Full red specimens command far greater premiums.

1864, Large Motto FS-02-1864-1301 (001.5)

VARIETY: Repunched Date LEONE: 64LG-100E
PUP: Date
URS-6 • I-4 • L-3

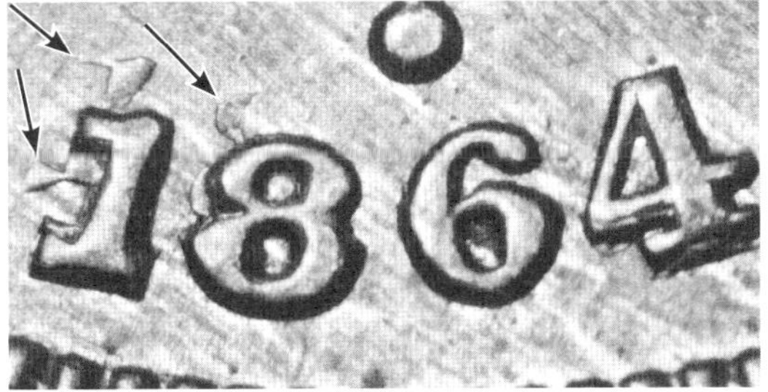

Description: The repunched date is evident as a tripled 1 and 8, with both secondary digits to the north of the primary numbers. There is no evident repunching easily visible on the 6, but the 4 is tripled, with both secondary digits very close to the primary.

Comments: This is one of the rarest repunched dates in the two-cent series and obviously very difficult to locate. This variety is found with two different reverses.

	VF-20	EF-40	AU-50	MS-60	MS-63	MS-65
VARIETY	$200	$350	$500	$650	$1,000	$1,500
NORMAL	$30	$50	$80	$110	$175	$650

Note: Values for MS-60 and MS-63 coins are for brown specimens; values for MS-65 coins are for red and brown specimens. Full red specimens command far greater premiums.

1864, Large Motto FS-02-1864-1302 (001.7)

VARIETY: Repunched Date LEONE: 64LG-24H
PUP: Date
URS-7 • I-3 • L-3

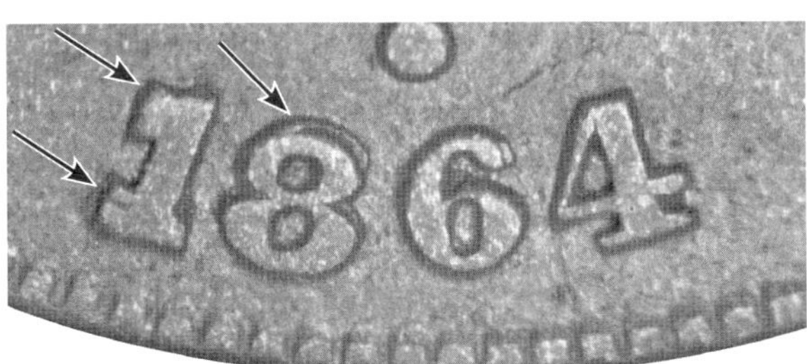

Description: The entire date was punched at least three times. Secondary digits are evident to the north of the 1 and 8, and to the southwest of the 6 and 4.

Comments: This is another nice and collectible repunched date in the two-cent series. It is often seen with a rotated reverse.

	VF-20	EF-40	AU-50	MS-60	MS-63	MS-65
VARIETY	$75	$150	$250	$350	$500	$900
NORMAL	$30	$50	$80	$110	$175	$650

Note: Values for MS-60 and MS-63 coins are for brown specimens; values for MS-65 coins are for red and brown specimens. Full red specimens commands far greater premiums.

1864 FS-02-1864-1303

VARIETY: Repunched Date
PUP: Date
URS-8 • I-3 • L-3

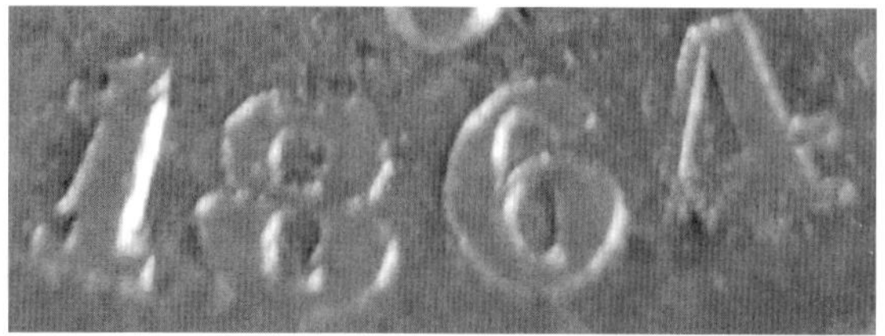

Description: The repunched date is clearly vertically doubled at the 1 and 8 of the date, with the serif and left base of the 1 nicely separated. The center top repunching of the 8 looks like two horns.

Comments: Early die states can show clashing of the obverse.

	VF-20	EF-40	AU-50	MS-60	MS-63	MS-65
VARIETY	$50	$90	$150	$220	$300	$1,300
NORMAL	$30	$50	$80	$110	$175	$650

Note: Values for MS-60 and MS-63 coins are for brown specimens; values for MS-65 coins are for red and brown specimens. Full red specimens command far greater premiums.

1864 FS-02-1864-1304

VARIETY: Repunched Date, Die Cracks
PUP: Date
URS-5 • I-3 • L-3

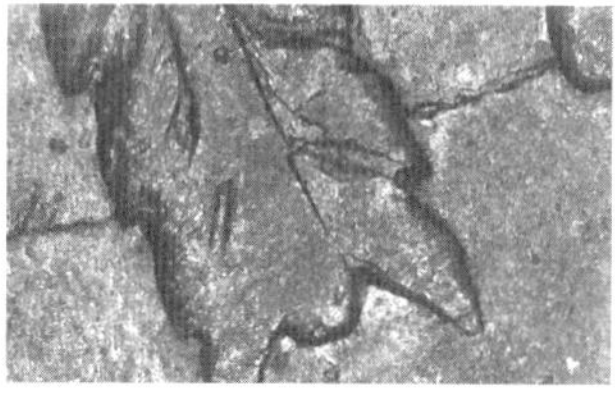

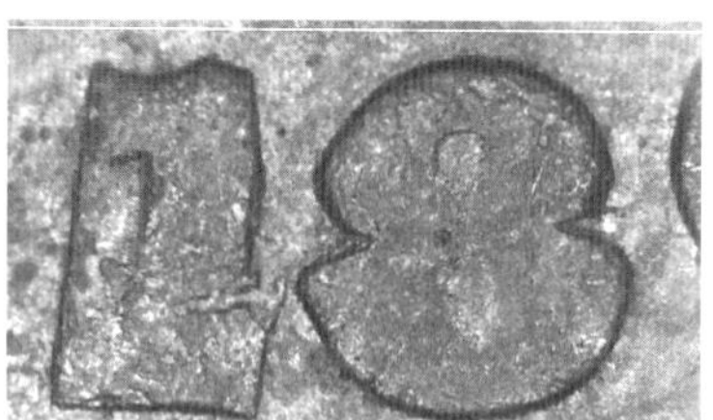

Description: The left side of the 1 in the date is closed by a vertical die crack, making it look like a box. The field portion of the "Box 1" fails and appears to progressively fill. A major die crack extends from near the top of the 4 through the right arrow feathers and to the right wreath.

Comments: Later die states extend the die failure to include filling the loops of the 8 and 6.

	VF-20	EF-40	AU-50	MS-60	MS-63	MS-65
VARIETY	$60	$100	$160	$225	$350	$1,300
NORMAL	$30	$50	$80	$110	$175	$650

Note: Values for MS-60 and MS-63 coins are for brown specimens; values for MS-65 coins are for red and brown specimens. Full red specimens command far greater premiums.

1864 — FS-02-1864-1401/1902

Variety: Obverse Die Clash, Reverse Die Clash
PUP: Upper obverse field, STATES OF
URS-6 • I-4 • L-4

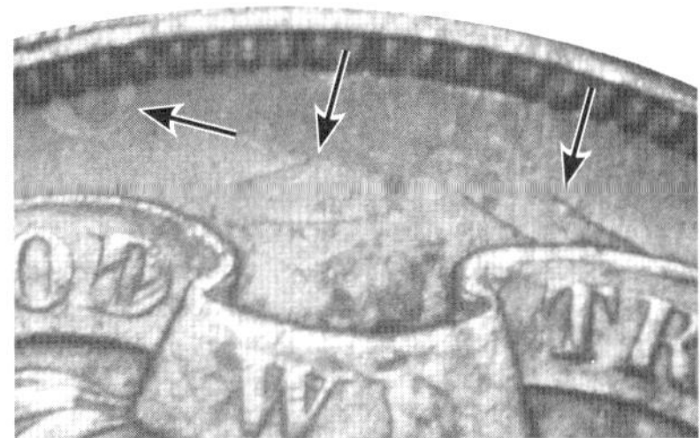

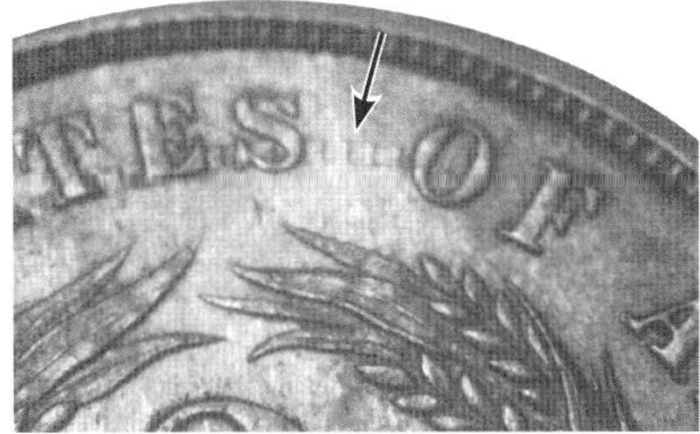

Description: This variety exhibits a major obverse clash from the leaves and bow of a reverse die, appearing above WE T. There is also a major reverse clash from the denticles of a misaligned die on the reverse, appearing from the base of the S through the O in OF.

	VF-20	EF-40	AU-50	MS-60	MS-63	MS-65
Variety	$200	$400	$700	$900	$1,500	$4,500
Normal	$30	$50	$80	$110	$175	$650

Note: Values for MS-60 and MS-63 coins are for brown specimens; values for MS-65 coins are for red and brown specimens. Full red specimens command far greater premiums.

1864, Large Motto — FS-02-1864-1901 (001.8)

Variety: Clashed Die — **Leone:** 64Lg-16B
PUP: Reverse field
URS-7 • I-4 • L-4

Description: Reminiscent of the mule clashed dies of 1857, this reverse die was clashed with an obverse die of an Indian Head cent. The profile of Miss Liberty is evident to the right of the 2, the chin at the bottom of the TS in CENTS, and the neck running south from the left side of that same T.

Comments: This is a wild die clash, and scarce.

	VF-20	EF-40	AU-50	MS-60	MS-63	MS-65
Variety	$175	$250	$350	$450	$975	$1,425
Normal	$30	$50	$80	$110	$175	$650

Note: Values for MS-60 and MS-63 coins are for brown specimens; values for MS-65 coins are for red and brown specimens. Full red specimens commands far greater premiums.

1865, Plain 5 — FS-02-1865-101 (002)

Variety: Doubled-Die Obverse — **Leone:** 65P-101R
PUP: TRUST
URS-7 • I-3 • L-3

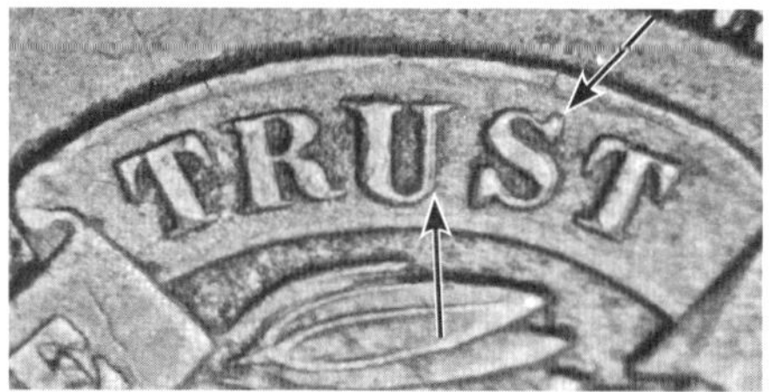

Description: The doubling is most visible on the upper half of the obverse, particularly on the word TRUST, the berry stems and leaves, and the horizontal lines of the shield.

Comments: Interestingly, there is a die gouge above IN on the banner, similar to that on the 1864 doubled die (FS-1101).

	VF-20	EF-40	AU-50	MS-60	MS-63	MS-65
Variety	$125	$250	$375	$500	$750	$1,000
Normal	$30	$50	$80	$110	$175	$650

Note: Values for MS-60 and MS-63 coins are for brown specimens; values for MS-65 coins are for red and brown specimens. Full red specimens command far greater premiums.

1865, Plain 5 — FS-02-1865-102

Variety: Doubled-Die Obverse
PUP: TRUST, arrow tip, leaves
URS-6 • I-3 • L-3

Description: This variety can be identified by the major doubling through TRUST and the right side of the wreath, as well as the arrow tip and the leaves. There is also a die scratch through the tops of the letters TRUS and a die chip at the right inside of the O in GOD, as well as some evidence of repunching on the 5.

Comments: Unlike many other coins of this issue, this variety does not show signs of a die gouge above the banner.

	VF-20	EF-40	AU-50	MS-60	MS-63	MS-65
Variety	$125	$250	$375	$500	$750	$1,000
Normal	$30	$50	$80	$110	$175	$650

Note: Values for MS-60 and MS-63 coins are for brown specimens; values for MS-65 coins are for red and brown specimens. Full red specimens command far greater premiums.

1865, Plain 5 — FS-02-1865-301 (002.3)

VARIETY: Repunched Date — LEONE: 65P-501R

PUP: Date

URS-6 • I-2 • L-2

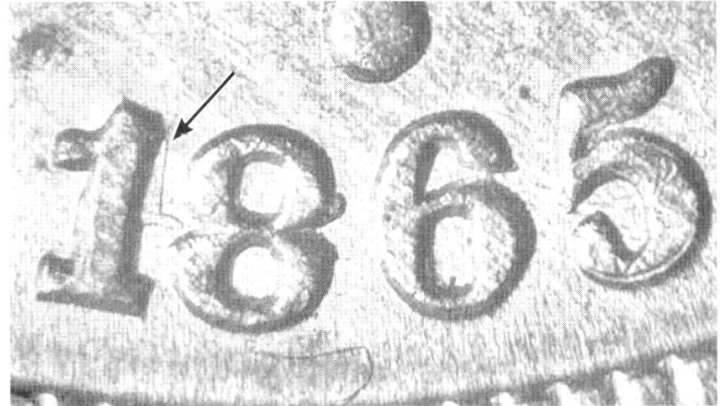

Description: The base of a secondary 1 is evident between the center of the primary 1 and the 8. Portions of the other digits are also visible.

Comments: Many examples of this variety have a rotated reverse. It is known with two different reverses. The latest die states have a small obverse cud at five o'clock.

	VF-20	EF-40	AU-50	MS-60	MS-63	MS-65
VARIETY	$100	$200	$350	$500	$750	$900
NORMAL	$30	$50	$80	$110	$175	$650

Note: Values for MS-60 and MS-63 coins are for brown specimens; values for MS-65 coins are for red and brown specimens. Full red specimens command far greater premiums.

1865, Plain 5 — FS-02-1865-401/901

VARIETY: Obverse Die Clash, Reverse Die Clash

PUP: Shield stripes, center of reverse

URS-7 • I-3 • L-3

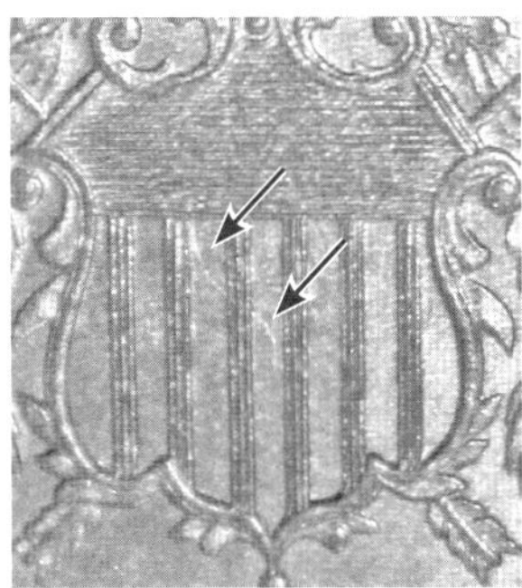

Description: The obverse shows heavy clash marks of an inverted 2 behind the shield stripes. The reverse shows clash marks of an inverted shield behind the central elements.

	VF-20	EF-40	AU-50	MS-60	MS-63	MS-65
VARIETY	$75	$125	$200	$250	$450	$1,650
NORMAL	$30	$50	$80	$110	$175	$650

Note: Values for MS-60 and MS-63 coins are for brown specimens; values for MS-65 coins are for red and brown specimens. Full red specimens command far greater premiums.

1865, Fancy 5 — FS-02-1865-1301 (002.5)

Variety: Repunched Date — Leone: 65F-101R
PUP: Date
URS-8 • I-3 • L-3

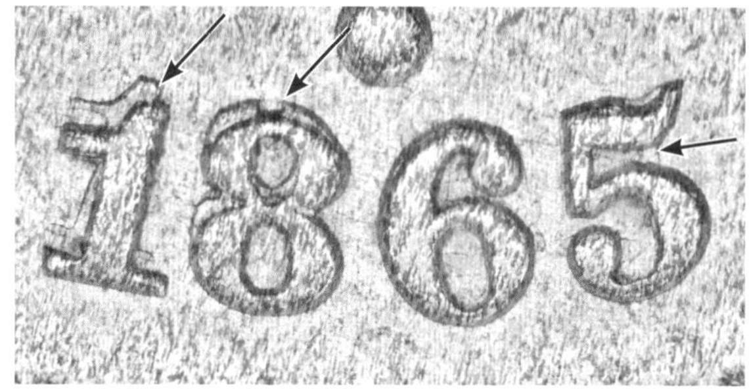

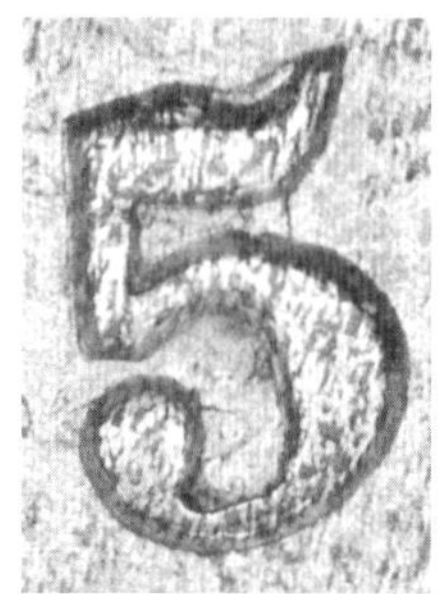

Description: A secondary 1 and 8 are evident to the northwest of the primary digits.

Comments: This variety was once believed to be an 1865, 5 Over 4 overdate. However, later research has proven that the image thought to be a 4 is actually an aberration to the date punch.

	VF-20	EF-40	AU-50	MS-60	MS-63	MS-65
Variety	$100	$200	$350	$500	$750	$900
Normal	$30	$50	$80	$110	$175	$650

Note: Values for MS-60 and MS-63 coins are for brown specimens; values for MS-65 coins are for red and brown specimens. Full red specimens command far greater premiums.

1865, Fancy 5 — FS-02-1865-1302 (002.7)

Variety: Repunched Date — Leone: 65F-201R
PUP: Date
URS-9 • I-3 • L-3

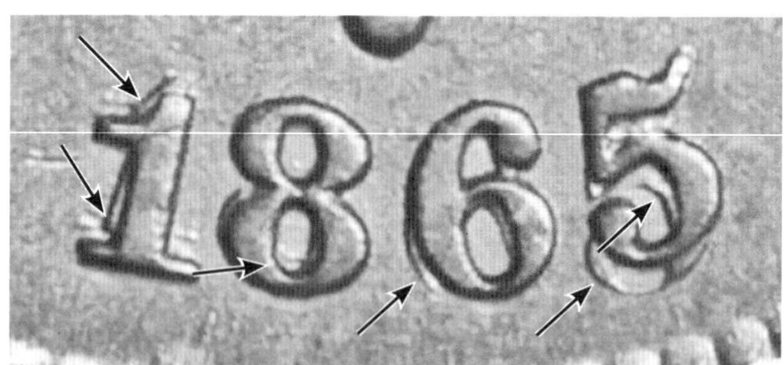

Description: A secondary 1 is evident slightly to the northwest of the primary 1, and a secondary 6 and 5 are evident to the southwest of the primary digits. Portions of a secondary 8 are evident within the lower loop of the primary 8.

Comments: A very similar variety exists, but the repunching is not quite as strong.

	VF-20	EF-40	AU-50	MS-60	MS-63	MS-65
Variety	$100	$200	$300	$400	$600	$800
Normal	$30	$50	$80	$110	$175	$650

Note: Values for MS-60 and MS-63 coins are for brown specimens; values for MS-65 coins are for red and brown specimens. Full red specimens command far greater premiums.

1865, Fancy 5 FS-02-1865-1303 (002.8)

VARIETY: Repunched Date
PUP: Date
URS-7 • I-3 • L-3

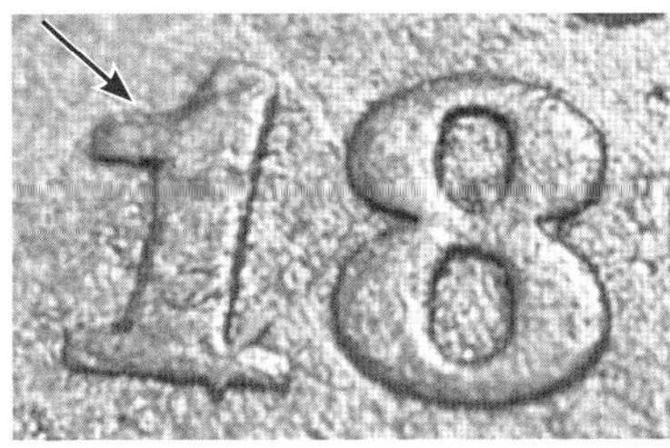

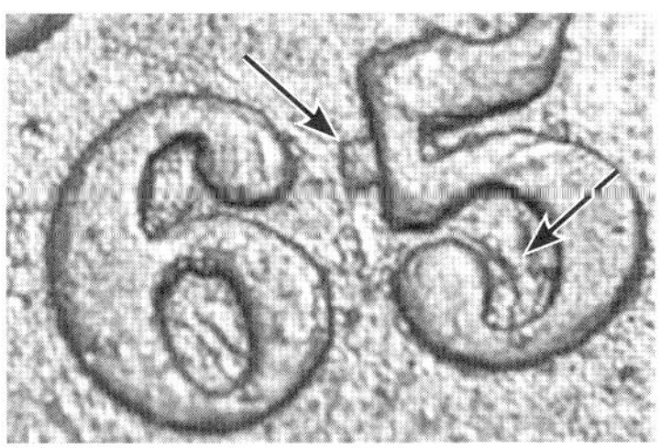

Description: This is one of the strongest repunched dates of the series, with a secondary 5 evident far to the southwest of the primary 5. A secondary 1 is visible slightly to the north of the primary 1.

Comments: A very similar variety exists, but the repunching is not quite as strong. This obverse is married to one of the few 1865 reverse dies with a complete upper serif on the D in UNITED.

	VF-20	EF-40	AU-50	MS-60	MS-63	MS-65
VARIETY	$150	$300	$450	$600	$800	$1,000
NORMAL	$30	$50	$80	$110	$175	$650

Note: Values for MS-60 and MS-63 coins are for brown specimens; values for MS-65 coins are for red and brown specimens. Full red specimens command far greater premiums.

1865, Fancy 5 FS-02-1865-1304 (002.9)

VARIETY: Misplaced Date
PUP: Denticles below date
URS-6 • I-3 • L-3

Description: The top of a digit, likely a 6, is evident in the denticles below and slightly to the right of the primary 8.

Comments: Strangely enough, there are relatively few misplaced dates known in this series. Certainly more exist. This variety is always softly struck at the center of the obverse.

	VF-20	EF-40	AU-50	MS-60	MS-63	MS-65
VARIETY	$50	$125	$200	$300	$500	$750
NORMAL	$30	$50	$80	$110	$175	$650

Note: Values for MS-60 and MS-63 coins are for brown specimens; values for MS-65 coins are for red and brown specimens. Full red specimens command far greater premiums.

1865, Fancy 5 — FS-02-1865-1305

Variety: Misplaced Date Digit
PUP: Left of date
URS-7 • I-4 • L-3

Description: The top serif of a misplaced 1 is located to the far left of the date, more than halfway to the left arrow feathers.

Comments: There is no evidence of any other digits from the date in the field.

	VF-20	EF-40	AU-50	MS-60	MS-63	MS-65
Variety	$75	$100	$200	$300	$500	$1,950
Normal	$30	$50	$80	$110	$175	$650

Note: Values for MS-60 and MS-63 coins are for brown specimens; values for MS-65 coins are for red and brown specimens. Full red specimens command far greater premiums.

1866 — FS-02-1866-801

Variety: Doubled-Die Reverse
PUP: Leaves of wreath, 2
URS-6 • I-4 • L-4

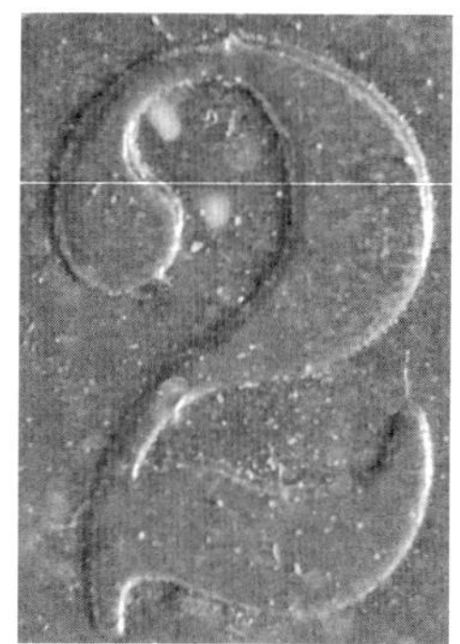

Description: The reverse wreath is doubled, most notably on the leaves at seven o'clock. The numeral 2 shows recutting.

	VF-20	EF-40	AU-50	MS-60	MS-63	MS-65
Variety	$75	$90	$150	$200	$425	$1,500
Normal	$35	$50	$80	$125	$175	$650

Note: Values for MS-60 and MS-63 coins are for brown specimens; values for MS-65 coins are for red and brown specimens. Full red specimens command far greater premiums.

1867 FS-02-1867-101 (003)

VARIETY: Doubled-Die Obverse
PUP: IN GOD WE TRUST
URS-7 • I-4 • L-4

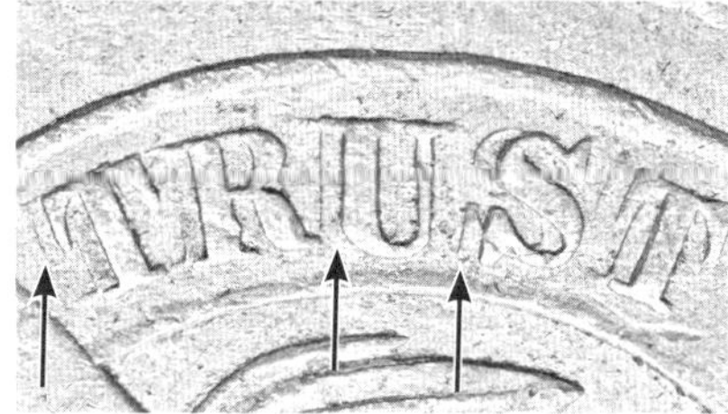

Description: This is by far the strongest doubled die known in the two-cent series. A secondary image is evident to the left of most of the primary devices.

Comments: This variety is somewhat common in low-end circulated grades, but is considered rare in Extremely Fine and About Uncirculated grades and very rare in Mint State.

	VF-20	EF-40	AU-50	MS-60	MS-63	MS-65
VARIETY	$300	$600	$800	$1,750	$4,000	$10,000
NORMAL	$35	$50	$80	$125	$175	$650

Note: Values for MS-60 and MS-63 coins are for brown specimens; values for MS-65 coins are for red and brown specimens. Full red specimens command far greater premiums.

1868 FS-02-1868-301 (003.5)

VARIETY: Misplaced Date
PUP: Denticles below date
URS-7 • I-3 • L-3

Description: The top of a digit, most likely a 6, is evident protruding from the denticles below the primary 6.

Comments: This is another of the few known misplaced dates in the two-cent series.

	VF-20	EF-40	AU-50	MS-60	MS-63	MS-65
VARIETY	$150	$250	$350	$500	$800	$1,750
NORMAL	$50	$75	$110	$150	$225	$1,150

Note: Values for MS-60 and MS-63 coins are for brown specimens; values for MS-65 coins are for red and brown specimens. Full red specimens command far greater premiums.

1868 — FS-02-1868-302

Variety: Possible Overdate
PUP: 8 of date
URS-1 • I-3 • L-3

Description: There is a diagonal bar evident at the lower-right side of the upper loop and the upper left side of the lower loop of the last 8. This diagonal bar matches the relative position of a 7.

Comments: The authors would like to be able to examine and study additional high-grade examples of this variety.

	VF-20	EF-40	AU-50	MS-60	MS-63	MS-65
Variety	(unique)					
Normal	$50	$75	$110	$150	$225	$1,150

Note: It would be impossible to place any value on this variety at this time, given the lack of a definitive attribution.

1868 — FS-02-1868-303

Variety: Repunched Date
PUP: Date
URS-7 • I-3 • L-3

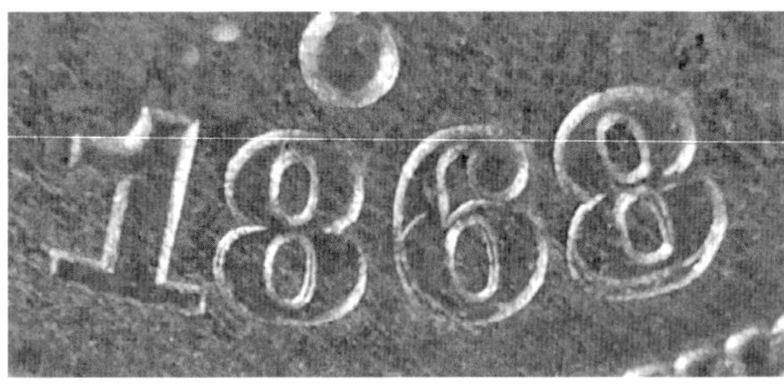

Description: This variety shows repunching on all digits, especially the 6 and 8; these show to the southwest of the primary location.

Comments: This variety comes with two different reverses, but these do not affect prices.

	VF-20	EF-40	AU-50	MS-60	MS-63	MS-65
Variety	$100	$125	$200	$300	$450	$1,750
Normal	$50	$75	$110	$150	$225	$1,150

Note: Values for MS-60 and MS-63 coins are for brown specimens; values for MS-65 coins are for red and brown specimens. Full red specimens command far greater premiums.

1869 — FS-02-1869-101 (004.2)

Variety: Doubled-Die Obverse
PUP: IN GOD
URS-6 • I-3 • L-3

Description: A secondary image is evident below and slightly right of IN GOD in the motto. The doubling is also evident on the leaves.

Comments: This coin was a pattern struck with Proof dies. This variety was discovered by Bob Grellman around 1991.

Note: This variety is slated to be removed from the coin-by-coin listings of future editions of the ***Cherrypickers' Guide*** due to lack of interest and/or unavailability. It will retain its Fivaz-Stanton number and continue to be listed in future editions' cross-reference appendix. A full list of varieties slated to be removed from each section appears after the introductory text of that section.

1869 — FS-02-1869-301 (003.9)

Variety: Repunched Date, Misplaced Date
PUP: Denticles below date
URS-8 • I-3 • L-3

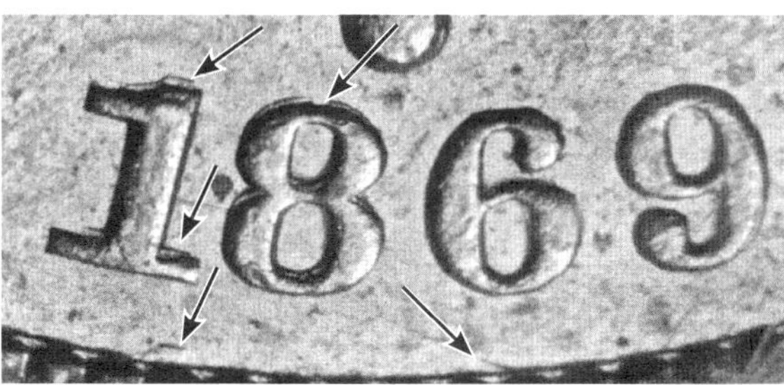

Description: The repunching is evident as a secondary 1 showing to the north of the primary 1. The top of a digit is protruding from the denticles below the 1.

Comments: There is a die scratch below the 6 of the date, once thought to possibly be portions of another digit.

	VF-20	EF-40	AU-50	MS-60	MS-63	MS-65
Variety	$150	$250	$350	$500	$900	$1,200
Normal	$55	$80	$125	$160	$225	$1,150

Note: Values for MS-60 and MS-63 coins are for brown specimens; values for MS-65 coins are for red and brown specimens. Full red specimens command far greater premiums.

1869 FS-02-1869-302 (004)

VARIETY: Repunched Date
PUP: Date
URS-9 • I-3 • L-3

Description: A secondary 1 and 8 are evident to the north of the primary digits.

Comments: This variety was once considered to be an overdate, but further research has proven that wrong. Later die states exhibit a die crack through the bottom of the date.

	VF-20	EF-40	AU-50	MS-60	MS-63	MS-65
VARIETY	$150	$250	$350	$500	$900	$1,200
NORMAL	$55	$80	$125	$160	$225	$1,150

Note: Values for MS-60 and MS-63 coins are for brown specimens; values for MS-65 coins are for red and brown specimens. Full red specimens command far greater premiums.

1870 FS-02-1870-101 (004.3)

VARIETY: Doubled-Die Obverse LEONE: 70B-1o1R
PUP: TRUST
URS-7 • I-2 • L-2

Description: Moderate doubling is evident on IN GOD WE TRUST, and there is slight doubling on the ribbon.

Comments: This variety was first reported in 1990.

	VF-20	EF-40	AU-50	MS-60	MS-63	MS-65
VARIETY	$175	$300	$500	$750	$1,000	$2,750
NORMAL	$85	$135	$200	$275	$300	$1,500

Note: Values for MS-60 and MS-63 coins are for brown specimens; values for MS-65 coins are for red and brown specimens. Full red specimens command far greater premiums.

1871 Proof FS-02-1871-102 (005)

VARIETY: Doubled-Die Obverse LEONE: 71N-1o1R
PUP: IN GOD WE TRUST
URS-16 • I-3 • L-3

Description: Very strong doubling is evident on IN GOD WE TRUST, the ribbon, the leaves, the shield, and the arrows.

Comments: All 1871 Proof two-cent pieces exhibit this doubled die, therefore it commands no premium. Note that Proof coins usually have sharp, squared rims. The 7 and 1 touch or nearly touch on all Proofs. The serif of the 1 is shorter on circulation strikes.

Note: This variety is slated to be removed from the coin-by-coin listings of future editions of the ***Cherrypickers' Guide*** due to lack of interest and/or unavailability. It will retain its Fivaz-Stanton number and continue to be listed in future editions' cross-reference appendix. **A full list of varieties slated to be removed from each section appears after the introductory text of that section.**

1871 FS-02-1871-103

VARIETY: Doubled-Die Obverse
PUP: IN GOD WE
URS-6 • I-4 • L-4

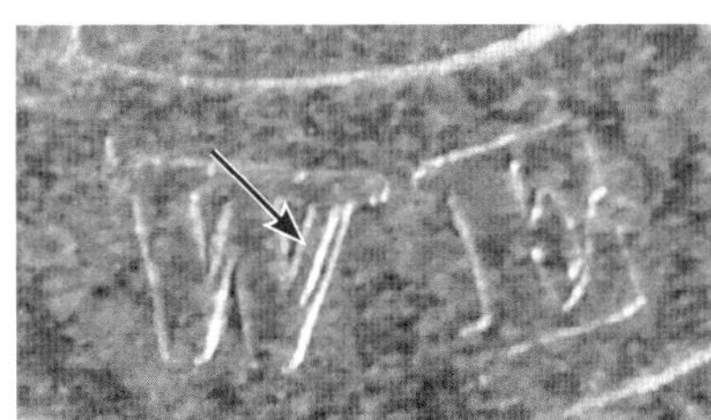

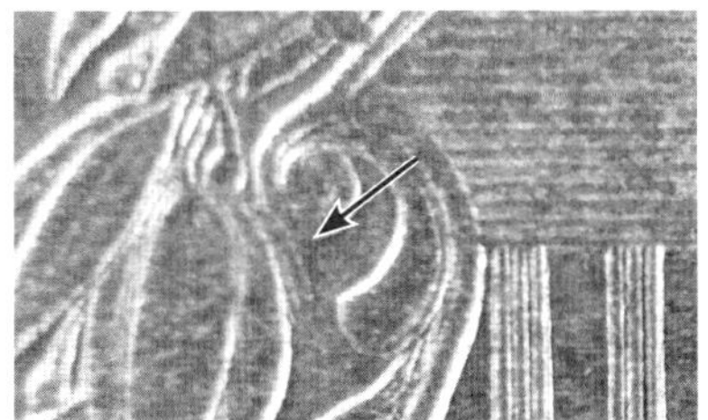

Description: The motto, especially at IN GOD WE, is doubled. There is a partial leaf showing to the left of the left ornament into the field below.

	VF-20	EF-40	AU-50	MS-60	MS-63	MS-65
VARIETY	$220	$300	$475	$750	$900	$2,500
NORMAL	$110	$150	$225	$300	$375	$1,700

Note: Values for MS-60 and MS-63 coins are for brown specimens; values for MS-65 coins are for red and brown specimens. Full red specimens command far greater premiums.

1871 — FS-02-1871-301

Variety: Repunched Date
PUP: Date
URS-7 • I-3 • L-3

Description: Repunching of the first 1 is slightly high. The 7 and second 1 are repunched low and left. The repunching at the base of the 7 is the first to fade out.

	VF-20	EF-40	AU-50	MS-60	MS-63	MS-65
Variety	$125	$175	$265	$365	$430	$1,950
Normal	$110	$150	$225	$300	$375	$1,700

Note: Values for MS-60 and MS-63 coins are for brown specimens; values for MS-65 coins are for red and brown specimens. Full red specimens command far greater premiums.

1872 — FS-02-1872-101 (006)

Variety: Doubled-Die Obverse — **Leone:** 72-1o1R
PUP: TRUST
URS-7 • I-3 • L-3

Description: The doubling is visible on the upper portion of the coin, with the spread growing stronger from left to right. It is most evident on TRUST.

Comments: As this is a very scarce date, remember the Fivaz axiom: "As the normal value of a coin increases, any premium one might expect for a variety on that coin will decrease." However, this doubled die is scarce in relation to the total 1872 population.

	VF-20	EF-40	AU-50	MS-60	MS-63	MS-65
Variety	$1,000	$1,250	$1,750	$3,000	$4,000	$12,500
Normal	$800	$1,050	$1,650	$2,800	$3,600	$11,000

Note: Values for MS-60 and MS-63 coins are for brown specimens; values for MS-65 coins are for red and brown specimens. Full red specimens command far greater premiums.

Silver Three-Cent Pieces, "Trimes," 1851–1873

The three-cent sections are the least populated in the entire *Cherrypickers' Guide*; trimes were not included until the fourth edition, published in 2000. Interest has gradually increased, and we hope that it will continue to expand.

Die clashes are widely known among trimes, more so for this series than any other. Die clashes are more likely on small coins than large ones, which made the tiny silver three-cent piece a prime target. A coin with clash marks will rarely bring a significant premium, if any at all.

A few three-cent die varieties (two repunched dates among the silver, and a fairly common Proof overdate in the nickel three-cent series) are listed in the regular-edition *Guide Book of United States Coins* (the hobby's famous "Red Book"). The *Deluxe Edition* of the Red Book includes several more. This kind of attention in widely promoted coin books helps keep the varieties on the hobby community's radar.

As of press date, no collector's club has been formed specifically for students of the three-cent denomination and its various types. If you're a fan of these historical little silver and copper-nickel coins, this could represent your chance to form a new specialty club.

Related articles occasionally appear in the larger hobby publications, such as *The Numismatist* (www.money.org/the-numismatist), *Coin World* (www.coinworld.com), *Numismatic News* (www.numismaticnews.net), *COINage Magazine* (www.coinagemag.com), and *Coins Magazine*. Three-cent pieces are sometimes discussed in online forums like the Collectors Universe Message Boards (forums.collectors.com) and the Collectors Society Message Boards (boards.collectors-society.com).

1851 — FS-3S-1851-301 (001)

Variety: Repunched Date — Breen-2902
PUP: Date
URS-9 • I-2 • L-2

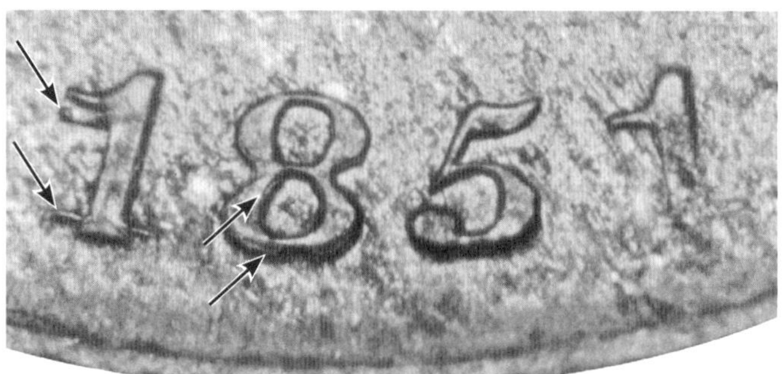

Description: For the first 1 and 8 only, secondary digits are evident to the south of the primary digits.

Comments: The secondary digits on this listing might not be visible on lower-grade specimens.

	VF-20	EF-40	AU-50	MS-60	MS-63	MS-65
Variety	$85	$100	$195	$240	$350	$1,000
Normal	$70	$80	$150	$200	$275	$850

1851 — FS-3S-1851-302 (001.5)

Variety: Repunched Date — Breen: N/L
PUP: Date
URS-7 • I-2 • L-2

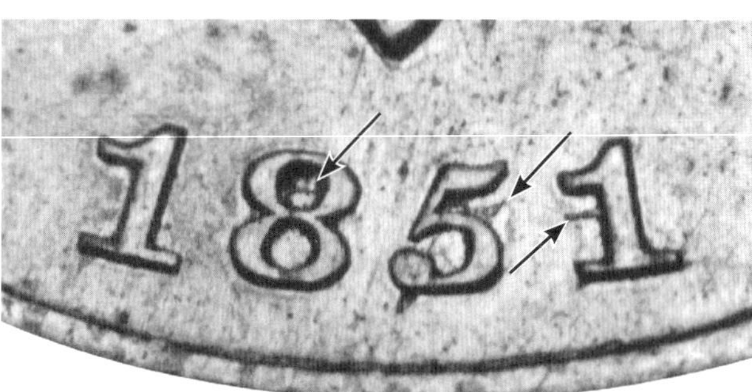

Description: Secondary digits are evident to the south of the primary digits on the 8, 5, and last 1.

Comments: This is a fairly strong repunched date for this series.

	VF-20	EF-40	AU-50	MS-60	MS-63	MS-65
Variety	$75	$95	$225	$275	$375	$1,100
Normal	$70	$80	$150	$200	$275	$850

1852 — FS-3S-1852-301 (002)

Variety: Repunched Date — Breen: N/L
PUP: First 1 of date
URS-4 • I-4 • L-4

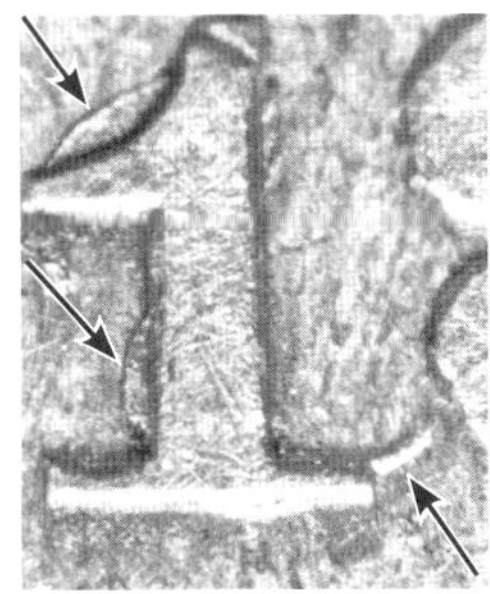

Description: An inverted 2 is evident underneath the primary 1. A secondary date punch was obviously punched into the die in an inverted orientation and then corrected after some effacing of the die.

Comments: Dan Brady discovered this variety in the mid-1990s.

	VF-20	EF-40	AU-50	MS-60	MS-63	MS-65
Variety	$600	$750	$900	$1,100	$1,350	$1,750
Normal	$70	$80	$150	$200	$275	$850

1852 — FS-3S-1852-302 (002.3)

Variety: Repunched Date — Breen: N/L
PUP: 5 and 2 of date
URS-4 • I-3 • L-3

Description: Secondary digits are evident to the east of the primary digits on the 5 and 2.

Comments: To date very few examples of this repunched date have been reported.

	VF-20	EF-40	AU-50	MS-60	MS-63	MS-65
Variety	$75	$95	$200	$300	$400	$1,050
Normal	$70	$80	$150	$200	$275	$850

1852 FS-3S-1852-801 (002.5)

VARIETY: Doubled-Die Reverse **BREEN:** N/L
PUP: Reverse stars
URS-5 • I-3 • L-3

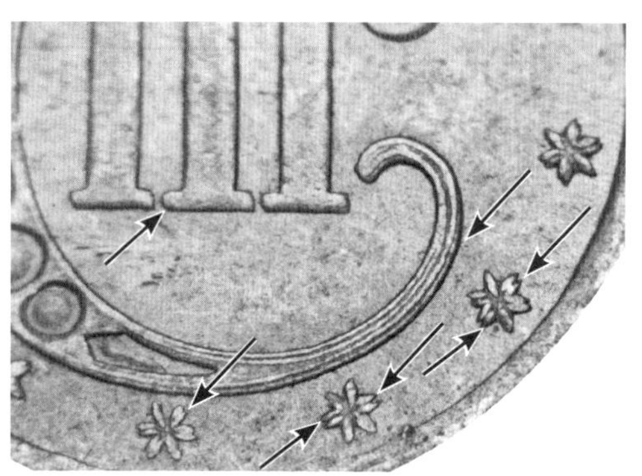

Description: Doubling is evident on the lower-right quadrant, especially the stars. Lesser doubling is also apparent on other reverse elements.

Comments: This is the only doubled die we have listed in the silver three-cent piece series.

	VF-20	EF-40	AU-50	MS-60	MS-63	MS-65
VARIETY	$115	$150	$340	$415	$600	$1,650
NORMAL	$70	$80	$150	$200	$275	$850

1853 FS-3S-1853-301 (003)

VARIETY: Repunched Date **BREEN**-2915
PUP: Date
URS-6 • I-2 • L-2

RB DE

Description: Secondary digits are evident to the north of the primary 1 and 8.

Comments: This repunched date can be detected on lower-grade specimens.

	VF-20	EF-40	AU-50	MS-60	MS-63	MS-65
VARIETY	$75	$95	$195	$250	$275	$1,000
NORMAL	$60	$80	$150	$200	$275	$850

1854 — FS-3S-1854-301 (004)

Variety: Repunched Date — Breen-2917
PUP: Date
URS-6 • I-3 • L-3

Description: Secondary digits are evident to the west of the primary 8 and 5.

Comments: This repunched date is one of the most evident in the entire silver three-cent piece series.

	VF-20	EF-40	AU-50	MS-60	MS-63	MS-65
Variety	$95	$175	$300	$450	$750	$3,500
Normal	$70	$120	$225	$350	$700	$3,000

1862 — FS-3S-1862-301 (007)

Variety: Overdate — Breen-2940
PUP: Date
URS-10 • I-4 • L-4

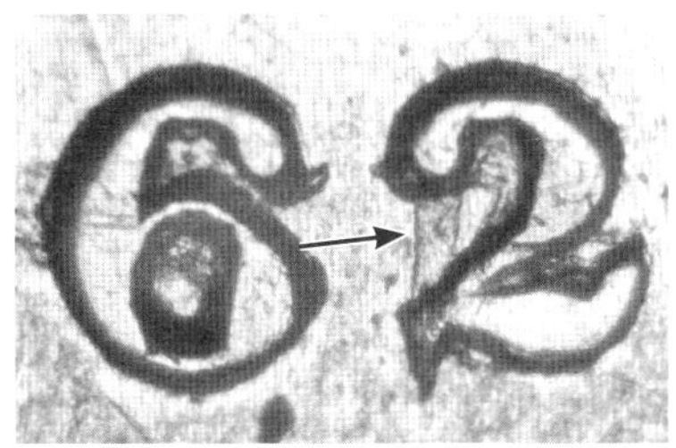

Description: There is a secondary 1 clearly visible beneath the 2 of the date.

Comments: This variety is well known and was originally discovered by John Cobb in 1963. The overdate is believed to be due more to economy (the Mint having used a good die another year) than to error.

	VF-20	EF-40	AU-50	MS-60	MS-63	MS-65
Variety	$65	$110	$200	$250	$350	$1,200
Normal	$60	$100	$175	$215	$285	$1,000

Nickel Three-Cent Pieces, 1865–1889

Any reference work of the magnitude of the *Cherrypickers' Guide* can be accomplished only with the help of outside sources—sources with detailed knowledge of the subject at hand. This section would not have been as complete or up-to-date without the selfless help and advice of Gary Rosner and Ed Fletcher. A big, hearty thanks to Ed and Gary for their contributions.

The nickel three-cent series is one of those few that have struggled for collectors over the years—at least when compared to most others. Yet the series is showing greater signs of popularity among collectors of "regular" coins and especially among those of us who enjoy the varieties.

As far as varieties go, the series contains many very nice repunched dates, misplaced dates, doubled-die obverses, doubled-die reverses, and even a nice overdate! Some of the misplaced dates are really dramatic, especially one with a 1 protruding from Miss Liberty's neck. Like many other series, some of the rarest varieties do not necessarily present the most eye appeal. Yet a couple of those varieties with super eye appeal are somewhat easy to find.

For those who have a greater interest in the varieties in the series, an excellent source is www.3centnickel.com. Gary Rosner has developed a terrific online source of information that can't be found anywhere else. Additionally, with the flexibility of Web-based information, the data is updated frequently, and new discoveries are published lightning-fast. You can be sure to read of new reference materials on Rosner's Web site. Pay him a visit and mention you heard of the site from the *Cherrypickers' Guide*.

As of press date, there is no collector's club dedicated to the small but significant three-cent piece. Here's a chance for active cherrypickers to band together and start a new numismatic society. Where to meet? The annual American Numismatic Association conventions, the Whitman Baltimore Expo, the Central States Numismatic Society convention, and the Florida United Numismatists shows would be excellent venues to gather for friendship, sharing research, and looking at coins.

1865 — FS-3N-1865-101 (003.5)

Variety: Doubled-Die Obverse
PUP: AMERICA
URS-5 • I-3 • L-3

Description: Secondary letters are evident to the left of the primary letters on AMERICA. Slight doubling is also visible on the hair and some of the other letters.

Comments: Many specimens exhibit an unusual obverse die crack across the bust and curls to the rim at 4:30. This has proven to be a very elusive variety.

	VF-20	EF-40	AU-50	MS-60	MS-63	MS-65
Variety	$50	$75	$125	$175	$250	$750
Normal	$30	$40	$65	$120	$160	$600

1865 — FS-3N-1865-102

Variety: Doubled-Die Obverse
PUP: UNITED STATES
URS-3 • I-3 • L-3

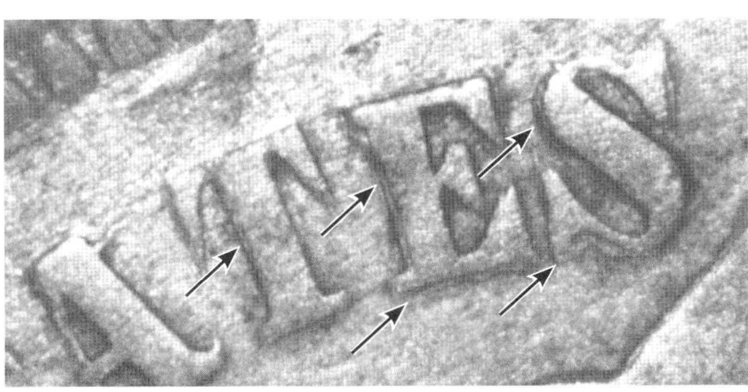

Description: Nice doubling is evident on UNITED STATES, LIBERTY, the nostril, the eyelid, and the front edge of the coronet.

Comments: There is a strong obverse cud at two o'clock and a triangular die gouge in the field below the denticles, above the T of STATES (which is evident in the photo). This variety is easy to spot as soon as you see the retained cud on the rim.

	VF-20	EF-40	AU-50	MS-60	MS-63	MS-65
Variety	$50	$75	$125	$175	$250	$750
Normal	$30	$40	$65	$120	$160	$600

1865 FS-3N-1865-301 (001)

VARIETY: Misplaced Date
PUP: Denticles below date
URS-7 • I-3 • L-3

Description: The top flag of a 5 is evident protruding from the denticles below and between the 6 and 5 of the date.

Comments: This variety usually exhibits a slightly rotated reverse. It was discovered by Tom Miller.

	VF-20	EF-40	AU-50	MS-60	MS-63	MS-65
VARIETY	$35	$50	$75	$150	$225	$725
NORMAL	$30	$40	$65	$120	$160	$600

1865 FS-3N-1865-302 (001.5)

VARIETY: Repunched Date
PUP: Date
URS-5 • I-3 • L-3

Description: Secondary digits are evident to the west of the primary digits on all four numbers.

Comments: Numerous heavy die cracks were on the specimens examined by the authors, indicating the die may have been short-lived. There is a similar repunched date on a Proof die, which may in fact have been used for a few circulation strikes.

	VF-20	EF-40	AU-50	MS-60	MS-63	MS-65
VARIETY	$50	$75	$125	$175	$250	$750
NORMAL	$30	$40	$65	$120	$160	$600

1865 — FS-3N-1865-303 (002)

VARIETY: Misplaced Date
PUP: Denticles below date
URS-7 • I-2 • L-2

Description: The top of what is believed to be a secondary 5 is visible within the denticles below the 6.

Comments: There are other 1865 dies with similar misplaced dates. This variety has proven to be one of the most difficult of all nickel three-cent varieties to locate! It was first reported to us in early 1989.

	VF-20	EF-40	AU-50	MS-60	MS-63	MS-65
VARIETY	$50	$75	$125	$175	$250	$750
NORMAL	$30	$40	$65	$120	$160	$600

1865 — FS-3N-1865-304 (002.5, 003)

VARIETY: Repunched Date
PUP: Date
URS-7 • I-3 • L-3

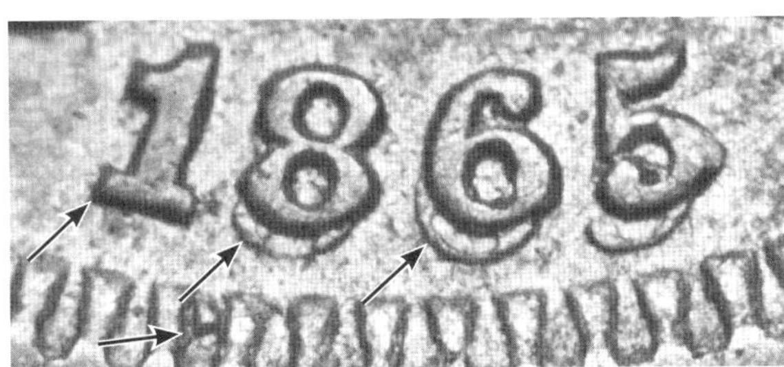

Description: Secondary digits of all four numbers are evident to the south of the primary digits.

Comments: This variety was incorrectly listed twice in the fourth edition. FS-003 was a very early die state, and FS-002.5 was a very late die state, which explains how the mistake occurred. There are two known reverse dies paired with this obverse. Strong clash marks are evident on mid- and late-die-state coins; this likely explains the change of reverse dies. Specimens are also known with a retained cud on the reverse at 11 o'clock.

	VF-20	EF-40	AU-50	MS-60	MS-63	MS-65
VARIETY	$50	$75	$125	$175	$250	$750
NORMAL	$30	$40	$65	$120	$160	$600

1865 FS-3N-1865-305

Variety: Repunched Date
PUP: Date
URS-3 • I-3 • L-3

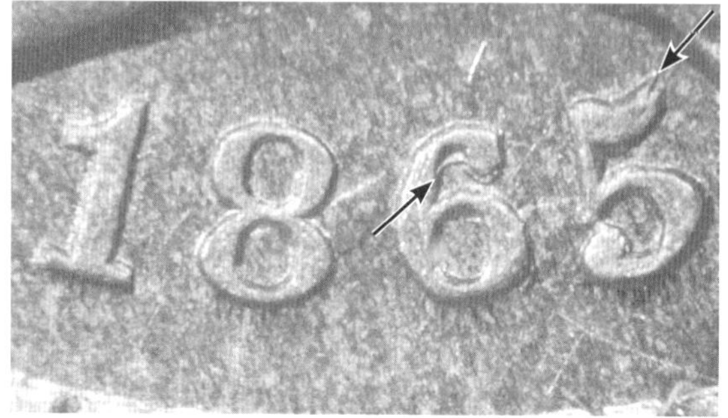

Description: Repunching is visible on the 6 to the south and the 5 to the north due to a date initially punched in a position rotated counterclockwise to the final date punch.

Comments: All known examples have a rotated reverse, turned approximately 190° clockwise.

	VF-20	EF-40	AU-50	MS-60	MS-63	MS-65
Variety	$50	$75	$125	$175	$250	$750
Normal	$30	$40	$65	$120	$160	$600

1866 FS-3N-1866-101 (004)

Variety: Doubled-Die Obverse
PUP: AMERICA
URS-5 • I-3 • L-3

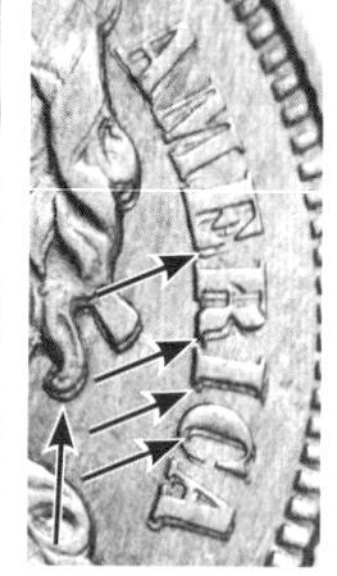

Description: Moderate doubling is evident on AMERICA and on portions of the hair.

Comments: The dies clashed midway through the obverse's life. Mid- and late-die-state coins exhibit the clash marks and die cracks as progression occurs. This variety has proven extremely scarce.

	VF-20	EF-40	AU-50	MS-60	MS-63	MS-65
Variety	$100	$150	$250	$350	$450	$900
Normal	$28	$40	$65	$120	$160	$600

1866 — FS-3N-1866-301

Variety: Repunched Date
PUP: Date
URS-3 • I-3 • L-3

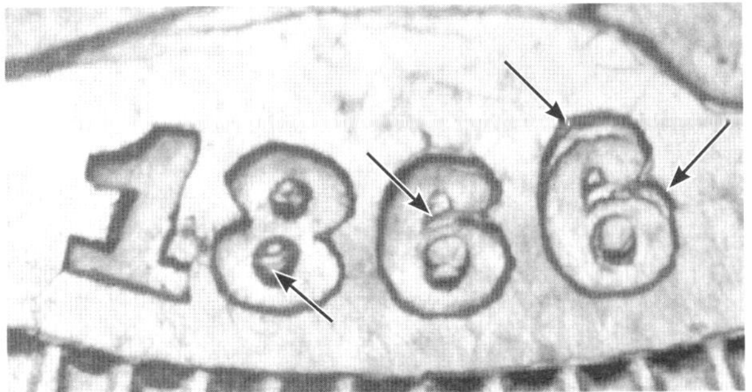

Description: Secondary digits are evident on the last three digits, strongest on the final 6. Slight repunching is visible on the 1.

Comments: This variety is a fairly new discovery.

	VF-20	EF-40	AU-50	MS-60	MS-63	MS-65
Variety	$50	$75	$125	$175	$250	$750
Normal	$28	$40	$65	$120	$160	$600

1869 — FS-3N-1869-301 (004.3)

Variety: Repunched Date
PUP: Date
URS-4 • I-3 • L-3

Description: A secondary 1 and 8 are evident to the north of the primary numbers.

Comments: This repunched date is scarcer than the other repunched dates for the date.

	VF-20	EF-40	AU-50	MS-60	MS-63	MS-65
Variety	$50	$75	$95	$150	$225	$850
Normal	$30	$40	$65	$135	$185	$750

1869 FS-3N-1869-302 (004.5)

Variety: Repunched Date
PUP: Date
URS-9 • I-3 • L-3

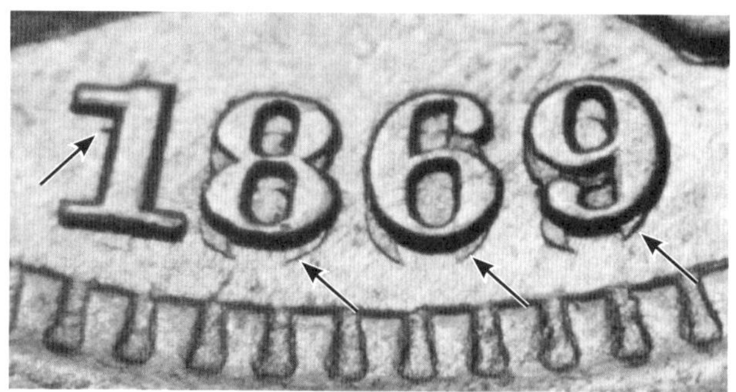

Description: Secondary digits are evident to the south of all four primary digits of the date.

Comments: Although stronger than the previous listing, and certainly holding more eye appeal, this variety has a slightly higher known population at this time. The obverse die is known paired with three reverse dies.

	VF-20	EF-40	AU-50	MS-60	MS-63	MS-65
Variety	$50	$75	$95	$150	$225	$850
Normal	$30	$40	$65	$135	$185	$750

1869 FS-3N-1869-801 (004.7)

Variety: Doubled-Die Reverse
PUP: Ribbon
URS-9 • I-2 • L-2

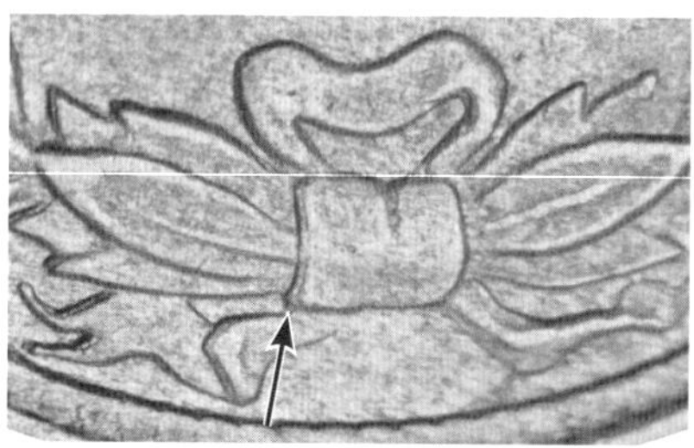

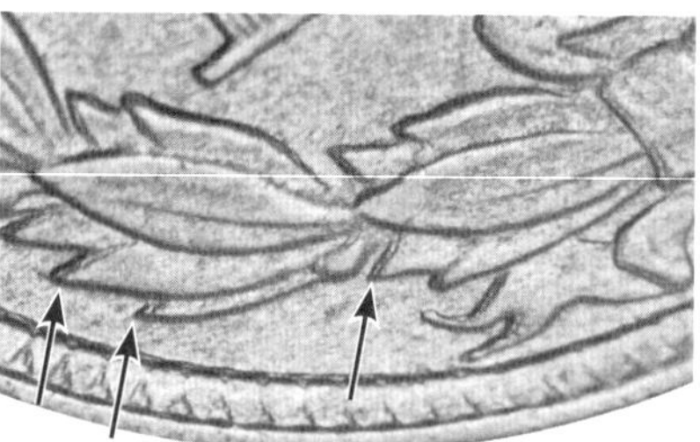

Description: The doubling is most evident in the lower-left quadrant of the reverse, especially on the ribbon bow.

Comments: This reverse die is known paired with two different obverse dies. This is not a very strong doubled die, but it is certainly worth the search.

	VF-20	EF-40	AU-50	MS-60	MS-63	MS-65
Variety	$45	$65	$95	$150	$200	$775
Normal	$30	$40	$65	$135	$185	$750

1870 FS-3N-1870-101 (005)

Variety: Repunched Date, Doubled-Die Obverse
PUP: Date
URS-6 • I-3 • L-3

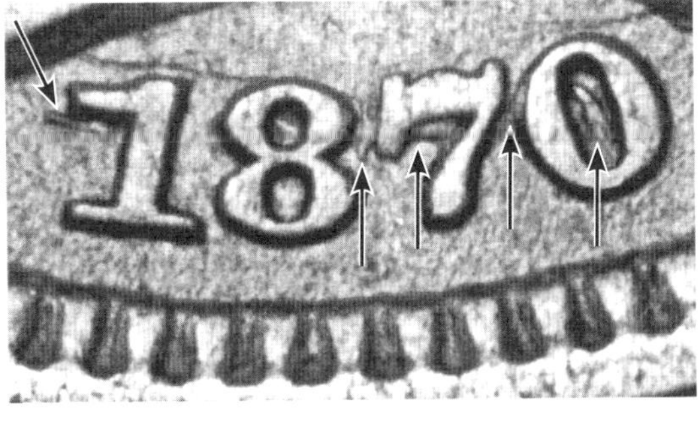

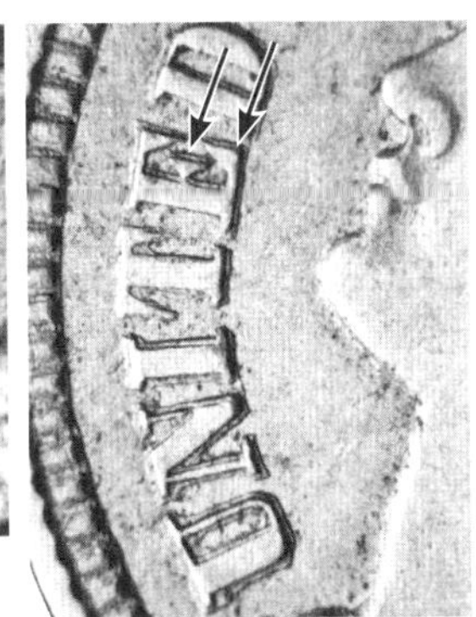

Description: Secondary digits are evident to the west of all four primary numbers.

Comments: This is also a minor doubled-die obverse, with doubling most noticeable on the second E of STATES. However, the repunched date is very strong and is the reason for the premium on this variety.

	VF-20	EF-40	AU-50	MS-60	MS-63	MS-65
Variety	$50	$75	$95	$150	$225	$850
Normal	$30	$40	$65	$140	$195	$725

1870 FS-3N-1870-301 (005.5)

Variety: Misplaced Date
PUP: Denticles below date
URS-4 • I-3 • L-3

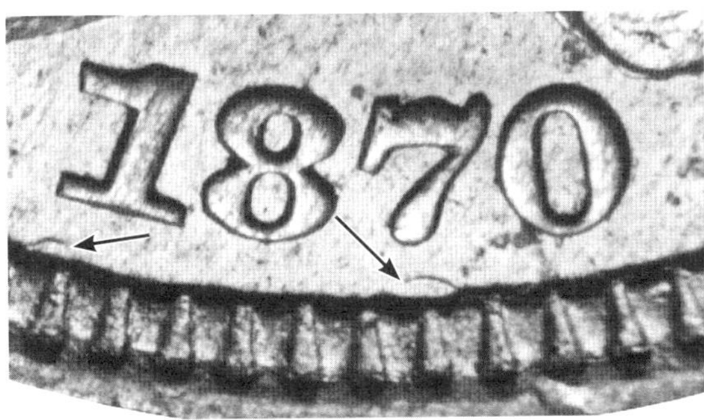

Description: The tops of two digits, supposedly a 1 and 0, are evident protruding from the denticles below the date.

	VF-20	EF-40	AU-50	MS-60	MS-63	MS-65
Variety	$65	$95	$125	$175	$300	$950
Normal	$30	$40	$65	$140	$195	$725

1870 FS-3N-1870-302 (005.6)

VARIETY: Misplaced Date, Doubled-Die Reverse
PUP: Denticles below date
URS-8 • I-3 • L-3

Description: Portions of several digits are evident in the denticles below the date. Minor doubling is evident on the reverse as split veins and leaf tips, mostly in the lower-left quadrant.

Comments: All the premium value in this variety comes from the misplaced date, not for the noted doubled-die reverse. In fact, the misplaced date die was paired with at least two reverses, only one of which is the doubled die. This variety is much more common than the previous listings for the date.

	VF-20	EF-40	AU-50	MS-60	MS-63	MS-65
VARIETY	$45	$65	$95	$150	$225	$795
NORMAL	$30	$40	$65	$140	$195	$725

1871 — FS-3N-1871-101 (006)

Variety: Tripled-Die Obverse
PUP: AMERICA
URS-7 • I-3 • L-3

Description: The tripling is very evident on the letters of UNITED STATES OF AMERICA, with light doubling evident on LIBERTY.

Comments: The highly visible tripled die makes this variety very impressive, though not quite as impressive as FS-3N-1866-101. Additionally, the variety is relatively easy to locate in circulated grades, yet tough in Mint State.

	VF-20	EF-40	AU-50	MS-60	MS-63	MS-65
Variety	$45	$65	$95	$175	$225	$850
Normal	$30	$40	$65	$140	$195	$750

1873, Close (or Closed) 3 — FS-3N-1873-301

Variety: Repunched Date
PUP: Date
URS-3 • I-3 • L-3

Description: A secondary 1 is evident to the south of the serif of the primary 1. A secondary 8 is also evident, inside the opening of the upper loop of the 8.

Comments: The repunched serif of the 1 is very strong, making this almost a naked-eye variety—if you can find one. So far they have been very elusive.

	VF-20	EF-40	AU-50	MS-60	MS-63	MS-65
Variety	$45	$65	$100	$200	$300	$1,750
Normal	$30	$40	$65	$150	$210	$1,400

1875 FS-3N-1875-301 (006.5)

VARIETY: Misplaced Date
PUP: Front of neck
URS-12 • I-3 • L-3

Description: The flag or base of a 1 is evident protruding from the front of Miss Liberty's neck.

Comments: This is likely the most readily available variety in the entire series. This being a very impressive misplaced date is the only reason it will command any premium.

	VF-20	EF-40	AU-50	MS-60	MS-63	MS-65
VARIETY	$40	$55	$95	$195	$260	$800
NORMAL	$35	$45	$80	$175	$225	$750

1881 FS-3N-1881-301 (006.8)

VARIETY: Repunched Date
PUP: Date
URS-10 • I-2 • L-2

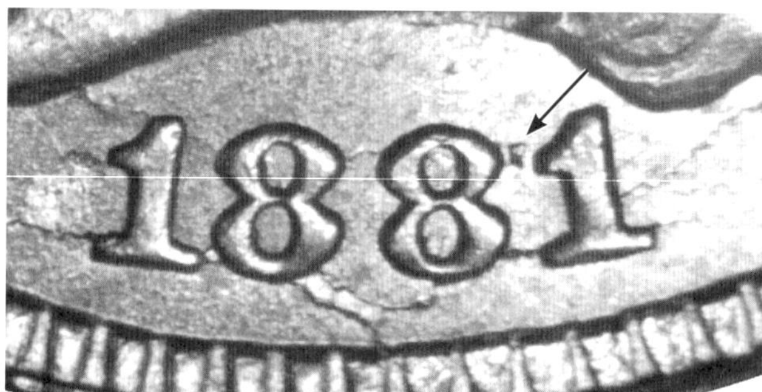

Description: This is an impressive repunched date, with a secondary 1 boldly evident between the final 8 and 1 of the date. The top of an 8 is visible between the top of the two 8's, and the top of another 8 shows inside the upper loop of the second 8.

Comments: There are several obverse die chips and cracks in various progressions, suggesting Mint personnel stretched the die's life further than normal. This variety has proven to be relatively easy to locate. There are many strong repunched dates of this date, none of which do the authors consider rare enough to command a significant premium.

	VF-20	EF-40	AU-50	MS-60	MS-63	MS-65
VARIETY	$35	$55	$85	$140	$200	$700
NORMAL	$30	$40	$65	$125	$185	$650

1887 — FS-3N-1887-301 (007)

Variety: Overdate
PUP: Date
URS-5 • I-4 • L-4

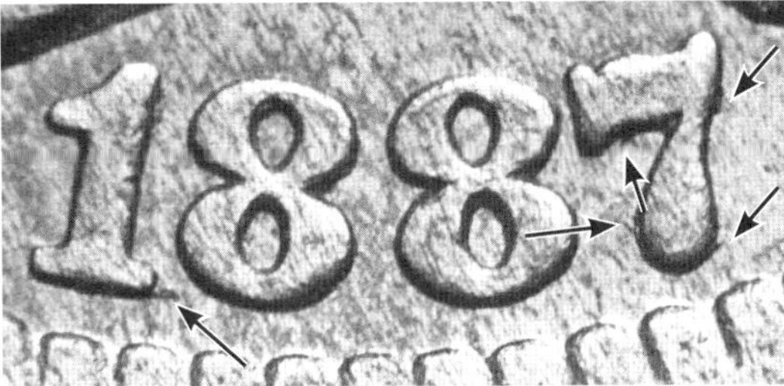
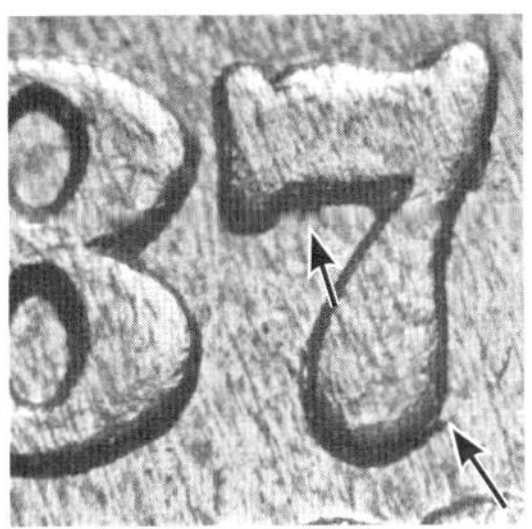

Description: The 1887 date was punched over a previously punched 1886 date. Faint remnants of the underlying 6 are evident on both lower sides of the 7. Secondary images are evident to the east of the primary 1 and both 8's.

Comments: Remember the Fivaz axiom: "As the value for a regular coin goes up, any premium one might expect for its variety will go down." This being an expensive "regular" coin, the percentage of premium for the variety is unimpressive.

	VF-20	EF-40	AU-50	MS-60	MS-63	MS-65
Variety	$425	$465	$595	$650	$800	$1,775
Normal	$350	$400	$500	$550	$675	$1,500

1887 Proof — FS-3N-1887-302

Variety: Overdate
PUP: Date
URS-7 • I-2 • L-2

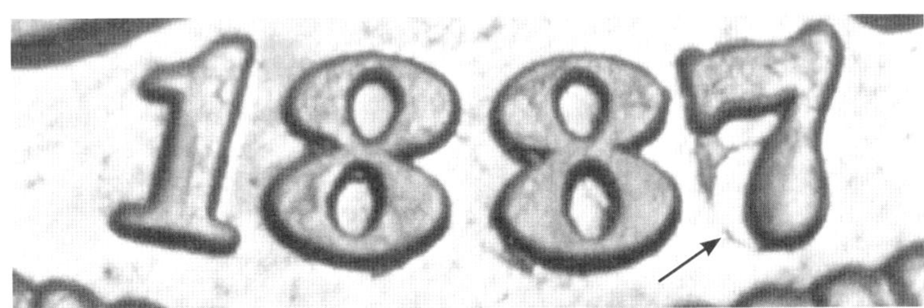

Description: This variety is similar to the previous listing, but on a Proof coin. The 1887 date was punched over a previously punched 1886 date. Strong remnants of the underlying 6 are visible on either side of the lower portion of the 7, with the 1 and both 8's clearly repunched.

Comments: According to many dealer price guides, the prices for PF-65 coins are the reverse of what one might expect. The non-overdate Proof coin can be valued higher than the overdate Proof coin in PF-65. The Proof overdate is relatively common. Compare this listing with the preceding.

	PF-60	PF-63	PF-64	PF-65
Variety	$475	$550	$600	$910
Normal	$400	$500	$575	$900

1888 — FS-3N-1888-301

VARIETY: Misplaced Date
PUP: Denticles below date
URS-3 • I-3 • L-3

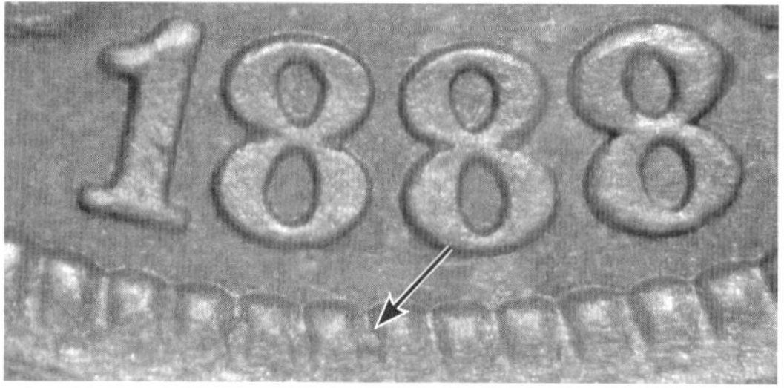
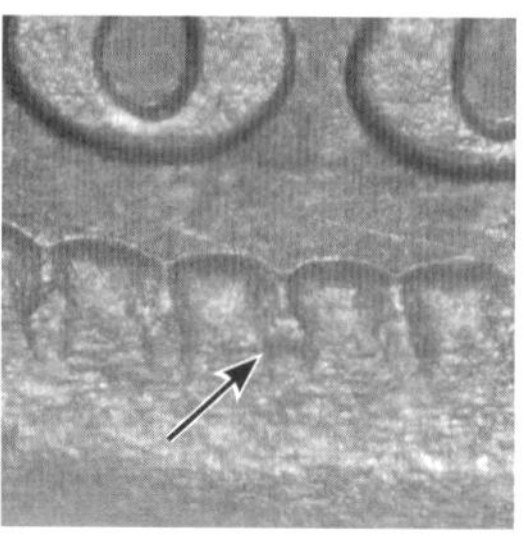

Description: The top of an 8 is evident protruding from the denticles below and between the first two 8's. Minor repunching of the last 8 is visible inside the upper loop.

Comments: This variety was discovered by Dick Osburn and reported by Gary Rosner. After the 1875 misplaced date, there are no reported misplaced dates in the series until this 1888. Then there is also a Proof 1889 with a misplaced date, which also has a repunched 1 to the south.

	VF-20	EF-40	AU-50	MS-60	MS-63	MS-65
VARIETY	$100	$125	$200	$350	$450	$955
NORMAL	$75	$100	$150	$300	$400	$850

THE CHERRYPICKERS' GUIDE HELPFUL HINTS

Over time, certain Cherrypickers' Guide *varieties have proven to be of low collector interest, and we have slated these for removal from the listings. However, these varieties will retain their Fivaz-Stanton number and continue to be listed in future editions' cross-reference appendix. Other varieties have been "debunked"—that is, they have been proven by experts to either not be true varieties, not be legitimate Mint issues, or not exist at all. These have been removed from the listings in this edition and will not retain their Fivaz-Stanton number. A full list of varieties either slated to be removed or debunked appears after the introductory text of each section.*

Shield Nickels, 1866–1883

Year for year, there are more varieties known in the Shield nickel series than in most others. In fact, with well over 100 listings (including many new additions in this volume), this is one of the largest sections in the *Cherrypickers' Guide*. It will undoubtedly continue to grow.

We have a theory as to why so many varieties are known in the Shield nickel series. The first circulating coin struck by the U.S. Mint in the very hard alloy of 75% copper and 25% nickel was the three-cent piece, which began production in 1865. The Shield design of the nickel five-cent piece, which is significantly larger, began production just a year later, in 1866.

The Mint was faced with a growing demand for minor coinage as commerce increased following the Civil War. Fractional silver coins (among others) had been hoarded by the nervous public during the war. The nickel five-cent piece was a very useful denomination and demand for it quickly increased. The Mint was faced with production of a coin made of an alloy with which it had very little experience.

The dies used to make the new nickel five-cent coins deteriorated much faster than Mint personnel had anticipated, due in part to the hardness of the metal. Dies cracked, chipped, and broke faster than Mint personnel could make new ones. Quality control suffered. Dies were hubbed with different or misaligned hubs, creating dramatic doubled dies. Dates were punched with less care, resulting in hundreds of repunched dates, overdates, and misplaced dates. According to numismatic researcher R.W. Julian, many blanks were not properly annealed before striking, further adding to the stresses the dies received. Many dies continued to be used after slight damage, as new dies were in short supply. Die cracks were abundant, creating many varieties in themselves that are eagerly sought by collectors today.

We suggest you look not only at the date of these coins, but also at the annulet (circle) under the cross, to check for doubled dies. And be sure to examine the lettering on the obverse and reverse, and the stars on the reverse, for possible doubled dies.

An excellent reference for this series is the *Guide Book of Shield and Liberty Head Nickels*, by Q. David Bowers. Additionally, Ed Fletcher studies the series in detail, listing all known varieties in his wonderful book entitled *The Shield Five Cent Series*. His is by far the best book available for detailed study. Howard Spindel, an avid collector and researcher, has developed an online club devoted to Shield nickels, at groups.yahoo.com/group/Shield_Nickels. Spindel also has a great Web site devoted to the series, shieldnickels.net. The information available on his Web site is invaluable. The cross-reference numbers with prefixes S1, S2, etc. that are listed in this section correspond to Spindel's Shield Nickel Viewer cataloging system, accessible via the aforementioned Web site.

There are many similar varieties within Shield nickel dates that are normally priced at about the same level. Also please ensure that the diagnostics of your coin match the illustration exactly.

Newly Listed Varieties

Fivaz-Stanton Number	Variety	Page No.
FS-05-1866-306/401	RPD, Obv Die Clash	226
FS-05-1866-307	RPD	227
FS-05-1866-308	RPD	228
FS-05-1867-1402/1901	Obv / Rev Die Clash	237
FS-05-1867-1902	Alt Rev	238
FS-05-1868-111	DDO	247
FS-05-1868-314	RPD	253
FS-05-1870-802	DDR	264
FS-05-1872-107/309	DDO / RPD / MPD	269
FS-05-1873-104	DDO	276
FS-05-1873-1103	DDO	277
FS-05-1876-104/301	DDO / RPD	286
FS-05-1876-401	Obv Die Var	286

Varieties to be Delisted

Fivaz-Stanton Number	Variety	Page No.
FS-05-1867-1101	DDO	231
FS-05-1867-1309	MPD	236
FS-05-1869-1104	DDO, RPD	257

Debunked Varieties

Fivaz-Stanton Number	Variety
FS-05-1868-110	DDO

Shield Nickel Missing Leaf Varieties

This section was contributed by Edward Fletcher.

When the master hub was produced for the Obverse Hub A, the outer leaf for the second right cluster was not engraved in the die. This missing leaf had to be hand engraved into each and every working die. This accounts for the many different shapes and sizes for the leaf in question. A handful of these dies passed through without the missing leaf being engraved into their surface. On these dies, the leaves on the right side of the shield are in clusters of 3/3/4/3 instead of the normal 3/4/4/3 clusters. They have been found on coins of 1866; 1867, Without Rays; 1868; and 1869, Wide Date. They are considered very rare.

Fewer than five of any Missing Leaf dies have been reported. Missing Leaf varieties that also have a repunched date or doubled-die obverse will command a higher premium.

Date	Number of dies known	With RPD	With DDO
1866	6	1	—
1867, With Rays	0	—	—
1867, Without Rays	9	—	—
1868	14	4	1
1868, Reverse of 1867	19	5	1
1868, Reverse of 1868	3	—	—
1869, Narrow Date	0	—	—
1869, Wide Date*	5	—	—
1869, Reverse of 1867	5	—	—
1869, Reverse of 1870	2	—	—

* Not all Missing Leaf varieties for the 1869, Wide Date, are found with the Reverse Hub IIb. One has also been found with Reverse Hub IIc.

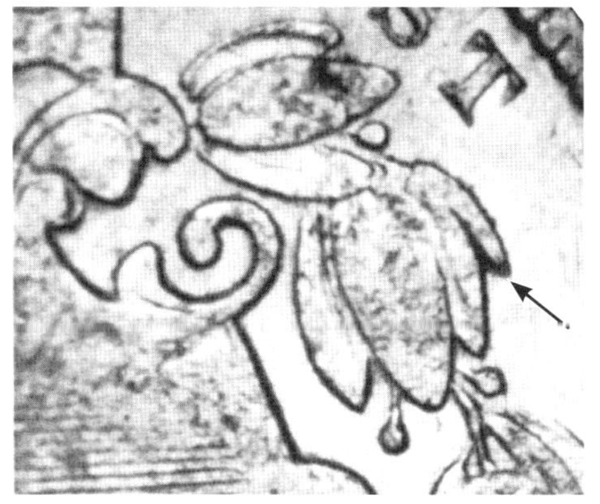

Normal leaf cluster

Missing leaf

Reverse Hubs of the Shield Nickel

This section was contributed by Edward Fletcher and has been revised by Howard Spindel.

Shield nickel reverse designs can be identified by the position of the stars in relation to the letters of UNITED STATES OF AMERICA. Use the outer point of the star for the identification. The star positions are as follows:

Reverse Hub I, With Rays

Below the left foot of the A in STATES
Below the right foot of the E in STATES
Below the left of the upright of the F in OF
Below the AM in AMERICA
Below the left foot of the R in AMERICA

Reverse Hub I has rays engraved between the stars, radiating out from the center of the design. Reverse Hub I is found on all 1866 and some 1867 Shield nickels.

Reverse Hub IIa, Without Rays

Below the left foot of the A in STATES
Below the right foot of the E in STATES
Below the left of the upright of the F in OF
Below the AM in AMERICA
Below the left foot of the R in AMERICA

Reverse Hub IIa is almost identical to Reverse Hub I, except the rays have been removed from the die. The star below the F has a broken point at 10 o'clock. This hub is found on all 1867, Without Rays; some 1868; all 1869, Narrow Date; and some 1869, Wide Date nickels. Three 1870 dies with this reverse exist, but only as a different hub doubled-die reverse. Two doubled-die reverses are IIa/IIc, one is IIc/IIa.

Reverse Hub IIb

Below the A in STATES
Below the left serif of the second S in STATES
To the center of the F in OF
Below the right edge of the foot of the M in AMERICA
Below the right of the upright of the R in AMERICA

Reverse Hub IIb is found with both solid and broken letters. It is found on some 1868 nickels.

Reverse Hub IIc

Below the left base of the A in STATES
Below the right foot of the E in STATES
Below the left of the upright of the F in OF
Below the M in AMERICA
Below the right side of the upright of the R in AMERICA

The first S in STATES is doubled slightly along the left side. The denticles are doubled, with the first set seen in the spaces between the final set. Reverse Hub IIc is found with both solid and broken letters. It is found on some 1869 and all 1870–1883 nickels. (Some 1868-dated nickels are said to exist with this reverse hub, but this has not been confirmed.)

Reverse Hub I

Reverse Hub IIa

Reverse Hub IIb

Reverse Hub IIc

Reverse Hub I

Reverse Hub IIa

Reverse Hub IIb

Reverse Hub IIc

Obverse and Reverse Hub Marriages

This chart was contributed by Edward Fletcher and has been revised by Howard Spindel.

Date	Obverse Hub	Reverse Hub
1866	A	I
1867, With Rays	A	I
1867, Without Rays	A	IIa
1868	A	IIa
	A	IIb
1869, Narrow Date	A	IIa
1869, Wide Date	A	IIa
	A	IIc
	B	IIa
	B	IIc
1870	B	IIa*
	B	IIc
1871	B	IIc
1872	B	IIc
	C	IIc
1873–1883	C	IIc

* 1870 Reverse IIa only exists as a doubled-die reverse.

1866 — FS-05-1866-101 (001.7)

Variety: Doubled-Die Obverse — **Fletcher-22, S1-1000**
PUP: Annulet
URS-3 • I-4 • L-4

Description: Strong doubling is evident on the classic area of this series, which is the annulet. A strong spread toward the southwest is evident on the annulet, the cross, the leaves, the scrolls, and the vertical lines in the shield.

Comments: Joseph Ambrulevich reportedly discovered this variety about 1988. This obverse die is paired with a very minor reverse doubled die.

	F-12	VF-20	EF-40	AU-50	MS-60	MS-63	MS-65
Variety	$80	$160	$240	$400	$480	$720	$4,000
Normal	$50	$100	$150	$250	$300	$450	$2,500

1866 — FS-05-1866-102 (001.5)

Variety: Doubled-Die Obverse, Repunched Date — **Fletcher-21, S1-7000**
PUP: IN GOD WE TRUST
URS-4 • I-4 • L-4

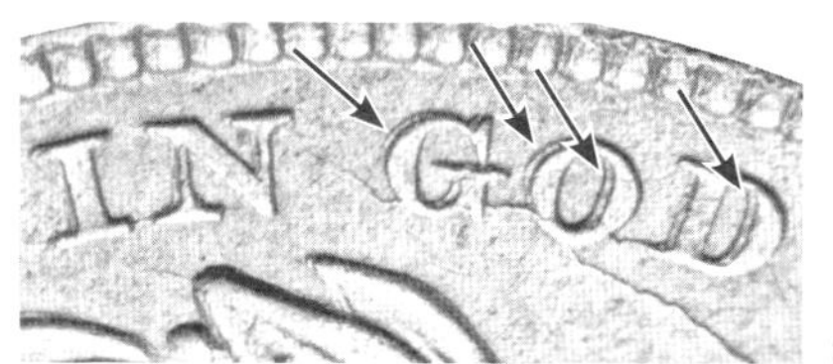

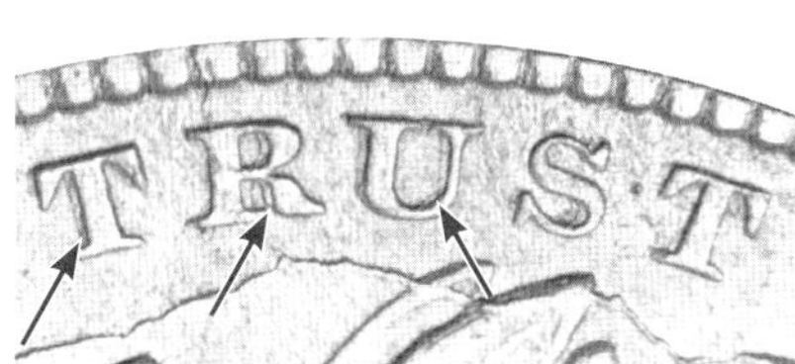

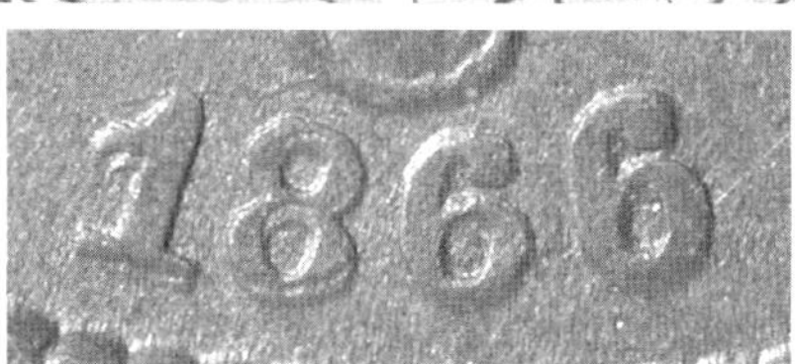

Description: Doubling is evident on all letters of IN GOD WE TRUST to the left of the primary image. There is also a repunched date to this variety. All four digits are repunched to the north.

Comments: This variety is unusual, as it is one of very few Shield nickels that has a doubled obverse die with no doubling evident anywhere on the shield.

	F-12	VF-20	EF-40	AU-50	MS-60	MS-63	MS-65
Variety	$63	$125	$190	$315	$375	$565	$3,125
Normal	$50	$100	$150	$250	$300	$450	$2,500

1866 — FS-05-1866-301 (001)

VARIETY: Repunched Date — FLETCHER-08, S1-3000

PUP: Date

URS-5 • I-4 • L-5

Description: All four digits are repunched, with secondary images clearly visible east of the primary digits.

Comments: Varieties in low grades can easily be cherrypicked. There are at least four other similar, very strong repunched dates for this year.

	F-12	VF-20	EF-40	AU-50	MS-60	MS-63	MS-65
VARIETY	$125	$250	$375	$625	$750	$1,125	$6,250
NORMAL	$50	$100	$150	$250	$300	$450	$2,500

1866 — FS-05-1866-302 (001.1)

VARIETY: Repunched Date — FLETCHER-10, S1-3001

PUP: Date

URS-5 • I-5 • L-5

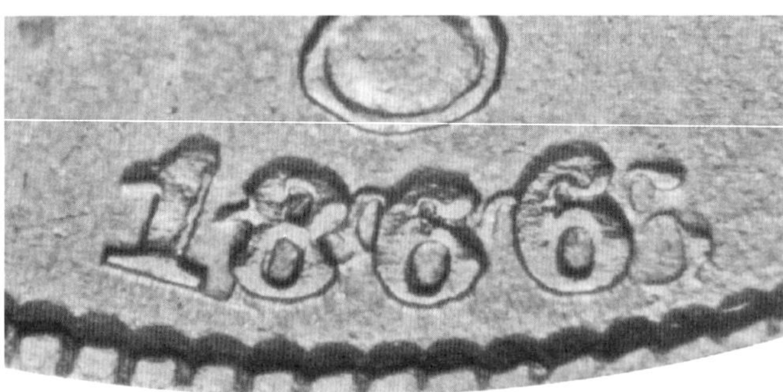

Description: All four digits are repunched, with secondary images clearly visible east of the primary digits.

Comments: Varieties in low grades can easily be picked. There are at least four other similar, very strong repunched dates for this year.

	F-12	VF-20	EF-40	AU-50	MS-60	MS-63	MS-65
VARIETY	$125	$250	$375	$625	$750	$1,125	$6,250
NORMAL	$50	$100	$150	$250	$300	$450	$2,500

1866 — FS-05-1866-303 (001.2)

VARIETY: Repunched Date — FLETCHER-20, S1-3002

PUP: Date

URS-4 • I-4 • L-5

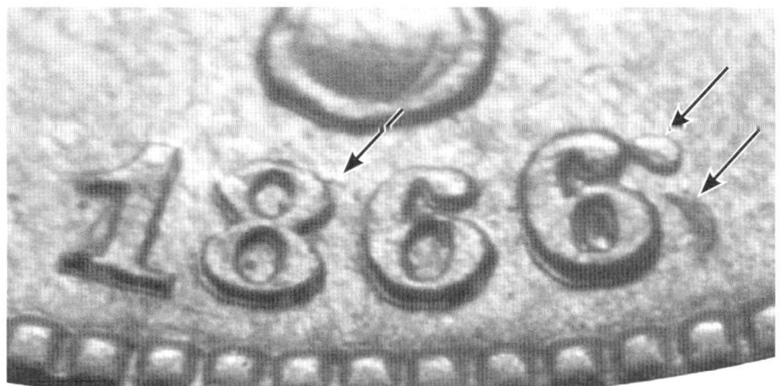

Description: All four digits are repunched, with secondary images clearly visible east of the primary digits.

Comments: Varieties in low grades can easily be picked. There are at least four other similar, very strong repunched dates for this year.

	F-12	VF-20	EF-40	AU-50	MS-60	MS-63	MS-65
VARIETY	$80	$160	$240	$400	$480	$720	$4,000
NORMAL	$50	$100	$150	$250	$300	$450	$2,500

1866 — FS-05-1866-304 (001.3)

VARIETY: Repunched Date — FLETCHER-16, S1-3003

PUP: Date

URS-4 • I-4 • L-5

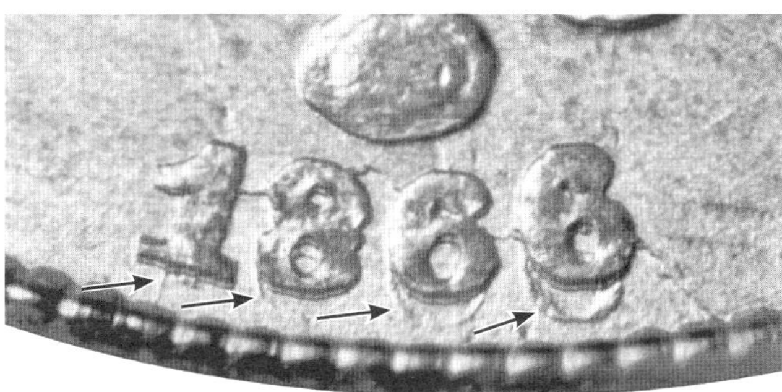

Description: All four digits are repunched, with secondary images clearly visible south of the primary digits.

Comments: Varieties in low grades can easily be picked. There are at least four other similar, very strong repunched dates for this year.

	F-12	VF-20	EF-40	AU-50	MS-60	MS-63	MS-65
VARIETY	$80	$160	$240	$400	$480	$720	$4,000
NORMAL	$50	$100	$150	$250	$300	$450	$2,500

1866 — FS-05-1866-305 (001.4)

VARIETY: Repunched Date — FLETCHER-13, S1-3006
PUP: Date
URS-4 • I-3 • L-3

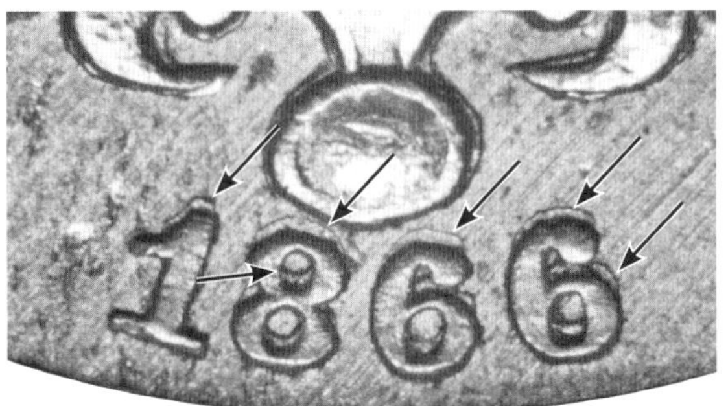

Description: All four digits are repunched, with secondary images clearly visible north of the primary digits.

Comments: Varieties in low grades can easily be picked. There are at least four other similar, very strong repunched dates for this year.

	F-12	VF-20	EF-40	AU-50	MS-60	MS-63	MS-65
VARIETY	$60	$120	$180	$300	$360	$540	$3,000
NORMAL	$50	$100	$150	$250	$300	$450	$2,500

1866 — FS-05-1866-306/401

VARIETY: Repunched Date, Obverse Clash — S1-3007.5
PUP: Date, shield, surrounding field
URS-5 • I-4 • L-4

Description: The date is repunched to the south on all four digits. The obverse shows very strong clash marks (the strongest in the Shield nickel series) from the reverse designs. The flag of the big 5 is visible within the lower shield, and reverse rays are visible around the periphery of the shield.

Notes: This is the same obverse die as used for FS-306/901, but a later die stage since the obverse of FS-306/901 shows no clashing. This coin does not show the reverse clash visible on FS-306/901.

	F-12	VF-20	EF-40	AU-50	MS-60	MS-63	MS-65
VARIETY	$88	$175	$265	$440	$525	$790	$4,375
NORMAL	$50	$100	$150	$250	$300	$450	$2,500

1866 — FS-05-1866-306/901

Variety: Misaligned Die Clash, Repunched Date — **Fletcher-09a, S1-3007**
PUP: Reverse below 5, date
URS-3 • I-4 • L-4

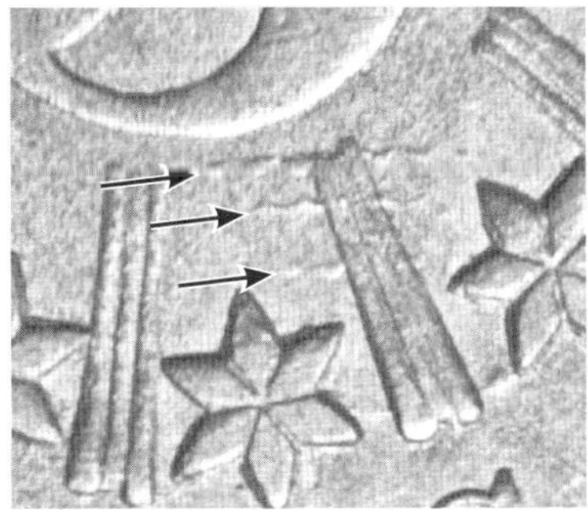

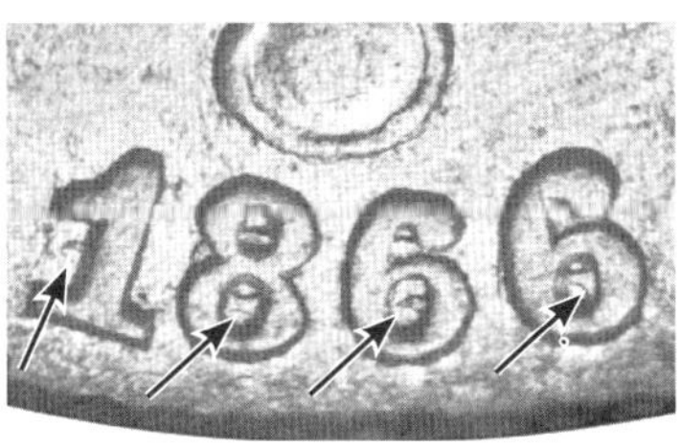

Description: The reverse die was clashed at least three times with what the authors feel were the denticles from another die, evident with three rows of images below and to the right of the 5. The date is also repunched, evident by a strong spread to the south on all four digits.

Comments: The value for this variety is primarily for the clashed die.

	F-12	VF-20	EF-40	AU-50	MS-60	MS-63	MS-65
Variety	$75	$150	$225	$375	$450	$675	$3,750
Normal	$50	$100	$150	$250	$300	$450	$2,500

1866 — FS-05-1866-307

Variety: Repunched Date — **Fletcher-10.01, S1-3004**
PUP: Date
URS-4 • I-5 • L-4

Description: All four digits are repunched far to the east. The second 6 is especially visible, while the head of the 1 and small amounts of the curves of the 8 and the first 6 are also visible.

Comments: Similar 1866 repunched dates exist. Careful attribution can ensure that the digit positioning matches this variety. Pay attention to the positioning of the repunch and the positioning of the date relative to the ball above.

	F-12	VF-20	EF-40	AU-50	MS-60	MS-63	MS-65
Variety	$125	$250	$375	$625	$750	$1,125	$6,250
Normal	$50	$100	$150	$250	$300	$450	$2,500

1866 — FS-05-1866-308

Variety: Repunched Date — Fletcher-11, S1-3016
PUP: Date
URS-5 • I-5 • L-4

Description: The date is repunched far to the east, with the second 6 very visible.

Comments: Similar 1866 repunched dates exist. Careful attribution ensures that the digit positioning matches. Pay attention to the positioning of the repunch and the positioning of the date relative to the ball above.

	F-12	VF-20	EF-40	AU-50	MS-60	MS-63	MS-65
Variety	$125	$250	$375	$625	$750	$1,125	$6,250
Normal	$50	$100	$150	$250	$300	$450	$2,500

1867, With Rays — FS-05-1867-301 (002.1)

Variety: Repunched Date — Fletcher-08, S1-3004
PUP: Date
URS-5 • I-4 • L-4

Description: The primary date is punched over a larger date logotype of a dime. The top of a 1 is evident far to the west of the primary 1, and the top of a 7 is evident far to the east of the primary 7. Portions of the other secondary digits are visible within the primary digits.

Comments: To date, a few specimens of this variety have been reported also with a reverse die rotated approximately 15° counterclockwise.

	F-12	VF-20	EF-40	AU-50	MS-60	MS-63	MS-65
Variety	$130	$260	$400	$600	$750	$1,000	$7,000
Normal	$65	$130	$200	$300	$375	$500	$3,500

1867, With Rays — FS-05-1867-302 (002.4)

VARIETY: Repunched Date, Doubled-Die Obverse — FLETCHER-09, S1-7000

PUP: Date, annulet

URS-5 • I-5 • L-4

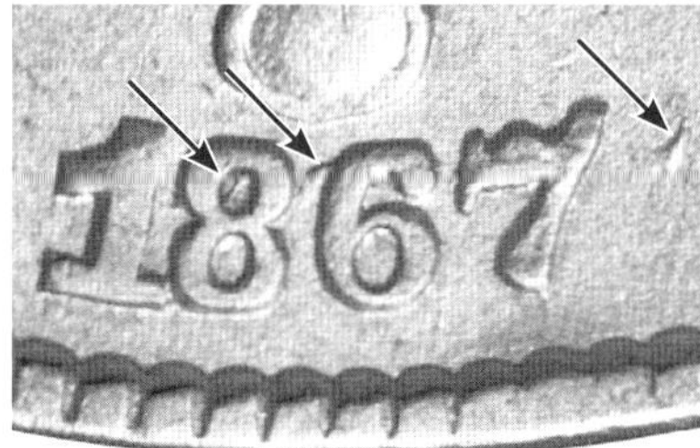

Description: The repunched date is evident with a secondary 7 evident far to the east of the primary 7. Other digits of the secondary date are evident within the numbers of the primary date. The doubled die is evident with the annulet, cross, leaves, and shield slightly doubled to the southeast.

Comments: Although the value for this variety is primarily for the repunched date, this is the only doubled die listed by Fletcher for the 1867, With Rays, type.

	F-12	VF-20	EF-40	AU-50	MS-60	MS-63	MS-65
VARIETY	$130	$260	$400	$600	$750	$1,000	$7,000
NORMAL	$65	$130	$200	$300	$375	$500	$3,500

1867, With Rays — FS-05-1867-303 (002.7)

VARIETY: Repunched Date — FLETCHER-02, S1-3002

PUP: Date

URS-5 • I-3 • L-3

Description: This repunched date exhibits a secondary 7 between the primary 6 and 7, as well as a secondary 6 between the primary 8 and 6.

Comments: Early and middle die states exhibit portions of a 1 to the left of the primary 1. This variety is known with a reverse rotated 155° counterclockwise.

	F-12	VF-20	EF-40	AU-50	MS-60	MS-63	MS-65
VARIETY	$100	$195	$300	$450	$565	$750	$5,250
NORMAL	$65	$130	$200	$300	$375	$500	$3,500

1867, With Rays — FS-05-1867-304 (002.6)

Variety: Misplaced Date (?) — Fletcher-01, S1-4002
PUP: Ball above date
URS-1 • I-4 • L-4

Description: An image that appears to be the base of a misplaced 1 is evident protruding from the left side of the ball above the date.

Comments: To date, this still is a unique specimen. Hundreds of dedicated Shield nickel enthusiasts are looking for this variety.

	F-12	VF-20	EF-40	AU-50	MS-60	MS-63	MS-65
Variety	(unique)						
Normal	$65	$130	$200	$300	$375	$500	$3,500

1867, With Rays — FS-05-1867-901

Variety: Clashed Reverse — Fletcher-11, S2-3009
PUP: Reverse at 12 o'clock
URS-1 • I-5 • L-5

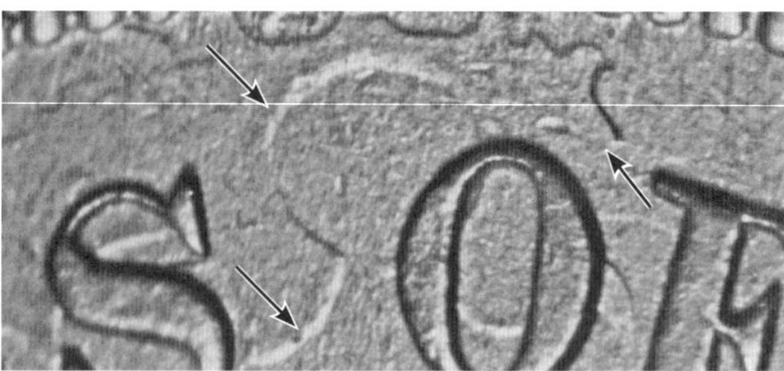

Description: The reverse die was clashed with an obverse die, evidenced by the image of the obverse ball at 12 o'clock on the reverse, between the S of STATES and the O in OF.

Comments: Only one specimen has been reported.

	F-12	VF-20	EF-40	AU-50	MS-60	MS-63	MS-65
Variety	(unique)						
Normal	$65	$130	$200	$300	$375	$500	$3,500

1867, No Rays — FS-05-1867-1101 (001.8)

Variety: Doubled-Die Obverse — Fletcher-59, S2-1002
PUP: IN GOD WE TRUST
URS-3 • I-3 • L-4

Description: Moderate doubling is evident on IN GOD WE TRUST, with the secondary image toward the center of the coin.

Comments: As of this writing, only a couple of specimens exist. However this is a rather minor doubled-die obverse.

Note: This variety is slated to be removed from the coin-by-coin listings of future editions of the ***Cherrypickers' Guide*** due to lack of interest and/or unavailability. It will retain its Fivaz-Stanton number and continue to be listed in future editions' cross-reference appendix. **A full list of varieties slated to be removed from each section appears after the introductory text of that section.**

1867, No Rays — FS-05-1867-1102 (002)

Variety: Doubled-Die Obverse, Repunched Date — Fletcher-54, S2-7000
PUP: Annulet, date
URS 5 • I 4 • L 4

Description: Doubling is evident on the annulet, the cross, and the leaves; the horizontal lines are encroaching into the vertical lines. The date is strongly repunched, with secondary digits south of the primary digits on all four numbers.

Comments: This remains a highly sought-after variety.

	F-12	VF-20	EF-40	AU-50	MS-60	MS-63	MS-65
Variety	$88	$125	$165	$275	$375	$565	$2,000
Normal	$35	$50	$65	$110	$150	$225	$800

1867, No Rays FS-05-1867-1301 (001.9)

Variety: Repunched Date Fletcher-23, S2-3002
PUP: Date
URS-5 • I-4 • L-4

Description: All four digits of the date are repunched, with the secondary digits south of the primary date.

Comments: This is one of the more popular repunched dates for this date.

	F-12	VF-20	EF-40	AU-50	MS-60	MS-63	MS-65
Variety	$70	$100	$130	$220	$300	$450	$1,600
Normal	$35	$50	$65	$110	$150	$225	$800

1867, No Rays FS-05-1867-1302 (002.15)

Variety: Repunched Date Fletcher-25
PUP: Date
URS-3 • I-3 • L-3

Description: All four digits of the date are repunched, with the secondary digits southeast of the primary date.

Comments: Late die states of this variety have a reverse cud.

	F-12	VF-20	EF-40	AU-50	MS-60	MS-63	MS-65
Variety	$44	$63	$80	$140	$190	$280	$1,000
Normal	$35	$50	$65	$110	$150	$225	$800

1867, No Rays — FS-05-1867-1303 (002.2)

VARIETY: Repunched Date — FLETCHER-21, S2-3001

PUP: Date

URS-4 • I-2 • L-3

Description: All four digits of the date are repunched, with the secondary digits to the southwest of the primary digits.

Comments: Ed Fletcher reports having examined three specimens, with all three having a die crack from the base of the 1 to the rim and a reverse rim cud at 4:30.

	F-12	VF-20	EF-40	AU-50	MS-60	MS-63	MS-65
VARIETY	$42	$60	$78	$135	$180	$270	$960
NORMAL	$35	$50	$65	$110	$150	$225	$800

1867, No Rays — FS-05-1867-1304 (002.25)

VARIETY: Repunched Date — FLETCHER-20, S2-3000

PUP: Date

URS-6 • I-3 • L-3

Description: This is a strong repunched date, with secondary digits evident to the west of the primary digits.

Comments: This variety is also rumored to have a 1 punched in the field above the primary 1, which we can't confirm at this time.

	F-12	VF-20	EF-40	AU-50	MS-60	MS-63	MS-65
VARIETY	$60	$85	$110	$190	$255	$385	$1,360
NORMAL	$35	$50	$65	$110	$150	$225	$800

1867, No Rays — FS-05-1867-1305 (002.3)

VARIETY: Repunched Date — FLETCHER-22, S2-3033
PUP: Date
URS-4 • I-4 • L-3

Description: A repunched date, with secondary digits (primarily the 6 and 7) evident far to the south of the primary digits.

Comments: This is another great repunched date.

	F-12	VF-20	EF-40	AU-50	MS-60	MS-63	MS-65
VARIETY	$70	$100	$130	$220	$300	$450	$1,600
NORMAL	$35	$50	$65	$110	$150	$225	$800

1867, No Rays — FS-05-1867-1306 (002.35)

VARIETY: Repunched Date, Doubled-Die Obverse — FLETCHER-08.01
PUP: Date
URS-5 • I-3 • L-3

Description: The repunched date is evident with a secondary 1 and 8 to the north of the primary digits. The doubled die is evident on the annulet, cross, shield, and leaves, with the secondary image southeast of the primary images.

Comments: The value is primarily for the repunched date.

	F-12	VF-20	EF-40	AU-50	MS-60	MS-63	MS-65
VARIETY	$42	$60	$78	$135	$180	$270	$960
NORMAL	$35	$50	$65	$110	$150	$225	$800

1867, No Rays — FS-05-1867-1307 (002.5)

VARIETY: Repunched Date — FLETCHER-38
PUP: Date
URS-3 • I-3 • L-3

Description: The date exhibits secondary digits south of the primary 6 and 7. (In the photo, the doubling on the 1 is the result of strike doubling.)

Comments: Notice the small die chip that connects the 8 to the ball.

	F-12	VF-20	EF-40	AU-50	MS-60	MS-63	MS-65
VARIETY	$50	$70	$90	$155	$210	$315	$1,120
NORMAL	$35	$50	$65	$110	$150	$225	$800

1867, No Rays — FS-05-1867-1308 (002.9)

VARIETY: Repunched Date — FLETCHER-46 S2-3012
PUP: Date
URS-4 • I-2 • L-3

Description: Secondary digits are evident south of the primary 6 and 7.

Comments: This is yet another very nice repunched date for this date. This obverse die is known paired with two different reverse dies.

	F-12	VF-20	EF-40	AU-50	MS-60	MS-63	MS-65
VARIETY	$42	$60	$78	$135	$180	$270	$960
NORMAL	$35	$50	$65	$110	$150	$225	$800

1867, No Rays — FS-05-1867-1309 (002.45)

VARIETY: Misplaced Date — FLETCHER-01.01
PUP: Bottom of shield, date
URS-4 • I-4 • L-3

Description: The top of an apparent 8 is evident protruding within the "V" of the shield, just above the ball.

Comments: The line between the 8 and 6 is a die crack.

Note: This variety is slated to be removed from the coin-by-coin listings of future editions of the ***Cherrypickers' Guide*** due to lack of interest and/or unavailability. It will retain its Fivaz-Stanton number and continue to be listed in future editions' cross-reference appendix. **A full list of varieties slated to be removed from each section appears after the introductory text of that section.**

1867, No Rays — FS-05-1867-1310 (002.75)

VARIETY: Misplaced Date — FLETCHER: N/L, S2-4002
PUP: Lower shield
URS-2 • I-5 • L-4

Description: The remnants of a 1 are evident errantly punched into the lower portion of the shield.

Comments: To date, only two specimens are known. Hundreds of dedicated Shield nickel enthusiasts are looking for this variety.

	F-12	VF-20	EF-40	AU-50	MS-60	MS-63	MS-65
VARIETY	$125	$175	$230	$385	$525	$790	$2,800
NORMAL	$35	$50	$65	$110	$150	$225	$800

1867, No Rays — FS-05-1867-1401

VARIETY: Misaligned Die Clash — FLETCHER-69
PUP: Center of shield
URS-1 • I-4 • L-4

Description: What was probably an unusual misaligned die clash of denticles is evident through the vertical lines of the shield, curving from upper right to lower left.

Comments: To the best of our knowledge, this is the only example reported to date.

	F-12	VF-20	EF-40	AU-50	MS-60	MS-63	MS-65
VARIETY	(unique)						
NORMAL	$35	$50	$65	$110	$150	$225	$800

1867, No Rays — FS-05-1867-1402/1901

VARIETY: Obverse Die Clash, Reverse Die Clash — S2-8000
PUP: Centers of obverse and reverse
URS-3 • I-4 • L-4

Description: Clashed dies are visible on both the obverse and reverse. The flag of the big 5 is clearly visible on the obverse, and vertical bars from the shield are clearly visible on the reverse.

Comments: This is the only Shield nickel known with clashes on both sides.

	F-12	VF-20	EF-40	AU-50	MS-60	MS-63	MS-65
VARIETY	$70	$100	$130	$220	$300	$450	$1,600
NORMAL	$35	$50	$65	$110	$150	$225	$800

1867, No Rays, Proof — FS-05-1867-1902

VARIETY: Alternate Reverse — S3-3000

PUP: Stars

URS-7 • I-5 • L-4

Description: This is the 1867 Proof with the prototype (J-507) reverse. These were the first 1867, No Rays, Proofs delivered. A star points directly to the T of STATES on the reverse (unlike the normal Hub IIa reverse).

Comments: It is thought that a prototype reverse hub was used on the first deliveries because the IIa hub was not yet available in early 1867.

	PF-63	PF-65	PF-66
VARIETY	$2,375	$11,250	$20,000
NORMAL	$475	$2,250	$4,000

Identifying the Varieties of Shield Nickel Reverse Dies of 1868

This section was contributed by Dennis Paulsen.

There are four known reverse hubs (types) used for Shield nickel circulation strikes. These are identified in detail in Ed Fletcher's book, *The Shield Five Cent Series*. However, there are five varieties for just one of these hubs, the reverse of 1868. It is the varieties from this type that are most interesting. (The term *type* generally refers to an intentional change in the design, while the term *variety* generally refers to an accidental change.)

The reverse hubs (types) of the Shield nickel are as follows:

With Rays
Reverse Hub I (all 1866 and some 1867 coins)

Without Rays
Reverse Hub IIa ("Reverse of 1867," some 1867, 1868, and 1869 coins)

Reverse Hub IIb ("Reverse of 1868," only on a very small percentage of 1868)

Reverse Hub IIc (some 1869 and all 1870–1883 coins)

The five varieties, plus a transitional sub-variety, of the reverses of the 1868 Shield nickels are distinguished by a certain number of broken letters.

To identify the "Reverse of 1868" varieties, simply look at the star at 12 o'clock. If the star points to the E of STATES, it is the more common "Reverse of 1867." If it points to the S, it is the "Reverse of 1868."

Reverse varieties of 1868 are as follows:

Variety 1—one broken letter (the C in CENTS); FS-05-1868-901 (002.94)

Variety 2—two broken letters (the C and the S in CENTS); FS-05-1868-902 (002.95)

Variety 3—three broken letters (the C and the S in CENTS; the first S in STATES); FS-05-1868-903 (002.96)

Variety 4—four broken letters (the C and the S in CENTS; the first S in STATES; the D in UNITED); FS-05-1868-904 (002.97)

Variety 5—no broken letters; FS-05-1868-905 (002.98)

Variety 5.5—a broken portion of the C in CENTS; FS-05-1868-906 (002.99)

Variety 1 (FS-05-1868-901)
Identified by the broken lower serif of the C in CENTS.

Variety 2 (FS-05-1868-902)
Identified by the broken C in CENTS (previously illustrated), and the broken lower loop of the S in CENTS.

Variety 3 (FS-05-1868-903)
Identified by the broken C and S in CENTS (previously illustrated), and a broken upper loop of the S in STATES.

Variety 4 (FS-05-1868-904)
Identified by the broken C and S in CENTS, the broken S in STATES (both previously illustrated), and a broken upper curve in the D in UNITED.

Variety 5 (FS-05-1868-905)
No broken letters.

Variety 5.5 (FS-05-1868-906)

This is a transition between Variety 5 and Variety 1. The top portion of the lower serif of the C in CENTS is only partially broken, indicated by a weak up-stroke of the lower serif of the C. This C is sometimes found with slight vestiges of the broken portions (three o'clock to five o'clock of the C). Bill Fivaz was the first to locate this transitional variety, and he refers to this as the "step-tail."

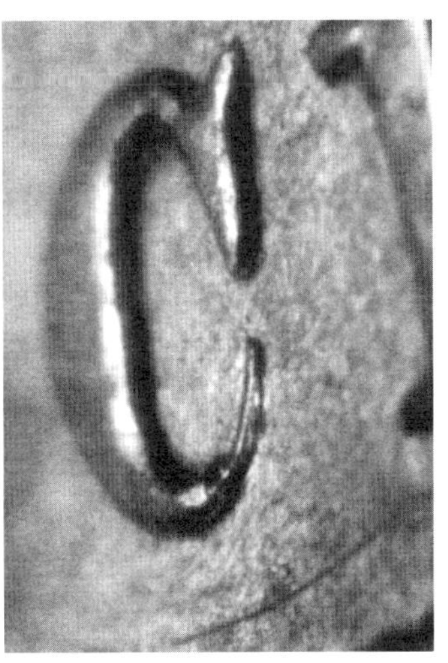

The rarest of the 1868 reverse varieties is FS-05-1868-905, "No Broken Letters." Examples are rarely encountered. They are the result of only one or two working reverse dies. FS-05-1868-901 and FS-05-1868-902, with one or two broken letters, are the most common, and represent almost 80 percent of all reverses of 1868.

Several years of study and examination of thousands of 1868 Shield nickels suggest that only about 10 percent of the 1868 Shield nickel population has the reverse type of 1868. Mint records indicate that 28,817,000 of the 1868 Shield nickel were struck. No one knows for sure the percentage minted with the reverse of 1868, but research indicates it to be 2,900,000. This chart shows estimates of value and rarity of the different varieties of the 1868 reverse.

	F-12	EF-40	AU-50	MS-60	Estimated Mintage	Percent of Total
FS-901	$20	$35	$75	$110	1,392,000	48%
FS-902	30	50	100	160	870,000	30%
FS-903	200	300	375	475	87,000	3%
FS-904	55	85	170	225	464,000	16%
FS-905	375	475	600	700	29,000	1%
FS-906	200	300	375	475	58,000	2%

Total Estimated Mintage: 2,900,000

1868 FS-05-1868-101 (003)

VARIETY: Doubled-Die Obverse FLETCHER-42, S1-1002
PUP: Annulet
URS-10 • I-4 • L-4

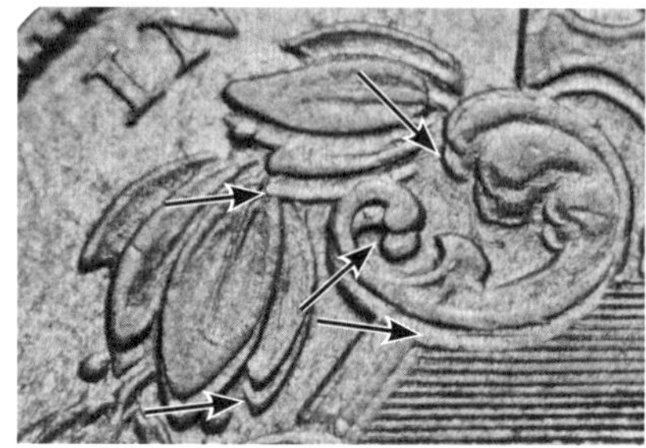

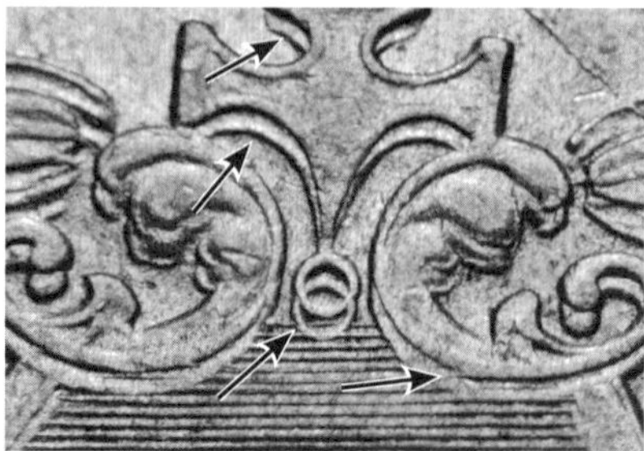

Description: Very strong doubling is evident on the upper portion of the design, including the annulet, the cross, the leaves, and the horizontal lines, which "bleed" into the vertical lines.

Comments: This is the Reverse of 1867, Hub IIa.

	F-12	VF-20	EF-40	AU-50	MS-60	MS-63	MS-65
VARIETY	$85	$120	$155	$265	$360	$540	$1,920
NORMAL	$35	$50	$65	$110	$150	$225	$800

THE CHERRYPICKERS' GUIDE HELPFUL HINTS

The state of the die at the time the coin was struck can be important. Almost across the board, early-die-state (EDS) coins are much more desirable and will sell for higher prices.

1868 — FS-05-1868-102 (003.65)

Variety: Tripled-Die Obverse — **Fletcher-111, S2-1004**
PUP: Annulet
URS-3 • I-5 • L-4

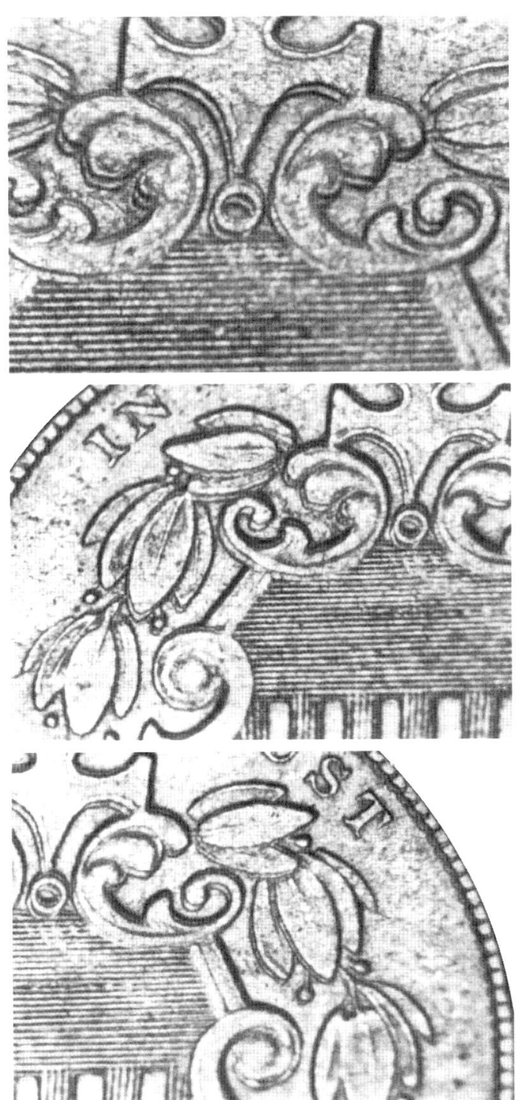

Description: Strong tripling is evident to the southwest and to the north on the annulet, cross, leaves, etc. A tripled die on the Shield nickel series is not typical.

Comments: This is the Reverse of 1868, Hub IIb. This variety was first reported to us in January 2000 by Howard Spindel. Ken Hill reports having two specimens. This was first discovered by Terry Searcy.

	F-12	VF-20	EF-40	AU-50	MS-60	MS-63	MS-65
Variety	$175	$250	$325	$550	$750	$1,125	$4,000
Normal	$35	$50	$65	$110	$150	$225	$800

1868 FS-05-1868-103 (003.8)

Variety: Doubled-Die Obverse
Fletcher-40, S1-1005
PUP: Annulet
URS-3 • I-4 • L-4

Description: Strong doubling is evident on the upper portion of the design, including the annulet, the shield, the leaves, the berries, and the cross.

Comments: This is the Reverse of 1867, Hub IIa.

	F-12	VF-20	EF-40	AU-50	MS-60	MS-63	MS-65
Variety	$70	$100	$130	$220	$300	$450	$1,600
Normal	$35	$50	$65	$110	$150	$225	$800

1868 FS-05-1868-104 (003.9)

Variety: Doubled-Die Obverse
Fletcher-34, S1-1013
PUP: Annulet
URS-4 • I-3 • L-4

Description: The doubling is evident slightly to the south of the primary image, most noticeably on the annulet, cross, and upper leaves.

Comments: This is the Reverse of 1867, Hub IIa. The date on this variety is punched high and slanted slightly to the right, with the first 8 touching the ball. Note also that the shape of the engraved leaf must match exactly for correct attribution.

	F-12	VF-20	EF-40	AU-50	MS-60	MS-63	MS-65
Variety	$53	$75	$100	$165	$225	$340	$1,200
Normal	$35	$50	$65	$110	$150	$225	$800

1868 — FS-05-1868-105 (003.95)

VARIETY: Doubled-Die Obverse, Doubled-Die Reverse — FLETCHER-45, S1-7000
PUP: IN GOD WE TRUST
URS-3 • I-3 • L-4

Description: On the obverse, moderate doubling is visible on IN GOD WE TRUST. On the reverse, slightly stronger doubling is visible on UNITED STATES OF AMERICA, CENTS, and some of the stars.

Comments: This is the Reverse of 1867, Hub IIa. This variety continues to be very elusive and in high demand by Shield nickel variety collectors.

	F-12	VF-20	EF-40	AU-50	MS-60	MS-63	MS-65
VARIETY	$75	$125	$175	$250	$300	$360	$1,000
NORMAL	$35	$50	$65	$110	$150	$225	$800

1868 — FS-05-1868-106 (003.96)

VARIETY: Doubled-Die Obverse — FLETCHER-107.01, S2-1007
PUP: Annulet
URS-3 • I-4 • L-2

Description: Strong doubling is evident to the southwest on the cross, annulet, and leaves, as well as on the horizontal lines and lower border of the shield.

Comments: This is the Reverse of 1868, Hub IIb. The date nearly touches the ball of the shield. Images appearing in previous editions for this coin were of a counterfeit coin.

	F-12	VF-20	EF-40	AU-50	MS-60	MS-63	MS-65
VARIETY	$85	$120	$155	$265	$360	$540	$1,920
NORMAL	$35	$50	$65	$110	$150	$225	$800

1868 — FS-05-1868-107 (003.97)

VARIETY: Doubled-Die Obverse, Repunched Date — FLETCHER-43, S1-7003

PUP: Date, annulet

URS-2 • I-4 • L-3

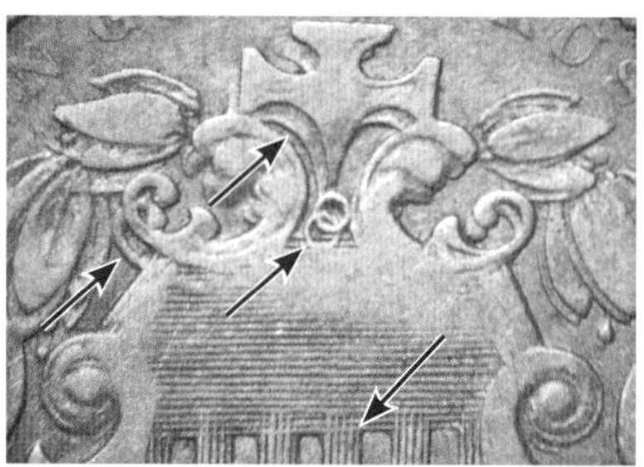

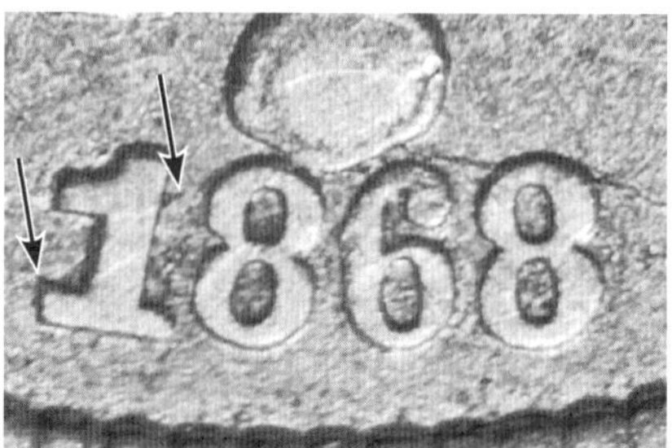

Description: Very strong doubling is evident on the annulet, cross, and leaves, as well as on the horizontal lines and lower border of the shield. The 1 of the date is repunched north and tilted slightly clockwise.

Comments: This is the Reverse of 1867, Hub IIa. The date is very high, with the 8 touching the ball. There is a clear die crack running from the 6 through the top of the second 8 and on to the denticles. The "engraved" leaf is almost completely separated from the adjacent leaf.

	F-12	VF-20	EF-40	AU-50	MS-60	MS-63	MS-65
VARIETY	$85	$120	$155	$265	$360	$540	$1,920
NORMAL	$35	$50	$65	$110	$150	$225	$800

1868 — FS-05-1868-109

VARIETY: Doubled-Die Obverse, Repunched Date — S2-1003

PUP: Annulet

URS-4 • I-4 • L-4

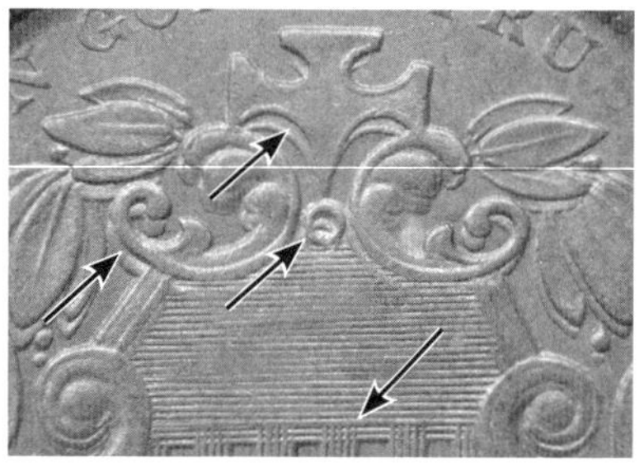

Description: Doubling is evident by a strong secondary image to the southwest of the primary image, most noticeable on the annulet, cross, shield, and leaves. The repunched date is visible as a secondary 1 closely north of the primary 1, evident mostly at the base.

Comments: This is the Reverse of 1868, Hub IIb. Images appearing in previous editions for this coin were of a counterfeit coin.

	F-12	VF-20	EF-40	AU-50	MS-60	MS-63	MS-65
VARIETY	$85	$120	$155	$265	$360	$540	$1,920
NORMAL	$35	$50	$65	$110	$150	$225	$800

1868 — FS-05-1868-111

VARIETY: Doubled-Die Obverse — S1-1010
PUP: Annulet
URS-3 • I-4 • L-4

Description: This is a doubled die clearly shown at the annulet, cross, and leaves. The doubling is nearly straight south.

Comments: Similar 1868 doubled-die obverses exist. Careful attribution can ensure that the doubled-die obverse matches exactly. This variety has the Reverse of 1867, Hub IIa.

	F-12	VF-20	EF-40	AU-50	MS-60	MS-63	MS-65
VARIETY	$85	$120	$155	$265	$360	$540	$1,920
NORMAL	$35	$50	$65	$110	$150	$225	$800

1868 — FS-05-1868-301 (003.2)

VARIETY: Repunched Date — FLETCHER-19, S1-3008
PUP: Date
URS-6 • I-3 • L-3

Description: This variety exhibits at least three date punches. Both secondary dates are evident starting north on the 1 and slanting downward from left to right. Secondary 6's and 8's (from the last 8) are evident south of the primary digits.

Comments: This is the Reverse of 1868, Hub IIa.

	F-12	VF-20	EF-40	AU-50	MS-60	MS-63	MS-65
VARIETY	$56	$80	$105	$175	$240	$360	$1,280
NORMAL	$35	$50	$65	$110	$150	$225	$800

1868 FS-05-1868-302 (003.3)

VARIETY: Repunched Date FLETCHER-106.01
PUP: Date
URS-6 • I-3 • L-3

Description: The initial date punch left the primary first 8 and 6 touching the ball of the shield. The subsequent date punch aligned the 1's of both, but like the previous listing, the last three digits are south, with a progressively stronger spread going from left to right.

Comments: This is the Reverse of 1868, Hub IIb. A die crack is evident on most specimens running from the rim west of the date, through the lower portion of the numbers, then downward to the rim southeast of the final 8.

	F-12	VF-20	EF-40	AU-50	MS-60	MS-63	MS-65
VARIETY	$56	$80	$105	$175	$240	$360	$1,280
NORMAL	$35	$50	$65	$110	$150	$225	$800

1868 FS-05-1868-303 (003.35)

VARIETY: Repunched Date FLETCHER-28.05
PUP: Date
URS-4 • I-3 • L-3

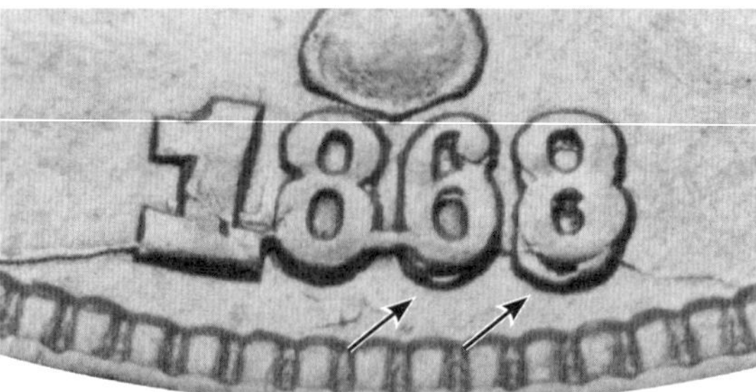

Description: This variety is extremely similar to the previous listing, except the 6 of the date does not touch the ball of the shield.

Comments: This is the Reverse of 1867, Hub IIa. Aside from the repunched date being almost identical to the previous listing, there is a die crack that is eerily similar to the one on the previous listing. The primary difference to the die crack is that on this variety the crack leaves the second 8 farther to the right.

	F-12	VF-20	EF-40	AU-50	MS-60	MS-63	MS-65
VARIETY	$53	$75	$100	$165	$225	$340	$1,200
NORMAL	$35	$50	$65	$110	$150	$225	$800

1868 — FS-05-1868-304 (003.4)

VARIETY: Repunched Date — FLETCHER-25, S1-3002
PUP: Date
URS-6 • I-3 • L-3

Description: The secondary date was punched to the southeast of the primary date. All four digits are visible.

Comments: This is the Reverse of 1867, Hub IIa. This variety was listed twice in the fourth edition of the ***Cherrypickers' Guide*** (003.75 as well as 003.4).

	F-12	VF-20	EF-40	AU-50	MS-60	MS-63	MS-65
VARIETY	$63	$90	$120	$200	$270	$405	$1,440
NORMAL	$35	$50	$65	$110	$150	$225	$800

1868 — FS-05-1868-305 (003.45)

VARIETY: Repunched Date — FLETCHER: N/L
PUP: Date
URS-3 • I-4 • L-4

Description: Secondary digits are evident for all four digits, to the north of the primary digits. A secondary 1 is also evident to the east of the primary 1, actually closer to the first 8 than the 1.

Comments: This is a really neat repunched date.

	F-12	VF-20	EF-40	AU-50	MS-60	MS-63	MS-65
VARIETY	$70	$100	$130	$220	$300	$450	$1,600
NORMAL	$35	$50	$65	$110	$150	$225	$800

1868 FS-05-1868-306 (003.5)

VARIETY: Repunched Date FLETCHER-24

PUP: Date

URS-4 • I-3 • L-4

Description: There are at least four 8's evident for the last digit. The first 8 touches the ball and is the result of a broken date punch.

Comments: This is the Reverse of 1867, Hub IIa.

	F-12	VF-20	EF-40	AU-50	MS-60	MS-63	MS-65
VARIETY	$56	$80	$105	$175	$240	$360	$1,280
NORMAL	$35	$50	$65	$110	$150	$225	$800

1868 FS-05-1868-307 (003.7)

VARIETY: Repunched Date FLETCHER-29.02

PUP: Date

URS-7 • I-3 • L-4

Description: A secondary 6 and secondary final 8 are evident south of the primary digits. The first 8 is touching the ball.

Comments: This is the Reverse of 1867, Hub IIa. Early die states of this variety are missing the die cracks through the date but do exhibit some file marks on the obverse at seven o'clock.

	F-12	VF-20	EF-40	AU-50	MS-60	MS-63	MS-65
VARIETY	$56	$80	$105	$175	$240	$360	$1,280
NORMAL	$35	$50	$65	$110	$150	$225	$800

1868 — FS-05-1868-309 (003.85)

VARIETY: Repunched Date FLETCHER-11
PUP: Date
URS-3 • I-2 • L-3

Description: Secondary digits are evident to the south of the primary digits on the 6 and the final 8.

	F-12	VF-20	EF-40	AU-50	MS-60	MS-63	MS-65
VARIETY	$42	$60	$78	$130	$180	$270	$960
NORMAL	$35	$50	$65	$110	$150	$225	$800

1868 — FS-05-1868-310 (003.98)

VARIETY: Repunched Date FLETCHER-20
PUP: Date
URS-3 • I-4 • L-3

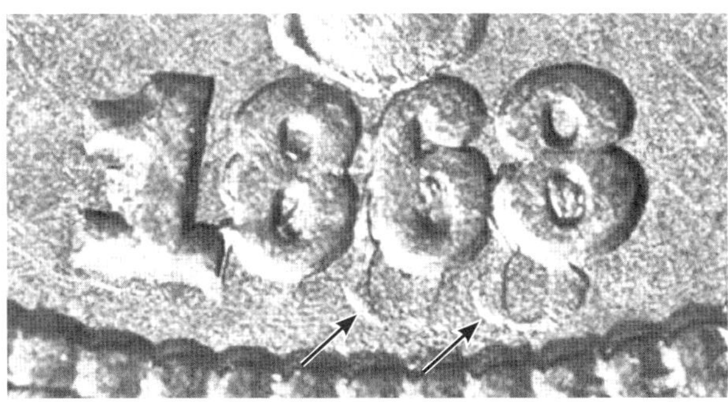

Description: This is a very strong repunched date, with secondary digits evident far to the south of the primary digits.

Comments: This is the Reverse of 1867, Hub IIa.

	F-12	VF-20	EF-40	AU-50	MS-60	MS-63	MS-65
VARIETY	$70	$100	$130	$220	$300	$450	$1,600
NORMAL	$35	$50	$65	$110	$150	$225	$800

1868 — FS-05-1868-311 (003.985)

VARIETY: Repunched Date, Missing Leaf — FLETCHER-29.03, S1-7014
PUP: Date
URS-4 • I-3 • L-3

Description: Secondary digits are evident to the north of the 1 and the first 8. This is also a Missing Leaf variety, of which there are several in the series.

Comments: This is the Reverse of 1867, Hub IIa. The retained cud by the date area would likely indicate that very few coins ultimately were struck from this die.

	F-12	VF-20	EF-40	AU-50	MS-60	MS-63	MS-65
VARIETY	$70	$100	$130	$220	$300	$450	$1,600
NORMAL	$35	$50	$65	$110	$150	$225	$800

1868 — FS-05-1868-312 (003.1)

VARIETY: Misplaced Date — FLETCHER-102, S2-4000
PUP: Ball above date
URS-4 • I-5 • L-3

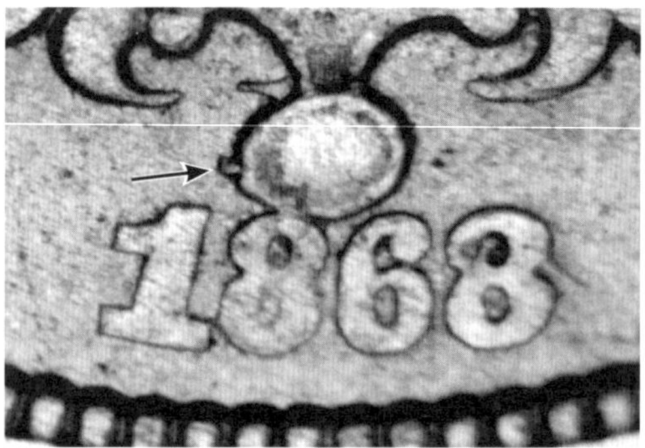

Description: A 1 is clearly evident protruding from the left side of the ball at the bottom of the shield.

Comments: This is the Reverse of 1868, Hub IIb.

	F-12	VF-20	EF-40	AU-50	MS-60	MS-63	MS-65
VARIETY	$105	$150	$195	$330	$450	$675	$2,400
NORMAL	$35	$50	$65	$110	$150	$225	$800

1868 — FS-05-1868-313 (003.6)

VARIETY: Misplaced Date — FLETCHER-02
PUP: Denticles below date
URS-1 • I-4 • L-4

Description: The top of a 6 or 8 is evident protruding from the denticles below the primary 6.

Comments: This is the Reverse of 1867, Hub IIa. The discovery coin is still the only known specimen.

	F-12	VF-20	EF-40	AU-50	MS-60	MS-63	MS-65
VARIETY	(unique)						
NORMAL	$35	$50	$65	$110	$150	$225	$800

1868 — FS-05-1868-314

VARIETY: Repunched Date — S1-3017
PUP: Date
URS-1 • I-4 • L-4

Description: The 8, 6, and 8 in the date are repunched far to the south.

Comments: The doubling seen on the leading edges of the digits is strike doubling. Only one example has been reported to date. This variety has the Reverse of 1867, Hub IIa.

	F-12	VF-20	EF-40	AU-50	MS-60	MS-63	MS-65
VARIETY	(unique)						
NORMAL	$35	$50	$65	$110	$150	$225	$800

1868 — FS-05-1868-401 (003.99)

VARIETY: Missing Leaf, Scribe Mark — FLETCHER-56
PUP: Second right leaf cluster
URS-2 • I-4 • L-4

Description: The second right leaf cluster has three leaves, unlike the normal four leaves. This variety also exhibits a circular "scribe mark," for lack of a better term, circumventing the shield on the top and through the shield near the bottom.

Comments: This is the Reverse of 1867, Hub IIa. All Missing Leaf varieties have only three leaves on the second cluster on the right.

	F-12	VF-20	EF-40	AU-50	MS-60	MS-63	MS-65
VARIETY	$80	$115	$145	$250	$340	$510	$1,800
NORMAL	$35	$50	$65	$110	$150	$225	$800

1869, Narrow Date — FS-05-1869-301 (005)

VARIETY: Narrow Date — FLETCHER-01, S1-0000

PUP: Date

URS-10 • I-2 • L-3

Description: The 1869, Narrow Date, Shield nickel variety is very scarce. Most dates for 1869 have wide digits. Previously referred to as the Tall Date, the name has been changed to Narrow Date by Shield nickel specialists because the digits for other Shield nickels are this same relative size.

Comments: All known Narrow Date varieties have the Reverse of 1867, Hub IIa. Those 1869, Narrow Date, varieties will have a three-digit Fivaz-Stanton number. All Wide Date Shield nickels will have a four-digit FS number.

	F-12	VF-20	EF-40	AU-50	MS-60	MS-63	MS-65
VARIETY	$39	$55	$72	$120	$155	$250	$880
NORMAL	$35	$50	$65	$110	$140	$225	$800

1869, Wide Date — FS-05-1869-1101 (004)

VARIETY: Doubled-Die Obverse — FLETCHER-413, S5-1002

PUP: Motto, annulet

URS 6 • I 3 • L 3

Description: Doubling is visible on IN GOD WE TRUST, rotated slightly counterclockwise. Doubling is also evident on the annulet, cross, leaves, and upper shield.

Comments: The date on this variety has the wide digits. This is the Reverse of 1867, Hub IIc.

	F-12	VF-20	EF-40	AU-50	MS-60	MS-63	MS-65
VARIETY	$56	$80	$105	$175	$225	$360	$1,280
NORMAL	$35	$50	$65	$110	$140	$225	$800

1869, Wide Date — FS-05-1869-1102 (004.5)

Variety: Doubled-Die Obverse, Repunched Date — Fletcher-414, S5-7000
PUP: Annulet, date
URS-3 • I-3 • L-3

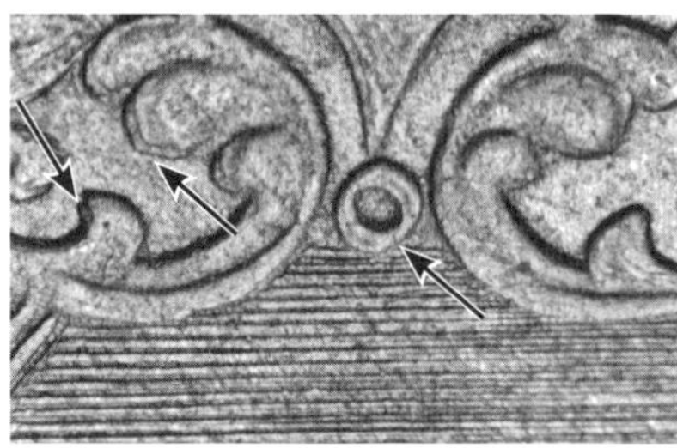

Description: Doubling is visible on IN GOD WE TRUST, the annulet, cross, leaves, and upper shield. The date is also repunched, with the secondary digits evident to the south of the primary digits.

Comments: Though this variety is very similar to the previous, compare the differences in the direction of the secondary annulet from the primary. The date on this variety has the wide digits.
This is the Reverse of 1867, Hub IIc.

	F-12	VF-20	EF-40	AU-50	MS-60	MS-63	MS-65
Variety	$70	$100	$130	$220	$280	$450	$1,600
Normal	$35	$50	$65	$110	$140	$225	$800

1869, Wide Date — FS-05-1869-1103 (005.67)

Variety: Doubled-Die Obverse, Repunched Date — Fletcher-411, S5-7001
PUP: Annulet, date
URS-3 • I-3 • L-3

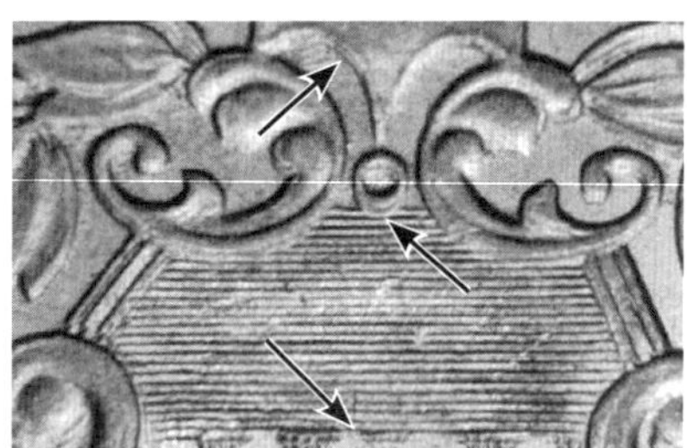

Description: Moderate doubling is evident to the south on the cross, annulet, and leaves, as well as at the horizontal lines and lower border of the shield. There is also doubling in the motto, rotated slightly counterclockwise. The date is also repunched, with a secondary 6 and 9 evident to the south of the primary digits, and a secondary 1 evident to the north of the primary digit.

Comments: The date on this variety has the wide digits. This is the Reverse of 1867, Hub IIc.

	F-12	VF-20	EF-40	AU-50	MS-60	MS-63	MS-65
Variety	$60	$88	$115	$195	$245	$395	$1,400
Normal	$35	$50	$65	$110	$140	$225	$800

1869, Wide Date — FS-05-1869-1104

VARIETY: Doubled-Die Obverse, Repunched Date — FLETCHER: N/L
PUP: Motto, annulet, date
URS-1 • I-4 • L-4

Description: Doubling is evident on IN GOD WE TRUST, the annulet, shield, and leaves. The date shows evidence of repunching, with a close secondary image to the south of the primary image.

Comments: To the best of our knowledge, this is the only example reported to date.

Note: This variety is slated to be removed from the coin-by-coin listings of future editions of the ***Cherrypickers' Guide*** due to lack of interest and/or unavailability. It will retain its Fivaz-Stanton number and continue to be listed in future editions' cross-reference appendix. **A full list of varieties slated to be removed from each section appears after the introductory text of that section.**

1869, Wide Date — FS-05-1869-1301

VARIETY: Wide Date — S2-0000, S3-0000, S4-0000, S5-0000
PUP: Date
URS-15 • I-1 • L-1

Description: This is the normal, common date punch for 1869.

Comments: The date on this variety has the wide digits. There is no significant value associated with the date style for this year.

	F-12	VF-20	EF-40	AU-50	MS-60	MS-63	MS-65
VARIETY	$35	$50	$65	$110	$140	$225	$800
NORMAL	$35	$50	$65	$110	$140	$225	$800

1869, Wide Date — FS-05-1869-1302 (005.3)

VARIETY: Repunched Date — FLETCHER-104, S2-3000
PUP: Date
URS-4 • I-3 • L-3

Description: Secondary digits are visible with a wide spread to the south of the primary digits. All four digits are repunched, though the 8 can be more difficult to see.

Comments: The date on this variety has the wide digits. This is the Reverse of 1867, Hub IIa.

	F-12	VF-20	EF-40	AU-50	MS-60	MS-63	MS-65
VARIETY	$70	$100	$130	$220	$280	$450	$1,600
NORMAL	$35	$50	$65	$110	$140	$225	$800

1869, Wide Date — FS-05-1869-1303 (005.4)

VARIETY: Repunched Date — FLETCHER-202, S3-3000
PUP: Date
URS-3 • I-3 • L-3

Description: A secondary 1 and 8 are evident to the north of the primary digits. Notice that the secondary 8 is clearly touching the ball of the shield.

Comments: The date on this variety has the wide digits. This is the Reverse of 1867, Hub IIc.

	F-12	VF-20	EF-40	AU-50	MS-60	MS-63	MS-65
VARIETY	$63	$90	$120	$200	$250	$405	$1,440
NORMAL	$35	$50	$65	$110	$140	$225	$800

1869, Wide Date — FS-05-1869-1304 (005.5)

VARIETY: Repunched Date — FLETCHER-408

PUP: Date

URS-4 • I-2 • L-3

Description: This date is actually triple-punched, with a set of secondary digits to the north and also to the east of the primary digits. The tops of the northern secondary 8 and 6 are touching the ball of the shield.

Comments: The date on this variety has the wide digits. This is the Reverse of 1867, Hub IIc.

	F-12	VF-20	EF-40	AU-50	MS-60	MS-63	MS-65
VARIETY	$46	$65	$85	$145	$180	$295	$1,040
NORMAL	$35	$50	$65	$110	$140	$225	$800

1869, Wide Date — FS-05-1869-1305 (005.6)

VARIETY: Repunched Date — FLETCHER-409, S5-3000

PUP: Date

URS-4 • I-2 • L-3

Description: Secondary digits are evident to the south of the primary digits. Early die states may show that certain digits are actually triple-punched.

Comments: The date on this variety has the wide digits. This is the Reverse of 1867, Hub IIc.

	F-12	VF-20	EF-40	AU-50	MS-60	MS-63	MS-65
VARIETY	$46	$65	$85	$145	$180	$295	$1,040
NORMAL	$35	$50	$65	$110	$140	$225	$800

1869, Wide Date — FS-05-1869-1306 (005.68)

VARIETY: Repunched Date — FLETCHER-105, S2-3002
PUP: Date
URS-4 • I-3 • L-3

Description: Secondary digits are evident to the northeast of the primary digits. The secondary 8 and 6 are touching the ball of the shield.

Comments: The date on this variety has the wide digits. This is the Reverse of 1867, Hub IIa.

	F-12	VF-20	EF-40	AU-50	MS-60	MS-63	MS-65
VARIETY	$70	$100	$130	$220	$280	$450	$1,600
NORMAL	$35	$50	$65	$110	$150	$225	$800

1869, Wide Date — FS-05-1869-1307 (005.2)

VARIETY: Misplaced Date
PUP: Ball of shield
URS-3 • I-3 • L-3

Description: A "spike" is evident protruding from the left side of the ball of the shield. We are not sure if this is a 1 or some other aberration.

Comments: The date on this variety has the wide digits. This is the Reverse of 1867, Hub IIa.

	F-12	VF-20	EF-40	AU-50	MS-60	MS-63	MS-65
VARIETY	$70	$100	$130	$220	$280	$450	$1,600
NORMAL	$35	$50	$65	$110	$150	$225	$800

1870 — FS-05-1870-101 (005.7)

VARIETY: Doubled-Die Obverse, Repunched Date — FLETCHER-03, S1-7001
PUP: Annulet, date
URS-5 • I-5 • L-5

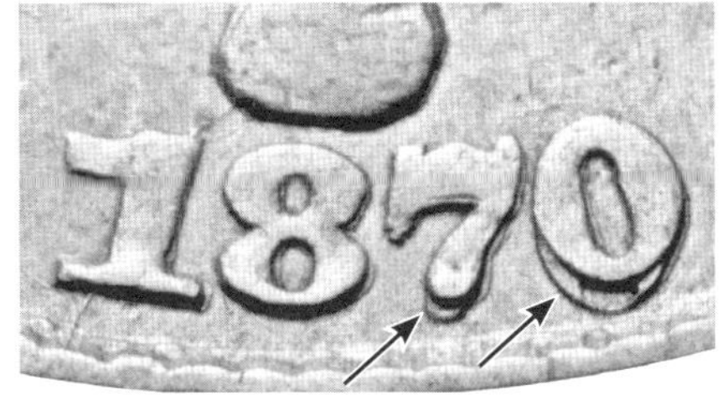

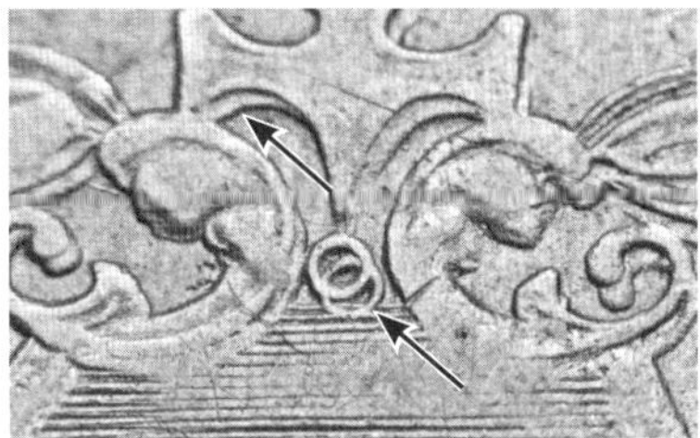

Description: This is an extremely strong doubled die, evident on the annulet, cross, upper shield, leaves, and berries. The date is also strongly repunched, with a secondary 7 and 0 evident to the south of the primary digits.

Comments: This is one of the Shield nickel varieties most actively sought by specialists.

	F-12	VF-20	EF-40	AU-50	MS-60	MS-63	MS-65
VARIETY	$180	$240	$300	$450	$750	$900	$5,250
NORMAL	$60	$80	$100	$150	$250	$300	$1,750

1870 — FS-05-1870-102 (005.74)

VARIETY: Doubled-Die Obverse — FLETCHER-12, S1-7000
PUP: Annulet
URS-4 • I-4 • L-4

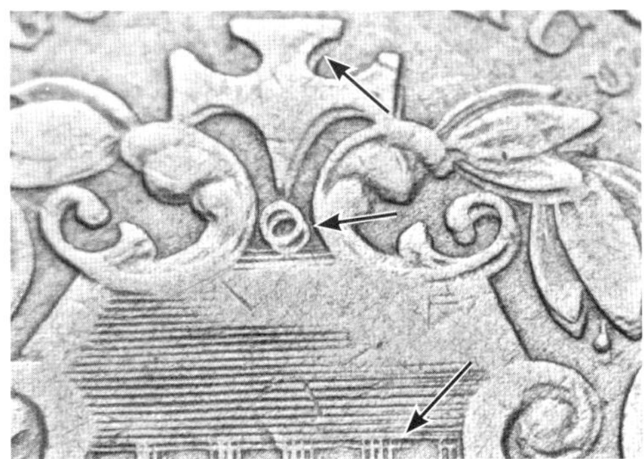

Description: Doubling is evident on the annulet, cross, upper shield, leaves, and berries. The horizontal lines also run into the vertical lines on the shield.

Comments: This is another of the many popular Shield nickel doubled dies.

	F-12	VF-20	EF-40	AU-50	MS-60	MS-63	MS-65
VARIETY	$135	$175	$220	$330	$550	$660	$3,850
NORMAL	$60	$80	$100	$150	$250	$300	$1,750

1870 — FS-05-1870-103 (005.75)

VARIETY: Doubled-Die Obverse, Repunched Date — FLETCHER-03.01, S1-7002
PUP: Annulet, date
URS-4 • I-5 • L-4

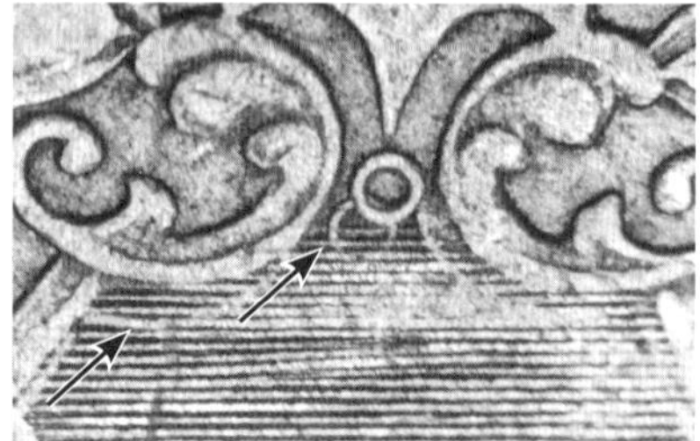

Description: This extremely strong doubled die is evident on the annulet, upper shield, and leaves, and shows the horizontal lines running into the vertical lines. The repunched date is evident with the remains of a 0 far to the right of the primary 0.

Comments: This is likely one of the most eagerly sought varieties within the series. It is a super variety, with the wide spread on the doubled die and the tremendous spread on the repunched date. It was first reported to us by Brian Greer in July of 1995.

	F-12	VF-20	EF-40	AU-50	MS-60	MS-63	MS-65
VARIETY	$300	$400	$500	$750	$1,250	$1,500	$8,750
NORMAL	$60	$80	$100	$150	$250	$300	$1,750

1870 — FS-05-1870-301 (005.77)

VARIETY: Repunched Date, Clash with Indian Head Cent — FLETCHER-15, S1-8001
PUP: Date, obverse
URS-4 • I-5 • L-4

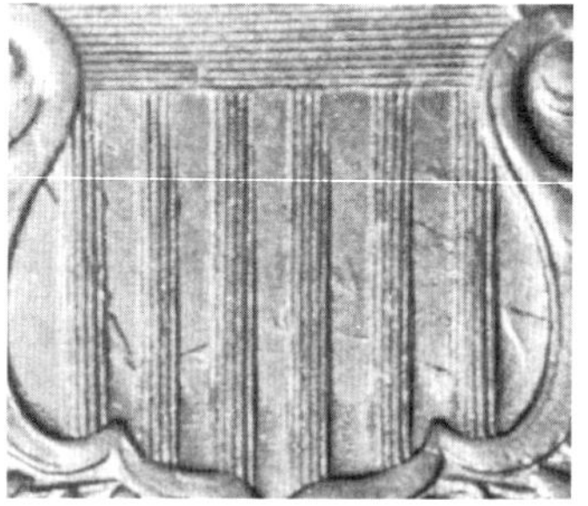

Description: The date is quadruple-punched, with secondary 1's evident to the southwest, the south, and the southeast of the primary 1. Other digits are also doubled. The obverse exhibits weak clash marks of an Indian Head cent obverse.

Comments: This is a super variety, with the clash of the Indian Head cent obverse and the strong repunched date.

	F-12	VF-20	EF-40	AU-50	MS-60	MS-63	MS-65
VARIETY	$600	$800	$1,000	$1,500	$2,500	$3,000	$17,500
NORMAL	$60	$80	$100	$150	$250	$300	$1,750

1870 — FS-05-1870-302 (005.76)

VARIETY: Repunched Date, Misplaced Date — FLETCHER-01
PUP: Date
URS-4 • I-1 • L-4

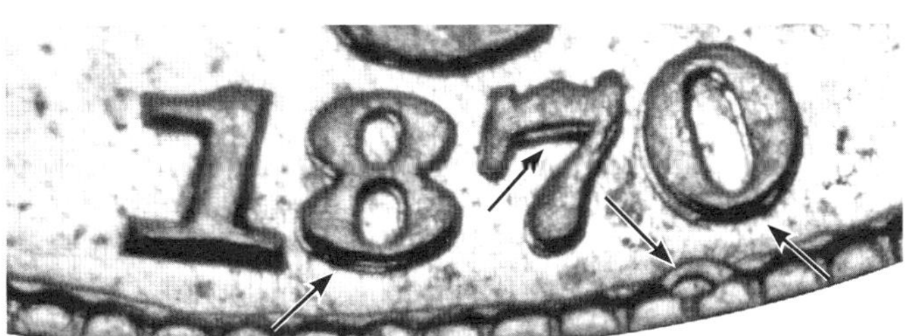

Description: The repunched date is evident with a close spread on the 8, 7, and 0 slightly to the south. The misplaced date is evident with the top of as many as three 0's protruding from the denticles.

Comments: The misplaced date is the primary feature of this variety.

	F-12	VF-20	EF-40	AU-50	MS-60	MS-63	MS-65
VARIETY	$78	$105	$130	$195	$325	$390	$2,275
NORMAL	$60	$80	$100	$150	$250	$300	$1,750

1870 — FS-05-1870-801 (005.9)

VARIETY: Doubled-Die Reverse — FLETCHER-14, S1-2002
PUP: Reverse lettering
URS-5 • I-4 • L-4

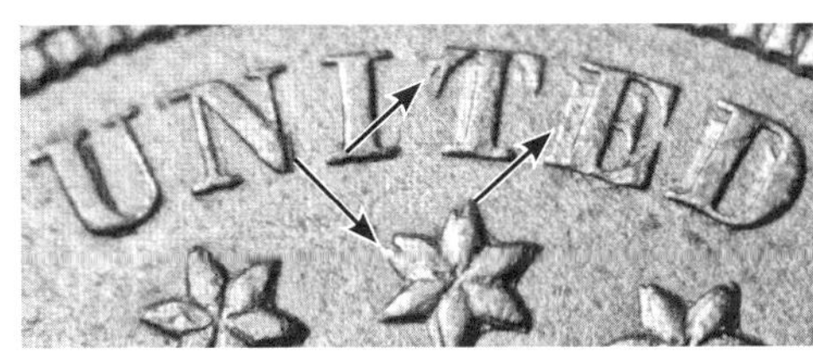

Description: Doubling is evident on all reverse lettering, most stars, and the 5 in the center of the design. The doubling is very unusual, as the spread between the images is in different directions. This doubled-die reverse was created when two different reverse hubs were used. First the die was impressed with Reverse Hub IIa, followed by Reverse Hub IIc.

Comments: This doubled-die reverse is known paired with three different obverse dies. Contrast with FS-802, which is also a dual-hub doubled-die reverse, but is Reverse Hub IIa Over Reverse Hub IIc.

	F-12	VF-20	EF-40	AU-50	MS-60	MS-63	MS-65
VARIETY	$150	$200	$250	$375	$625	$750	$4,375
NORMAL	$60	$80	$100	$150	$250	$300	$1,750

1870 — FS-05-1870-802

VARIETY: Doubled-Die Reverse S1-2001
PUP: Reverse stars, letters
URS-3 • I-5 • L-4

Description: Many reverse stars and letters are doubled. This doubled-die reverse was created when two different reverse hubs were used. First the die was impressed with Reverse Hub IIc, followed by Reverse Hub IIa.

Comments: This variety accounts for the "thought to exist" 1870 with Reverse Hub IIa. In fact, the 1870 Reverse Hub IIa does not exist ***except*** as a doubled-die reverse. There is a second 1870 Reverse Hub IIc over Reverse Hub IIa doubled-die reverse that is slightly less dramatic and slightly more available. Compare the doubling carefully to attribute properly. Contrast this variety with FS-801, which is also a dual-hub doubled-die reverse, but is Reverse Hub IIc Over Reverse Hub IIa.

	F-12	VF-20	EF-40	AU-50	MS-60	MS-63	MS-65
VARIETY	$180	$240	$300	$450	$750	$900	$5,250
NORMAL	$60	$80	$100	$150	$250	$300	$1,750

1871 — FS-05-1871-101 (006)

Variety: Doubled-Die Obverse — **Fletcher:** N/L
PUP: Annulet
URS-4 • I-4 • L-3

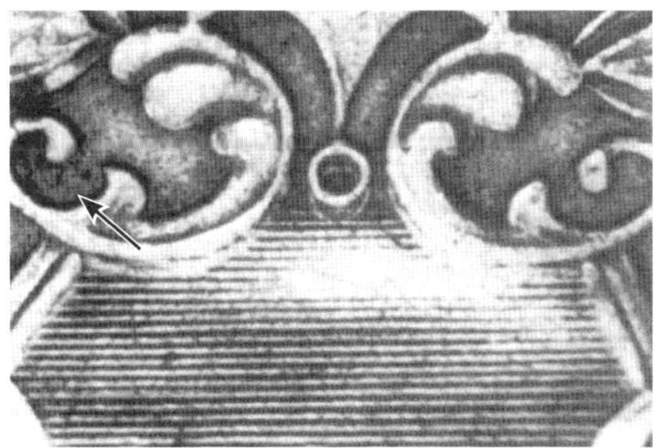

Description: Doubling is evident on the annulet, cross, leaves, and upper shield.

Comments: This is another typical Shield nickel doubled-die obverse.

	F-12	VF-20	EF-40	AU-50	MS-60	MS-63	MS-65
Variety	$450	$645	$840	$1,050	$1,350	$1,875	$6,750
Normal	$150	$215	$280	$350	$450	$625	$2,250

1871 — FS-05-1871-301 (006.5)

Variety: Repunched Date — **Fletcher-02, S1-3000**
PUP: Date
URS-5 • I-3 • L-3

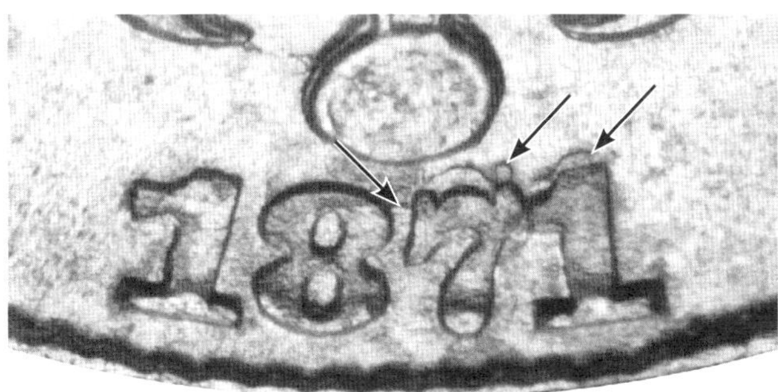

Description: All four digits are evidently repunched, with the secondary digits to the north of the primary digits. Later die states may show on only the 7 and the last 1.

Comments: There is a small, curved, raised line connecting the top of the 8 and the 7. This is likely a small die crack.

	F-12	VF-20	EF-40	AU-50	MS-60	MS-63	MS-65
Variety	$300	$430	$560	$700	$900	$1,250	$4,500
Normal	$150	$215	$280	$350	$450	$625	$2,250

1872 — FS-05-1872-101 (007)

VARIETY: Doubled-Die Obverse — FLETCHER-121, S2-1005
PUP: Annulet
URS-5 • I-3 • L-3

Description: Moderate doubling is evident on the annulet, cross, leaves, and shield, with the secondary image south-southeast of the primary image.

Comments: This date is well known with several doubled dies and repunched dates.

	F-12	VF-20	EF-40	AU-50	MS-60	MS-63	MS-65
VARIETY	$120	$160	$200	$280	$375	$480	$2,400
NORMAL	$75	$100	$125	$175	$235	$300	$1,500

1872 — FS-05-1872-102 (007.1)

VARIETY: Doubled-Die Obverse — FLETCHER-123, S2-1008
PUP: Annulet
URS-5 • I-4 • L-4

Description: Very strong doubling is evident on the annulet, upper shield, and leaves. The horizontal lines protrude into the vertical lines.

Comments: This is a fabulous doubled die, as are many in the Shield nickel series. Date position is essential for correct attribution.

	F-12	VF-20	EF-40	AU-50	MS-60	MS-63	MS-65
VARIETY	$180	$240	$300	$420	$565	$720	$3,600
NORMAL	$75	$100	$125	$175	$235	$300	$1,500

1872 — FS-05-1872-103 (007.2)

VARIETY: Doubled-Die Obverse — FLETCHER-124, S2-1009
PUP: Annulet
URS-5 • I-4 • L-4

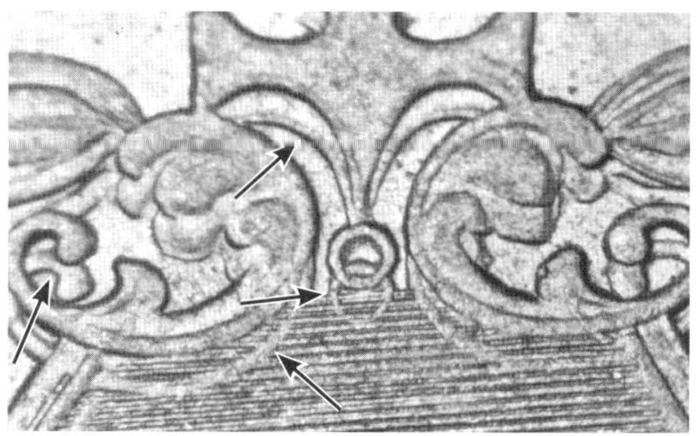
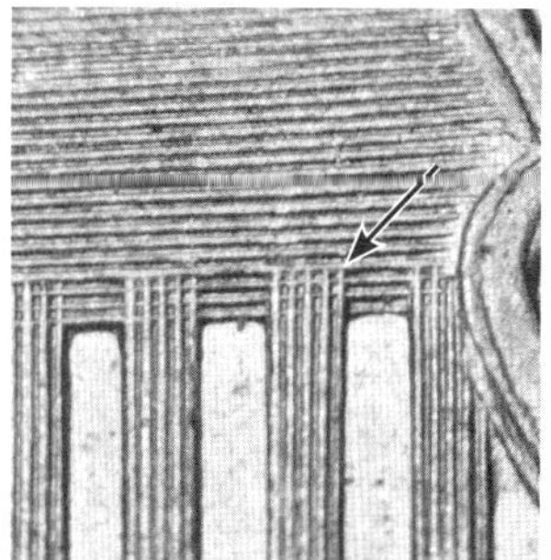

Description: Very strong doubling is evident on the annulet, upper shield, and leaves. The horizontal lines protrude into the vertical lines.

Comments: Compare the photos of the doubling on the annulet for the differences in these varieties.

	F-12	VF-20	EF-40	AU-50	MS-60	MS-63	MS-65
VARIETY	$180	$240	$300	$420	$565	$720	$3,600
NORMAL	$75	$100	$125	$175	$235	$300	$1,500

1872 — FS-05-1872-104 (007.3)

VARIETY: Doubled-Die Obverse — FLETCHER-109, S2-7002
PUP: Annulet
URS-4 • I-4 • L-4

Description: Very strong doubling is evident on the annulet, upper shield, leaves, and berries. The horizontal lines protrude into the vertical lines.

Comments: Compare the photos of the doubling on the annulet for the differences in these varieties.

	F-12	VF-20	EF-40	AU-50	MS-60	MS-63	MS-65
VARIETY	$180	$240	$300	$420	$565	$720	$3,600
NORMAL	$75	$100	$125	$175	$235	$300	$1,500

1872 — FS-05-1872-105 (007.4)

VARIETY: Tripled-Die Obverse — FLETCHER-05, S1-7000
PUP: Annulet, upper shield
URS-4 • I-5 • L-4

Description: Very strong tripling is evident on the annulet, with doubling evident on the upper shield and leaves.

Comments: This was the second tripled-die obverse reported in the series, after the 1876. Others have since been reported.

	F-12	VF-20	EF-40	AU-50	MS-60	MS-63	MS-65
VARIETY	$600	$800	$1,000	$1,400	$1,880	$2,400	$12,000
NORMAL	$75	$100	$125	$175	$235	$300	$1,500

1872 — FS-05-1872-106 (007.5)

VARIETY: Doubled-Die Obverse — FLETCHER-116, S2-1002
PUP: Annulet
URS-4 • I-5 • L-5

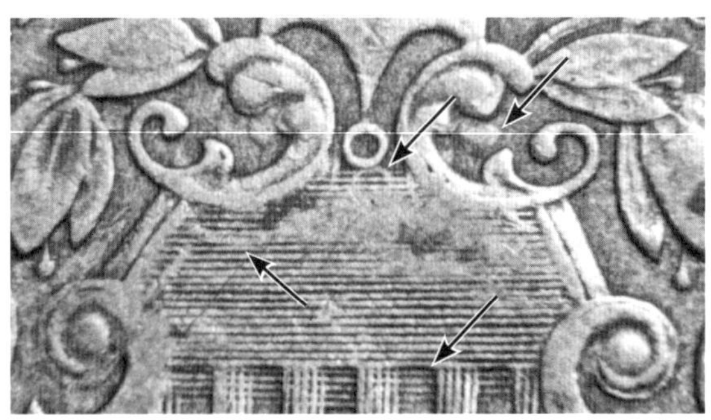

Description: Extremely strong doubling is evident on the annulet, with the top of the secondary annulet barely touching the bottom of the primary annulet. Strong doubling is also visible on the upper shield, leaves, and berries. The horizontal lines protrude far south into the vertical lines.

Comments: This variety was first reported by Dave Brody.

	F-12	VF-20	EF-40	AU-50	MS-60	MS-63	MS-65
VARIETY	$225	$300	$375	$525	$705	$900	$4,500
NORMAL	$75	$100	$125	$175	$235	$300	$1,500

1872 FS-05-1872-107/309

VARIETY: Doubled-Die Obverse, Repunched Date, Misplaced Date S2-7003
PUP: Annulet, date, ball above date
URS-3 • I-5 • L-4

Description: This is probably the wildest variety in the entire Shield nickel series. It has strong doubling on the obverse to the southeast (visible at the annulet, cross, and leaves), a repunched 2 (very far west), and an apparent misplaced 2 in the denticles below the date.

Comments: What more could you ask for in a variety?

	F-12	VF-20	EF-40	AU-50	MS-60	MS-63	MS-65
VARIETY	$225	$300	$375	$525	$705	$900	$4,500
NORMAL	$75	$100	$125	$175	$235	$300	$1,500

1872 FS-05-1872-301 (007.6)

VARIETY: Repunched Date FLETCHER-104, S2-3001
PUP: Date
URS-4 • I-4 • L-4

Description: The secondary digits are evident to the north of the primary digits. The separation increases from left to right.

	F-12	VF-20	EF-40	AU-50	MS-60	MS-63	MS-65
VARIETY	$135	$180	$225	$315	$425	$540	$2,700
NORMAL	$75	$100	$125	$175	$235	$300	$1,500

1872 — FS-05-1872-302 (007.65)

Variety: Repunched Date — S2-4001
PUP: Date
URS-4 • I-4 • L-4

Description: Several secondary 2's are evident behind the 7 and the primary 2. There are at least three 2's in the wrong position.

	F-12	VF-20	EF-40	AU-50	MS-60	MS-63	MS-65
Variety	$135	$180	$225	$315	$425	$540	$2,700
Normal	$75	$100	$125	$175	$235	$300	$1,500

1872 — FS-05-1872-303 (007.7)

Variety: Repunched Date — Fletcher-103, S2-3004
PUP: Date
URS-4 • I-4 • L-4

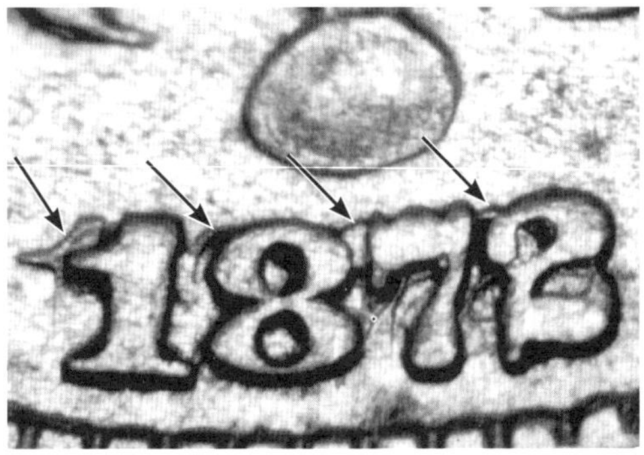

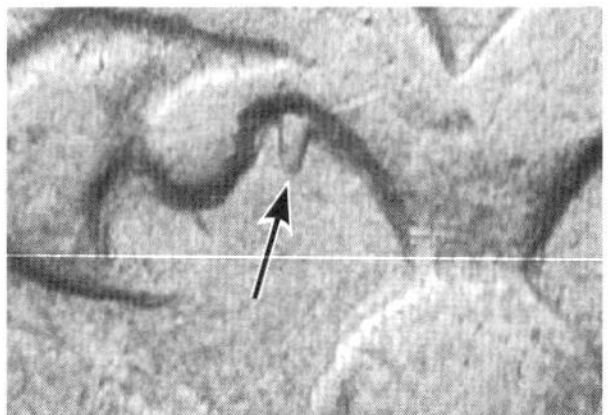

Description: All four secondary digits from the first date punch are evident to the west of the primary digits.

Comments: A "spike" protrudes from the bottom of the shield, just above the left side of the ball. This could be the lower serif of a 7, or simply be a die chip.

	F-12	VF-20	EF-40	AU-50	MS-60	MS-63	MS-65
Variety	$150	$200	$250	$350	$470	$600	$3,000
Normal	$75	$100	$125	$175	$235	$300	$1,500

1872 — FS-05-1872-304 (007.76)

Variety: Repunched Date — Fletcher-03.01, S1-3000
PUP: Date
URS-5 • I-2 • L-3

Description: Secondary digits are evident to the north of the primary 7 and 2.

	F-12	VF-20	EF-40	AU-50	MS-60	MS-63	MS-65
Variety	$120	$160	$200	$280	$376	$480	$2,400
Normal	$75	$100	$125	$175	$235	$300	$1,500

1872 — FS-05-1872-305 (007.77)

Variety: Repunched Date — Fletcher-101.01
PUP: Date
URS-4 • I-2 • L-3

Description: Secondary digits are evident to the west of the primary 7 and 2. Also, the top of an apparent 1 is evident protruding from the denticles below the 8.

	F-12	VF-20	EF-40	AU-50	MS-60	MS-63	MS-65
Variety	$150	$200	$250	$350	$470	$600	$3,000
Normal	$75	$100	$125	$175	$235	$300	$1,500

1872 FS-05-1872-306 (007.9)

VARIETY: Repunched Date FLETCHER-02

PUP: Date

URS-3 • I-3 • L-3

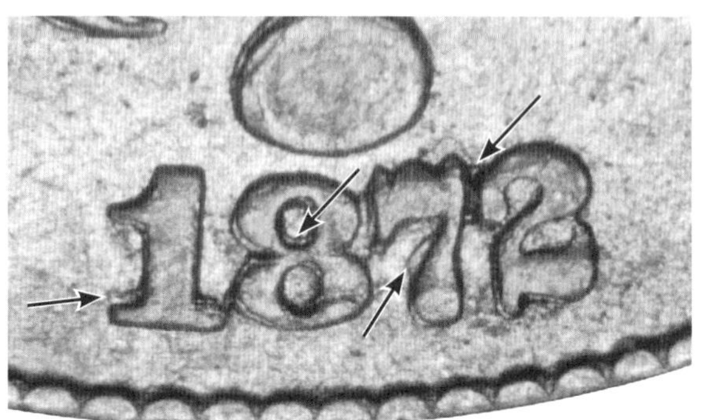

Description: Portions of the secondary digits are evident to the north of the primary 1, 8, and 7.

Comments: Strike doubling is also evident on the digits of the date.

	F-12	VF-20	EF-40	AU-50	MS-60	MS-63	MS-65
VARIETY	$100	$130	$165	$230	$305	$390	$1,950
NORMAL	$75	$100	$125	$175	$235	$300	$1,500

1872 FS-05-1872-307 (007.75)

VARIETY: Misplaced Date FLETCHER-101.02, S2-4000

PUP: Date

URS-4 • I-5 • L-3

Description: Portions of a misplaced 2 are evident in the field immediately to the right of the ball.

	F-12	VF-20	EF-40	AU-50	MS-60	MS-63	MS-65
VARIETY	$300	$400	$500	$700	$940	$1,200	$6,000
NORMAL	$75	$100	$125	$175	$235	$300	$1,500

1872 — FS-05-1872-308 (007.8)

Variety: Small Over Large Date — Fletcher-102, S2-3000

PUP: Date

URS-4 • I-5 • L-5

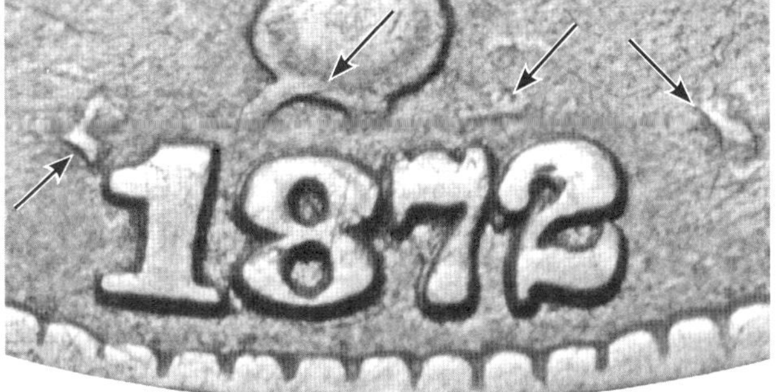

Description: A secondary, larger date punch was first placed into the die, then corrected with the normal date punch for the series. The flag of a 1 is evident northwest of the primary 1, the top of the secondary 8 is evident touching the ball, the top of the secondary 7 is evident northeast of the primary 7, and the upper right curve of a secondary 2 is evident far to the east of the primary 2.

Comments: It has been determined that the secondary, larger date punch was intended for a Liberty Seated dime. As of mid-2015, there are six known examples, the finest graded Extremely Fine.

	F-12	VF-20	EF-40	AU-50	MS-60	MS-63	MS-65
Variety	$750	$1,000	$1,250	*$1,750*	*$2,350*	*$3,000*	*$15,000*
Normal	$75	$100	$125	$175	$235	$300	$1,500

The Cherrypickers' Guide HELPFUL HINTS

Prices provided for varieties are for raw (unslabbed) coins. Varieties correctly attributed, certified, and graded by a third-party grading service may *command higher premiums—but not necessarily. Ultimately, the marketplace of variety collectors determines a coin's value.*

1873, Close (or Closed) 3 — FS-05-1873-101 (008, 008.85)

VARIETY: Doubled-Die Obverse — FLETCHER-04, S1-1002

PUP: Annulet

URS-5 • I-3 • L-3

Description: The secondary image is evident on the annulet, leaves, and cross. The horizontal lines barely encroach into the vertical lines.

Comments: This variety was listed twice in the fourth edition of the ***Cherrypickers' Guide***, as FS-008 and FS-008.85.

	F-12	VF-20	EF-40	AU-50	MS-60	MS-63	MS-65
VARIETY	$95	$160	$225	$320	$520	$935	$4,400
NORMAL	$60	$100	$140	$200	$325	$585	$2,750

1873, Close (or Closed) 3 — FS-05-1873-102 (008.7)

Variety: Doubled-Die Obverse — Fletcher-05, S1-1000
PUP: Annulet
URS-3 • I-5 • L-5

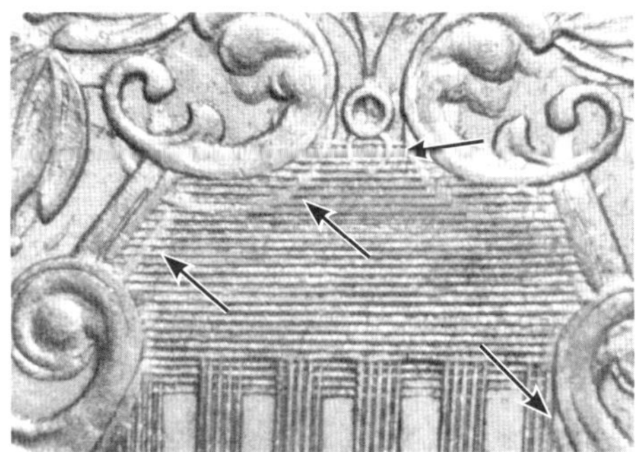

Description: Extremely strong doubling is evident, with the secondary annulet far to the south of the primary annulet, barely touching it. Doubling is also evident on the cross, leaves, shield, and berries.

Comments: This is one of the stronger doubled dies in the Shield nickel series and is on the want-list of virtually every collector. This variety is frequently mistaken for FS-1103. This variety is a Close (or Closed) 3, while FS-1103 is an Open 3.

	F-12	VF-20	EF-40	AU-50	MS-60	MS-63	MS-65
Variety	$180	$300	$420	$600	$975	$1,755	$8,250
Normal	$60	$100	$140	$200	$325	$585	$2,750

1873, Close (or Closed) 3 — FS-05-1873-103 (008.8)

Variety: Doubled-Die Obverse — Fletcher-06, S1-1001
PUP: Horizontal lines below primary lines
URS-3 • I-5 • L-5

Description: Extremely strong doubling is evident, with the secondary annulet far to the south of the primary annulet, not touching it. Very strong doubling is also evident on the cross, leaves, shield, and berries. The horizontal lines protrude far into the vertical lines.

Comments: This is the largest known spread in the series. This variety is frequently mistaken for FS-104. While FS-103 shows a die crack running northwest from the top of the 3, FS-104 shows a die crack running northeast through the ball.

	F-12	VF-20	EF-40	AU-50	MS-60	MS-63	MS-65
Variety	$180	$300	$420	$600	$975	$1,755	$8,250
Normal	$60	$100	$140	$200	$325	$585	$2,750

1873, Close (or Closed) 3 — FS-05-1873-104

Variety: Doubled-Die Obverse — S1-1003
PUP: Annulet
URS-3 • I-5 • L-4

Description: Extremely strong doubling is clearly visible at the annulet, cross, and leaves.

Comments: This variety is frequently mistaken for FS-103. While FS-103 shows a die crack running northwest from the top of the 3, this coin shows a die crack running northeast through the ball.

	F-12	VF-20	EF-40	AU-50	MS-60	MS-63	MS-65
Variety	$145	$240	$335	$480	$780	$1,400	$6,600
Normal	$60	$100	$140	$200	$325	$585	$2,750

1873, Open 3 — FS-05-1873-1101 (008.3)

Variety: Doubled-Die Obverse — Fletcher-113, S2-1002
PUP: Annulet
URS-4 • I-4 • L-4

Description: Very strong doubling is evident on the annulet, cross, leaves, and shield, with the spread to the west.

	F-12	VF-20	EF-40	AU-50	MS-60	MS-63	MS-65
Variety	$210	$280	$350	$490	$735	$1,050	$7,000
Normal	$60	$80	$100	$140	$210	$300	$2,000

1873, Open 3 — FS-05-1873-1102 (008.5)

VARIETY: Doubled-Die Obverse, Misplaced Date — FLETCHER-102, S2-7001
PUP: Annulet, date
URS-5 • I-5 • L-5

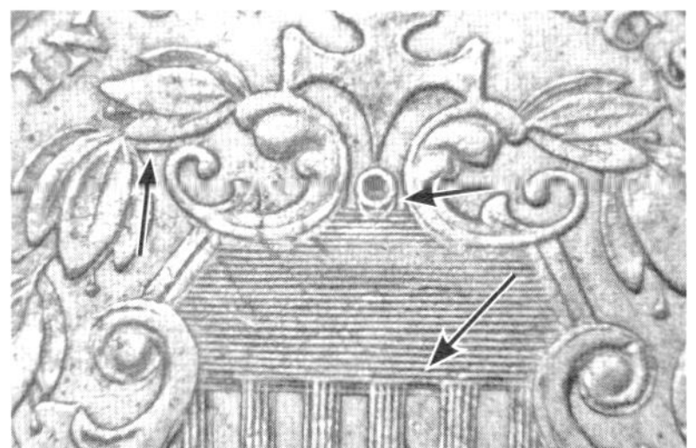

Description: The doubling is typical for the series, with a secondary annulet evident to the south of the primary. Doubling is also visible on the leaves, cross, and shield. Portions of several digits are evident protruding from the denticles below the date.

	F-12	VF-20	EF-40	AU-50	MS-60	MS-63	MS-65
VARIETY	$180	$240	$300	$420	$630	$900	$6,000
NORMAL	$60	$80	$100	$140	$210	$300	$2,000

1873, Open 3 — FS-05-1873-1103

VARIETY: Doubled-Die Obverse — S2-1003
PUP: Annulet
URS-2 • I-5 • L-4

Description: Extremely strong doubling is clearly visible at the annulet, cross, and leaves.

Comments: This variety is frequently mistaken for FS-102. FS-102 is a Close (or Closed) 3 while this is an Open 3.

	F-12	VF-20	EF-40	AU-50	MS-60	MS-63	MS-65
VARIETY	$145	$190	$240	$335	$505	$720	$4,800
NORMAL	$60	$80	$100	$140	$210	$300	$2,000

1873, Open 3 — FS-05-1873-1301 (009)

Variety: Repunched Date (Large Over Small) — Fletcher-106, S2-3000
PUP: Date
URS-3 • I-5 • L-5

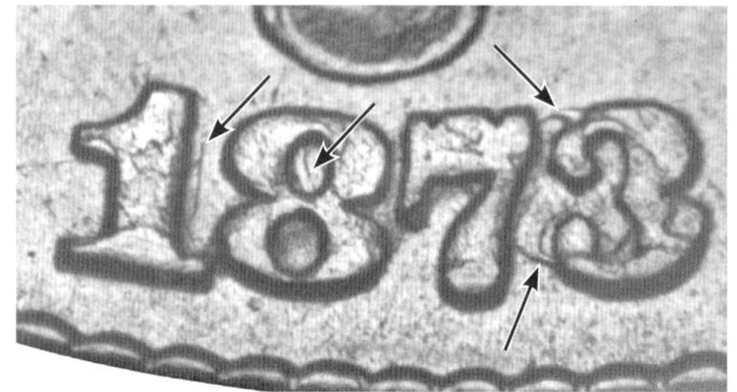

Description: The initial date punch was likely that intended for a three-cent piece or half dime. The primary date punch was normal for the date, creating a Large Date Over Small Date variety. The secondary 1 is evident between the primary 1 and 8, and a secondary 3 is evident between the primary 7 and 3.

Comments: This is a very rare variety, always sought by the many Shield nickel specialists.

	F-12	VF-20	EF-40	AU-50	MS-60	MS-63	MS-65
Variety	$600	$800	$1,000	$1,400	$2,100	$3,000	$20,000
Normal	$60	$80	$100	$140	$210	$300	$2,000

1873, Open 3 — FS-05-1873-1302 (009.3)

Variety: Repunched Date — Fletcher-103, S2-3003
PUP: Date
URS-3 • I-3 • L-3

Description: The flag of a secondary 1 is evident high between the primary 1 and 8.

	F-12	VF-20	EF-40	AU-50	MS-60	MS-63	MS-65
Variety	$120	$160	$200	$280	$420	$600	$4,000
Normal	$60	$80	$100	$140	$210	$300	$2,000

1873, Open 3 — FS-05-1873-1303 (009.5)

VARIETY: Repunched Date — FLETCHER-110, S2-3001
PUP: Date
URS-4 • I-4 • L-4

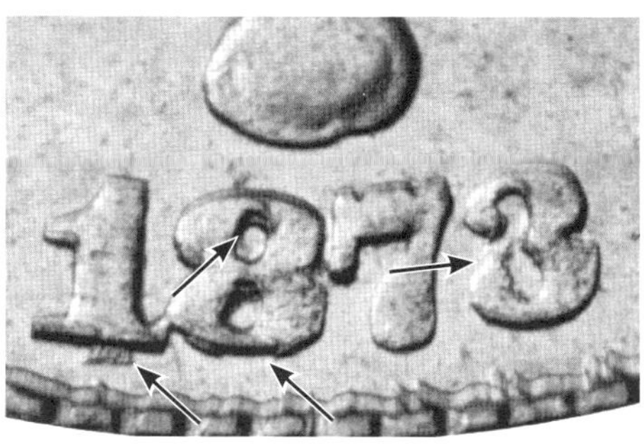
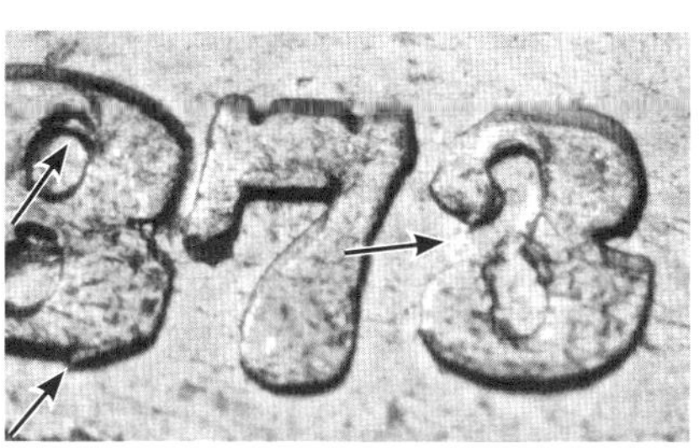

Description: A secondary 1 protrudes from the bottom of the primary 1, a secondary 8 barely protrudes from the bottom of the primary 8, and what appears to be a secondary 3 is evident inside the primary 3.

Comments: This is a very interesting repunched date. It may, in time, prove to be an 1873, 3 Over 2 overdate.

	F-12	VF-20	EF-40	AU-50	MS-60	MS-63	MS-65
VARIETY	$110	$145	$180	$250	$380	$540	$3,600
NORMAL	$60	$80	$100	$140	$210	$300	$2,000

1873, Open 3 — FS-05-1873-1304 (009.7)

VARIETY: Repunched Date — FLETCHER-108.01, S2-3002
PUP: Date
URS-2 • I-3 • L-4

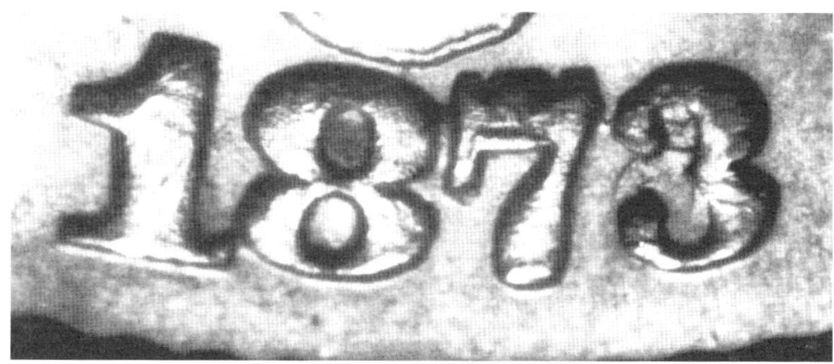

Description: A secondary 7 is evident between the primary 7 and 3. A secondary 3 is evident far to the south but within the opening of the primary 3.

Comments: This is a very unusual repunched date.

	F-12	VF-20	EF-40	AU-50	MS-60	MS-63	MS-65
VARIETY	$120	$160	$200	$280	$420	$600	$4,000
NORMAL	$60	$80	$100	$140	$210	$300	$2,000

1874 — FS-05-1874-101 (010)

VARIETY: Doubled-Die Obverse — FLETCHER-05, S1-1001
PUP: Annulet
URS-6 • I-3 • L-3

Description: Typical Shield nickel doubling is evident on the annulet, cross, upper shield, and leaves. The horizontal lines barely creep into the vertical lines.

	F-12	VF-20	EF-40	AU-50	MS-60	MS-63	MS-65
VARIETY	$105	$130	$200	$270	$400	$520	$2,400
NORMAL	$65	$80	$125	$170	$250	$325	$1,500

1874 — FS-05-1874-102 (010.4)

VARIETY: Doubled-Die Obverse — FLETCHER-12, S1-1003
PUP: Annulet, motto
URS-4 • I-3 • L-3

Description: Typical Shield nickel doubling is evident on the annulet, cross, upper shield, and leaves. The horizontal lines barely creep into the vertical lines. Doubling is also evident on IN GOD WE TRUST.

Comments: This particular variety exhibits the strongest known doubling of the motto (IN GOD WE TRUST) of any Shield nickel doubled die.

	F-12	VF-20	EF-40	AU-50	MS-60	MS-63	MS-65
VARIETY	$260	$320	$500	$680	$1,000	$1,300	$6,000
NORMAL	$65	$80	$125	$170	$250	$325	$1,500

1874 — FS-05-1874-103 (010.5)

VARIETY: Doubled-Die Obverse — FLETCHER-08, S1-1002
PUP: Annulet
URS-3 • I-4 • L-3

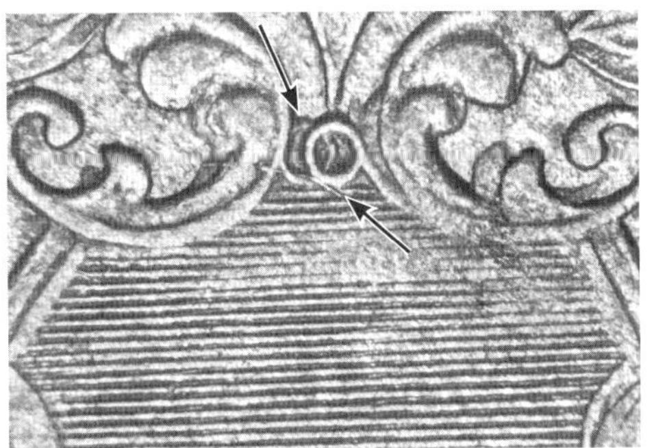

Description: Very strong doubling is evident to the west on the annulet, cross, upper shield, leaves, and berries.

Comments: This variety was discovered by J.T. Stanton in January of 1990. There is a die scratch on the lower portion of the annulet. It is unusual for the doubling to be to the west, as on this example.

	F-12	VF-20	EF-40	AU-50	MS-60	MS-63	MS-65
VARIETY	$260	$320	$500	$680	$1,000	$1,300	$6,000
NORMAL	$65	$80	$125	$170	$250	$325	$1,500

1874 — FS-05-1874-104 (010.6)

VARIETY: Doubled-Die Obverse — FLETCHER-09.01, S1-1007
PUP: Annulet
URS-3 • I-4 • L-5

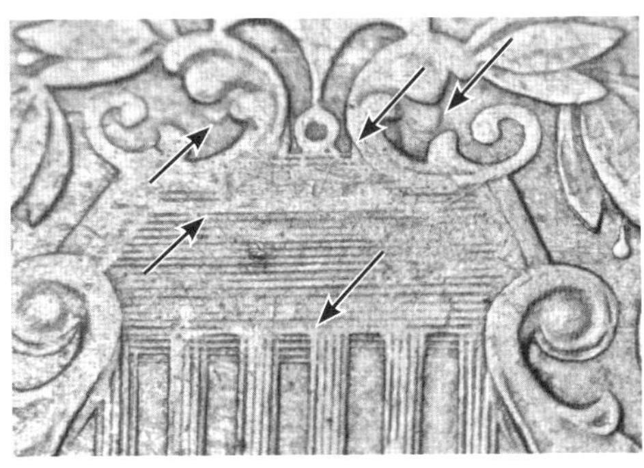

Description: This is a very strong doubled die, with the top of the secondary annulet barely touching the lower portion of the primary annulet. The doubling is also evident on the upper shield, cross, leaves, and berries. The horizontal lines protrude into the vertical lines.

	F-12	VF-20	EF-40	AU-50	MS-60	MS-63	MS-65
VARIETY	$155	$195	$300	$410	$600	$780	$3,600
NORMAL	$65	$80	$125	$170	$250	$325	$1,500

1874 — FS-05-1874-301 (010.7)

Variety: Repunched Date — Fletcher-02, S1-3001
PUP: Date
URS-6 • I-2 • L-3

Description: A secondary 1 and secondary 8 are evident to the north of the primary digits. The primary 8 touches the ball, with the secondary 8 "broken" around the ball.

Comments: The date is punched farther right than a normal position.

	F-12	VF-20	EF-40	AU-50	MS-60	MS-63	MS-65
Variety	$100	$120	$190	$255	$375	$490	$2,250
Normal	$65	$80	$125	$170	$250	$325	$1,500

1874 — FS-05-1874-302 (010.8)

Variety: Repunched Date — Fletcher-01
PUP: Date
URS-2 • I-3 • L-3

Description: The top serif or "flag" of a secondary 1 is evident protruding from the left side of the primary 1's upright.

Comments: The specimens we've seen exhibit very strong strike doubling on the date.

	F-12	VF-20	EF-40	AU-50	MS-60	MS-63	MS-65
Variety	$120	$145	$225	$305	$450	$585	$2,700
Normal	$65	$80	$125	$170	$250	$325	$1,500

1875 — FS-05-1875-101 (011)

VARIETY: Doubled-Die Obverse — FLETCHER-04, S1-1002

PUP: Annulet

URS-5 • I-4 • L-4

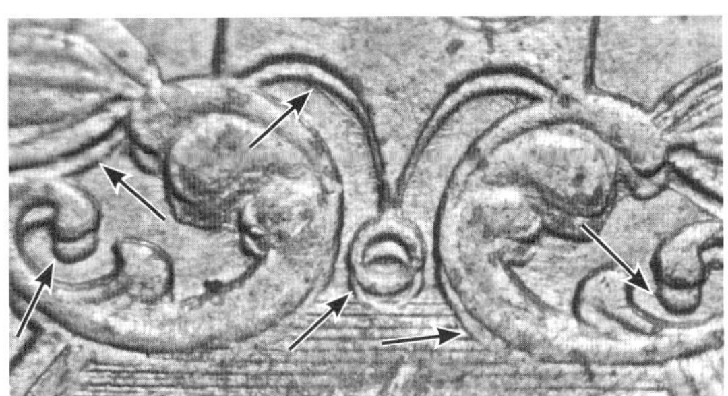

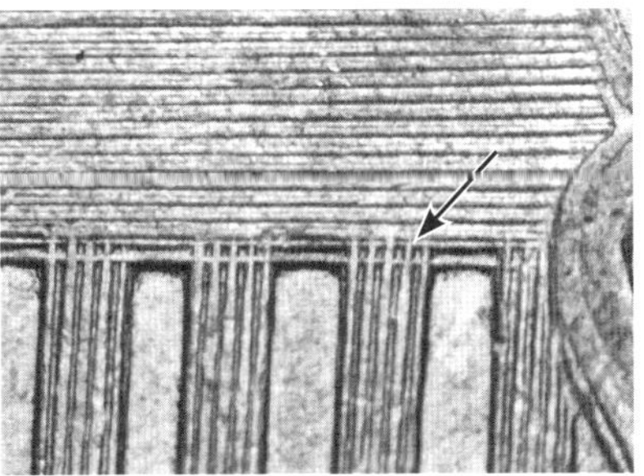

Description: Doubling is evident on the annulet, cross, leaves, berries, and upper shield. The horizontal lines protrude into the vertical lines.

	F-12	VF-20	EF-40	AU-50	MS-60	MS-63	MS-65
VARIETY	$170	$220	$270	$375	$470	$615	$2,890
NORMAL	$100	$130	$160	$220	$275	$360	$1,700

1875 — FS-05-1875-102 (011.3)

VARIETY: Doubled-Die Obverse — FLETCHER-05, S1-1000

PUP: Annulet

URS-4 • I-4 • L-4

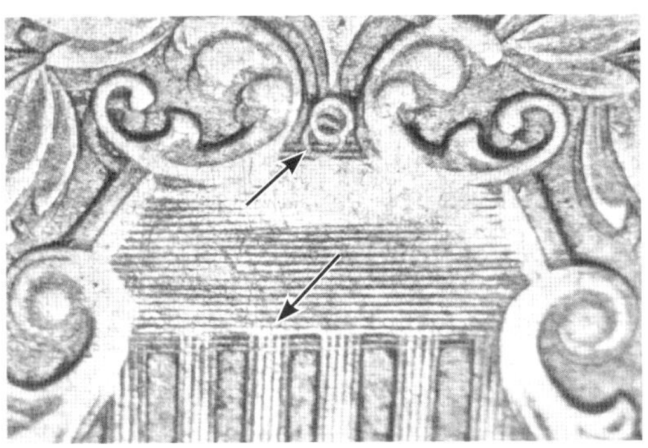

Description: Doubling is evident on the annulet, cross, upper shield, leaves, and berries. The horizontal lines protrude into the vertical lines.

Comments: This is a typical but very strong doubled die for the Shield nickel series.

	F-12	VF-20	EF-40	AU-50	MS-60	MS-63	MS-65
VARIETY	$240	$315	$385	$530	$660	$865	$4,080
NORMAL	$100	$130	$160	$220	$275	$360	$1,700

1875 — FS-05-1875-103 (011.5)

Variety: Doubled-Die Obverse, Repunched Date — Fletcher-03, S1-7000
PUP: Annulet, date
URS-4 • I-3 • L-3

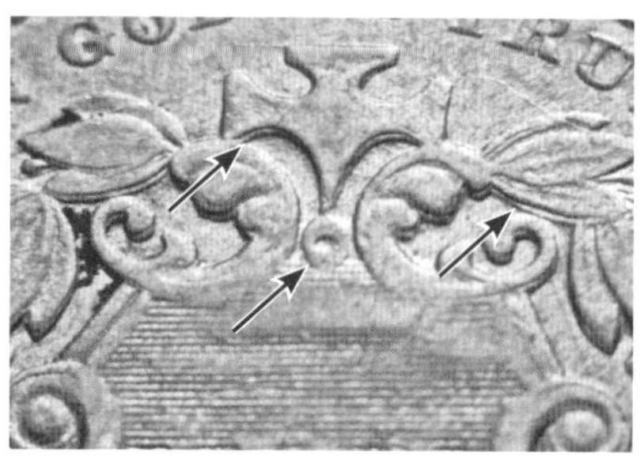

Description: Moderate doubling is evident on the annulet, upper shield, cross, leaves, and berries. The horizontal lines protrude into the vertical lines. A secondary 7 and 5 are visible protruding from the tops of the primary digits.

	F-12	VF-20	EF-40	AU-50	MS-60	MS-63	MS-65
Variety	$200	$260	$320	$440	$550	$720	$3,400
Normal	$100	$130	$160	$220	$275	$360	$1,700

1876 — FS-05-1876-101 (012)

Variety: Tripled-Die Obverse — Fletcher-04, S1-1000
PUP: Annulet
URS-6 • I-5 • L-5

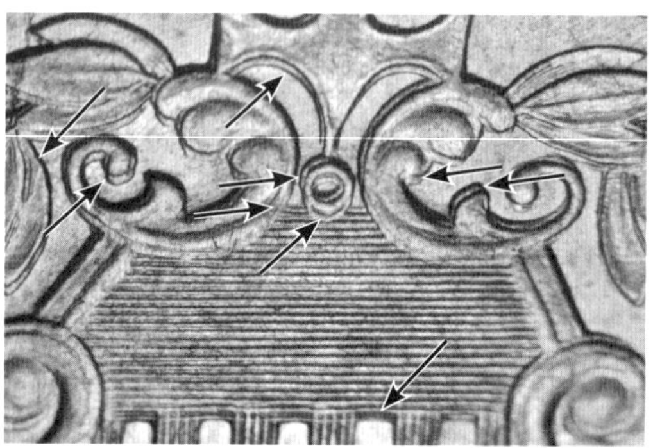

Description: This is a spectacular variety with the tripled image most evident on the annulet to the north and south. Doubling is evident on the upper shield, cross, leaves, and berries. The horizontal lines protrude into the vertical lines.

	F-12	VF-20	EF-40	AU-50	MS-60	MS-63	MS-65
Variety	$400	$575	$750	$1,000	$1,250	$1,625	$6,250
Normal	$80	$115	$150	$200	$250	$325	$1,250

1876 — FS-05-1876-102 (012.1)

VARIETY: Doubled-Die Obverse — FLETCHER-05, S1-1001
PUP: Annulet
URS-5 • I-3 • L-3

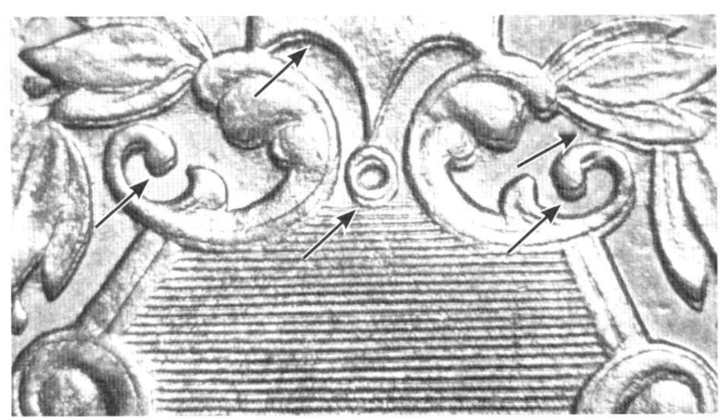

Description: Secondary images are evident on the annulet, cross, upper shield, leaves, and berries. The horizontal lines protrude into the vertical lines.

Comments: This is another typical doubled die for the series.

	F-12	VF-20	EF-40	AU-50	MS-60	MS-63	MS-65
VARIETY	$130	$185	$240	$320	$400	$520	$2,000
NORMAL	$80	$115	$150	$200	$250	$325	$1,250

1876 — FS-05-1876-103

VARIETY: Doubled-Die Obverse, Repunched Date — FLETCHER-08, S1-7000
PUP: Annulet, Date
URS-3 • I-3 • L-3

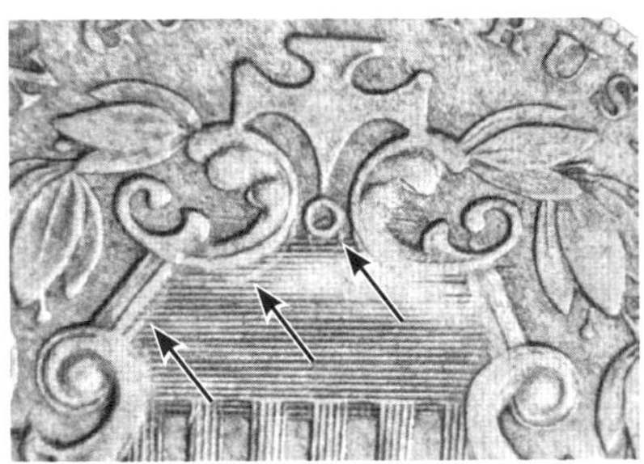

Description: Moderate doubling is evident on the annulet, the lower right of the cross, the right leaf clusters, and very slightly on the right side of the shield. The repunched date is evident by the base of a secondary 1 visible to the west of the primary 1's base.

Comments: To the best of our knowledge, there are only four specimens known.

	F-12	VF-20	EF-40	AU-50	MS-60	MS-63	MS-65
VARIETY	$145	$210	$270	$360	$450	$585	$2,250
NORMAL	$80	$115	$150	$200	$250	$325	$1,250

1876 FS-05-1876-104/301

VARIETY: Doubled-Die Obverse, Repunched Date FLETCHER-08, S1-7000
PUP: Annulet, date
URS-1 • I-5 • L-4

Description: Extremely strong doubling to the southeast is clearly visible at the annulet, cross, and leaves. This variety also has a repunched date, with the foot of the secondary 1 visible to the west of the primary 1. There are so many die polishing lines behind the area of the cross that it looks like extra shield lines.

Comments: So far, this is a unique variety in two ways. Only one example has been reported, and no other Shield nickel shows die polishing lines like this one.

	F-12	VF-20	EF-40	AU-50	MS-60	MS-63	MS-65
VARIETY	(unique)						
NORMAL	$80	$115	$150	$200	$250	$325	$1,250

1876 FS-05-1876-401

VARIETY: Engraver Error ("The Bleeder") FLETCHER-09, S1-8000
PUP: Horizontal shield lines
URS-5 • I-4 • L-4

Description: Multiple vertical lines cut through the horizontal lines of the shield due to an engraver slipping and cutting the die.

Comments: This variety is popularly called "The Bleeder." It is the only known variety of its kind in the Shield nickel series.

	F-12	VF-20	EF-40	AU-50	MS-60	MS-63	MS-65
VARIETY	$160	$230	$300	$400	$500	$650	$2,500
NORMAL	$80	$115	$150	$200	$250	$325	$1,250

1882 — FS-05-1882-101

VARIETY: Doubled-Die Obverse — FLETCHER-19, S1-1000
PUP: Annulet
URS-1 • I-4 • L-3

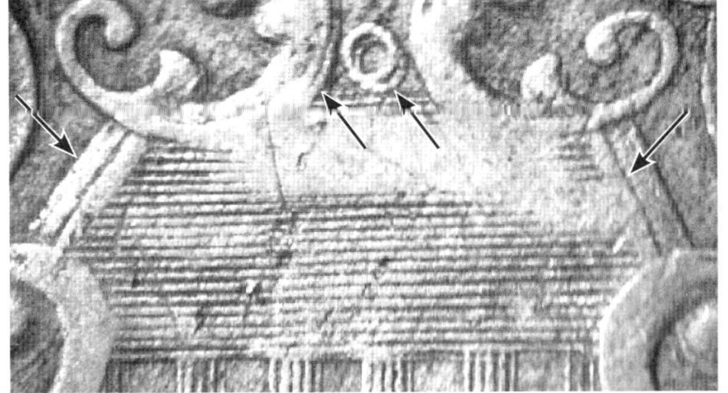

Description: Moderate doubling is evident on the annulet, the lower right of the cross, the right leaf clusters, and very slightly on the right side of the shield.

Comments: To the best of our knowledge, the discovery specimen is the only known example of this variety.

	F-12	VF-20	EF-40	AU-50	MS-60	MS-63	MS-65
VARIETY	(unique)						
NORMAL	$35	$50	$65	$110	$150	$225	$725

1882 — FS-05-1882-301 (012.5)

VARIETY: Repunched Date — FLETCHER-17.01
PUP: Date
URS-4 • I-3 • L-3

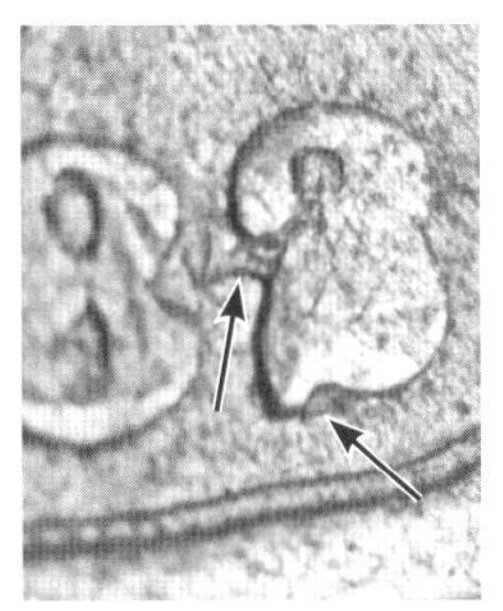

Description: The upper portion of a secondary 2 is evident low between the primary 8 and 2.

Comments: This repunched date (and other 1882 nickels with filled 2's) is often incorrectly identified as an 1883, 3 Over 2 overdate. Don't be confused!

	F-12	VF-20	EF-40	AU-50	MS-60	MS-63	MS-65
VARIETY	$88	$125	$165	$275	$375	$565	$1,815
NORMAL	$35	$50	$65	$110	$150	$225	$725

1882 — FS-05-1882-302

VARIETY: Repunched Date — FLETCHER-02, S1-3009

PUP: Date

URS-3 • I-2 • L-3

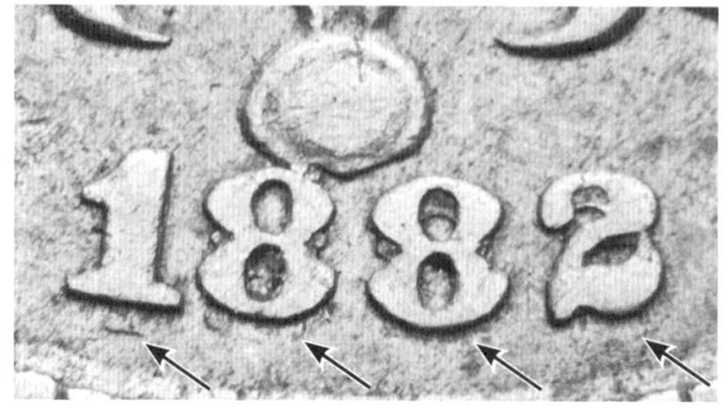

Description: This is a very strong repunched date, with secondary digits evident far to the south of the primary digits.

Comments: This is a relatively new discovery, located shortly after publication of the fourth edition of the ***Cherrypickers' Guide***.

	F-12	VF-20	EF-40	AU-50	MS-60	MS-63	MS-65
VARIETY	$42	$60	$78	$135	$180	$270	$870
NORMAL	$35	$50	$65	$110	$150	$225	$725

1882 — FS-05-1882-999

VARIETY: Die Chip — FLETCHER: N/L, S1-8001

PUP: Date

URS-50 • I-0 • L-0

Description: The 2 of the date is filled, caused by a die chip. Various stages are known, and more than one die was affected.

Comments: This is a common die chip on a common coin and is not an 1883, 3 Over 2 overdate! We list this common variety solely to help collectors avoid purchasing it or a similar coin errantly attributed as an 1883, 3 Over 2 overdate. This coin is worth no more than a normal 1882 Shield nickel! The photos show two different coins with different stages of filling on the 2.

	F-12	VF-20	EF-40	AU-50	MS-60	MS-63	MS-65
VARIETY	$35	$50	$65	$110	$150	$225	$725
NORMAL	$35	$50	$65	$110	$150	$225	$725

1883 — FS-05-1883-301 (013)

Variety: Overdate — Fletcher-08, S1-5001
PUP: Date
URS-4 • I-5 • L-5

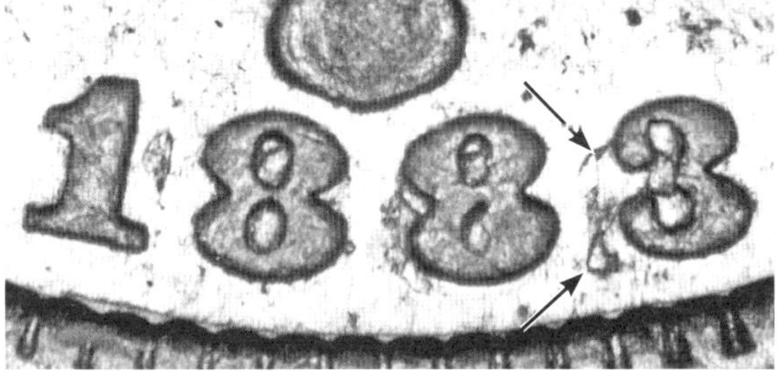

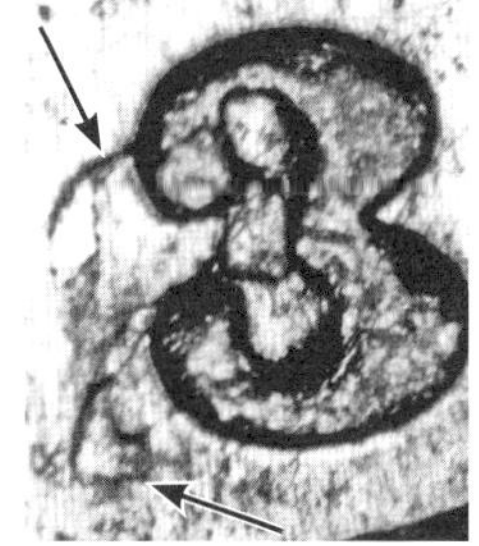

Description: The left half of an underlying 2 is evident between the last 8 and the 3. Secondary digits are also visible on the two 8's.

Comments: Compare this and the four other listed varieties. Additionally, read the text associated with FS-05-1882-999 on the previous page. This is the most visible and desirable of the overdate varieties.

	F-12	VF-20	EF-40	AU-50	MS-60	MS-63	MS-65
Variety	$410	$650	$925	$1,400	$1,800	$2,000	$5,000+
Normal	$35	$50	$65	$110	$150	$225	$725

1883 — FS-05-1883-302 (013.1)

Variety: Overdate — Fletcher-09, S1-5002
PUP: Date
URS-8 • I-5 • L-5

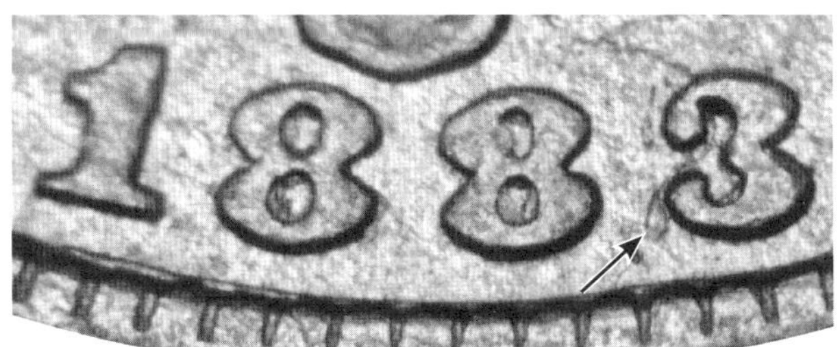

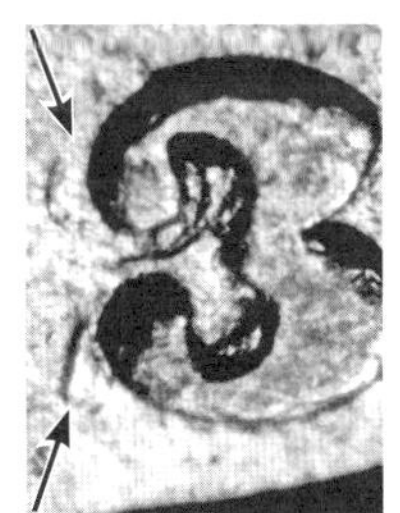

Description: The underlying 2 on this variety is evident to the west of the 3, but not as far left as on FS-301. The lower-left curve of the 2 is most evident. Secondary digits are also visible on the two 8's.

Comments: Compare this and the four other listed varieties. Additionally, read the text associated with FS-05-1882-999 on the previous page.

	F-12	VF-20	EF-40	AU-50	MS-60	MS-63	MS-65
Variety	$410	$650	$925	$1,400	$1,800	$2,000	$5,000+
Normal	$35	$50	$65	$110	$150	$225	$725

1883 — FS-05-1883-303 (013.2)

VARIETY: Overdate — FLETCHER-10, S1-5003
PUP: Date
URS-7 • I-5 • L-5

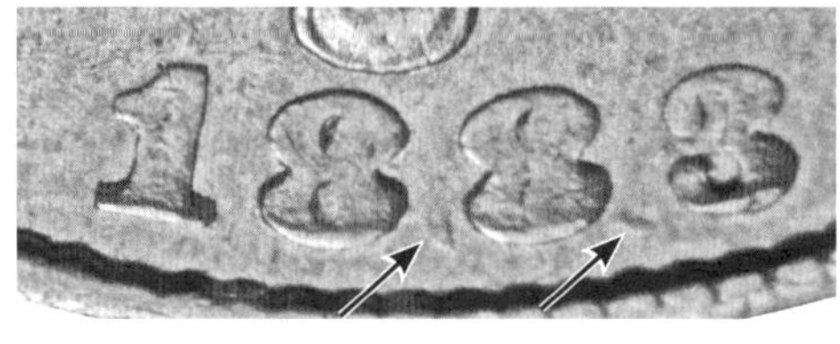

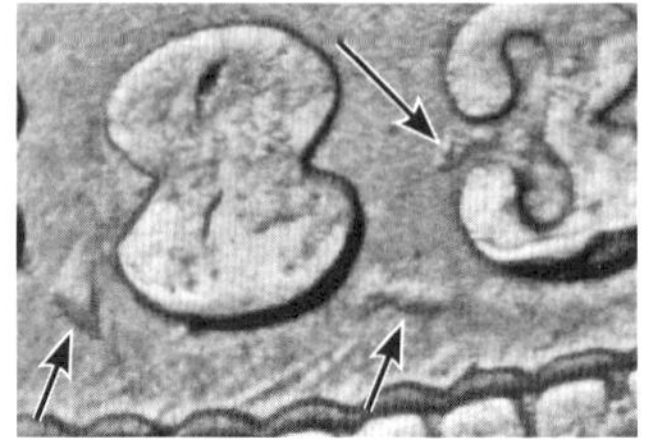

Description: The underlying 2 on this variety is evident far to the west of the 3; the lower-left portion of the 2 is most evident, almost touching the 8. The lower portion of a secondary 8 is also evident between the two primary 8's. Some specimens have a die crack running from the rim at seven o'clock to the rim at six o'clock, and touching the bottom of the 1 and the first 8. Still-later die states show a full cud in this area.

Comments: This is likely the most common of the five known varieties. Some specialists feel this die may represent as much as 75 percent of all 1883, 3 Over 2 overdates. Compare this and the other four listed varieties. Additionally, read the text associated with FS-05-1882-999.

	F-12	VF-20	EF-40	AU-50	MS-60	MS-63	MS-65
VARIETY	$410	$650	$925	$1,400	$1,800	$2,000	$5,000+
NORMAL	$35	$50	$65	$110	$150	$225	$725

1883 — FS-05-1883-304 (013.3)

VARIETY: Overdate — FLETCHER-08.01, S1-5004
PUP: Date
URS-6 • I-5 • L-5

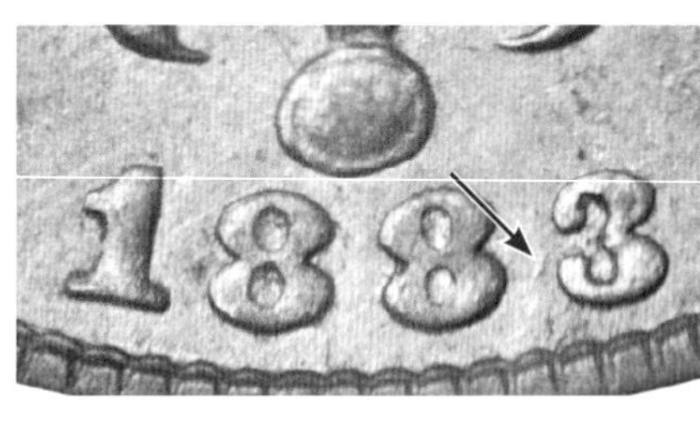

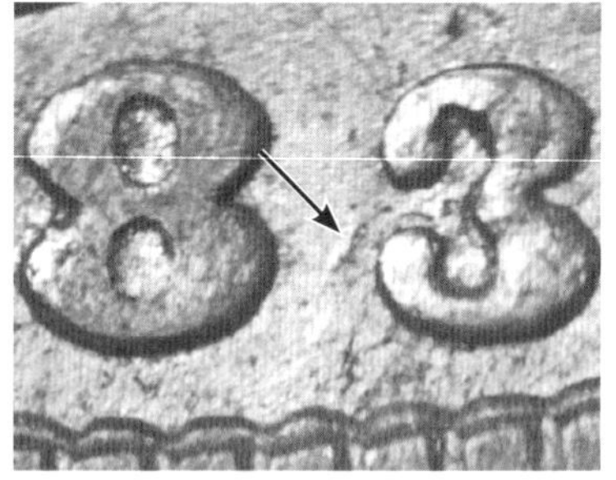

Description: The underlying 2 on this variety is weak but visible to the west of the 3. This is similar to the previous listing, but the 2 is not quite as far west. The lower-left curve of the 2 is most evident. Secondary digits are also visible on the two 8's.

Comments: Compare this and the four other listed varieties. Additionally, read the text associated with FS-05-1882-999. Evidence of the overdate diminishes in lower grades.

	F-12	VF-20	EF-40	AU-50	MS-60	MS-63	MS-65
VARIETY	$410	$650	$925	$1,400	$1,800	$2,000	$5,000+
NORMAL	$35	$50	$65	$110	$150	$225	$725

1883 — FS-05-1883-305

VARIETY: Overdate — FLETCHER-07, S1-5000
PUP: Date
URS-6 • I-4 • L-5

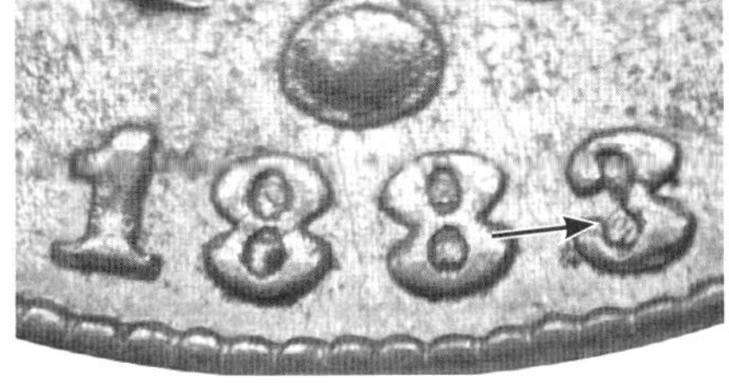

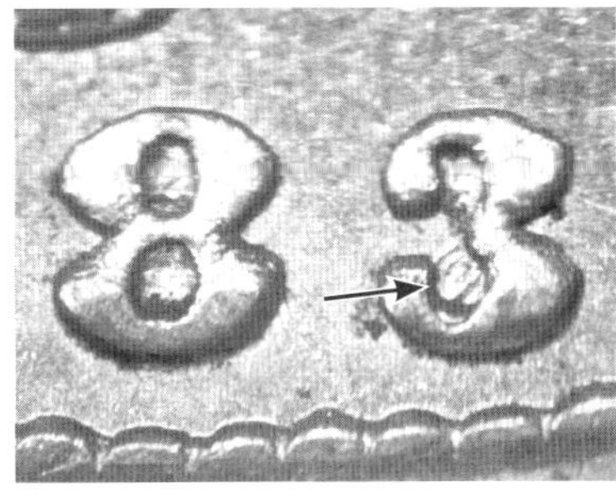

Description: The 2 is centered under the 3. The left curve of the 2 is visible connecting the center point of the 3 with the tip of the lower serif. The lower-left corner of the 2 is visible protruding from the lower-left portion of the 3. This is the only one of the five known overdates where the 2 is not between the last 8 and the 3.

Comments: Compare this and the four other listed varieties. Additionally, read the text associated with FS-05-1882-999.

	F-12	VF-20	EF-40	AU-50	MS-60	MS-63	MS-65
VARIETY	$410	$650	$925	$1,400	$1,800	$2,000	$5,000+
NORMAL	$35	$50	$65	$110	$150	$225	$725

1883 — FS-05-1883-311 (012.8)

VARIETY: Repunched Date — FLETCHER-04, S1-3000
PUP: Date
URS-4 • I-4 • L-3

Description: The base of a secondary 1 is evident slightly below and between the 1 and the first 8.

	F-12	VF-20	EF-40	AU-50	MS-60	MS-63	MS-65
VARIETY	$70	$100	$130	$220	$300	$450	$1,450
NORMAL	$35	$50	$65	$110	$150	$225	$725

1883 — FS-05-1883-312 (012.9)

Variety: Repunched Date — Fletcher-02, S1-3001
PUP: Date
URS-7 • I-3 • L-3

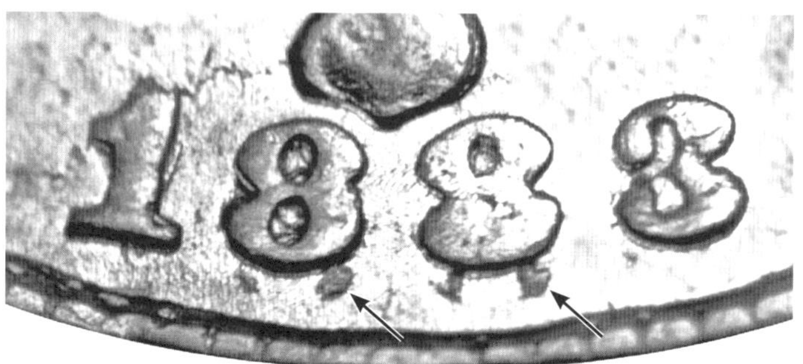

Description: Repunching is evident south of the primary date.

Comments: This variety can be found with some searching.

	F-12	VF-20	EF-40	AU-50	MS-60	MS-63	MS-65
Variety	$53	$75	$100	$165	$225	$340	$1,090
Normal	$35	$50	$65	$110	$150	$225	$725

The Cherrypickers' Guide HELPFUL HINTS

Over time, certain Cherrypickers' Guide *varieties have proven to be of low collector interest, and we have slated these for removal from the listings. However, these varieties will retain their Fivaz-Stanton number and continue to be listed in future editions' cross-reference appendix. Other varieties have been "debunked"—that is, they have been proven by experts to either not be true varieties, not be legitimate Mint issues, or not exist at all. These have been removed from the listings in this edition and will not retain their Fivaz-Stanton number. A full list of varieties either slated to be removed or debunked appears after the introductory text of each section.*

Liberty Head Nickels, 1883–1912

The first edition of the *Cherrypickers' Guide*, published in 1990, included a single Liberty Head nickel variety—the 1887 doubled-die reverse.

Since then, the number of listed Liberty Head nickel die varieties has slowly grown. By the fourth edition, 10 were listed. The fifth edition included a few more, and, as predicted in that book, the section is larger again in the current volume. We expect this section to expand as the hobby community catches on to this 30-year series and its notable repunched dates, doubled dies, and other varieties.

Interest in the series has risen with the publication of references including the *Complete Guide to Shield and Liberty Head Nickels*, by Gloria Peters and Cynthia Mohon, and the *Guide Book of Shield and Liberty Head Nickels*, by Q. David Bowers. The regular edition of the *Guide Book of United States Coins* (the hobby's best-selling "Red Book") doesn't include any Liberty Head nickel die varieties in its listings, but the *Guide Book of United States Coins, Deluxe Edition* does. That kind of publicity in a widely distributed coin-collecting publication helps spread the word about the more popular die varieties.

The Barber Coin Collectors' Society is a nonprofit group of collectors interested in the coins designed by Charles E. Barber, who was chief engraver of the U.S. Mint from 1879 to 1917. Barber's best-known designs might be those of the suite of dimes, quarters, and half dollars that were minted from 1892 to 1916 (or 1915 for the halves). But he was also the designer of the Liberty Head nickel, so the BCCS is a club for collectors of this series, as well. Explore its Web site at www.barbercoins.org; you'll find a membership application there. The Society's annual meeting is at the American Numismatic Association World's Fair of Money (the ANA's summer show, held in August). It also holds regional meetings at the winter Florida United Numismatists show, the Whitman Baltimore Expo, and other coin conventions. Its meetings frequently include educational programs. In addition, the Society publishes a quarterly journal with informative articles, detailed photographs, real-world advice for collectors, member stories, and other valuable content.

Articles related to Liberty Head nickels sometimes appear in the larger hobby publications, such as *The Numismatist* (www.money.org/the-numismatist), *Coin World* (www.coinworld.com), *Numismatic News* (www.numismaticnews.net), *COINage Magazine* (www.coinagemag.com), and *Coins Magazine*. These coins are also sometimes discussed in online forums like the Collectors Universe Message Boards (forums.collectors.com) and the Collectors Society Message Boards (boards.collectors-society.com).

Newly Listed Varieties

Fivaz-Stanton Number	Variety	Page No.
FS-05-1906-801	DDR	302

1883, No Cents / With Cents FS-05-1883-1301 (013.7)

Variety: Repunched Date Breen: N/L
PUP: Date
URS-4 • I-3 • L-3

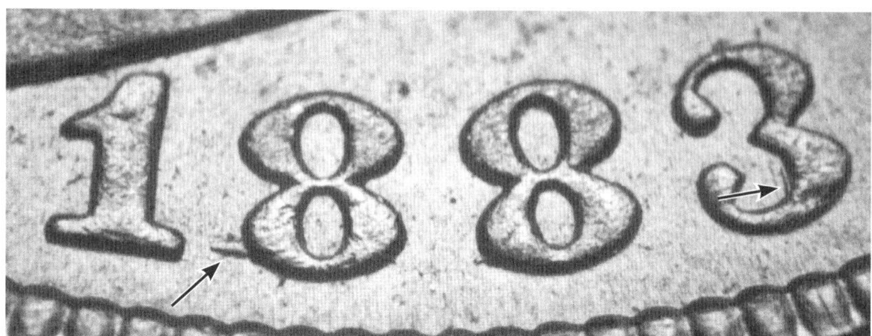

Description: The base of a secondary 1 is evident protruding from the lower-left side of the first 8.

Comments: This is a really interesting repunched date, with the position one digit off to the right. This die variety is known on both No Cents and With Cents issues, with the latter being more common.

	VF-20	EF-40	AU-50	MS-60	MS-63	MS-65
Variety	$20	$35	$50	$75	$100	$275
Normal	$11	$15	$18	$35	$50	$225

1883, No Cents FS-05-1883-1302

Variety: Repunched Date Breen: N/L
PUP: Date
URS-3 • I-3 • L-3

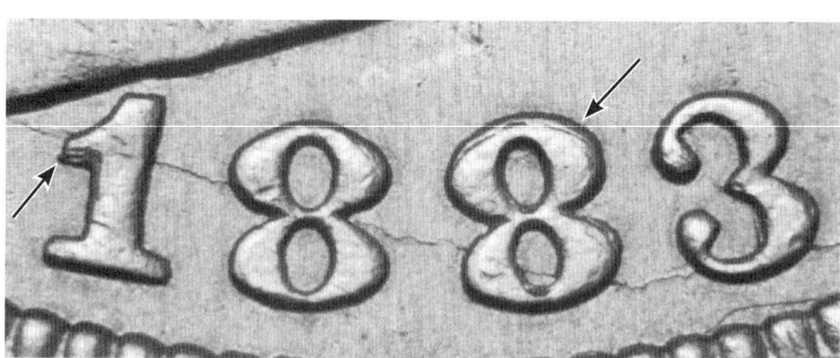

Description: The 1 of the date is actually triple-punched, with secondary digits evident barely to the south, under the flag of the primary 1. A secondary 8 is evident slightly north of the primary second 8.

Comments: It is very likely that more examples of this specimen will be located by observant collectors.

	VF-20	EF-40	AU-50	MS-60	MS-63	MS-65
Variety	$20	$35	$50	$75	$100	$275
Normal	$11	$15	$18	$35	$50	$225

1884 — FS-05-1884-301 (013.8)

Variety: Repunched Date — **Breen:** N/L

PUP: Date

URS-7 • I-3 • L-3

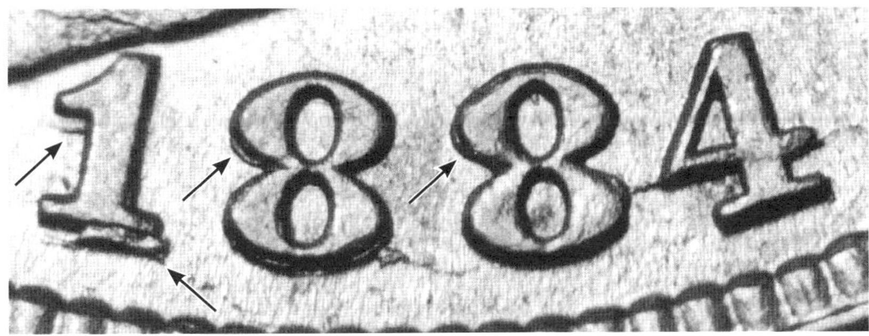

Description: All four digits exhibit secondary digits south, with the spread strongest on the 1 and weaker from left to right.

Comments: The secondary digits of the 8, 8, and 4 may not be visible on late-die-state specimens.

	VF-20	EF-40	AU-50	MS-60	MS-63	MS-65
Variety	$65	$100	$135	$200	$335	$2,000
Normal	$55	$85	$130	$190	$300	$1,800

1886 — FS-05-1886-301 (013.9)

Variety: Repunched Date — **Breen:** N/L

PUP: Date

URS-6 • I-3 • L-3

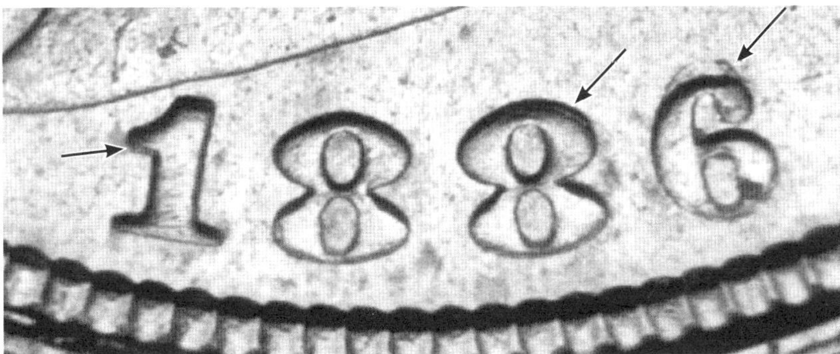

Description: There is a secondary 1 slightly to the south of the primary 1, and a strong secondary 6 to the north of the primary 6.

Comments: Occurring on what is itself a scarce coin, this Liberty Head nickel variety likely will have a very low total certified population, but a high percentage of total date population.

	VF-20	EF-40	AU-50	MS-60	MS-63	MS-65
Variety	$515	$720	$850	$1,030	$2,675	$7,200
Normal	$500	$700	$825	$1,000	$2,600	$7,000

1887 FS-05-1887-801 (014)

VARIETY: Doubled-Die Reverse BREEN: N/L
PUP: STATES OF AMERICA
URS-6 • I-3 • L-3

Description: Moderate doubling is evident on UNITED STATES OF AMERICA and E PLURIBUS UNUM.

Comments: This variety was first reported by Guy Araby, and very few specimens have been reported since.

	VF-20	EF-40	AU-50	MS-60	MS-63	MS-65
VARIETY	$75	$150	$200	$250	$350	$1,250
NORMAL	$50	$75	$110	$140	$195	$950

1888 FS-05-1888-101

VARIETY: Doubled-Die Obverse BREEN: N/L
PUP: Ear
URS-2 • I-3 • L-3

Description: Moderate doubling is evident in the form of a doubled earlobe.

Comments: Certainly more examples of this neat variety exist than have been reported.

	VF-20	EF-40	AU-50	MS-60	MS-63	MS-65
VARIETY	$125	$195	$245	$315	$375	$1,550
NORMAL	$120	$175	$220	$275	$340	$1,200

1889 — FS-05-1889-301

Variety: Repunched Date — **Breen:** N/L
PUP: Date
URS-4 • I-3 • L-3

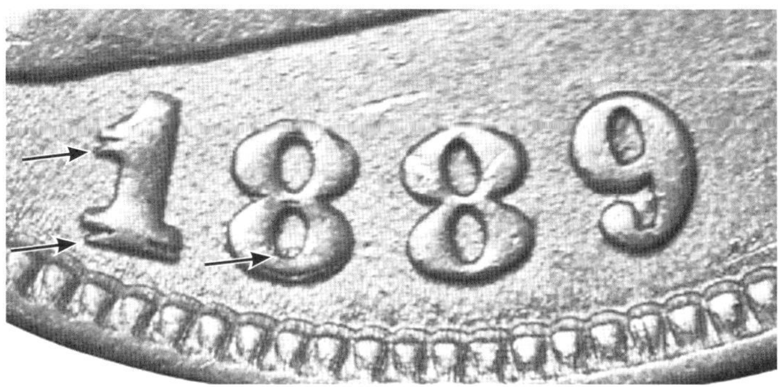

Description: There is a secondary 1 to the southeast of the primary 1, and the first 8 shows a secondary 8 to the southwest of the primary digit.

Comments: To date, only a couple examples of this very nice repunched date have been reported.

	VF-20	EF-40	AU-50	MS-60	MS-63	MS-65
Variety	$65	$100	$150	$175	$250	$1,050
Normal	$50	$75	$120	$140	$175	$800

1890 — FS-05-1890-301 (014.3)

Variety: Repunched Date — **Breen:** N/L
PUP: Date
URS-4 • I-3 • L-3

Description: Secondary digits are evident to the south of the primary digits on the 1, 8, and 9.

Comments: Though the first punch was fairly weak, the width of separation is fairly strong.

	VF-20	EF-40	AU-50	MS-60	MS-63	MS-65
Variety	$50	$75	$125	$195	$225	$1,500
Normal	$40	$65	$110	$160	$200	$1,000

1897 FS-05-1897-301 (014.48)

Variety: Repunched Date **Breen:** N/L
PUP: Date
URS-3 • I-3 • L-3

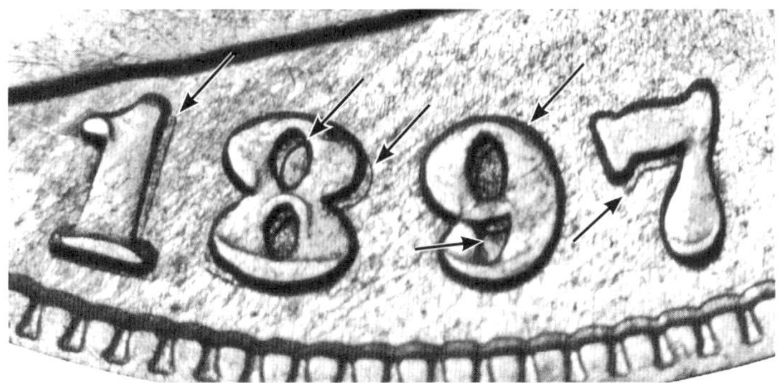

Description: All four digits of the date exhibit secondary digits to the east and south of the primary digits.

Comments: It is our belief that the Liberty Head nickel series is ripe for new finds.

	VF-20	EF-40	AU-50	MS-60	MS-63	MS-65
Variety	$35	$65	$100	$125	$195	$950
Normal	$27	$45	$70	$100	$160	$900

1898 FS-05-1898-301 (014.49)

Variety: Repunched Date **Breen:** N/L
PUP: Date
URS-4 • I-2 • L-2

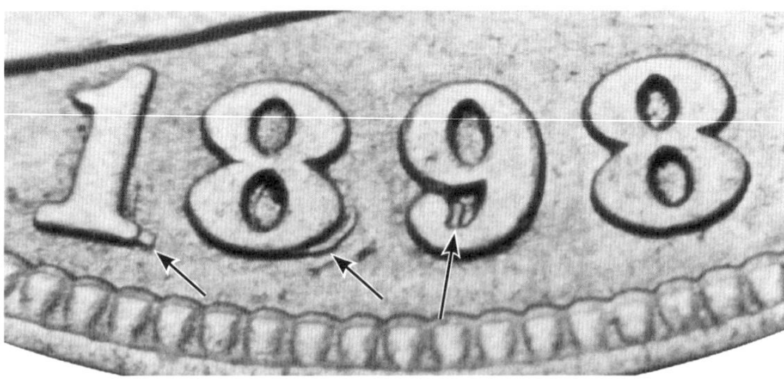

Description: Secondary digits are evident southeast of the 1, 8, and 9.

Comments: Compare this listing with the next.

	VF-20	EF-40	AU-50	MS-60	MS-63	MS-65
Variety	$35	$65	$95	$195	$240	$1,100
Normal	$27	$45	$75	$150	$185	$950

1898 — FS-05-1898-302 (014.495)

VARIETY: Repunched Date — BREEN: N/L

PUP: Date

URS-3 • I-2 • L-2

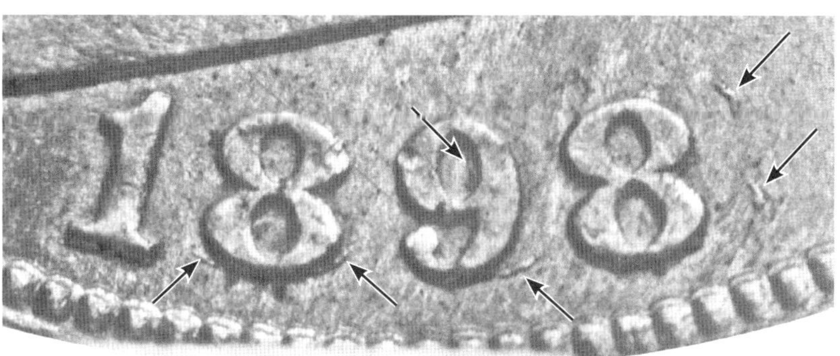

Description: This is actually a triple-punched date. A secondary digit is evident to the west of the lower curve of the first 8. There is a wide spread to the east on the last three primary digits.

Comments: An early-die-state specimen is a neat find!

	VF-20	EF-40	AU-50	MS-60	MS-63	MS-65
VARIETY	$45	$75	$100	$175	$200	$1,100
NORMAL	$27	$45	$75	$150	$185	$950

THE CHERRYPICKERS' GUIDE HELPFUL HINTS

The sixth edition, volume I of the Cherrypickers' Guide *introduces a new symbol for use in the coin-by-coin listings. Coins marked with the symbol to the right are listed in the most recent edition of R.S. Yeoman's* Guide Book of United States Coins, Deluxe Edition *(a greatly expanded version of the classic known as the "Red Book").*

RB DE

1899 — FS-05-1899-301 (014.5)

Variety: Repunched Date — Breen: N/L
PUP: Date
URS-4 • I-3 • L-3

Early Die State

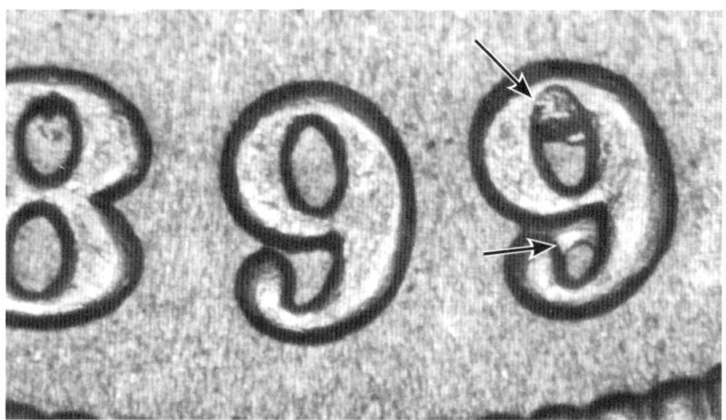

Late Die State

Description: The loop of a 9, or possibly (but unlikely) an 8, is evident within the lower loop of the second 9.

Comments: Some specialists believe this to be a 1899, 9 Over 8 overdate. However, we feel it is simply a repunched date, with the secondary 9 far to the south of the primary 9 at the last digit.

	VF-20	EF-40	AU-50	MS-60	MS-63	MS-65
Variety	$35	$75	$125	$175	$225	$750
Normal	$20	$30	$60	$90	$130	$600

1900 FS-05-1900-801 (014.7)

VARIETY: Doubled-Die Reverse BREEN: N/L

PUP: CENTS

URS-5 • I-3 • L-3

Description: Doubling is evident on all reverse design elements, including the V, with a stronger spread on the lower quadrant of the reverse.

Comments: This variety is very popular among specialists.

	VF-20	EF-40	AU-50	MS-60	MS-63	MS-65
VARIETY	$65	$100	$150	$225	$300	$850
NORMAL	$15	$30	$65	$90	$140	$525

1906 FS-05-1906-801

VARIETY: Doubled-Die Reverse
PUP: Lower wreath, reverse lettering
URS-1 • I-4 • L-4

Description: Doubling is evident on the lower part of the wreath and much of the reverse lettering, most notably on the U in UNITED and all letters of CENTS.

Comments: This variety was recently discovered and remains unique as of this printing.

	VF-20	EF-40	AU-50	MS-60	MS-63	MS-65
VARIETY	(unique)					
NORMAL	$13	$30	$60	$75	$125	$700

Buffalo Nickels, 1913–1938

The Buffalo nickel is one of the most widely collected series of American numismatics. It is very popular with collectors as well as the general public, in large part due to a great, all-American design concept.

Many collectors, dealers, and other specialists have contributed to the Buffalo nickel section of the *Cherrypickers' Guide* over the years. The active participation of so many enthusiasts shows us just how popular these coins are.

While there is no club specifically for collectors of the Buffalo nickel, we can easily see one becoming one of the more active groups in the hobby. All it would take is a passionate cherrypicker or two to spread the word and encourage others to join the Buffalo herd. The larger regional and national coin shows would be good places for such a group to meet to exchange ideas, share knowledge and discoveries, examine coins, and enjoy the camaraderie of the hobby. We recommend the American Numismatic Association's annual conventions, the Whitman Baltimore Expo, the Central States Numismatic Society convention, and the Florida United Numismatists show as some of the larger and more popular venues, where thousands of collectors gather every year.

More than a half dozen of the most widely collected Buffalo nickel die varieties are included in the regular-edition *Guide Book of United States Coins* (the "Red Book," published since 1946, with more than 23 million copies sold to date). Even more are featured in the *Guide Book of United States Coins, Deluxe Edition*. This level of publicity in widely distributed, high-visibility coin books guarantees that Buffalo nickel varieties will continue to be a rock-solid segment of the hobby.

The coins are frequently discussed in online forums like the Collectors Society Message Boards (boards.collectors-society.com) and the Collectors Universe Message Boards (forums.collectors.com). Articles related to Buffalo nickels can be found in hobby publications such as *The Numismatist* (www.money.org/the-numismatist), *Numismatic News* (www.numismaticnews.net), *Coin World* (www.coinworld.com), *COINage Magazine* (www.coinagemag.com), and *Coins Magazine*.

There are some good reference books on the series, as well. One excellent work is *Treasure Hunting Buffalo Nickels*, by John Wexler, Ron Pope, et al. Another is David W. Lange's *Complete Guide to Buffalo Nickels*. And Q. David Bowers covers the type and its more popular varieties in *A Guide Book of Buffalo and Jefferson Nickels*. Finally, *Buffalo Nickels—The Abraided Die Varieties*, by Ron Pope, is also a very valuable reference.

NEWLY LISTED VARIETIES

FIVAZ-STANTON NUMBER	VARIETY	PAGE NO.
FS-05-1913-1802	DDR	306
FS-05-1913S-401	2 Feathers	307–310
FS-05-1915D-401	2 Feathers	307–310
FS-05-1916-402	2 Feathers	307–310
FS-05-1916S-401	2 Feathers	307–310
FS-05-1919D-401	2 Feathers	307–310
FS-05-1919S-401	2 Feathers	307–310
FS-05-1920-401	2 Feathers	307–310
FS-05-1920D-401	2 Feathers	307–310
FS-05-1923-401	2 Feathers	307–310
FS-05-1926D-401	2 Feathers	307–310
FS-05-1927D-401	2 Feathers	307–310
FS-05-1927S-401	2 Feathers	307–310
FS-05-1928S-401	2 Feathers	307–310
FS-05-1929S-401	2 Feathers	307–310
FS-05-1916D-901	3-1/2-Legged Buffalo	315

FIVAZ-STANTON NUMBER	VARIETY	PAGE NO.
FS-05-1919-101	DDO	318
FS-05-1920D-502	RPM	318
FS-05-1926-101/801	DDO / DDR	319
FS-05-1926D-901	3-1/2-Legged Buffalo	320
FS-05-1927S-101	DDO	321
FS-05-1930-102	DDO	323
FS-05-1930-103	DDO	323
FS-05-1930S-101	DDO	325
FS-05-1931S-801	DDR	326
FS-05-1931S-802	DDR	327
FS-05-1936-102	DDO	330
FS-05-1938D-512	OMM	334
FS-05-1938D-513	OMM	334
FS-05-1938D-514	OMM	334
FS-05-1938D-515	OMM	334

VARIETIES TO BE DELISTED

FIVAZ-STANTON NUMBER	VARIETY	PAGE NO.
FS-05-1914S-101	Overdate	311

DEBUNKED VARIETIES

FIVAZ-STANTON NUMBER	VARIETY
FS-05-1920D-501	RPM

1913, Type I — FS-05-1913-901 (014.85)

VARIETY: 3-1/2-Legged Buffalo — CONECA: N/L

PUP: Front leg

URS-6 • I-4 • L-4

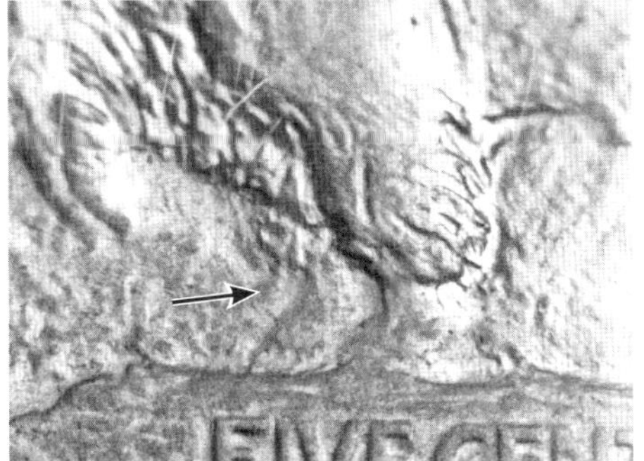

Description: The reverse die was heavily polished, possibly to remove clash marks. The result was a die with most of the bison's front leg missing, hence the nickname "3-1/2-Legged Buffalo."

Comments: This variety was reportedly discovered by Joseph Ambrulevich about 1988. An MS-65 example sold at auction for $47,050 in recent years.

	VF-20	EF-40	AU-50	MS-60	MS-63	MS-65
VARIETY	$900	$1,250	$1,750	$2,650	$5,000	—
NORMAL	$20	$25	$35	$45	$60	$170

1913, Type II — FS-05-1913-1101 (014.8)

VARIETY: Doubled-Die Obverse — CONECA: DDO-001

PUP: Date

URS-5 • I-4 • L-3

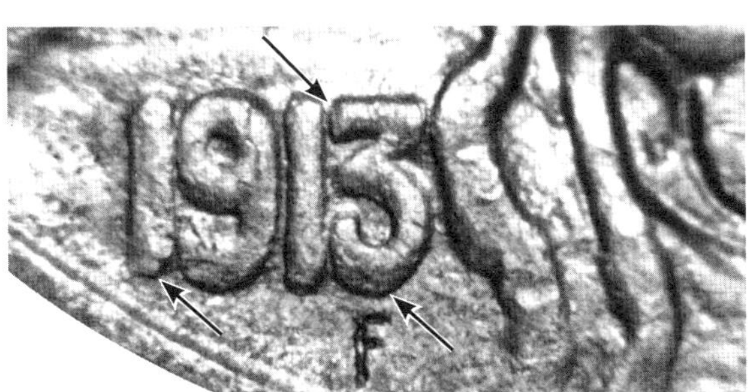

Description: Moderate doubling is evident on the date, with the secondary image visible south of the primary digits.

Comments: As a Class VI doubled die, doubling may not be evident on late stages or coins below Fine, but such coins would show extra-thick numerals.

	VF-20	EF-40	AU-50	MS-60	MS-63	MS-65
VARIETY	$75	$100	$150	$200	$300	—
NORMAL	$17	$22	$30	$40	$80	$320

1913, Type II — FS-05-1913-1801 (014.86)

Variety: Doubled-Die Reverse — CONECA: DDR-001
PUP: FIVE CENTS
URS-5 • I-3 • L-3

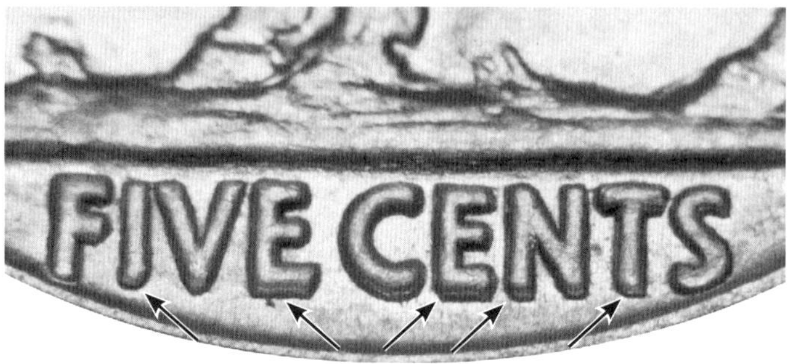

Description: Doubling is evident to the south on FIVE CENTS.

Comments: The doubling on this variety is very similar to that on a variety from 1930 listed as FS-05-1930-801.

	VF-20	EF-40	AU-50	MS-60	MS-63	MS-65
Variety	$35	$50	$75	$150	$300	$700
Normal	$17	$22	$30	$40	$80	$320

1913, Type II — FS-05-1913-1802

Variety: Doubled-Die Reverse
PUP: UNITED STATES OF AMERICA and FIVE CENTS
URS-9 • I-3 • L-3

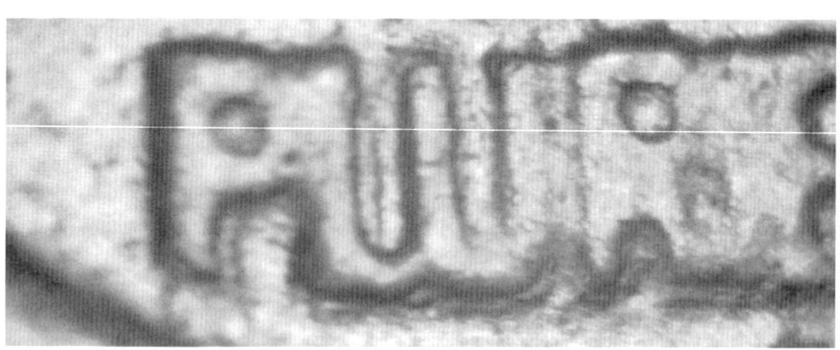

Description: This variety exhibits a light spread on E PLURIBUS UNUM.

	VF-20	EF-40	AU-50	MS-60	MS-63	MS-65
Variety	$30	$40	$60	$100	$200	$600
Normal	$17	$22	$30	$40	$80	$320

1913-D–1930-S FS-05-[Year]-40X

VARIETY: Two Feathers
PUP: Small innermost feather

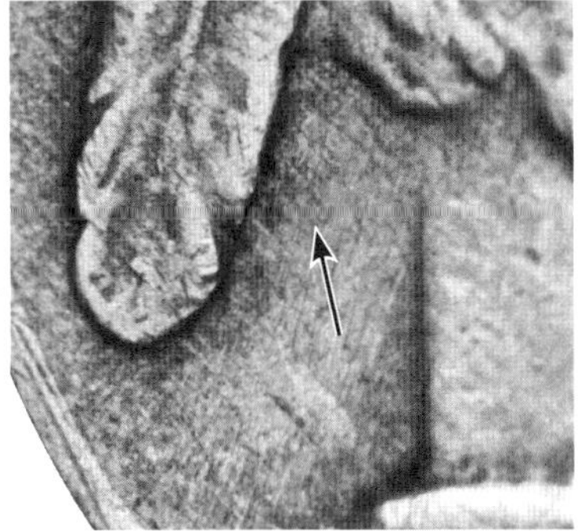

Description: The obverse die was heavily polished, probably to remove clash marks. The result was a die with the innermost feather missing, hence the name "Two Feathers." A second, similar variety that both lacks the third feather and the designer's initials has been known for some years.

Comments: This variety is identical in cause and effect to the famous "3-Legged" nickels. Some examples are the "true" Two Feathers varieties, which will show no trace of the feather; these are the most sought-after of the variety. Others show a small portion of the feather still remaining.

1913-D, FS-05-1913D-401

	VF-20	EF-40	AU-50	MS-60	MS-63
VARIETY	$60	$125	$150	$175	$250
NORMAL	$34	$42	$60	$75	$80

1913-S, FS-05-1913S-401

	VF-20	EF-40	AU-50	MS-60	MS-63
VARIETY	$350	$550	$950	$1,250	$1,400
NORMAL	$70	$90	$110	$130	$180

1915, FS-05-1915-401

	VF-20	EF-40	AU-50	MS-60	MS-63
VARIETY	$175	$375	$500	$1,000	$1,250
NORMAL	$15	$25	$45	$60	$90

1915-D, FS-05-1915D-401

	VF-20	EF-40	AU-50	MS-60	MS-63
VARIETY	$200	$300	$400	*$650*	*$850*
NORMAL	$70	$130	$160	$270	$350

1913-D–1930-S (continued) FS-05-[Year]-40X

VARIETY: Two Feathers
PUP: Small innermost feather

1916, FS-05-1916-402

	VF-20	EF-40	AU-50	MS-60	MS-63
VARIETY*	$20	$40	$75	$135	$275
NORMAL	$10	$15	$25	$50	$85

1917, FS-05-1917-401

	VF-20	EF-40	AU-50	MS-60	MS-63
VARIETY	$65	$115	$180	$325	$2,000
NORMAL	$12	$16	$35	$60	$150

1917-D, FS-05-1917D-401

	VF-20	EF-40	AU-50	MS-60	MS-63
VARIETY	$200	$300	$400	$600	$1,150
NORMAL	$85	$150	$275	$350	$750

1917-S, FS-05-1917S-401

	VF-20	EF-40	AU-50	MS-60	MS-63
VARIETY*	$135	$300	$525	$650	*$1,750*
NORMAL	$115	$200	$375	$450	$1,200

1918, FS-05-1918-401

	VF-20	EF-40	AU-50	MS-60	MS-63
VARIETY*	$100	$225	$500	$1,000	*$1,750*
NORMAL	$16	$32	$50	$125	$325

1918-S, FS-05-1918S-401

	VF-20	EF-40	AU-50	MS-60	MS-63
VARIETY*	$275	$450	$750	*$1,150*	*$3,000*
NORMAL	$110	$200	$325	$585	$2,750

1919, FS-05-1919-401

	VF-20	EF-40	AU-50	MS-60	MS-63
VARIETY*	$85	$175	$225	$300	*$375*
NORMAL	$8	$15	$32	$55	$125

1919-D, FS-05-1919D-401

	VF-20	EF-40	AU-50	MS-60	MS-63
VARIETY	$275	$425	$600	*$850*	*$2,000*
NORMAL	$135	$260	$350	$600	$1,500

Note: Varieties marked with an asterisk (*) are sometimes found missing the designer's initial as well as the third feather.

1913-D–1930-S (continued) FS-05-[Year]-40X

VARIETY: Two Feathers
PUP: Small innermost feather

1919-S, FS-05-1919S-401

	VF-20	EF-40	AU-50	MS-60	MS-63
VARIETY	$300	*$500*	*$750*		
NORMAL	$125	$260	$375	$625	$1,800

1920, FS-05-1920-401

	VF-20	EF-40	AU-50	MS-60	MS-63
VARIETY*	$50	$85	$115	$200	*$400*
NORMAL	$7	$14	$30	$65	$145

1920-D, FS-05-1920D-401

	VF-20	EF-40	AU-50	MS-60	MS-63
VARIETY	$350	$500	$850	$1,250	*$1,800*
NORMAL	$115	$275	$325	$585	$1,400

1920-S, FS-05-1920S-401

	VF-20	EF-40	AU-50	MS-60	MS-63
VARIETY	$200	$400	$700	*$1,500*	*$3,500*
NORMAL	$100	$200	$300	$575	$1,850

1921, FS-05-1921-401

	VF-20	EF-40	AU-50	MS-60	MS-63
VARIETY	$40	$100	$150	$200	$400
NORMAL	$24	$50	$75	$150	$320

1921-S, FS-05-1921S-401

	VF-20	EF-40	AU-50	MS-60	MS-63
VARIETY*	$650	$1,350	$1,950	$2,250	$3,000
NORMAL	$550	$950	$1,200	$1,600	$2,100

1923, FS-05-1923-401

	VF-20	EF-40	AU-50	MS-60	MS-63
VARIETY	*$150*	*$200*	*$300*	*$400*	*$625*
NORMAL	$6	$13	$35	$65	$160

1925-D, FS-05-1925D-401

	VF-20	EF-40	AU-50	MS-60	MS-63
VARIETY	$225	$450	*$650*		
NORMAL	$95	$185	$265	$400	$750

Note: Varieties marked with an asterisk (*) are sometimes found missing the designer's initial as well as the third feather.

1913-D–1930-S (continued) FS-05-[Year]-40X

VARIETY: Two Feathers
PUP: Small innermost feather

1925-S, FS-05-1925S-401

	VF-20	EF-40	AU-50	MS-60	MS-63
VARIETY	$175	$275	$400	*$750*	*$2,250*
NORMAL	$90	$180	$250	$475	$1,850

1926-D, FS-05-1926D-401

	VF-20	EF-40	AU-50	MS-60	MS-63
VARIETY	$225	$450	*$525*	*$625*	*$1,000*
NORMAL	$110	$185	$300	$350	$500

1927-D, FS-05-1927D-401

	VF-20	EF-40	AU-50	MS-60	MS-63
VARIETY	$75	*$200*			
NORMAL	$32	$80	$135	$180	$310

1927-S, FS-05-1927S-401

	VF-20	EF-40	AU-50	MS-60	MS-63
VARIETY	$150	$250	$425		
NORMAL	$34	$95	$185	$550	$2,000

1928-S, FS-05-1928S-401

	VF-20	EF-40	AU-50	MS-60	MS-63
VARIETY	$65	$175	$400	*$600*	*$850*
NORMAL	$11	$26	$110	$260	$550

1929-S, FS-05-1929S-401

	VF-20	EF-40	AU-50	MS-60	MS-63
VARIETY	*$40*	*$75*	*$150*	*$400*	*$625*
NORMAL	$4	$12	$25	$55	$80

1930-S, FS-05-1930S-401

	VF-20	EF-40	AU-50	MS-60	MS-63
VARIETY	$300	$400	*$750*	*$1,000*	
NORMAL	$4	$14	$35	$65	$120

Note: Varieties marked with an asterisk (*) are sometimes found missing the designer's initial as well as the third feather.

1914 — FS-05-1914-101 (014.87)

VARIETY: Overdate — CONECA: N/L

PUP: Date

URS-7 • I-5 • L-4

Description: The overdate is seen as the straight top bar of the underlying 3 at the top of the 4 and the start of the 3's diagonal on the upper right outside of the 4. On some, a hint of the curve of the lower portion of the 3 shows just above the crossbar of the 4.

Comments: Since first being reported in January of 1997, many specimens have been found. Additionally, another overdate on the 1914-S has been confirmed (see FS-05-1914S-101), and a 1914-D is reported. More study is being conducted. This was first reported by R.A. Medina, with confirmation from Roger Alexander. There are several different overdate dies known for the Philadelphia Mint issue. The one illustrated here is the strongest. Some controversy surrounds this variety, but the authors feel that the overdate theory best fits the evidence. A leading third-party grading service recognizes this as a true overdate and will slab two dies that exhibit heavy abrasion lines over the 1 and 4, as seen in the image above.

	VF-20	EF-40	AU-50	MS-60	MS-63
VARIETY	$275	$450	$800	$1,500	$3,000
NORMAL	$30	$35	$45	$60	$85

1914-S — FS-05-1914S-101 (014.89)

VARIETY: Overdate — CONECA: N/L

PUP: Date

URS-6 • I-5 • L-5

Description: See the description for FS-05-1914-101, as both descriptions are the same.

Comments: See the comments for FS-05-1914-101.

Note: This variety is slated to be removed from the coin-by-coin listings of future editions of the ***Cherrypickers' Guide*** due to lack of interest and/or unavailability. It will retain its Fivaz-Stanton number and continue to be listed in future editions' cross-reference appendix. **A full list of varieties slated to be removed from each section appears after the introductory text of that section.**

1915 — FS-05-1915-101 (014.9)

Variety: Doubled-Die Obverse — CONECA: DDO-001
PUP: Eye, nostril
URS-4 • I-4 • L-3

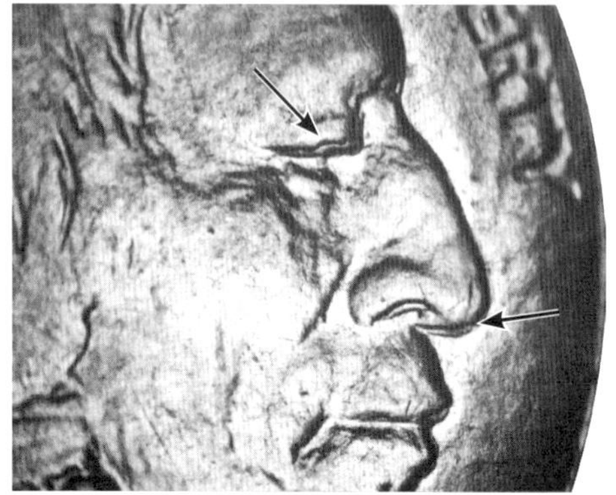

Description: The doubling is evident as a secondary image on the eyelid, nose, and nostril.

Comments: The doubling on this variety is very similar to that on FS-05-1930-101 (017). This variety is extremely rare and seldom found.

	VF-20	EF-40	AU-50	MS-60	MS-63
Variety	$250	$500	$1,000	—	—
Normal	$15	$25	$45	$60	$90

1915-D — FS-05-1915D-501 (015)

Variety: Repunched Mintmark — CONECA: RPM-001
PUP: Mintmark
URS-6 • I-5 • L-3

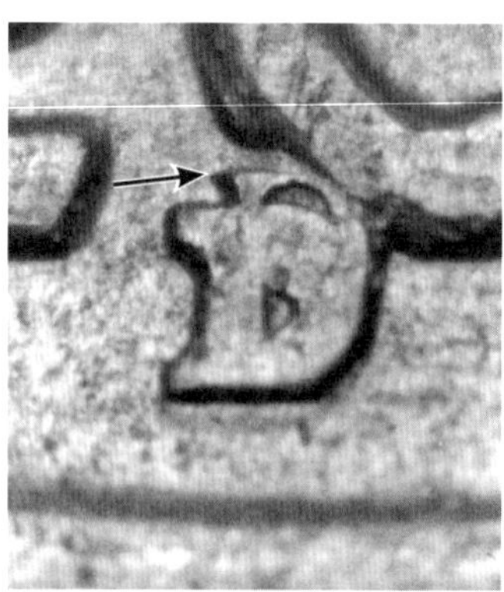

Description: The second D is northeast of the primary image.

Comments: This is a very rare variety, especially in high grade.

	VF-20	EF-40	AU-50	MS-60	MS-63
Variety	$225	$320	$500	$750	$1,000
Normal	$70	$130	$160	$270	$350

1915-S — FS-05-1915S-501 (015.5)

VARIETY: Repunched Mintmark — CONECA: RPM-001
PUP: Mintmark
URS-4 • I-4 • L-3

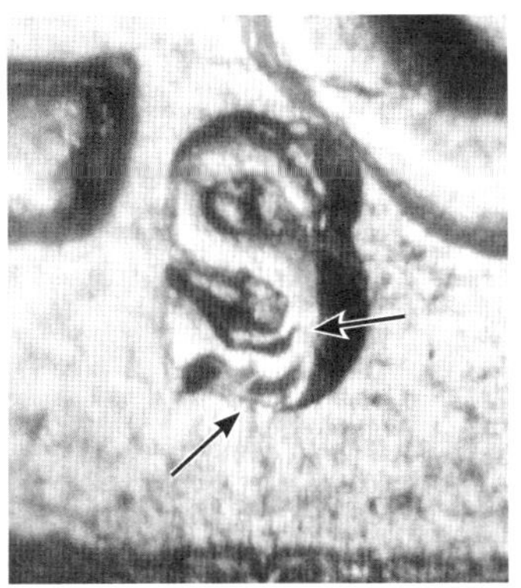

Description: The mintmark was actually triple punched, with the secondary S's to the north and south of the primary image.

Comments: This is a very rare variety, especially in high grade.

	VF-20	EF-40	AU-50	MS-60	MS-63
VARIETY	$250	$750	$1,000	$1,500	
NORMAL	$200	$400	$500	$650	$1,000

1915-S — FS-05-1915S-502 (015.6)

VARIETY: Repunched Mintmark — CONECA: RPM-002
PUP: Mintmark
URS-1 • I-4 • L-3

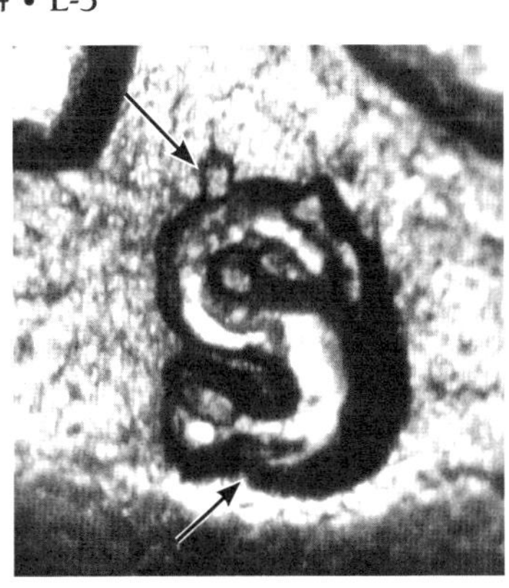

Description: The mintmark was actually triple punched, with the secondary S's to the northeast and south of the primary image.

Comments: Further study could prove that the mintmark has four or more punchings!

	VF-20	EF-40	AU-50	MS-60	MS-63
VARIETY	$250	$485	$650	$1,000	$1,300
NORMAL	$200	$400	$500	$650	$1,000

1916 FS-05-1916-101 (016)

VARIETY: Doubled-Die Obverse CONECA: DDO-001
PUP: Date
URS-9 • I-5 • L-5

Description: The date, chin, throat, feathers, and the tie on the braids are all doubled. The date is doubled to the southeast, with the top two-thirds of the 1 and 6 quite strong, and the lower two-thirds of the 1 and 9 virtually missing.

Comments: Although well known, this variety is quite rare. Beware of 1916 nickels with strike doubling on the date offered as this variety. Please read the appendix on other forms of doubling. The true doubled die must look like the coin shown here. This variety can sometimes be identified even without a visible date by the doubling to the right on the long feather behind the neck.

	VF-20	EF-40	AU-50	MS-60	MS-63
VARIETY	*$11,000*	*$18,500*	*$32,000*	*$60,000*	*$140,000*
NORMAL	$10	$15	$25	$50	$85

1916 FS-05-1916-401 (016.3)

VARIETY: Missing Designer's Initial CONECA: N/L
PUP: Date area
URS-7 • I-3 • L-3

Description: The designer's initial, F, normally below the date, is obviously missing.

Comments: There are some dies with a partially missing or weak initial, but these do not command the premium of this variety with no trace showing.

	VF-20	EF-40	AU-50	MS-60	MS-63
VARIETY	$50	$100	$175	$275	$400
NORMAL	$10	$15	$25	$50	$85

1916-D — FS-05-1916D-901

VARIETY: 3-1/2-Legged Buffalo
PUP: Right front leg
URS-9 • I-3 • L-3

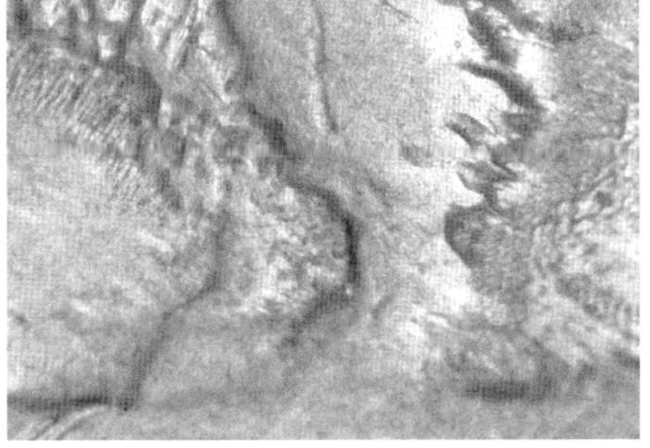

Description: The reverse die was heavily polished, probably to remove clash marks. This resulted in a die where the right front leg just above the hoof was severely weakened.

Comments: The strength of the leg varies widely on this variety. Only those coins showing a similar weakness to the image should command a premium.

	VF-20	EF-40	AU-50	MS-60	MS-63
VARIETY	*$250*	*$425*	*$675*	*$1,000*	*$1,800*
NORMAL	$45	$90	$120	$175	$260

1917 — FS-05-1917-801 (016.4)

VARIETY: Doubled-Die Reverse — CONECA: DDR-001
PUP: E PLURIBUS UNUM
URS-6 • I-4 • L-3

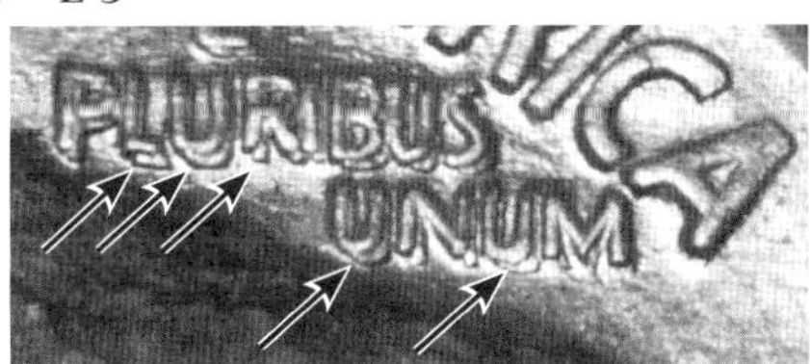

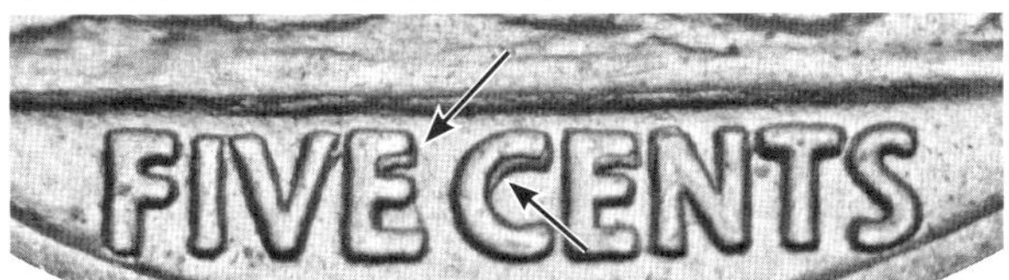

Description: Doubling is clearest on E PLURIBUS UNUM; the VE CE of FIVE CENTS; the lower ground; and the legs, horn, beard, and mane of the buffalo.

Comments: Another doubled-die reverse variety has been discovered, but it is far less dramatic. (See FS-05-1917-802.) In January 2007, a PCGS MS-64 sold for $10,925. This coin would likely bring a higher price if sold today. No other Mint State pieces have been reported.

	VF-20	EF-40	AU-50	MS-60	MS-63
VARIETY	$1,300	$2,000	$3,500	—	—
NORMAL	$12	$16	$35	$60	$150

1917 — FS-05-1917-802 (016.41)

Variety: Doubled-Die Reverse — CONECA: DDR-002
PUP: E PLURIBUS UNUM
URS-4 • I-3 • L-3

Description: Doubling is clearest to the northeast on E PLURIBUS UNUM.

Comments: This is the weaker of the two reported 1917 doubled-die reverses. See FS-05-1917-801 for the other.

	VF-20	EF-40	AU-50	MS-60	MS-63
Variety	$75	$120	$315	$400	$475
Normal	$12	$16	$35	$60	$150

1917-D — FS-05-1917D-901 (016.42)

Variety: 3-1/2-Legged Buffalo — CONECA: N/L
PUP: Right front leg
URS-9 • I-4 • L-4

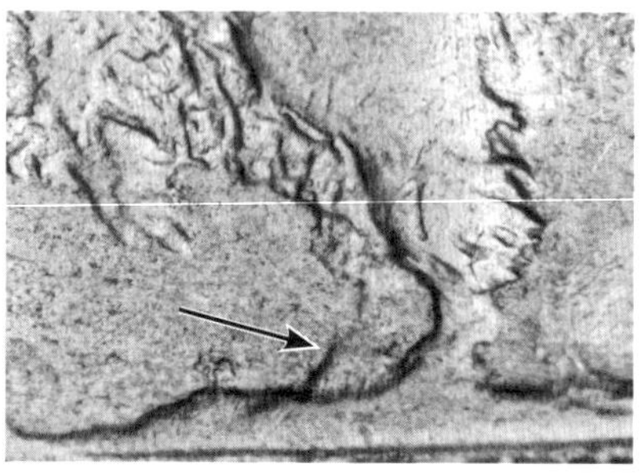

Description: The reverse die was heavily polished, probably to remove clash marks. The result was a die with portions of the buffalo's front leg missing, hence the nickname "3-1/2-Legged Buffalo."

Comments: This is the most recent discovery of a 3- or 3-1/2-Legged Buffalo, having been first reported in 1999 by Bob White. There is also a possibility that this has a doubled-die obverse. The die state of the discovery piece makes it difficult to tell. We would love to see an earlier die state.

	VF-20	EF-40	AU-50	MS-60	MS-63
Variety	$250	$400	$1,000	$2,650	$3,500
Normal	$85	$150	$275	$350	$750

1918 — FS-05-1918-801 (016.45)

VARIETY: Doubled-Die Reverse — CONECA: DDR-001

PUP: E PLURIBUS UNUM

URS-4 • I-3 • L-4

RB DE

Description: Doubling is clearest to the north on E PLURIBUS UNUM.

Comments: We anticipate the interest in this relative newcomer will increase. Some specimens show a die crack on the reverse from the rim to the bison's rump, just below the tail.

	VF-20	EF-40	AU-50	MS-60	MS-63
VARIETY	$500	$750	$1,250	$1,750	*$2,500*
NORMAL	$16	$32	$50	$125	$325

1918-D — FS-05-1918D-101 (016.5)

VARIETY: Overdate — CONECA: DDO-001

PUP: Date

URS-9 • I-5 • L-5

RB RB DE

Description: This is a very rare overdate, with the top of the 8 extending halfway up into the horizontal bar of the 7. The two "ears" of the 7 show clearly, as well as the flat top surface of the 7. The diagonal of the 7 is straight, not curved, and appears on the right portion of the upperloop and the left half of the lower loop.

Comments: Look for the small die crack immediately above the tie on the braid, leading slightly downward to the Indian's jaw. The beginning of this die break can usually be seen even on lower-grade coins.

	VF-20	EF-40	AU-50	MS-60	MS-63
VARIETY	$5,500	$8,500	$12,000	$34,000	$57,500
NORMAL	$135	$225	$350	$450	$1,050

1919 FS-05-1919-101

VARIETY: Doubled-Die Obverse
PUP: Date, feathers, ribbon tie
URS-2 • I-3 • L-3

Description: Doubling can be seen on the date, the small feather behind the neck, the tip of the large feather, and the ribbon tie closest to the date.

Comments: This is a recent discovery, so rarity ratings will surely change as more are found.

	VF-20	EF-40	AU-50	MS-60	MS-63
VARIETY	$25	$50	$90	$150	$350
NORMAL	$8	$15	$32	$55	$125

1920-D FS-05-1920D-502

VARIETY: Repunched Mintmark
PUP: Mintmark
URS-1 • I-4 • L-4

Description: The secondary D mintmark is seen to the southeast of the primary D.

Comments: This variety was discovered by Dr. Eugene Bruder of California in 2010. The variety remains unique.

	VF-20	EF-40	AU-50	MS-60	MS-63
VARIETY	(unique)				
NORMAL	$115	$275	$325	$585	$1,400

1925-S FS-05-1925S-501 (016.64)

Variety: Repunched Mintmark CONECA: RPM-001
PUP: Mintmark
URS-4 • I-3 • L-3

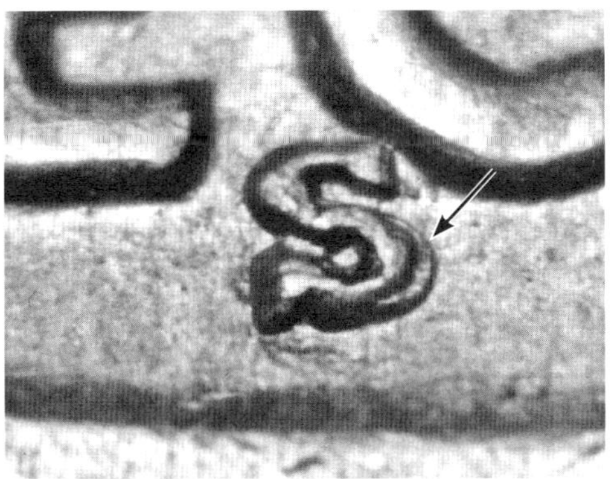

Description: The secondary S is visible to the east of the primary S.

Comments: Known for a long time, this variety has received very little publicity.

	VF-20	EF-40	AU-50	MS-60	MS-63
Variety	$380	$750	*$900*		
Normal	$90	$180	$250	$475	$1,850

1926 FS-05-1926-101/801

Variety: Doubled-Die Obverse and Reverse CONECA: DDO-002/DDR-002
PUP: LIBERTY, E PLURIBUS UNUM
URS-1 • I-4 • L-4

Description: This coin shows a medium spread on LIBERTY and light spread on E PLURIBUS UNUM.

Comments: This is one of the nicest doubled-die obverses in the series.

	VF-20	EF-40	AU-50	MS-60	MS-63
Variety	(unique)				
Normal	$5	$10	$20	$32	$75

1926-D FS-05-1926D-901

VARIETY: 3-1/2-Legged Buffalo
PUP: Right front leg
URS-9 • I-4 • L-4

Description: The reverse die was heavily polished, probably to remove clash marks. This resulted in a die where the right front leg just above the hoof was severely weakened.

Comments: The strength of the leg can vary, but not to the degree of some other dates of this variety. Only those coins showing a similar weakness to the image should command a premium.

	VF-20	EF-40	AU-50	MS-60	MS-63
VARIETY	$175	$400	$1,150	—	—
NORMAL	$110	$185	$300	$350	$500

1927-D FS-05-1927D-501 (016.7)

VARIETY: Repunched Mintmark
CONECA: RPM-001
PUP: Mintmark
URS-5 • I-4 • L-4

Description: There are remnants of two secondary mintmarks, one to the north and one to the south of the primary mintmark.

	VF-20	EF-40	AU-50	MS-60	MS-63
VARIETY	$110	$225	$340	$375	$475
NORMAL	$32	$80	$135	$180	$310

1927-D — FS-05-1927D-901 (016.65)

VARIETY: 3-1/2-Legged Buffalo — CONECA: N/L

PUP: Right front leg

URS-4 • I-4 • L-3

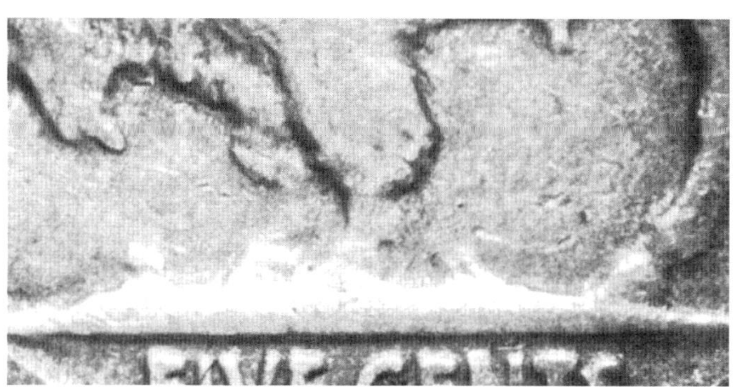

Description: The reverse die was heavily polished, possibly to remove clash marks. The result was a die with most of the bison's front leg missing, hence the nickname "3-1/2-Legged Buffalo."

Comments: This variety was first reported by Ron Pope.

	VF-20	EF-40	AU-50	MS-60	MS-63
Variety	$200	$500	$850	$6,500	$9,000
Normal	$32	$80	$135	$180	$310

1927-S — FS-05-1927S-101

VARIETY: Doubled-Die Obverse

PUP: Date

URS-7 • I-3 • L-3

Description: Doubling is evident on the bottoms of the lower two feathers and especially on the date.

Comments: A very similar 1927-D is also known.

	VF-20	EF-40	AU-50	MS-60	MS-63
Variety	$100	$200	$400	$1,000	$3,000
Normal	$34	$95	$185	$550	$2,000

1929 — FS-05-1929-101 (016.8)

VARIETY: Doubled-Die Obverse — CONECA: DDO-001
PUP: Date
URS-5 • I-3 • L-2

Description: The doubling is visible on the date, neck, and hair braid.

	VF-20	EF-40	AU-50	MS-60	MS-63
VARIETY	$45	$95	$165	$250	$400
NORMAL	$4	$12	$25	$55	$80

1930 — FS-05-1930-101 (017)

VARIETY: Doubled-Die Obverse — CONECA: DDO-001
PUP: Eyelid, nostril
URS-9 • I-3 • L-2

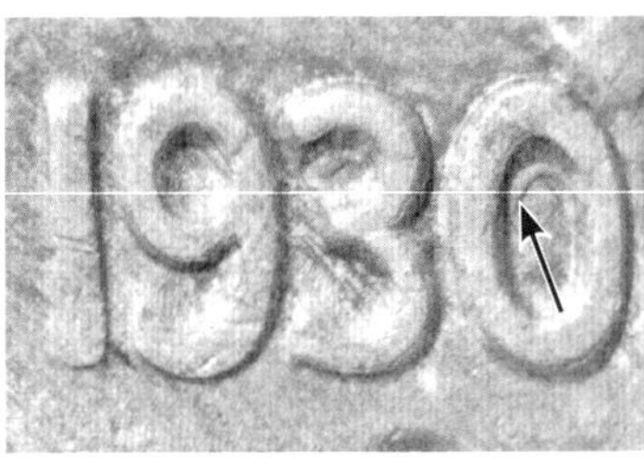

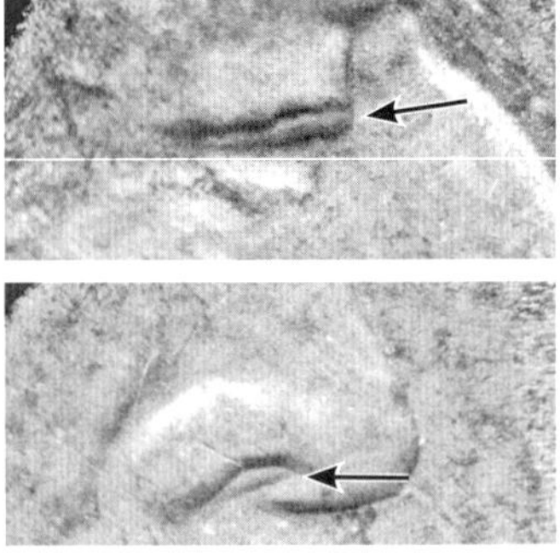

Description: There are at least six different varieties of doubled obverse dies for this date, the strongest pictured here. The doubling may be picked up on the upper eyelid, nostril, and upper lip. The date is also slightly doubled.

Comments: The doubling on one of the other varieties of this date is very similar to this one but not as strong. On a third, a strongly doubled brow on the Indian is the pick-up point.

	VF-20	EF-40	AU-50	MS-60	MS-63
VARIETY	$50	$75	$125	$175	$350
NORMAL	$4	$11	$20	$35	$75

1930 — FS-05-1930-102

VARIETY: Doubled-Die Obverse — CONECA: DDO-004
PUP: Eyelid
URS-5 • I-4 • L-4

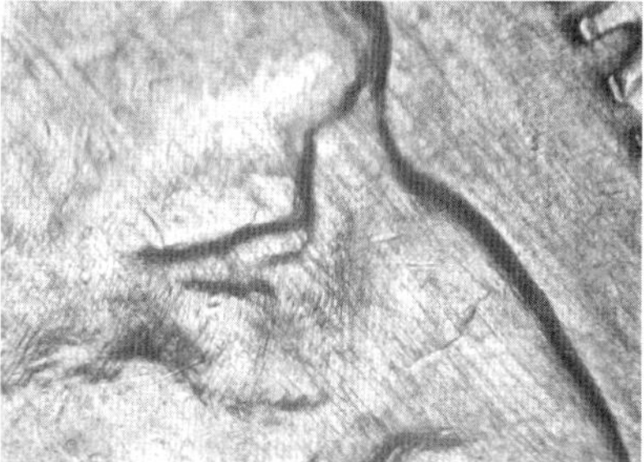

Description: This coin shows a strong spread on the eyelid and the lower vertical feather.

Comments: Several doubled-eye dies are known for this date. Check the attribution guides for diagnostic markers.

	VF-20	EF-40	AU-50	MS-60	MS-63
VARIETY	$15	$30	$60	$100	$200
NORMAL	$4	$11	$20	$35	$75

1930 — FS-05-1930-103

VARIETY: Doubled-Die Obverse — CONECA: DDO-006
PUP: Eyelid
URS-5 • I-4 • L-4

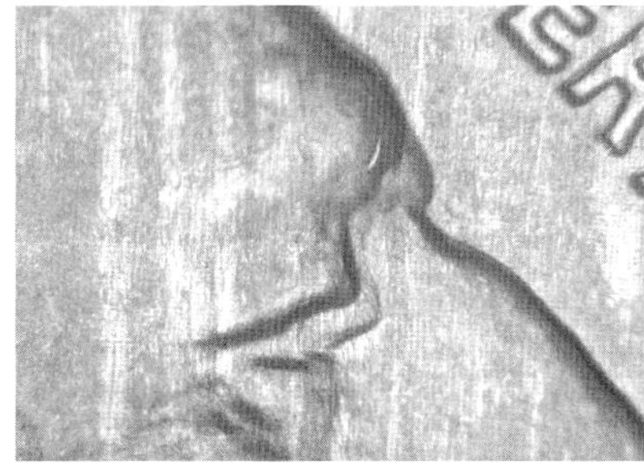

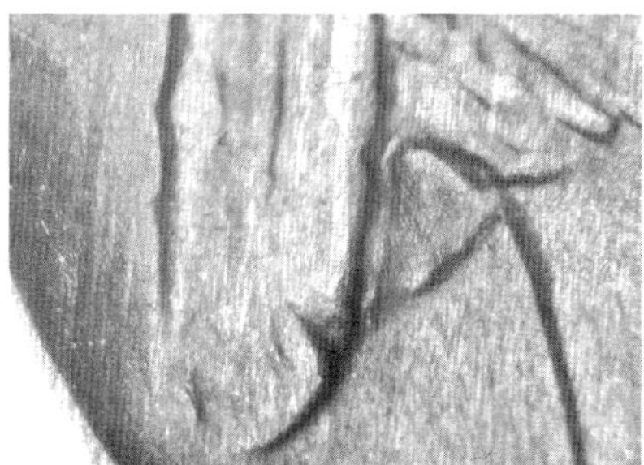

Description: This variety has a very strong spread northwest on the eyelid, brow, nostril, and lower vertical feather.

Comments: This is the strongest of the doubled-eye doubled dies.

	VF-20	EF-40	AU-50	MS-60	MS-63
VARIETY	$20	$40	$80	$150	$300
NORMAL	$4	$11	$20	$35	$75

1930 FS-05-1930-801 (017.5)

Variety: Doubled-Die Reverse ("5-Legged Buffalo") CONECA: DDR-001
PUP: Left front leg
URS-9 • I-3 • L-3

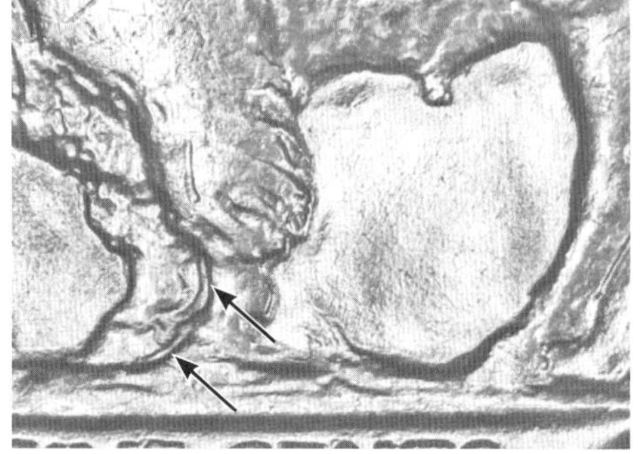

Description: Doubling is slight on E PLURIBUS UNUM, but most noticeable as an extra left front leg, hence the nickname "5-Legged Buffalo."

Comments: This coin was discovered by Marilyn and Leroy Van Allen.

	VF-20	EF-40	AU-50	MS-60	MS-63
Variety	$50	$100	$150	$250	$400
Normal	$4	$11	$20	$35	$75

1930 FS-05-1930-802 (017.3)

Variety: Doubled-Die Reverse CONECA: DDR-002
PUP: E PLURIBUS UNUM
URS-4 • I-3 • L-2

Description: Doubling is evident to the west on the PL of PLURIBUS and the first U of UNUM.

Comments: Though only portions are doubled, it is a very nice spread.

	VF-20	EF-40	AU-50	MS-60	MS-63
Variety	$275	$500	$750	*$1,000*	*$1,750*
Normal	$4	$11	$20	$35	$75

1930 — FS-05-1930-803 (017.4)

Variety: Doubled-Die Reverse — **CONECA:** DDR-003
PUP: E PLURIBUS UNUM, buffalo's appendage
URS-5 • I-2 • L-2

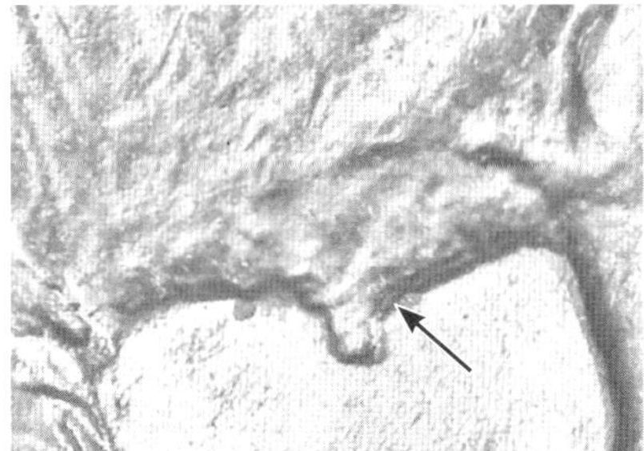

Description: Doubling is evident to the southeast on portions of E PLURIBUS UNUM and the bison's appendage.

Comments: The coin shown here is a rather late die state. We would like to see a much earlier die state.

	VF-20	EF-40	AU-50	MS-60	MS-63
Variety	$50	$75	$100	$150	$250
Normal	$4	$11	$20	$35	$75

1930-S — FS-05-1930S-101

Variety: Doubled-Die Obverse
PUP: Date, LIBERTY
URS-8 • I-4 • L-3

Description: Extra thickness can be easily seen on the date and LIBERTY.

Comments: This variety closely resembles the 1936 doubled-die obverse, but this one isn't quite as strong.

	VF-20	EF-40	AU-50	MS-60	MS-63
Variety	$50	$75	$125	$175	$250
Normal	$4	$14	$35	$65	$120

1930-S FS-05-1930S-501 (017.71)

Variety: Repunched Mintmark CONECA: RPM-002
PUP: Mintmark
URS-4 • I-3 • L-3

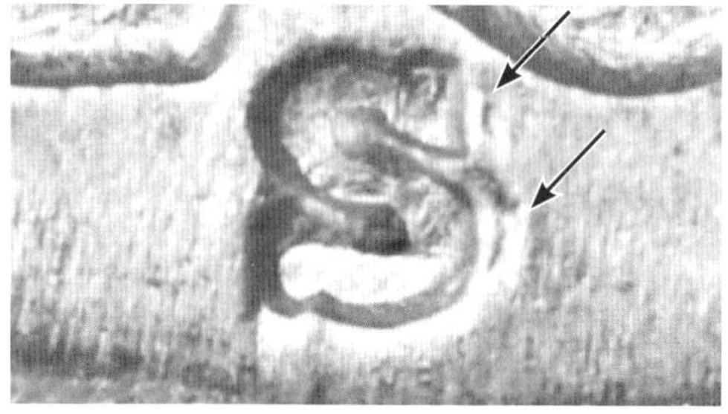

Description: The secondary mintmark is visible to the east of the primary mintmark.

Comments: This variety has been known for some time but seldom is seen.

	VF-20	EF-40	AU-50	MS-60	MS-63
Variety	$50	$75	$110	$150	$200
Normal	$4	$14	$35	$65	$120

1931-S FS-05-1931S-801

Variety: Doubled-Die Reverse CONECA: DDR-002
PUP: Left front leg
URS-4 • I-3 • L-4

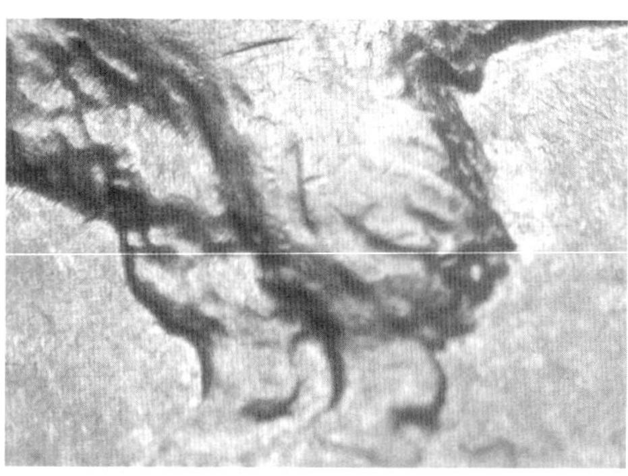

Description: This variety exhibits a medium spread below the neck, behind the top of the left front leg, and behind the middle of the left rear leg.

Comments: The doubling makes it appear as though the buffalo has five legs.

	VF-20	EF-40	AU-50	MS-60	MS-63
Variety	$75	$100	$150	$175	$300
Normal	$25	$35	$55	$65	$100

1931-S — FS-05-1931S-802

VARIETY: Tripled-Die Reverse — CONECA: DDR-003
PUP: E PLURIBUS UNUM
URS-4 • I-3 • L-4

Description: This coin has tripling of a medium spread on PL of PLURIBUS and the first U of UNUM, plus doubling on UR of PLURIBUS and the left front leg.

Comments: This one is tough to locate and eagerly sought after.

	VF-20	EF-40	AU-50	MS-60	MS-63
VARIETY	$75	$100	$150	$175	$300
NORMAL	$25	$35	$55	$65	$100

1935 — FS-05-1935-801 (018)

VARIETY: Doubled-Die Reverse — CONECA: DDR-001
PUP: FIVE CENTS
URS-10 • I-5 • L-5

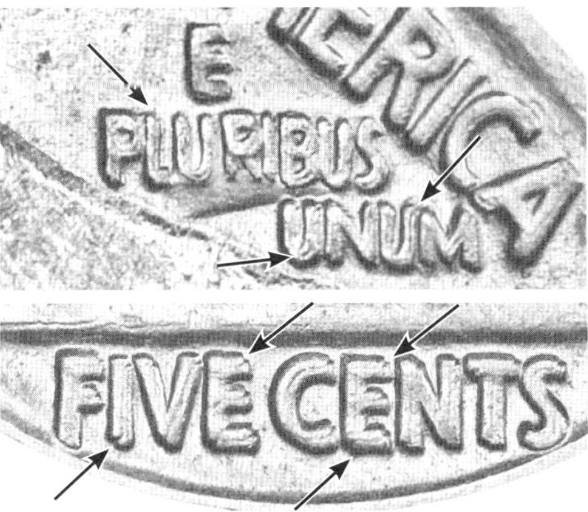

Description: There is a strong doubling on FIVE CENTS and E PLURIBUS UNUM, as well as at the eye, horn, and mane of the buffalo.

Comments: This variety is rare in any grade above Very Fine. About 10 are known in Mint State. Early-die-state coins are very rare and command significant premiums.

	VF-20	EF-40	AU-50	MS-60	MS-63
VARIETY	$170	$450	$1,400	$7,000	$15,500
NORMAL	$2	$3	$10	$22	$45

1935 — FS-05-1935-803 (018.1)

Variety: Doubled-Die Reverse — CONECA: DDR-003
PUP: FIVE CENTS
URS-4 • I-3 • L-3

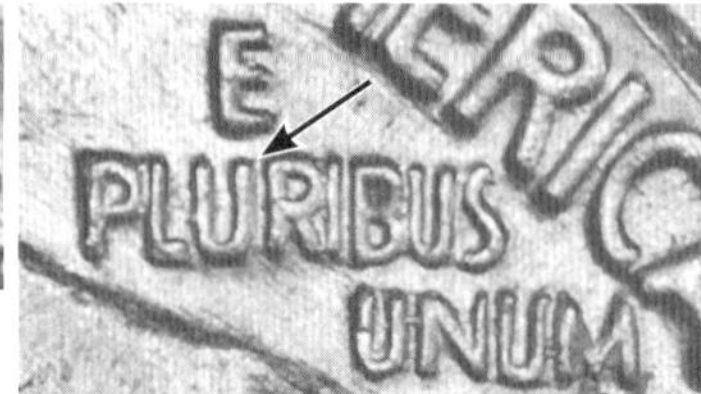

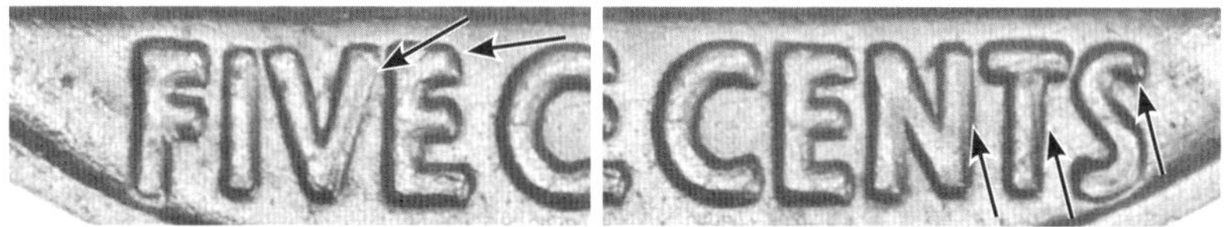

Description: This variety shows moderate doubling on FIVE CENTS, and to a lesser degree on UNITED and E PLURIBUS UNUM.

Comments: Though perhaps more rare than FS-05-1935-801, be careful not to confuse this with that listing, as the premiums are not nearly as high for this variety.

	VF-20	EF-40	AU-50	MS-60	MS-63
Variety	$50	$100	$250	$400	$500
Normal	$2	$3	$10	$22	$45

1935-D — FS-05-1935D-502 (018.5)

Variety: Repunched Mintmark — CONECA: RPM-002
PUP: Mintmark
URS-4 • I-4 • L-4

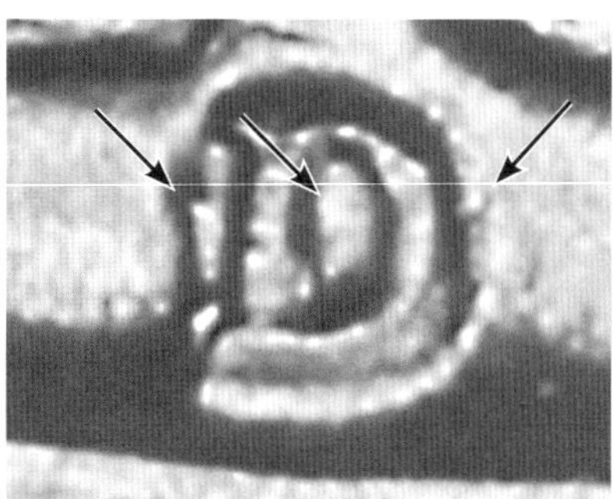

Description: This is, without a doubt, one of the nicer repunched mintmarks of this series. There are at least four mintmark punches, with two to the west and one to the east of the primary mintmark.

Comments: This coin was first reported to us by Denny Polly about 1987.

	VF-20	EF-40	AU-50	MS-60	MS-63
Variety	$100	$150	$225	$350	$500
Normal	$6	$18	$42	$75	$85

1935-S — FS-05-1935S-801 (018.6)

Variety: Doubled-Die Reverse — CONECA: DDR-001
PUP: E PLURIBUS UNUM, FIVE CENTS
URS-5 • I-2 • L-2

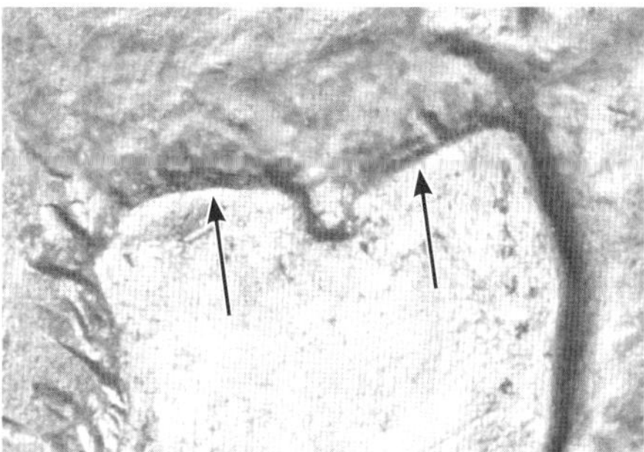

Description: Doubling is seen to the southeast on portions of E PLURIBUS UNUM and FIVE CENTS. It is also evident on the buffalo's belly.

Comments: More and more doubled-die reverses with similar doubling are being reported.

	VF-20	EF-40	AU-50	MS-60	MS-63
Variety	$200	$500	$750	$1,500	$1,750
Normal	$2.50	$4	$18	$55	$70

1936 — FS-05-1936-101 (018.7)

Variety: Doubled-Die Obverse — CONECA: DDO-001
PUP: Date, LIBERTY
URS-10 • I-3 • L-4

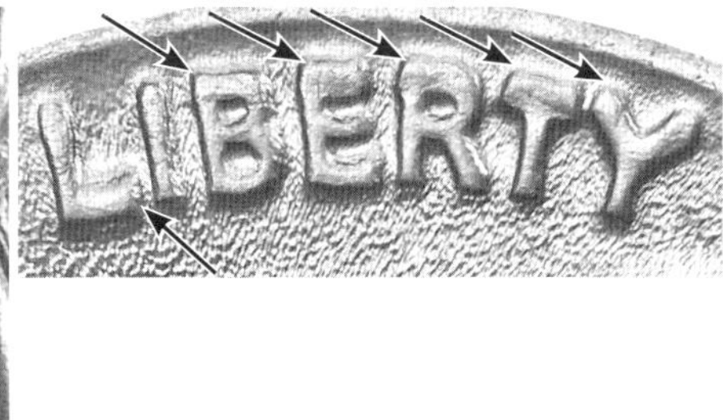

Description: Doubling is seen as extreme thickness primarily on the date and LIBERTY.

Comments: This is one of the strongest known Class VI doubled-die obverses for the series.

	VF-20	EF-40	AU-50	MS-60	MS-63
Variety	$25	$50	$125	$200	$350
Normal	$2	$3	$9	$22	$40

1936 — FS-05-1936-102

VARIETY: Doubled-Die Obverse — CONECA: DDO-002
PUP: LIBERTY
URS-6 • I-3 • L-4

Description: This variety is identified by strong extra thickness on LIBERTY and the date.

Comments: The doubling is not as strong as FS-101, but is very nice nonetheless.

	VF-20	EF-40	AU-50	MS-60	MS-63
VARIETY	$20	$40	$100	$175	$300
NORMAL	$2	$3	$9	$22	$40

1936 — FS-05-1936-801 (018.8)

VARIETY: Doubled-Die Reverse — CONECA: DDR-001
PUP: UNITED STATES, CENTS
URS-6 • I-3 • L-3

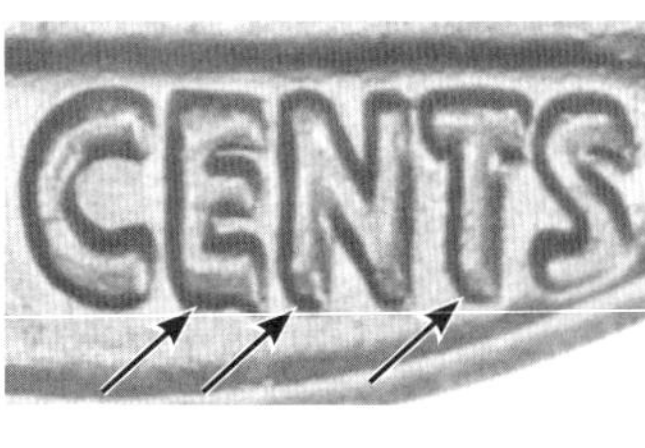

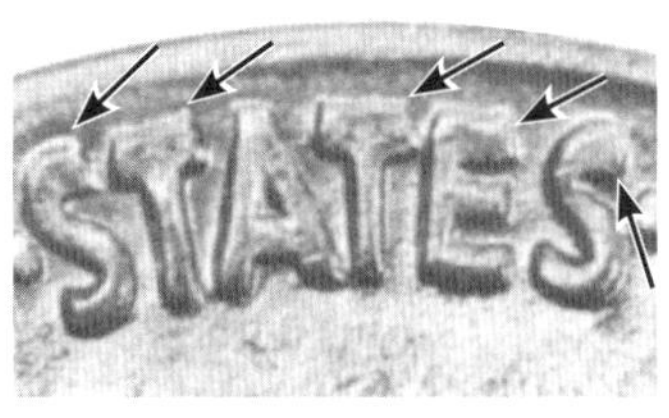

Description: Doubling is seen as extreme thickness on all reverse lettering, with near separation on the dot between UNITED and STATES.

Comments: This is perhaps the strongest known Class VI doubled-die reverse for the series and would make a great companion to FS-05-1936-101.

	VF-20	EF-40	AU-50	MS-60	MS-63
VARIETY	$75	$150	$300	$450	$750
NORMAL	$2	$3	$9	$22	$40

1936-D FS-05-1936D-502 (019.5)

VARIETY: Repunched Mintmark CONECA: RPM-002
PUP: Mintmark
URS-12 • I-3 • L-4

Description: The secondary mintmark is visible to the northwest of the primary mintmark.

Comments: This is a very popular repunched mintmark.

	VF-20	EF-40	AU-50	MS-60	MS-63
VARIETY	$25	$50	$75	$125	$200
NORMAL	$2	$4	$12	$38	$45

1936-D FS-05-1936D-511 (019.8)

VARIETY: Repunched Mintmark (D/D/D) CONECA: RPM-004
PUP: Mintmark
URS-4 • I-4 • L-4

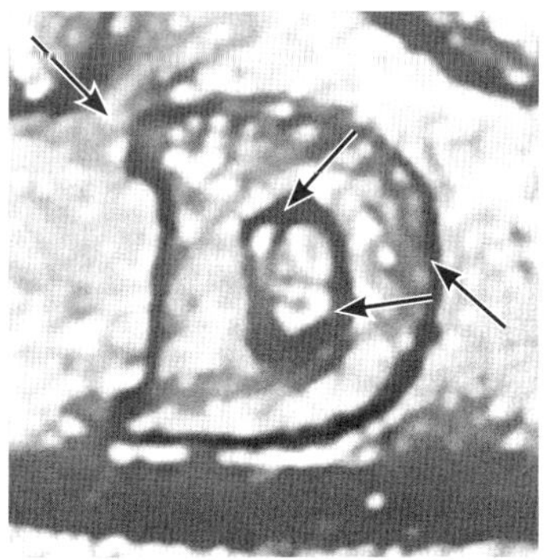

Description: A D mintmark was initially punched into the die, followed by two subsequent D mintmark punches.

Comments: This variety has been proven to be a D Over D Over D mintmark and not a D Over D Over S.

	VF-20	EF-40	AU-50	MS-60	MS-63
VARIETY	$40	$60	$125	$200	$350
NORMAL	$2	$4	$12	$38	$45

1936-D — FS-05-1936D-901 (019)

Variety: 3-1/2-Legged Buffalo — CONECA: N/L
PUP: Right front leg
URS-7 • I-5 • L-5

Description: The right front leg of the buffalo on this variety has been partially polished off the die—similar to the famous 1937-D 3-Legged variety, but not as severe. It is not from the same die as the 1937-D variety.

Comments: This is an extremely rare variety. This was incorrectly listed by Breen as 1936-P.

	VF-20	EF-40	AU-50	MS-60	MS-63
Variety	$1,500	$2,500	$4,000	$12,500	*$20,000*
Normal	$2	$4	$12	$38	$45

1936-S — FS-05-1936S-501 (020)

Variety: Repunched Mintmark — CONECA: RPM-001
PUP: Mintmark
URS-11 • I-4 • L-3

Description: This is a very strong repunched mintmark, with the secondary S almost half a letter south of the primary S.

Comments: This variety is very scarce in grades above Extremely Fine, and rare in Mint State.

	VF-20	EF-40	AU-50	MS-60	MS-63
Variety	$25	$40	$75	$150	$300
Normal	$2	$4	$12	$38	$45

1937-D — FS-05-1937D-901 (020.2)

VARIETY: 3-Legged Buffalo — CONECA: N/L
PUP: Right front leg
URS-14 • I-5 • L-5

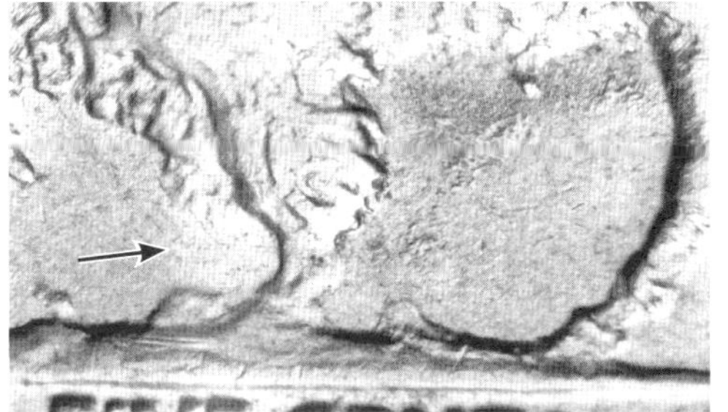

Description: This reverse die was heavily polished, possibly to remove clash marks. The result was a die with portions of the bison's right front leg missing, hence the nickname "3-Legged Buffalo."

Comments: There are many altered specimens passed as the genuine coin. Look for a line of raised dots from the middle of the bison's belly to the ground as one of the diagnostics on the genuine specimen.

	VF-20	EF-40	AU-50	MS-60	MS-63
VARIETY	$750	$900	$1,000	$2,250	$4,500
NORMAL	$3	$4	$10	$32	$42

1938-D — FS-05-1938D-511 (020.5)

VARIETY: Over Mintmark (D/D/D/S) — CONECA: OMM-001
PUP: Mintmark
URS-13 • I-5 • L-4

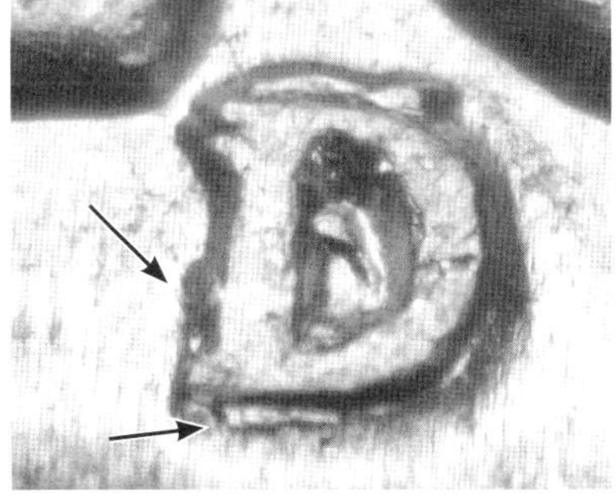

Description: An S mintmark was initially punched into the die, followed by three subsequent D mintmark punches. The alteration was deliberate, as the Mint was preparing the new Jefferson design dies, and it was cheaper to recycle dies marked for the San Francisco Mint but never shipped than to hub new dies and scrap the S-mintmark dies.

Comments: There are five different D Over S dies for this date. OMM-001, the variety illustrated here, is the variety listed in most major pricing guides. The other varieties command less of a premium.

	VF-20	EF-40	AU-50	MS-60	MS-63
VARIETY	$14	$20	$32	$55	$80
NORMAL	$4.75	$5	$8	$22	$36

1938-D — FS-05-1938D-512, 513, 514, 515

VARIETY: Over Mintmark (D Over S)
PUP: Mintmark
URS-7 • I-3 • L-3

CONECA: OMM-002, OMM-003, OMM-004, OMM-005

FS-05-1938D-512

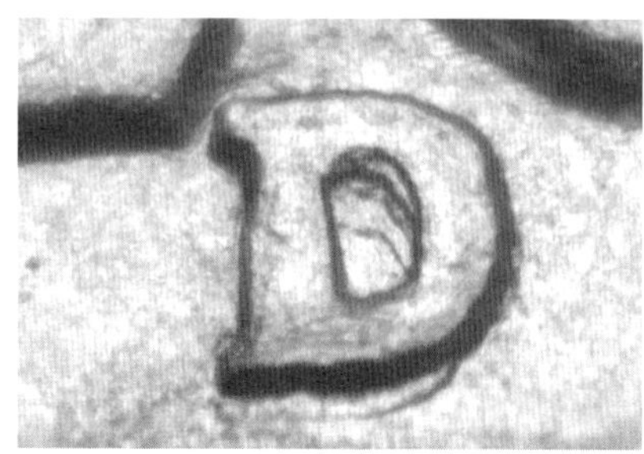

FS-05-1938D-513

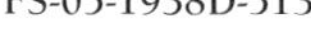

FS-05-1938D-514

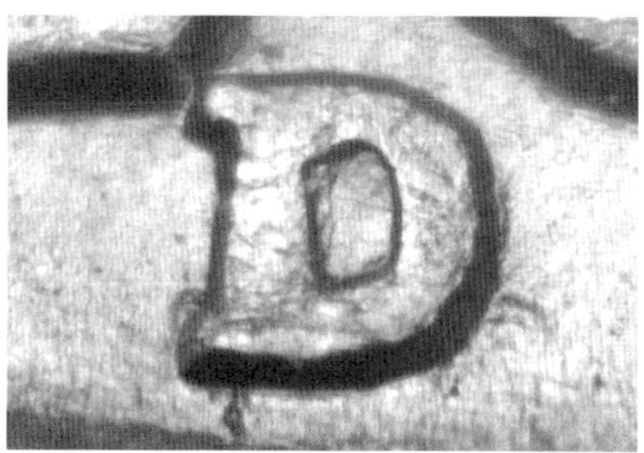

FS-05-1938D-515

Description: Besides FS-511, listed separately, there are four additional dies considered to be D Over S over mintmarks.

Comments: Note that FS-513 is also a doubled-die reverse, showing doubling on E PLURIBUS UNUM.

	VF-20	EF-40	AU-50	MS-60	MS-63
VARIETY, FS-512	$15	$30	$50	$75	$100
VARIETY, FS-513	$15	$30	$50	$75	$100
VARIETY, FS-514	$15	$30	$50	$75	$100
VARIETY, FS-515	$15	$30	$50	$75	$100
NORMAL	$4.75	$5	$8	$22	$36

Jefferson Nickels, 1938 to Date

The Jefferson nickel series is one of the most widely collected of all modern coin designs and most certainly as far as varieties are concerned. The popularity of collecting these varieties started full force with the beginning of PAK, the Full Steps Jefferson nickel club that originated in the 1970s. (Its name derived from the initials of founders Philip Petrillo, Adolf Weiss, and Karl Nenninger.)

Due in large part to PAK, most of the varieties listed in the *Cherrypickers' Guide* have been well known to specialists for several decades, yet still may be somewhat new to more novice collectors. In the earlier days of PAK, there was a list of the "10 Most Wanted" varieties within the series:

1. 1939 Doubled-Die Reverse (FS-801)
2. 1942-D, D Over Horizontal D (FS-501)
3. 1943-P, 3 Over 2 Overdate (FS-101)
4. 1943-P "Doubled Eye" Doubled-Die Obverse (FS-106)
5. 1945-P Doubled-Die Reverse (FS-801)
6. 1946-D, D Over Inverted D (FS-501)
7. 1949-D, D Over S (FS-501)
8. 1954-S, S Over D (FS-501)
9. 1955 Proof Tripled-Die Reverse (FS-801)
10. 1955-D, D Over S (FS-501, CONECA OMM-001)

These 10 are still popular today, though there have been many additions to collectors' "must have" lists.

An excellent reference for general information on the series is *A Guide Book of Buffalo and Jefferson Nickels* by Q. David Bowers. Included is a complete history of the series, price guidelines, grading information, variety information, and much more. A detailed date-by-date analysis defines strike characteristics, availability by grade, and many facts not available in any other reference. Add to this the accurate, interesting, and at times colorful writing by the best numismatic author of our time, and you will have the most interesting and informative book on the series.

There are several other books devoted to Jefferson nickel varieties which we can recommend to those interested in obtaining more information. *The Jefferson Nickel RPM Book – An Attribution Guide* by James Wiles describes and illustrates all known repunched and over mintmarks within the series. A second edition was produced in 2003 to include discoveries made after the initial publication. *The Best of the Jefferson Nickel Doubled Dies* by John A. Wexler and Brian A. Ribar describes and illustrates many of the doubled dies within the series. There is another important book by Bernard A. Nagengast entitled *The Jefferson Nickel Analyst*. This reference offers a date-by-date analysis of the series, and also describes and rates rarity of Full Steps nickels.

A previously popular collector's club, the Jefferson Full Step Nickel Club, has been defunct for a few years. Given the popularity of these coins, we encourage cherrypickers to organize a new club to keep the excitement going.

Newly Listed Varieties

Fivaz-Stanton Number	Variety	Page No.
FS-05-1938-106	DDO	338
FS-05-1938-401	Re-Engraved Die	338
FS-05-1938-402	Re-Engraved Die	339
FS-05-1938-403	Re-Engraved Die	339
FS-05-1939-101	DDO	340
FS-05-1940S-501	RPM	342
FS-05-1942P-501	RPM	346
FS-05-1942S-501	RPM	346
FS-05-1942S-502	MM Location	347
FS-05-1943P-102	DDO	348
FS-05-1943P-103	DDO	348
FS-05-1943D-501	RPM	349
FS-05-1944D-501	RPM	350
FS-05-1945D-101	DDO	352
FS-05-1945D-501	RPM	352
FS-05-1946-801	DDR	353
FS-05-1952-401	Re-Engraved Die	356
FS-05-1952-402	Re-Engraved Die	356

Fivaz-Stanton Number	Variety	Page No.
FS-05-1952-403	Re-Engraved Die	356
FS-05-1952-404	Re-Engraved Die	356
FS-05-1953-401	Re-Engraved Die	357
FS-05-1953D-501	RPM	358
FS-05-1954-401	Re-Engraved Die	358
FS-05-1954S-801	DDR	360
FS-05-1958D-501	RPM	364
FS-05-1964-801	DDR	366
FS-05-1969S-501	RPM	367
FS-05-1971S-501	No MM	368
FS-05-1971S-801	DDR	368
FS-05-1979S-501	Type 2 MM	369
FS-05-1981S-501	Type 2 MM	369
FS-05-1990S-101	DDO	369
FS-05-2004P-101	DDO	370
FS-05-2005P-101	DDO	370

Varieties to be Delisted

Fivaz-Stanton Number	Variety	Page No.
FS-05-1956-102	DDO	362
FS-05-1961-801	DDR	365

Debunked Varieties

Fivaz-Stanton Number	Variety
FS-05-1941S-503	IMM

1938 — FS-05-1938-101 (021)

VARIETY: Doubled-Die Obverse — CONECA: DDO-002
PUP: Date
URS-10 • I-3 • L-2

Description: A moderate spread is evident on the motto, star, and date. The secondary image is rotated slightly counterclockwise.

Comments: Once a very popular Jefferson nickel variety, this doubled die can still be cherrypicked with some searching.

	EF-40	AU-50	MS-60	MS-63	MS-65
VARIETY	$30	$45	$60	$75	$105
NORMAL	$1	$1.50	$3	$4	$16

1938 — FS-05-1938-105 (021.5)

VARIETY: Quadrupled-Die Obverse — CONECA: DDO-005
PUP: Date, LIBERTY
URS-10 • I-3 • L-3

Description: This is a moderate quadrupled die, with secondary images evident toward the center of the coin on LIBERTY, IN GOD WE TRUST, the date, and the star.

Comments: Early-die-state specimens especially are quite attractive, with the four images very clear on all the lettering and the date.

	EF-40	AU-50	MS-60	MS-63	MS-65
VARIETY	$40	$60	$80	$100	$140
NORMAL	$1	$1.50	$3	$4	$16

1938 FS-05-1938-106

Variety: Doubled-Die Obverse CONECA: DDO-008
PUP: LIBERTY
URS-5 • I-4 • L-4

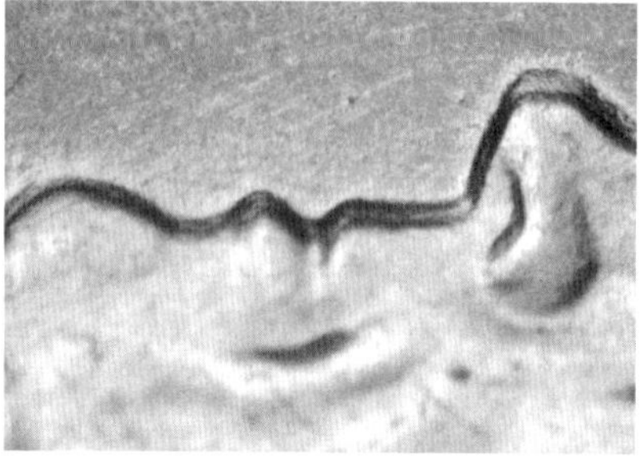

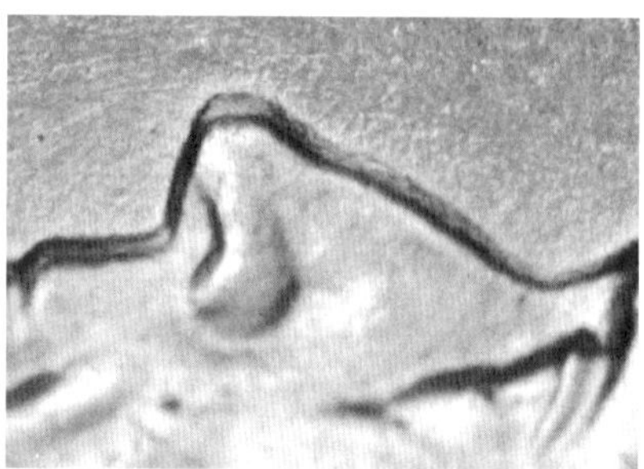

Description: This variety shows a strong spread on LIBERTY, the date, IN GOD WE TRUST, and the profile.

Comments: No early-die-state coins have been reported yet.

	EF-40	AU-50	MS-60	MS-63	MS-65
Variety	$50	$75	$100	$175	$250
Normal	$1	$1.50	$3	$4	$16

1938 Proof FS-05-1938-401

Variety: Re-engraved Obverse Design CONECA: RED-001
PUP: IN GOD WE TRUST, LIBERTY, ribbon
URS-6 • I-3 • L-3

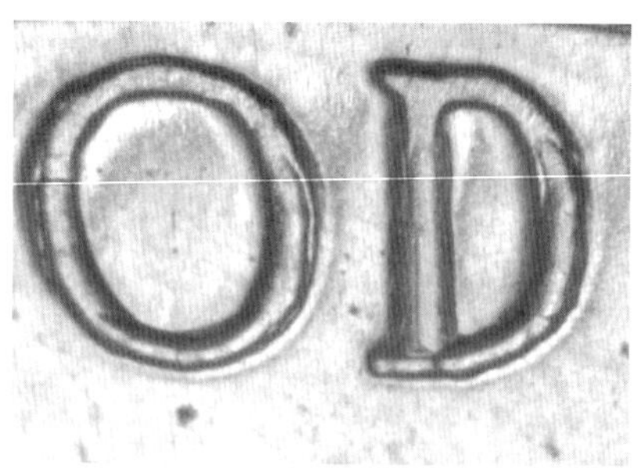

Description: All the letters of IN GOD WE TRUST, LIBERTY, and the 1 and 9 of the date have been hand-engraved to strengthen their relief. A serif has been added to the lower S of TRUST.

Comments: In addition to the three 1938 re-engraved die varieties listed here, at least two more re-engraved dies are known to exist. Research is ongoing. There is also some re-engraving on the reverse dies.

	PF-63	PF-65	PF-67
Variety	$100	$150	$450
Normal	$50	$125	$400

1938 Proof — FS-05-1938-402

VARIETY: Re-engraved Obverse Design — CONECA: RED-003
PUP: IN GOD WE TRUST, LIBERTY, ribbon
URS-6 • I-3 • L-3

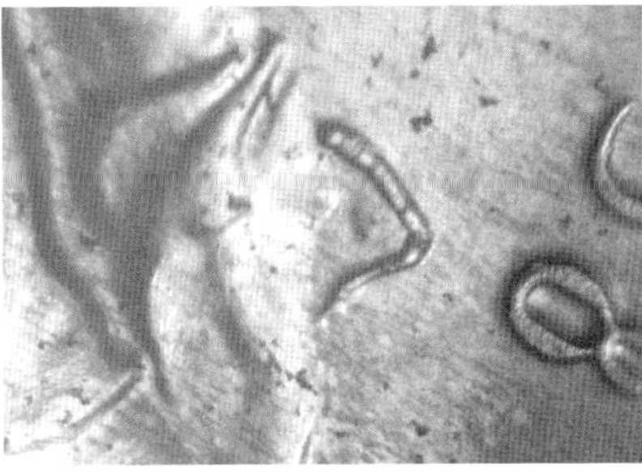

Description: This variety is identified by a strongly re-engraved ribbon.

Comments: In addition to the three 1938 re-engraved die varieties listed here, at least two more re-engraved dies are known to exist. Research is ongoing. There is also some re-engraving on the reverse dies.

	PF-63	PF-65	PF-67
VARIETY	$100	$150	$450
NORMAL	$50	$125	$400

1938 Proof — FS-05-1938-403

VARIETY: Re-engraved Obverse Design — CONECA: RED-004
PUP: IN GOD WE TRUST, LIBERTY, ribbon
URS-6 • I-3 • L-3

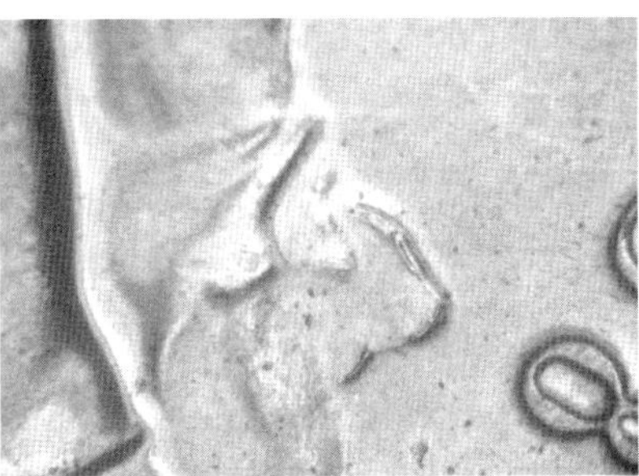

Description: This variety has a lightly re-engraved ribbon. IN GOD and LIB have been enhanced. No serif is present on the lower S of TRUST.

Comments: In addition to the three 1938 re-engraved die varieties listed here, at least two more re-engraved dies are known to exist. Research is ongoing. There is also some re-engraving on the reverse dies.

	PF-63	PF-65	PF-67
VARIETY	$100	$150	$450
NORMAL	$50	$125	$400

1939 FS-05-1939-101

VARIETY: Doubled-Die Obverse CONECA: DDO-007
PUP: LIBERTY
URS-4 • I-3 • L-4

Description: There is strong extra thickness on all lettering around the rim, the star, and the date.

Comments: Several dies exhibit these extra-thick letters, so check the attribution guides for distinguishing markers.

	EF-40	AU-50	MS-60	MS-63	MS-65
VARIETY	$40	$60	$100	$125	$200
NORMAL	$0.50	$1	$2	$2.50	$12

1939 FS-05-1939-801 (022)

VARIETY: Doubled-Die Reverse CONECA: DDR-001
PUP: MONTICELLO, CENTS
URS-10 • I-5 • L-5

Description: Very strong doubling is evident to the east of the primary letters, most noticeably on MONTICELLO and FIVE CENTS. Lesser doubling is also visible on UNITED STATES OF AMERICA and the right side of the building.

Comments: Early-die-state specimens especially are quite attractive. This variety is only seen on issues using the reverse of 1940.

	EF-40	AU-50	MS-60	MS-63	MS-65
VARIETY	$100	$200	$250	$400	$1,000
NORMAL	$0.50	$1	$2	$2.50	$12

1939 — FS-05-1939-802 (022.5)

VARIETY: Quadrupled-Die Reverse — CONECA: DDR-002
PUP: MONTICELLO, CENTS
URS-10 • I-4 • L-3

Description: Strong multiple images are evident on all reverse lettering, with a close spread. The final O of MONTICELLO is almost egg-shaped.

Comments: This variety is still fairly scarce to rare in Mint State. This variety is only seen on issues using the reverse of 1940.

	EF-40	AU-50	MS-60	MS-63	MS-65
VARIETY	$25	$50	$100	$150	$250
NORMAL	$0.50	$1	$2	$2.50	$12

1939 Proof — FS-05-1939-901 (023)

VARIETY: Reverse of 1940 — CONECA: RDV-002
PUP: Steps of Monticello
URS-9 • I-4 • L-4

Description: The vast majority of the 1939 Proof Jefferson mintage was produced with the reverse of 1938, which had "wavy," ill-defined steps on Monticello. However, a very few of the Proof coins were produced using the new, enhanced design of 1940, with sharp, well-defined steps. The photo here is of the steps of 1940.

Comments: Circulation-strike coins produced in 1939 from all three mints are known with both reverse designs, but the Proof coins from 1939 are rare with the "type II" steps of 1940.

	PF-63	PF-65	PF-67
VARIETY	$300	$750	$3,000
NORMAL	$50	$125	$400

1940 Proof — FS-05-1940-901 (024)

VARIETY: Reverse of 1938 — CONECA: RDV-001
PUP: Steps of Monticello
URS-5 • I-5 • L-5

Description: The vast majority of the 1940 Proof Jefferson mintage was produced with the reverse of 1940, which had sharp, well-defined steps. However, a very few of the Proof coins were produced using the older hub, with ill-defined steps of 1938. The photo here is of the reverse of 1938. The coin also exhibits doubling on the reverse.

Comments: This is an extremely rare variety. There are no known circulation strikes with the reverse of 1938. This reverse is also known on pieces dated 1939.

	PF-63	PF-65	PF-67
VARIETY	$500	$1,000	$3,500
NORMAL	$50	$125	$600

1940-S — FS-05-1940S-501

VARIETY: Repunched Mintmark — CONECA: RPM-001
PUP: Mintmark
URS-6 • I-3 • L-3

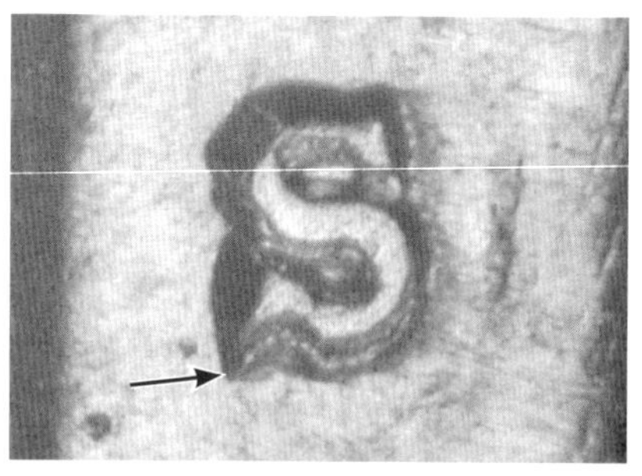

Description: The additional S appears to the south.

Comments: This one has been known for ages, but Mint State specimens are elusive.

	EF-40	AU-50	MS-60	MS-63	MS-65
VARIETY	$20	$30	$40	$50	$75
NORMAL	$0.50	$1	$2.25	$3	$12

1941-D — FS-05-1941D-501 (024.3)

VARIETY: Repunched Mintmark — CONECA: RPM-003
PUP: Mintmark
URS-5 • I-2 • L-2

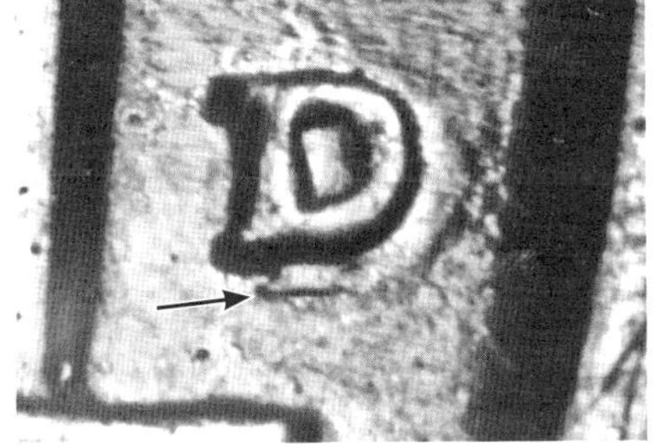

Description: A secondary D is evident to the southeast of the primary D.

Comments: This variety is included primarily to remind novices that repunched mintmarks are known and available in this series for almost any dated coin bearing a mintmark through the 1950s, and with many dates later.

	AU-50	MS-63	MS-65
VARIETY	$25	$50	$95
NORMAL	$1.50	$3.50	$10

Note: Please note that relatively minor varieties such as this are very difficult to sell in grades below About Uncirculated.

1941-S — FS-05-1941S-501 (024.5)

VARIETY: Large S Mintmark — CONECA: MMS-002
PUP: Mintmark
URS-5 • I-4 • L-4

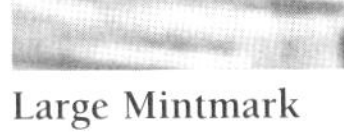

Large Mintmark

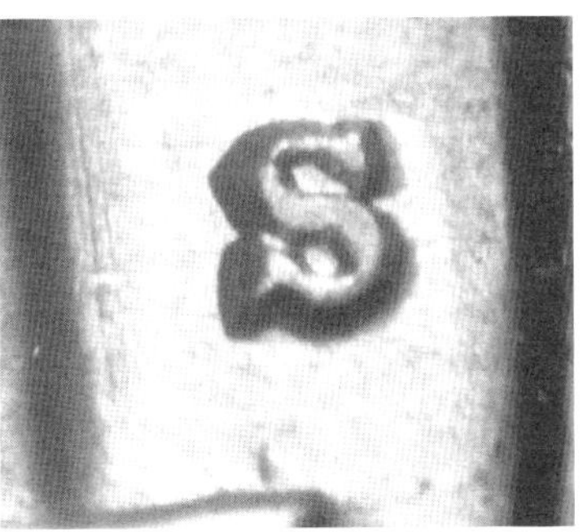

Small Mintmark

Description: Two mintmark styles were used on 1941-S nickels; the Large S (shown on the left) is far rarer than the normal or Small S (shown on the right).

Comments: This variety is extremely difficult to locate in any grade. Several repunched mintmarks are known for this variety.

	AU-50	MS-63	MS-65
VARIETY	$38	$115	$190
NORMAL	$1.50	$4	$12

1941-S — FS-05-1941S-502

Variety: Repunched Mintmark — CONECA: RPM-002
PUP: Mintmark
URS-5 • I-3 • L-3

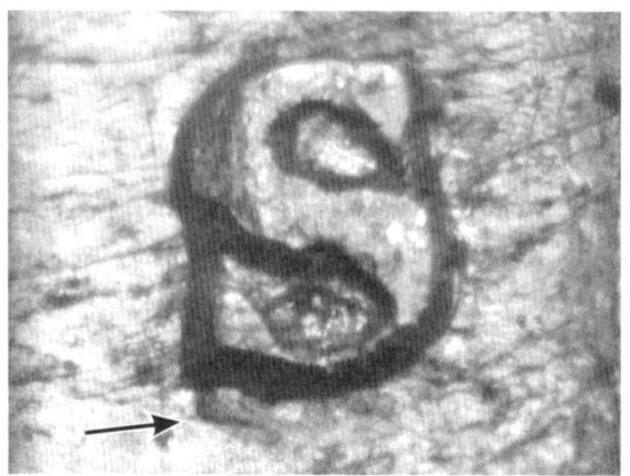

Description: A secondary S is evident to the south of the primary S. This is the Large S variety.

Comments: Most of the value for this repunched mintmark is for the Large S–style mintmark.

	AU-50	MS-63	MS-65
Variety	$100	$150	$250
Normal	$1.50	$4	$12

1942, Copper-Nickel Alloy — FS-05-1942-101 (025)

Variety: Doubled-Die Obverse — CONECA: DDO-002
PUP: Nose, date, GOD
URS-5 • I-4 • L-4

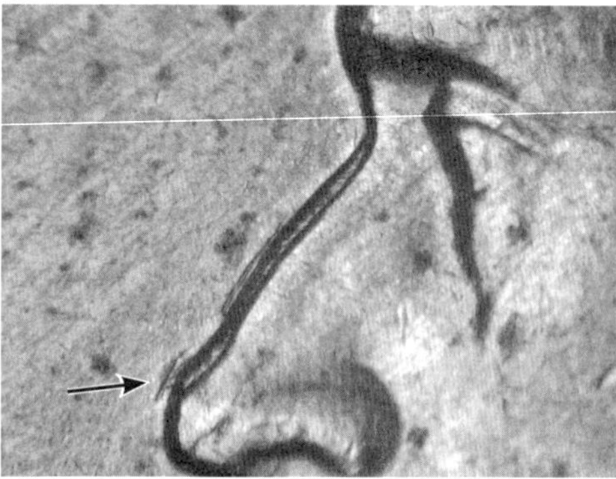

Description: Strong doubling is evident on Jefferson's profile, especially the nose, and on the date, the motto, and LIBERTY.

Comments: This is a much underrated variety and extremely difficult to locate. This variety appears only on coins of the copper-nickel issue.

	EF-40	AU-50	MS-60	MS-63	MS-65
Variety	$75	$100	$250	$500	$1,000
Normal	$0.45	$1.25	$4	$6	$15

1942, Copper-Nickel Alloy — FS-05-1942-102 (026)

VARIETY: Doubled-Die Obverse — CONECA: DDO-003
PUP: Eye, nose
URS-9 • I-3 • L-3

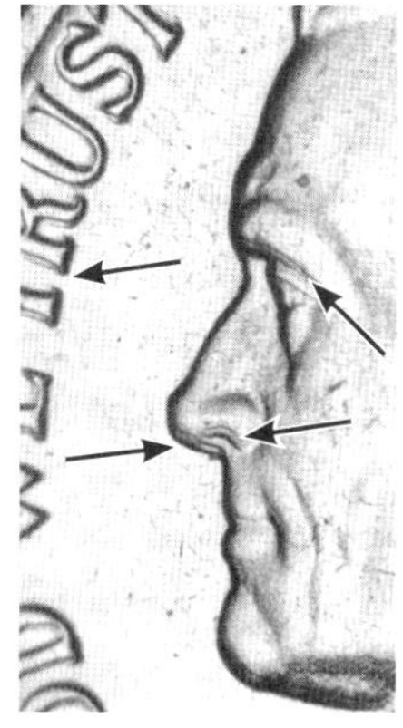

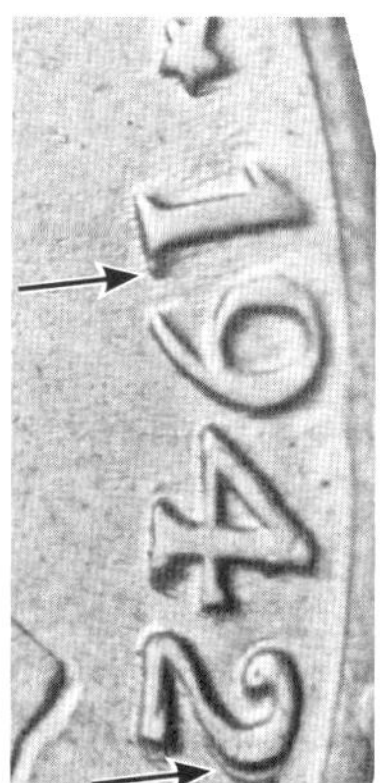

Description: Strong doubling is evident on Jefferson's eyebrow, lower nose, lips, and jaw, as well as on all the obverse lettering.

Comments: This and the previous listings can be difficult to locate, and are not well known. This variety appears only on coins of the copper-nickel issue.

	EF-40	AU-50	MS-60	MS-63	MS-65
VARIETY	$25	$35	$60	$100	$300
NORMAL	$0.45	$1.25	$4	$6	$15

1942-D, Copper-Nickel Alloy — FS-05-1942D-501 (027)

VARIETY: D Over Horizontal D — CONECA: RPM-001
PUP: Mintmark
URS-11 • I-5 • L-5

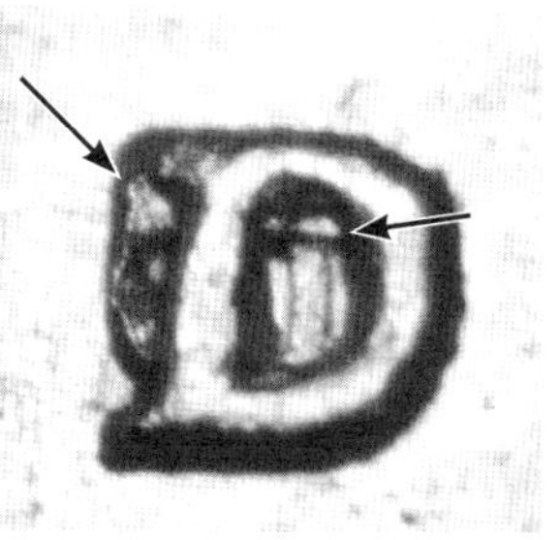

Description: The initial D mintmark was punched into the die horizontally, then corrected, creating the D Over Horizontal D variety.

Comments: This is one of the rarest of the major Jefferson nickel varieties in Mint State. Coins below the grade of About Uncirculated have moderate interest only.

	EF-40	AU-50	MS-60	MS-63	MS-65
VARIETY	$75	$100	$1,400	$2,000	$4,000
NORMAL	$2	$5	$28	$38	$60

1942-P, Silver Alloy — FS-05-1942P-501

VARIETY: Repunched Mintmark — CONECA: RPM-008
PUP: Mintmark
URS-5 • I-3 • L-3

Description: The additional P appears to the east.

Comments: Repunched mintmarks abound on nickels from the World War II years. Be sure to check the attribution guides for distinguishing markers.

	EF-40	AU-50	MS-60	MS-63	MS-65
VARIETY	$10	$20	$30	$50	$75
NORMAL	$2.50	$3.25	$7	$12	$20

1942-S, Silver Alloy — FS-05-1942S-501

VARIETY: Repunched Mintmark — CONECA: RPM-001
PUP: Mintmark
URS-5 • I-3 • L-3

Description: Two additional S mintmarks appear to the west.

Comments: This variety belongs in any short set of wartime nickel repunched mintmarks.

	EF-40	AU-50	MS-60	MS-63	MS-65
VARIETY	$10	$20	$30	$50	$75
NORMAL	$2.50	$3.25	$7	$12	$25

1942-S, Silver Alloy — FS-05-1942S-502

Variety: Mintmark Location
PUP: Field right of Monticello
URS-1 • I-5 • L-5

Description: All other 1942-S Jefferson nickels are known with the mintmark location typical of silver-composition wartime nickels—above Monticello. This variety was discovered in 1961 by Ken Frith and to date is the only known silver example with the mintmark location of prior years' coins. It has been analyzed by the Campus Electron Optics Facility at Ohio State University and was found to be, in their opinion, a genuine Mint product.

Comments: Confirmation of this variety would necessitate the finding of at least one more example.

	EF-40	AU-50	MS-60	MS-63	MS-65
Variety	(unique)				
Normal	$2.50	$3.25	$7	$12	$25

1943-P — FS-05-1943P-101 (028)

Variety: Doubled-Die Obverse, Overdate — CONECA: DDO-003
PUP: Date
URS-13 • I-5 • L-5

Description: This popular variety was created when the die was first hubbed with a 1942-dated hub, then subsequently hubbed with a 1943-dated hub. The diagonal of the 2 is visible within the lower opening of the 3. Doubling is also visible on LIBERTY and IN GOD WE TRUST. Most of the high-grade specimens available are late die states with heavy metal flow lines toward the rim and somewhat "mushy" numbers and letters. The reverse is also a tripled die.

Comments: There is at least one 1943-P five-cent piece that has a faint, short die gouge extending upward from the lower ball of the 3; this is often mistaken for the overdate. The true overdate must look like the variety pictured here. Although this is an overdate, there is low interest in examples of this variety in grades below About Uncirculated. It was discovered by Del Romines.

	EF-40	AU-50	MS-60	MS-63	MS-65
Variety	$50	$100	$200	$350	$750
Normal	$2.50	$3	$5	$8	$20

1943-P FS-05-1943P-102

VARIETY: Doubled-Die Obverse CONECA: DDO-005
PUP: LIBERTY
URS-4 • I-3 • L-4

Description: There is strong extra thickness on IN GOD WE TRUST, LIBERTY, the star, and the date.

Comments: This is one of the nicer Class VI doubled dies.

	EF-40	AU-50	MS-60	MS-63	MS-65
VARIETY	$10	$20	$30	$50	$75
NORMAL	$2.50	$3	$5	$8	$20

1943-P FS-05-1943P-103

VARIETY: Doubled-Die Obverse CONECA: DDO-013
PUP: LIBERTY
URS-6 • I-3 • L-4

Description: This variety shows a strong spread on the date, the star, LIBERTY, and IN GOD WE TRUST. This coin also has a very light doubled-die reverse, visible on UNUM and AMERICA.

Comments: All 1943 nickels are both series doubled on TRUST and master die doubled on LIBERTY. In addition, there are many rotational doubled dies listed in the CONECA files, so check the attribution files for diagnostic markers.

	EF-40	AU-50	MS-60	MS-63	MS-65
VARIETY	$10	$20	$30	$50	$75
NORMAL	$2.50	$3	$5	$8	$20

1943-P — FS-05-1943P-106 (029)

VARIETY: Doubled-Die Obverse ("Doubled Eye") — CONECA: DDO-006

PUP: Eye

URS-7 • I-5 • L-5

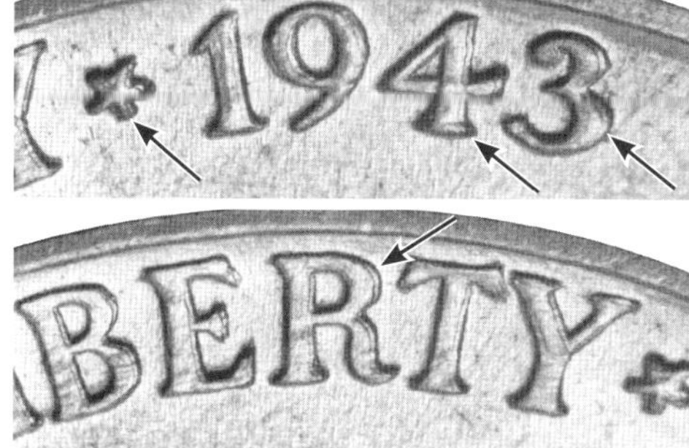

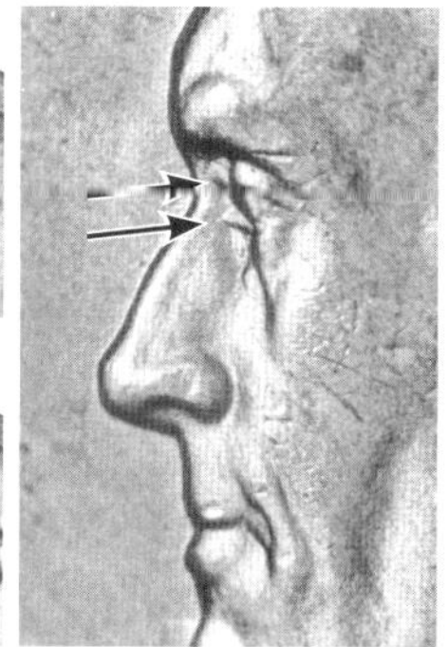

Description: The doubling is visible on the date, LIBERTY, the motto, and (most noticeably) the eye. There is a secondary eye below the primary eye, hence the nickname "Doubled Eye" variety.

Comments: This is one of the Jefferson nickel original "Top 10" varieties. It is becoming more and more difficult to locate.

	EF-40	AU-50	MS-60	MS-63	MS-65
VARIETY	$50	$95	$125	$300	$500
NORMAL	$2.50	$3	$5	$8	$20

1943-D — FS-05-1943D-501

VARIETY: Repunched Mintmark — CONECA: RPM-001

PUP: Mintmark

URS-5 • I-3 • L-3

Description: The additional D appears to the south.

Comments: The giant mintmark used for the wartime issues produced a lot of repunched mintmarks.

	EF-40	AU-50	MS-60	MS-63	MS-65
VARIETY	$10	$20	$30	$50	$75
NORMAL	$3.50	$4	$6	$12	$20

1944-D — FS-05-1944D-501

Variety: Repunched Mintmark — CONECA: RPM-001, DDO-002, DDR-001
PUP: Mintmark
URS-6 • I-3 • L-3

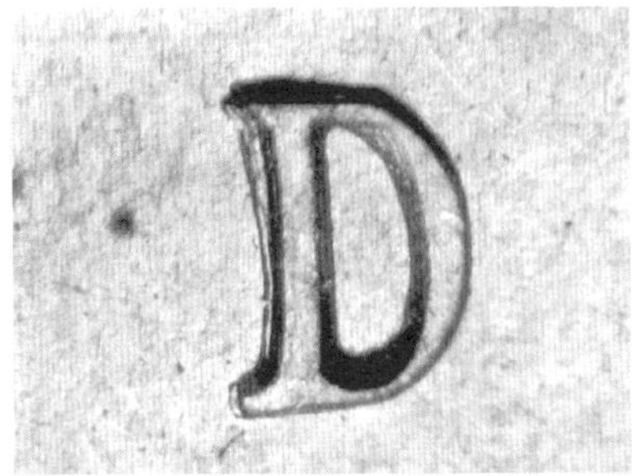

Description: The additional D appears to the west.

Comments: This variety comes both with and without a doubled-die obverse. Be sure to check the attribution guides for marker details.

	EF-40	AU-50	MS-60	MS-63	MS-65
Variety	$10	$20	$30	$50	$75
Normal	$2.50	$3	$6	$12	$25

1945-P — FS-05-1945P-501/804 (030.5)

Variety: Tripled-Die Reverse — CONECA: DDR-004, RPM-001
PUP: AMERICA, mintmark
URS-9 • I-3 • L-3

Description: The tripling is evident on the final O of MONTICELLO, CENTS, UNITED STATES OF AMERICA, and on portions of E PLURIBUS UNUM. The mintmark is punched at least three times.

Comments: Aside from the tripled die, this is one of the nicer repunched mintmarks of 1945.

	EF-40	AU-50	MS-60	MS-63	MS-65
Variety	$25	$50	$75	$150	$200
Normal	$2.50	$3	$5	$8	$20

1945-P — FS-05-1945P-801 (030)

Variety: Doubled-Die Reverse — **CONECA:** DDR-001
PUP: Last O of MONTICELLO
URS-10 • I-5 • L-4

Description: The reverse is strongly doubled, with the spread increasing from left to right.

Comments: There are at least two other collectible doubled-die reverses for this date.

	EF-40	AU-50	MS-60	MS-63	MS-65
Variety	$35	$55	$80	$150	$340
Normal	$2.50	$3	$5	$8	$20

1945-P — FS-05-1945P-803 (030.3)

Variety: Tripled-Die Reverse — **CONECA:** DDR-003
PUP: UNUM, AMERICA
URS-10 • I-3 • L-3

Description: Tripling is evident on all reverse lettering, especially E PLURIBUS UNUM, UNITED STATES OF AMERICA, FIVE CENTS, and the LLO of MONTICELLO.

Comments: This variety is not as dramatic as the preceding or following listings, but it is still a nice tripled die.

	EF-40	AU-50	MS-60	MS-63	MS-65
Variety	$25	$50	$90	$150	$250
Normal	$2.50	$3	$5	$8	$20

1945-D FS-05-1945D-101

Variety: Doubled-Die Obverse CONECA: DDO-006, RPM-005, RPM-020
PUP: LIBERTY
URS-6 • I-3 • L-4

Description: This variety exhibits strong extra thickness on all lettering and the date. This coin comes with two different reverses, both of which exhibit a repunched mintmark.

Comments: This is another nice Class VI doubled die as well as a combination variety coin.

	EF-40	AU-50	MS-60	MS-63	MS-65
Variety	$25	$50	$75	$100	$150
Normal	$2.50	$3	$5	$8	$20

1945-D FS-05-1945D-501

Variety: Repunched Mintmark CONECA: RPM-014
PUP: Mintmark
URS-3 • I-3 • L-3

Description: The additional D appears to the east.

Comments: This one is the widest spread of all the war nickel repunched mintmarks.

	EF-40	AU-50	MS-60	MS-63	MS-65
Variety	$10	$20	$30	$50	$75
Normal	$2.50	$3	$5	$8	$20

1946 — FS-05-1946-801

VARIETY: Doubled-Die Reverse — CONECA: DDR-003
PUP: Steps
URS-4 • I-4 • L-4

Description: There is a very strong spread south appearing as an extra set of steps in the letters of MONTICELLO, as well as extreme extra thickness on E PLURIBUS UNUM, UNITED STATES OF AMERICA, MONTICELLO, and FIVE CENTS.

Comments: The coin pictured is an early-die-state specimen. Late-die-state coins show only the step above the N of MONTICELLO.

	EF-40	AU-50	MS-60	MS-63	MS-65
VARIETY	$50	$75	$150	$250	$350
NORMAL	$0.30	$0.35	$0.75	$2.50	$15

1946-D — FS-05-1946D-501 (031)

VARIETY: Repunched Mintmark — CONECA: RPM-002
PUP: Mintmark
URS-7 • I-5 • L-5

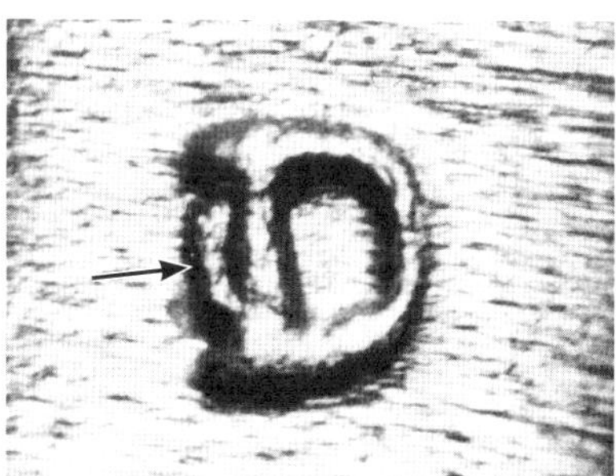

Description: The initial mintmark punch was inverted, with the subsequent punch in the correct position.

Comments: This is considered the second rarest of the original Jefferson "Top 10" in Mint State, second only to the 1942-D, D Over Horizontal D. Even in circulated grades, this is a very difficult variety to find.

	EF-40	AU-50	MS-60	MS-63	MS-65
VARIETY	$50	$200	$300	$700	$1,000
NORMAL	$0.40	$0.45	$1	$2.50	$12

1946-S — FS-05-1946S-101 (031.5)

Variety: Doubled-Die Obverse — CONECA: DDO-001
PUP: LIBERTY, date
URS-5 • I-4 • L-4

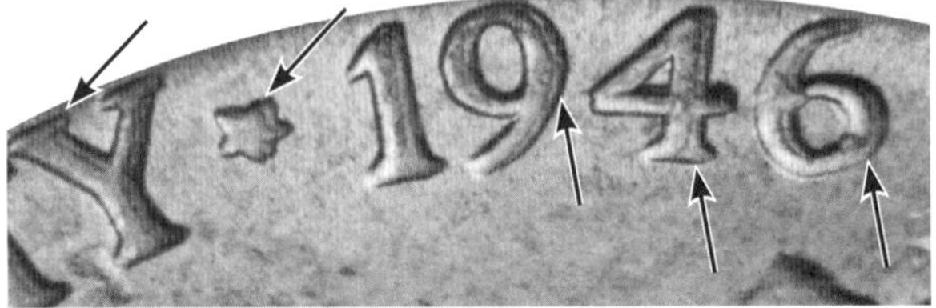

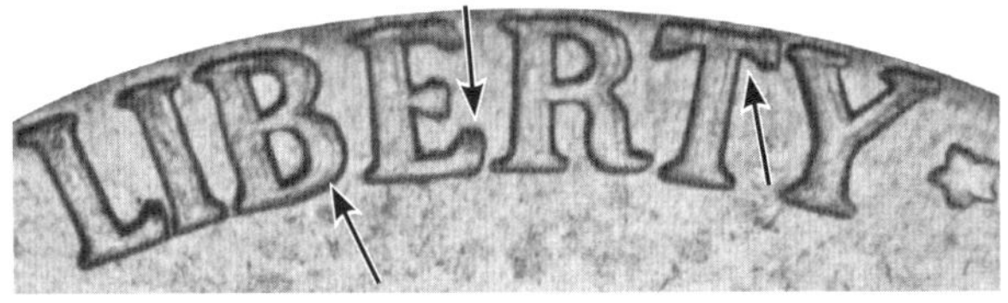

Description: The doubling is evident as a counterclockwise spread primarily on LIBERTY, the star, and the date.

Comments: John Wexler first reported this variety in 1979.

	EF-40	AU-50	MS-60	MS-63	MS-65
Variety	$50	$150	$350	$700	$950
Normal	$0.45	$0.50	$1	$2	$11

1949-D — FS-05-1949D-501 (032)

Variety: Over Mintmark (D Over S) — CONECA: OMM-001
PUP: Mintmark
URS-7 • I-5 • L-5

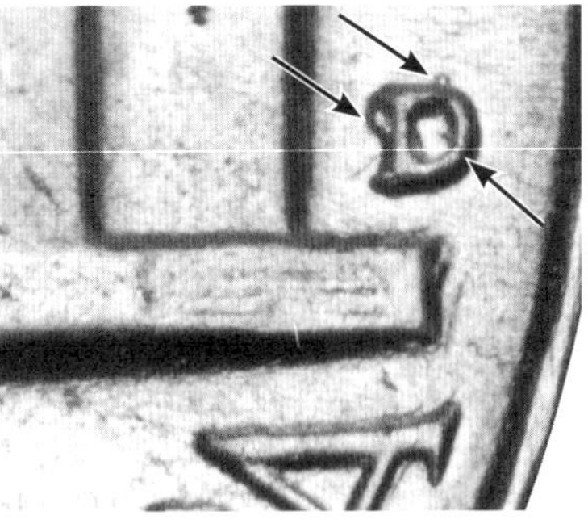

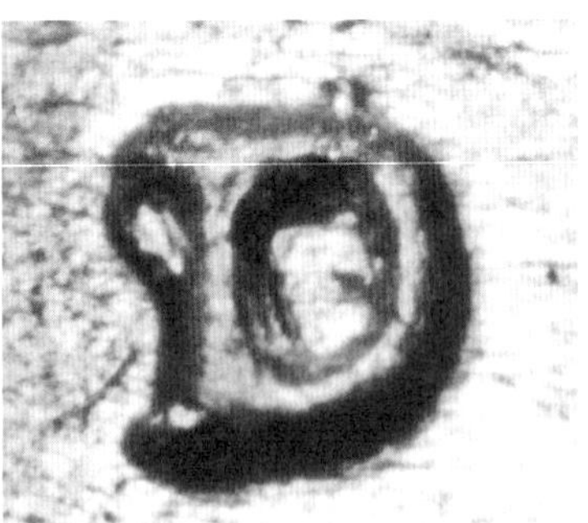

Description: The die initially received an S mintmark punch and later received a D mintmark on top of that. The top serif of the S is visible to the north of the D, with the upper left loop of the S visible to the west of the D.

Comments: This variety is quite rare in Mint State and highly sought after. Some may still be found in circulated grades. Some specimens have been located in original Mint sets.

	MS-60	MS-63	MS-65
Variety	$200	$300	$500
Normal	$1.50	$6	$10

1951 Proof — FS-05-1951-101 (032.5)

VARIETY: Doubled-Die Obverse — CONECA: DDO-001
PUP: Eye, chin, TRUST
URS-6 • I-3 • L-3

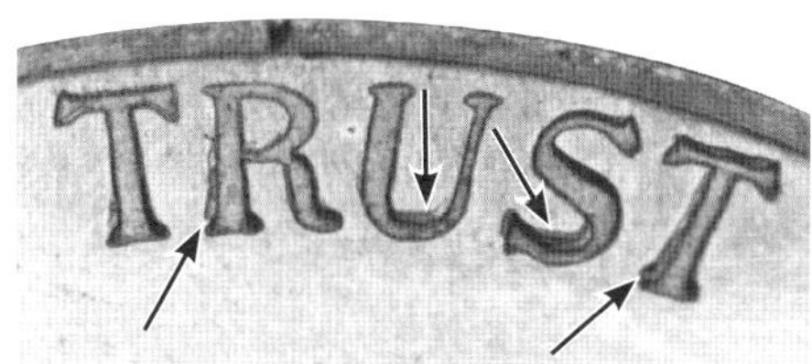

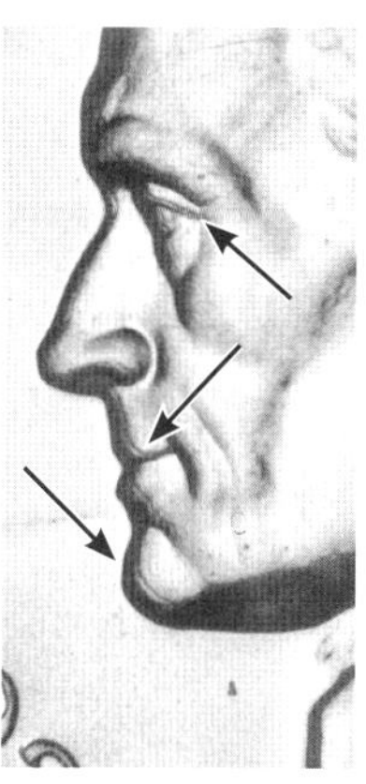

Description: The doubling is evident on the entire profile, including the chin, lips, nose, and eye. Some letters also show doubling, especially TRUST.

	PF-63	PF-64	PF-65
VARIETY	$100	$125	$175
NORMAL	$20	$40	$65

THE CHERRYPICKERS' GUIDE HELPFUL HINTS

The state of the die at the time the coin was struck can be important. Almost across the board, early-die-state (EDS) coins are much more desirable and will sell for higher prices.

1952 Proof — FS-05-1952-401, 402, 403, 404

Variety: Re-Engraved Obverse Design
PUP: Ribbon and lower queue
URS-1 • I-3 • L-3

CONECA: RED-001, RED-002, RED-003, RED-004

FS-05-1952-401

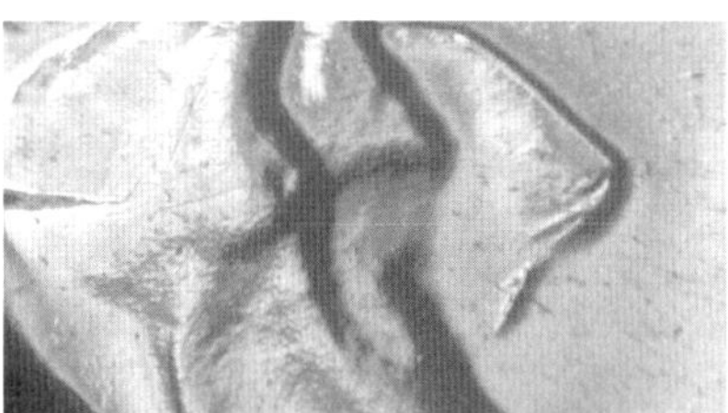

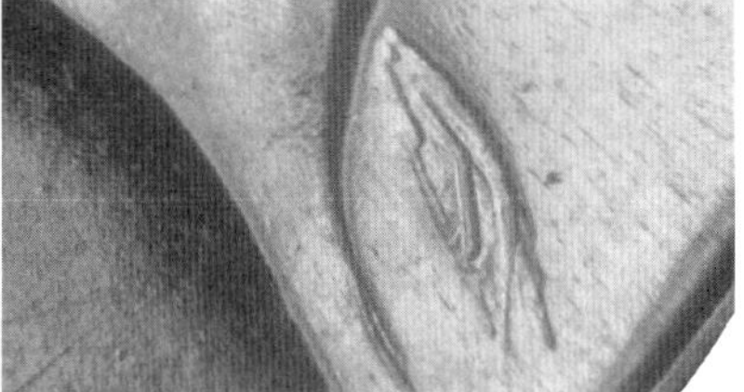

FS-05-1952-403

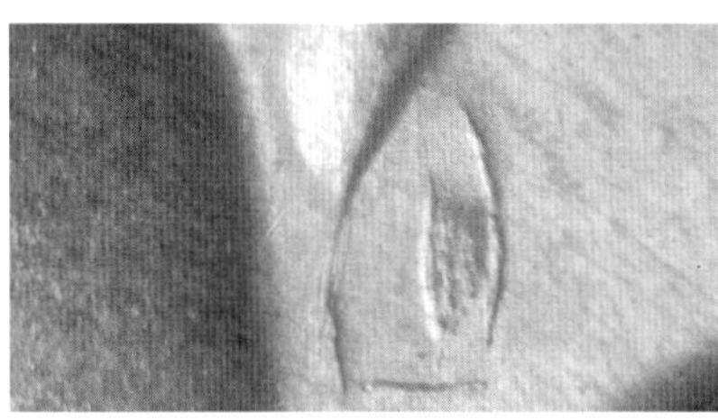

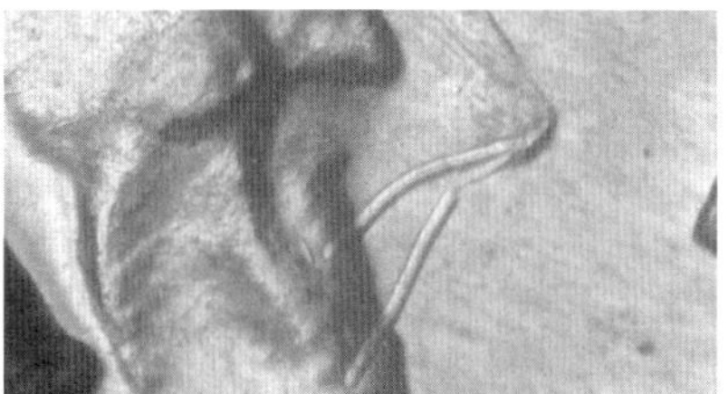

FS-05-1952-403

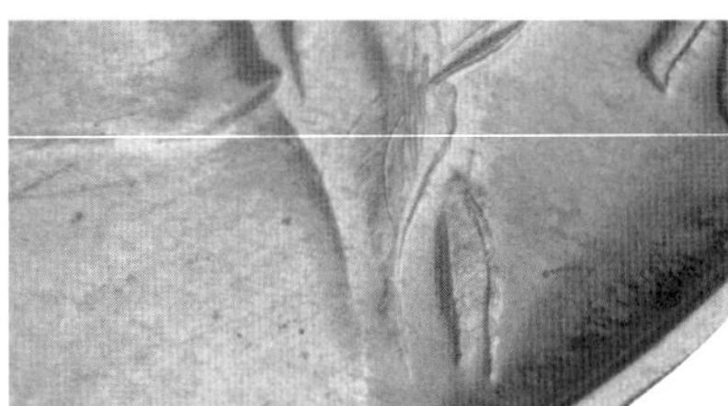

FS-05-1952-404

Description: These coins are identified by a re-engraved ribbon and lower queue.

Comments: All of these are unique design changes, because they were hand-engraved.

	PF-63	PF-64	PF-65
Variety, FS-401	(unique)		
Variety, FS-402	(unique)		
Variety, FS-403	(unique)		
Variety, FS-404	(unique)		
Normal	$12	$25	$45

1953 Proof — FS-05-1953-101 (032.7)

VARIETY: Doubled-Die Obverse — CONECA: DDO-001
PUP: IN GOD WE TRUST
URS-6 • I-3 • L-3

Description: The doubling is evident on all the letters of IN GOD WE TRUST.

	PF-63	PF-64	PF-65
VARIETY	$75	$100	$150
NORMAL	$12	$25	$45

1953 Proof — FS-05-1953-401

VARIETY: Re-Engraved Obverse Design — CONECA: RED-001
PUP: Ribbon
URS-1 • I-3 • L-3

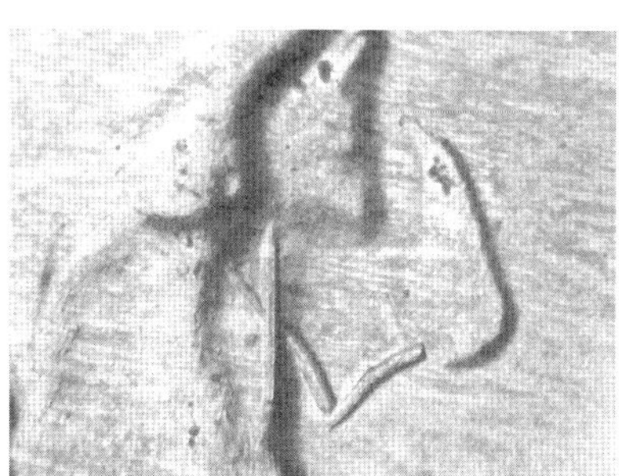

Description: This variety can be identified by a re-engraved ribbon.

Comments: Whereas there are multiple known re-engraved dies for 1952, this is the only one known for 1953.

	PF-63	PF-64	PF-65
VARIETY	(unique)		
NORMAL	$12	$25	$45

1953-D FS-05-1953D-501

VARIETY: Repunched Mintmark CONECA: RPM-001
PUP: Mintmark
URS-5 • I-4 • L-4

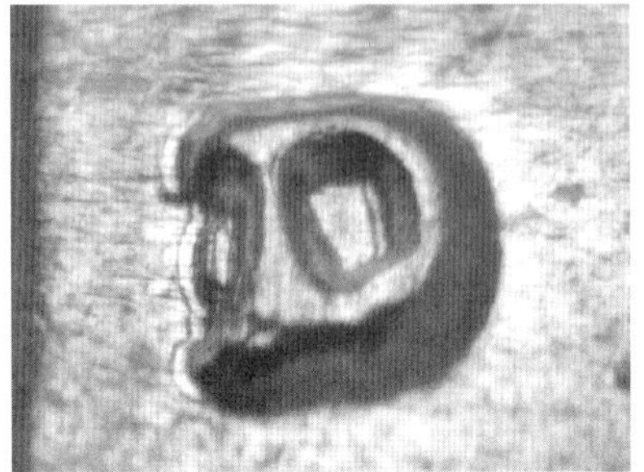

Description: The D mintmark is repunched over an inverted D.

Comments: This variety is very elusive and desirable.

	MS-60	MS-63	MS-65
VARIETY	$300	$500	$750
NORMAL	$0.25	$0.75	$9

1954 Proof FS-05-1954-401

VARIETY: Re-Engraved Design CONECA: RED-001
PUP: Ribbon
URS-4 • I-3 • L-3

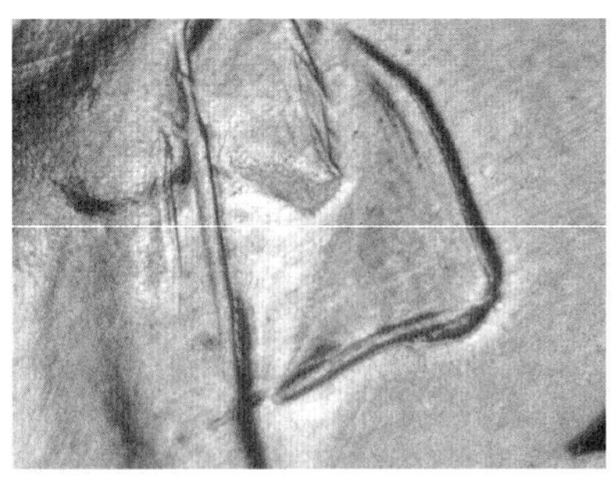

Description: The re-engraved ribbon is the pickup point here.

Comments: This variety is known in all three die states.

	PF-63	PF-64	PF-65
VARIETY	$25	$50	$90
NORMAL	$5	$10	$22

1954-D FS-05-1954D-501 (032.9)

VARIETY: Repunched Mintmark CONECA: RPM-003
PUP: Mintmark
URS-6 • I-4 • L-2

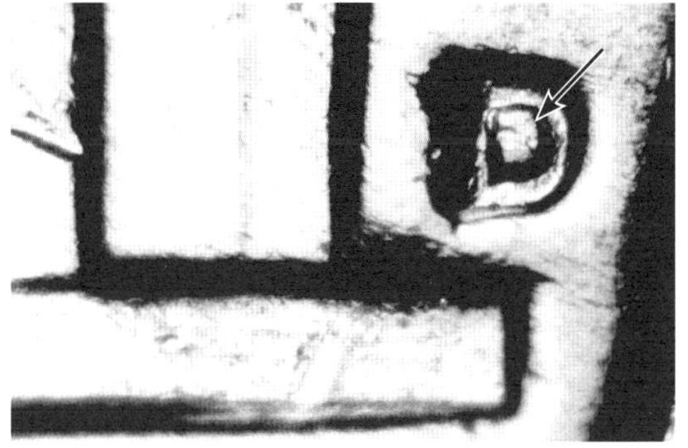

Description: This variety has been confirmed as a repunched mintmark and not an over mintmark.

	MS-60	MS-63	MS-65
VARIETY	$25	$50	$100
NORMAL	$0.60	$1	$30

1954-S FS-05-1954S-501 (033)

VARIETY: Over Mintmark (S Over D) CONECA: OMM-001
PUP: Mintmark
URS-10 • I-5 • L-5

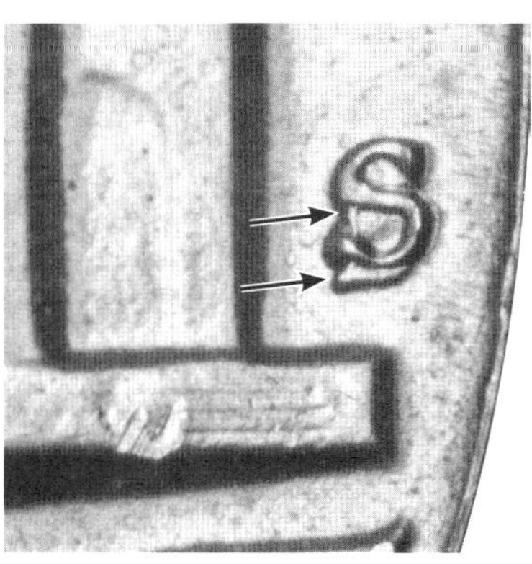

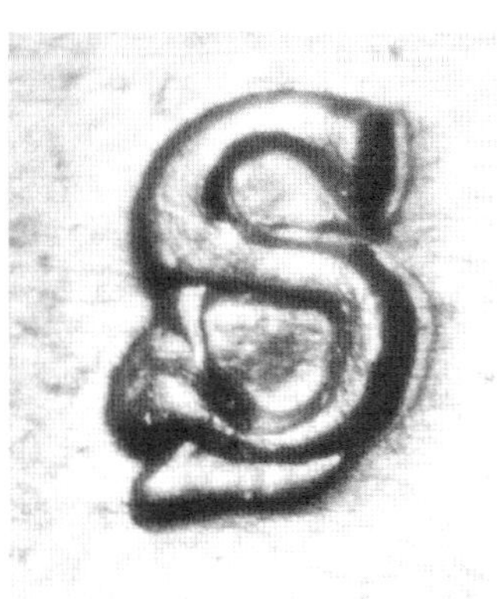

Description: The die initially received a D mintmark and later was punched with an S mintmark.

Comments: Finding an early-die-state specimen that is well struck is quite difficult, and such a coin would command a high premium. The overall strength of the strike is the important factor in the value of this over mintmark. This variety is unknown with Full Steps.

	MS-60	MS-63	MS-65
VARIETY	$25	$50	$100
NORMAL	$1.75	$2	$15

1954-S FS-05-1954S-502 (033.1)

VARIETY: Repunched Mintmark CONECA: RPM-001
PUP: Mintmark
URS-10 • I-2 • L-2

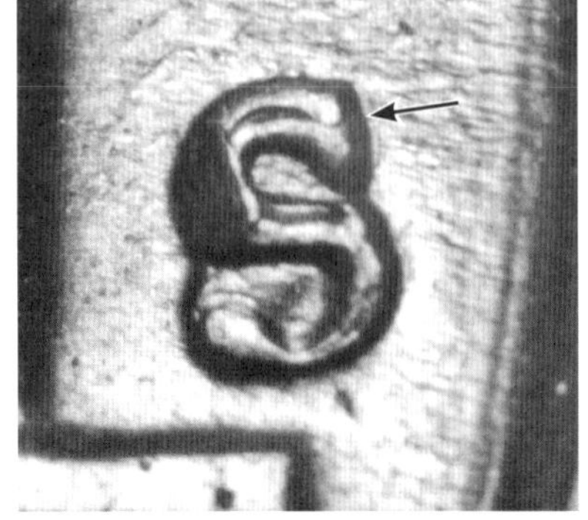

Description: The secondary S is visible to the north of the primary S.

Comments: This is one of the more popular Jefferson nickel repunched mintmarks.

	MS-60	MS-63	MS-65
VARIETY	$15	$25	$50
NORMAL	$1.75	$2	$15

1954-S FS-05-1954S-801

VARIETY: Doubled-Die Reverse CONECA: DDR-002
PUP: Steps
URS-4 • I-4 • L-4

Description: This variety exhibits a very strong spread of the left steps between the tops of the N and T of MONTICELLO.

Comments: This is a nice example of a tilted first hubbing.

	MS-60	MS-63	MS-65
VARIETY	$100	$150	$250
NORMAL	$1.75	$2	$15

1955 Proof — FS-05-1955-801 (035)

VARIETY: Tripled-Die Reverse — CONECA: DDR-001
PUP: MONTICELLO
URS-11 • I-4 • L-3

Description: The reverse die is tripled, which is most evident on the last O of MONTICELLO and the lower portions of the letters in UNITED STATES OF AMERICA.

Comments: There are several doubled reverse dies for this date, but they do not command the premium of this variety. This variety was discovered by Frank Capper in 1978.

	PF-63	PF-64	PF-65
VARIETY	$30	$40	$50
NORMAL	$6	$12	$18

1955-D — FS-05-1955D-501 (034)

VARIETY: Over Mintmark (D Over S) — CONECA: OMM-001
PUP: Mintmark
URS-13 • I-4 • L-4

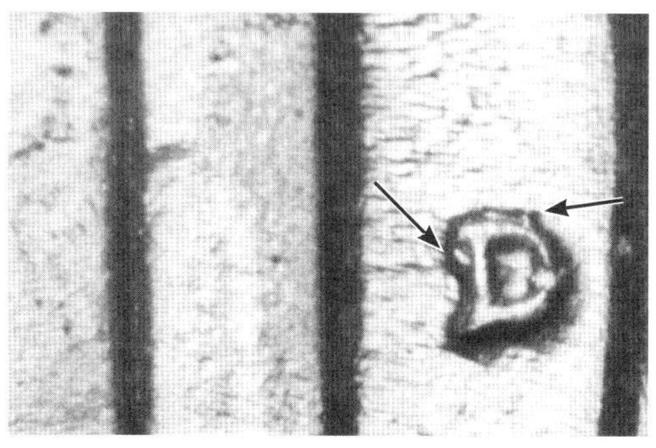

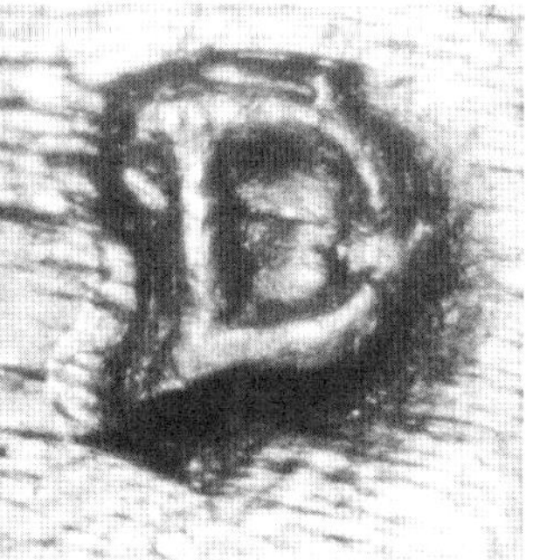

Description: A D mintmark was punched over an S mintmark. The top curve of the S is visible slightly to the north of the D. This probably occurred as production ceased in San Francisco and remaining usable reverse dies were repunched in Philadelphia.

Comments: There are some 10 different D Over S varieties for 1955-D, but the strongest (OMM-001), shown here, is the most sought after. Others bring less than the prices listed and can be difficult to attribute.

	MS-60	MS-63	MS-65
VARIETY	$38	$60	$95
NORMAL	$0.50	$0.75	$20

1956 Proof — FS-05-1956-102 (035.4)

Variety: Doubled-Die Obverse — CONECA: DDO-002
PUP: IN GOD WE TRUST
URS-6 • I-3 • L-2

Description: The doubling is evident on all the letters of IN GOD WE TRUST.

Comments: There are many different doubled dies, both obverse and reverse, on Proof Jefferson nickels. Many are outstanding multiple hubbings.

Note: This variety is slated to be removed from the coin-by-coin listings of future editions of the ***Cherrypickers' Guide*** due to lack of interest and/or unavailability. It will retain its Fivaz-Stanton number and continue to be listed in future editions' cross-reference appendix. A full list of varieties slated to be removed from each section appears after the introductory text of that section.

1956 — FS-05-1956-801 (035.2)

Variety: Quadrupled-Die Reverse — CONECA: DDR-018
PUP: E PLURIBUS UNUM, AMERICA
URS-6 • I-3 • L-2

Description: The reverse die is at least quadrupled, which is most evident on the last O of MONTICELLO and the lower portions of the letters of UNITED STATES OF AMERICA and E PLURIBUS UNUM.

Comments: This variety was first reported to us by Frank Baumann.

	MS-60	MS-63	MS-65
Variety	$25	$75	$150
Normal	$0.50	$0.75	$20

1956 — FS-05-1956-802 (035.6)

VARIETY: Tripled-Die Reverse — CONECA: DDR-024
PUP: AMERICA, UNUM
URS-6 • I-3 • L-2

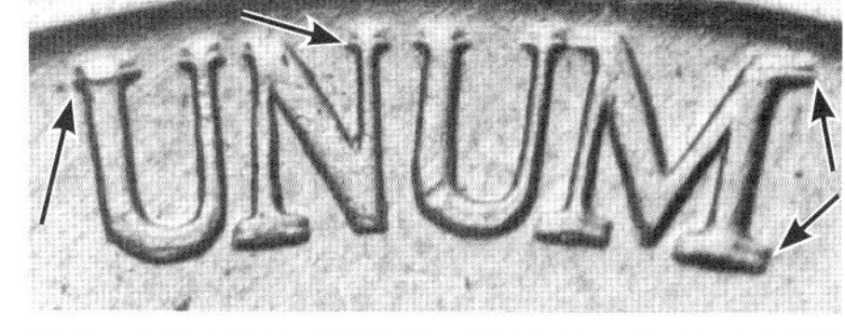

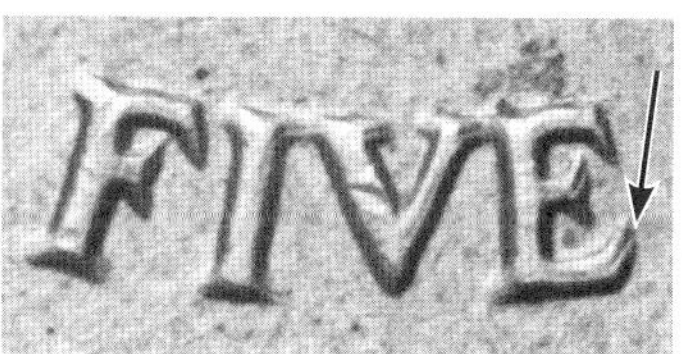

Description: The reverse die is tripled; this is most evident on the letters of UNITED STATES OF AMERICA and E PLURIBUS UNUM.

Comments: There are many very nice doubled-die reverses known for late-1950s to early-1960s circulation-strike Jefferson nickels.

	MS-60	MS-63	MS-65
VARIETY	$25	$75	$150
NORMAL	$0.50	$0.75	$20

1957 Proof — FS-05-1957-101 (035.8)

VARIETY: Quadrupled-Die Obverse — CONECA: DDO-004
PUP: LIBERTY, date, star
URS-7 • I-3 • L-2

Description: The quadrupling is most evident on all the letters of LIBERTY, the date, and the star.

Comments: There are many different doubled dies, both obverse and reverse, on Proof Jefferson nickels. Many are outstanding multiple hubbings.

	PF-63	PF-64	PF-65
VARIETY	$50	$75	$100
NORMAL	$1	$1.50	$3

1958-D FS-05-1958D-501

VARIETY: Repunched Mintmark CONECA: RPM-005
PUP: Mintmark
URS-5 • I-4 • L-4

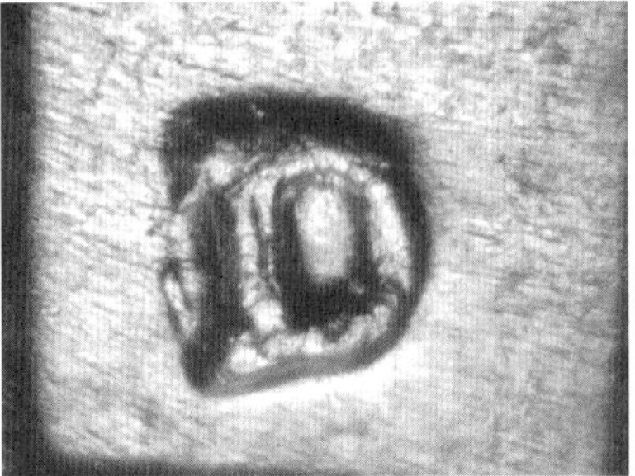

Description: The D mintmark is repunched over an inverted D.

Comments: This variety was first reported about 15 years ago, and few have been found since.

	MS-60	MS-63	MS-65
VARIETY	$300	$700	$1,000
NORMAL	$0.40	$0.50	$12

1960 Proof FS-05-1960-801 (036)

VARIETY: Quadrupled-Die Reverse CONECA: DDR-001
PUP: AMERICA, O in MONTICELLO
URS-9 • I-3 • L-2

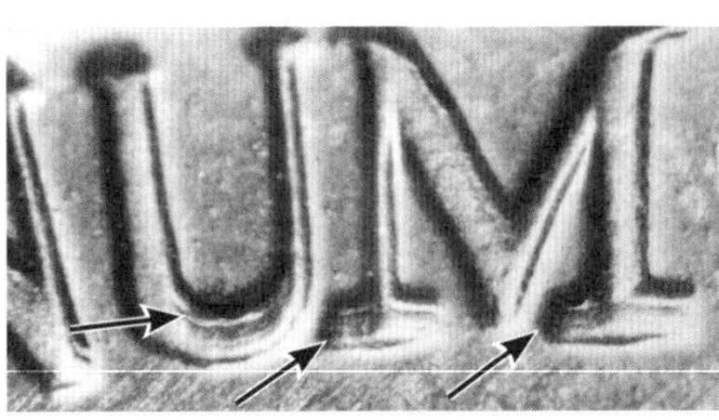
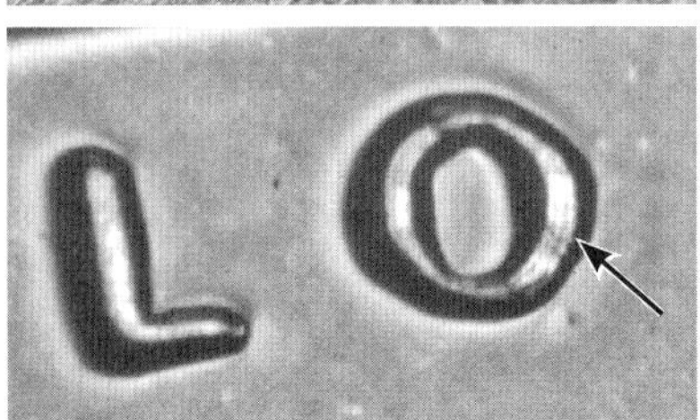

Description: The reverse die is quadrupled, most evident on MONTICELLO and most of the lettering around the rim, especially on UNUM and AMERICA.

Comments: There are also several doubled-die reverses for this date.

	PF-63	PF-64	PF-65
VARIETY	$50	$75	$100
NORMAL	$1	$1.50	$3

1961 Proof — FS-05-1961-801 (037)

VARIETY: Tripled-Die Reverse — CONECA: DDR-013
PUP: UNUM, OF AMERICA
URS-7 • I-2 • L-2

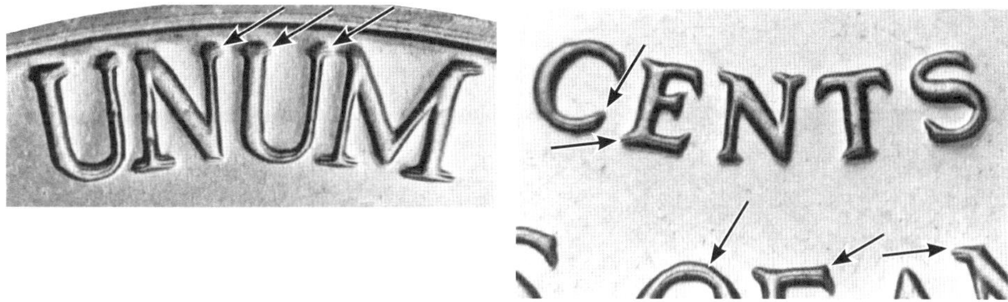

Description: The reverse die is tripled, most evident on UNUM, OF AMERICA, and CENTS.

Comments: There are many different doubled dies, both obverse and reverse, on Proof Jefferson nickels. Many are outstanding multiple hubbings.

Note: This variety is slated to be removed from the coin-by-coin listings of future editions of the ***Cherrypickers' Guide*** due to lack of interest and/or unavailability. It will retain its Fivaz-Stanton number and continue to be listed in future editions' cross-reference appendix. A full list of varieties slated to be removed from each section appears after the introductory text of that section.

1963 — FS-05-1963-801 (037.3)

VARIETY: Tripled-Die Reverse — CONECA: DDR-080
PUP: E PLURIBUS UNUM
URS-6 • I-2 • L-2

Description: The reverse die is tripled, most evident on E PLURIBUS UNUM, with doubling to a lesser extent on most reverse lettering.

Comments: There are many doubled-die reverses for early-1960s circulation-strike Jefferson nickels. This is one of the nicer ones.

	MS-60	MS-63	MS-65
VARIETY	$25	$75	$150
NORMAL	$0.25	$0.50	$10

1964 Proof — FS-05-1964-801

VARIETY: Tripled-Die Reverse — CONECA: DDR-024
PUP: STATES
URS-6 • I-3 • L-4

Description: This variety shows a strong triple spread on UNITED STATES OF AMERICA decreasing from left to right, a double spread on MONTICELLO and FIVE CENTS, and light spread on E PLURIBUS.

Comments: Proof doubled-die reverses abound from 1960 through 1964. This is one of the nicer tripled dies.

	PF-63	PF-64	PF-65
VARIETY	$25	$75	$100
NORMAL	$1	$1.50	$3

1964-D — FS-05-1964D-501 (037.5)

VARIETY: Repunched Mintmark — CONECA: RPM-005
PUP: Mintmark
URS-5 • I-3 • L-4

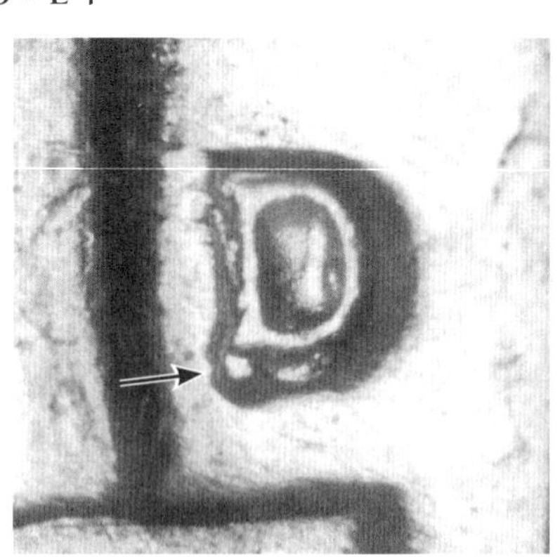

Description: The secondary D is visible to the south of the primary D.

Comments: If you like Jefferson nickel repunched mintmarks, we strongly recommend James Wiles's ***Jefferson Nickel RPM Book***.

	MS-60	MS-63	MS-65
VARIETY	$100	$200	$300
NORMAL	$0.25	$0.50	$5

1968-S Proof

FS-05-1968S-501 (038)

VARIETY: Repunched Mintmark — CONECA: RPM-002
PUP: Mintmark
URS-5 • I-3 • L-3

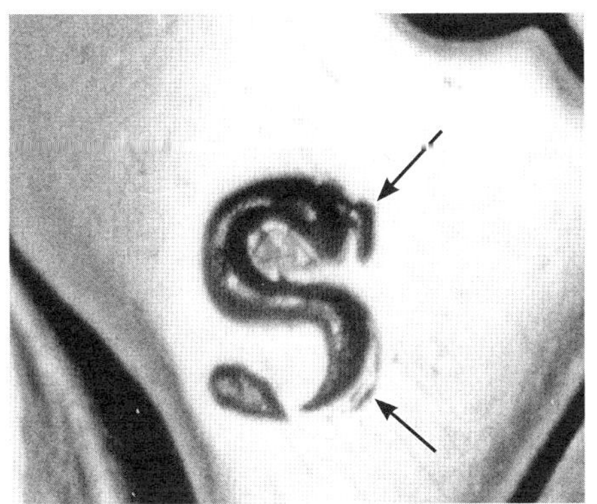

Description: The secondary S is visible to the southeast of the primary S.

Comments: This is one of only a few nice repunched mintmarks found on Proof coinage.

	PF-63	PF-64	PF-65
VARIETY	$150	$200	$250
NORMAL	$1	$2	$4

1969-S Proof

FS-05-1969S-501

VARIETY: Repunched Mintmark — CONECA: RPM-001
PUP: Mintmark
URS-5 • I-3 • L-3

Description: The additional S appears to the east.

Comments: This is one of the nicer Proof repunched mintmarks.

	PF-63	PF-64	PF-65
VARIETY	$25	$75	$100
NORMAL	$1	$1.50	$3

1971-S Proof — FS-05-1971S-501

VARIETY: Missing Mintmark — CONECA: MMO-001
PUP: Mintmark
URS-11 • I-5 • L-5

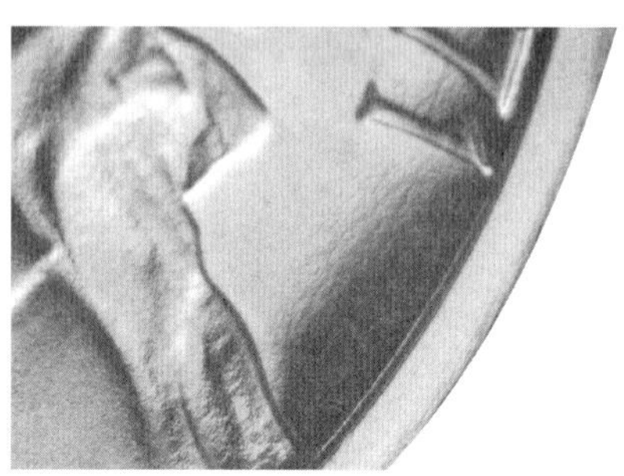

Description: This variety is identified by its missing mintmark.

	PF-63	PF-64	PF-65
VARIETY	$1,300	$1,400	$1,500
NORMAL	$1	$1.25	$2

1971-S Proof — FS-05-1971S-801

VARIETY: Doubled-Die Reverse — CONECA: DDR-028
PUP: E PLURIBUS UNUM, right side of building
URS-3 • I-3 • L-3

Description: There is strong extra thickness on E PLURIBUS UNUM and the right building edge, with medium extra thickness on UNITED STATES OF AMERICA, FIVE CENTS, and MONTICELLO.

Comments: This coin's reverse is RDV-006 (weak railings).

	PF-63	PF-64	PF-65
VARIETY	$25	$75	$100
NORMAL	$1	$1.25	$2

1979-S, 1981-S Proof — FS-05-[Year]S-501

VARIETY: Type 2 Mintmark
PUP: Mintmark
URS-14 • I-3 • L-3

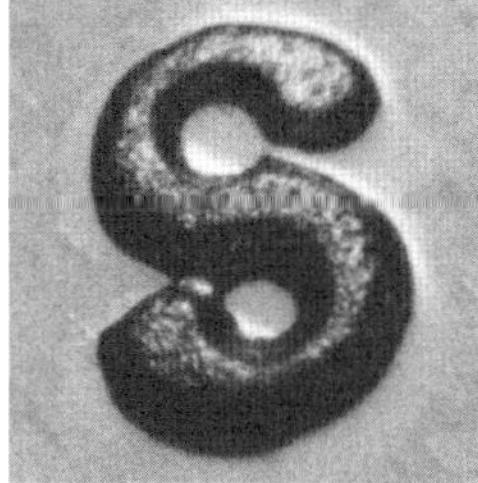

1979-S Type II Mintmark

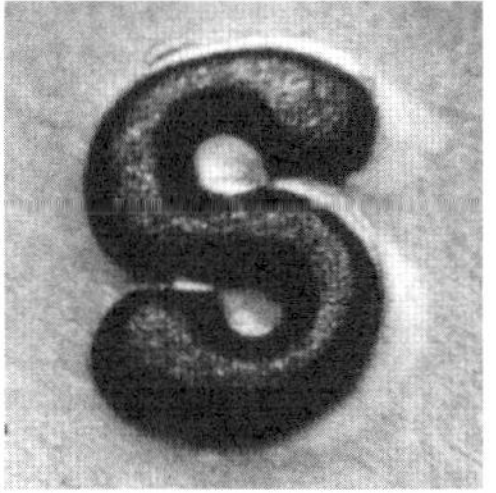

1981-S Type II Mintmark

Description: Two S mintmark styles were used on both 1979 and 1981 Proof Jefferson nickels. The second mintmark style used (referred to as "Type 2") appears about as frequently as the first (referred to as "Type 1") on 1979-dated Proof nickels. Meanwhile, coins with the Type 2 mintmark of 1981 are rarer and slightly more valuable than those with Type 1.

Comments: Interestingly, the Type 2 mintmark of 1979 is the same style as the Type 1 of 1981.

1979-S, FS-05-1979S-501

	PF-63	PF-64	PF-65
Variety, Type 2 MM	$4	$5	$6
Normal, Type 1 MM	$4	$5	$6

1981-S, FS-05-1981S-501

	PF-63	PF-64	PF-65
Variety, Type 2 MM	$5	$6	$7
Normal, Type 1 MM	$4	$5	$6

1990-S Proof — FS-05-1990S-101

VARIETY: Doubled-Die Obverse — CONECA: DDO-001
PUP: IN GOD WE
URS-4 • I-4 • L-4

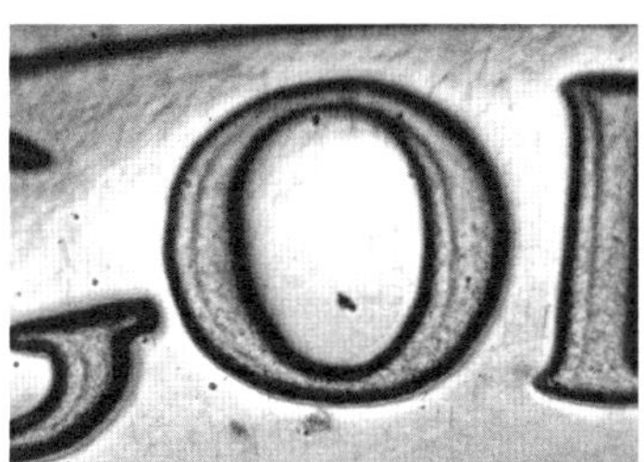

Description: This variety has a medium spread on IN GOD WE TRUST and the designer's initials.

Comments: This one is hard to obtain and eagerly sought after by specialists.

	PF-63	PF-64	PF-65
Variety	$250	$500	$750
Normal	$1	$2	$4

2004-P (Peace) FS-05-2004P-101

Variety: Doubled-Die Obverse CONECA: DDO-001
PUP: Date
URS-6 • I-3 • L-4

Description: There is a medium spread with extra thickness on IN GOD WE TRUST, LIBERTY, the star, the date, and the designer's initials.

Comments: Many late-die-state examples exist, which show mushy, indistinct doubling. Early-die-state coins will command a significant premium.

	MS-60	MS-63	MS-65
Variety	$25	$50	$75
Normal	$0.10	$0.25	$0.75

2005-P (American Bison) FS-05-2005P-101

Variety: Doubled-Die Obverse CONECA: DDO-001
PUP: LIBERTY
URS-6 • I-3 • L-3

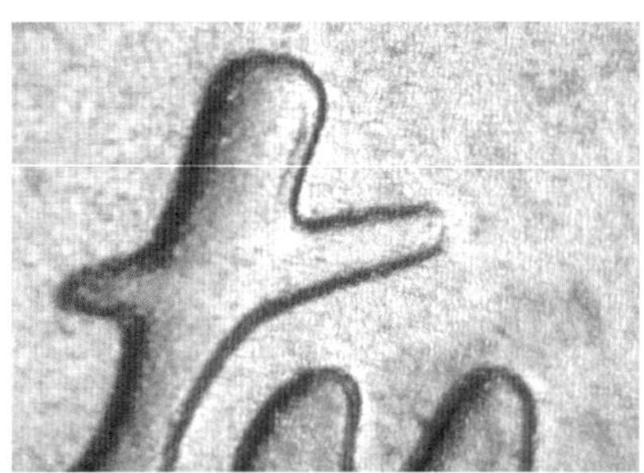

Description: This variety shows a medium spread on IN GOD WE TRUST, the ERTY of LIBERTY, the mintmark, and the date.

Comments: This coin has a satin finish and can be found in Westward Journey sets.

	MS-60	MS-63	MS-65
Variety	$25	$50	$75
Normal	$0.10	$0.35	$1.25

Appendix A

Doubled Dies vs. Other Forms of Doubling

The difference between die doubling (doubled dies, repunched dates, and repunched mintmarks, among others) and the more confusing forms of doubling can be very challenging to explain, and even more difficult for a novice to comprehend. Additionally, there are times when determining the difference can be frustrating even for a very experienced collector. This section will help you learn the differences. But reading alone will not do it all; you must examine numerous coins before you can expect to have a solid grasp of the differences between die doubling and other forms of doubling.

Die Doubling: Those Abnormalities We Love to Collect!

Die doubling is the type of doubling that exhibits a doubled image on the die itself, even before the coin is struck. Die doubling includes doubled dies, repunched dates, repunched mintmarks, overdates, over mintmarks, and repunched letters. It almost always exhibits splits in the serifs of the letters and/or numerals, with rounded, secondary images.

On this Jefferson nickel, the distinctive splits in the serifs are evident, and the secondary images are "rounded" and can easily be detected.

The photograph shown here of a true 1969-S doubled-die Lincoln cent exhibits the typical rounded secondary images. Notice also the "crease" between the images.

Many 19th-century coins have letters and numerals that are flat on their top surfaces as compared to the rounded appearance of most 20th-century letters and numerals. Therefore, the key to identifying true die doubling on 19th-century coins is the distinctive splits in the serifs.

There is one class of doubled die that would not exhibit the normal characteristics mentioned for die doubling. Known as Class VI doubled dies, these exhibit extra thickness on

The splits in the serifs on this 1887 Indian Head cent doubled-die obverse are typical of what one would expect for most 19th-century coins with true die doubling.

some letters and numbers. Most widely known on Lincoln cents, the doubling sometimes exhibits letters that are slightly misshapen, such as the lower bar of an E being curved. This curved shape often is convex. Although some specialists may disagree, Class VI doubled dies *generally* command very small premiums—except in rare cases.

Notice the extra thickness of the letters in LIBERTY. This is typical of a Class VI doubled die, shown here on a Lincoln cent.

STRIKE DOUBLING

Strike doubling is the type of doubling most often confused with, and very often misidentified as, a doubled die or repunched mintmark. Not only do novices confuse this type of doubling with doubled dies, but specialists disagree as to what the correct terminology should be.

This LIBERTY on a Lincoln cent exhibits typical strike doubling. Notice the flat, shelf-like appearance of the secondary image.

Strike doubling (the term we prefer) is generally accepted to be caused by die bounce due to looseness in the tooling-to-die assembly, the die holder, or the die(s) within that holder. This causes excessive vibration during press operation, much as excessive vibration may set up in a running automobile with a broken motor mount. In effect, the vibration causes a coin to bounce or slide against the die within the split second after it is struck, just before or during ejection. In its most common form, strike doubling is characterized by a flat, shelf-like area of doubling bordering a design; this represents metal from the original raised image that has been smashed by the die down into the field of the coin. According to Mint technicians, strike doubling is usually eliminated when loose bolts, etc., are tightened.

Some might argue that the striking of the coin ends when the hammer die reaches the very end of its stroke. By this argument, this should not be called *strike doubling,* but rather *mechanical* or *machine doubling.* In our opinion, this is like trying to split a hair. Additionally, we feel that *machine* or *mechanical* doubling can be even more confusing, as neither term indicates in which part of the minting process this happens. Either of those terms could refer to the coin counters at the end of the process! We feel *strike doubling* is best suited to indicate the point of the minting process in which this doubling occurs.

Furthermore, numismatists agree there are three basic areas of the minting process: planchet, die, and striking. This doubling occurs during the striking process, and not in the die-making or planchet-making process. (We don't refer to incomplete planchets as a machine problem, although a machine causes them.)

Whether you refer to this as *strike doubling, machine doubling, mechanical doubling,* or *ejection doubling,* your primary focus should be to understand the differences and educate others.

Typically, strike doubling exhibits a flat, shelf-like secondary image, not like the rounded secondary images of true die doubling. Usually this secondary image is low to the field. There are no splits in the serifs. On most Uncirculated and Proof coins, strike doubling gives the appearance that the metal has been "moved," much like that on hobo nickels or love tokens, and has a very shiny appearance. (Other less common forms of strike doubling exist that are not covered here.)

Strike doubling can affect all lettering on one or both sides, or could be detected on only one letter or a small portion of a device. Proof coins often exhibit strike doubling due to the excessive force employed in their manufacture. Strike doubling can also be evident on a coin with a true doubled die or true repunched mintmark.

On this 1937 Buffalo nickel, the secondary images exhibit the flat, shelf-like doubling typical of strike doubling. The secondary image is low, close to the field.

There are several dates (and runs of dates) in several series that are well known for strike doubling. Examples include Mercury dimes from 1936 through 1942 and Lincoln cents from 1968 through 1972.

Compare this 1969-S Lincoln cent doubled die with the strike-doubling specimen to the right.

In this 1969-S cent, strike doubling is evident on the date and mintmark. Whenever the date and mintmark both are doubled, odds are that the doubling is strike doubling.

Although it can be difficult for a novice to understand, strike doubling might affect only the mintmark on a coin, creating what some may interpret as a repunched mintmark. In fact, this is fairly common, especially on Franklin halves and Washington quarters. This is often because strike doubling first affects the deepest part of the die (the highest part of the coin), which in many cases is the deeply punched mintmark.

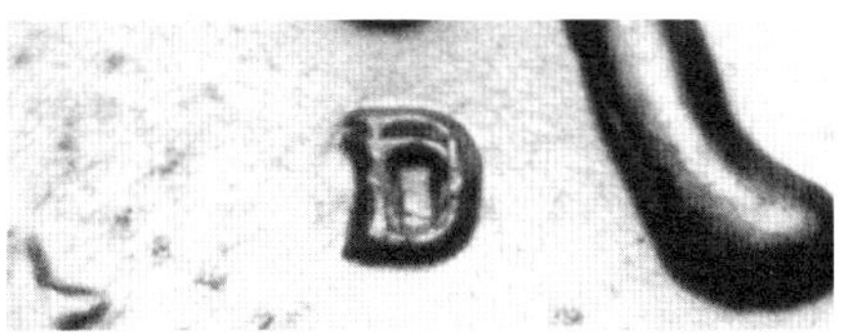

This is a genuine repunched mintmark on a Kennedy half dollar. Compare the doubling here with the next, which was caused by strike doubling.

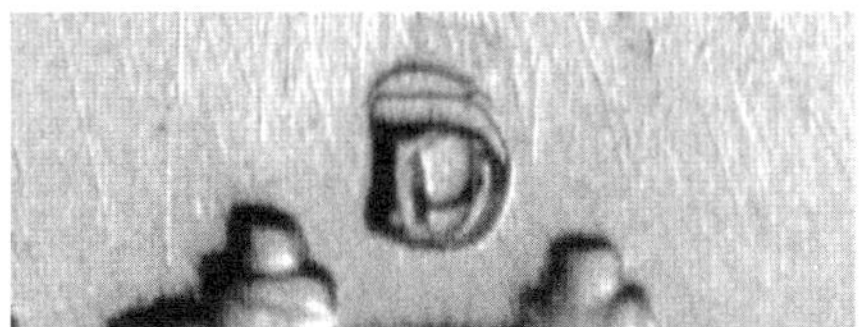

This mintmark on a Franklin half dollar is the result of strike doubling. Notice the flat, shelf-like doubling, which is the primary characteristic of strike doubling.

Other Forms of Doubling

In addition to strike doubling, there are other forms of doubling that are often mistaken for die doubling. Among these are doubling caused by die deterioration, and doubling that is typical on coins designed by James B. Longacre, possibly intentionally.

Die Deterioration

Die deterioration doubling is very often confused with doubled dies, repunched mintmarks, and other collectible forms of die doubling. In general, as a die deteriorates, its letters and numerals (among other design elements) will develop doubling, twisting, mushrooming, and similar effects. The exact result often depends on the type of die steel used, composition of planchets struck, geometry of die design, and length of time the die(s) remain in service. These effects normally begin on elements closest to the rim and move inward to a point of leaving random die-deterioration patches that may appear to be misplaced mintmarks in strange places (e.g., on Roosevelt's cheek). This is due to stress in the metal of the die. This doubling will often, but not always, occur in combination with an "orange-peel" effect on the fields of the coin, created by the stress in the metal on the dies.

Die deterioration is very common on Washington quarters from the 1980s and 1990s, Jefferson nickels from 1955 to date, and Roosevelt dimes from 1965 to date. Die deterioration is a prime example of what can happen when the Mint tries to get maximum production out of every single die.

Die deterioration is very evident and extreme in this Jefferson nickel. Notice the secondary images on both sides of the letters, and the "orange-peel" effect on the field.

Here is another example of die deterioration. Notice the edges of the I and T appearing to merge into the field. Also, the letters have less definition than one would expect.

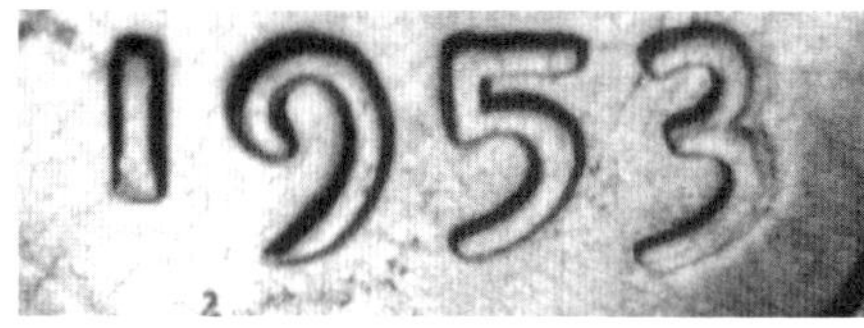

Die deterioration doubling is found on many Lincoln cents, in particular those of the 1950s and earlier. One such deteriorated 1955 cent was often promoted by dealers as "the poor man's doubled die."

"Longacre" Doubling

In this Indian Head cent, the doubling that is typical on many of Longacre's designs is evident. Notice that the secondary image is visible on both sides of the letters.

This term was coined by J.T. Stanton as an easy way to describe the doubling that is typical on many coins designed by James Barton Longacre. These include Indian Head cents, nickel three-cent pieces, Shield nickels, and many gold issues. We're certain many readers have seen this doubling before; almost all of the letters are doubled, with the secondary image appearing on both sides of the letters. Some specialists believe this is from the shoulder of the punch penetrating the die, causing the secondary step. Others feel it was an intentional design on Longacre's part, to help the metal flow into the tight crevices of the die. Although this doubling is evident on many of the coins that Longacre designed, it is not seen on all of his coins. This would likely remove the theory that the secondary or "stepped" image was planned to help with metal flow.

Longacre doubling does not add premium to a coin's value.

Summary

We hope this long, but educational, article will help our readers learn the difference between die doubling and other forms of doubling. However, the best learning tool is experience. In that light, we suggest that you look—and look carefully—at as many coins as possible, especially in the date ranges mentioned. Look especially carefully at Proof quarters from 1968 and 1969 for strike doubling, Indian Head cents from the 1860s, 1870s, and 1880s for "Longacre" doubling, nickels from the 1980s for die deterioration, and Franklin half dollars for strike doubling on the mintmark. Don't pass up the opportunity to buy a good example of one of these for your reference, if it's not too expensive.

Die-Doubling I.Q. Test

The 10 photographs here exhibit some examples of die doubling, strike doubling, and even some other forms of doubling. Take a few minutes to see for yourself whether you can accurately identify the various forms of doubling.

Note: Most variety collectors feel coins exhibiting other forms of doubling should not command a premium. However, some collectors believe they are collectible and actively seek them. We feel there is absolutely nothing wrong with this and encourage those who decide to take this course. The question is and should be, "Are you having *fun* in your collecting pursuits?"

Test photo 1

Test photo 2

Test photo 3

Test photo 4

Test photo 5

Test photo 6

Test photo 7

Test photo 8

Test photo 9

Test photo 10

Answers to the test photographs:

1. strike doubling; 2. strike doubling; 3. doubled die; 4. strike doubling; 5. doubled die; 6. die deterioration; 7. strike doubling; 8. repunched mintmark; 9. doubled die; 10. strike doubling.

In test photo 10, notice that the date and the mintmark both exhibit similar doubling. This should be a red flag. There are very few examples on which a doubled die and a repunched mintmark both are evident on the same side of the same coin. Keep in mind that until very recently, the mintmark was punched into the die after the die was made. Therefore, if the die is doubled, the mintmark is not necessarily doubled.

Appendix B
The Minting Process

Why Study the Minting Process?

In the study of Mint errors and varieties—and the study of the "regular" segment of numismatics, as well—a basic knowledge of the minting process is vital. If you do not understand how an error or variety occurred, you will not be able to determine whether it is genuine. The description that follows is an abbreviated one, but the basics remain the same.

There are three basic processes that take place at the U.S. Mint, and in each process errors and varieties can occur. First is the die-making process, in which the coin is designed, a model is engraved, and the design is transferred to a "die steel" to strike the coin. The second process is the making of planchets—coin blanks that are created and specially prepared for striking. The last process is the striking of these planchets to make them into coins.

These three processes—die making, planchet production, and striking—are where errors and varieties occur. Some have described this trio of areas as "P-D-S" (planchets, dies, and striking); the resemblance of these initials to the P, D, and S mintmarks of the three primary minting facilities (Philadelphia, Denver, and San Francisco) makes it easy to remember these areas of production.

Error vs. Variety

Occasionally there is disagreement as to whether a certain aberrant coin is an error or a variety. Generally speaking, most specialists consider an error a one-time occurrence that is not repeated in exactly the same way, and a variety an occurrence that *is* repeated in exactly the same way. An off-center strike, therefore, would be considered an error. True, some off-center strikes look quite similar, but generally speaking, each one will be different. However, a doubled die will repeat exactly with each strike, and is thus considered a variety.

The Die-Making Process

Sculptors and engravers are employed by the Mint to design coins and medals and to sculpt and engrave other designs into workable subjects for coining. These highly trained specialists take a design from a drawing, painting, or other two-dimensional object and transform it onto a plaster model, approximately 15 inches in diameter, that will ultimately be transferred to a coin or medal. The design on the model is always raised above the surrounding area (i.e., it is "positive" or "in relief"), just as it will appear on the finished coin. This plaster sculpture, after slight changes and improvements, is coated with epoxy resins that act as a preservative and a hardener. The epoxy-coated plaster sculpture is called a *galvano* and is forwarded to the die-making area of the Mint.

Technology has developed tremendously in the last few years. As a result many modern coin designs are developed with the use of CAD (Computer Aided Design) programs. In fact some short-run coins have the designs cut directly into the steel dies by laser.

Since the galvano is usually many times larger than the intended coin, its design must be reduced. To accomplish this, the galvano is placed onto a Janvier transfer-reducing machine. This machine traces the design on the galvano and, using the principle of the fulcrum, transfers the design onto the end of a piece of steel bar the actual size of the coin to be produced. This is called the *reducing* stage of die production, and this finished piece of steel is called the *master hub*. When the master hub has been produced, it is heated to extreme temperature, then quenched (cooled) quickly in a vat of oil. This heating-and-cooling process, called *tempering*, hardens the steel even further.

The large galvano is reduced on a Janvier transfer-reducing machine to create a master hub (a "positive") that is the actual size of the coin.

The master hub has the design in the same relief design as on the galvano and as it will appear on the finished coin. It is placed into a hydraulic hubbing press, opposite a piece of die steel that is about four inches long. When each is seated into the press, hydraulic force brings the two together, transferring the image from the master hub onto the end of the die steel. When complete, this is called the *master die*, with the design pressed (incused) into its surface.

This operation, known as *hubbing*, used to take several impressions to bring the design to the depth specifications. After each hubbing, the die would be annealed to make the steel soft for the next hubbing. If the die were to receive the image deep enough in the first hubbing, stress on the die steel would result and very likely create cracks, or at least would weaken the die. Strength and durability are stringent requirements. This process is now done by the "single-squeeze method," using one high-pressure compression.

Initially, it was thought that this would ring the death knell to doubled dies. Cherrypickers, however, have found this to be false. The single-squeeze–hubbing method still produces doubled dies, but they are generally located in the center of the coin with limited spreads. Hundreds of doubled dies have been cataloged on coins produced by this new hubbing method.

After the master die is produced, it is placed into the hubbing press to create the working hub in the same manner. Several working hubs are produced. These working hubs then produce working dies in the manner described before. The working dies are then placed into the coining presses to strike coins and medals.

Traditionally, all dies were made in the Philadelphia Mint. Until 1985 the dies were produced without mintmarks, which were added by hand with punches before the dies were shipped to the branch-mint facilities for completion. However, beginning in 1985 the mintmark was added to the master die for Proof coinage, and in 1989–90 it was added to the master dies for circulation coinage. In the late 1990s the mintmark was made part of the original plaster sculpture and a reduction was made for each mint. Subsequently, the mintmark is transferred to the master hub and on down the die-production chain. Beginning in 1996, the Denver Mint started producing dies for its own use and for the San Francisco Mint's production facilities.

Remember that the plaster sculpture, the galvano, the master hub, and the working hub all have the image of the coin in relief, or positive, just as the finished coin will appear. Master dies and working dies have the image coin incuse, or negative—a mirror image of the finished coin.

Planchet Making

Cent and nickel planchets are primarily made outside the Mint, as is the sheet metal for the other denominations. However, the process is much the same as when the Mint produced its own planchets and metal. Raw metal, after being melted, is rolled into long sheets until it is the proper thickness for the intended coin. These long sheets are then coiled for storage, shipping, and eventual use. The sheets are uncoiled and fed into a blanking press—which is nothing more than a series of punches that cut blanks out of the metal coils—either at the outside facility or at the Mint. Notice the word "blank" instead of "planchet": Technically speaking, a *blank* is a disc of metal that has not yet been prepared for striking, whereas a *planchet* is a blank that has been further prepared for striking, as described below.

Once the blanks are produced, they pass through what is known as a *riddler,* which passes the blanks over a three-tiered, vibrating screen, with holes in the first tier slightly larger than the intended blanks. The blanks that are of proper diameter drop through, and blanks that are too large are retained on the upper tier and carried to a scrap bin. The second-tier screen has holes slightly smaller than a proper-sized blank. Blanks that are too small pass through these holes to the third tier, from which they are carried away to the scrap bin. The blanks that remain on the second tier are presumed to be of accurate size, and are forwarded to the next process.

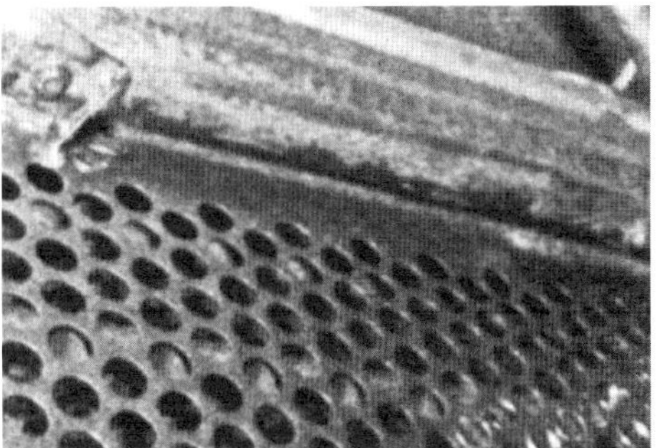

Once the blanks are produced, they pass through what is known as a riddler, which removes imperfectly-sized blanks.

At this point, the blanks must be annealed and cleaned. The annealing process softens the blanks to improve striking and reduce wear on the dies. The blanks are fed into a furnace. This furnace is much like a long dryer with the blanks being fed in one end and tumbled as they travel through the furnace. When the blanks exit the furnace, they are washed in a chemical bath and slowly tumbled dry.

The blanks are then ready for the *upset mill.* This is a machine with two primary components: (1) a stationary die with V-shaped grooves, and (2) a rotating die in the center, also with V-shaped grooves. Blanks are fed into one end of the upset mill, fitting into the grooves. As the center die rotates, the blanks pass between the outer, stationary die and the inner, rotating die. As the blanks go through the mill, the spacing between the two dies is gradually reduced, forcing the metal on the edge of the blank to be raised above the flat surfaces. When the disc of metal exits the upset mill, generally with raised metal all around the edge, it is considered a planchet.

The reason for putting raised edges on planchets before striking is that it greatly helps in coin production: it helps force the metal, during striking, toward the center of the coin and then into the crevices of the die; it also helps the coins stack neatly for use in commerce.

A blank remains a blank until it has been through the upsetting mill and received a raised edge, at which time it becomes a planchet. Blanks are frequently (and erroneously) referred to as "Type 1 planchets," but because they do not have raised edges, they should not be called planchets of any kind. There are no Type 1 or Type 2 planchets; the disc of metal is either a blank or a planchet, period.

STRIKING

The striking process begins with the planchets being brought to the coining presses via overhead conveyors with small bins. These conveyors deposit the planchets into a hopper above the coining presses. From that point the planchets are fed by gravity through feeder tubes and down into the *coining chamber* (the area of the coining press where striking takes place).

The planchets drop from the feeder tubes into *feeder fingers*, each of which has a slot in the end to push out the struck coin and a hole a couple of inches back that holds the next planchet to be deposited into the chamber. These fingers slide back and forth over a smooth steel surface.

The coining chamber consists primarily of the anvil (lower) die, hammer (upper) die, collar, and feeder fingers. The *anvil die,* which usually strikes the reverse of the coin, moves only when coins are being ejected and planchets received. The *hammer die,* which usually strikes the obverse, comes down and strikes the planchet. The *collar* is a metal ring that retains the planchet during the strike, preventing the metal from expanding outside the desired diameter. The collar also serves as a third die, creating the reeding or lettering on coins intended to have reeded or lettered edges.

When the planchet is deposited on the anvil die and within the collar by the feeder finger, the finger retracts and the hammer die comes down and strikes the planchet. As the hammer die retracts, the anvil die (riding on a cam) rises; the feeder finger pushes the struck coin out of the chamber, continues forward, and deposits another planchet onto the anvil die. The feeder finger retracts and the striking process begins again. The finished coins pass through an additional riddler to catch errors; this has greatly reduced the number of error coins escaping the Mint.

COUNTING AND BAGGING

Once the coins are ejected from the coining press, they fall down a chute and are carried to the counting room on conveyors. In the counting room, the coins are counted, packaged, and weighed. Some coins are bagged in the well-known Mint-sewn bags, while others (usually cents) are placed in large totes containing 1,500 pounds of coins within a heavy plastic liner. The bagged coins are then shipped to the various Federal Reserve banks.

Appendix C

What Are the Best Magnifiers?

"What level of magnification should I use when searching for varieties?" "Which magnifier is the best to use?" "Do I need a microscope?" These are three of the more common questions ever broached concerning this subject. All too often a collector will believe *more* magnification is better—when in fact less is usually best. With coin collecting in general and variety collecting in particular, the strength of the magnification is not as important as the *quality*.

Virtually every variety of any significance can be detected with a 7x glass, if it's of good quality. (A good 7x magnifier is also the recommended loupe for the most accurate coin grading.) A lesser-quality magnifier will only distort the image, making proper identification even more difficult. On the other hand, a good-quality glass with too much magnification is almost always overkill, as it can cause you to overlook key identification points.

An H.E. Harris magnifier (or *loupe*, pronounced "loop") is a common sight at coin shows. You will see dealers and collectors slip them out of their pocket to examine interesting coins. (Some wear them on a chain or string around their neck, for constant easy access.) These magnifiers fold into their chrome cases to protect the lens, which is usually 4x to 8x or greater strength.

Most serious collectors and almost all dealers use a Hastings triplet magnifier; usually a 7x or 10x power is preferred. "Hastings" is not a brand but a method of manufacture. The Hastings triplet has a three-glass (or plastic) optic, which ensures clarity throughout the entire lens and produces virtually no distortion.

Some manufacturers use 10x or 17x designations. However, without good-quality optics, the 10x or 17x means nothing. We've seen some magnifiers marked as 17x, compared to which a 10x Hastings triplet provides more detail, better clarity, and a wider field of view. And remember, if you can't see a variety with a 7x glass, it's likely not worth searching for.

A good 7x Bausch & Lomb Hastings triplet will normally run about $45. However, with some searching on the Internet, you can find a good 7x Hastings triplet for less than $25.

Stereoscopes (microscopes) are handy, fun, and very educational, but these are not absolutely necessary for the study of varieties. Should you have the desire to add one to your array of collecting tools, a good stereoscope can be obtained for as little as $200 (though most will run around $500 or more). Be sure to get a stereoscope—one that has two eyepieces. This will allow the very best in clarity and use. A stereoscope is great for taking photographs, and for studying the minute differences evident on every coin.

Check with your local supplier or favorite online dealers. See what they recommend. We strongly advise spending a little more for a good-quality product. You'll reap the rewards soon afterward.

Appendix D

Popular Varieties From Proof and Mint Sets

This list of Proof sets and Mint sets that contain significant varieties should be useful for all collectors. Beginning with those modern Mint sets from 1947, and Proof sets from 1950, there are many years of one or the other that are absent of a significant variety. Not all of the known varieties are significant. Should you encounter a significant variety that is not listed, please contact the publisher so the list can be updated. Again, this list is just to be used as a guide. Those Proof listings in bold type are considered the most desirable.

Mint Sets

1948	1¢	S/S—repunched mintmark
1949	5¢	D/S—over mintmark (although known, most have already been removed)
1954	5¢	doubled-die reverse
1959	1¢	D/D—repunched mintmark
1960	1¢	D/D—repunched mintmark (RPM-001, RPM-023)
1961	50¢	D/D—repunched mintmark
1963	1¢	D/D—repunched mintmark (RPM-012, RPM-016)
1963	5¢	D—doubled-die reverse
1963	10¢	(P)—doubled-die obverse
1963	25¢	(P)—doubled-die obverse (DDO-001, DDO-008)
1963	25¢	(P)—doubled-die obverse and doubled-die reverse (DDO-007 and DDR-001)
1963	25¢	D—doubled-die obverse (DDO-001, DDO-002)
1963	50¢	(P)—doubled-die obverse
1963	50¢	(P)—doubled-die reverse (DDR-001, DDR-004)
1968	10¢	(P)—doubled-die obverse
1968	25¢	D—doubled-die reverse
1969	10¢	D/D—repunched mintmark
1969	25¢	D/D—repunched mintmark
1969	50¢	D—doubled-die reverse (DDR-001, DDR-004)
1970	1¢	D/D—repunched mintmark
1970	1¢	S/S—repunched mintmark
1970	10¢	D—doubled-die reverse (DDR-001, DDR-003, DDR-004, DDR-005)
1970	25¢	D—doubled-die reverse (DDR-001, DDR-002, DDR-004)
1970	50¢	D—doubled-die reverse (DDR-001, DDR-002, DDR-003, DDR-004, DDR-005, DDR-006, DDR-007, DDR-008, DDR-009)
1971	5¢	D/D—repunched mintmark (RPM-001, RPM-004)
1971	10¢	D/D—repunched mintmark
1971	10¢	D—doubled-die reverse
1971	50¢	D—doubled-die obverse (DDO-004, DDO-006, DDO-007)
1972	5¢	D—doubled-die reverse
1972	50¢	D—doubled-die reverse
1973	50¢	(P)—doubled-die reverse
1973	50¢	D—doubled-die obverse

Mint Sets

1974	50¢	D—doubled-die obverse
1974	50¢	D—doubled-die reverse
1976	25¢	D—doubled-die obverse
1976	50¢	D—doubled-die obverse
1981	5¢	D—doubled-die reverse
1981	25¢	P—doubled-die obverse
1984	50¢	D/D—repunched mintmark
1987	10¢	D/D—repunched mintmark
1989	5¢	D—doubled-die reverse
1989	10¢	P—doubled-die reverse
1989	25¢	P—doubled-die obverse
1989	50¢	D/D—repunched mintmark
1991	5¢	D—doubled-die reverse (DDR-001, DDR-002, DDR-003, DDR-004)
2005	5¢ Bison	P—doubled-die obverse (DDO-001, DDO-002, DDO-003, DDO-004)
2005	5¢ Ocean in View	P—doubled-die reverse (many)
2005	25¢ Minnesota	P—doubled-die reverse (many)
2005	25¢ Oregon	P—doubled-die reverse (many)
2005	25¢ Oregon	D—doubled-die reverse (many)
2007	25¢ Wyoming	P—doubled-die reverse (many)
2008	25¢ New Mexico	D—doubled-die reverse (many)
2009	1¢ Formative Years	D—doubled-die reverse (many)
2009	25¢ Washington, D.C.	P—doubled-die reverse

Proof Sets

1950	10¢	doubled-die reverse
1950	50¢	doubled-die obverse
1951	1¢	doubled-die obverse
1951	**5¢**	**doubled-die obverse**
1952	**25¢**	**"Superbird"**
1953	1¢	doubled-die obverse
1953	**5¢**	**doubled-die obverse**
1953	25¢	doubled-die obverse
1953	25¢	recut tail feathers
1954	5¢	doubled-die obverse
1954	10¢	doubled-die obverse
1954	50¢	doubled-die obverse
1955	1¢	doubled-die obverse
1955	1¢	doubled-die reverse
1955	**5¢**	**tripled-die reverse**
1956	1¢	doubled-die obverse
1956	1¢	doubled-die reverse
1956	10¢	doubled-die obverse
1956	50¢	doubled-die obverse
1956	50¢	doubled-die reverse
1957	**5¢**	**quadrupled-die obverse**
1957	50¢	doubled-die reverse
1959	25¢	doubled-die obverse
1960, Small Date	**1¢**	**doubled-die obverse (Large/Small)**
1960, Small Date	**1¢**	**doubled-die obverse (Small/Large)**
1960	5¢	doubled-die reverse
1960	10¢	doubled-die obverse
1960	**10¢**	**doubled-die reverse**
1960	**25¢**	**doubled-die reverse**

Proof Sets

1960	50¢	doubled-die obverse
1961	5¢	doubled-die reverse
1961	25¢	doubled-die obverse
1961	**50¢**	**doubled-die reverse**
1962	50¢	doubled-die obverse
1963	**10¢**	**doubled-die reverse**
1963	25¢	doubled-die reverse
1964	10¢	doubled-die obverse
1964	50¢	doubled-die obverse
1968-S	1¢	doubled-die obverse
1968-S	5¢	repunched mintmark
1968-S	10¢	doubled-die obverse
1968-S	**10¢**	**doubled-die reverse**
1968-S	**10¢**	**doubled-die obverse**
1968-S	**10¢**	**No S**
1968-S	**25¢**	**doubled-die reverse**
1968-S	**50¢**	**doubled-die obverse**
1969-S	5¢	repunched mintmark
1969-S	25¢	doubled-die obverse
1969-S	**25¢**	**repunched mintmark**
1970-S	**10¢**	**No S**
1970-S	50¢	doubled-die obverse
1971-S	1¢	doubled-die obverse
1971-S	**5¢**	**No S**
1971-S	50¢	doubled-die obverse
1975-S	**10¢**	**No S**
1979-S	1¢	Type II mintmark
1979-S	5¢	Type II mintmark
1979-S	10¢	Type II mintmark
1979-S	25¢	Type II mintmark
1979-S	50¢	Type II mintmark
1979-S	$1	Type II mintmark
1981-S	1¢	Type II mintmark
1981-S	5¢	Type II mintmark
1981-S	10¢	Type II mintmark
1981-S	25¢	Type II mintmark
1981-S	50¢	Type II mintmark
1981-S	$1	Type II mintmark
1983-S	**10¢**	**No S**
1988-S	**50¢**	**doubled-die obverse**
1990-S	**1¢**	**No S**
1990-S	5¢	doubled-die obverse
1990-S	25¢	doubled-die obverse
1992-S	50¢	doubled-die obverse
1995-S	25¢	doubled-die obverse

Appendix E

When Cherrypickin', Use Courtesy and Respect!

Many years ago, a dealer friend of ours indicated he would never let anyone, other than a few people, cherrypick his stock (fortunately, we were among that select group). He had legitimate complaints regarding most of those who try to cherrypick varieties. His experiences are not unlike those of many dealers. Too often, collectors who are most interested in cherrypickin' varieties disregard the dealer's other (and potentially more profitable) customers. Many cherrypickers will take up space and time, and then walk away without a single purchase. Is that right? Is that fair to the dealer?

Before we get directly into the *courtesy* aspect of this article, we would like to remind you that there is nothing wrong with cherrypickin'. We use our knowledge just as another dealer or collector would use their knowledge to buy the best deal. A dealer trying to buy an 1892-S Barber quarter in Fine condition for a client will usually cherrypick to get the best possible value. Dealers with excellent grading skills can cherrypick undergraded coins, making a nice profit in a later sale. That has been occurring for decades in our hobby.

When the term *cherrypick* is used today, most hobbyists automatically think of those who search for varieties among a stock of normal coins. Those of us involved with varieties have studied long and hard for our knowledge. However, to make the most of this knowledge, we must use some common sense, and we must *always* respect a dealer's main objective—to earn a living. Dealers are at shows and in the coin business to make money to support their families. This is their livelihood, and we must always respect their time and space. If you don't feel you can afford them this courtesy, don't consider cherrypickin' for varieties. Those of us who do respect a dealer's time and space do not want a few inconsiderate people to ruin the pickings for the rest of us.

There are a few "courtesy" pointers that we'd like you to keep in mind. Remember that you are very likely a small customer for the typical dealer. They can almost certainly make more money from another customer in a tenth of the time they might spend with you. Remember that *you need the dealers* for cherrypickin'—they could make their living without cherrypickers!

If you're at a show and you've spotted a dealer whose stock you would like to search, and that dealer is busy, simply go to another dealer for a while. If you are seated at a dealer's table looking over their stock, and they start to get busy, let them know in a respectful way that you realize you're taking up their space and time, and that you will come back when they aren't as busy. We promise the dealer will remember your courtesy and respect, and you're more likely to be welcomed back when time permits.

We've often had dealers ask what we're looking for. We generally tell them that we're looking for various varieties, and that will usually suffice. Don't lie. Never lie! But you don't have to tell everything. If the dealer persists, you might tell them about a few of the more scarce varieties, and explain that there is a market for those varieties. Remember most dealers couldn't care less about the popular varieties that aren't listed in the Red Book. They will usually say "fine," and you can continue looking.

However, the best-case scenario is that you can teach this dealer something about varieties. As you become better acquainted, the dealer might start to look for some of the varieties, and save them for you. Sure, you'll likely pay a little more for them than the price of the normal coin, but far less than the actual value of the variety. In short, you'll have added a pair of eyes to *your* cherrypickin'. You'll get a new supply for varieties and at prices that will enable you to realize a very nice profit. We've even had dealers tell us to name the price, and we've had dealers ask for only the value of the normal coin.

Here's a tip that we think is extremely important. If you're at a dealer's table, and if for some reason you need to reach into your pocket or lap, plainly open your hands above the table, turn them over and rub them together, then do what you need to do. You don't need to say anything, and don't make a big deal of it, but make sure it's obvious. Why? The dealer will know for sure that you are not "palming" a coin. Do this with dealers you know well, and with dealers you don't know. Make it a habit. The main point here is to *never* give any dealer any opportunity to even think you are doing something wrong. We've seen people who hold a want list or magnifier in their lap, then take the coin below the table's surface, out of view of the dealer. That is very wrong, whether cherrypickin' or not, and will often discourage a dealer from welcoming you back. Always think of how you would want a customer to act if you were the dealer, and *always be respectful*—even if the dealer may seem rude.

Here are some other important points: Never let a dealer feel cheated when you buy a coin, or you'll never be welcomed back. Never brag about what you've purchased from a dealer if there is any way possible it could get back to the dealer. Always be polite and courteous—and being friendly doesn't hurt, either. Try to put yourself in their shoes once in a while. Usually, a dealer's main objective is to sell for a profit coins they have and know best. Many dealers specialize in certain areas, and leave other coins to others. We cherrypickers are the ones who know varieties best, and so they will usually leave this area for us.

One last tip: Suppose you find a super variety for the price of a regular coin, and for some reason you don't want the dealer to key in on that one coin. You might buy a few other coins at the same time to draw less attention to the coin you really want. Who cares about the added expense? You'll make a bundle on that nice cherry! And if the extra coins are ones with firm markets, such as an MS-63 Morgan dollar or a Proof set, you'll be able to turn around and sell them quickly.

Above all, *always use courtesy and respect* in all your dealings, be honest, and always act in a professional manner. You'll make some friends along the way, and we guarantee you'll come out ahead in the long run!

Appendix F
1979-S and 1981-S Proof-Mintmark Varieties

The Type I and Type II mintmark varieties for the 1979-S and 1981-S Proof sets are very well known, yet many people become confused when trying to differentiate them. This appendix illustrates the four mintmark styles for each denomination.

Compare these descriptions to the photos, and you'll be able to identify the correct types:

- The *1979-S Type I* mintmark has a squared, filled S, very indistinct.
- The *1979-S Type II* mintmark is clear and well formed.
- The *1981-S Type I* is a worn version of the 1979-S Type II.
- The *1981-S Type II,* although somewhat similar to the Type I, is distinguishable by the flattened top surface of the S. Some specialists argue that the S must be clear in both loops. Most agree that the S can show some slight filling, but the mintmark punch must show that flattened top surface. This is usually the most difficult type to comprehend. But the key is really very simple—that flatness on the top surface.

Cents

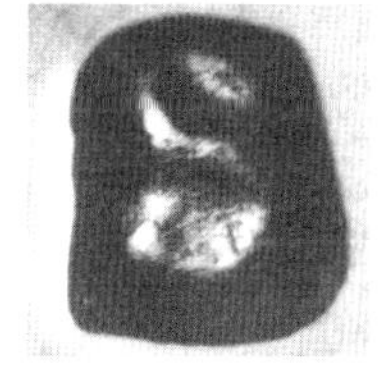
1979-S Type I

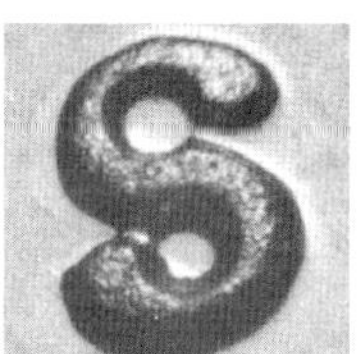
1979-S Type II

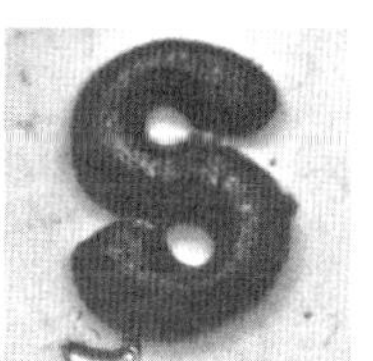
1981-S Type I

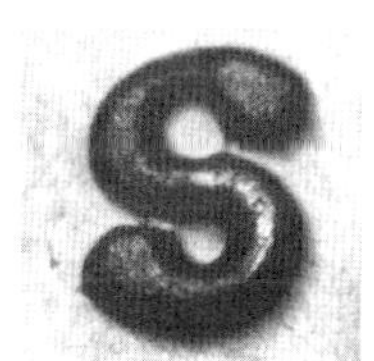
1981-S Type II

Nickels

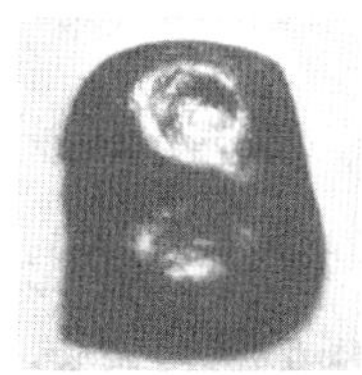
1979-S Type I

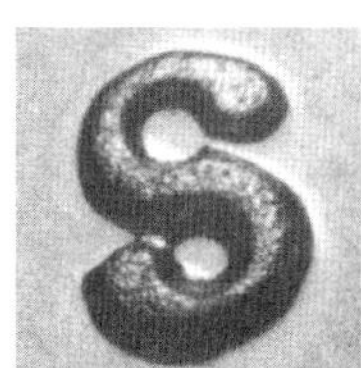
1979-S Type II

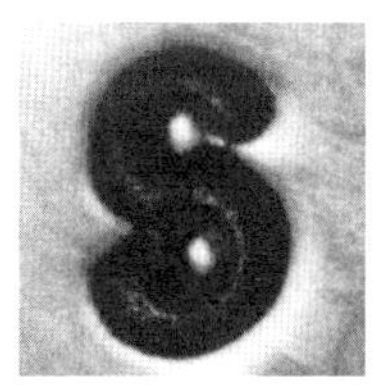
1981-S Type I

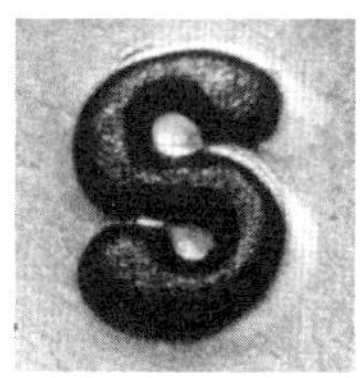
1981-S Type II

Dimes

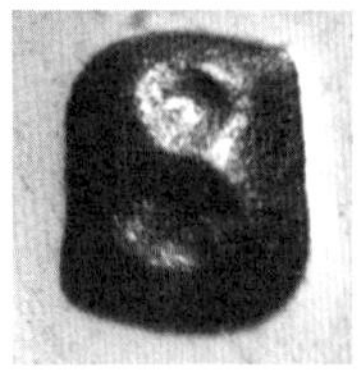
1979-S Type I

1979-S Type II

1981-S Type I

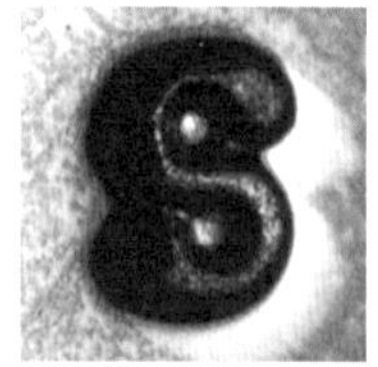
1981-S Type II

Quarter Dollars

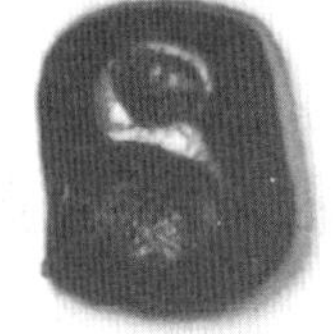
1979-S Type I

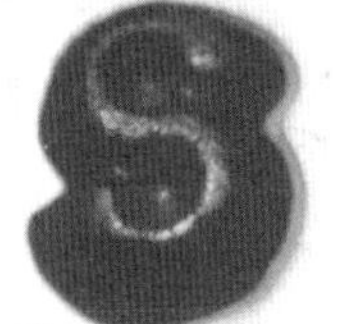
1979-S Type II

1981-S Type I

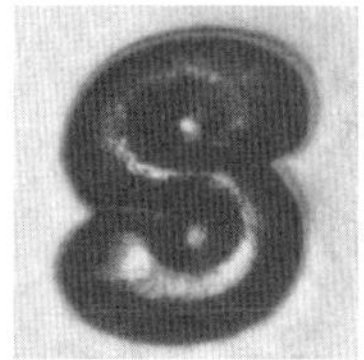
1981-S Type II

Half Dollars

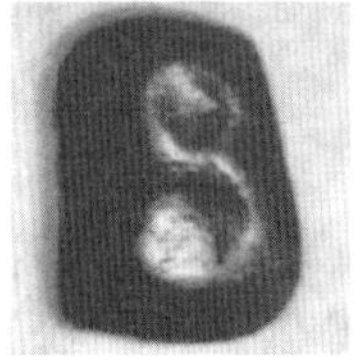
1979-S Type I

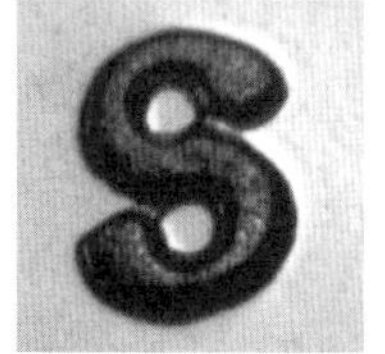
1979-S Type II

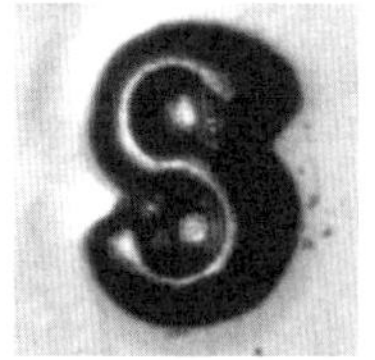
1981-S Type I

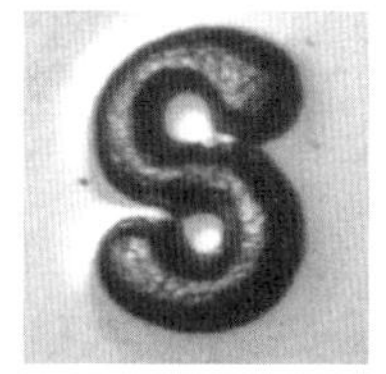
1981-S Type II

Dollars

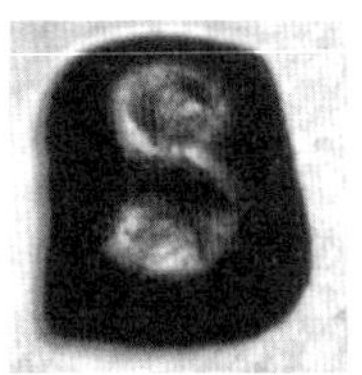
1979-S Type I

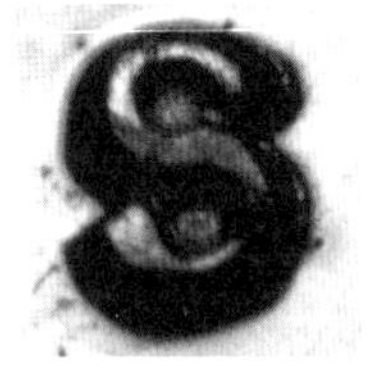
1979-S Type II

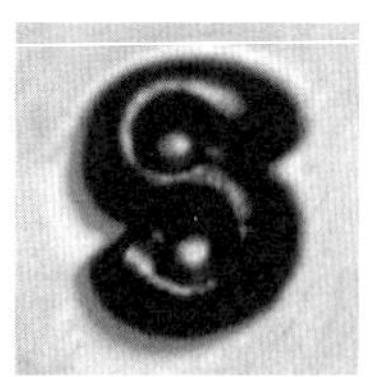
1981-S Type I

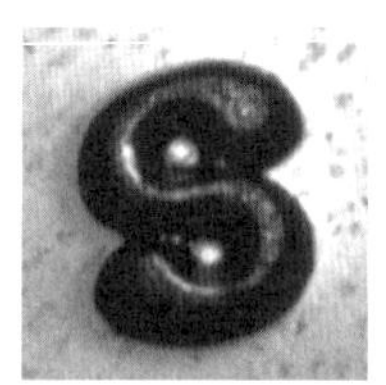
1981-S Type II

Appendix G

Recommended Reading

The axiom "Buy the book before the coin" applies even more strongly to the error/variety collector than to the regular segment of the hobby. The following is a list of recommended readings. It can by no means stay complete—new books become available regularly—but it gives you an excellent foundation for building your knowledge. Most of these books are available online, or through any coin dealer. The abbreviation OOP indicates the reference is out of print.

General

The following books cover not only errors and varieties, but regular coins as well. These books should be included in any numismatist's library:

A Guide Book of United States Coins, by R.S. Yeoman, edited by Kenneth Bressett. Popularly known as the "Red Book," this is the book with which any numismatic library should begin.

Walter Breen's Complete Encyclopedia of U.S. and Colonial Coins. (OOP) This is an excellent early reference book for anyone interested in die varieties. It's not cheap, but much of the information it contains cannot be found anywhere else.

Walter Breen's Encyclopedia of Early United States Cents, 1793–1814. (OOP)

Walter Breen's Encyclopedia of United States Half Cents, 1793–1857. (OOP)

Series Topics

The following books highlight a specific series or subject. Each is a tremendous asset for anyone seriously interested in the particular topic. Also take note, all references by James Wiles are cataloging the CONECA variety files.

The Flying Eagle and Indian Cent Attribution Guide, third ed., vols. 1–2, by Richard E. Snow.

Flying Eagle and Indian Cent Die Varieties, by Larry R. Steve et al. (OOP)

A Guide Book of Flying Eagle and Indian Head Cents, second ed., by Richard Snow.

The Authoritative Reference on Lincoln Cents, by John Wexler et al. (OOP)

The Complete Guide to Lincoln Cents, by David Lange. (OOP)

The Complete Price Guide and Cross Reference to Lincoln Cent Mint Mark Varieties, by Brian Allen and John A. Wexler. (OOP)

The Comprehensive Guide to Lincoln Memorial Cent Repunched Mintmark Varieties: 1959, by John A. Wexler and John W. Bordner. (OOP)

The Comprehensive Guide to Lincoln Repunched Mintmark Varieties: Wheat Cents, 1909–1939, by John A. Wexler, Brian Allen, and John W. Bordner.

A Detailed Analysis of Lincoln Cents, vol. 1, by Billy Crawford. 2003. (OOP)

A Guide Book of Lincoln Cents, by Q. David Bowers.

The Lincoln Cent Doubled Die, by John Wexler. (OOP)

The Lincoln Cent Doubled Die Book, Vol. 1: 1909–1958, by James Wiles. (e-Book)

The Lincoln Cent RPM Book, Vol. 1, 1909–1958, third ed., by James Wiles. (e-Book)

The Lincoln Cent RPM Book, Vol. 2, 1959–1989, third ed., by James Wiles. (e-Book)

The Lincoln Cent RPM Book Update, 1997–2002, by James Wiles. (OOP)

Lincoln Cent Varieties, 1909–2009, by Billy G. Crawford. (e-Book)

Looking Through Lincoln Cents, second ed., by Charles Daughtrey.

A Quick Reference to the Top Lincoln Cent Varieties, by Gary Wagnon et al. (OOP)

The RPM Book: Lincoln Cents, second ed., by James Wiles. (OOP)

The Top 100 Lincoln Cent RPMs and OMMs, by James Wiles. (e-Book)

The Wexler Doubled Die Files: Lincoln Cents, vols. 1–3, by John A. Wexler.

Longacre's Two-Cent Piece, 1864: Attribution Guide, by Frank Leone. (OOP)

The Complete Guide to Shield and Liberty Nickels, by Gloria Peters and Cynthia Mohon. (OOP)

A Guide Book of Shield and Liberty Head Nickels, by Q. David Bowers.

The Shield Five Cent Series, by Ed Fletcher. (OOP)

Buffalo Nickels: The Abraded Die Varieties, by Ron Pope.

The Complete Guide to Buffalo Nickels, second ed., by David W. Lange.

A Guide Book of Buffalo and Jefferson Nickels, by Q. David Bowers.

Treasure Hunting Buffalo Nickels, by John Wexler et al. (OOP)

The Best of the Jefferson Nickel Doubled Dies, by John Wexler and Brian Ribar. (OOP)

The Jefferson Nickel Analyst, second ed., by Bernard A. Nagengast.

The Jefferson Nickel RPM Book and *The Jefferson Nickel RPM Book Update: 2001–2002*, by James Wiles. (OOP)

The Complete Guide to Liberty Seated Half Dimes, by Al Blythe. (OOP)

The Complete Guide to Liberty Seated Dimes, by Brian Greer. (OOP)

The Complete Guide to Barber Dimes, by David Lawrence. (OOP)

A Guide Book of Barber Silver Coins, by Q. David Bowers.

The Complete Guide to Mercury Dimes, second ed., by David W. Lange.

The Authoritative Reference on Roosevelt Dimes, by John Wexler et al.

Richard's Roosevelt Dime Review: The Silver Years, 1946–1965, by Richard Bateson.

The Early Quarter Dollars of the United States, 1796–1838, by A.W. Browning.

The Comprehensive Encyclopedia of United States Liberty Seated Quarters, by Larry Briggs. (OOP)

Standing Liberty Quarters, third ed., by J. H. Cline.

A Guide Book of Mercury Dimes, Standing Liberty Quarters, and Liberty Walking Half Dollars, by Q. David Bowers.

Standing Liberty Quarters: Varieties and Errors, by Robert H. Knauss.

The Complete Guide to Barber Quarters, by David Lawrence. (OOP)

The Best of the Washington Quarter Doubled Dies, by John Wexler et al. (OOP)

A Guide Book of Washington and State Quarters, by Q. David Bowers.

The Washington Quarter Dollar Book, vols. 1–3, by James Wiles. (OOP)

Early Half Dollar Varieties, fifth ed., by Al C. Overton (now credited to Don L. Parsley as author).

Bust Half Fever, 1807–1836, by Edgar E. Sounders.

The Top 100 R4 and R5 Capped Bust Half Dollar Varieties and Sub-Varieties, by Edgar E. Sounders.

The Ultimate Guide to Attributing Bust Half Dollars, by Glenn R. Peterson.

The Complete Guide to Liberty Seated Half Dollars, by Randy Wiley and Bill Bugert. (OOP)

A Guide Book of Liberty Seated Silver Coins, by Q. David Bowers.

The Complete Guide to Barber Halves, by David Lawrence. (OOP)

The Complete Guide to Walking Liberty Half Dollars, by Bruce Fox. (OOP)

A Guide Book of Franklin and Kennedy Half Dollars, second ed., by Rick Tomaska.

The Kennedy Half Dollar, by James Wiles. (OOP)

Comprehensive Catalog and Encyclopedia of Morgan and Peace Dollars, fourth ed., by Leroy C. Van Allen and George Mallis.

A Guide Book of Morgan Silver Dollars, fourth ed., by Q. David Bowers.

Top 100 Morgan Dollar Die Varieties: The VAM Keys, fourth ed., by Michael Fey and Jeff Oxman.

A Guide Book of Peace Dollars, second ed., by Roger W. Burdette.

The Authoritative Reference on Eisenhower Dollars, second ed., by John Wexler et al.

Collectable Ike Varieties: Facts—Photos—Theories, by the Ike Group

Little Book of Collectible Eisenhower Dollars, by the Ike Group, edited by Bill Sanders.

A Guide Book of Gold Dollars, second ed., by Q. David Bowers.

The United States $3 Gold Pieces, 1854–1889, by Douglas Winter and Q. David Bowers.

An Insider's Guide to Collecting Type One Double Eagles, by Douglas Winter and Adam Crum.

Type Three Double Eagles, 1877–1907: A Numismatic History and Analysis, by Mike Fuljenz.

Gold Coins of the Carson City Mint: 1870–1893, by Douglas Winter.

Gold Coins of the Charlotte Mint: 1838–1861, third ed., by Douglas Winter.

Gold Coins of the Dahlonega Mint: 1838–1861, second ed., by Douglas Winter.

Gold Coins of the New Orleans Mint: 1839–1909, second ed., by Douglas Winter.

Commemorative Coins of the United States—A Complete Encyclopedia, by Q. David Bowers. (OOP)

A Guide Book of United States Commemorative Coins, by Q. David Bowers.

100 Greatest U.S. Error Coins, by Nicholas P. Brown, David J. Camire, and Fred Weinberg.

Error Coins From A to Z, by Arnold Margolis. (OOP)

The Error Coin Encyclopedia, by Arnold Margolis. (OOP)

Error-Variety News Classics, books I and II, by John A. Wexler and Robert Wilharm. (OOP)

Official Price Guide to Mint Errors, seventh ed., by Alan Herbert. (OOP)

World's Greatest Mint Errors, by Mike Byers. (OOP)

The Cud Book, by Sam Thurman and Arnold Margolis. (OOP)

The Encyclopedia of Doubled Dies, vols. 1 and 2, by John Wexler. (OOP)

The RPM Book, by John Wexler and Tom Miller. (OOP)

Strike It Rich With Pocket Change: Error Coins Bring Big Money, third ed., by Ken Potter and Brian Allen.

Ultra Modern Doubled Dies (1996–2012), by James Wiles. (e-Book)

What Are Die Varieties? by James Wiles. (e-Book)

Periodicals

These magazines regularly feature varieties and errors.

ErrorScope. The bi-monthly magazine of CONECA (Combined Organizations of Numismatic Error Collectors of America), the national error/variety club. Membership information is available online at www.conecaonline.org

Error Trends Coin Magazine. This highly educational monthly magazine was devoted to the error/variety hobby, weighted toward errors. (OOP)

The Hub. This was the bi-monthly magazine of the National Collectors Association of Die Doubling. (OOP)

Appendix H
Coin Clubs

Joining a coin club is an important part of your hobby fulfillment. Membership brings many advantages, most important of which are camaraderie and the accumulation of knowledge. We all need both.

Even if you can't travel to meeting locations and shows, most clubs produce newsletters that are highly educational and encourage members to contribute articles. This is one of the best ways to learn about a specific numismatic subject. With every article you write, you'll travel new avenues of research and add to your numismatic knowledge. It never fails.

Many specialized coin clubs have been born in the virtual environment of the Internet. These clubs often are interactive, offering all members a great opportunity to ask questions of specialists, share knowledge, and meet others with similar interests.

This appendix lists numismatic organizations dedicated to subjects that should interest most of our readers. The information noted, including membership fees and addresses, is as accurate as possible at the time of publication. A visit to a group's Web site can provide the latest information.

Nationwide Clubs and Groups

The American Numismatic Association. This is the largest coin-collecting group in the world. The monthly magazine, *The Numismatist*, contains articles submitted by members on a wide array of topics. Additionally, the ANA's library is second to none and is available to all members. Other great benefits are also included as a part of your membership.

American Numismatic
Association
818 N. Cascade Ave.
Colorado Springs, CO 80903-3279
Phone: 800-367-9723
Fax: 719-634-4085
E-mail: ana@money.org
Web site: www.money.org

CONECA (Combined Organizations of Numismatic Error Collectors of America). CONECA is a worldwide organization that specializes in the study of errors and varieties. Its bimonthly newsletter, *ErrorScope*, is filled with educational topics. Additionally, CONECA's Web site has a huge listing with descriptions of several thousand repunched mintmarks and doubled dies. And access to that is free to all! Finally, there are also members-only sections with still more for your error and variety education.

CONECA
c/o Rachel Irish
3807 Belmont Rd.
Coeur d'Alene, ID 83815
Web site: www.conecaonline.org

SPECIALIZED CLUBS AND GROUPS

Barber Coin Collectors' Society. Serving collectors of the many U.S. coins designed by Charles Barber, chief engraver of the Mint from 1879 to 1917, this group offers myriad resources for the interested numismatist. It publishes the *Journal of the Barber Coin Collectors' Society* on a quarterly basis. A membership application is available via its Web site.

Dave Earp
BCCS Membership
P.O. Box 1723
Decatur, IL 62525

Early American Coppers. Founded in 1967, this not-for-profit numismatic organization serves as a point of contact for collectors of early U.S. copper coins, including colonial issues and Hard Times tokens in addition to U.S. half cents and large cents. The group's publication, *Penny-Wise*, is renowned as a great source of information. A membership application is available via its Web site.

EAC
P.O. Box 2462
Heath, OH 43056
Web site: www.eacs.org

Fly-In Club. This specialty group, formed in 1991, is for collectors of Flying Eagle and Indian Head small cents. *Longacre's Ledger* is the group's award-winning publication. A membership application is available via its Web site.

Fly-In Club
P.O. Box 559
Sandwich, IL 60548
Web site: www.fly-inclub.org

John Reich Collectors Society. The purpose of the John Reich Collectors Society is to encourage the study of numismatics, particularly United States gold and silver coins minted before the introduction of the Liberty Seated design, and to provide technical and educational information concerning such coins. JRCS has a great newsletter and conducts meetings at various times throughout the year.

John Reich Collectors Society
Attn: Stephen A. Crain
P.O. Box 1680
Windham, ME 04062
Web site: http://logan.com/jrcs

Liberty Seated Collectors Club. LSCC is one of the strongest groups dedicated to any coin design or series. LSCC members receive the quarterly *Gobrecht Journal,* which is filled with some of the most educational numismatic articles available anywhere.

LSCC
Dennis Fortier
LSCC New Member Dues
P.O. Box 1841
Pawtucket, RI 02862
Web site: www.lsccweb.org

Lincoln Cent Forum. An active online community for Lincoln cent collectors to discuss America's smallest circulating denomination, this forum also provides various resources for Lincoln cent collectors, including detailed explanation of the series and various aspects of the design, a glossary, and tips on coin photography. Creating an account is free.

Web site: www.lincolncentforum.com

Shield Nickels. This is another excellent online group, this one for enthusiasts of Shield nickels. Like many of the others, the discussion groups are filled with excellent information. There is no better discussion group available for the variety enthusiast. And best of all, you can join free!

Web site: groups.yahoo.com/group/Shield_Nickels

Appendix I

Fivaz-Stanton Numbers Cross-Reference Chart

The Fivaz-Stanton numbering system changed in the fourth edition of the *Cherrypickers' Guide*. The earlier numbering system was very confined, limiting the number of new listings that could be added. The newer system is rational and infinite. For details, consult the "How to Use This Book" section.

This chart cross-references the current FS numbers assigned to all previous listings. The first column indicates the *new* FS number, with other columns showing the old FS number (if there was a listing), the date and mint of the coin, and a brief description. Due to space limitations, the description is very short and should not be used in an attempt to identify a variety.

These numbers can easily be used in an abbreviated format, by using only the final three or four digits in the full number. A variety is always described with the denomination and date, so duplicating that number in a description is not really necessary. The final digits will describe the variety's FS number when the denomination and date are identified.

FS#	Old FS#	Issue	Brief Description
HALF CENTS			
HC-1804-301	001	1804	Date Orientation; Cohen-2
HC-1804-302	002	1804	Date Orientation; Cohen-4
HC-1805-301	003	1805	Date Orientation; Cohen-2
HC-1806-301	004	1806	Date Orientation; Cohen-3
HC-1808-301	005	1808	Overdate (8 Over 7); Cohen 1
HC-1809-301	006	1809	Date Orientation; Cohen-1
LARGE CENTS			
LC-1843-301	001	1843	Date Orientation; Newcomb-17
LC-1846-301	002	1846	Date Orientation; Newcomb-23
LC-1846-302	002.5	1846	Date Orientation; Newcomb-25
LC-1847-301	003	1847	Date Orientation; Newcomb-36
LC-1847-302	004	1847	Date Orientation; Newcomb-43
LC-1849-301	005	1849	Date Orientation; Newcomb-25
LC-1850-301	005.5	1850	Date Orientation; Newcomb-24
LC-1851-301	006	1851	Date Orientation; Newcomb-42
LC-1851-302	006.5	1851	Date Orientation; Newcomb-44
LC-1856-301	007	1856	Date Orientation; Newcomb-22
FLYING EAGLE CENTS			
01-1857-101	002	1857	DDO (UNITED STATES OF AMERICA, beak, eye, tail); Snow-4
01-1857-102	002.3	1857	DDO (UNITED STATES OF AMERICA, beak, eye, tail); Snow-15
01-1857-103	002.7	1857	DDO (UNITED STATES OF AMERICA, beak, and eye; also RPD); Snow-10
01-1857-104	002.8	1857	DDO (UNITED STATES OF AMERICA, beak, and wing); Snow-5
01-1857-105	002	1857	DDO (UNITED STATES OF AMERICA, beak, eye, and tail); Snow-3
01-1857-301	001.5	1857	RPD (all digits); Snow-11
01-1857-401	001	1857	Obv of '56 (rectangular opening of O, long center serifs of F)
01-1857-402	003	1857	Obv Die Clash (with Liberty Seated half dollar obv)
01-1857-403	004	1857	Obv Die Clash with Liberty Head $20 gold obv)
01-1857-901	005	1857	Rev Die Clash (with Liberty Seated quarter rev)
01-1858-101	005.5	1858 LL	DDO; Snow-2
01-1858-301	006	1858 LL	Overdate (8 Over 7; Die 1); Snow-1
01-1858-302	006.1	1858 LL	Overdate (8 Over 7; Die 2); Snow-7
01-1858-901		1858 LL	Low Leaves
01-1858-1901		1858 SL	High Leaves

FS#	Old FS#	Issue	Brief Description
INDIAN HEAD CENTS			
01-1859-301	006.3	1859	RPD; Snow-1
01-1859-302	006.2	1859	RPD; Snow-2
01-1859-303	006.35	1859	RPD; Snow-3
01-1860-401	006.4	1860	Transitional Design (pointed bust of 1860)
01-1861-301	006.45	1861	RPD; Snow-1
01-1862-301		1862	MPD; Snow-2
01-1862-801		1862	DDR; Snow-5
01-1862-802		1862	DDR; Snow-6
01-1863-301		1863	RPD; Snow-2
01-1863-302		1863	MPD
01-1863-801	006.46	1863	DDR; Snow-10
01-1864-401		1864	Polished Die; Snow-5
01-1864-1101	006.47	1864 BR	DDO (also RPD); Snow-4
01-1864-1301	006.48	1864 BR	RPD; Snow-2
01-1864-1401		1864 BR	Lathe Lines; Snow-11
01-1864-2301	006.7	1864 L	RPD; Snow-1
01-1864-2302	006.71	1864 L	RPD; Snow-3
01-1864-2303	006.72	1864 L	RPD; Snow-4
01-1864-2304	006.5, 006.55	1864 L	RPD; Snow-5
01-1864-2305		1864 L	RPD; Snow-2
01-1864-2306	006.73	1864 L	RPD; Snow-10
01-1865-301	007.4	1865 P5	RPD; Snow-1
01-1865-302	007.45	1865 P5	RPD
01-1865-303	007.5	1865 P5	RPD; Snow-3
01-1865-304	007.56	1865 P5	MPD; Snow-2
01-1865-1301	007.3	1865 F5	RPD; Snow-1
01-1865-1302	007.55	1865 F5	RPD; Snow-4
01-1865-1401	007.2	1865 F5	Obv Die Gouge; Snow-14
01-1865-1801	007	1865 F5	DDR; Snow-2
01-1866-101	007.6	1866	DDO (also multiple MPDs); Snow-1
01-1866-301	007.7	1866	RPD; Snow-2
01-1866-302	007.9	1866	RPD; Snow-3
01-1866-303	007.8	1866	RPD; Snow-9
01-1867-301	008	1867	RPD; Snow-1
01-1867-302	008.1	1867	RPD; Snow-4
01-1867-303		1867	RPD; Snow-2
01-1868-101	008.2	1868	DDO; Snow-1
01-1868-102	008.26	1868	DDO (also RPD); Snow-4
01-1868-103	008.25	1868	DDO (also RPD); Snow-5
01-1868-301	008.23	1868	MPD; Snow-8
01-1868-302/901		1868	RPD, Die Gouge; Snow-13
01-1869-301	008.3	1869	RPD; Snow-3
01-1869-302	008.5	1869	RPD; Snow-1
01-1869-303		1869	RPD; Snow-4
01-1870-101	008.6	1870	DDO; Snow-1, 2, 13, 22, 28
01-1870-102	008.82	1870	DDO (also RPD); Snow-5
01-1870-301	008.81	1870	RPD; Snow-4
01-1870-302	008.8	1870	MPD (also DDR); Snow-8
01-1870-303		1870	"Pick Axe" Die Gouge; Snow-7

FS#	Old FS#	Issue	Brief Description
01-1870-801	008.7	1870	DDR; Snow-2, 3, 14
01-1870-901		1870	Shallow N Rev
01-1871-301		1871	MPD; Snow-2
01-1871-901		1871	Shallow N Rev
01-1872-301	008.9	1872	RPD; Snow-1
01-1872-901		1872	Shallow N Rev
01-1873-101	009	1873 C3	DDO; Snow-1
01-1873-102	009.1	1873 C3	DDO; Snow-2
01-1873-1301	009.3	1873 O3	RPD; Snow-1
01-1873-1302		1873 O3	MPD; Snow-6
01-1874-101	009.33	1874	DDO; Snow-1
01-1875-301		1875	RPD; Snow-1
01-1875-302		1875	RPD; Snow-2
01-1875-303		1875	RPD; Snow-3
01-1875-801		1875	Die Alteration; Snow-16
01-1878-301	009.4	1878	MPD; Snow-2
01-1880-101	009.41	1880	DDO (also Misaligned Die Clash Rev); Snow-1
01-1882-301		1882	Broken 2; Snow-2
01-1882-302	009.43	1882	MPD; Snow-6
01-1883-301	009.45	1883	MPD; Snow-8
01-1883-302		1883	MPD; Snow-7
01-1883-303		1883	MPD; Snow-1
01-1883-401		1883	Misaligned Die Clash; Snow-11
01-1883-801	009.46	1883	DDR; Snow-6
01-1884-301	009.48	1884	MPD; Snow-1
01-1887-101	009.5	1887	DDO; Snow-1
01-1888-301	010	1888	Overdate (8 Over 7); Snow-1
01-1888-302	010.7	1888	RPD; Snow-2
01-1888-303	010.73	1888	MPD (base of 1 in ribbon)
01-1888-304	010.74	1888	MPD (8 in hair curl)
01-1888-305	010.75	1888	MPD (two 8's in hair curl)
01-1889-301	010.8	1889	RPD; Snow-3
01-1889-302		1889	MPD; Snow-4
01-1889-801	010.81	1889	DDR; Snow-1
01-1889-802		1889	DDR; Snow-11
01-1889-901		1889	Misaligned Die Clash; Snow-31
01-1890-101	010.85	1890	TDO; Snow-1
01-1890-401	010.82	1890	MPD; Snow-3
01-1890-402	010.84	1890	MPD; Snow-6
01-1890-901		1890	Misaligned Die Clash; Snow-16
01-1891-101	010.88	1891	DDO; Snow-1
01-1891-301	010.87	1891	RPD; Snow-3
01-1892-301	010.89	1892	RPD; Snow-8
01-1892-302	010.9	1892	RPD (also DDR); Snow-1
01-1892-401	010.91	1892	Heavy Die Scratches
01-1893-301	010.95	1893	RPD; Snow-2
01-1894-301	011	1894	RPD; Snow-1
01-1894-402	011.2	1894	MPD; Snow-2
01-1895-301	011.3	1895	RPD; Snow-1

FS#	Old FS#	Issue	Brief Description
01-1895-302	011.31	1895	RPD; Snow-9
01-1895-303		1895	RPD; Snow-20
01-1896-301	011.4	1896	RPD; Snow-1
01-1896-302		1896	Date Variety; Snow-21
01-1897-401	011.5	1897	MPD; Snow-1
01-1897-402	011.6	1897	RPD; Snow-8
01-1898-401	011.65	1898	MPD (8 in denticles)
01-1898-402	011.66	1898	MPD; Snow-5
01-1899-301	011.7	1899	RPD; Snow-1
01-1899-302	011.75	1899	RPD; Snow-13
01-1899-303		1899	RPD; Snow-9
01-1900-301	011.751	1900	RPD; Snow-1
01-1900-302		1900	RPD; Snow-3
01-1901-301		1901	RPD; Snow-19
01-1902-401		1902	Die Gouge; Snow-4
01-1903-301	011.76	1903	MPD; Snow-10
01-1903-302	011.765	1903	MPD; Snow-6
01-1903-303		1903	RPD; Snow-7
01-1903-304		1903	RPD; Snow-3
01-1904-301		1904	RPD; Snow-10
01-1905-301		1905	RPD; Snow-1
01-1906-301		1906	RPD; Snow-7
01-1906-302		1906	RPD, MPD; Snow-14
01-1906-303		1906	RPD; Snow-20
01-1907-301		1907	RPD; Snow-1
01-1907-302		1907	RPD; Snow-2
01-1907-303		1907	RPD; Snow-20
01-1907-304		1907	RPD; Snow-27
01-1908-301	011.77	1908	MPD; Snow-4
01-1908-302	011.79	1908	MPD; Snow-9
01-1908S-501		1908-S	RPM; Snow-1
01-1909-101	011.9	1909	DDO (L); Snow-1

LINCOLN CENTS

FS#	Old FS#	Issue	Brief Description
01-1909-1101	012	1909 V.D.B.	DDO-001
01-1909-1102	012.1	1909 V.D.B.	DDO-002
01-1909S-1501	012.2	1909-S	RPM (S Over S)
01-1909S-1502	012.3	1909-S	RPM (S Over Horizontal S)
01-1910S-501		1910-S	RPM
01-1910S-502	012.7	1910-S	RPM (S Over S)
01-1911D-501	012.8	1911-D	RPM (D Over D)
01-1911D-502	012.81	1911-D	RPM (D Over D)
01-1911D-503	012.82	1911-D	RPM (D Over D)
01-1911D-504	012.83	1911-D	RPM (D Over D)
01-1911S-501	012.85	1911-S	RPM
01-1917-101	013	1917	DDO-001
01-1922-401	013.2	1922	"No D" (Die Pair #2 only) and "Weak D"
01-1925S-101	013.3	1925-S	DDO-001
01-1925S-501	013.31	1925-S	RPM (S Over S)
01-1927-101	013.5	1927	DDO-001
01-1927D-501	013.51	1927-D	RPM (D Over D)
01-1928S-501	013.6	1928-S	Large S Mintmark
01-1929S-501	013.65	1929-S	RPM (S Over S)

FS#	Old FS#	Issue	Brief Description
01-1930D-501		1930-D	RPM
01-1930D-502	013.7	1930-D	RPM (D Over D)
01-1930S-501	013.73	1930-S	RPM (S Over S)
01-1934-101	013.79	1934	DDO
01-1934D-101		1934-D	DDO-001
01-1934D-503	013.81	1934-D	RPM (D/D/D/D)
01-1934D-504	013.8	1934-D	RPM (D Over D)
01-1935-101	013.9	1935	DDO-001
01-1936-101	014	1936	DDO-001
01-1936-102	015	1936	DDO-002
01-1936-103	016	1936	DDO-003
01-1938D-501	016.4	1938-D	RPM (D Over D)
01-1938S-501	016.51	1938-S	RPM (S Over S)
01-1938S-502	016.5	1938-S	RPM (S Over S Over S)
01-1939-101	017	1939	DDO-001
01-1941-101	018	1941	DDO-001
01-1941-102	018.1	1941	DDO-002
01-1941-103	018.3	1941	DDO-005
01-1942-101		1942	DDO-002
01-1942-102	018.7	1942	DDO-004
01-1942-103	018.9	1942	DDO-006
01-1942-104		1942	DDO-008
01-1942D-502	018.91	1942-D	RPM (D Over D)
01-1942D-504	018.92	1942-D	RPM (D Over D)
01-1942S-101/301	018.94	1942-S	DDO-001, RPM (S Over S)
01-1942S-512	018.93	1942-S	RPM (S Over S Over S)
01-1943-101	018.97	1943	DDO-001
01-1943-801		1943	DDR-001
01-1943D-501	019	1943-D	RPM (D Over D)
01-1943D-513	019.1	1943-D	RPM (D Over D)
01-1943S-101	019.5	1943-S	DDO-001
01-1944D-101		1944-D	DDO-001
01-1944D-502	021.1	1944-D	RPM (D Over D)
01-1944D-507	021.11	1944-D	RPM (D Over D)
01-1944D-511	020	1944-D	OMM (D Over S)
01-1944D-512	021	1944-D	OMM (D Over S)
01-1945-101		1945	DDO-013
01-1946S-501		1946-S	IMM-101
01-1946S-511	021.2	1944-S	OMM (S Over D)
01-1947-101	021.3	1947	DDO-001
01-1947S-504	021.31	1947-S	RPM (S Over S)
01-1949D-501	021.33	1949-D	RPM (D Over D Over D)
01-1949S-101		1949-S	DDO-001
01-1950S-504	021.34	1950-S	RPM (S Over S)
01-1951-101	021.35	1951 PF	DDO-001
01-1951D-101	021.4	1951-D	DDO-001
01-1951D-511	021.5	1951-D	OMM (D Over S)
01-1951D-512	021.52	1951-D	OMM (D Over S)
01-1952D-511	021.6	1952-D	OMM (D Over S)
01-1953-101	021.7	1953 PF	DDO-001
01-1953-401		1953 PF	Re-Engraved Die; RED-001
01-1953-402		1953 PF	Re-Engraved Die; RED-002
01-1953D-501	021.73	1953-D	RPM (D Over D)
01-1953D-502		1953-D	RPM-028

FS#	Old FS#	Issue	Brief Description
01-1954D-501	021.76	1954-D	RPM (D Over D Over D)
01-1955-101	021.8	1955	DDO-001
01-1955-102	021.9	1955	DDO-002
01-1955-103/801		1955 PF	DDO-004, DDR-004
01-1955D-101	021.93	1955-D	DDO-001
01-1955D-503	021.94	1955-D	RPM (D Over D Over D)
01-1955D-504	021.95	1955-D	RPM (D Over Horizontal D)
01-1955S-501	021.97	1955-S	RPM (S Over S Over S)
01-1956-101		1956 PF	DDO-002
01-1956-801		1956 PF	DDR-004
01-1956D-501	022.1	1956-D	RPM (D Over D)
01-1956D-502		1956-D	RPM-016
01-1956D-508	022	1956-D	RPM (D Over D)
01-1958-101	022.15	1958	DDO-001
01-1959-101	022.2	1959	DDO-001
01-1959-104	022.3	1959	DDO-004
01-1959D-501	022.5	1959-D	RPM (D Over D Over D)
01-1960-101	025	1960 PF	DDO-001, Large/Small Date
01-1960-102	024	1960 PF	DDO-002, Small/Large Date
01-1960-103	023	1960 PF	DDO-003, Large/Small Date
01-1960-801		1960 PF	DDR-009
01-1960D-101/501	025.5	1960-D	DDO, Small/Large Date, RPM
01-1960D-502		1960-D	RPM-001
01-1961D-501		1961-D	RPM (D Over Horizontal D)
01-1962-801		1962 PF	DDR-020
01-1963-801		1963 PF	DDR-006
01-1963D-101	025.8	1963-D	DDO-001
01-1964-801	026	1964	DDR-001
01-1964-802	027	1964	DDR-058
01-1966-101		1966	DDO-001
01-1966-801		1966	DDR-001
01-1968D-501	027.3	1968-D	RPM-001
01-1968D-801	027.4	1968-D	DDR-001
01-1968S-101	027.5	1968-S PF	DDO-005
01-1969S-101	028	1969-S	DDO-001
01-1970S-101	029	1970-S	DDO-001
01-1970S-102	030	1970-S PF	DDO-003, Large/Small Date
01-1970S-103	030.1	1970-S	DDO-005
01-1970S-107	030.4	1970-S PF	DDO-007
01-1970S-113	030.6	1970-S PF	DDO-013
01-1970S-1401		1970-S	Small Date
01-1970S-1402	030.2	1970-S PF	Small Date
01-1971-101	031	1971	DDO-001
01-1971S-101	032	1971-S PF	DDO-001
01-1971S-102	033	1971-S PF	DDO-002
01-1971S-103	033.1	1971-S PF	DDO-004
01-1972-101	033.3	1972	DDO-001
01-1972-102	033.52	1972	DDO-002
01-1972-103	033.53	1972	DDO-003
01-1972-104	033.54	1972	DDO-004
01-1972-105	033.55	1972	DDO-005
01-1972-106	033.56	1972	DDO-006
01-1972-107	033.57	1972	DDO-007
01-1972-108	033.58	1972	DDO-008
01-1972-109	033.59	1972	DDO-009
01-1972S-101	033.7	1972-S PF	DDO-001
01-1979S-501		1979-S	Type 2 MM
01-1980-101	034	1980	DDO-001
01-1981S-501		1981-S	Type 2 MM
01-1982-101	034.5	1982 CLD	DDO-002
01-1982-1801		1982 ZSD	DDR-002
01-1983-101	035	1983	DDO-001
01-1983-102	035.1	1983	DDO-002
01-1983-103	035.2	1983	DDO-003
01-1983-401	035.3	1983	Obv Die Clash
01-1983-801	036	1983	DDR-001
01-1983-802		1983	DDR-002
01-1983D-101		1983-D	DDO-001
01-1984-101	037	1984	DDO-001
01-1984-102	038	1984	DDO-002
01-1984D-101	039	1984-D	DDO-001
01-1987D-501		1987-D	RPM-003
01-1988-101		1988	DDO-003
01-1988-901		1988	Proof Rev (Wide AM); RDV-006
01-1988D-901		1988-D	Proof Rev (Wide AM); RDV-006
01-1990-101		1990-(S) PF	Missing Mintmark
01-1992-901		1992 PF	Circ Strike Rev (Close AM); RDV-007
01-1992D-901		1992-D PF	Circ Strike Rev (Close AM); RDV-007
01-1994-801	039.9	1994	DDR-001
01-1995-101	040	1995	DDO-001
01-1995D-103	041	1995-D	DDO-003
01-1996-101		1996	DDO-001
01-1997-101	043	1997	DDO (ear)
01-1998-901		1998	Proof Rev (Wide AM); RDV-006
01-1998S-901		1998-S PF	Circ Strike Rev (Close AM); RDV-007
01-1999-901		1999	Proof Rev (Wide AM); RDV-006
01-1999S-901		1999-S PF	Circ Strike Rev (Close AM); RDV-007
01-2000-901		2000	Proof Rev (Wide AM); RDV-006
01-2004-801		2004	DDR-001
01-2006-101		2006	DDO-004
01-2009-801		2009	DDR-043
01-2009-802		2009	DDR-001

FS#	Old FS#	Issue	Brief Description
01-2009-803		2009	DDR-002
01-2009-804		2009	DDR-050
01-2009-805		2009	DDR-026
01-2009-806		2009	DDR-021
01-2009-807		2009	DDR-012
01-2009-808		2009	DDR-009
01-2009S-801		2009-S PF	DDR-003
01-2014-101		2014	DDO-001

TWO-CENT PIECES

FS#	Old FS#	Issue	Brief Description
02-1864-401	000.5	1864	Small Motto
02-1864-1101	001	1864	DDO; Leone-64Lg-06G
02-1864-1301	001.5	1864	RPD; Leone-64Lg-100E
02-1864-1302	001.7	1864	RPD; Leone-64Lg-24H
02-1868-1303		1864	RPD
02-1868-1304		1864	RPD
02-1864-1401/1902		1864	Obv & Rev Die Clash
02-1864-1901	001.8	1864	Rev Die Clash (with obv of Indian Head cent)
02-1865-101	002	1865 P5	DDO; Leone-65P-1o1r
02-1865-102		1865 P5	DDO
02-1865-301	002.3	1865 P5	RPD; Leone-65P-5o1r
02-1865-401/901		1865 P5	Obv & Rev Die Clash
02-1865-1301	002.5	1865 F5	RPD; Leone-65F-1o1r
02-1865-1302	002.7	1865 F5	RPD; Leone-65F-2o1r
02-1865-1303	002.8	1865 F5	RPD
02-1865-1304	002.9	1865 F5	MPD (6 or 8 in digits below primary 8)
02-1865-1305		1865 F5	MPD
02-1866-801		1866	DDR
02-1867-101	003	1867	DDO
02-1868-301	003.5	1868	MPD (6 below primary 6)
02-1868-302		1868	Possible overdate
02-1868-303		1868	RPD
02-1869-101	004.2	1869	DDO
02-1869-301	003.9	1869	RPD, MPD (6 below primary 6)
02-1869-302	004	1869	RPD
02-1870-101	004.3	1870	DDO
02-1871-102		1871 PF	DDO
02-1871-103		1871	TDO
02-1871-301		1871	RPD
02-1872-101	006	1872	DDO

THREE-CENT SILVER PIECES

FS#	Old FS#	Issue	Brief Description
3S-1851-301	001	1851	RPD
3S-1851-302	001.5	1851	RPD
3S-1852-301	002	1852	RPD
3S-1852-302	002.3	1852	RPD
3S-1852-801	002.5	1852	DDR
3S-1853-301	003	1853	RPD
3S-1854-301	004	1854	RPD
3S-1862-301	007	1862	Overdate (2 Over 1)

NICKEL THREE-CENT PIECES

FS#	Old FS#	Issue	Brief Description
3N-1865-101	003.5	1865	DDO
3N-1865-102		1865	DDO
3N-1865-301	001	1865	MPD (flag of 5 in denticles)
3N-1865-302	001.5	1865	RPD (wide west)
3N-1865-303	002	1865	MPD (flag of 5 deep in denticles)
3N-1865-304	002.5, 003	1865	RPD (blunt tip 5)
3N-1865-305		1865	RPD
3N-1866-101	004	1866	DDO
3N-1866-301		1866	RPD
3N-1869-301	004.3	1869	RPD
3N-1869-302	004.5	1869	RPD
3N-1869-801	004.7	1869	DDR
3N-1870-101	005	1870	DDO, RPD
3N-1870-301	005.5	1870	MPD
3N-1870-302	005.6	1870	MPD, DDR
3N-1871-101	006	1871	TDO
3N-1871-301		1871	RPD
3N-1875-301	006.5	1875	MPD (1 in neck)
3N-1881-301	006.8	1881	RPD
3N-1887-301	007	1887	Overdate (7 Over 6)
3N-1887-302	007	1887 PF	Overdate (7 Over 6)
3N-1888-301		1888	MPD

SHIELD NICKELS

FS#	Old FS#	Issue	Brief Description
05-1866-101	001.7	1866	DDO; F-22
05-1866-102	001.5	1866	DDO; F-21
05-1866-301	001	1866	RPD; F-08
05-1866-302	001.1	1866	RPD; F-10
05-1866-303	001.2	1866	RPD; F-20
05-1866-304	001.3	1866	RPD; F-16
05-1866-305	001.4	1866	RPD; F-13
05-1866-306/401		1866	RPD, Obv Die Clash
05-1866-307		1866	RPD
05-1866-308		1866	RPD
05-1866-901		1866	Rev Die Clash (also RPD); F-09a
05-1867-301	002.1	1867 WR	RPD; F-8
05-1867-302	002.4	1867 WR	RPD; F-9
05-1867-303	002.7	1867 WR	RPD; F-2
05-1867-304	002.6	1867 WR	MPD; F-01
05-1867-901		1867 WR	Rev Die Clash (with obv die)
05-1867-1101	001.8	1867 NR	DDO; F-59
05-1867-1102	002	1867 NR	DDO, RPD
05-1867-1301	001.9	1867 NR	RPD; F-23
05-1867-1302	002.15	1867 NR	RPD; F-25
05-1867-1303	002.2	1867 NR	RPD; F-21
05-1867-1304	002.25	1867 NR	RPD; F-20
05-1867-1305	002.3	1867 NR	RPD; F-22
05-1867-1306	002.35	1867 NR	RPD (also DDO); F-08.01
05-1867-1307	002.5	1867 NR	RPD; F-38
05-1867-1308	002.9	1867 NR	RPD; F-46
05-1867-1309	002.45	1867 NR	MPD; F-01.01
05-1867-1310	002.75	1867 NR	MPD (1 punched in shield)
05-1867-1401		1867 NR	Obv Die Clash; F-69

FS#	Old FS#	Issue	Brief Description
05-1867-1402/1901		1867 NR	Obv & Rev Die Clash
05-1867-1902		1867 NR PF	Alt Rev
05-1868-101	003	1868	DDO
05-1868-102	003.65	1868	TDO (also Rev of '68)
05-1868-103	003.8	1868	DDO
05-1868-104	003.9	1868	DDO
05-1868-105	003.95	1868	DDO (also DDR)
05-1868-106	003.96	1868	DDO (also Rev of '68)
05-1868-107	003.97	1868	DDO (also RPD)
05-1868-109		1868	DDO (also RPD)
05-1868-111		1868	DDO
05-1868-301	003.2	1868	RPD; F-19
05-1868-302	003.3	1868	RPD (also Rev of '68)
05-1868-303	003.35	1868	RPD; F-28.05
05-1868-304	003.4	1868	RPD; F-25
05-1868-305	003.45	1868	RPD
05-1868-306	003.5	1868	RPD; F-24
05-1868-307	003.7	1868	RPD
05-1868-309	003.85	1868	RPD
05-1868-310	003.98	1868	RPD; F-20
05-1868-311	003.985	1868	RPD (also Missing Leaf)
05-1868-312	003.1	1868	MPD (1 in ball of shield; Rev of '68)
05-1868-313	003.6	1868	MPD (digit in denticles); F-2
05-1868-314		1868	RPD
05-1868-401	003.99	1868	Missing Leaf and Circular Scribe Mark
05-1868-901	002.94	1868	Fully Broken C of CENTS
05-1868-902	002.95	1868	Broken C and S of CENTS
05-1868-903	002.96	1868	Broken C and S of CENTS, S of STATES
05-1868-904	002.97	1868	Broken C and S of CENTS, S of STATES, D of UNITED
05-1868-905	002.98	1868	No Broken Letters
05-1868-906	002.99	1868	Partially Broken C of CENTS
05-1869-301	005	1869 ND	Narrow Date
05-1869-1101	004	1869 WD	DDO
05-1869-1102	004.5	1869 WD	DDO (also RPD)
05-1869-1103	005.67	1869 WD	DDO (also RPD)
05-1869-1104		1869 WD	DDO (also RPD)
05-1869-1301		1869 WD	Normal "Wide Date"
05-1869-1302	005.3	1869 WD	RPD; F-104
05-1869-1303	005.4	1869 WD	RPD; F-202
05-1869-1304	005.5	1869 WD	RPD; F-408
05-1869-1305	005.6	1869 WD	RPD; F-408
05-1869-1306	005.68	1869 WD	RPD; F-105
05-1869-1307	005.2	1869 WD	MPD (1 in ball above date)
05-1870-101	005.7	1870	DDO (also RPD); F-03
05-1870-102	005.74	1870	DDO; F-12
05-1870-103	005.75	1870	DDO, RPD

FS#	Old FS#	Issue	Brief Description
05-1870-301	005.77	1870	RPD, Die Clash
05-1870-302	005.76	1870	MPD (0 in denticles)
05-1870-801	005.9	1870	DDR (Rev of '70 Over Rev of '67)
05-1870-802		1870	DDR
05-1871-101	006	1871	DDO
05-1871-301	006.5	1871	RPD; F-02
05-1872-101	007	1872	DDO; F-121
05-1872-102	007.1	1872	DDO; F-123
05-1872-103	007.2	1872	DDO; F-124
05-1872-104	007.3	1872	DDO; F-109
05-1872-105	007.4	1872	TDO; F-05
05-1872-106	007.5	1872	DDO; F-116
05-1872-107/309		1872	DDO, RPD, MPD
05-1872-301	007.6	1872	RPD; F-104
05-1872-302	007.65	1872	RPD (7 of date)
05-1872-303	007.7	1872	RPD; F-103
05-1872-304	007.76	1872	RPD (72 repunched north)
05-1872-305	007.77	1872	RPD, MPD
05-1872-306	007.9	1872	RPD; F-02
05-1872-307	007.75	1872	MPD (2 north right of ball)
05-1872-308	007.8	1872	RPD (Small Date Over Large Date)
05-1873-101	008, 008.85	1873 C3	DDO; F-04
05-1873-102	008.7	1873 C3	DDO; F-05
05-1873-103	008.8	1873 C3	DDO; F-06
05-1873-104		1873 C3	DDO
05-1873-1101	008.3	1873 O3	DDO; F-113
05-1873-1102	008.5	1873 O3	DDO, MPD; F-102
05-1873-1103		1873 O3	DDO
05-1873-1301	009	1873 O3	RPD (Large Date Over Small Date)
05-1873-1302	009.3	1873 O3	RPD; F-103
05-1873-1303	009.5	1873 O3	RPD; F-110
05-1873-1304	009.7	1873 O3	RPD
05-1874-101	010	1874	DDO; F-05
05-1874-102	010.4	1874	DDO (shield, motto); F-12
05-1874-103	010.5	1874	DDO; F-08
05-1874-104	010.6	1874	DDO (annulet)
05-1874-301	010.7	1874	RPD; F-02
05-1874-302	010.8	1874	RPD; F-01
05-1875-101	011	1875	DDO; F-04
05-1875-102	011.3	1875	DDO; F-05
05-1875-103	011.5	1875	DDO, RPD; F-03
05-1876-101	012	1876	TDO; F-04
05-1876-102	012.1	1876	DDO
05-1876-103		1876	DDO, RPD; F-08
05-1876-104/301		1876	DDO, RPD
05-1876-401		1876	Obv Die Variety
05-1882-101		1882	DDO; F-19
05-1882-301	012.5	1882	RPD
05-1882-302		1882	RPD; F-02
05-1882-999		1882	Die chip

FS#	Old FS#	Issue	Brief Description
05-1883-301	013	1883	Overdate (3 Over 2, Die #1); F-08
05-1883-302	013.1	1883	Overdate (3 Over 2, Die #2); F-09
05-1883-303	013.2	1883	Overdate (3 Over 2, Die #3); F-10
05-1883-304	013.3	1883	Overdate (3 Over 2, Die #4); F-08.01
05-1883-305		1883	Overdate (3 Over 2, Die #5); F-07
05-1883-311	012.8	1883	RPD; F-04
05-1883-312	012.9	1883	RPD; F-02
LIBERTY HEAD NICKELS			
05-1883-1301	013.7	1883 NC	RPD (base of 1 low and left from first 8)
05-1883-1302		1883 NC	RPD (base of 1 low and left from first 8)
05-1884-301	013.8	1884	RPD
05-1886-301	013.9	1886	RPD
05-1887-801	014	1887	DDR
05-1888-101		1888	DDO (ear)
05-1889-301		1889	RPD
05-1890-301	014.3	1890	RPD
05-1897-301	014.48	1897	RPD
05-1898-301	014.49	1898	RPD
05-1898-302	014.495	1898	RPD (east)
05-1899-301	014.5	1899	RPD (possible Overdate, 9 Over 8)
05-1900-801	014.7	1900	DDR (all elements)
05-1906-801		1906	DDR
BUFFALO NICKELS			
05-1913-901	014.85	1913 T1	3-1/2-Legged Buffalo
05-1913-1101	014.8	1913 T2	DDO-001
05-1913-1801	014.86	1913 T2	DDR-001
05-1913-1802		1913 T2	DDR
05-1913D-401	014.861	1913-D	Two Feathers
05-1913S-401		1913-S	Two Feathers
05-1914-101	014.87	1914	DDO, Overdate (4 Over 3)
05-1914S-101	014.89	1914-S	DDO, Overdate (4 Over 3)
05-1915-101	014.9	1915	DDO-001
05-1915-401	014.91	1915	Two Feathers
05-1915D-401		1915-D	Two Feathers
05-1915D-501	015	1915-D	RPM (D Over D)
05-1915S-501	015.5	1915-S	RPM
05-1915S-502	015.6	1915-S	RPM
05-1916-101	016	1916	DDO (also RPD)
05-1916-401	016.3	1916	Missing Designer's Initial
05-1916-402		1916	Two Feathers
05-1916D-901		1916-D	3-1/2-Legged Buffalo
05-1916S-401		1916-S	Two Feathers
05-1917-401	016.411	1917	Two Feathers
05-1917-801	016.4	1917	DDR-001
05-1917-802	016.41	1917	DDR-002
05-1917D-401	016.43	1917-D	Two Feathers
05-1917D-901	016.42	1917-D	3-1/2-Legged Buffalo
05-1917S-401	016.44	1917-S	Two Feathers
05-1918-401	016.46	1918	Two Feathers
05-1918-801	016.45	1918	DDR-001
05-1918D-101	016.5	1918-D	Overdate (8 Over 7)
05-1918S-401	016.6	1918-S	Two Feathers
05-1919-101		1919	DDO-001
05-1919-401	016.61	1919	Two Feathers, Missing Designer's initial
05-1919D-401		1919-D	Two Feathers
05-1919S-401		1919-S	Two Feathers
05-1920-401		1920	Two Feathers
05-1920D-401		1920-D	Two Feathers
05-1920D-502		1920-D	RPM
05-1920S-401	016.631	1920-S	Two Feathers
05-1921-401	016.633	1921	Two Feathers
05-1921S-401	016.635	1921-S	Two Feathers
05-1923-401		1923	Two Feathers
05-1925D-401	016.638	1925-D	Two Feathers
05-1925S-401	016.641	1925-S	Two Feathers
05-1925S-501	016.64	1925-S	RPM
05-1926-101/801		1926	DDO-002, DDR-002
05-1926D-401		1926-D	Two Feathers
05-1926D-901		1926-D	3-1/2-Legged Buffalo
05-1927D-401		1927-D	Two Feathers
05-1927D-501	016.7	1927-D	RPM
05-1927D-901	016.65	1927-D	3-1/2-Legged Buffalo
05-1927S-101	016.75	1927-S	DDO-001
05-1927S-401		1927-S	Two Feathers
05-1928S-401		1928-S	Two Feathers
05-1929-101	016.8	1929	DDO
05-1929S-401		1929-S	Two Feathers
05-1930-101	017	1930	DDO-001
05-1930-102		1930	DDO-004
05-1930-103		1930	DDO-006
05-1930-801	017.5	1930	DDR-001
05-1930-802	017.3	1930	DDR-002
05-1930-803	017.4	1930	DDR-003
05-1930S-101		1930-S	DDO-001
05-1930S-401	017.711	1930-S	Two Feathers
05-1930S-501	017.71	1930-S	RPM (S Over S)
05-1931S-801		1931-S	DDR-002
05-1931S-802		1931-S	DDR-003
05-1935-801	018	1935	DDR-001
05-1935-803	018.1	1935	DDR-003
05-1935D-502	018.5	1935-D	RPM (D/D/D/D)
05-1935S-801	018.6	1935-S	DDR-001
05-1936-101	018.7	1936	DDO-001
05-1936-102		1936	DDO-002
05-1936-801	018.8	1936	DDR-001
05-1936D-502	019.5	1936-D	RPM (D Over D Over D)
05-1936D-511	019.8	1936-D	OMM (D/D/D/S)
05-1936D-901	019	1936-D	3-1/2-Legged Buffalo

FS#	Old FS#	Issue	Brief Description
05-1936S-501	020	1936-S	RPM (S Over S)
05-1937D-901	020.2	1937-D	3-Legged Buffalo
05-1938D-511	020.5	1938-D	OMM (D/D/D/S)
05-1938D-512		1938-D	OMM (D Over S)
05-1938D-513		1938-D	OMM (D Over S)
05-1938D-514		1938-D	OMM (D Over S)
05-1938D-515		1938-D	OMM (D Over S)

JEFFERSON NICKELS

FS#	Old FS#	Issue	Brief Description
05-1938-101	021	1938	DDO-001
05-1938-105	021.5	1938	DDO-005
05-1938-106		1938	DDO-008
05-1938-401		1938 PF	Re-Engraved Die; RED-001
05-1938-402		1938 PF	Re-Engraved Die; RED-003
05-1938-403		1938 PF	Re-Engraved Die; RED-004
05-1939-101		1939	DDO-007
05-1939-801	022	1939	DDR-001
05-1939-802	022.5	1939	DDR-002
05-1939-901	023	1939 PF	Reverse of 1940 (Type II Steps)
05-1940-901	024	1940 PF	Reverse of 1938 (Type I Steps)
05-1940 S-501		1940-S	RPM-001
05-1941D-501	024.3	1941-D	RPM (D Over D)
05-1941S-501	024.5	1941-S	Large S Mintmark
05-1941S-502		1941-S	RPM (S Over S)
05-1942-101	025	1942 CN	DDO-002
05-1942-102	026	1942 CN	DDO-003
05-1942D-501	027	1942-D CN	RPM (D Over Horizontal D)
05-1942P-501		1942-P SA	RPM-008
05-1942S-501		1942-S SA	RPM-001
05-1942S-502		1942-S SA	Mintmark Location
05-1943P-101	028	1943-P	DDO (also Overdate, 3 Over 2)
05-1943P-102		1943-P	DDO-005
05-1943P-103		1943-P	DDO-013
05-1943P-106	029	1943-P	DDO-006 (eye)
05-1943D-501		1943-D	RPM-001
05-1944D-501		1944-D	RPM-001
05-1945P-801	030	1945-P	DDR-001
05-1945P-803	030.3	1945-P	DDR-003
05-1945P-804	030.5	1945-P	DDR-004, RPM
05-1945D-101		1945-D	DDO-006
05-1945D-501		1945-D	RPM-014
05-1946-801		1946	DDR-003
05-1946D-501	031	1946-D	RPM (D Over Inverted D)
05-1946S-101	031.5	1946-S	DDO-001
05-1949D-501	032	1949-D	OMM (D Over S)
05-1951-101	032.5	1951 PF	DDO-001
05-1952-401		1952 PF	Re-Engraved Die; RED-001
05-1952-402		1952 PF	Re-Engraved Die; RED-002
05-1952-403		1952 PF	Re-Engraved Die; RED-003
05-1952-404		1952 PF	Re-Engraved Die; RED-004
05-1953-101	032.7	1953 PF	DDO-001
05-1953-401		1953 PF	Re-Engraved Die; RED-001
05-1953D-501		1953-D	RPM-001
05-1954-401		1954 PF	Re-Engraved Die; RED-001
05-1954D-501	032.9	1954-D	RPM (possible OMM, D Over S)
05-1954S-501	033	1954-S	OMM (D Over S)
05-1954S-502	033.1	1954-S	RPM (S Over S)
05-1954S-801		1954-S	DDR-002
05-1955D-501		1955-D	OMM
05-1955-801	035	1955 PF	DDR-001
05-1956-102	035.4	1956 PF	DDO
05-1956-801	035.2	1956	DDR-018 (quadrupled)
05-1956-802	035.6	1956	TDR
05-1957-101	035.8	1957 PF	QDO
05-1958D-501		1958-D	RPM-001
05-1960-801	036	1960 PF	DDR-001
05-1961-801	037	1961 PF	DDR-013
05-1963-801	037.3	1963	TDR
01-1964-801		1964 PF	DDR-024
05-1964D-501	037.5	1964-D	RPM
05-1968S-501	038	1968-S PF	RPM (S Over S)
05-1969S-501		1969-S PF	RPM-001
05-1971S-501		1971-S PF	MMO-001
05-1971S-801		1971-S PF	DDR-028
05-1979S-501		1979-S PF	Type 2 MM
05-1981S-501		1981-S PF	Type 2 MM
05-1990S-101		1990-S PF	DDO-001
05-2004P-101		2004-P (Peace)	DDO-001
05-2005P-101		2005-P (Buffalo)	DDO-001

BUST HALF DIMES

FS#	Old FS#	Issue	Brief Description
H10-1829-301	000.1	1829	Overdate (9 Over 8)
H10-1834-301	000.3	1834	Overdate (3 Over Inverted 3)
H10-1836-301		1836	RPD; Breen-3003

LIBERTY SEATED HALF DIMES

FS#	Old FS#	Issue	Brief Description
H10-1838-901		1838	Rusted Die Rev
H10-1839O-501		1839-O	Rev of '38 (Large O Mintmark; also "Blundered Date" variety); Breen-3414
H10-1840O-901	000.5	1840-O	Transitional Rev (Large Letter reverse with open buds)
H10-1842O-301		1842-O	RPD (8 and 2)
H10-1843-301	000.6	1843	RPD (1, 8, and 4 south)
H10-1844-301	000.63	1844	RPD (1, 8, and 4 south , also 1 north)
H10-1845-301	000.65	1845	RPD (84 protruding south from base of rock)
H10-1845-302	000.66	1845	RPD (all digits northwest)
H10-1848-301	001	1848	Large Date
H10-1848-302	001.3	1848	Overdate (8 Over 7 Over 6)
H10-1849-301	001.5	1849	Overdate (9 Over 8)
H10-1849-302	001.55	1849	Overdate (possibly 9 Over 6)
H10-1853-301	001.8	1853	MPD (date protruding from rock)

FS#	Old FS#	Issue	Brief Description
H10-1853-401		1853	Arrows; Dot Below 5 of Date
H10-1855-101		1855	DDO (lower edge of skirt; also Obv Die Clash)
H10-1856-301	001.9	1856	MPD (8 in rock above primary 8)
H10-1858-301	002	1858	RPD; Breen-3090
H10-1858-302	003	1858	RPD (Date Over Inverted Date)
H10-1861-301	003.6	1861	Overdate (1 Over 0)
H10-1865-301	003.8	1865	RPD (circulation strike of V-1)
H10-1871-301	003.9	1871	MPD (portion of a digit in rock)
H10-1872-101	004	1872	DDO
H10-1872S-301	005	1872-S	MPD (1 in skirt right of ribbon end)
H10-1872S-302		1872-S	MPD (left of and below pendant; also Mintmark Below Bow)
BUST DIMES			
10-1824-901		1824	"Broken Wing" Rev
10-1829-301	001	1829	Curl Base 2
10-1829-901	002	1829	Small/Large 10 C.
10-1830-301	003	1830	Overdate (30 Over 29)
LIBERTY SEATED DIMES—NO STARS (1838 ONLY)			
10-18380-501		1838-O	Normal Mintmark
10-18380-502		1838-O	RPM
LIBERTY SEATED DIMES—SMALL STARS OBVERSE, NO DRAPERY, CLOSED BUD REVERSE—1838–1840			
10-1838-801	003.27	1838	DDR (all of this type are the DDR)
LIBERTY SEATED DIMES—LARGE STARS OBVERSE, NO DRAPERY, CLOSED BUD REVERSE—1838–1840			
10-1838-401		1838	Cracked Obv Die #1
10-1838-402		1838	Cracked Obv Die #2
10-1838-403		1838	Cracked Obv Die #3
10-1838-802	003.27	1838	DDR (same reverse die as FS-801)
10-1838-901		1838	Die Flaw Rev (chip between N and M of ONE DIME)
10-1840-401		1838	Die Clash/Break ("Whiskers" at Liberty's chin)
LIBERTY SEATED DIMES—LARGE STARS OBVERSE, PARTIAL DRAPERY, CLOSED BUD REVERSE—1838–1839			
10-1839o-501	003.28	1839-O	RPM (O Over O)
10-1839o-502		1839-O	Huge O Mintmark
LIBERTY SEATED DIMES—LARGE STARS OBVERSE, WITH DRAPERY, OPEN BUD REVERSE—1840–1853, 1856–1860-S			
10-1841-301		1841	RPD (184)
10-1841-302		1841	RPD (841)
10-1841o-301		1841-O	Small O Mintmark
10-1841o-302		1841-O	Large O Mintmark
10-1841o-901	003.3	1841-O	Transitional Rev (closed bud; Small O Mintmark)
10-1841o-902		1841-O	Transitional Rev (closed bud; Large O Mintmark)
10-1843-301		1843	RPD
LIBERTY SEATED DIMES—ARROWS ADDED			
10-1853-1301		1853	RPD
10-1854o-501		1854-O	Incomplete Mintmark Punch ("U" shaped); Breen-3286
10-1856-1101		1856 SD	DDO, Small date
10-1856-301		1856	RPD
10-1856o-2301		1856-O	RPD (also Large O Mintmark)
10-1872-301	003.45	1872	RPD
10-1872-302		1872	MPD (outer curve of 2)
10-1872-801		1872	DDR (reverse rotated about 175 degrees)
LIBERTY SEATED DIMES—NO ARROWS, CLOSE 3			
10-1873-301		1873	RPD
LIBERTY SEATED DIMES—WITH ARROWS			
10-1873-2101	003.5	1873	DDO
10-1875-301		1875	MPD (1 in denticles)
10-1876CC-101	004	1876-CC	DDO (level CC mintmark)
10-1876CC-102	004	1876-CC	DDO (right C high)
10-1876CC-103	004	1876-CC	DDO (right C low)
10-1876CC-301	003.7	1876-CC	MPD (digits in skirt by shield)
10-1876CC-901	005	1876-CC	Type II Rev
10-1876S-301		1876-S	RPD (18 of date)
10-1877CC-301		1877-CC	Overdate (7 Over 6)
10-1887S-501		1887-S	RPM (S Over S)
10-1888S-501		1888-S	RPM (S Over S); Greer-101
10-1889-801	005.3	1889	DDR (also RPD)
10-1890-301	005.5	1890	MPD
10-1890-302	005.6	1890	MPD (digits in drapery)
10-1890S-501		1890-S	RPM; Greer-105
10-1890S-502		1890-S	RPM
10-1891-301		1891	MPD (digits in denticles)
10-18910-501	008	1891-O	RPM (O Over Horizontal O)
10-1891S-501	007	1891-S	RPM; Greer-101
BARBER DIMES			
10-1892-301	008.3	1892	RPD
10-1892-302	008.4	1892	RPD
10-18920-301	008.5	1892-O	RPD
10-1893S-501	009	1893-S	RPM
10-1895S-301	009.2	1895-S	RPD (9 and 5)
10-1896-301	009.3	1896	RPD (8, 9, and 6)
10-1897-301		1897	RPD
10-1897-302		1897	RPD
10-1897-303		1897	RPD
10-18990-501		1899-O	RPM
10-19000-501		1900-O	RPM
10-19010-501	010	1901-O	RPM

FS#	Old FS#	Issue	Brief Description
10-1903-301		1903	RPD
10-1903O-301		1903-O	RPD
10-1904S-501		1904-S	Slanted S Mintmark
10-1906-301		1906	RPD
10-1906D-301		1906-D	RPD (also RPM)
10-1906D-302		1906-D	RPD (also RPM)
10-1906D-303		1906-D	RPD, MPD
10-1906O-301		1906-O	RPD, MPD
10-1906S-301		1906-S	RPD (also RPM); Breen-3552
10-1907-301		1907	RPD
10-1907D-301		1907-D	RPD
10-1907O-501		1907-O	RPM
10-1908-301		1908	RPD
10-1908-302		1908	Possible Overdate (08 Over 07)
10-1908-303		1908	RPD (multiple punches)
10-1908D-301	010.220	1908-D	RPD (possible overdate)
10-1908D-302	010.210	1908-D	RPD
10-1908D-303	010.200	1908-D	Overdate
10-1908D-304	010.225	1908-D	RPD
10-1908D-305	010.230	1908-D	RPD
10-1908D-306	010.235	1908-D	RPD
10-1908D-307	010.240	1908-D	RPD
10-1908O-301	010.250	1908-O	RPD
10-1908O-302	010.260	1908-O	RPD
10-1912S-101		1912-S	DDO (obv letters, date, ribbon ends)
MERCURY DIMES			
10-1928S-501		1928-S	Large S Mintmark
10-1929S-101	010.3	1929-S	DDO
10-1931D-101		1931-D	DDO (also DDR)
10-1931S-101		1931-S	DDO
10-1934D-501		1934-D	RPM-001
10-1935S-501		1935-S	RPM (also strike doubling on north side of mintmark)
10-1936-101	010.5	1936	DDO
10-1936S-110		1936-S	Possible Overdate (193 Over 192)
10-1937-101		1937	DDO
10-1937S-101		1937-S	DDO
10-1939-101		1939	DDO
10-1939D-501		1939-D	RPM (D Over D)
10-1940S-501		1940-S	RPM (S/S/S/S)
10-1940S-901		1940-S	DDO-002, DDR-001
10-1941-101		1941	DDO
10-1941D-101	010.58	1941-D	DDO-001, DDR-001
10-1941S-501	010.6	1941-S	RPM
10-1941S-502		1941-S	RPM
10-1941S-511	010.65	1941-S	Large S Mintmark
10-1941S-801		1941-S	DDR
10-1942-101	010.7	1942/41	DDO
10-1942D-101	010.8	1942/41-D	DDO (also RPM)
10-1942D-501		1942-D	RPM

FS#	Old FS#	Issue	Brief Description
10-1942S-501		1942-S	IMM
10-1943S-501		1943-S	RPM (S Over S)
10-1943S-511		1943-S	Large, Trumpet Tail S Mintmark
10-1944D-501		1944-D	RPM
10-1945-901		1945	DDO-002 (date)
10-1945D-501		1945-D	RPM (D Over D)
10-1945D-506	010.95	1945-D	RPM (D Over Horizontal D)
10-1945S-503	011	1945-S	RPM (S Over Horizontal S)
10-1945S-511		1945-S	RPM (possible S Over D)
10-1945S-512		1945-S	Micro S Mintmark
ROOSEVELT DIMES			
10-1946-101	011.4	1946	DDO-004, DDR-003
10-1946-102		1946	DDO (same obv die as above, but no DDR)
10-1946-103	011.5	1946	DDO
10-1946-104		1946	DDO
10-1946-801		1946	DDR
10-1946-802		1946	DDR
10-1946D-501		1946-D	RPM (D Over D)
10-1946D-502		1946-D	RPM (D Over D)
10-1946D-503		1946-D	RPM (D Over D)
10-1946S-501	011.7	1946-S	RPM (also DDR-001)
10-1946S-502	011.6	1946-S	RPM (also DDR-002)
10-1946S-503		1946-S	RPM (S Over S Over S, possibly RPM-013)
10-1946S-504		1946-S	Sans Serif S Mintmark
10-1947-101	011.9	1947	DDO
10-1947D-101		1947-D	DDO-003
10-1947D-102		1947-D	DDO-001 (LIBERTY, IN GOD WE TRUST)
10-1947S-501	013	1947-S	OMM (S Over D)
10-1947S-502	012	1947-S	OMM (S Over D)
10-1947S-503		1947-S	RPM (S Over S)
10-1947S-504		1947-S	RPM (S Over Horizontal S)
10-1947S-801	013.5	1947-S	DDR
10-1948-801		1948	DDR
10-1948S-501		1948-S	RPM-001
10-1950-801		1950 PF	DDR
10-1950D-501		1950-D	OMM (D Over S)
10-1950D-801	014	1950-D	DDR
10-1950S-501	014.5	1950-S	RPM (S Over Inverted S)
10-1951D-501		1951-D	RPM-001
10-1952S-501		1952-S	RPM-001
10-1953D-501		1953-D	RPM (D Over Horizontal D)
10-1953S-501		1953-S	RPM-002
10-1954-101		1954 PF	DDO
10-1954-801		1954	DDR (base of torch and oak stem)
10-1954S-501		1954-S	RPM
10-1954S-901		1954-S	Missing Designer's Initials; Breen-3736
10-1956-101		1956 PF	DDO
10-1959D-501	014.8	1959-D	RPM (D Over Inverted D)

FS#	Old FS#	Issue	Brief Description
10-1959D-502		1959-D	RPM (D Over D)
10-1959D-503		1959-D	RPM (D Over D)
10-1959D-504		1959-D	RPM-001
10-1960-101		1960 PF	DDO
10-1960-102A	015	1960 PF	DDO (early die state)
10-1960-102B	015	1960 PF	DDO (late die state)
10-1960-103		1960 PF	DDO-004 (designer's initials, TRUST)
10-1960-104		1960 PF	DDO-007 (like FS-101 but stronger on N)
10-1960-105		1960 PF	DDO-008 (TRUST)
10-1960-801	015.5	1960 PF	DDR
10-1960D-501		1960-D	RPM (D Over D Over D)
10-1961D-801	015.8	1961-D	DDR
10-1962D-505		1962-D	RPM (D Over Horizontal D)
10-1963-101	016	1963	DDO
10-1963-801	017	1963 PF	DDR
10-1963-802	017.5	1963 PF	DDR
10-1963-803	018	1963 PF	DDR
10-1963-804		1963 PF	DDR
10-1963-805		1963	DDR
10-1963D-801	018.2	1963-D	DDR
10-1964-101	018.4	1964 PF	DDO
10-1964-801		1964	DDR
10-1964-802	018.3	1964	DDR
10-1964D-101	018.45	1964-D	DDO
10-1964D-501		1964-D	RPM (D Over D northeast)
10-1964D-502	018.7	1964-D	Misplaced Mintmark (D protruding from torch)
10-1964D-503		1964-D	RPM (D Over D south)
10-1964D-504		1964-D	RPM (D Over D south)
10-1964D-505		1964-D	RPM (D Over D south)
10-1964D-506		1964-D	RPM (D Over D south)
10-1964D-801	018.5	1964-D	DDR
10-1964D-802		1964-D	DDR
10-1964D-803		1964-D	DDR
10-1967-101	019	1967	DDO
10-1968-101	019.5	1968	DDO
10-1968S-101	020	1968-S PF	DDO
10-1968S-102	020.2	1968-S PF	DDO
10-1968S-501		1968-S PF	Missing Mintmark
10-1968S-502		1968-S PF	RPM (also minor DDO)
10-1968S-801	020.3	1968-S PF	DDR
10-1968S-802		1968-S PF	DDR
10-1969-901		1969	Rev of '68 (deeper lines in flame); RDV-002
10-1969D-501	020.4	1969-D	RPM (D Over D northeast)
10-1970-801	020.6	1970	DDR
10 -1970-901		1970	Rev of '68 (deeper lines in flame); RDV-002
10-1970D-801		1970-D	DDR
10-1970D-802		1970-D	DDR
10-1970D-901		1970-D	Rev of '68 (deeper lines in flame); RDV-002

FS#	Old FS#	Issue	Brief Description
10-1975S-501		1975-S PF	RPM (S Over S)
10-1982-501	021	1982	Missing Mintmark
10-1982-501		1982	Missing Mintmark
10-1983D-501		1983-D	RPM (D Over D)
10-1985P-501		1985-P	Possible Misplaced Mintmark ("ghost" in neck; similar to a P)
10-1986P-501		1986-P	Possible Misplaced Mintmark ("ghost" in neck; similar to a P)
10-1987P-501		1987-P	Possible Misplaced Mintmark ("ghost" in neck; similar to a P)
10-2004D-101		2004-D	DDO (ear, rotated die)
TWENTY-CENT PIECES			
20-1875S-301		1875-S	MPD (8 in denticles; also RPM)
20-1875S-302		1875-S	Possible MPD (denticles below 7; also RPM)
BUST QUARTERS			
25-1831-301		1831	RPD (1 and 8 south)
25-1833-801		1833	DDR
25-1834-901		1834	Recut "OF A" in UNITED STATES OF AMERICA
LIBERTY SEATED QUARTERS			
25-18400-501		1840-O	Large O Mintmark
25-18410-101	001	1841-O	DDO-001
25-18430-301		1843-O	RPD (1 and 8 north)
25-18430-501	001.5	1843-O	Large O Mintmark
25-1845-301		1845	RPD (Large 5 Over Small 5)
25-1847-301	002.3	1847	MPD (8 protruding from base of rock)
25-1847-801	002	1847	DDR-001 (also RPD)
25-1850-301		1850	RPD (1 in denticles)
25-1853-301		1853	RPD (5 and 3 below the primary digits, slanted)
LIBERTY SEATED QUARTERS—ARROWS AND RAYS			
25-1853-1301	003	1853	Overdate (3 Over 4)
25-18530-501		1853-O	RPD (O Over Horizontal O)
25-18540-501	004	1854-O	Huge O Mintmark
25-1856-301		1856	MPD (1 and 6 punched in gown)
25-1856S-501	005	1856-S	Large S / Small S Mintmark
25-1857-401		1857	Die Gouge (Liberty's fingers; resembles a cigar)
25-1857-901	006	1857	Rev Die Clash (with reverse of Flying Eagle cent)
25-18570-301	006.2	1857-O	MPD (1 and 8 in denticles)
25-1872-301		1872	RPD (1 and 8 repunched south)
25-1875-301	006.75	1875	MPD (1 and 7 in denticles)
25-1876-301		1876	MPD (top of a 6 in denticles below 6)

FS#	Old FS#	Issue	Brief Description
25-1876-302	006.8	1876	MPD (1 southwest of primary 1)

LIBERTY SEATED QUARTERS

FS#	Old FS#	Issue	Brief Description
25-1876-303	06.85	1876	MPD (6 in rock)
25-1876-304		1876	RPD (triple 6)
25-1876-305		1876	MPD (top of 1 and 8 in denticles)
25-1876CC-301		1876-CC	RPD (1, 8, and 7 close south)
25-1876S-301	006.88	1876-S	MPD (7 and 6 in denticles)
25-1876S-302		1876-S	MPD (digit in denticles under 8)
25-1877CC-301		1877-CC	RPD (1, 8, and 7 close south)
25-1877S-501	007	1877-S	RPM (S Over Horizontal S)
25-1891-301	007.5	1891	MPD

BARBER QUARTERS

FS#	Old FS#	Issue	Brief Description
25-1892-101	007.7	1892	DDO (IN GOD WE TRUST)
25-1892-301		1892	RPD (also minor TDO)
25-1892-801		1892	TDR
25-1892O-101	007.8	1892-O	DDO (IN GOD WE TRUST)
25-1892O-301	007.9	1892-O	RPD
25-1892o-901		1892-O, Covered E Reverse	Obv Die Clash (Liberty's profile)
25-1899-901		1899	DDR (DOLLAR, arrows, claws)
25-1892S-501		1892-S	RPM (S Over S)
25-1902O-301		1902-O	MPD (denticles)
25-1907D-301		1907-D	RPD (also DDO)
25-1907S-501		1907-S	RPM
25-1908D-301		1908-D	MPD (denticles)
25-1914D-101	007.99	1914-D	DDO
25-1916D-501	008	1916-D	RPM

STANDING LIBERTY QUARTERS

FS#	Old FS#	Issue	Brief Description
25-1917D-801		1917-D, Type 1	DDR-001 (motto)
25-1918S-101	008.5	1918-S	DDO-001 (also Overdate, 8 Over 7)
25-1920-401		1920	Obv Die Clash (drapery)
25-1920S-401		1920-S	Obv Die Clash (drapery)
25-1928S-501		1928-S	IMM
25-1928S-502		1928-S	RPM
25-1929S-401		1929-S	Obv Die Clash
25-1930S-501		1930-S	RPM (likely Small S Over Large S)

WASHINGTON QUARTERS

FS#	Old FS#	Issue	Brief Description
25-1932-101		1932	DDO (earlobe)
25-1934-101	009	1934	DDO-001
25-1934-401		1934	Light Motto
25-1934-402		1934	Medium Motto
25-1934-403		1934	Large Motto
25-1934D-501	009.5	1934-D	Small D (D of 1932)
25-1935-101	010	1935	DDO-001
25-1936-101	011	1936	DDO-001
25-1937-101	012	1937	DDO-001
25-1939D-501	012.3	1939-D	OMM (D Over S)
25-1939S-101		1939-S	DDO
25-1940D-101	012.5	1940-D	DDO-001
25-1940D-501	012.4	1940-D	RPM (D Over D to left)
25-1941-101	012.7	1941	DDO
25-1941-102	012.9	1941	DDO
25-1941-103		1941	DDO-004 (date and IN GOD WE TRUST)
25-1941-801	013	1941	DDR-004 (tripled)
25-1941D-101		1941-D	DDO-001 (date and IN GOD WE TRUST); Breen-4309
25-1941D-801		1941-D	DDR-001 (OF AMERICA, QUARTER DOLLAR)
25-1941S-501		1941-S	Large Mintmark (Trumpet Tail style)
25-1941S-502		1941-S	RPM (S Over S north; Small Mintmark)
25-1942-101		1942	DDO
25-1942-801	014	1942	DDR
25-1942-802	014.3	1942	DDR
25-1942-803		1942	DDR
25-1942D-101	015	1942-D	DDO
25-1942D-801	016	1942-D	DDR
25-1943-101	016.5	1943	DDO (motto, LIB, and date)
25-1943-102		1943	DDO (LIBERTY, motto, and date)
25-1943-103	016.7	1943	DDO (motto, LIB, and date)
25-1943D-101		1943-D	DDO (eye, hair curls, initials, lip, chin)
25-1943S-101	017	1943-S	DDO
25-1943S-401		1943-S	Die Deformation (Washington's throat; "Goiter" variety)
25-1943S-501	017.3	1943-S	Mintmark Style (Trumpet Tail S)
25-1943S-502		1943-S	Slightly smaller and slightly different S (Large S is common)
25-1943S-503		1943-S	RPM (south; filled upper loop of primary mintmark)
25-1943S-504		1943-S	RPM (knob south of primary mintmark)
25-1944-101		1944	DDO (IN GOD WE TRUST, date, and LIB)
25-1944D-101		1944-D	DDO (LIBERTY)
25-1944S-101	017.5	1944-S	DDO
25-1945-101	018	1945	DDO
25-1945S-101		1945-S	DDO (IN GOD WE TRUST, date, and TY of LIBERTY)
25-1945S-102		1945-S	DDO (IN GOD WE TRUST, LIBERTY)
25-1946-101		1946	DDO (IN GOD WE TRUST, date, and LIBERTY)

FS#	Old FS#	Issue	Brief Description
25-1946-801		1946	DDR (lettering; also DDO)
25-1946D-501		1946-D	RPM (north of primary)
25-1946S-501		1946-S	RPM (S Over S)
25-1947-101		1947	DDO (LIBERTY)
25-1947S-501		1947-S	RPM (S Over S)
25-1947S-502		1947-S	RPM (S Over S)
25-1948S-501	018.4	1948-S	RPM (S/S/S/S)
25-1949D-501		1949-D	RPM (D Over D Over D)
25-1949D-601		1949-D	Possible OMM (D Over S)
25-1950-801	019	1950	DDR (eagle's beak, wings)
25-1950D-801	020	1950-D	DDR (talons, feathers, and arrow tips)
25-1950D-802		1950-D	DDR (lettering, esp. QUARTER DOLLAR)
25-1950D-502		1950-D	RPM (D Over D)
25-1950D-601	021	1950-D	OMM (D Over S)
25-1950S-501		1950-S	RPM (S Over S north)
25-1950S-601	022	1950-S	OMM (S Over D)
25-1950S-801		1950-S	DDR
25-1951D-101		1951-D	DDO (LIBERTY, IN GOD WE TRUST, date)
25-1951D-501		1951-D	RPM-004
25-1952-901		1952 PF	"Superbird" (unusual S evident on breast of eagle)
25-1952-902		1952 PF	"Superbird" plus Recut Tail Feathers and DDO
25-1952D-101		1952-D	DDO
25-1952D-501		1952-D	Huge D Mintmark
25-1952S-501		1952-S	RPM (S Over S Over S)
25-1952S-502		1952-S	RPM (S Over S)
25-1953-101		1953 PF	DDO
25-1953-901		1953 PF	Recut Tail Feathers
25-1953D-801	022.2	1953-D	DDR (UNITED STATES OF AMERICA, E PLURIBUS UNUM)
25-1953D-501		1953-D	RPM (Inverted D Over D)
25-1953D-601		1953-D	OMM (D/D/D/S/S)
25-1956-701		1956 PF	Rev Die Gouges
25-1956-701		1956	Rev Die Gouge
25-1956-901		1956	Type B Rev on Circ Strike (intended for Proofs)
25-1956D-501		1956-D	RPM (D Over Inverted D)
25-1957-901		1957	Type B Rev on Circ Strike (intended for Proofs)
25-1957D-501		1957-D	RPM (master die; separate D above olive branch)
25-1957D-901		1957-D	Recut Tail Feathers
25-1958-901		1958	Type B Rev on Circ Strike (intended for Proofs)
25-1959-101	022.45	1959 PF	DDO (IN GOD WE TRUST)
25-1959-901		1959	Type B Rev on Circ Strike (intended for Proofs)
25-1959D-501		1959-D	RPM (D Over D)
25-1960-801	022.5	1960 PF	DDR

FS#	Old FS#	Issue	Brief Description
25-1960-901		1960	Type B Rev on Circ Strike (intended for Proofs)
25-1961-101		1961 PF	DDO (IN GOD WE TRUST)
25-1961-901		1961	Type B Rev on Circ Strike (intended for Proofs)
25-1961D-501		1961-D	RPM (D Over D northeast)
25-1961D-502		1961-D	RPM (D Over D)
25-1962-101		1962 PF	DDO (lettering)
25-1962-901		1962	Type B Rev on Circ Strike (intended for Proofs)
25-1962D-501		1962-D	RPM (D Over D)
25-1963-101	023	1963	DDO (date, motto, and LIBERTY)
25-1963-102		1963	DDO
25-1963-103		1963	DDO (63 of date)
25-1963-801		1963	DDR (C and M of AMERICA, first T of STATES)
25-1963-802		1963 PF	DDR (AMERICA)
25-1963-901		1963	Type B Rev on Circ Strike (intended for Proofs)
25-1963D-101		1963-D	DDO-004 (lettering and date)
25-1964-101		1964	DDO (IN GOD WE TRUST)
25-1964-801		1964	DDR (lettering)
25-1964-802	024.5	1964	DDR (QUARTER DOLLAR)
25-1964-803		1964	DDR (STATES OF AMERICA)
25-1964-804		1964	DDR (UNITED)
25-1964-901		1964	Type B Rev on Circ Strike (intended for Proofs)
25-1964-902		1964	Type C Rev (intended for production beginning in 1965)
25-1964D-101		1964-D	DDO (IN GOD WE TRUST)
25-1964D-501		1964-D	RPM (D Over D)
25-1964D-502		1964-D	RPM (D Over D)
25-1964D-801	025	1964-D	DDR (STATES OF AMERICA, QUARTER DOLLAR)
25-1964D-901		1964-D	Type B Rev on Circ Strike (intended for Proofs)
25-1964D-902		1964-D	Type C Rev (intended for production beginning in 1965)
25-1965-101	026	1965	DDO (lettering)
25-1965-102		1965	DDO (LIBERTY)
25-1965-801		1965	DDR (QUARTER DOLLAR)
25-1966-801	026.3	1966	DDR (lettering)
25-1967-101	026.5	1967 SMS	DDO (lettering)
25-1967-801		1967 SMS	DDR (lower branches, leaves, QUARTER DOLLAR)
25-1968D-801		1968-D	DDR (lettering)
25-1968S-101		1968-S PF	DDO (lettering)
25-1968S-501		1968-S PF	RPM (S Over S north)
25-1968S-801	027	1968-S PF	DDR (lettering)
25-1969D-501	027.06	1969-D	RPM (D Over D)
25-1969D-502		1969-D	RPM (D Over D)
25-1969S-101	027.08	1969-S PF	DDO (lettering and date)
25-1969S-501	027.1	1969-S PF	RPM (S Over S Over S)

FS#	Old FS#	Issue	Brief Description
25-1970D-101	027.3	1970-D	DDO (lettering)
25-1970D-102		1970-D	DDO (LIBERTY)
25-1970D-801		1970-D	DDR (lettering)
25-1970D-802		1970-D	DDR (lettering)
25-1971-801	027.7	1971	DDR (lettering)
25-1971D-801	027.8	1971-D	DDR (UNITED STATES OF AMERICA)
25-1976D-101	028	1976-D	DDO (LIBERTY)
25-1976D-102		1976-D	DDO-002 (LIBERTY)
25-1979S-501		1979-S PF	Type II Mintmark
25-1981S-501		1981-S PF	Type II Mintmark
25-1982S-101		1982-S PF	DDO (IN GOD WE TRUST, date)
25-1989D-501		1989-D	RPM (D Over D)
25-1990S-101		1990-S PF	DDO (date and mintmark)
25-1995S-101		1995-S PF	DDO (date, mintmark, ribbon, hair, west on LIBERTY and IN GOD WE TRUST)
25-1996P-701		1996-P	Abraded Die (bust)
25-2004D-5901		2004-D, WI	Extra Leaf High (lines pointing up)
25-2004D-5902		2004-D, WI	Extra Leaf Low (lines pointing down)
25-2005P-MN-801		2005-P, MN	DDR-001 (right of 4th tree)
25-2005P-MN-802		2005-P, MN	DDR-002 (right of 4th tree)
25-2005P-MN-803		2005-P, MN	DDR-004 (right of 4th tree)
25-2005P-MN-804		2005-P, MN	DDR-006 (left of 4th tree)
25-2005P-MN-805		2005-P, MN	DDR-007 (right of 4th tree)
25-2005P-MN-806		2005-P, MN	DDR-008 (right of 4th tree)
25-2005P-MN-807		2005-P, MN	DDR-012 (right of 4th tree)
25-2005D-MN-801		2005-D, MN	DDR-001 (left of 4th tree)
25-2005D-MN-802		2005-D, MN	DDR-003 (left of 4th tree)
S25-2005S-KS-901		2005-S, KS, PF, 90% Silver	Large Die Dent Rev (bison's hindquarter)
25-2005P-OR-801		2005-P, OR	DDR-001 (tallest tree, right side of coin)
25-2005P-OR-802		2005-P, OR	DDR-002 (two trees on right side of coin)
25-2007P-WY-801		2007-P, WY	DDR-018 (saddle horn)
25-2007P-WY-802		2007-P, WY	DDR (saddle horn)
25-2007P-WY-803		2007-P, WY	DDR (saddle horn)
25-2009D-DC-801		2009-D, DC	DDR-001 (ELL of ELLINGTON)
25-2009P-DC-801		2009-P, DC	DDR-012 (piano keys)
25-2009P-DC-802		2009-P, DC	DDR-004 (piano key below ELL)
BUST HALF DOLLARS			
50-1806-301		1806	RPD (6 Over Inverted 6)
50-1806-901		1806	STATES Over STATAS (A under E of STATES)
50-1808-301		1808	RPD
50-1812-101		1812	DDO (LIBERTY)
50-1812-901		1812	Rev Die Clash (BER of LIBERTY evident)
50-1829-301		1829	RPD (curled-base 2 of date over flat-based 2)
LIBERTY SEATED HALF DOLLARS			
50-1840-301		1840, Rev. of '39	RPD (4 and 0 south; also Rev of '39)
50-1840-302		1840, Rev. of '39	RPD (1 and 8 west, 4 and 0 north; also small letters)
50-1840-401		1840, Rev. of '39	Obv Die Crack, Open Claw (on branch)
50-1842-301		1842 MD	RPD (842 south)
50-1842-801	000.5	1842 MD	DDR (UNITED STATES OF AMERICA, eagle)
50-18430-301		1843-O	RPD (1, 8, and 4 south; 3 north)
50-18440-301	001	1844-O	RPD (rock)
50-18450-301	001.5	1845-O	RPD (5 in date)
50-18450-302	002	1845-O	RPD (tripled south)
50-18450-303		1845-O	RPD (west)
50-18450-501	002.5	1845-O	RPM (O Over Horizontal O)
50-1846-301	003	1846	RPD (6 Over Horizontal 6)
50-1847-101		1847	DDO (shield, LIBERTY)
50-1847-301	004	1847	Overdate (7 Over 6)
50-1849-301	004.5	1849	RPD (west)
50-1853-401		1853	Obv Die Clash (rays of rev at rock)
50-1853-801	004.7	1853	DDR (UNITED, HALF)
50-1853-802		1853	DDR (HALF DOL, AMERICA, and arrows)
50-1853-803		1853	DDR (STATES)
50-1855-301	005	1855	Overdate (5 Over 4)
50-18550-501	006	1855-O	RPM (O Over Horizontal O)
50-18560-301		1856-O	RPD (1 south, 5 and 6 north)
50-1858-101		1858	DDO (drapery, skirt, foot, and rock)
50-1858-301		1858	RPD (right of first 8 and 5)
50-1858-302		1858	MPD (8 protruding from skirt above first 8)
50-18580-301		1858-O	MPD (8 protruding from rock above of second 8)
50-18580-901		1858-O	Rev Die Clash (leg of eagle)
50-18590-301		1859-O	RPD (1 south, 9 north)
50-18610-401	007	1861-O	Obv Die Crack (Confederate obv die)
50-1865-301		1865	RPD (1 north, 5 south)
50-1866-301		1866	MPD (6 in rock above last 6)
50-1866-302	007.01	1866	MPD (6 in denticles after last 6)
50-1867-801		1867	DDR (motto, beak, eye, and wings)

LIBERTY SEATED HALF DOLLARS—ARROWS AT DATE

FS#	Old FS#	Issue	Brief Description
50-1873-101	007.1	1873	DDO (shield, gown, foot, scroll, lower stars)
50-1873-301		1873	MPD (denticles below arrows)
50-1876-301	007.4	1876	RPD (Large Over Small Date)
50-1876-302		1876	RPD (two secondary digits west of 7 and 6)
50-1876-303	007.3	1876	MPD (digit in denticles below 7)
50-1876-304		1876	MPD (denticles below 8)
50-1876-401		1876 PF	Obv Die Variety (top of letter C matching mintmark style punched in Liberty's neck)
50-1877-301	007.5	1877, 7 Over 6	Overdate (7 Over 6)

BARBER HALF DOLLARS

FS#	Old FS#	Issue	Brief Description
50-1892-301	007.7	1892	RPD (south)
50-1892-801	007.8	1892	DDR (lettering, arrows, ribbon, leaves, stars)
50-1892O-501	007.9	1892	Micro O Mintmark
50-1893-801		1893	DDR-001 (tripled lettering on rim, esp. HALF)
50-1909S-501		1909-S	IMM
50-1911S-501		1911-S	RPM (west)

LIBERTY WALKING HALF DOLLARS

FS#	Old FS#	Issue	Brief Description
50-1916D-501	008	1916-D	RPM (D Over D southwest)
50-1936-101	008.4	1936	DDO (date)
50-1936-102		1936	DDO-001 (date, IN GOD WE TRUST, shoe, skirt, rays)
50-1936D-101		1936-D	DDO-001 (date, shoe, skirt, ground)
50-1936S-101		1936-S	DDO (date, shoe, skirt, ground)
50-1939D-101	008.45	1939-D	DDO (date, IN GOD WE TRUST, shoe, skirt)
50-1939D-501		1939-D	RPM-001 (D Over D north)
50-1941D-501		1941-D	RPM-001 (D Over D northwest)
50-1941S-501		1941-S	RPM (S Over S southwest)
50-1942-101	009	1942	DDO (breast; master die DDO)
50-1942-801	008.5	1942	DDR (AMERICA, HALF DOLLAR, feathers)
50-1942D-101		1942-D	DDO (breast; master die DDO)
50-1942D-501	010	1942-D	Mintmark Variety (formerly believed to be OMM, D Over S)
50-1942S-101		1942-S	DDO (breast; master die DDO)
50-1943-101	010.5	1943	DDO (date, IN GOD WE TRUST, LIBERTY, skirt)
50-1943D-101	010.5	1943-D	DDO (date, IN GOD WE TRUST, LIBERTY, skirt)
50-1943D-501		1943-D	Mintmark Variety (formerly believed to be OMM, D Over S)
50-1943S-101	010.5	1943-S	DDO (date, IN GOD WE TRUST, LIBERTY, skirt)
50-1944D-901		1944-D	Hand-Engraved Designer's Initials
50-1944S-501	010.6	1944-S	RPM (S Over S north)
50-1944S-502	010.7	1944-S	RPM (S Over S southwest)
50-1944S-511		1944-S	Possible IMM
50-1945-901		1945	Missing Designer's Initials
50-1946-101		1946	DDO (breast, robe, IN GOD WE TRUST)
50-1946-801	011.1	1946	DDR-001 (E PLURIBUS UNUM, branches, feathers)

FRANKLIN HALF DOLLARS

FS#	Old FS#	Issue	Brief Description
50-1948-801		1948	DDR (lettering, clapper)
50-1948D-801		1948-D	DDR (lettering, clapper)
50-1949S-501	011.3	1949-S	RPM (S Over S south)
50-1950-101		1950 PF	DDO (date, LIBERTY, IN GOD WE TRUST)
50-1950D-501		1950-D	RPM-001 (possible OMM, secondary S or D)
50-1951-801		1951 PF	DDR-010 (PASS AND STOW, feathers, etc.)
50-1951S-501		1951-S	RPM-001
50-1951S-801	011.5	1951-S	DDR (E PLURIBUS UNUM)
50-1952-402		1952	Die Cracks (face and lapel)
50-1952S-501		1952-S	RPM-001
50-1953S-501		1953-S	RPM (S Over S northwest)
50-1954-101		1954 PF	DDO (date, IN GOD WE TRUST, LIBERTY)
50-1955-401		1955	Obv Die Clash ("Bugs Bunny")
50-1956-101		1956 PF	DDO (date, IN GOD WE TRUST)
50-1956-801		1956 PF	DDR (lettering, esp. E PLURIBUS UNUM)
50-1956-802		1956 PF	DDR (eagle; Type II Over Type I)
50-1956-901		1956 PF	Type 1 Rev (low-relief eagle); RDV-001
50-1957-801		1957 PF	DDR (lettering, eagle, ri ght of bell)
50-1957D-501		1957-D	RPM (D Over Horizontal D)
50-1959-402		1959	Obv Die Break (throat; "Goiter" variety)
50-1959-801		1959	DDR (E PLURIBUS UNUM, eagle)
50-1960-101	012	1960 PF	DDO (date, TRUST, and LIBERTY)
50-1961-801	013	1961 PF	DDR (E PLURIBUS UNUM, UNITED, and HALF)

FS#	Old FS#	Issue	Brief Description
50-1961-802		1961 PF	DDR (outer lettering, E PLURIBUS UNUM, tail feathers)
50-1961-803		1961 PF	DDR (outer lettering, eagle, E PLURIBUS UNUM)
50-1962-101		1962 PF	DDO (2 of date and lettering)
50-1962-901		1962 PF	Possible Misplaced Mintmark (apparent D southwest of STOW)
50-1963-801		1963	DDR-001 (E PLURIBUS UNUM)
KENNEDY HALF DOLLARS			
50-1964-101	013.2	1964 PF	DDO (WE TRUST, RTY, date)
50-1964-102		1964	DDO (WE TRUST, LIBERTY, and date)
50-1964-103		1964 PF	DDO (IN GOD WE TRUST, LIBERTY, date, and hair)
50-1964-104		1964 PF, Nml Hair	DDO-021 (IN GOD WE TRUST, date, etc.)
50-1964-105		1964 PF, Nml Hair	DDO-035 (quadrupled WE TRUST)
50-1964-401		1964 PF	Accented Hair
50-1964-402		1964 PF	Normal Hair
50-1964-801		1964	DDR (UNITED STATES OF AMERICA, stars, ribbon, E PLURIBUS UNUM)
50-1964-802		1964 PF, Acc Hair	DDR-003 (quadrupled stars, designer's initials)
50-1964D-101	013.4	1964-D	DDO (IN GOD WE TRUST, LIBERTY, initials, hair)
50-1964D-102		1964-D	(reserved for future listing)
50-1964D-103	013.5	1964-D	TDO (IN GOD WE TRUST, RTY, and date)
50-1964D-104		1964-D	DDO (IN GOD, LI, and 19)
50-1964D-105	013.6	1964-D	TDO (IN GOD WE TRUST, TY, and hair)
50-1964D-106		1964-D	DDO (WE TRUST, TY, and hair)
50-1964D-107		1964-D	(reserved for future listing)
50-1964D-108		1964-D	TDO (IN GOD WE TRUST, date, initials, RTY)
50-1964D-501		1964-D	RPM (D Over D south)
50-1964D-502		1964-D	RPM (D Over D north)
50-1964D-503		1964-D	RPM (D Over D northeast)
50-1964D-504		1964-D	RPM (D Over D Over Horizontal D)
50-1965-801		1965 (BS)	DDR (outer lettering, stars)
50-1965-802		1965	DDR-004 (stars, E PLURIBUS UNUM)
50-1966-101	013.8	1966 (BS)	DDO (IN GOD WE TRUST, profile, date)
50-1966-102		1966 SMS	DDO (IN GOD WE TRUST, profile, eye)
50-1966-103		1966 SMS	DDO (IN GOD WE TRUST, LIBERTY, profile, tripled WE TRUST)
50-1966-104		1966 SMS	DDO (IN GOD WE TRUST, LIBERTY, date, profile)
50-1966-105		1966, SMS	DDO-007 (profile, ear)
50-1966-106		1966, SMS	DDO-020 (profile, ear)
50-1966-901		1966 SMS	Missing Designer's Initials
50-1967-101		1967 SMS	DDO (quintupled IN GOD WE TRUST, LIBERTY, date)
50-1967-102		1967	DDO (IN GOD WE TRUST, LIBERTY, date)
50-1967-103		1967	DDO-001 (GOD, LIB)
50-1967-801		1967	DDR (lettering, stars, rays; also minor DDO)
50-1968D-101		1968-D	TDO (IN GOD WE TRUST, date, and LIBERTY)
50-1968S-101	014	1968-S PF	DDO (IN GOD WE TRUST, LIBERTY, date)
50-1968S-511		1968-S PF	IMM
50-1968S-801		1968-S PF	DDR (all elements)
50-1970S-101		1970-S PF	DDO (lettering)
50-1970S-102		1970-S PF	DDO-002 (TRUST)
50-1971D-101	014.3	1971-D	DDO (LIBERTY, 71, GOD WE TRUST)
50-1971D-102		1971-D	DDO (IN GOD WE TRUST, hair)
50-1971S-101		1971-S PF	DDO (WE TRUST and date)
50-1971S-102	014.5	1971-S PF	DDO (lettering, date, and upper hair)
50-1971S-103		1971-S PF	DDO-008 (TRUST)
50-1971S-801		1971-S PF	DDR (lettering, stars)
50-1972-101		1972	DDO (IN GOD WE TRUST, Y of LIBERTY, and date)
50-1972D-901		1972-D	Missing Designer's Initials
50-1973D-101	014.8	1973-D	DDO (lettering, date, and hair)
50-1974D-101	015	1974-D	DDO (letters, esp. WE TRUST, and date)
50-1976S-101	016	1976-S	DDO (WE TRUST; 40% silver)
50-1976S-801		1976-S PF, Clad	DDR-001 (designer's initials)
50-1977D-101		1977-D	DDO (WE TRUST)
50-1979S-501		1979-S PF	Type II Mintmark
50-1981S-501		1981-S PF	Type II Mintmark
50-1988S-101		1988-S PF	DDO (lettering, esp. WE TRUST, and date and mintmark; silver)
50-1992S-101		1992-S PF	DDO (lettering, esp. WE TRUST, and date and mintmark; silver)
LIBERTY SEATED DOLLARS			
S1-1865-801		1865	DDR (U of UNITED)
S1-1868-301		1868	MPD (top of 6 or 8 in denticles below 6)

FS#	Old FS#	Issue	Brief Description
S1-1869-301		1869	RPD (1 south)
S1-1869-302		1869	RPD (base of 1 is midway between 1 and 8)
S1-1869-303		1869	MPD (top of 6 or 9 in denticles below 6)
S1-1871-301		1871	MPD (top of 8 in denticles below 8)

TRADE DOLLARS

FS#	Old FS#	Issue	Brief Description
T1-1873CC-301	012.3	1873-CC	MPD (digit in denticles below 8 and 7)
T1-1873CC-302		1873-CC	MPD (top of 8 and 7 in denticles below 8 and 7)
T1-1875S-501	012.5	1875-S	OMM (S Over CC)
T1-1875S-502		1875-S	OMM (S Over CC; similar to FS-501)
T1-1876-301		1876	RPD (6 within loop of 6)
T1-1876CC-801	014	1876-CC	DDR (all rev elements, esp. branch, talons, wing)
T1-1876S-101	013	1876-S	DDO (all obv elements)
T1-1877-101		1877	DDO (LIBERTY and wheat)
T1-1877S-301		1877-S	RPD (final 7 south)
T1-1877S-801	014.5	1877-S	DDR (E PLURIBUS UNUM, ribbon, UNITED STATES OF AMERICA, top of eagle)
T1-1877S-802		1877-S	DDR (lower rev elements, TRADE DOLLAR, 420 GRAINS)
T1-1878S-801	015	1878-S	DDR (all rev elements)
T1-1878S-802		1878-S	DDR (UNITED STATES and E PLURIBUS UNUM)

MORGAN DOLLARS

FS#	Old FS#	Issue	Brief Description
S1-1878-005		1878 8TF	DDO; VAM-5
S1-1878-009		1878 8TF	First Die Pair; VAM-9
S1-1878-014.11		1878 8TF	Obv Die Gouge; VAM-14.11
S1-1878-015		1878 8TF	DDO (LIBERTY); VAM-15
S1-1878-032		1878 7/8TF	DDR (tail feathers); VAM-32
S1-1878-044	001	1878 7/8TF	TDO, DDR; VAM-44
S1-1878-115		1878 7TF	TDO, DDR; VAM-115
S1-1878-145		1878 7TF	Broken Letters Obv (M); VAM-145
S1-1878-162		1878 7TF	Broken Letters Obv (N and M of UNUM broken, R of TRUST); VAM-162
S1-1878-166		1878 7TF	TDO ("Spikes" at eyelid); VAM-166
S1-1878-168		1878 7TF	DDO, DDR (eye, R of TRUST); VAM-168
S1-1878-188		1878 7TF	Polished Die (L of LIBERTY); VAM-188
S1-1878-220		1878 7TF	TDO (R of PLURIBUS); VAM-220
S1-1878-901		1878 7TF	Rev of '78 (flat breast, parallel arrow feathers)
S1-1878-902		1878 7TF	Rev of '79 (round breast, slanted feathers)
S1-1878CC-006		1878-CC	DDO (headdress and ear; also wide, level CC on rev)
S1-1878CC-018		1878-CC	DDO (headdress and ear; also close, uneven CC on rev)
S1-1878S-050		1878-S	TDO (eyelid)
S1-1879O-004		1879-O	RPM (O Over O Over O)
S1-1879O-028		1879-O	RPM (O Over O Over O)
S1-1879S-301		1879-S	Rev of '78; several VAM listings
S1-1880-006		1880	Overdate (80 Over 79, "spikes")
S1-1880-007		1880	Overdate (80 Over 79, "crossbar")
S1-1880-008		1880	Overdate (80 Over 79, "ears")
S1-1880-023		1880	Overdate (80 Over 79)
S1-1880CC-004		1880-CC 8/L7	Overdate, Second Rev; VAM-4
S1-1880CC-005		1880-CC 8/L7	Overdate, Third Rev; VAM-5
S1-1880CC-006		1880-CC 8/L7	Overdate, Third Rev; VAM-6
S1-1880CC-007		1880-CC 8/L7	Overdate, Second Rev; VAM-7
S1-1880O-004		1880-O	Overdate; VAM-4
S1-1880O-005		1880-O	Overdate; VAM-5
S1-1880O-049		1880-O	RPD ("Hangnail"); VAM-49
S1-1880O-016		1880-O	Checkmark
S1-1880O-017		1880-O	Checkmark
S1-1880O-021		1880-O	Checkmark
S1-1881O-005		1881-O	RPM (O Over O); VAM-5
S1-1881O-027		1881-O	DDO; VAM-27
S1-1882O-003		1882-O	OMM (O Over S, early die state); VAM-3
S1-1882O-003		1882-O	OMM (O Over S, late die state); VAM-3
S1-1882O-004		1882-O	OMM (O Over S, recused, early die state); VAM-4
S1-1882O-004		1882-O	OMM (O Over S, recused, late die state); VAM-4
S1-1882O-005		1882-O	OMM (O Over S, Broken S, early die state); VAM-5
S1-1882O-005		1882-O	OMM (O Over S, Broken S, late die state); VAM-5
S1-1883-010		1883	DDO
S1-1884-003		1884	Large Dot; VAM-3
S1-1884-004		1884	Small Dot; VAM-4
S1-1884-005		1884	DDO
S1-1885-022		1885	Die Chip; VAM-22
S1-1885CC-004		1885-CC	Die Chip; VAM-4
S1-1886-001C		1886	Rev Die Clash; VAM-1C
S1-1886-020		1886	RPD; VAM-20
S1-1886O-001A		1886-O	Rev Die Clash (E); VAM-1A
S1-1887-001B		1887	Rev Die Clash (E); VAM-1B
S1-1887-002		1887	Overdate (7 Over 6); VAM-2
S1-1887-012		1887	DDO (front of eye; "Alligator Eye" variety); VAM-12, VAM-12A

FS#	Old FS#	Issue	Brief Description
S1-18870-002		1887-O	RPD; VAM-2
S1-18870-003		1887-O	Overdate (7 Over 6); VAM-3
S1-18870-030		1887-O	Rev Die Clash; VAM-30
S1-18880-001A		1888-O	Rev Die Clash (E); VAM-1A
S1-18880-001B		1888-O	Die Crack ("Scarface)"); VAM-1B
S1-18880-004		1888-O	DDO ("Hot Lips"); VAM-4
S1-18880-015		1888-O	DDR, RPM
S1-18880-301		1888-O	Mintmark Variety (Oval O); various VAM listings
S1-1889-019		1889	Die Break ("Bar Wing"); VAM-19A
S1-1889-022		1889	Die Break ("Bar Wing"); VAM-22
S1-1889-023a		1889	Obv Die Clash; VAM-23A
S1-18890-001a		1889-O	Rev Die Clash (E); VAM-1A
S1-18890-002		1889-O	Mintmark Variety (Oval O); various VAM listings
S1-18890-017		1889-O	Mintmark Variety (Oval O)
S1-1890CC-004		1890-CC	Die Gouge ("Tailbar"); VAM-4
S1-18900-010		1890-O	Die Gouges ("Comet"); VAM-10
S1-18900-020		1890-O	DDO
S1-1891CC-003		1891-CC	Die Gouge ("Spitting Eagle"); VAM-3
S1-18910-001a		1891-O	Rev Die Clash (E); VAM-1A
S1-18910-001b		1891-O	Pitted Rev Die; VAM-1B
S1-1895S-003		1895-S	RPM (S Over S); VAM-3
S1-1895S-004		1895-S	RPM (S Over S)
S1-1896-020		1896	RPD; VAM-20
S1-18960-004		1896-O	Micro O; VAM-4
S1-18960-019		1896-O	RPD; VAM-19
S1-18980-020		1898-O	RPD; VAM-20
S1-18990-501		1899-O	Micro O; various VAM listings
S1-1900-011		1900	DDR; VAM-16
S1-1900-016		1900	C4 Over C3 Rev
S1-19000-005		1900-O	Micro O; VAM-5
S1-19000-029a		1900-O	Die Break; VAM-29A
S1-19000-501		1900-O	OMM (O Over CC); various VAM listings
S1-1901-003		1901	DDR ("Shifted Eagle"); VAM-3
S1-1902-004		1902	DDO
S1-19020-003		1902-O	Micro O; VAM-3
S1-1903S-002		1903-S	Small S; VAM-2
S1-1921-301		1921	Wide Reeding
S1-1921D-001a		1921-D	Over-Polished Die
S1-1921D-001x		1921-D	Large Cud; VAM-1X
S1-1921S-001a		1921-S	Die Scratch
S1-1921S-001b		1921-S	Die Gouges
S1-1921S-001b7		1921-S	Die Gouges ("Thornhead"); VAM-1B7

PEACE DOLLARS

FS#	Old FS#	Issue	Brief Description
S1-1921-003		1921	Rev Variety (line through L of DOLLAR); VAM-3
S1-1921-1003		1921	DDR (line through R)
S1-1922-001f		1922	Die Break; VAM-1F
S1-1922-002a		1922	Die Break ("Earring"); VAM-2A
S1-1922-002c		1922	Die Break ("Extra Hair"); VAM-2C
S1-1922-005a		1922	Die Break ("Scar Cheek"); VAM-5A
S1-1922-012a		1922	Die Break ("Moustache"); VAM-12A
S1-1922-401		1922	High Relief (Design Type of 1921)
S1-1923-001a		1923	Die Break ("Whisker Jaw"); VAM-1A
S1-1923-001b1		1923	Die Break ("Extra Hair"); VAM-1B
S1-1923-001b2		1923	Die Break ("Extra Hair," plus extra die breaks); VAM-1B
S1-1923-001c		1923	Die Break (tail on O); VAM-1C
S1-1923-001d		1923	Die Break ("Whisker Cheek"); VAM-1D
S1-1923-002		1923	DDO ("Double Tiara"); VAM-2
S1-1923S-001c		1923-S	Pitted Rev; VAM-1C
S1-1924-005a		1924	Die Break ("Broken Wing"); VAM-5A
S1-1925-005		1925	Over-Polished Die ("Missing Ray"); VAM-5
S1-1926S-004		1926-S	Dot ("Extra Berry"); VAM-4
S1-1927S-101		1927-S	RPM-001 (S Over Rotated S); VAM-4
S1-1928S-003		1928-S	DDO; VAM-3
S1-1934D-003		1934-D	DDO; Medium D Mintmark; VAM-3
S1-1934D-004		1934-D	DDO; Small D Mintmark; VAM-4

EISENHOWER DOLLARS

FS#	Old FS#	Issue	Brief Description
C1-1971D-901		1971-D	Low-Relief Rev ("Friendly Eagle"); RDV-006
S1-1971S-103	015.8	1971-S PF, 40% Silver	DDO (clad Proof)
S1-1971S-106		1971-S PF, 40% Silver	DDO-006 (lettering and date)
S1-1971S-401		1971-S, 40% Silver	Polished Die ("Pegleg R")
S1-1971S-501		1971-S, 40% Silver	RPM (S Over S, 40% silver, "Blue Pack")

FS#	Old FS#	Issue	Brief Description
S1-1971S-801		1971-S PF, 40% Silver	DDR-005 (UNITED STATES OF AMERICA, E PLURIBUS UNUM, denomination)
C1-1972-901		1972, Variety II	B Rev ("King of Ikes"); RDV-002, Breen-5749
S1-1972S-101		1972-S PF, 40% Silver	TDO (IN GOD WE TRUST, LIBERTY, date)
S1-1973S-101		1973-S PF, 40% Silver	DDO (IN GOD WE TRUST)

SUSAN B. ANTHONY AND GOLDEN DOLLARS

FS#	Old FS#	Issue	Brief Description
C1-1979P-301	016	1979-P	Wide Rim ("Near Date"); ODV-002
C1-1979S-501		1979-S PF	Type II Mintmark; MMS-002
C1-1980S-501		1980-S PF	RPM (S Over S)
C1-1981S-501		1981-S PF	Type II Mintmark; MMS-003
C1-2000P-901		2000-P	Rev Die Alterations ("Speared Eagle")
C1-2000P-902		2000-P	Enhanced Rev Die ("Cheerios")
C1-(2007)-GW-701		(2007), Washington	Missing Edge Inscription ("Plain Edge")
C1-(2007)-TJ-701		(2007), Jefferson	Missing Edge Inscription ("Plain Edge")
C1-(2007)-JA-701		(2007), Adams	Missing Edge Inscription ("Plain Edge")
C1-(2010)-NA-701		(2010), Native Am., Satin	Missing Edge Inscription ("Plain Edge")
C1-2007S-TJ-701		2007-S, Jeff PF	Out-of-Sequence Edge Inscription

GOLD DOLLARS

FS#	Old FS#	Issue	Brief Description
G1-1854-101		1854 Ty 2	DDO (lettering; also Rev Die Clash)
G1-1854-301		1854 Ty 2	RPD (all digits)
G1-1856S-501		1856-S	RPM-001 (S Over S)
G1-1862-101	G-001	1862	DDO-001 (UNITED STATES OF AMERICA, top of crown, beads, hair)

QUARTER EAGLES

FS#	Old FS#	Issue	Brief Description
G2-1851-301		1851	RPD (1, 5, and 1)
G2-1853-301		1853	RPD (1 and 8)
G2-18540-301		1854-O	MPD (crosslet of 4 in hair curl above 4)
G2-1862-301	G-002	1862/1	Overdate (2 Over 1)
G2-1891-801		1891	DDR-001 (AMERICA, arrow tips, D of 2-1/2 D)

$3 GOLD

FS#	Old FS#	Issue	Brief Description
G3-1882-301		1882	RPD (2)

HALF EAGLES

FS#	Old FS#	Issue	Brief Description
G5-1802-301		1802	Overdate (2 Over 1)
G5-1819-901		1819	Repunched Denomination ("5D Over 50")
G5-1847-301	003	1847	MPD (top of 7 in denticles below 4)
G5-1847-302	004	1847	MPD (1 in neck of Liberty)
G5-1847-303		1847	RPD (1 and 8 south, 7 right)
G5-1847-304		1847	MPD (base of 1 in bust)
G5-1848D-501		1848-D	RPM-001
G5-1854-101	004.5	1854	DDO-001 (hair and ear; "Earring")
G5-1881-301	005	1881	Overdate (1881 Over 1880)
G5-1881-302		1881	RPD (881)
G5-1881-303		1881	RPD (all digits north)
G5-1881-304		1881	RPD (all digits west)
G5-1881-305		1881	RPD (all digits north and west)
G5-1899-301		1899	RPD (899)
G5-1901S-301		1901-S	Overdate (1 Over 0)
G5-1901S-501		1901-S	RPM-002 (S Over S)
G5-1905S-501	006.5	1905-S	RPM-001 (S Over S)
G5-1906-301		1906	RPD (6)
G5-1911S-501		1911-S	RPM-001 (S Over S south)
G5-1911S-502		1911-S	RPM (S Over S); VP-001

EAGLES

FS#	Old FS#	Issue	Brief Description
G10-18460-301		1846-O	RPD (6; also RPM, O Over O)
G10-1853-301	007	1853	Overdate (3 Over 2)
G10-1854S-301		1854-S	MPD (base of 1 below 1 and 8)
G10-1883S-301		1883-S	MPD (3 in denticles below 3)
G10-1889S-501		1889-S	RPM-001 (S Over S; also DDR-001, STATES OF AMERICA, arrows)
G10-1891CC-501		1891-CC	RPM-001 (extra C to right)
G10-1892CC-501		1892-CC	TDR (IN GOD WE TRUST); VP-001

DOUBLE EAGLES

FS#	Old FS#	Issue	Brief Description
G20-1852-301		1852	RPD (all digits north)
G20-1853-301	G-008	1853	Overdate (3 Over 2)
G20-1857-301		1857	MPD (digit, likely 1), at center right of 5)
G20-1859S-101		1859-S	DDO-001 (LIBERTY, hair curl, eye, neck, and profile)
G20-1865-301		1865	MPD (digits in denticles)
G20-1866-801		1866	DDR (dual hub, small IN over large IN of motto)
G20-1866S-301		1866-S	MPD (digit in denticles left of 1)
G20-1871S-301		1871-S	MPD (digit, likely 7, in denticles)
G20-1873-101		1873 O3	DDO-001 (LIBERTY)
G20-1879-801		1879	DDR-001 (most lettering)
G20-1883S-301		1883-S	MPD (digit in denticles below second 8)

FS#	Old FS#	Date/Mint	Brief Description
G20-1888-801		1888	DDR-001 (TWENTY DOLLARS and lower ribbon)
G20-1896-301		1896	RPD (all digits north)
G20-1908-801		1908	DDR (eagle's beak, upper lettering)
G20-1909-301		1909	Overdate (9 Over 8)
G20-1909S-501		1909-S	RPM-001 (S Over S)
G20-1911D-501		1911-D	RPM-001 (D Over D east)
G20-1922-801		1922	DDR-001 (motto, lettering, rays, talons)
G20-1925-801		1925	DDR (eagle's feathers, rays, IN GOD WE TRUST)
G20-1926-101		1926	DDO-001 (tripled rays, date, stars, etc.)
CLASSIC COMMEMORATIVES			
C50-1892-301	C-000.5	1892	Columbian Expo half dollar; RPD (2 north)
C50-1892-302		1892	Columbian Expo half dollar; RPD (2 northeast)
C50-1892-303		1892	Columbian Expo half dollar; RPD (89 east)
C50-1893-301		1893	Columbian Expo half dollar; RPD (3 north)
C50-1915S-501		1915-S	Pan-Pac half dollar; RPM-002 (S Over S east)
C50-1915S-502		1915-S	Pan-Pac half dollar; RPM-001
C50-1920-901		1920	Pilgrim half dollar; Die Crack/Break (between masts)
C50-1925-101	C-001	1925	Stone Mountain half dollar; DDO-002
C50-1925-102		1925	Vancouver half dollar; DDO
C50-1933D-101		1933-D	Oregon Trail half dollar; DDO-001 (tripling)
C50-1935-101		1935	Boone half dollar; DDO-001 (possibly a master die DDO)
C50-1936D-101		1936-D	California Pacific Expo half dollar; QDO (LIBERTY), RPM
C50-1936D-501		1936-D	California Pacific Expo half dollar; RPM-001 (D Over D south)
C50-1951-801		1951	Carver/Washington half dollar; DDR (possibly a master die DDR)
C50-1953S-801		1953-S	Carver/Washington half dollar; DDR-001 (possibly a master die DDR)
BULLION COINAGE, 1986 TO DATE			
SE1-2008W-901		2008-W	Silver Eagle, Burnished; Rev of '07 (no spur on U of UNITED)
G5-1999W-401		1999-W Unc.	.10-oz.; Proof W-Mintmark Obverse
G10-1999W-401		1999-W Unc.	.25-oz.; Proof W-Mintmark Obverse
P25-2007W-901		2007-W PF	.25-oz.; FREEDOM on Shield Frosted
P50-2007W-901		2007-W PF	.50-oz.; FREEDOM on Shield Frosted
P100-2007W-901		2007-W PF	1-oz.; FREEDOM on Shield Frosted

ABOUT THE AUTHORS AND EDITORS

Bill Fivaz

Bill Fivaz, a coin collector since 1950, has earned recognition as one of the country's most respected authorities on numismatic errors and die varieties. His awards include the highest recognition of the American Numismatic Association, which presented him its top honor, the Farran Zerbe Memorial Award, in 1995. He was elected to the ANA Hall of Fame in 2002.

Bill is widely known as an engaging teacher and a speaker on numismatic topics. He has written hundreds of articles on a wide array of numismatic topics, and has been a consultant to several coin-authentication services. His contributions are noted in many of today's most popular and respected hobby books, including the *Guide Book of United States Coins* (the "Red Book").

Bill has served on the board of governors of the ANA and on the board of directors of CONECA (the Combined Organizations of Numismatic Error Collectors).

To honor his reputation as a teacher and writer, in 2010 the ANA and Whitman Publishing endowed the Bill Fivaz Young Numismatist Literary Award, for young numismatists aged 8 to 12.

J.T. Stanton

J.T. Stanton has collected coins since 1959 and began specializing in errors and varieties in 1982. Well known as a teacher and lecturer in the die-variety field, he instructed American Numismatic Association Summer Seminar courses for 11 years and started the ANA's annual "Errors and Varieties and Modern Minting Process" class.

The ANA has recognized J.T.'s contributions to the hobby with awards including the Medal of Merit, the Glenn Smedley Memorial Award, the Outstanding Adult Supervisor Award, and two Presidential Awards.

J.T. has taken leadership positions in the hobby community over the years. He served on the board of governors of the ANA from 1995 to 1997. His dedication to CONECA includes terms on the board of directors and as the group's president. He was elected to CONECA's Hall of Fame.

Mike Ellis

Mike Ellis, NLG has been a coin collector since age 8 in 1968, and he never completely stopped collecting, as many do during their early adulthood. Once he fully immersed himself in numismatics in the 1980s, he developed a powerful interest in error and variety coins, which inspired him to look closer at coins and learn the minting process. This naturally led to proficiency in authentication of coins, grading, and attribution of die varieties, as well as a strong desire to teach others, as he does today. He is a life member of both CONECA and the American Numismatic Association and has shared his expertise through leadership roles in both organizations: vice president (for six years) and then president (for eight years) of CONECA, and a member of the Board of Governors of the ANA.

Mike has been teaching at the ANA Summer Seminar on behalf of the ANA since 1996, and he shared his numismatic knowledge independently before that. Classes he has led for the ANA include "Modern Minting and Varieties and Errors," "Early Minting," "Counterfeit and Altered Coins," and "Coin Grading," the last of which he teaches on a regular basis to this day. He has also taught many short classes at the Summer Seminar and across the nation.

Mike has been writing even longer than he has been teaching. Besides articles for numerous numismatic periodicals of all kinds, he has been a columnist for *Numismatic News* and for *ErrorScope*, the official publication of CONECA. He has also edited numismatic references, including the *Cherrypickers' Guide to Rare Varieties*, fourth edition, volume I, and the ANA's *Modern Minting Process and U.S. Minting Errors and Varieties*, and has contributed to dozens of others. He also served as editor of both *ErrorScope* and *Cherrypickers' News*.

For all his efforts, Mike has received every award CONECA has to offer, including the Lyndon King Award, and is the eighth entry into their Hall of Fame. From the ANA, he has received the Glenn Smedley Memorial Award and a Presidential Award. Outside of the numismatic community he is a Georgia Master 4-Her (a member of the Georgia Master 4-H Club) and recipient of two U.S. Navy Achievement Medals. Currently a senior grader for QA Check, he has previously worked with both ANACS and ICG.

Ken Potter started collecting coins in 1959, and has been an active coin and exonumia dealer since 1973. His focus on errors and die varieties began in earnest in 1979.

Ken Potter

Hobbyists know Ken Potter as a prolific researcher and writer whose columns and articles are regularly featured in *Coin World, Numismatic News, World Coin News, Canadian Coin News,* and numerous club publications. His work has won awards from the Numismatic Literary Guild and induction into CONECA's Hall of Fame. He is an active member of nearly a dozen hobby organizations, and has served in leadership positions in many of them, including as CONECA's longest-serving doubled-die attributor. He often speaks to coin clubs, schools, and treasure-hunting clubs on the topics of minting varieties and errors.

While Ken is a longtime contributor to the *Cherrypickers' Guide to Rare Die Varieties*, the fifth edition, volume II, marked his first effort as the book's main editor. In this position he coordinated resources including a network of specialists from around the country, and contributed his own original research and photography.

CONECA

New Member Application / Renewal Form

Today's Date: ______/______/______

Membership Type: _____ Regular/Annual Member - $25.00
_____ Young Numismatist (under 18) - $7.50

Mailing Options: _____ U.S. bulk rate - No extra charge
_____ First Class or Outside the U.S.A. - $12.50 additional

Total: _____ Amount Due

Name: ______________________________________

Address: ______________________________________

City: ________________________State: ______

Zip +4 Code: __________________________

Phone: ________________ Email: ______________________________________

Recommended by: *The Cherrypickers' Guide*

Comments/Interests:

____

____

Send application and check/money order (payable to CONECA) to:

CONECA
c/o Rachel Irish, CONECA Membership Coordinator
3807 Belmont Rd.
Couer d'Alene, ID 83815

Your membership is subject to approval by the Membership Committee and subject to the rules and regulations set forth in the CONECA Constitution and By-Laws.

A PDF version of the CONECA membership application, which includes 2-year and life memembership options, as well as more options for alternate delivery of the ErrorScope *publication, is available at conecaonline.org/join.html.*